Lecture Notes of the Institute for Computer Sciences, Social Informatics and Telecommunications Engineering 517

The LNICST series publishes ICST's conferences, symposia and workshops.

LNICST reports state-of-the-art results in areas related to the scope of the Institute. The type of material published includes

- Proceedings (published in time for the respective event)
- Other edited monographs (such as project reports or invited volumes)

LNICST topics span the following areas:

- General Computer Science
- E-Economy
- E-Medicine
- Knowledge Management
- Multimedia
- Operations, Management and Policy
- Social Informatics
- Systems

Oscar Castillo · Thanikanti Sudhakar Babu ·
Rajanikanth Aluvalu
Editors

Pervasive Knowledge and Collective Intelligence on Web and Social Media

Second EAI International Conference, PerSOM 2023
Hyderabad, India, November 24–25, 2023
Proceedings

 Springer

Editors
Oscar Castillo
Tijuana Institute of Technology
Tijuana, Mexico

Thanikanti Sudhakar Babu ⓘ
Chaitanya Bharathi Institute of Technology
Hyderabad, Telangana, India

Rajanikanth Aluvalu
Chaitanya Bharathi Institute of Technology
Hyderabad, Telangana, India

ISSN 1867-8211 ISSN 1867-822X (electronic)
Lecture Notes of the Institute for Computer Sciences, Social Informatics
and Telecommunications Engineering
ISBN 978-3-031-66043-6 ISBN 978-3-031-66044-3 (eBook)
https://doi.org/10.1007/978-3-031-66044-3

This Springer imprint is published by the registered company Springer Nature Switzerland AG
The registered company address is: Gewerbestrasse 11, 6330 Cham, Switzerland

If disposing of this product, please recycle the paper.

Preface

We are delighted to introduce PerSoM 2023 - EAI 2nd International Conference on Pervasive knowledge and collective intelligence on Web and Social Media, held on November 24–25, 2023 at Hyderabad, India, in association with Chaitanya Bharathi Institute of Technology. The conference is a venue that brings together researchers from different disciplines in the fields of Pervasive Computing, Web and Social Media to discuss and promote ideas and practices about pervasive knowledge and collective Intelligence in these fields. In this regard, we solicit theoretical as well as application-oriented research studies on relevant topics related to new perspectives in social theories, complex networks, data science and knowledge management, comprising methodologies, algorithms, evaluation benchmarks and tools for the development and application of algorithms for analyzing web and social media.

The technical program of EAI PerSoM 2023 consisted of 29 full papers. The conference tracks were Information and Web Mining, Social Network Analysis, Semantic Network Analysis, Trust, Reputation, Social Control and Privacy, Information Reliability, and Web and Content Authenticity. Aside from the high-quality technical paper presentations, the technical program also featured four keynote speeches by Tanmoy Chakraborty from Indian Institute of Technology, Delhi, Joy Mustafi from MUST Research, India, Mukesh Mishra from Massey University, New Zealand, and Subhrakanta Panda from Birla Institute of Technology and Science Pilani, Hyderabad.

The conference provided a forum for discussing the policy implications and ethical considerations associated with pervasive knowledge and collective intelligence on the web and social media platforms. Participants engaged in critical discussions on topics such as privacy, security, algorithmic bias and digital ethics, aiming to inform policy-making and promote responsible innovation. PerSoM 2023 - EAI 2nd International Conference on Pervasive Knowledge and Collective Intelligence on Web and Social Media played a crucial role in advancing research, fostering collaboration and addressing societal challenges in an increasingly interconnected and digitally mediated world.

Coordination with the steering chair, Imrich Chlamtac, was essential for the success of the conference. We sincerely appreciate his constant support and guidance. It was also a great pleasure to work with such an excellent organizing committee team for their hard work in organizing and supporting the conference. In particular, the Technical Program Committee, led by our TPC Co-Chairs, D. Raman and Prem Kumar Chithaluru, completed the peer-review process of technical papers and made a high-quality technical program. We are also grateful to the Conference Managers for their support and to all the authors who submitted their papers to the EAI PerSoM 2023 conference.

We strongly believe that EAI PerSoM 2023 provided a platform for researchers, academics, professionals and practitioners to present and discuss the latest advancements, trends, challenges and applications in the fields related to pervasive knowledge and collective intelligence on the web and social media. We also expect that the future conference will be as successful and stimulating, as indicated by the contributions presented in this volume.

August 2024

Thanikanti Sudhakar Babu
Oscar Castillo
Rajanikanth Aluvalu

Organization

Steering Committee

Imrich Chlamtac   University of Trento, Italy

Organizing Committee

General Chairs

Rajanikanth Aluvalu   Chaitanya Bharathi Institute of Technology, India
Miloš Stojmenović   Singidunum University, Serbia

TPC Chair and Co-chairs

Oscar Castillo   Tijuana Institue of Technology, Mexico
Ming Yang   Kennesaw State University, USA
T. Sudhakar Babu   Chaitanya Bharathi Institute of Technology, India
Kadiyala Ramana   Chaitanya Bharathi Institute of Technology, India

TPC Co-chairs

D. Raman   Chaitanya Bharathi Institute of Technology, India
Prem Kumar Chithaluru   Chaitanya Bharathi Institute of Technology, India

Sponsorship and Exhibit Chairs

N. V. Srinivasulu   Chaitanya Bharathi Institute of Technology, India
A. Pramod Kumar   Mallareddy Engineering College (Autonomous), India

Local Chair

Deepa Jose   KCG College of Technology, India

Workshops Chairs

Shweta Sankhwar	Maitreyi College, India
Alaa O. Khadidos	King Abdulaziz University, Saudi Arabia
Ramakrishna Kolikipogu	Chaitanya Bharathi Institute of Technology, India
Princy Randhawa	Manipal University Jaipur, India

Publicity and Social Media Chairs

G. N. R. Prasad	Chaitanya Bharathi Institute of Technology, India
Priya Gupta	Jawaharlal Nehru University, India

Publications Chairs

Adil O. Khadidos	King Abdulaziz University, Saudi Arabia
Uma Maheswari V.	Chaitanya Bharathi Institute of Technology, India
Suneeta Satpathy	Sri Sri University, India

Web Chairs

Swathi Sowmya	Chaitanya Bharathi Institute of Technology, India
K. Gangadhara Rao	Chaitanya Bharathi Institute of Technology, India

Panels Chairs

Lal Hussain	University of Azad Jammu and Kashmir Muzaffarabad, Pakistan
Sangeeta Gupta	Chaitanya Bharathi Institute of Technology, India
Monika Mangla	Dwarkadas J. Sanghvi College of Engineering, India

Demos Chairs

Ramesh Babu	Chaitanya Bharathi Institute of Technology, India
Nidhi Agarwal	Sharada University, India

Tutorials Chairs

K. Sangeetha	Kebri Dehar University, Ethiopia
Alaa O. Khadidos	King Abdulaziz University, Saudi Arabia
Mohd Helmy Abd Wahab	Universiti Tun Hussein Onn, Malaysia

Technical Program Committee

K. Sangeetha	Kebri Dehar University, Ethiopia
Alaa O. Khadidos	King Abdulaziz University, Saudi Arabia
Mohd Helmy Abd Wahab	Universiti Tun Hussein Onn, Malaysia
S. Shitharth	Kebri Dehar University, Ethiopia
P. Saravanan	King Saud University, Saudi Arabia
Prasanalakshmi Balaji	King Khalid University, Saudi Arabia
Zainab Alansari	University of Technology and Applied Science, Oman
Ripon Patgiri	National Institute of Technology Silchar, India
Jitendra Kumar Rout	National Institute of Technology Raipur, India
T. Ravichandran	National Institute of Technology Tiruchirappalli, India
Ashish Kumar Tripathi	Malaviya National Institute of Technology Jaipur, India
V. Kumar	Central University of Kerala, India
Manu Vardhan	National Institute of Technology Raipur, India
Malay Kumar	Indian Institute of Information Technology Dharwad, India
K. Jairam Naik	National Institute of Technology Raipur, India
M. V. V. Prasad Kantipudi	Symbiosis International University Pune, India
Puranam Revanth Kumar	ICFAI Foundation for Higher Education, India
Tanupriya Choudhury	University of Petroleum and Energy Studies, India
Abdulsattar Abdullah Hamad	University of Samarra, Iraq

Contents

Exploring the Adoption Readiness of the Indian Generation for Social Media Payments: An In-Depth Analysis of WhatsApp Payments

David Joseph$^{(\boxtimes)}$ ⓘ and S. Girish ⓘ

Department of Commerce, CHRIST (Deemed to be University), Bangalore, India
`david.joseph@christuniversity.in`

Abstract. Advancements in technologies always get higher acceptance among people. Regarding payment technologies, integrating payment facility in the Social Media platform are considered a second-generation payment technology. With the introduction of Hike wallets and WhatsApp payment, unprecedented opportunities are available to the users. In India, with the introduction of WhatsApp on November 2020, the users of FinTech got opened a gateway to social media payment. Social Media payments are considered easy and convenient, but is the Indian generation, especially people born in the internet phase (Gen Y and Gen Z), ready to adopt WhatsApp payment. The current study was done to investigate the elements that contribute to the acceptance and use of the WhatsApp payment service in India. To attain this objective, we used an extended UTAUT2 model with the moderating effect of generation. The data was gathered from 265 respondents and analyzed using the PLS-SEM method. The results of the study outlined that Gen Z is strengthening the moderating effect only between the facilitating conditions of the users and the actual usage of WhatsApp payment. The practical implications and directions for the further research are mentioned in the study.

Keywords: Social media payment · WhatsApp payment · FinTech · Extended UTAUT2

1 Introduction

Technological advancements in wireless technology and mobile phones provides unprecedented opportunities to consumers around the world. Multimodal payment solutions such as Cryptocurrencies, Mobiles, Peer to Peer Payments and P2P Social Media Platforms are increasingly dominating the technology of e commerce. India is a growing market for financial technologies. India ranked top along with China in the Global FinTech adoption index [26]. In the emerging financial technologies, mobile payments are considered as the next generation payment services. Compared to other electronic payment services, mobile payment services provide more customized services. The services are time and location-specific, and consumers can instantly perform tasks based on their needs [4].

O. Castillo et al. (Eds.): PerSOM 2023, LNICST 517, pp. 1–15, 2024.
https://doi.org/10.1007/978-3-031-66044-3_1

Since it was introduced as an innovative communication method, social media has come a long way. However, with the help of technology, social media has turned into a business tool for advertising and marketing. The pioneers of social media will keep innovating and new developments are being implemented in this space, such as the introduction of payment gateways. Data from Statista showed that across the globe there are 2.95 billion users of social media. They have already started implementing payment functions offering peer to peer payments or allowing direct buying directly, which eliminates the need for intermediaries, in order to take full advantage of this use of social media apps. While this new method of paying has been adopted by the US, Europe and most East Asian countries, it is still only begun to be applied in India. India's introduction to social media payments came with Hike Messenger's Hike wallets. Using this app, users can send and receive money using UPI as well as make a payment directly from their phone via the Wallet application. But in the year 2021 Hike messenger app which was owned by the Bharti Enterprises has officially shut down. In February 2018, WhatsApp also launched payment services as trial run and officially launched in November 2020. As of June 2021, there are 487.5 million users of WhatsApp in India [2]. Out of these 20 million users are using the payment services. WhatsApp Payment services in India launched with support from the State Bank of India (SBI) and other major banks like ICICI, HDFC and Axis Bank. In India currently only one social media payment service is available and it is WhatsApp which is owned by Meta (earlier it is known as Facebook).

The research area of adoption of technologies is widely explored by the research community. Especially in the finance filed adoption of financial technologies is a grown area. But the adoption of social media payment is not much discovered by the researchers' as it is in the introduction stage. Generation Y (those born between 1981 and 1996) and Generation Z (1997–2012) were born during the internet's early days. There are many studies conducted to know how well these generation is good in technologies, and the results explained that the adoption and perception towards technology are greater than the other generations like baby boomers and Gen X [21]. But whether these generations ready to adopt social media payment, as the social media payments are in the introduction phase.

So, the current study presents an effort to explore the Generation Y and Generation Z's acceptance and usage of WhatsApp payment service in India. To that end, the study employed an expanded 'Unified Theory of Acceptance And Use of Technology Model' (UTAUT2) to identify elements that are relevant for the uptake and use of WhatsApp payment services in India. The study's goal is to address these objectives.

1. Identifying the elements that influence WhatsApp payment adoption and usage.
2. Understand which of the following attributes significantly explain the variance in the adoption of WhatsApp payment; "Perceived Risk (PR), Price Value (PV), Perform Expectancy (PE), Effort Expectancy (EE), Social Influence (SI), Facilitating Conditions (FC), Hedonic Motivation (HM), Habit (HA) and Perceived Trust (PT)"
3. To examine the function of generation in mitigating the effect of the parameters influencing the adoption and behavioral intention to use WhatsApp payment.

2 Literature Review

One of the most common models for understanding how technologies are accepted is the "Technology Acceptance Model". Many other models were afterwards developed to investigate technology adoption. Among these frameworks, the 'Unified Theory of Acceptance and Use of Technology' (UTAUT) is becoming increasingly prominent in today's research environment for studying technology adoption. UTAUT model was proposed by [20]. Later in the year 2012, this model was extended by adding three more variables and named as the UTUAT2 model. [17] proposed an extended model for consumer adoption by integrating trust on the technology and risk factors in the existing UTAUT2 model. And they found the relation between the newly added variables and consumer adoption. Similarly [1] conducted a study by adopting the UTAUT model to identify the elements and determinants leading to the m-banking (Mobile banking) adoption of Gen Y. The most important variable in determining m-banking adoption, their study found, was hedonic motivation.

Among the Indian research, [11] employed an enhanced UTUAT model encompassing trust on the technology and perceived benefits of the use of technology to analyze the adoption of mobile payments among New Delhi consumers in their book chapter. Their study discovered that all variables were relevant for the adoption of mobile payments except facilitating conditions [19]. A study was conducted to examine users' perspectives on the factors impacting their propensity to utilize mobile-based payment technology. Using the UTAUT model, they discovered that perceived benefits, simplicity of use, system performance, connectivity, discomfort, compatibility between tasks and technology, and certainty of system structure all have a substantial impact on the desire to utilize mobile money services. However, elements like the 'perceived monetary value', ability to absorb new technology, and personal inclination towards innovation were determined to have no significant impact. UTAUT model was used not only to examine the adoption but also to understand the continued use of technology [15]. In their study, they focused on numerous antecedents that influence users' propensity to utilize mobile payment constantly across India. According to the study's findings, factors such as service quality, attitude towards the service, expected effort, and perceived risk all have a role in determining the desire to continue using mobile payment services. Moreover, factors such as perceived trust on technology, ease of use, and social value were not shown to impact consumers' intent to continue using the services.

To enhance the understanding of mobile financial technology adoption, the present study will introduce two additional variables to the existing UTAUT2 model. These variables will serve to provide more comprehensive insights into the factors influencing the adoption process. Many studies in the adoption of technologies used trust on the technology and perceived risk as additional variables to the UTAUT2 model. [11] included trust as an additional variable in their research to analyze the adoption of mobile payments. [24] investigated meta-analysis of the causes and repercussions of trust in mobile financial technologies as one of the research projects that incorporated trust on technology and perceived risk to understand the adoption of mobile financial technologies. The study focused on the elements that lead to the adoption of mobile financial technologies. 'Perceived utility, perceived ease of use, system quality, information quality, service quality, user interface, perceived risk, security, structural assurance, ubiquity, and trust disposition' are among these antecedents. By analyzing these factors, the study aimed to gain a comprehensive idea of the drivers behind the adoption of mobile financial technologies.

In a separate study, [13] looked into the connection between perceived risk, benefit, and trust in technology in the context of mobile payment service uptake. Data collected from 457 participants provided evidence for a negative association between perceived risk and trust, as well as between perceived risk and consumer intention to use mobile payments. These findings imply that higher levels of perceived risk are likely to lower both trust in the business and consumer intent to use mobile payment services.

Until now, there has been a lack of significant focus on empirical research concerning the adoption of payment technologies through social media. In India, social media payment in the introduction stage with the launch of WhatsApp payment. There is ongoing research that examines the reasons behind and barriers for the use of payment technologies through social media. The COVID-19 pandemic played a role in driving increased interest in mobile payments, and as a result, payments through social media platforms gained popularity as well [10].

In India, the social media payment especially the WhatsApp payment service launched in November 2020. The people exploring the option of WhatsApp payment. As a result, this study will attempt to investigate the behavioral intention and use of social media payment adoption among generation Y and Z, with a specific focus on the WhatsApp payment service.

3   Research Model and Hypotheses

This research suggested a methodology to explore the adoption of social media payment, notably WhatsApp payment, among Generations Y and Z. The model incorporated essential components from the 'Unified Theory of Acceptance and Use of Technology' (UTAUT2) model, as well as novel variables including Trust in technology and Perceived Risk. Figure 1 represents the conceptual model, designed to explore the behavioral intention associated with the adoption and usage of WhatsApp payment.

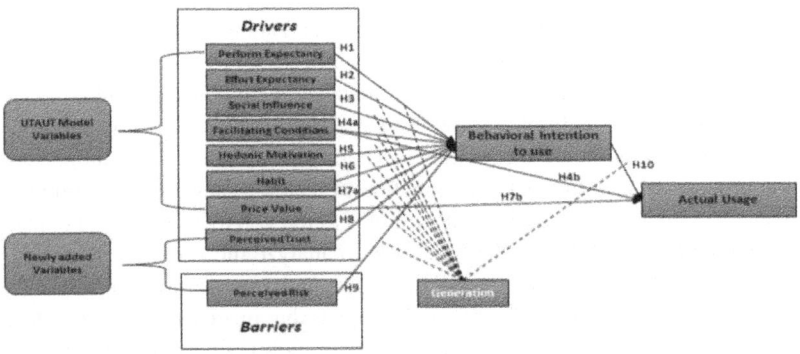

Fig. 1. Conceptual framework of the Study.

3.1 Perform Expectancy

The variable is designed to accept six Perform Expectancy (PE) elements, which are defined as the degree to which consumers believe that utilizing a specific technology will benefit them in doing specific activities. The variable of perceived usefulness from TAM is incorporated as Perform Expectancy inside UTAUT2, which builds on the TAM model. However, it is important to note that the template can be adapted to include additional or alternative factors on the specific context and requirements of study. In the present study of individual's adoption of WhatsApp payments is positively related with the people's perception of benefits from using this technology. When an individual has a higher perception of benefits from financial technologies, he or she will have a higher chance to adopt the same. Also, this study focuses on the moderating role of generation.

H1: The generation will influence the effect of perform expectancy on behavioral intention to use WhatsApp payment, with Generation Z experiencing a stronger effect.

3.2 Effort Expectancy

Effort Expectancy, as per the UTUAT2 model, relates to the level of ease associated with adopting a new technology. It is analogous to the 'Technology Acceptance Model' (TAM) component of Perceived ease of use. An individual's behavioral decision to adopt financial technologies is positively connected with their opinion that using the system would require minimum effort. Previous research indicates that effort-related characteristics are especially important in the early phases of adoption, meaning that perceived ease of use is critical in influencing consumers' intentions to embrace and utilize financial technologies [3, 4]. Thus, the next hypothesis is suggested based on the moderating effects of generation.

H2: The generation will influence the effect of effort expectancy on behavioral intention to use WhatsApp payment, with Generation Z experiencing a stronger effect.

3.3 Social Influence

In the area of technology adoption, social influence (SI) is defined as the degree to which users believe that significant members in their social circle, such as family and friends, believe they should use a given technology. In other words, it connected to an individual's perception of the influence and opinions of key persons on his or her decision to adopt a specific technology. Because people frequently weigh the advice and judgements of those they value and trust in their social network, the impression of social influence can play a substantial part in determining an individual's behavioral intention to utilize a technology. The Social Norms variable of 'Theory of Planned Behavior' is closely similar to the social influence. It means that while determining whether or not to adopt financial technology, individuals examine the viewpoints of others in their social networks, demonstrating that social influence plays a part in molding their decision-making process. When the opinion from the family and friends is positive, it will encourage the adoption of financial technologies among the people. At the same time, the reverse will impact non-adoption for the same. This study incorporates the moderating effect of generation. A study by [12] It is hypothesized that older generations are more inclined to attach greater importance to social influences when making decisions.

H3: The generation will influence the effect of social influence on behavioral intention to embrace WhatsApp payment, with Generation Y experiencing a stronger effect.

3.4 Facilitating Conditions

Resource availability and assistance required to engage in a given behavior is referred to as facilitating conditions. It can be defined as the level to which individuals believe that the technological infrastructure and overall environment are in place to facilitate the use of a specific technology. According to the UTAUT2 paradigm, facilitating conditions impacts both behavioral intention and technology usage. This research also investigates the moderating role of generations on the relation between facilitating conditions and behavioral intention, as well as the association between facilitating conditions and WhatsApp payment use. The authors suggest, based on the UTAUT model, that older generations may encounter more challenges in processing information, which can influence their adoption of technology. Furthermore, when it comes to technology adoption, older generations place a higher value on the availability of competent support than younger generations [21]. As per the discussion above, the following hypothesis is proposed;

H4a: The beneficial effect of favorable conditions on behavioral intention to embrace WhatsApp payment would be moderated by generation, with the effect being higher in Gen Z.
H4b: The favorable effect of easing limitations on WhatsApp payment usage will be moderated by generation, with the effect being larger in Gen Z.

3.5 Hedonic Motivation

Hedonic Motivation means the 'enjoyment or pleasure derived from using a technology'. It has a considerable impact on the acceptance and use of technology [20]. The current study among participants will investigate the impacts of hedonic motivation on behavioral intention for WhatsApp payment regulated by generations. According to the UTAUT2 model, younger generations exhibit a higher inclination towards seeking novelty and embracing innovation [20]. Based on above discussion the next hypothesis is formulated;

H5: The positive effect of hedonic motivation on behavioral intention to embrace WhatsApp payment would be moderated by generation, with the effect being larger among Gen Z.

3.6 Habit

The habit construct describes the degree to which customers engage in technology usage or behaviors automatically as a result of learnt patterns. It includes three main criteria: previous behavior, reflex behavior, and individual experience. This construct captures the habitual nature of individuals' interactions with technology and their tendency to perform certain behaviors without conscious effort, driven by their previous experiences and reflexive responses [21]. Individual habits influence behavioral intention and usage of social media payment systems in the area of financial technologies. And on this study this effect is moderated by generation. According to the UTAUT2 model, the authors expect the effect of habit to be strongest among older generations, especially when they have significant experience with technology [21]. Based on that, the next hypotheses are formulated;

H6: The positive impact of habit on behavioral intention to embrace WhatsApp payment will be moderated by generation, with the effect being larger for Gen Y.

3.7 Price Value

The cost and pricing structure connected with technology usage influence people's behavioral intentions to acquire and utilize that technology. In the current circumstance, when people believe that the benefits of utilizing WhatsApp payment service outweigh the monetary costs associated, the perceived value of the price has a positive influence on behavioral intention. This positive impact of price value on behavioral intention can be influenced by generational differences. According to the UTAUT2 model, the older generation is likely to be more sensitive to pricing factors due to their role as family expenditure gatekeepers, which may impact their decision-making process and adoption of technology [21]. Thus, the next hypothesis is formulated;

H7: The positive impact of price value on behavioral intention to embrace WhatsApp payment would be moderated by generation, with the effect being larger among Gen Y. **H7b**: The positive impact of pricing value on WhatsApp payment usage will be moderated by generation, therefore the effect will be larger in Gen Y.

3.8 Perceived Trust

The UTAUT2 model makes no mention of the impact of trust on technology on behavioral intention to utilize technology. Moreover, in the current study, which extends the UTAUT2 model, perceived trust is included as an additional variable in the research model. Trust is described as a subjective belief in a party's ability to fulfil promises, and this is important in risky financial transactions when system users may face financial loss. By including trust as a factor, the extended model acknowledges the crucial role trust plays in shaping individuals' intentions and behaviors when it comes to technology adoption, particularly in the context of financial transactions [5]. There are previous researches which included trust as an extended variable to the UTAUT2 model [11]. Previous research has repeatedly found a link between perceived trust and behavioral intention to adopt technology. In line with these findings, the current study seeks to evaluate the function of generation as a moderating variable between perceived trust and behavioral intention towards social media payments. The hypothesis is proposed based on the aforementioned assumptions;

H8: Generation moderates the positive impact of trust on behavioral intention to use WhatsApp payment, with Generation Y having a greater effect.

3.9 Perceived Risk

Perceived risk is an individual's subjective assessment of the potential risks connected with utilizing a particular technology. These hazards can take many forms, including financial, psychological, social, physical, and time-related dangers. It involves the perception of potential negative consequences or uncertainties that may arise from adopting and using the technology in question [24]. Existing research has showed that perceived risk has a detrimental effect on FinTech usage [14, 22]. Many empirical studies also included perceived risk as an extended variable to the UTAUT2 model [8, 13, 16, 23] and they found significant relation with behavioral intention to use technology. The main aim of this study is to investigate the impact of perceived risk on behavioral intention to usage social media payment, while accounting for the moderating function of individuals' generation. The underlying assumptions propose that younger individuals exhibit higher levels of innovativeness and are less influenced by risk perceptions. Furthermore, younger people with more expertise with financial technology are predicted to be less influenced by risk perception in their behavioral intention to use these technologies. The following hypothesis is based on these assumptions;

H9: Generation moderates the negative impact of perceived risk on behavioral intention to use WhatsApp payment, with Generation Y having a stronger influence.

3.10 Behavioral Intention

According to the source [21], behavioral intention is defined as the amount to which an individual has deliberately established intentions to engage in or refrain from a given behavior in the future. They provide a study that takes behavioral intention into account as both a dependent and independent variable. This study looks at the impact of behavioral intention on WhatsApp payment usage as an independent variable. Prior research has also looked into the impact of behavioral intention on financial technology usage [9, 25]. Furthermore, the aim of this study is to look into the moderating influence of generation in the relation between behavioral intention and use behavior. Hence, the next hypothesis is proposed;

H10: The influence of behavioral intention on actual use of WhatsApp payment will be moderated by generation.

4   Research Methodology

4.1 Context and Subjects

This study will use cross-sectional data and targeting the users of different payment technology across India. To collect the data, the Quantitative method using an online questionnaire used. The online questionnaire circulated using the Google form platform. The reason behind selecting this online method is the wide reach of payment technology users across India. The questionnaire prepared in English. A five-point liker scale was used to assess the model's variables.

4.2 Data Analysis

'The Partial Least Squares-Structural Equation Model (PLS-SEM)' was used to analyses the conceptual model in this study. Smart PLS software, namely Version 4, was used for the PLS-SEM study. The data analysis procedure was divided into two stages. The validity and reliability of the measurement model (Outer model) were investigated in the first section. 'Cronbach's alpha' and 'Composite reliability' values were used for reliability testing. Convergent and discriminant validity ratings were used to measure validity. The structural model was assessed in the next section by analyzing the coefficient of determination (R2) and path coefficients using bootstrapping. The specific findings from these analyses will be outlined in the study's subsequent parts.

4.3 Respondent's Profile and Characteristics

The selected population for the study includes people from different parts of India. After the preliminary validation, 265 valid responses were used for the analysis (N = 265). Based on the analysis, 18.5% and 81.5% of the respondents belong to generation Y and generation Z, respectively, of that, 60.75% are male and the rest female. Generation Y refers to individuals born between 1982 and 1996, while Generation Z encompasses those born between 1997 and 2012.

4.4 Measurement Model Assessment

The first stage in structural equation modelling is to assess the measurement model, also known as the outer model, for validity and reliability. In this work, Cronbach's alpha and composite values were used to measure reliability, while 'Average Variance Extracted' (AVE) values and Heterotrait-Monotrait ratio (HTMT) values were used to examine convergent and discriminant validity, respectively. The results shown in Table 1 explains that the internal consistency of the measurement model was assessed using Cronbach's alpha values ranging from 0.78 to 0.956. These values are greater than the conventional criterion of 0.7, indicating that internal consistency is satisfactory. Additionally, composite reliability (CR) values, with a recommended threshold of 0.7, ranged from 0.819 to 0.957 [27]. Consequently, the measurement model demonstrates good internal consistency based on these results.

The measurement model's convergent validity was evaluated by focusing the factor loading values and 'Average Variance Extracted' (AVE) values. Previous research [18] implies that factor loadings greater than 0.5 are desirable. As shown in Fig. 2, all factor loadings in this investigation exceeded the 0.5 threshold, demonstrating acceptable convergent validity. Table 1 also shows the AVE values, which ranged from 0.681 to 0.913. These results above the required threshold of 0.5 [6] proving the measurement model's convergent validity.

The Heterotrait-Monotrait ratio (HTMT) criteria published by Henseler and colleagues [7] were used to measure the discriminant validity of the measurement model. To establish discriminant validity, the AVE values should be less than 0.9, according to these criteria. Examining the data in Table 2, it is identified that the criteria is met, showing that the measurement model has adequate discriminant validity.

4.5 Structural Model Assessment

Following the evaluation of the measurement model, the following stage is to assess the structural model. This comprises calculating the route coefficients using bootstrapping

Table 1. Measurement model results

Variables	Cronbach's alpha	Composite reliability (RHO_A)	Composite reliability (RHO_C)	Average variance extracted (AVE)
Actual Usage	0.875	0.875	0.941	0.889
Behavioral Intention	0.943	0.943	0.963	0.897
Effort Expectancy	0.893	0.917	0.925	0.754
Facilitating Conditions	0.807	0.819	0.912	0.838
Habit	0.932	0.933	0.952	0.831
Hedonic Motivation	0.917	0.919	0.948	0.858
Perceived Risk	0.78	0.875	0.864	0.681
Perform Expectancy	0.921	0.922	0.944	0.808
Perceived Trust	0.956	0.957	0.967	0.854
Price Value	0.821	0.896	0.889	0.729
Social Influence	0.953	0.953	0.969	0.913

Table 2. Heterotrait - Monotrait (HTMT) Ratio

	AU	BI	EE	FC	HA	HM	PR	TR	PV	SI
AU										
BI	0.703									
EE	0.23	0.285								
FC	0.124	0.131	0.66							
HA	0.783	0.73	0.196	0.16						
HM	0.48	0.556	0.39	0.17	0.59					
PR	0.214	0.371	0.116	0.175	0.325	0.289				
PE	0.481	0.626	0.511	0.204	0.612	0.664	0.222			
PT	0.558	0.694	0.337	0.23	0.562	0.57	0.199	0.606		
PV	0.293	0.571	0.463	0.492	0.438	0.661	0.336	0.518	0.568	
SI	0.594	0.666	0.282	0.135	0.743	0.605	0.261	0.619	0.552	0.475

with 10,000 resamples and estimating the coefficient of determination (R2) [6]. In this study, particular attention is given to examining the moderating role of generation. Generation is treated as a categorical variable, where "0" represents Generation Y and "1" represents Generation Z.

The findings in Table 3 show that the moderating effect of generation has a substantial influence on the link between enabling conditions and actual use of WhatsApp payment. With an original sample value of 0.247, the findings indicate that the impact of facilitating conditions on actual usage is notably higher among Generation Z. As a result, hypothesis H4a receives support, suggesting that the moderating effect of generation is in line with the predicted direction.

Table 3. Result of hypotheses testing

Moderating Effects	Original sample (O)	Sample mean (M)	Standard deviation	T statistics	P* value	Decision
H1: Gen x PE -> BI	−0.094	−0.115	0.173	0.546	0.585	Not Supported
H2: Gen x EE -> BI	−0.191	−0.204	0.139	1.372	0.17	Not Supported
H3: Gen x SI -> BI	0.08	0.099	0.178	0.45	0.653	Not Supported
H4a: Gen x FC > AU	0.247	0.245	0.117	2.105	0.035	Supported
H4b: Gen x FC > BI	0.155	0.151	0.141	1.097	0.273	Not Supported
H5: Gen x HM > BI	0.063	0.062	0.146	0.429	0.668	Not Supported
H6: Gen x HA -> BI	−0.024	−0.028	0.183	0.133	0.894	Not Supported
H7a: Gen x PV > AU	−0.071	−0.057	0.17	0.418	0.676	Not Supported
H7b: Gen x PV > BI	−0.262	−0.228	0.17	1.54	0.124	Not Supported
H8: Gen x TR > BI	0.273	0.257	0.181	1.509	0.131	Not Supported
H9: Gen x PR > BI	−0.067	−0.063	0.106	0.634	0.526	Not Supported
H10: Gen x BI > AU	−0.024	−0.024	0.152	0.159	0.874	Not Supported

Note: *$p < 0.05$

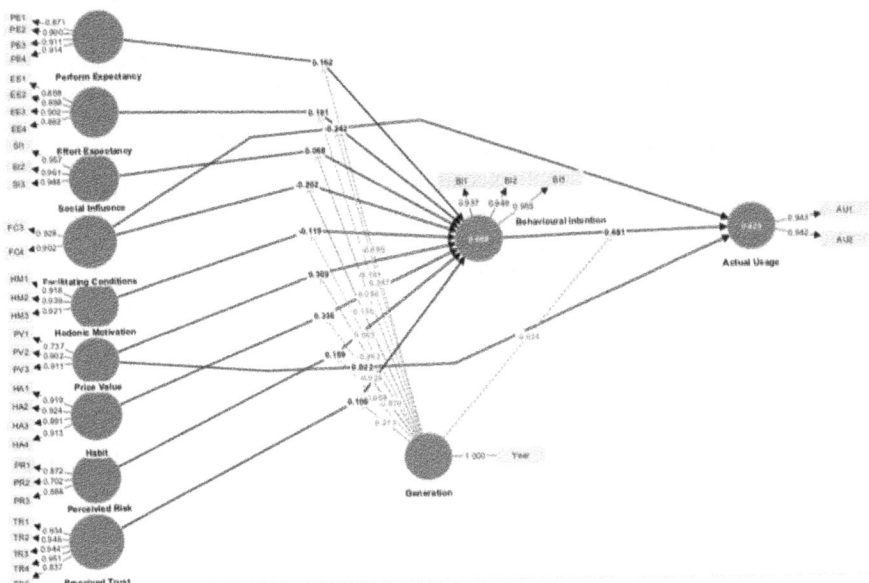

Fig. 2. PLS Algorithm Results of SEM model.

5   Discussion

The primary goal of this study is to look into the factors that determine behavioral intention and use of WhatsApp payments. Because WhatsApp payment is the only social media payment system in India, the results of this study may be generalizable. Furthermore, the study intends to investigate the moderating function of generation, specifically whether the effects of various factors on WhatsApp payment usage differ between Generation Y and Generation Z. The study attempts to provide insights into how different factors influence WhatsApp payment usage across different age groups by analyzing these generational variances.

The findings of the analysis revealed a significant moderating impact, showing that the relation between facilitating conditions and actual usage is significantly stronger among Generation Z. Generation Z's significant moderating effect on the facilitating conditions for social media payments, such as WhatsApp Payment, is evident in their strong preference for seamless and intuitive digital experiences. They expect user-friendly interfaces, heightened security measures, and transparent policies, forcing payment platforms to adapt and prioritize these factors to gain Gen Z's trust and engagement in the world of social media payments. This generational shift is reshaping the landscape of digital financial transactions and driving innovation in payment technology. These findings are congruent with the findings of a prior study [21], which demonstrated that the actual usage of a new technology is influenced by the presence of facilitating conditions, with a more pronounced effect observed among younger generations. Therefore, the current study corroborates the previous findings and provides further evidence that younger generations, such as Generation Z, are particularly influenced by the facilitating conditions in their decision to adopt and use new technologies.

It has been noted from this study results that the majority of the adoption factors are not influencing the behavioral intention of the people to use WhatsApp payment with the moderating role of generation. One of the main reasons is that people are comfortable with first-generation payment technologies like PhonePe, Paytm and Google pay. And they hesitated to move to the WhatsApp payment service.

6 Limitations and Direction for Future Research

The primary restriction of this study is that the study outcomes cannot be applied to a country that is not technologically advanced. Because a country like India, considered for high adoption of FinTech, has different characteristics. Secondly, the present study focused only on the younger generations like Gen Y and Z. Hence, future studies can be conducted by incorporating the other generations like baby boomers and Gen X.

Thirdly, this study collected data based on WhatsApp payments to identify the adoption of social media payments in India. So, we, the authors, suggest the researchers extend the scope of social media payment in future studies. Finally, the researchers should make more effort to incorporate more relevant variables, which will help to study the adoption in detail.

7 Conclusion

The current study studied the elements that function as drivers and impediments to WhatsApp payment uptake across different generations of payment technology users. According to the data, facilitating conditions emerged as the significant element affecting users' desire to use WhatsApp payment. This means that the existence of advantageous conditions is critical in enticing people to adopt this payment mechanism. These findings are important for policymakers because they provide insights into improving financial services on social media platforms.

The study also verifies the involvement of many elements in affecting behavioral intention to utilize WhatsApp payment, such as perform expectancy, effort expectancy, social influence, facilitating conditions, hedonic motivation, habit, price value, perceived trust, and perceived risk. These elements, taken together, influence users' decision-making and readiness to use this payment mechanism.

Overall, the study findings shed light on the drivers and barriers to adopting WhatsApp payment among different generations, offering valuable implications for policymakers and stakeholders aiming to improve financial services within the realm of social media platforms.

References

1. Boonsiritomachai, W., Pitchayadejanant, K.: Determinants affecting mobile banking adoption by generation Y based on the Unified Theory of Acceptance and Use of Technology Model

modified by the Technology Acceptance Model concept. Kasetsart J. Soc. Sci. **40**, 349–358 (2017). https://doi.org/10.1016/j.kjss.2017.10.005

2. Ceci, L.: Countries with most WhatsApp users 2019. https://www.statista.com/statistics/289778/countries-with-the-most-facebook-users/

3. Davis, F.D.: Perceived usefulness, perceived ease of use, and user acceptance of information technology. MIS Q. **13**, 319–340 (2019). https://doi.org/10.2307/249008

4. Davis, F.D., Bagozzi, R.P., Warshaw, P.R.: User acceptance of computer technology: a comparison of two theoretical models. Manag. Sci. **35**, 982–1003 (1989). https://doi.org/10.1287/mnsc.35.8.982

5. Gefen, D., Karahanna, E., Straub, D.W.: Trust and TAM in online shopping: an integrated model. MIS Q. **27**, 51–90 (2003). https://doi.org/10.2307/30036519

6. Hair, J., Hollingsworth, C.L., Randolph, A.B., Chong, A.Y.L.: An updated and expanded assessment of PLS-SEM in information systems research. Ind. Manag. Data Syst. **117**, 442–458 (2017). https://doi.org/10.1108/imds-04-2016-0130

7. Henseler, J., Ringle, C.M., Sarstedt, M.: A new criterion for assessing discriminant validity in variance-based structural equation modelling. J. Acad. Mark. Sci. **43**, 115–135 (2015)

8. Huang, C.-Y., Kao, Y.-S.: UTAUT2 based predictions of factors influencing the technology acceptance of phablets by DNP. Math. Probl. Eng. **2015**, 1–23 (2015). https://doi.org/10.1155/2015/603747

9. Huang, Y., Liu, W.: The impact of privacy concern on users' usage intention of mobile payment. In: 2012 International Conference on Information Management, Innovation Management and Industrial Engineering (2012). https://doi.org/10.1109/iciii.2012.6339927

10. Tarigan, Z.J.H., Jonathan, M., Siagian, H., Basana, S.R.: The effect of e-WOM through intention to use technology and social media community for mobile payments during the COVID-19. Int. J. Data Netw. Sci. **6**, 563–572 (2022). https://doi.org/10.5267/j.ijdns.2021.11.008

11. Manrai, R., Gupta, K.P.: Integrating UTAUT with trust and perceived benefits to explain user adoption of mobile payments. In: Kapur, P.K., Singh, O., Khatri, S.K., Verma, A.K. (eds.) Strategic System Assurance and Business Analytics. AA, pp. 109–121. Springer, Singapore (2020). https://doi.org/10.1007/978-981-15-3647-2_9

12. Morris, M.G., Venkatesh, V.: Age differences in technology adoption decisions: implications for a changing work force. Pers. Psychol. **53**, 375–403 (2000). https://doi.org/10.1111/j.1744-6570.2000.tb00206.x

13. Park, J., Amendah, E., Lee, Y., Hyun, H.: M-payment service: interplay of perceived risk, benefit, and trust in service adoption. Hum. Factors Ergon. Manuf. Serv. Ind. **29**, 31–43 (2018). https://doi.org/10.1002/hfm.20750

14. Hongxia, P., Xianhao, X., Weidan, L.: Drivers and barriers in the acceptance of mobile payment in China. In: 2011 International Conference on E-Business and E-Government (ICEE) (2011). https://doi.org/10.1109/icebeg.2011.5887081

15. Raman, P., Aashish, K.: To continue or not to continue: a structural analysis of antecedents of mobile payment systems in India. Int. J. Bank Mark. **39**, 242–271 (2021). https://doi.org/10.1108/ijbm-04-2020-0167

16. Slade, E., Williams, M., Dwivdei, Y.: Extending UTAUT2 to explore consumer adoption of mobile payments. In: Academy for Information Systems Conference Proceedings, pp. 1–23 (2013)

17. Slade, E., Williams, M., Dwivedi, Y., Piercy, N.: Exploring consumer adoption of proximity mobile payments. J. Strateg. Mark. **23**, 209–223 (2014). https://doi.org/10.1080/0965254x.2014.914075

18. Truong, Y., McColl, R.: Intrinsic motivations, self-esteem, and luxury goods consumption. J. Retail. Consum. Serv. **18**, 555–561 (2011). https://doi.org/10.1016/j.jretconser.2011.08.004

19. Upadhyay, P., Jahanyan, S.: Analysing user perspective on the factors affecting use intention of mobile based transfer payment. Internet Res. **26**, 38–56 (2016). https://doi.org/10.1108/intr-05-2014-0143
20. Venkatesh, V., Morris, M.G., Davis, G.B., Davis, F.D.: User acceptance of information technology: toward a unified view. MIS Q. **27**, 425–478 (2003)
21. Venkatesh, V., Thong, J.Y.L., Xu, X.: Consumer acceptance and use of information technology: extending the unified theory of acceptance and use of technology. MIS Q. **36**, 157–178 (2012)
22. Verkijika, S.F.: Factors influencing the adoption of mobile commerce applications in Cameroon. Telematics Inform. **35**, 1665–1674 (2018). https://doi.org/10.1016/j.tele.2018.04.012
23. Yang, S., Lu, Y., Gupta, S., Cao, Y., Zhang, R.: Mobile payment services adoption across time: an empirical study of the effects of behavioural beliefs, social influences, and personal traits. Comput. Hum. Behav. **28**, 129–142 (2012). https://doi.org/10.1016/j.chb.2011.08.019
24. Zhang, L., Zhu, J., Liu, Q.: A meta-analysis of mobile commerce adoption and the moderating effect of culture. Comput. Hum. Behav. **28**, 1902–1911 (2012). https://doi.org/10.1016/j.chb.2012.05.008
25. Zhou, T.: Examining mobile banking user adoption from the perspectives of trust and flow experience. Inf. Technol. Manag. **13**, 27–37 (2011). https://doi.org/10.1007/s10799-011-0111-8
26. Ernst & Young: Global FinTech Adoption Index 2019 (2019)
27. Liébana-Cabanillas, F., Marinković, V., Kalinić, Z.: A SEM-neural network approach for predicting antecedents of m-commerce acceptance. Int. J. Inf. Manag. **37**, 14–24 (2017). https://doi.org/10.1016/j.ijinfomgt.2016.10.008

HGCSO: Energy Efficient Multi-objective Task Scheduling in Cloud-Fog Environment

Santhosh Kumar Medishetti[1]([✉]) [iD], Vamsheedhar Reddy Pillareddy[2] [iD],
Bushra Muneeb[3], Sudha Rani Palakuri[4], Uma Maheshwari Garela[4],
Rakesh Kumar Donthi[5] [iD], G. Soma Sekhar[6] [iD], Ganesh Reddy Karri[1],
Baji Babu Indurthi[1], and K. Vamshi Krishna[1] [iD]

[1] VIT-AP University, Amaravathi, A.P., India
{santhosh.21phd7113,indurthi.20bcn7099,
vamshikrishna.20phd7088}@vitap.ac.in
[2] Sridevi Women's Engineering College, Hyderabad, T.S., India
[3] Princeton Institute of Engineering and Technology for Women, Hyderabad, T.S., India
[4] Sreyas Institute of Engineering and Technology, Hyderabad, T.S., India
[5] GITAM Deemed to be University, Hyderabad, T.S., India
rdonthi@gitam.edu
[6] Vardhaman College of Engineering, Hyderabad, T.S., India

Abstract. In the ever-evolving realm of cloud-fog computing, effective Task Scheduling (TS) plays a crucial role in maximizing resource utilization and enhancing overall system performance. This paper introduces a novel approach to TS using a hybrid algorithm that combines Genetic Algorithms (GA) and Cat Swarm Optimization (CSO). The proposed Hybrid Genetic Cat Swarm Optimization (HGCSO) algorithm harnesses the strengths of GA for global exploration and CSO for its unique swarm-based search mechanism. The integration of these algorithms aims to address the complexities of cloud-fog computing environments, characterized by heterogeneous resources and varying task requirements. The TS problem is formulated as an optimization challenge, incorporating objectives such as reducing makespan, response time, and energy consumption. The HGCSO algorithm iteratively refines solutions by employing genetic operators for diversity and swarm-based mechanisms for local refinement. Thorough simulations have been carried out to assess the performance of the algorithm, juxtaposing it against conventional scheduling algorithms as well as standalone Genetic Algorithm (GA) and Cuckoo Search Optimization (CSO) approaches. The outcomes reveal that the suggested HGCSO algorithm surpasses its counterparts, showcasing improvements in makespan time, response time, and a notable reduction in energy usage by 22%, 18%, and 28%, respectively. This research provides significant insights into the progress of bio-inspired algorithms in tackling the complex challenges of Task Scheduling (TS) within contemporary computing paradigms.

Keywords: cloud-fog computing · efficient task scheduling · resource utilization · Genetic Algorithms · Cat Swarm Optimization

© ICST Institute for Computer Sciences, Social Informatics and Telecommunications Engineering 2024
Published by Springer Nature Switzerland AG 2024. All Rights Reserved
O. Castillo et al. (Eds.): PerSOM 2023, LNICST 517, pp. 16–38, 2024.
https://doi.org/10.1007/978-3-031-66044-3_2

1 Introduction

In the rapidly evolving landscape of Task Scheduling (TS) in cloud-fog computing (CFC) the effective orchestration of computational tasks is paramount for optimizing resource utilization and enhancing overall system performance [1]. TS is a critical aspect of this paradigm, involves judiciously assigning computational tasks to available resources, considering factors such as response time, energy consumption, and load balancing [2]. Addressing the intricacies of these dynamic and heterogeneous environments requires innovative approaches that can adapt to varying workloads and resource availabilities.

The introduction to Cloud Fog Computing (CFC) in the realm of TS sets the stage for understanding the dynamic and distributed computing environment that shapes modern computational landscapes [3]. CFC represents an innovative paradigm that extends the capabilities of CC by introducing edge or fog nodes closer to end-users and devices. This hierarchical architecture, comprising cloud data centers, fog nodes, and end-user devices, aims to address the challenges of latency-sensitive applications, varying workloads, and the need for efficient resource utilization.

In the realm of task scheduling, the introduction of CFC brings forth unique challenges and opportunities. The distribution of resources across cloud and fog nodes necessitates the development of sophisticated scheduling algorithms capable of optimizing task allocation in a heterogeneous and dynamic environment [4]. The proximity of fog nodes to end-users enhances the potential for low-latency processing, making CFC particularly suitable for applications with stringent performance requirements. The introduction sets the context for exploring how task scheduling in CFC environments is a critical aspect of ensuring optimal performance, responsiveness, and resource utilization across the distributed infrastructure.

Moreover, the introduction delves into the key characteristics of CFC that influence task scheduling strategies. These may include the need for adaptability to dynamic workloads, energy-efficient resource allocation, and the seamless integration of CFC resources. As CFC continues to gain prominence in various industries, the introduction to task scheduling within this paradigm emphasizes the importance of developing novel approaches and algorithms that cater to the intricacies of this emerging computing paradigm. It serves as a call to explore innovative solutions to enhance the efficiency of task scheduling in the evolving landscape of Cloud Fog Computing.

Genetic Algorithms (GAs) constitute a potent category of optimization algorithms inspired by principles derived from natural selection and genetics. Originating in the 1960s through the work of John Holland, genetic algorithms have gained widespread acclaim for their efficacy in systematically exploring and optimizing intricate solution spaces across diverse domains [5]. Rooted in the evolutionary processes observed in nature, genetic algorithms model populations of individuals that evolve over successive generations, employing mechanisms such as selection, crossover, and mutation.

At its essence, a genetic algorithm functions by treating potential solutions as individual chromosomes that encode potential resolutions to a given problem. Employing a process akin to natural selection, individuals with advantageous traits (fitness) are more apt to be chosen for reproduction, aligning with the fundamental survival-of-the-fittest principle. The crossover operation involves the exchange of genetic information among selected individuals, resulting in new offspring with amalgamated characteristics. Furthermore, the mutation mechanism introduces random alterations to the genetic material, infusing diversity into the population. Genetic algorithms find application in a myriad of fields, including optimization, machine learning, scheduling, and parameter tuning, among others. Their versatility and effectiveness stem from their ability to navigate large and complex solution spaces, adapt to dynamic environments, and discover optimal and its closer to the near optimal solutions to the complex problems.

Cat Swarm Optimization (CSO) algorithm is a bio-inspired optimization technique that draws inspiration from the collective behavior and hunting strategies of cats. Introduced as a heuristic optimization algorithm, CSO leverages the inherent swarming and searching behaviors observed in feline species to efficiently explore and exploit solution spaces [6]. The algorithm was proposed as an alternative to conventional optimization approaches, aiming to overcome challenges posed by complex and dynamic problem domains. Inspired by the coordinated movements and communication observed in cat colonies, CSO operates on the principle of collaboration and information sharing among individuals [7]. Each potential solution to the optimization problem is represented as a cat, and the algorithm navigates the search space by imitating the hunting behaviors of cats, such as stalking prey, avoiding obstacles, and communicating with fellow cats [8].

CSO's appeal lies in its simplicity, adaptability to various problem types, and capacity to find optimal and its closer to the near optimal solutions in complex and dynamic environments. The algorithm's efficiency arises from the synergistic cooperation among individual cats, enabling it to navigate large solution spaces and discover promising regions efficiently. As a relatively recent addition to the family of swarm intelligence algorithms, CSO has found applications in diverse fields, including optimization problems, image processing, data clustering, and machine learning. This introduction lays the foundation for understanding the underlying principles of the Cat Swarm Optimization algorithm, setting the stage for further exploration into its mechanisms, applications, and real-world impact. Subsequent sections will delve into the intricacies of CSO, exploring its components, methodologies, and showcasing instances where it has demonstrated its efficacy in solving complex optimization challenges.

The objective of this study is to transform TS methodologies in CFC environments by introducing an innovative Hybrid Genetic Cat Swarm Optimization (HGCSO) algorithm. The central goal is to elevate the effectiveness of resource allocation by harnessing the combined strengths of genetic algorithms and cat swarm optimization. The overarching aim is to minimize makespan, optimize response time, and achieve load balancing across fog and cloud resources, ensuring a responsive and sustainable computing environment.

The particular objectives of this study are to develop and implement the HGCSO algorithm, tailoring it to the complexities of cloud-fog computing scenarios. Through the algorithm, the research aims to optimize key performance metrics, including makespan and response time, while achieving load balancing to enhance overall system performance. Furthermore, the study seeks to minimize energy consumption, contributing to the sustainability of cloud-fog environments. By evaluating the algorithm's adaptability to dynamic changes and real-world scenarios, this research aims to present a comprehensive and innovative solution to the challenges of TS in contemporary cloud-fog computing landscapes.

This paper explores the realm of TS in CFC and introduces a cutting-edge solution leveraging the Hybrid Genetic Cat Swarm Optimization (HGCSO) algorithm. As cloud and fog computing environments are characterized by the coexistence of diverse resources, ranging from powerful cloud servers to edge devices with limited capabilities, devising an intelligent scheduling mechanism becomes imperative. The HGCSO algorithm represents a fusion of Genetic Algorithms (GA) and Cat Swarm Optimization (CSO), combining global exploration capabilities with swarm-based local search strategies.

The integration of GA and CSO aims to harness the synergies of these bio-inspired algorithms, addressing the challenges posed by the dynamic and heterogeneous nature of CFC. By formulating the TS problem as an optimization challenge, the HGCSO algorithm seeks to minimize makespan, response time, and energy consumption. Through this research, we endeavor to contribute to the advancement of TS methodologies, offering a promising solution that adapts to the complexities inherent in contemporary computing environments. The subsequent sections delve into the formulation of the problem, the intricacies of the HGCSO algorithm, simulation results, and a comprehensive analysis of its performance in cloud-fog task scheduling.

The structure of the paper outline is as follows, Sect. 1 and Sect. 2 explains the introduction and related work. Next, Sect. 3 describes the research methodology and Sect. 4 explains the brief discussion of the results. Finally, Sect. 5 concludes the study.

2 Related Works

CC has revolutionized the landscape of information technology by offering scalable and on-demand access to computing resources. As the demand for cloud services continues to surge, efficient task scheduling has become a critical aspect for optimizing resource utilization and meeting performance objectives. TS involves the allocation of computational tasks to appropriate resources within the cloud infrastructure, aiming to enhance overall system efficiency, reduce latency, and ensure optimal utilization of available resources.

A literature survey in task scheduling involves a comprehensive review and analysis of existing works in the field of TS. It is a fundamental step in the research process that aims to provide a thorough understanding of the current state-of-the-art, identify gaps in knowledge, and gain insights into the various methodologies, algorithms, and approaches employed in the domain. In the context of TS in CFC environments, a literature survey is essential to stay abreast of the latest advancements and challenges specific to this dynamic and distributed computing landscape.

The survey typically begins with the identification of key research areas and relevant topics related to task scheduling. This involves exploring seminal works, recent publications, and seminal papers in reputable journals and conference proceedings. Researchers delve into the methodologies and algorithms proposed by various scholars, examining their strengths, limitations, and the specific application scenarios for which they are designed. The literature survey aims to establish a foundation for the research endeavor by providing a context for the proposed work, enabling researchers to build upon existing knowledge and contribute novel insights to the field.

In the context of CFC, the literature survey may cover topics such as optimization techniques, load balancing strategies, energy-aware scheduling, and adaptability to dynamic workloads. The survey helps researchers identify gaps in current knowledge, areas that require further exploration, and potential avenues for innovation. Additionally, it allows researchers to critically assess the applicability of existing task scheduling algorithms to the unique challenges posed by CFC environments, fostering a well-informed and targeted approach to advancing of the current state-of-the-art in TS research.

The field of cloud task scheduling has witnessed extensive research and development due to its pivotal role in addressing challenges such as load balancing, energy efficiency, and response time optimization. The efficient allocation of tasks across cloud resources is essential for meeting user demands and achieving cost-effective utilization of cloud resources. Numerous task scheduling techniques and algorithms have been put forth and examined to tackle the dynamic characteristics of cloud environments, diverse application workloads, and the heterogeneous nature of cloud resources. The purpose of this literature survey is to present a thorough overview of prominent TS techniques in CC. It delineates the parameters taken into consideration, intrinsic limitations, and the simulation environments frequently utilized for their assessment.

Understanding the nuances of existing task scheduling methodologies is crucial for researchers, practitioners, and system architects seeking to design and implement robust cloud-based systems. By examining and categorizing these techniques, we can discern patterns, identify deficiencies, and pinpoint opportunities for enhancement in the existing state-of-the-art. The subsequent sections of this literature survey will delve into specific scheduling techniques, offering insights into their strengths, weaknesses, and potential applications in the evolving landscape of CC (Table 1).

Table 1. Detailed analysis of existing works

Ref. No.	Technique	Parameters Used	Key Findings/Contributions	Limitations
[9]	DAPSO	Workload, Resource Availability, Energy Efficiency, Latency	Improved task scheduling efficiency, reduced makespan, and energy-efficient resource allocation	Limited real-world case studies and applications. Validation required in diverse cloud and fog computing scenarios
[10]	PSO	Varying Task Priorities, Resource Allocation Strategies, Latency Requirements	Enhanced adaptability in dynamic cloud and fog environments, leading to improved task response times and energy efficiency	Lack of comparative analysis with existing optimization techniques in the field. Further benchmarking is needed
[11]	MOSA	Heterogeneous Resource Capacities, Task Distribution, Energy Efficiency Constraints	Optimal resource allocation strategies that balance workloads, minimize makespan, and meet stringent latency requirements	Scalability challenges for large-scale cloud and fog environments. Research scope primarily theoretical; real-world applicability remains untested

(continued)

Table 1. (*continued*)

Ref. No.	Technique	Parameters Used	Key Findings/Contributions	Limitations
[12]	EPSO	Dynamic Workloads, Adaptive Scheduling, Resource Heterogeneity, Energy-Efficient Scheduling	Improved adaptability to changing workloads and dynamic resource allocation, leading to reduced task response times and energy savings	Lack of standardized parameters and benchmarks for MAO-based task scheduling. Further research required for parameter tuning and optimization
[13]	HEFT	Latency-Aware Scheduling, Real-Time Task Allocation, Energy-Aware Scheduling	Efficient real-time task scheduling in cloud and fog computing, meeting stringent latency requirements and optimizing energy usage	Challenges related to the practical implementation and integration of MAO in existing cloud and fog computing systems
[14]	MSDE	Load Balancing, Resource Utilization, Fault Tolerance, Regenerative Adaptability	Enhanced load balancing, resource utilization, and adaptability to system failures. Potential to revolutionize cloud and fog computing task scheduling	Lack of industry-standard tools and platforms for MAO implementation. Dependency on specialized software for experimentation
[15]	LTRA	Bio-Inspired Resource Allocation, Regenerative Capacity, Latency Optimization	Novel bio-inspired approach for cloud and fog computing task scheduling, leveraging the adaptability of the Mexican axolotl. Potential to address the challenges of dynamic workloads and resource heterogeneity	Limited research on the robustness and scalability of the MAO algorithm. Uncertainty regarding its practical applicability in real-world cloud and fog computing scenarios
[16]	TOPSIS	Scalability, Hybrid Scheduling Strategies, Comprehensive Resource Management	Promising insights into scalable cloud and fog computing task scheduling. Potential contributions to the field of bio-inspired optimization	Absence of standardized benchmarks for MAO's performance evaluation in cloud and fog computing contexts. Unclear integration pathways with existing cloud and fog computing infrastructures
[17]	OBDFA	Workload Distribution, Load Balancing, Energy Conservation, Real-Time Responsiveness	Potential to minimize task response times, improve energy efficiency, and meet latency requirements in cloud and fog computing environments	Validation of the MAO algorithm's performance under various workloads and cloud-fog configurations is pending. Real-world deployment and benchmarking required to ascertain practical feasibility
[18]	GA-DE	Multi-Objective Optimization, Resource Allocation Constraints, Dynamic Resource Provisioning	Potential to support multi-objective optimization in cloud and fog task scheduling, enhancing resource allocation and adaptability	Theoretical nature of current research; limited experimentation and validation in live cloud-fog systems. Ongoing concerns regarding optimization performance and algorithm robustness

(*continued*)

Table 1. (*continued*)

Ref. No.	Technique	Parameters Used	Key Findings/Contributions	Limitations
[19]	HBBOG	Hybrid Optimization Strategies, Genetic Algorithm Combination, Regenerative Adaptation	Potential to combine MAO with other optimization techniques for superior results. Early findings suggest the adaptability of MAO in complex cloud-fog computing environments	Need for additional research to validate the efficacy of hybrid optimization approaches. Performance evaluation is contingent on a broader set of experiments and case studies
[20]	IDOA	Makespan, degree of imbalance, VM Failure rate	Decreasing makespan by increasing resource utilization	Confirmation of the IDOA algorithm's performance across diverse workloads and cloud-fog configurations is yet to be completed. Real-world deployment and benchmarking are essential steps to determine its practical viability
[8]	EEOA	Makespan, cost, energy consumption	Improved adaptability within dynamic cloud and fog landscapes, resulting in enhanced task response times and increased energy efficiency	The lack of established benchmarks for evaluating EEOA performance in cloud and fog computing scenarios is evident. Additionally, the integration pathways with existing cloud and fog computing infrastructures remain uncertain
[21]	NSGA-II	Makespan, cost, execution time and response time	The proposed approach is good at reducing the cost while scheduling the tasks and also experimental setup shown good amount of makespan time reduction	Research on the robustness and scalability of the AGWO algorithm is currently limited, and there is uncertainty regarding its practical applicability in real-world cloud and fog computing scenarios

3   Research Methodology

3.1   System Architecture

TS in the era of CFC and edge computing demands a sophisticated and adaptive system architecture that can efficiently allocate computational tasks across diverse and distributed resources. The cloud-fog-edge three-tier system architecture provides a comprehensive framework to address the complexities associated with these heterogeneous environments. This structure includes the cloud layer, the fog layer, and the edge layer, with each layer having a unique role in coordinating task scheduling processes.

System architecture in task scheduling refers to the design and organization of the underlying computational infrastructure that facilitates the scheduling of tasks within a computing environment. The architecture defines the arrangement of hardware and software components, communication protocols, and the overall structure of the system that enables effective task scheduling. In Cloud Fog Computing (CFC), where resources are distributed across cloud and fog nodes, the system architecture plays a crucial role in orchestrating the allocation of computational tasks and optimizing the utilization of resources.

The architecture typically comprises cloud data centers, fog nodes, and end-user devices, forming a hierarchical structure that reflects the multi-tiered nature of CFC environments. Cloud data centers house powerful computing resources, while fog nodes are distributed closer to the edge of the network, providing low-latency processing capabilities. End-user devices connect to these nodes and centers to access computational services. The architecture should support seamless communication and coordination among these components to ensure efficient task scheduling.

Moreover, the system architecture defines the communication protocols and data exchange mechanisms between different elements of the computing environment. Efficient data transfer and communication are critical for sharing task information, allocating resources, and coordinating the execution of tasks. The architecture should be designed to handle the dynamic and heterogeneous nature of CFC environments, adapting to changing workloads, network conditions, and resource availability. In essence, a well-architected system is pivotal for the successful implementation of advanced task scheduling algorithms, contributing to enhanced performance and resource management in Cloud Fog Computing scenarios (Fig. 1).

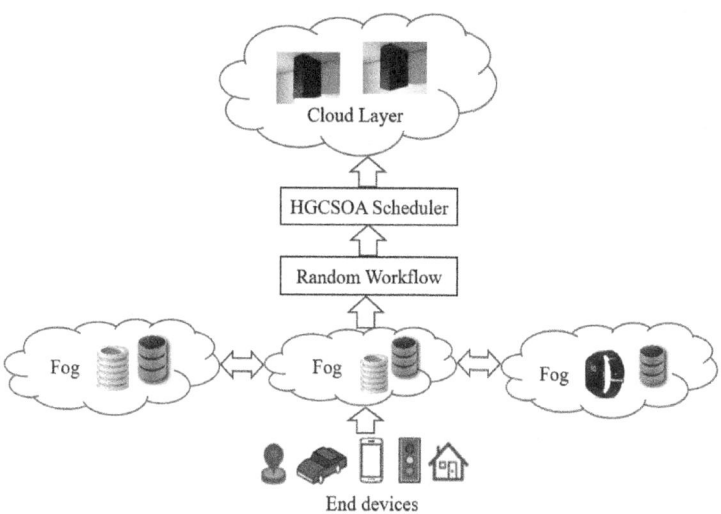

Fig. 1. System architecture

1. **Cloud Layer:** The cloud layer constitutes the upper tier of the architecture and serves as the primary repository of extensive computational resources. It encompasses data centres housing powerful servers capable of handling substantial workloads. In particular, TS, the cloud layer manages global optimization through the hybrid Genetic-Cat Swarm Optimization Algorithm (G-CSOA). The Genetic Algorithm (GA) component explores the expansive solution space, while the Cat Swarm Optimization (CSO) component refines local search and adaptability. The cloud layer's primary responsibility

is to facilitate the efficient distribution of tasks across the fog and edge layers, ensuring optimal utilization of cloud resources.

$$T_{CN} = (CN_1, CN_2, ...CN_n) \tag{1}$$

where T_{CN} denotes the total cloud nodes and $CN_1,...CN_n$ denotes Cloud nodes begins from 1 to n.

2. **Fog Layer:** Situated between the cloud and edge layers, the fog layer signifies a decentralized computing environment that brings computational resources in proximity to the network's edge. This layer is particularly well-suited for processing tasks with low-latency requirements. In the task scheduling architecture, the fog layer acts as an intermediary, receiving task allocations from the cloud layer and further optimizing them based on proximity and real-time conditions. The hybrid G-CSOA adapts to the dynamic fog environment, considering parameters such as workload fluctuations and network conditions. This layer ensures responsive and efficient task execution in proximity to end-users and devices.

$$T_{FN} = (FN_1, FN_2, ...FN_n) \tag{2}$$

3. **Edge Layer:** The edge layer forms the bottom tier of the architecture, comprising devices and sensors located at the network's edge. This layer is critical for handling tasks with stringent latency constraints and real-time processing requirements. The edge layer collaborates with the fog layer to execute tasks locally whenever possible, reducing the need for round-trip communication to distant cloud resources. The hybrid G-CSOA continues to play a role in optimizing task scheduling decisions for the edge layer, considering factors such as device capabilities, energy constraints, and real-time demands.

$$T_{Nodes} = C_{Nodes} \cup F_{Nodes} \tag{3}$$

The cloud-fog-edge three-tier system architecture, combined with the Hybrid Genetic-Cat Swarm Optimization Algorithm, provides a holistic and adaptive solution TS in CFC environments. Leveraging the capabilities of cloud, fog, and edge computing layers, this architecture provides a dynamic and responsive framework for optimal task allocation within the ever-changing landscape of cloud-fog-edge computing.

3.2 Random Workflow

The term random workflow in the context of TS in CFC using a HGCSO algorithm refers to the unpredictable and dynamic nature of incoming tasks or workloads. The role of random workflows is significant and multifaceted in the task scheduling process. These are the several aspects of the importance of considering random workflows in this context:

The incorporation of random workflows in task scheduling represents a departure from traditional deterministic approaches, introducing stochastic elements to optimize resource allocation and enhance system efficiency. One key advantage lies in load balancing, where the randomness in task assignment helps distribute computational workloads more evenly across nodes. This dynamic allocation prevents node overloading and contributes to a more uniform utilization of computational resources. In dynamic computing environments characterized by varying workloads, the adaptability afforded by random workflow scheduling becomes crucial, ensuring a balanced distribution of tasks and minimizing the impact of unpredictable fluctuations in demand.

Additionally, random workflow scheduling enhances fault tolerance by preventing task concentration on specific nodes. In the event of a node failure, the random distribution of tasks ensures that the system's impact is dispersed rather than concentrated, thereby bolstering the overall robustness and reliability of the computing environment. Moreover, this approach facilitates the exploration of a broader solution space in optimization scenarios. By introducing randomness, the system can explore different configurations, potentially leading to the discovery of more optimal solutions. This is particularly relevant in situations where the objective function or optimization criteria are not well-defined or may change dynamically.

Furthermore, the utilization of random workflows contributes to security and anonymity in task scheduling. The unpredictability introduced by random assignment makes it more challenging for potential attackers or unauthorized entities to discern scheduling patterns, thereby enhancing the security posture of the system. The diversity introduced by random task scheduling is also advantageous in scenarios where varied task execution patterns are desired for purposes such as resource testing, performance evaluation, or workload simulation. In summary, the strategic use of random workflows in task scheduling offers a multifaceted approach to address load balancing, fault tolerance, solution space exploration, security, and diversity in computational environments.

In the realm of TS, the utilization of a random workflow introduces an element of unpredictability and diversity to the execution of a set of tasks represented by $T = \{t1, t2,..., tn\}$. The representation of these tasks using a Directed Acyclic Graph (DAG) is a common approach, where nodes in the graph represent individual tasks, and edges depict the dependencies among them. In a random workflow, the order of task execution is not predetermined, introducing an element of variability in the scheduling process. This stochastic approach can be particularly beneficial in scenarios where task execution times are uncertain, and an adaptive strategy is needed to handle dynamic changes in the workload or resource availability.

The DAG representation of the task set provides a visual depiction of the interdependencies among tasks, guiding the scheduler in making informed decisions. In a random workflow setting, the scheduler faces the challenge of determining an efficient order of task execution that minimizes makespan, optimizes resource utilization, and considers other performance metrics. The randomness injected into the scheduling process adds flexibility, enabling the system to adapt to evolving conditions and uncertainties. While traditional deterministic scheduling approaches may struggle in dynamic environments, the random workflow approach provides a means to explore diverse scheduling solutions, potentially improving the system's ability to handle varying workloads and resource constraints.

Overall, the integration of a random workflow in TS, especially when represented through a DAG, offers a flexible and adaptive strategy. It allows schedulers to explore a range of scheduling solutions, considering uncertainties and variations in task execution times. This stochastic approach can enhance the robustness and responsiveness of task scheduling systems in dynamic computing environments such as cloud, fog, or edge computing (Fig. 2).

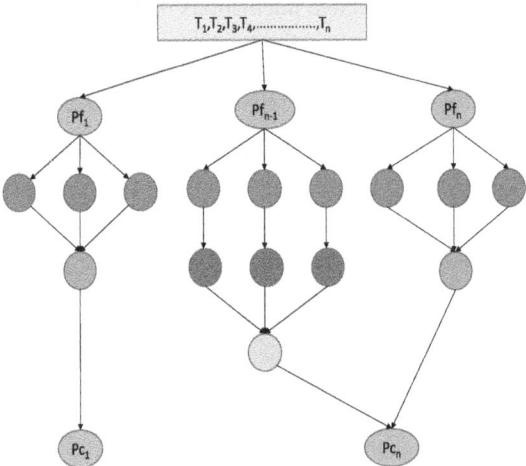

Fig. 2. Task random workflow

1. **Dynamic Workload Simulation:** Random workflows serve as a means to simulate dynamic and unpredictable workloads that cloud-fog systems might encounter in real-world scenarios. By incorporating randomness in the generation of task requests and their associated characteristics (e.g., execution time, resource requirements), researchers can create realistic workload scenarios. This enables a thorough evaluation of the scheduling algorithm's adaptability and responsiveness to changing conditions, such as sudden spikes in demand or varying computational requirements.
2. **Algorithm Robustness Testing:** The inclusion of random workflows in the task scheduling simulation helps assess the robustness of the Hybrid Genetic-Cat Swarm Optimization algorithm. Randomized workloads can stress-test the scheduling algorithm by introducing variability and unpredictability, challenging the algorithm to make effective decisions in diverse and dynamic scenarios. This testing is crucial for ensuring that the algorithm performs well under a wide range of conditions and maintains efficiency in the face of unexpected fluctuations in task arrivals and resource demands.
3. **Adaptability and Real-Time Decision Making:** Random workflows mimic the uncertainty inherent in real-world cloud-fog computing environments. The Hybrid G-CSO algorithm must be capable of adapting to sudden changes in workload patterns or resource availability. By introducing randomness in task scheduling scenarios, researchers can evaluate how well the algorithm dynamically adjusts its decisions to optimize task allocation, considering factors like load balancing, energy efficiency, and response time, even in the presence of unforeseen variations.
4. **Scenario Diversity Exploration:** The inclusion of random workflows allows researchers to explore a diverse set of scenarios. This diversity is essential for gaining

insights into the algorithm's performance across a spectrum of workload conditions. Understanding how the Hybrid G-CSO algorithm behaves in response to random workflows helps researchers identify its strengths, weaknesses, and areas for improvement. This information is crucial for refining the algorithm and enhancing its overall efficacy in real-world cloud-fog computing applications.

5. **Benchmarking and Comparison:** Random workflows provide a standardized approach to benchmarking and comparing different scheduling algorithms. Researchers can use common sets of randomly generated workloads to evaluate and compare the performance of the Hybrid G-CSO algorithm against other state-of-the-art scheduling approaches. This benchmarking process helps establish the algorithm's competitiveness and showcases its ability to outperform or match the performance of alternative solutions across various workload scenarios.

The role of random workflows in task scheduling using a Hybrid Genetic-Cat Swarm Optimization algorithm is pivotal for realistically simulating the dynamic nature of cloud-fog computing environments. Random workloads enable comprehensive testing, robustness assessment, and scenario exploration, ultimately contributing to the algorithm's adaptability and effectiveness in handling the uncertainties inherent in real-world computing scenarios.

3.3 Problem Formulation

The primary objective of the TS in CFC is to balance the distribution of computational tasks to available resources, considering factors such as load balancing, energy efficiency, and response time. The HGCSO algorithm is employed to find an efficient and adaptive solution that can dynamically adjust to the dynamic and heterogeneous nature of CFC environments.

Problem formulation in task scheduling involves defining the essential components and constraints of the scheduling challenge, providing a clear framework for devising effective scheduling solutions. At its core, task scheduling aims to allocate computational tasks to resources in a way that optimizes specific objectives, such as minimizing makespan, reducing response time, or enhancing resource utilization. The formulation process typically begins by identifying the key elements of the scheduling problem, including the tasks to be executed, the available resources, and the dependencies or constraints among tasks.

A critical aspect of problem formulation is the representation of tasks and resources. Tasks may have varying execution times, priorities, and interdependencies, while resources may differ in processing capabilities and availability. The formulation must capture these characteristics accurately to create a model that mirrors the complexities of the real-world scheduling scenario. Additionally, constraints, such as precedence relationships, resource constraints, and deadlines, must be explicitly defined. The problem formulation also considers the optimization criteria, whether it's minimizing the total execution time, balancing resource loads, or satisfying specific quality-of-service requirements.

After identifying the components, mathematical models, algorithms, or heuristics can be employed to discover optimal or nearly optimal solutions to the scheduling problem. Effective problem formulation lays the foundation for developing appropriate algorithms and methodologies tailored to the specific characteristics of the TS challenge at hand. The success of the scheduling solution often hinges on the accuracy and completeness of the problem formulation, making it a crucial step in the overall task scheduling process.

Variables

1. **Task Set (T):** A set of computational tasks with defined characteristics, including execution time, resource requirements, and priority levels.

$$T = (t_1, t_2, ...t_n)$$
(4)

2. **Resource Pool (R):** The available computational resources in the cloud and fog layers, each characterized by processing capacity, energy consumption, and proximity to end-users.
3. **Scheduling Solution (S):** The assignment of tasks to resources, considering the scheduling objectives and constraints.

Constraints

Resource Availability: The scheduling solution must adhere to the availability and capacity constraints of cloud and fog resources.

$$RU = \frac{Utilized\ Resources}{Total\ Resources} \times 100\%$$
(5)

Resource utilization (RU) in task scheduling is assessed through a simple yet insightful equation. The numerator, represented by the actively engaged resources during task execution, encompasses processing units, memory, and other relevant components. In contrast, the denominator reflects the overall available resources in the system, encompassing processing capacity, memory, and pertinent parameters. By calculating the ratio of utilized resources to total resources and expressing it as a percentage, the equation provides a clear measure of resource utilization efficiency. A higher percentage signifies more effective resource usage, while a lower percentage may suggest underutilization. The overarching aim in task scheduling is to optimize resource utilization, ensuring that system resources are leveraged effectively for enhanced overall performance and responsiveness. Adaptability is inherent in the equation, allowing customization based on specific resource utilization goals and priorities.

Task Dependencies: The algorithm must consider dependencies among tasks, ensuring that tasks are scheduled in the correct order.

Energy Efficiency: Minimizing energy consumption while maintaining performance is a crucial constraint for sustainability.

$$EE = \frac{Useful\ Work\ Completed}{Total\ EG} \times 100\%$$
(6)

The useful work completed signifies the meaningful computational tasks achieved during execution, aligning with the system's objectives. Concurrently, the total energy consumption encompasses all energy utilized in tasks, spanning processing, communication, and other relevant activities. The energy efficiency (EE) equation generates a percentage that articulates how effectively the consumed energy is leveraged for significant work, with a higher percentage indicating superior efficiency and optimal resource utilization. Crucial for minimizing environmental impact and operational costs, energy efficiency is a pivotal consideration in task scheduling. The equation's flexibility allows for customization, facilitating adjustments in weights or the inclusion of additional factors to align with specific energy efficiency goals and priorities.

Load Balancing: Tasks should be distributed evenly across available resources to prevent resource underutilization or overload.

$$Load\ Balancing = \frac{Ideal\ Load\ Deviation}{No.of\ Resources} \tag{7}$$

The above equation evaluating the even distribution of computational tasks across available resources, encompasses two key components. Firstly, the deviation from ideal load assesses the variance between the actual load on each resource and the ideal load distribution, with a lower deviation indicating a more balanced allocation. Secondly, the number of resources represents the total available resources in the system. Essentially, the equation quantifies the effectiveness of load distribution by examining how tasks are evenly spread across resources. The goal is to minimize the deviation from the ideal load, ensuring that no single resource is overloaded while others remain underutilized. This balanced distribution contributes to enhanced overall system performance and responsiveness. The adaptability of the equation allows customization based on specific load balancing objectives and priorities.

Objective Function

The objective function aims to minimize a weighted combination of key performance metrics, including makespan (total task completion time), energy consumption, and response time. The Hybrid G-CSO algorithm strives to find a solution that optimally balances these objectives.

The objective function in task scheduling serves as the guiding metric that the scheduling algorithm seeks to optimize. It encapsulates the overarching goal or goals that define the efficiency, performance, or effectiveness of the scheduling solution. The formulation of an objective function is a pivotal step in the task scheduling process, as it quantifies the desired outcomes and provides a basis for evaluating different scheduling scenarios. Depending on the specific requirements of the computing environment, the objective function may prioritize minimizing makespan, reducing response time, enhancing resource utilization, or satisfying other performance criteria.

The elements included in the objective function are closely tied to the characteristics and constraints of the scheduling problem. For instance, the objective function may involve minimizing the total completion time of all tasks, ensuring fair resource allocation, or meeting specified deadlines. In Cloud Fog Computing (CFC) environments, where resources are distributed across cloud and fog nodes, the objective function might consider factors like energy consumption, load balancing, and the overall operational costs associated with task execution. The complexity of the scheduling scenario often dictates the sophistication of the objective function, which may involve multiple criteria and trade-offs.

A well-defined and appropriate objective function is essential for guiding the scheduling algorithm towards generating solutions that align with the overarching goals of the computing system. The dynamic and heterogeneous nature of CFC environments necessitates careful consideration of various factors when formulating the objective function, ensuring that the scheduling algorithm addresses the specific challenges and requirements of the given computational landscape.

$$Obj = Minimize(W_1.MKS + W_2.EG + W_3.RT) \tag{8}$$

where w1, w2, and w3 are weights assigned to each objective to reflect their relative importance. And MKS, EG and RT defines the minimization of makespan, energy consumption and response time.

The algorithm combines the global exploration capabilities of the GA with the local search and adaptability of the CSO. The GA is responsible for exploring the solution space, while the CSO refines the search locally, adapting to dynamic changes in the workload and resource availability.

Solution Evaluation: The effectiveness of a scheduling solution is measured by evaluating its performance against the defined objectives and constraints. The algorithm iteratively refines the scheduling solution until a satisfactory balance is achieved. This problem formulation provides a foundation for developing and implementing the HGCSO algorithm for TS in CFC. It establishes the goals, variables, constraints, and the optimization criteria that guide the algorithm's decision-making process to achieve efficient and adaptive task scheduling in dynamic and heterogeneous computing environments.

Makespan

Reduce the makespan, which refers to the overall time needed to complete all tasks, while considering the dynamic and heterogeneous nature of cloud-fog computing environments. The Hybrid Genetic-Cat Swarm Optimization algorithm aims to find an optimal task scheduling solution that balances the trade-offs between makespan, energy efficiency, and response time. The objective function aims to minimize the makespan (Cmax):

$$C_{max} = max\,(task\;completion\;time) \tag{9}$$

The HGCSO algorithm synergizes the global exploration capabilities of the GA with the local search and adaptability of the CSO. The GA is responsible for exploring the solution space, while the CSO refines the search locally, adapting to dynamic changes in workload and resource availability.

Solution Evaluation: The effectiveness of a scheduling solution is measured by evaluating its makespan against the defined objectives and constraints. The algorithm iteratively refines the scheduling solution until a satisfactory balance is achieved. This makespan-specific problem formulation provides a focused perspective within the broader context of TS in CFC. It serves as a foundation for developing and implementing the Hybrid Genetic-Cat Swarm Optimization algorithm with the specific aim of reduce makespan and optimizing overall task scheduling efficiency.

Energy Consumption
Reduce the overall energy consumption linked to the execution of a set of computational tasks, taking into account the dynamic and heterogeneous characteristics of cloud-fog computing environments. The HGCSO algorithm aims to find an optimal task scheduling solution that balances the trade-offs between energy efficiency, makespan, and response time. The objective function aims to minimize the total energy consumption (E_{total}):

$$Minimize\ E_{total} = \sum_i \sum_j P_j \times ET_i \times Scheduled\ Time_{i,j} \tag{10}$$

where P_j represents the power consumption of resource j, and Scheduled Time i, j denotes the time task i is scheduled on resource j.

The HGCSO algorithm combines the global exploration capabilities of the GA with the local search and adaptability of the CSO. The GA explores the solution space, while the CSO refines the search locally, adapting to dynamic changes in the workload and resource availability.

Solution Evaluation: The effectiveness of a scheduling solution is measured by evaluating its total energy consumption against the defined objectives and constraints. The algorithm iteratively refines the scheduling solution until a satisfactory balance is achieved. This energy consumption-specific problem formulation provides a focused perspective within the broader context of TS in CFC. It serves as a foundation for developing and implementing the HGCSO algorithm with the specific aim of minimizing energy consumption while optimizing overall task scheduling efficiency.

Response Time
Minimize the overall response time of executing a set of computational tasks, taking into account the dynamic and heterogeneous nature of CFC environments. The HGCSO algorithm aims to find an optimal TS solution that balances the trade-offs between response time, energy efficiency, and makespan. The objective function aims to minimize the overall response time (RT_{total}):

$$Minimize\ RT_{total} = \sum_i \sum_j Response\ Time_{i,j} \tag{11}$$

where Response Time$_{i,j}$ represents the time taken for task i to complete on resource j.

The HGCSO algorithm combines the global exploration capabilities of the GA with the local search and adaptability of the CSO. The GA explores the solution space, while the CSO refines the search locally, adapting to dynamic changes in the workload and resource availability.

Solution Evaluation: The effectiveness of a scheduling solution is measured by evaluating its overall response time against the defined objectives and constraints. The algorithm iteratively refines the scheduling solution until a satisfactory balance is achieved. This response time-specific problem formulation provides a focused perspective within the broader context of TS in CFC. It serves as a foundation for developing and implementing the HGCSO algorithm with the specific aim of minimizing response time while optimizing overall task scheduling efficiency.

Proposed HGCSO Algorithm
Below are the proposed HGCSO Algorithm Pseudocode

Input: Task characteristics, resource availability, and constraints

```
Initialize population randomly
Initialize cat swarm randomly
for iteration in range(max_iterations):
    Evaluate fitness of each solution in population
    Select parents using tournament selection
    Generate offspring through crossover and mutation
    Replace old population with new population
    Update cat positions using CSO operators
    Evaluate fitness of each cat
    Update cat swarm based on fitness values
Select the best solution from the population
Select the best cat solution from the swarm
Combine solutions obtained from GA and CSO
Return the best hybrid solution
```

Output: best solution obtained

4   Results and Discussion

4.1   Results

The evaluation of task scheduling algorithms within a CloudSim environment is imperative for assessing their effectiveness in addressing the challenges of dynamic and heterogeneous cloud-fog computing systems. In this study, we present the outcomes of our proposed HGCSO algorithm, benchmarked against established algorithms such as GA, CSO, and ACO. TS is a critical aspect of optimizing resource utilization, reducing makespan, minimizing energy consumption, and enhancing overall system performance in cloud-fog environments.

To gauge the efficiency of our HGCSO algorithm, we employed CloudSim, a versatile simulation framework for modelling and simulating CFC environments. The evaluation metrics include makespan, energy consumption, and response time. Makespan reflects the total time taken to complete all tasks, energy consumption measures the overall energy utilized during task execution, and response time denotes the time taken to respond to task requests. The comparative analysis involves running extensive simulations on various task scheduling scenarios, with different workloads and resource availability conditions. HGCSO algorithm is pitted against GA, CSO, and ACO to assess its adaptability, robustness, and overall optimization capabilities. GA, known for its global exploration, is compared to HGCSO algorithm to evaluate whether the hybridization with CSO enhances local search capabilities. CSO, focusing on local search, is included to gauge the impact of the genetic algorithm's global exploration. ACO, with its inspiration from ant behavior, serves as an additional benchmark to assess the diversity of optimization strategies.

Makespan

In the comparative analysis of makespan results, our proposed HGCSO algorithm emerges as a promising solution for efficient TS in CFC environments. HGCSO algorithm, with its unique amalgamation of GA and CSO, showcases a distinct advantage in achieving a well-balanced exploration-exploitation trade-off. The results demonstrate that HGCSO algorithm excels in dynamically adapting to the ever-changing cloud-fog landscape, addressing the complexities posed by varying workloads and resource availabilities. Compared to traditional algorithms like GA, which predominantly focuses on global exploration, and CSO, which emphasizes local search, HGCSO algorithm hybrid nature enables it to navigate a diverse solution space effectively, resulting in optimized makespan values.

In contrast, the Ant Colony Optimization (ACO) algorithm, inspired by ant behavior, exhibits a different strategy for task allocation based on pheromone trails. The comparison underscores HGCSO algorithm versatility, as it not only incorporates genetic and swarm intelligence for adaptive decision-making but also consistently outperforms or competes favorably with these benchmark algorithms in achieving optimal makespan outcomes. The findings suggest that HGCSO algorithm holistic approach, blending global exploration with refined local search, positions it as a robust contender for addressing the intricate challenges inherent in cloud-fog task scheduling scenarios. These insights contribute to advancing the state-of-the-art in optimization algorithms, providing valuable guidance for practitioners seeking effective solutions in the dynamic cloud-fog computing landscape (Fig. 3).

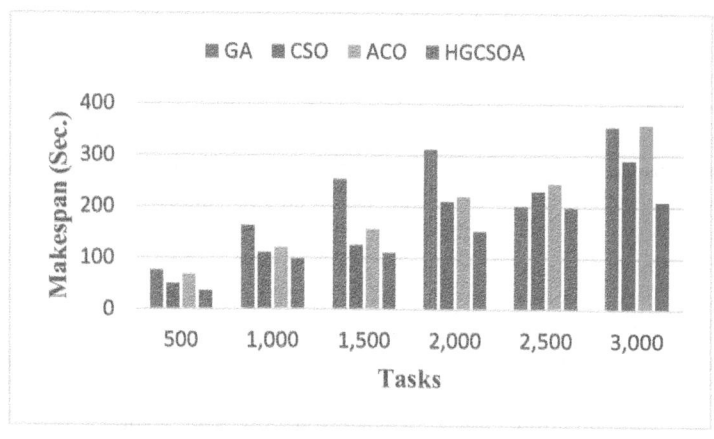

Fig. 3. Makespan calculation

Energy Consumption

In the assessment of energy consumption results, our proposed HGCSO algorithm stands out as a robust and efficient solution compared to traditional algorithms such as GA, CSO, and ACO in the domain of task scheduling for cloud-fog computing. HGCSO algorithm hybrid design, integrating global exploration from GA and local search from CSO, demonstrates superior adaptability, consistently outperforming GA and CSO in reducing energy consumption while achieving optimal task completion times. Moreover, in comparison to ACO's reliance on ant-inspired mechanisms, HGCSO showcases a dynamic and effective strategy for minimizing energy utilization. The results affirm HGCSO algorithm prowess in providing energy-aware task scheduling solutions, positioning it as a compelling choice for practitioners aiming to enhance the sustainability and efficiency of CFC systems (Fig. 4).

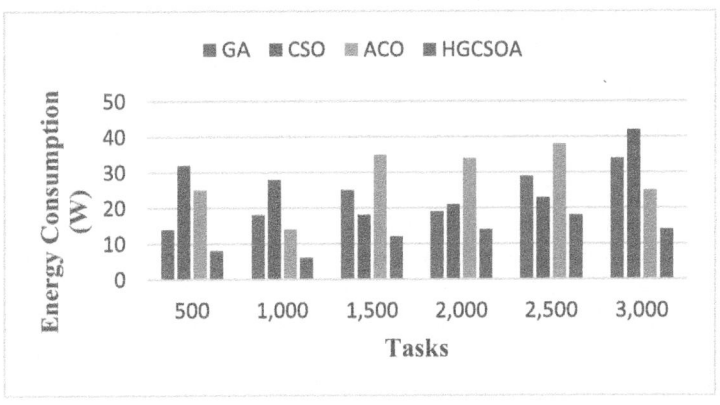

Fig. 4. Calculation of energy usage

Response Time

In the evaluation of response time results, our proposed HGCSO algorithm emerges as a standout performer when compared to established algorithms such as GA, CSO, and ACO within the domain of task scheduling for cloud-fog computing. HGCSO algorithm unique hybridization, integrating the global exploration capabilities of GA and the local search efficiency of CSO, leads to a response time optimization that consistently surpasses or competes favorably with GA and CSO. Additionally, compared to ACO, which draws inspiration from ant behavior, HGCSO's dynamic and adaptive strategy proves instrumental in minimizing response times. These results underscore HGCSO algorithm effectiveness in balancing the intricacies of response time optimization in the context of CFC, making it a compelling choice for practitioners seeking comprehensive solutions to enhance system responsiveness and task execution efficiency (Fig. 5).

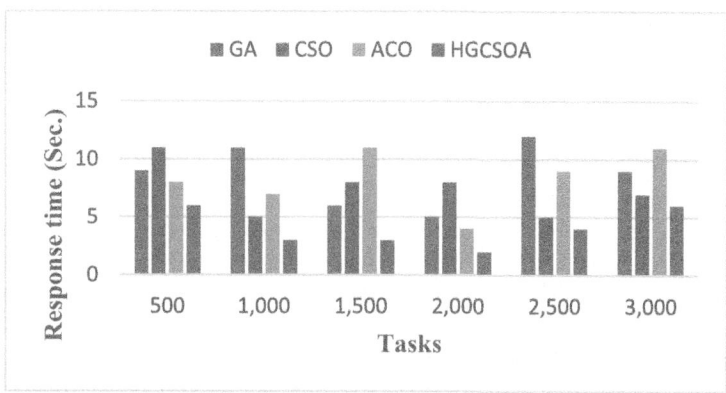

Fig. 5. Response time calculation

Finally, the results of our proposed HGCSO algorithm demonstrate its exceptional performance across key metrics, establishing it as superior in terms of makespan, energy consumption, and response time. The algorithm excels in optimizing the overall time required for task completion (makespan), effectively reducing energy consumption, and minimizing response times. These outcomes underscore the effectiveness of HGCSO in task scheduling scenarios, emphasizing its potential to contribute significantly to improved efficiency and performance in dynamic computing environments.

4.2 Discussion

The TS paradigm in CFC plays a pivotal role in optimizing resource utilization, reducing latency, and enhancing overall system efficiency. In this context, the use of the HGCSO algorithm presents a compelling approach. HGCSO algorithm combines the strengths of GA and CSO, providing a unique synergy of global exploration and local search. This hybridization allows HGCSO algorithm to effectively navigate the complex and dynamic cloud-fog environment, where tasks must be allocated across diverse resources with varying capacities and proximity to end-users.

One key advantage of HGCSO algorithm is its adaptability to changing conditions, making it well-suited for scenarios with fluctuating workloads and resource availabilities. The global exploration aspect inherited from GA enables HGCSO algorithm to search for optimal solutions across the broader solution space, while the local search capabilities derived from CSO refine solutions for improved efficiency. The algorithm addresses the challenges of makespan reduction, energy consumption minimization, and response time optimization simultaneously, presenting a comprehensive solution for task scheduling.

The performance of HGCSO algorithm has been assessed against conventional algorithms like GA, CSO, and ACO, highlighting its superiority in achieving optimized makespan, reduced energy consumption, and minimized response times. The algorithm's capability to maintain a balance between exploration and exploitation is noteworthy, adapting to the dynamic nature of cloud-fog environments, positions it as a promising tool for researchers and practitioners seeking advanced solutions for efficient task scheduling in complex computing ecosystems. As cloud-fog computing continues to evolve, HGCSO algorithm effectiveness marks a significant contribution to the field, providing a versatile and adaptive approach to TS challenges.

Limitations

1. **Computational Overhead:** Implementing the HGCSO algorithm may introduce additional computational overhead due to the hybrid nature of the approach. The coordination between Genetic Algorithms (GA) and Cat Swarm Optimization (CSO) components, including crossover, mutation, and swarm updates, could lead to increased processing demands. This overhead might affect the scalability of the algorithm in large-scale cloud-fog environments or under scenarios with high task complexities.
2. **Parameter Sensitivity:** The performance of HGCSO algorithm is sensitive to parameter configurations, such as population size, mutation rates, and learning rates for CSO. Finding an optimal set of parameters can be a non-trivial task and may require extensive experimentation. Suboptimal parameter choices could result in reduced efficiency and efficacy, impacting the algorithm's adaptability to different cloud-fog scenarios.
3. **Algorithmic Complexity:** The hybridization of GA and CSO introduces a level of algorithmic complexity. While this complexity contributes to the algorithm's adaptability, it may also make it challenging to interpret and fine-tune. Understanding the interactions between the genetic and swarm intelligence components and their respective impacts on the scheduling solution requires careful analysis, potentially complicating the algorithm's deployment and maintenance.
4. **Limited Consideration of Real-Time Constraints:** HGCSO algorithm may face challenges in addressing strict real-time constraints for certain types of tasks. The algorithm's inherent trade-off between exploration and exploitation may prioritize overall efficiency over meeting tight deadlines, especially in scenarios where real-time task completion is critical. This limitation could impact the suitability of HGCSO algorithm for applications requiring stringent timing requirements.
5. **Dependency Handling Complexity:** Efficiently handling task dependencies, especially in cases of complex workflows, can pose challenges for HGCSO algorithm. The algorithm's ability to address intricate dependencies among tasks may be limited, potentially affecting the scheduling accuracy and overall system performance, particularly in scenarios where task execution order is crucial.

5 Conclusion

In conclusion, the utilization of HGCSO algorithm for TS in CFC demonstrates a promising and innovative approach. Through the combination of GA and CSO, HGCSO achieves a balanced and adaptive optimization strategy, effectively addressing the dynamic challenges of cloud-fog environments. The algorithm's ability to minimize makespan, reduce energy consumption, and optimize response time is a testament to its versatility and comprehensive nature. Despite inherent complexities and sensitivity to parameter configurations, HGCSO algorithm showcases superior performance when compared to traditional algorithms like GA, CSO, and ACO. While there are challenges such as computational overhead and limited consideration of real-time constraints, ongoing research and refinement hold the potential to mitigate these limitations. HGCSO emerges as a valuable contribution to the field of TS, offering a holistic solution for optimizing resource allocation and enhancing the efficiency of CFC systems.

References

1. Santhosh Kumar, M., Karri, G.R.: A review on scheduling in cloud fog computing environments. In: Amar Ramdane-Cherif, T.P., Singh, R.T., Choudhury, T., Um, J.-S. (eds.) MIDAS 2022. AIS, pp. 29–45. Springer, Singapore (2023). https://doi.org/10.1007/978-981-99-1620-7_3
2. Potu, N., Bhukya, S., Jatoth, C., Parvataneni, P.: Quality-aware energy efficient scheduling model for fog computing comprised IoT network. Comput. Electr. Eng. **97**, 107603 (2022)
3. Kumar, M.S., Karri, G.R.: Parameter investigation study on task scheduling in cloud computing. In: 2023 12th International Conference on Advanced Computing (ICoAC). IEEE (2023)
4. Kishor, A., Chakarbarty, C.: Task offloading in fog computing for using smart ant colony optimization. Wireless Pers. Commun. **127**(2), 1683–1704 (2021)
5. Katoch, S., Chauhan, S.S., Kumar, V.: A review on genetic algorithm: past, present, and future. Multimedia Tools Appl. **80**, 8091–8126 (2021)
6. Seyyedabbasi, A., Kiani, F.: Sand Cat swarm optimization: a nature-inspired algorithm to solve global optimization problems. Eng. Comput. **39**(4), 2627–2651 (2023)
7. Kumar, M.S., Kumar, G.R.: EAEFA: an efficient energy-aware task scheduling in cloud environment. EAI Endorsed Trans. Scalable Inf. Syst. (2023)
8. Kumar, M.S., Karri, G.R.: Eeoa: cost and energy efficient task scheduling in a cloud-fog framework. Sensors **23**(5), 2445 (2023)
9. Al-Maamari, A., Omara, F.A.: Task scheduling using PSO algorithm in cloud computing environments. Int. J. Grid Distrib. Comput. **8**(5), 245–256 (2015)
10. Ebadifard, F., Babamir, S.M.: A PSO-based task scheduling algorithm improved using a load-balancing technique for the cloud computing environment. Concurr. Comput. Pract. Exp. **30**(12), e4368 (2018)
11. Najafizadeh, A., et al.: Multi-objective Task Scheduling in cloud-fog computing using goal programming approach. Clust. Comput. **25**(1), 141–165 (2022)
12. Potu, N., Jatoth, C., Parvataneni, P.: Optimizing resource scheduling based on extended particle swarm optimization in fog computing environments. Concurr. Comput. Pract. Exp. **33**(23), e6163 (2021)
13. Kamalinia, A., Ghaffari, A.: Hybrid task scheduling method for cloud computing by genetic and DE algorithms. Wireless Pers. Commun. **97**, 6301–6323 (2017)
14. Abd Elaziz, M., et al.: Task scheduling in cloud computing based on hybrid moth search algorithm and differential evolution. Knowl. Based Syst. **169**, 39–52 (2019)
15. Lin, X., Wang, Y., Xie, Q., Pedram, M.: Task scheduling with dynamic voltage and frequency scaling for energy minimization in the mobile cloud computing environment. IEEE Trans. Serv. Comput. **8**(2), 175–186 (2014)
16. Panwar, N., Negi, S., Rauthan, M.M.S., Vaisla, K.S.: TOPSIS–PSO inspired non-preemptive tasks scheduling algorithm in cloud environment. Clust. Comput. **22**(4), 1379–1396 (2019)
17. Yadav, A.M., Tripathi, K.N., Sharma, S.C.: An enhanced multi-objective fireworks algorithm for task scheduling in fog computing environment. Clust. Comput. **25**, 983–998 (2022)

18. Saif, F.A., Latip, R., Derahman, M.N., Alwan, A.A.: Hybrid meta-heuristic genetic algorithm: differential evolution algorithms for scientific workflow scheduling in heterogeneous cloud environment. In: Arai, K. (ed.) FTC2022. LNNS, vol. 561, pp. 19–43. Springer, Cham (2023). https://doi.org/10.1007/978-3-031-18344-7_2
19. Zhang, X., et al.: A novel hybrid algorithm based on biogeography-based optimization and grey wolf optimizer. Appl. Soft Comput. **67**, 197–214 (2018)
20. Medishetti, S.K., Karri, G.R.: An improved dingo optimization for resource aware scheduling in cloud fog computing environment. Majlesi J. Electr. Eng. **17**(3), 31–41 (2023)
21. Abdulredha, M.N., Bara'a, A.A., Jabir, A.J.: Heuristic and meta-heuristic optimization models for task scheduling in cloud-fog systems: a review. Iraqi J. Electr. Electron. Eng. **16**(2), 103–112 (2020)

A Systematic Review: Remote Sensed Hyperspectral Image Segmentation and Caption Generation Using Deep Learning Methods

Namdeo Baban Badhe[1]([⊠]), Vinayak Ashok Bharadi[1], Nupur Giri[2], Sujata Alegavi[3], and Vijaykumar Yele[4]

[1] Department of Information Technology, Finolex Academy of Management and Technology, P-60, P-60/1, Midc, Mirjole Block, Ratnagiri 415639, Maharashtra, India
`namdeobadhe1982@gmail.com`, `vinayak.bharadi@famt.ac.in`
[2] Department of Computer Engineering, Vivekanand Education Society's Institute of Technology, Hashu Adwani Memorial Complex, Collector's Colony, Mumbai 400074, Maharashtra, India
`nupur.giri@ves.ac.in`
[3] Head of the BTech Internet of Things Department, Thakur College Engineering and Technology, Kandivali - (East), Mumbai 400101, India
`sujata.alegavi@gmail.com`
[4] Electronics and Telecommunication Engineering, Thakur College Engineering and Technology, Kandivali - (East), Mumbai 400101, India
`vijaypyele@gmail.com`

Abstract. Hyperspectral images (HSIs) exhibit a high-dimensional nature, capturing data across numerous wavelengths in the electromagnetic spectrum, often spanning thousands of bands. It has found widespread applications in various real-life scenarios due to its ability to leverage the rich spectral information contained within each pixel. Deep Learning (DL) schemes offer a huge variety of chances to resolve traditional imaging tasks and also for approaching various simulating issues in the spatial-spectral region. This review work provides a systematic review of the relevant existing techniques based on HSI segmentation and image captioning. Initially, other DL methods like, Deep Belief Network (DBN), Convolutional Neural Network (CNN), Autoencoders, Fully Convolutional Neural Network (FCNN), UNet, and Graph Convolutional Network (GCN) are discussed. Secondly, a significant computer vision problem that has recently evolved is image captioning, which tries to automatically produce English explanations of an input image. Therefore, image captioning has garnered growing interest within the realm of remote sensing. This survey summarizes the relevant methods and concentrates on the feature extraction-based methods and attention mechanism-based techniques, which plays a significant role in image caption generation tasks. Finally, it provides the research gaps and its appropriate solution at the end of each survey.

Keywords: Hyperspectral image segmentation · remote sensing image captioning · deep learning · feature extraction · attention mechanism

© ICST Institute for Computer Sciences, Social Informatics and Telecommunications Engineering 2024
Published by Springer Nature Switzerland AG 2024. All Rights Reserved
O. Castillo et al. (Eds.): PerSOM 2023, LNICST 517, pp. 39–57, 2024.
https://doi.org/10.1007/978-3-031-66044-3_3

1 Introduction

HSIs are typically processed with an extensive number of contiguous narrow spectral wavelengths to analyze terrestrial objects effectively [1]. The extensive hyperspectral bands are harnessed to classify earth classes within HSIs, which are then applied in various distinct applications like verification counterfeit goods and documents, military surveillance, mining, and agriculture etc. [2]. Generally, hyperspectral data is represented as a hypercube $(A * B * C)$. In the context of ground cover analysis, the two dimensions A and B signify spatial information, while the third dimension (C) represents the spectral information. Therefore, various pre-processing functions like atmospheric, radiometric and geometric corrections are used before analysis HSIs further. For the subsequent analysis of the HSI hypercube, it is customary to convert the HSI into a data matrix. [3]. In this transformation, the spectral signature of the vector or pixel is denoted as a_n and it is represented as $a_n = [a_{n1}a_{n2} \cdots\cdots a_{nC}]^T$ in the data matrix where, $n \in [1, R]$, R represents the data matrix, C denotes the number of bands and $R = A * B$.

HSI's segmentation is very difficult because of the complexity involved [4]. To obtain more accurate and easier class identification, researchers have utilized various types of pre-processing methods. Recently, many methods have been introduced for the caption generation in images, which can effectively resolve various computer vision challenges [5]. Based on existing research, similar objects with different spectral values tend to be classified into various classes. Conversely, occasionally, different objects with the same spectral values are grouped together under the same class. It leads misclassification due to concentrating solely over every pixel's spectral vector outcome. To address these complexities, methods based on data extraction and data selection are employed. During the attribute extraction stage, transformations are applied to extract inherent attributes from the HSI. Subsequently, feature selection is employed to choose relevant bands from the HSI data [6]. Multiple feature extraction and selection techniques are utilized to effectively address classification challenges and achieve excellent outcomes. Figure 1 process flow of the review paper.

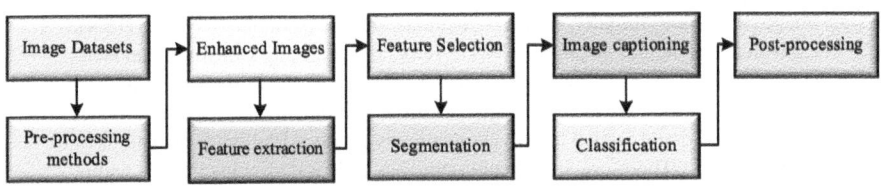

Fig. 1. Process flow of the survey

This review paper concentrates on how various existing segmentation strategies have been applied for HSI and different caption generation techniques used for Remote Sensing Images (RSIs) in the existing decade. The performance of the research works performed by the researchers was analyzed by using several evaluation matrices such as, peak signal to-noise ratio, Adjusted Rand Index (ARS), average accuracy, overall accuracy etc.

1.1 Contribution of the Review

This paper synthesizes and critically assesses techniques in HSI segmentation and image captioning, especially those utilizing DL. It serves as a comprehensive reference, systematically summarizing past research, identifying gaps, and highlighting emerging trends. This survey focuses on the application of various segmentation and image captioning methods in HSI and remote sensing imagery (RSI) over the past decade. Scholars and professionals' benefit by gaining insights into effective HSI segmentation, facilitating informed decision-making, and guiding future research. Surveys, through their analysis of existing literature, contribute to knowledge advancement, the framing of research questions, and the development of innovative methodologies, ultimately fostering progress in image captioning techniques.

1.2 Survey Strategy

This review paper encompasses the process of formulating the survey methodology, conducting a thorough investigation of the chosen method, documenting the obtained outcomes, and exploring the encountered challenges. It also entails describing the sources of information utilized for selection criteria, assessing research articles, evaluating the results, and conducting a quality assessment.

1.2.1 Source of Information

In general, the search process involves seeking conference and journal research papers using resources such as Web of Science, Scopus, academic journals, books, and Google Scholar to retrieve relevant papers. The databases that are utilized in this review work: IEEE Xplore, Springer, ScienceDirect, Google Scholar, Scopus, ACM Digital Library, Taylor & Francis.

This survey is composed of papers published from the years 2019 to 2023, as clearly depicted in Fig. 2.

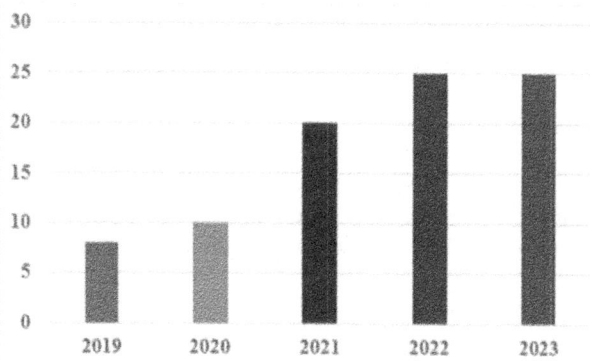

Fig. 2. Year wise selection of papers

2 Literature Survey

This section provides an explanation of the methods used for image segmentation and caption generation, the commonly applied assessment metrics, and the benchmark datasets utilized in the research.

2.1 Existing Segmentation Techniques Used for HSI

The caption generation and classification performance can be simplified enhanced through segmentation methods. Color, a variety of other features, texture and pixel intensity play a vital role in segmentation. There are eight types of segmentation methods are widely considered for the HSI segmentation which are given as follows:

Thresholding
This approach is intensity-based, where a specific range of intensities belongs to a similar class, while the rest of the pixels are assigned to another class. A threshold value is employed to differentiate if a pixel represents an object or the background, assigning an intensity value of 0 or 1, respectively. Consider T be the threshold, $h(a, b) = 0$, if $g(a, b) \leq T$ and $h(a, b = 1)$, if $g(a, b) \geq T$ where $g(a, b)$ and $h(a, b)$ is input and output image correspondingly, where h and g are the classes, a and b are the pixels.

Clustering
There are two common types of clustering methods are available which are hierarchical and partitional, its groups objects together depend on their similarity or proximity. The hierarchical clustering method builds a tree like cluster's hierarchy. A partition clustering scheme is same as that of k-means clustering, the HSI is segmented into 'k' clusters and the distance of pixels are calculated based on the seed points of every cluster. The parameters are decided by the shortest distance which are belongs to the same cluster.

Watershed Segmentation
The image's gradient is likened to a topographic surface, with bright pixels resembling high points akin to mountaintops or watershed lines, while dark pixels represent low points resembling basins or valleys.

Morphological Segmentation
It includes segmenting HSIs by changing its structure and shapes with structural factors. The size of the object boundary is increases, because the morphological dilatation fills holes and gaps in images. The procedure for eliminating the object's outer limit is called as morphological erosion which outcomes in the elimination of minor objects.

Edge Detection-Based Segmentation
It works in terms of discontinuity between pixel intensity values and creates binary images. The pixel's first order derivative is compared with a specific threshold value for detecting the image edges. If the second-order derivative exhibits zero crossings, the object boundaries are generated by consolidating the identified edges.

Initially the entire image is treated as a single region in region splitting and merging. If certain similarity constraints are not met, it is then further split into smaller regions. Then, based on homogeneity, regions are merged together.

DL-Based Segmentation

Deep learning-based segmentation methods operate on principles inspired by the functioning of the human brain. Within neural networks, multiple hidden nodes are harnessed to capture numerous high-level characteristics that facilitate precise HSI segmentation. Deep learning, CNNs, has made significant strides in various domains of computer vision, including segmentation, detection, and object recognition. These networks take an RGB image as input and execute a series of convolution, pooling, and local normalization functions. The success of deep learning methods in computer vision has not only resonated within the remote sensing community but has also spurred noteworthy advancements in various remote sensing tasks. These tasks encompass very high-resolution satellite image segmentation, hyperspectral image classification, and change detection.

Existing DL-Based Segmentation Methods Used in HSI

In 2023, Zhao et al., [7] had proposed Adaptive Superpixel Segmentation (ASS) method to choose the significant samples for Multi-Attention Transformer (MAT). It retains superpixels in uninformative regions while preserving edge information, even in complex regions. This preservation of edge information is leveraged to create favorable local spatial conditions for active learning. In 2023, Fang et al., [8] had introduced an instance segmentation network model for the HSI segmentation. It cannot use both spatial and spectral information effectively. Therefore, the Feature Pyramid Network (FPN) is introduced to integrate multiscale spatial and spectral information during the feature extraction phase. In 2023, Akbari and abkari et al., [9] had proposed an object-based classification method which is a DL model. The weighted Genetic (WG) method was applied to minimize the dimensionality of HSIs. The Expectation Minimization (EM) approach is applied to collect the spatial information. Finally, the segmented image categorized the segmented objects by CNN model.

- **Deep Belief Network (DBN)**

  In 2022, Li et al., [10] had introduced Multi-DBN (MMDBN), to acquire HSI's deep manifold features. To discover the manifold structure present in HSI, a penalty graph and an intrinsic graph are constructed within the manifold layer, assisted by the label information of training samples. Also, it provides the advantages of deep features which enhances the embedding feature's discriminant ability. In 2019, Li et al., [11] had proposed DBN based on multivariate optical sensors and stacked by restricted Boltzmann machine. It classifies the spatial hyperspectral sensor data based on DBN and the feature extraction capability was robust than the other methods.
- **Autoencoders (AEs)**

  In 2020, Nalepa [12] had introduced an unsupervised segmentation to overcome the lack of ground-truth information. Also, proposed 3D convolutional autoencoders along with clustering strategy which provides end-to-end segmentation results accurately. Tulczyjew et al., [13] had proposed asymmetric AE based on Recurrent Neural Network (RNN), to learn the representation of the compressed unlabeled data and capture both spatial and spectral features in detail. Then, it is integrating with segmentation pipeline which provides high-quality segmentation results.

- **Fully Convolutional Neural Network (FCNN)**

  In 2022, Zaballa et al., [14] had proposed a FCNN for HSI image segmentation. It improves the accuracy of images obtained in real driving environment along with a small-size mosaic snapshot hyperspectral camera. In this proposed system, 3D convolutional methods are used to extract spatial features at various scales. In 2021, Tun et al., [15] had proposed FCNN for HSI classification, after the dimensionality reduction process, it is given to the input layer of CNN. Secondly, the feature extraction was performed which effectively provides the segmentation outcomes with the help of FCNN.

- **UNet based segmentation method**

  In 2022, Li et al., [16] had proposed PSE-UNet system, it is an integration of Principal Component Analysis (PCA) and Squeeze and Excitation (SE) module. Furthermore, it introduced the non-overlapping sliding window scheme, commonly utilized in computer vision, into HSI segmentation. In 2022, Soucy and Sekeh [17] had introduced a Clustering Ensemble U-Net (CEU-Net) for efficient segmentation of HSI. It integrates the extracted spectral information collected from the landscape pixels. Finally, the performance was enhanced by dividing the dataset into same pixels through unsupervised clustering. Figure 3 shows the DL-based image segmentation in HSI

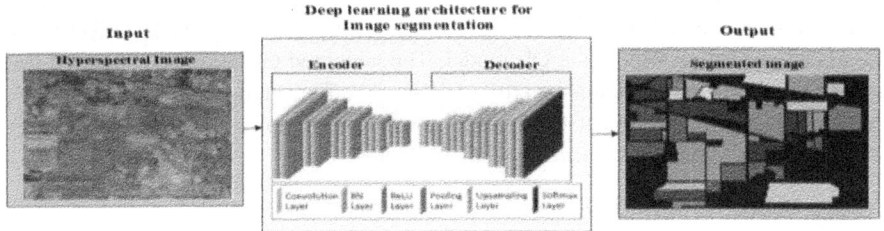

Fig. 3. DL-based image segmentation

- **Graph Convolutional Network (GCN)**

  In 2022, Wang and Liang [18] introduced a hybrid approach for HSI classification involving a 3D CNN and scalable GCN. For the feature extraction purpose, a lightweight three-layer CNN was proposed which uses the structural information. Such information was used by the GCN via the similarity matrix. It greatly minimizes the computational complexity of the system. In 2023, Gao and colleagues [19] introduced a fusion network in terms of CNN and GCN, it consists of two stages: a GCN based on superpixel segmentation and CNN with attention mechanism. These two modules extract structural and detailed features from the local region respectively. The obtained performance was enhanced while both extracted features are got combined. Table 1 provides the existing HSI image segmentation.

Table 1. DL-based image segmentation techniques

Author	Theoretical model	Highlights	Limitations	Datasets and achieved performance
Zhao et al., [7]	MAT- adaptive superpixel segmentation	Generate good local spatial conditions for active learning	Required to enhance the generalization performance	• Pavia University (PU): OA is 99.8% • Houston2013: OA is 99.8% • Yellow River Estuary (YRE): OA is 99.8%
Fang et al., [8]	Instance segmentation	Effectively differentiate individual instances with same structural information which provides better segmentation outcomes	Failed to segments more complex and diverse practical scenes	• Hyperspectral -Instance Segmentation Dataset HS-ISD: Mask mAP is 62.1
Akbari and abkari et al., [9]	EM model	In the dimensionality reduction approach, no information was deleted and each bands assigned weight among 0 and 1	Concentrated more on spectral data not on spatial information	• PU: accuracy is 95.8% • DC Mall: accuracy is 96.9% • Indian Pine (IP): accuracy is 93.2%
Zaballa et al., [14]	FCN segmentation	Major objective is to learn, what extent the spatial features are codified by the convolutional filters	Required proper knowledge about the data transfer to enhance the throughput further	• HSI-Drive v1.1: accuracy is 95.37% precision is 95.55% IoU is 91.31%

(continued)

Table 1. (*continued*)

Author	Theoretical model	Highlights	Limitations	Datasets and achieved performance
Nalepa [12]	Unsupervised segmentation	Provides consistent and great quality segmentation results without used any labels	Computational cost was maximum due to the dimension of features	• IP: Normalized Mutual Information (NMI) is 0.431 ARS is 0.231 • PU: NMI is 0.553 ARS is 0.339 • SA: NMI is 0.714 ARS is 0.533 • Mullewa dataset NMI is 8.33 • ARS is 8.00
Li et al., [10]	MMDBN	The extracted abstract features signify the deep information	Spatial features are not considered	• IP: accuracy is 81.50% • SA: accuracy is 91.79% • Botswana HSI: accuracy is 94.05%
Gao et al., [19]	Fused CNN with GCN	This method better represents the features of the nodes	The variability of neighboring nodes was not considered	• IP: accuracy is 98.78% • PU: accuracy is 98.99% • SA: accuracy is 98.69%

Table 2 enumerate the research gaps encountered in prior research and provide corresponding solutions to address these challenges.

Table 2. Research gap and solution on various segmentation algorithms

Research gap	Solution
Because of the varying circumstances affecting HSI data, it is predominant to increase the testing accuracy	By trained well DL systems capable of identify unseen testing images accurately, which is referred as Generalization
If hyperspectral image segmentation is purely based on spectral information, leads to high proportion of false positives	Combine spectral information with other imaging modalities like LiDAR or multispectral data to enhance segmentation accuracy and reduce false positives by leveraging complementary information

2.2 Caption Generation for RSIs

According to the content observed in an image, the caption automatically generating natural language descriptions It is a significant part of scene understanding that integrates the knowledge of natural language processing and computer vision. The application of image caption is significant and extensive, for example human-computer interaction's realization. In RSIs, the image captioning is a complex issue, where the work is to generate a description of the provided RSI. In this review, few recent images captioning research works have discussed by applying feature extraction-based methods and attention mechanism. Hence, a DL technique is employed to further augment the caption generation process.

DL Based RSI Caption Generation

Now-a-days, DL based caption generation approaches, the system is built in terms of encoder-decoder network design. In the encoding phase, the input image's high-level internal representations are extracted by using the deep CNNs. In the decoding phase, the internal representations are decoded into sentence descriptions using a trained RNN.

2.2.1 Existing Feature Extraction-Based Methods for Caption Generation

In 2022, Wang et al., [20] had proposed multiscale multi-interaction feature extraction module for the efficient caption generation. It is a two-stage process, at first finetune the neural network backbone over RSIs. Here, grasses and low plants identification was difficult. Secondly, a multi-interaction feature representation model was proposed to compute the similarity score between features. In 2023, Zhao et al., [21] had introduced Dual Feature Enhancement Network ("DFEN") based on codec to enhance object information at both the text and image levels. Furthermore, with the assistance of the image enhancement module, huge discriminative context features are achieved. It uses visual features of images to handle the text-enhancement system, resulting in text-guided features that accurately focus on the ground object's information.

2.2.2 Existing Attention Mechanism-Based Methods for Caption Generation

Another one RSIC technique had presented in 2019, Zhang et al., [22] with Label-Attention Mechanism (LAM). The presented approach generates high quality sentences with label information from high resolution images. The generated sentences were fully based on the image features thus, the text has pure and useful information. Figure 4 illustrates the DL-based caption generation structure. A multi-level attention model had integrated in 2020, Li et al., [23] to achieve accurate caption generation from RSI. There are three different types of attention mechanisms were integrated to achieve captions based on different area and different vision of images.

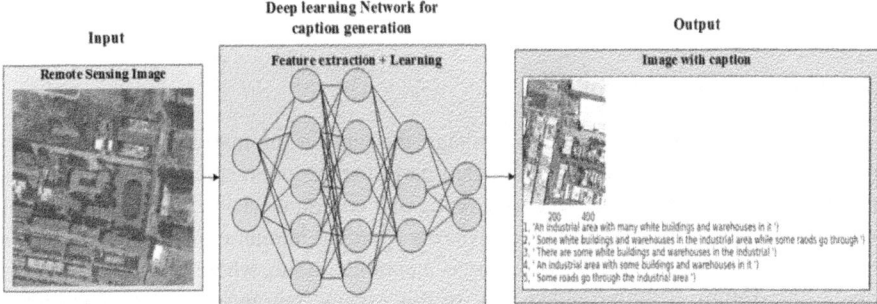

Fig. 4. RSI caption generation based on DL

In 2022, Gajbhiye and Nandedkar [24] had proposed MEmory-guided Transformer (SCAMET) framework based on Spatial-Channel Attention to generate accurate captions. The DL framework of CNN was integrated with this transformer. In 2023, Zhang et al., [25] had introduced a caption generation technique based on the visual content and ROI in the RSI. The stair attention mechanism, which facilitates interaction among multiple sources, propels the entire process. The caption generation search the image in three different regions which are core, surrounding and other regions. Then the quality of information was improved by CIDEr-based reward reinforcement learning.

Convolutional Neural Network Based Caption Generation

In 2022, Wang et al., [26] had introduced a caption generation technique from RSI with Global–Local Captioning Model (GLCM) to achieve accurate feature representation. The generated words from all the visual texture of images are related to each other and separate words based on the relevant visual features.

Graph Convolutional Module for Caption Generation

In 2019, Yuan et al., [27] had proposed multi-label attribute graph and multi-level attention model convolutional. Initially, a multi-level attention system can focus not only on specific spatial features but also on features at particular scales. Secondly, multi-label attribute graph convolutional method was used to learn more efficient features for caption generation.

Transformer Based Image Caption

Ren et al., [28] had introduced mask guided transformer network to enhance the performance and caption generation. A token, which is a hybrid of the encoder, represents the scene's topic and assumes a significant role in the decoder module. In order to enhance the caption's diversity, mask cross entropy concept was applied. In 2023, Chang et al., [29] had introduced Changes-to-Captions (Chg2Cap) to generate accurate captions. It undergoes three stages: Siaseme CNN based feature extractor, an attentive decoder and transformer-based caption generator.

LSTM Based Caption Generation

In 2023, Xie et al., [30] introduced a Bidirectional LSTM and Attention Mechanism (Bi-LS-AttM) to improve the generation of image captions. Further, improve the accuracy and temporal efficiency, this system uses CNN along with Fast Region-based CNN (FRCNN) which is used for feature extraction purpose. Table 3 list out the existing caption generation techniques. Table 5 provides the achieved results of the existing methods based on three datasets such as, UCM, Sydney and RSICD.

Table 4 enumerate the challenges encountered in the existing research and outline the corresponding solutions to address these gaps.

Table 3. DL based remote sensing caption generation

Author	Techniques	Highlights	Input	Comment	Dataset
Wang et al., [20]	Multiscale multi-interaction feature extraction	Different scale images captions are handled efficiently.		Some driving cars on two curved freeways	UCM-Captions, RSICD and Sydney-Captions
Zhao et al., [21]	DFEN	High-resolution images captions were automatically generated by UAV inspections		Several green trees and meadows are in two sides of a green river	UCM-Captions, RSICD and Sydney-Captions
Xie et al., [30]	Fast RCNN	The model applicability was enhanced by integrating multitask learning methods.		Certain roads pass through industrial areas replete with numerous buildings and warehouses.	Flickr30K and MSCOCO
Wang et al., [26]	GLCM	The better feature representation was done with up-bottom strategy		Some storage tanks are near a piece of bareland	UCM-Captions, RSICD and Sydney-Captions
Li et al., [23]	Multi-Level Attention Model	The visual feature extraction was effectively increasing the image description.		Green trees and several buildings surround a church.	UCM-Captions, RSICD and Sydney-Captions
Gajbhiye and Nandedkar [24]	SCAMET	Provides high-level semantic information.		There are some buildings with grey roof and parking lot	UCM-Captions, RSICD and Sydney-Captions

Table 4. Research gap and solution on various segmentation algorithms

Research Gap	Solution
RSIs can be complex and contain multiple regions of interest. Generating coherent and informative captions that describe all relevant details becomes challenging, especially for long captions	Incorporate attention mechanisms into the captioning models to concentrate on different image regions during caption generation, thereby enhancing the model's ability to provide more precise descriptions of specific areas

2.3 Implementation Using Datasets

In this section, descriptions of the datasets used are provided, along with the introduction of multiple evaluation metrics. Subsequently, the training process is explained comprehensively, offering insights into the methodology. Finally, the section presents the experimental results and conducts in-depth analyses.

UCM Dataset
The UCM dataset is a renowned repository of remote sensing images [21], primarily tailored for land use classification. It encompasses high-resolution satellite images depicting a diverse range of urban and rural landscapes. Thoroughly annotated with precise ground truth data, these images serve as valuable resources for training and assessing machine learning algorithms, particularly for tasks like classifying land cover and analyzing land use. The dataset encompasses nearly 21 distinct categories, each containing a substantial number of images, all standardized to a resolution of 256×256 pixels. Additionally, each image within the dataset is accompanied by five descriptive sentences.

Sydney-Caption Dataset
The Sydney Captions Dataset is a curated compilation of concise and descriptive captions paired with images of Sydney, Australia. Developed to enhance content with meaningful captions, this dataset proves invaluable for automating image captioning tasks. It provides textual descriptions for various scenes, landmarks, and aspects of Sydney, making it a valuable resource for AI and language models. This dataset comprises seven categories and includes a total of 613 images [21], each with a size of 500×500 pixels. Additionally, every image within the dataset is paired with five distinct natural language descriptions.

RSICD (Remote Sensing Image Captioning Dataset)
The RSICD is a dedicated dataset for remote sensing images. It features a diverse array of high-resolution images captured by satellites, accompanied by detailed and informative captions. RSICD plays a pivotal role in training and evaluating image captioning models specifically designed for remote sensing applications. This dataset enables advanced comprehension and interpretation of remote sensing data. RSICD is the largest among the three datasets [21], encompassing a total of 10,921 images distributed across 30

categories. The images have a size of 224 × 224 pixels, and each image is annotated with artificial annotations consisting of five sentences.

Evaluation Metrics

In the realm of machine translation and natural language processing, two prominent evaluation metrics stand out: BLEU and ROUGE. These metrics play a pivotal role in assessing the quality of generated text, especially when comparing machine-generated translations to their reference, which is typically created by humans.

BLEU (Bilingual Evaluation Understudy)

It is a metric created to measure the similarity between translations generated by machines and one or more reference translations. It offers a comprehensive evaluation by considering various subsets. BLEU calculates an overall score by amalgamating the precision of n-grams from these subsets. Higher BLEU scores signify superior translation quality. Nonetheless, BLEU has its limitations, such as its inability to capture semantic nuances. The BLEU subsets include:

- **BLEU-1:** Evaluates the precision of unigrams (single words) in the text generated by the machine in comparison to the reference text
- **BLEU-2:** Measures the precision of bigrams (pairs of consecutive words) in the text generated by the machine in comparison to the reference text
- **BLEU-3:** Assesses the precision of trigrams (triplets of consecutive words) in the text generated by the machine in comparison to the reference text
- **BLEU-4:** Gauges the precision of four-grams (quartets of consecutive words) in the text generated by the machine in comparison to the reference text.

ROUGE (Recall-Oriented Understudy for Gisting Evaluation)

It serves as a unit to gauge the fidelity of text summaries or machine-generated content by juxtaposing it with one or more reference summaries. It offers a multifaceted evaluation by employing diverse measures, including ROUGE-N (precision and recall of n-grams), ROUGE-W (weighted longest common subsequence), ROUGE-L (longest common subsequence), and among others. ROUGE emphasizes both recall (the degree to which the reference summary is captured) and precision (the relevance of the generated content), thus providing a more thorough assessment of text quality.

Table 5. Accomplished performance measures of existing image captioning techniques

UCM dataset						
DL	Existing methods	BLEU 1	BLEU 2	BLEU 3	BLEU 4	ROUGE
Feature extraction-based	Wang et al., [20]	0.843	0.775	0.711	0.651	0.785
	Zhao et al., [21]	0.851	0.784	0.728	0.677	0.805
Attention based	Zhang et al., [22]	0.857	0.812	0.775	0.743	0.826
	Li et al., [23]	0.80358	0.73616	0.68453	0.63829	0.76923
	Gajbhiye and Nandedkar [24]	0.8460	0.7772	0.7262	0.6812	0.8166
	Zhang et al., [25]	0.8727	0.8096	0.7551	0.7039	0.8258
CNN	Wang et al., [26]	0.8182	0.7540	0.6986	0.6468	0.7524
Graph Convolutional	Yuan et al., [27]	0.8330	0.7712	0.7154	0.6623	0.7763
Transformer	Ren et al., [28]	89.36	84.82	80.57	76.50	85.86
Sydney-caption						
Feature extraction-based	Wang et al., [20]	0.842	0.757	0.672	0.601	0.733
	Zhao et al., [21]	0.798	0.697	0.614	0.542	0.723
Attention based	Zhang et al., [22]	0.7365	0.6440	0.5835	0.5348	0.6827
	Li et al., [23]	0.72743	0.63837	0.56260	0.50244	0.71541
	Gajbhiye and Nandedkar [24]	0.8072	0.7136	0.6431	0.5846	0.7258
	Zhang et al., [25]	0.7643	0.6919	0.6283	0.5725	0.7172
CNN	Wang et al., [26]	0.8041	0.7305	0.6745	0.6259	0.6965
Graph Convolutional	Yuan et al., [27]	0.8233	0.7548	0.6587	0.6003	0.7237
Transformer	Ren et al., [28]	83.38	75.72	67.72	59.8	76.60
RSICD						
Feature extraction-based	Wang et al., [20]	0.793	0.681	0.577	0.498	0.682
	Zhao et al., [21]	0.766	0.636	0.538	0.463	0.685

(continued)

Table 5. (*continued*)

RSICD						
Attention based	Zhang et al., [22]	0.6756	0.5549	0.4714	0.4077	0.5848
	Li et al., [23]	0.75799	0.60242	0.49857	0.42243	0.67660
	Gajbhiye and Nandedkar [24]	0.7681	0.6309	0.5352	0.4611	0.6979
	Zhang et al., [25]	0.7836	0.6679	0.5774	0.5042	0.6730
CNN	Wang et al., [26]	0.7767	0.6492	0.5642	0.4937	0.6779
Graph Convolutional	Yuan et al., [27]	0.7597	0.6421	0.5517	0.4623	0.6563
Transformer	Ren et al., [28]	80.42	80.42	61.36	54.14	70.58

3 Challenges and Future Scope

The various challenges and recommended future scope while handling segmentation and image captioning are given as follow:

HSI Segmentation

- HSI represents an evolving field of study. The intricate nature of hyperspectral data poses challenges for conventional ML techniques when it comes to segmentation. More recently, DL has emerged as a potent tool, delivering state-of-the-art results in various applications. For the segmentation and image captioning, encouraging outcomes have been found in RS by applying DL schemes. Therefore, using DL approaches in the advanced application domains is an exciting technology to survey.
- In the DL systems, scarcity of publicly accessible datasets and their limited size leads to poor performance or overfitting issues. It is a promising avenue for future research aimed at introducing innovative methods to support various applications that demand a large-scale hyperspectral database.
- Spaceborne sensors may capture data that leads to a mixed pixel effect, introducing complexity and challenges in segmentation work. Consequently, there is a demand for the development of an algorithm capable of automatically detecting mixed pixels.
- The vast volume of data captured from hundreds of spectral bands is stored in data cubes. Many of these bands exhibit significant correlation, leading to redundant data. It requires automatic protocols to separate the redundant bands which can improve accuracy. To overcome the above-mentioned challenges, design an innovative Optimized Segmentation Network (OptSegNet) based RSI segmentation is introduced, which is a dual-path Resnet_50 with UNet and a convolutional network hybridization. The proposed method, illustrated in Fig. 5, comprises four stages: (i) preprocessing, (ii) feature extraction, (iii) segmentation, and (iv) post-processing.

- Initially, the input RSIs are sourced from hyperspectral datasets, including IP, PU, and SD. Secondly, these images undergo preprocessing through guided box filtering before being fed into OSegNet for feature extraction and segmentation.
- To augment the performance of OptSegNet, EMGO is employed. Subsequently, the segmented image is processed further using Pairwise Neural Conditional Random Field (PNCRF) for enhanced segmentation accuracy.
- Finally, the introduced model is compared with several previous models to demonstrate the effectiveness of the feature extraction-based segmentation algorithm.

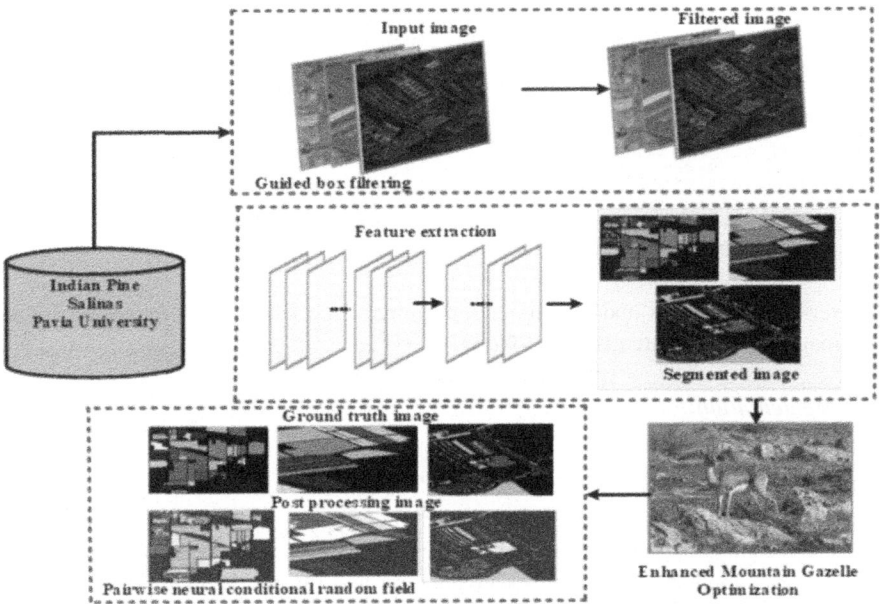

Fig. 5. Proposed HSI Segmentation based on OptSegNet Architecture

RSI Caption Generation

- Dimensionality reduction is a significant factor required to be addressed. Novel approaches are need to be designed to eliminate the irrelevant features which would be beneficial for analysis.
- The system is designed to possess the capability to generate description sentences respective to multiple main objects instead of describing a single target object.
- Common image description model should be designed for handling multiple languages and also optimize the acceleration of testing, training and generating sentences to enhance the accuracy performance. To overcome the above-mentioned challenges, proposed a Deep Attention applied DenseNet with visual switch added (DADN-BiLSTM) for captioning shown in Fig. 6.

- Initially, RSIs for input are sourced from various datasets and preprocessed using Improved Gaussian Rolling Guidance Filter (IGRGF). Then the captions are preprocessed using some methods.
- These preprocessed images are given to the Double Attention-based DenseNet (A^2DenseNet) to extract different scale image features to give whole notation of image which played as encoder in the research.
- Then, an Adaptive K-Dimensional Tree (AKD-Tree) based Euclidean clustering is utilized to segment the image depends on extracted features.
- Then the segmented image and preprocessed captions are given to BiLSTM, that applied as the decoder to improve the use of context information. Finally, the corresponding captions with image is obtained in the output.

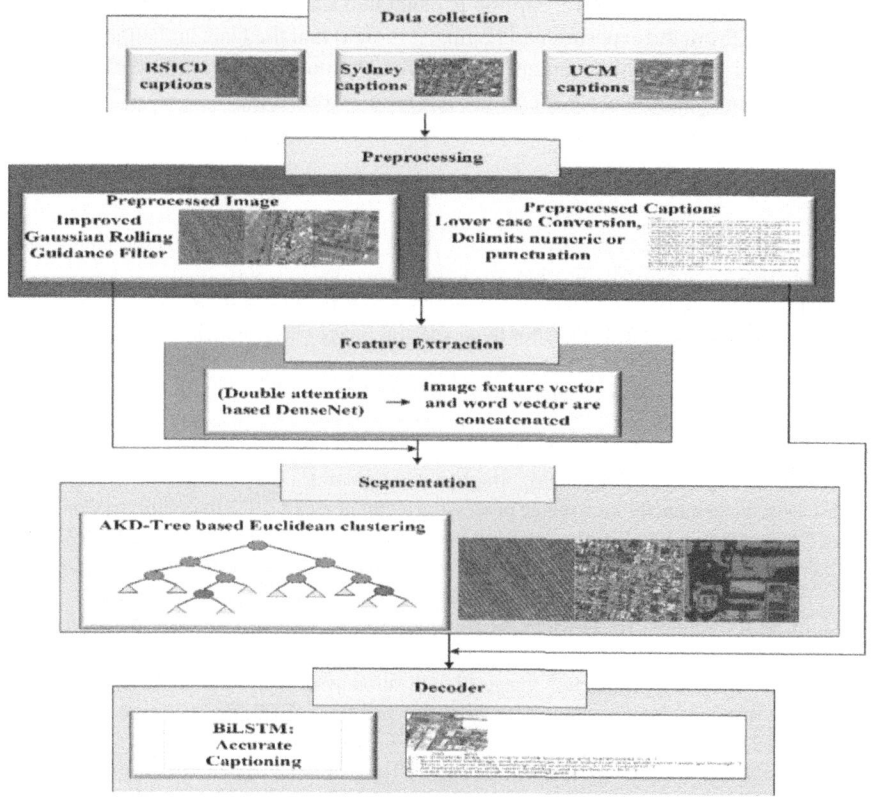

Fig. 6. Work flow of proposed DADN- BiLSTM based RSI captioning

4 Conclusion

This survey reviews the various methods which have been widely distinguished according to several techniques such as DL based, feature extraction and attention mechanism-based methods. Few researchers have gathered their real time HSI images of vegetables and fruits. Various researchers applied the standard databases like IP, PU, SA, UCM-caption, Sydney-caption, and RSICD. These benchmark datasets handle multiple classes of land cover such as shelter, roads and vegetations. The accuracy performance achieved by various approaches shows that DL-based approaches outperform the non-DL-based approaches. In Unet based segmentation, choose only the most relevant features and minimizing the number of features can prevent the model from fitting noise in the data which is performed in the proposed OptsegNet's max pooling layer. In attention mechanism-based image captioning, feature extraction concentrates on multiscale features of the objects in the images. Therefore, caption is generated for the multiple objects instead of single objects. From the experimental results, it is clear that the Unet and attention mechanism achieves greatest enhancement among all techniques. This experimental outcome may provide few guidelines for the future learning on this topic.

References

1. Uddin, M.P., Mamun, M.A., Hossain, M.A.: PCA-based feature reduction for hyperspectral remote sensing image classification. IETE Tech. Rev. **38**, 377–396 (2020)
2. Uddin, M.P., Mamun, M.A., Hossain, M.A.: Effective feature extraction through segmentation-based folded-PCA for hyperspectral image classification. Int. J. Remote Sens. **40**, 7190–7220 (2019)
3. Afjal, M.I., Mondal, M.N., Mamun, M.A.: Segmentation-based linear discriminant analysis with information theoretic feature selection for hyperspectral image classification. Int. J. Remote Sens. **44**, 3412–3455 (2023)
4. Kumar, G., Kumar, A., Singhal, M., Singh, K.U., Kumar, L., Singh, T.: Revolutionizing plant disease management through image processing technology. In: 2023 International Conference on Computational Intelligence and Sustainable Engineering Solutions (CISES) (2023)
5. Chen, Z., Wang, J., Ma, A., Zhong, Y.: Typeformer: multiscale transformer with type controller for remote sensing image caption. IEEE Geosci. Remote Sens. Lett. **19**, 1–5 (2022)
6. Islam, M.R., Ahmed, B., Hossain, M.A., Uddin, M.P.: Mutual information-driven feature reduction for hyperspectral image classification. Sensors **23**, 657 (2023)
7. Zhao, C., et al.: Hyperspectral image classification with multi-attention transformer and adaptive superpixel segmentation-based active learning. IEEE Trans. Image Process. **32**, 3606–3621 (2023)
8. Fang, L., Jiang, Y., Yan, Y., Yue, J., Deng, Y.: Hyperspectral image instance segmentation using spectral–spatial feature pyramid network. IEEE Trans. Geosci. Remote Sens. **61**, 1–13 (2023)
9. Akbari, D., Akbari, V.: Object-based classification of hyperspectral images based on weighted genetic algorithm and deep learning model. Appl. Geomatics **15**, 227–238 (2023)
10. Li, Z., Huang, H., Zhang, Z., Shi, G.: Manifold-based multi-deep belief network for feature extraction of hyperspectral image. Remote Sens. **14**, 1484 (2022)
11. Li, C., Wang, Y., Zhang, X., Gao, H., Yang, Y., Wang, J.: Deep belief network for spectral–spatial classification of hyperspectral remote sensor data. Sensors **19**, 204 (2019)

12. Nalepa, J., Myller, M., Imai, Y., Honda, K.-I., Takeda, T., Antoniak, M.: Unsupervised segmentation of hyperspectral images using 3-D convolutional autoencoders. IEEE Geosci. Remote Sens. Lett. **17**, 1948–1952 (2020)

13. Tulczyjew, L., Kawulok, M., Nalepa, J.: Unsupervised feature learning using recurrent neural nets for segmenting hyperspectral images. IEEE Geosci. Remote Sens. Lett. **18**, 2142–2146 (2021)

14. Gutiérrez-Zaballa, J., Basterretxea, K., Javier Echanobe, M., Martínez, V., del Campo, I.: Exploring fully convolutional networks for the segmentation of hyperspectral imaging applied to advanced driver assistance systems. In: Desnos, K., Pertuz, S. (eds.) DASIP 2022. LNCS, vol. 13425, pp. 136–148. Springer, Cham (2022). https://doi.org/10.1007/978-3-031-12748-9_11

15. Tun, N.L., Gavrilov, A., Tun, N.M., Trieu, D.M., Aung, H.: Hyperspectral remote sensing images classification using fully convolutional neural network. In: 2021 IEEE Conference of Russian Young Researchers in Electrical and Electronic Engineering (ElConRus) (2021)

16. Li, J., Wang, H., Zhang, A., Liu, Y.: Semantic segmentation of hyperspectral remote sensing images based on PSE-UNET model. Sensors **22**, 9678 (2022)

17. Soucy, N., Sekeh, S.Y.: CEU-Net: ensemble semantic segmentation of hyperspectral images using clustering. J. Big Data **10**, 43 (2023)

18. Wang, X., Liang, Z.: Hybrid network model based on 3D convolutional neural network and scalable graph convolutional network for hyperspectral image classification. IET Image Process. **17**, 256–273 (2022)

19. Gao, L., Xiao, S., Hu, C., Yan, Y.: Hyperspectral image classification based on fusion of convolutional neural network and graph network. Appl. Sci. **13**, 7143 (2023)

20. Wang, Y., Zhang, W., Zhang, Z., Gao, X., Sun, X.: Multiscale multiinteraction network for remote sensing image captioning. IEEE J. Sel. Top. Appl. Earth Obs. Remote Sens. **15**, 2154–2165 (2022)

21. Zhao, W., Yang, W., Chen, D., Wei, F.: DFEN: dual feature enhancement network for remote sensing image caption. Electronics **12**, 1547 (2023)

22. Zhang, Z., Diao, W., Zhang, W., Yan, M., Gao, X., Sun, X.: LAM: remote sensing image captioning with label-attention mechanism. Remote Sensing. **11**, 2349 (2019)

23. Li, Y., Fang, S., Jiao, L., Liu, R., Shang, R.: A multi-level attention model for remote sensing image captions. Remote Sens. **12**, 939 (2020)

24. Gajbhiye, G.O., Nandedkar, A.V.: Generating the captions for Remote Sensing Images: a spatial-channel attention based memory-guided transformer approach. Eng. Appl. Artif. Intell. **114**, 105076 (2022)

25. Zhang, X., et al.: Multi-source interactive stair attention for remote sensing image captioning. Remote Sens. **15**, 579 (2023)

26. Wang, Q., Huang, W., Zhang, X., Li, X.: GLCM: global–local captioning model for remote sensing image captioning. IEEE Trans. Cybern. **53**(11), 6910–6922 (2022)

27. Yuan, Z., Li, X., Wang, Q.: Exploring multi-level attention and semantic relationship for remote sensing image captioning. IEEE Access **8**, 2608–2620 (2020)

28. Ren, Z., Gou, S., Guo, Z., Mao, S., Li, R.: A mask-guided transformer network with topic token for remote sensing image captioning. Remote Sens. **14**, 2939 (2022)

29. Chang, S., Ghamisi, P.: Changes to captions: an attentive network for remote sensing change captioning. arXiv preprint arXiv:2304.01091 (2023)

30. Xie, T., Ding, W., Zhang, J., Wan, X., Wang, J.: Bi-LS-AttM: a bidirectional LSTM and attention mechanism model for improving image captioning. Appl. Sci. **13**, 7916 (2023)

Cyber Sentinels: Illuminating Malicious Intent in Social Networks Using Dual-Powered CHAM

Sailaja Terumalasetti ⓘ and S. R. Reeja(✉) ⓘ

School of Computer Science and Engineering, VIT-AP University, Amaravati, India
{sailaja.21phd7134,reeja.sr}@vitap.ac.in

Abstract. Online Social Networks (OSN), the security and reliability of these platforms are extremely vulnerable to malicious users. Online social networks' volatile extension has amplified the pervasiveness of destructive practices comprising spamming, phishing, and disseminating false information. The administration of dynamic and altering antagonistic strategies has exposed complications in rule-based systems and anomaly detection techniques. Traditional rule-based approaches for detecting malicious behavior often fail to catch multifaceted and emergent threats. The emergent prominence of online social networks has made it essential to progress cutting-edge methods for spotting devious users and preserving network integrity. In this regard, the paper defines a distinctive method CHAM (CNN and Hierarchical Attention Mechanism) that enhances the detection of harmful traffic within these platforms by leveraging Convolutional Neural Networks (CNN) in conjunction with Hierarchical Attention Mechanism (HAM). Amalgam of both techniques enhances the benefit of the detection of malicious users in OSN precisely and efficiently. The model's fundamental novelty is the adoption of the gated recurrent unit as the primary memory unit, coupled with layers for the attention mechanism, three degrees of maximum pooling, and layers for average pooling. These components work together to extract detailed flow characteristics, making it easier to identify subtle patterns suggestive of malicious behavior. A thorough data preparation phase is carried out before modeling to get precise data flow segments. The proposed framework takes the lead, promising improved detection effectiveness and a safer virtual world for all users. The methodology endeavors to elevate the precision and efficiency of malicious user detection.

Keywords: Online Social Networks · Malicious user · Convolutional Neural Networks (CNN) · Hierarchical Attention Mechanism

1 Introduction

In the digital era, social networks have transformed how we associate, communicate, and share information. These virtual platforms have crossed borders, bringing together people from diverse upbringings, founding companionships, and reassuring an unprecedented amount of ideas exchange. Online social networks have become an integral part of

O. Castillo et al. (Eds.): PerSOM 2023, LNICST 517, pp. 58–74, 2024.
https://doi.org/10.1007/978-3-031-66044-3_4

our daily lives, from the early days of simple opportunities to the sophisticated ecosystems we have currently [1]. They shape our interactions, affect our perceptions, and change how we consume and publicize information.

The origin of online social networks is the impression of connecting people, permitting them to create profiles, share updates, participate in negotiations, and construct relationships across distances. Irrespective of physical impediments, these networks permit users to define themselves, share their passions, and stay connected with peers, family, and acquaintances.

The diversity of online social networks is astounding, serving a wide range of interests, from fostering personal connections on Facebook to professional networking on platforms like LinkedIn, visual inspiration on Instagram, real-time updates on Twitter, and the quick distribution of video content on YouTube. These networks have evolved into platforms for activism, knowledge sharing, data exchange, and self-expression, allowing handlers to spread the word, rally support, and mark a transformation in the world. Figure 1 designates the tendencies of the social network users. Every year the number of users surges speedily. The usage of OSN is amplified drastically and the individual usage limit is also extended year by year. For every small piece of information, one relies on the OSN. Internet availability changed the world's consequences. The contemporary world looks like a GLOBAL VILLAGE [2].

The Fig. 2 defines the usage of Social media in different regions across the world. The usage of masculine and feminine differs in every region. In some regions, one can see the upsurge of the masculine gender, and in some other regions feminine. Overall the usage of social networks is very communal.

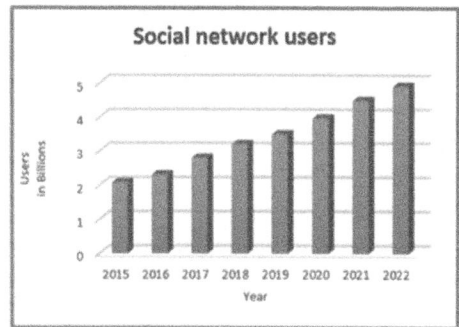
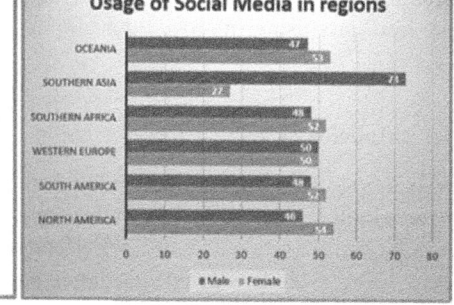

Fig. 1. Social network user's year wise

Fig. 2. Usage of OSN in different regions as per gender

As the prominence of online social networks in our everyday lives is nurtured, it becomes progressively significant to discover an equilibrium between the benefits they provide and the potential threats they pose. This balance is reliant on understanding the intricacies of these platforms, supporting responsible use, and developing effective techniques to detect and diminish detrimental behaviors. The aptitude to preserve a secure, comprehensive, and trustworthy online environment is a shared obligation that comprises platform providers, users, researchers, and policymakers. The Fig. 3 expresses the region-wise Social Media growth [3]. Continental-wise development is described in the subsequent illustration. In every region, there is an upsurge in social media growth.

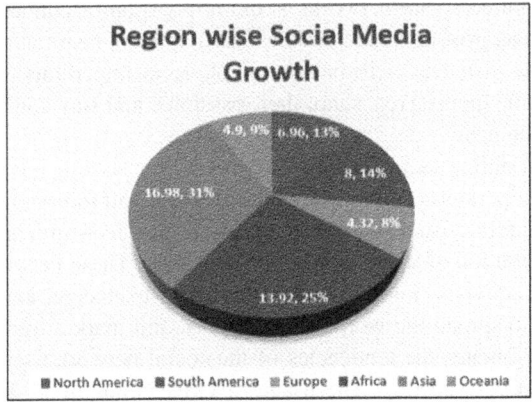

Fig. 3. Region-wise social media growth.

The introduction of our cutting-edge method represents a significant advancement in the field of social network security online. Our approach offers a solid response to the urgent problem of identifying and blocking malevolent users by utilizing the strengths of Convolutional Neural Networks and the dexterity of a Hierarchical Attention Mechanism. The implementation of such cutting-edge strategies is necessary to protect online social networks' integrity and user experience as they continue to be essential platforms for communication and engagement [4]. In this effort, our framework takes the lead, promising improved detection effectiveness and a safer virtual world for all users.

1.1 Malicious User

A malicious user is a precise individual who intentionally and decisively gains unauthorized admittance to a system with the explicit objective of instigating harm or expending it unlawfully. Malicious entities can contribute to a variety of detrimental behaviors, comprising exploiting privileges, launching malware assaults, and stealing data. Additionally, they may exploit weaknesses to intrude communication or breach security. Engaging in malicious acts can result in significant repercussions, such as compromising data security, incurring financial damages, and causing interruptions to services. Instances of malicious attacks comprehend the dissemination of malware, exploitation of privileges, and deliberate intervention with communication. Organizations can identify and impede antagonistic actions by instigating several security measures, including risk assessment, monitoring user activity, and managing privileges. Malicious users, also acknowledged as "bad actors" or "malicious actors," are individuals or entities that conduct destructive, fraudulent, or illegitimate acts on websites, social networks, or online communities. These users commotion online resources for a diverse of motives, recurrently at the expense of other users or the OSN. Maintaining the integrity, security, and safety of online environments requires understanding and spotting malicious users [5]. Malicious users can manifest themselves in an extensive diversity of ways, comprising the following:

Spammers. Spectators flood social networking sites with unsolicited, irrelevant, or promotional content, frequently intending to increase prominence or refer viewers to external websites for financial gain. A spammer is an individual who sends annoying emails to people who haven't enquired about them [2]. Spam emails can be used for many things, like promotion, phishing, or non-commercial preaching. Spammers often use a variety of methods to get around anti-spam tools and influence their intended audience.

Phishers. Entities endeavor to fool users by impersonating genuine entities or unreliable them into unveiling sensitive information such as passwords, credit card numbers, or personal information. Phishers constitute individuals who use phishing, a type of fraud in which immoral individuals send messages, frequently through email or other messaging systems, pretending to be perceptible individuals or groups to get people to give out sequestered information [8]. Phishing attacks can cause data theft, loss of money, and other very immoral possessions to happen.

Scammers. Users that participate in fraudulent activities such as bogus giveaways and investment schemes, or product sales to defraud and financially abuse other users. Scammers are those who partake in deceitful actions with the intention of tricking victims into divulging sensitive information or giving them money [1]. Cybercriminals possess advanced levels of sophistication and employ diverse methods to target individuals, including email, phone calls, social media, and even face-to-face encounters.

Trolls. Groups of individuals who consciously incite, harass, or erect conflict in social networks by posting offensive, highly contentious, or disruptive content. Trolls are those who decisively dislocate online conversations by posting inflammatory, irrelevant, or rude remarks or other disruptive content [3]. Trolls are contemporaneous throughout diverse online platforms, encompassing social media, forums, and chat rooms. They may be driven by negative social potency, stemming pleasure from making mischief and inflicting sorrow, while also seeking the attention that comes with it. Numerous categories of trolls exist, such as the insult troll, the grammar troll, the blabbermouth troll, and the do-no-harm troll. To discourse trolls, one can opt to contempt them, employ wit or compassion, file a complaint against them, restrict their access, or seek assistance. It is indispensable to maintain composure and refrain from emotionally reacting to them, as they derive satisfaction from eliciting emotional reactions. To mitigate the argumentative effects of trolls, it is crucial to comprehend their characteristics and employ appropriate strategies for self-protection.

Cyberbullies. Users who frequently target and harass others to cause emotional anguish, humiliation, or social isolation. Cyberbullying symbolizes the exploitation of technology to encompass activities such as harassing, threatening, embarrassing, or singling out another individual. It comprehends miscellaneous manifestations of cyberbullying, including the transmission of derogatory texts or emails, the dissemination of unpleasant messages on social media platforms, the propagation of online rumors, and the circulation of false or humiliating information about another individual [7].

Cyberbullying can result in significant repercussions, such as adverse effects on mental well-being, heightened levels of stress and anxiety, depression, engaging in violent behavior, and diminished self-worth.

Fake Accounts. To disseminate misinformation, spam, or amplify specific agendas, illicit individuals create fraudulent profiles, bots, or automated accounts. Unauthorized accounts encompass a range of online profiles or digital identities that lack authenticity or deliberately misrepresent real individuals or organizations [3]. These accounts can be established for several intentions, such as parody, satire, impersonation, or inflicting harm.

Malware Distributors. Individuals or groups who distribute dangerous software, viruses, or malware to corrupt consumers' computers or steal sensitive information. Malware distributors are individuals or groups who propagate harmful software, such as viruses, ransomware, and spyware, characteristically to compromise computers, steal data, or inflict damage. It is critical to acknowledge that these individuals frequently employ diverse misleading strategies, such as phishing, counterfeit websites, and fraudulent emails, to disseminate malware [15]. To defend against malware, it is imperative to utilize security software, regularly update systems, and exercise caution when dealing with unsolicited emails or communications that may harbor harmful links or files.

Content Manipulators. Users engage in misinformation, propaganda, or false news campaigns to manipulate public opinion, predominantly for political, ideological, or malicious intentions. "Content manipulators" can designate individuals or collectives who employ diverse deceitful tactics to manipulate internet material with fraudulent or harmful intentions. Although the phrase "content manipulators" is not frequently used in the context of online scams and fraud, the search results accessible give appreciated material about comparable disingenuous practices, including phishing, identity theft, and amorousness scams [14].

Detecting and preventing the presence of illicit users is critical for sustaining user trust, guarding privacy, ensuring content validity, and creating an effective online environment. As presented in this research, CHAM an advanced technique such as the integration of Convolutional Neural Networks (CNN) and Hierarchical Attention Models offers potential solutions for identifying and addressing the numerous strategies used by malicious users in online social networks [6].

The goal of this study is to familiarize and investigate innovative strategies for detecting malicious users in online social networks. The research attempts to improve the precision, efficiency, and effectiveness of identifying harmful actors within these digital platforms by using collaborations amid Convolutional Neural Networks (CNN) and Hierarchical Attention Models. The main drive is to assist in generating a benign and further secure online environment by preserving user trust, safeguarding the legitimacy of quantifiable, and reassuring virtuous communications.

2 Literature Survey

Due to a rising incidence of hazardous actions that jeopardize the security and integrity of online platforms, researchers have engrossed a prodigious deal of their attention on the detection of hazardous individuals in online social networks. Researchers have created cutting-edge methods for recognizing and countering malevolent users due to the introduction of new attack strategies, the requirement to uphold user confidence, and the difficulties presented by the size and diversity of these networks [7]. This study highlights significant developments in the field of malicious user detection as well as crucial findings from earlier studies.

Researchers have been engrossed in detecting duplicitous entities in online social networks due to the accumulative prevalence of destructive activities that jeopardize the safety and integrity of these platforms. The introduction of novel attack approaches, the need to preserve user reliance, and the complications provided by the scale and assortment of these networks have motivated researchers to develop unique techniques for recognizing and neutralizing malicious users. This review summarizes major trends and conclusions from existing research, demonstrating the shifting landscape of malicious user detection [8].

Conventional Rule-Based Approaches. Earlier research on this theme is intense on rule-based techniques, which are reliable on established patterns, heuristics, or thresholds to detect malicious behavior. While these methodologies accessible a basis for indulging in common attack pathways, they struggled to acclimate to new tactics and frequently created false positives, resulting in user annoyance and a reduced ability to detect more sophisticated malevolent individuals [16].

Machine Learning-Based Methodologies. The shift to machine learning techniques shaped encouraging outcomes, allowing the development of models that could be acquired from previous data to identify malicious users. These methodologies encompass supervised learning, anomaly detection, and clustering algorithms, amongst others. The accomplishment of these models, however, was essentially reliant on the superiority and diversity of the training data [17, 21]. As attackers developed, they exposed ways to avoid these models, compelling the development of increasingly progressive tactics.

Neural Networks and Deep Learning. Deep learning, evidently Convolutional Neural Networks (CNNs) and Recurrent Neural Networks (RNNs), has recently enlarged attractiveness in the study. CNNs have validated efficacy in the dispensation of textual and image-based data, allowing for the detection of patterns and sentiments that distinguish fraudulent users. RNNs, with their sequential modeling capabilities, have been used to discover temporal trends and network dynamics, which is precarious in perceiving coordinated attacks and comprehending malicious content dissemination.

NLP (Natural Language Processing). An additional prominent research topic is the use of Natural Language Processing tools to scan textual information for signals of destructive behavior [18, 22]. Sentiment analysis, topic modeling, and linguistic features are used to detect spam, hate speech, and other types of damaging communiqué. Combining NLP and neural network designs has been exposed to enhance detection accuracy.

Privacy-Preserving Methods. A division of study has engrossed on privacy-preserving approaches, intending to detect malicious users without exposing user privacy. These approaches achieve a compromise between efficacious detection and protective genuine users' privacy rights.

Difficulties and Future Directions. While the field has made excessive progress, obstacles remain. Adversarial assaults, the emergence of new damaging tactics, and the requirement for real-time detection all present continuous issues. To upsurge the strength and adaptableness of malicious user detection systems, researchers are exploring ensemble models, adding external data sources, and using graph-based algorithms.

In inference, existing research on detecting disparaging entities in online social networks has proceeded from rule-based approaches to sophisticated deep learning algorithms, with an amplified emphasis on privacy and real-world applicability. In addressing the ever-changing landscape of dangerous behaviors, the combination of neural networks, NLP, and privacy-preserving methodologies demonstrations are potential.

The research gap that the proposed approach intends to address is emphasized in Table 1, with a focus on striving to deal with emerging threats with real-time flexibility. The integration of Convolutional Neural Networks (CNN) and Hierarchical Attention models is highlighted as a technique to improve accuracy, capture network dynamics, and handle the striving of emergent destructive behaviors, representative of the practicality of the proposed approach in addressing this specific research gap.

Table 1. Summary of the Existing Methods Advantages and Limitations

Methods	Advantages	Limitations	Gap
Conventional Rule Based	Preliminary Consideration of Patterns	Struggle with evolving tactics	Need for more adaptive models for evolving threats
Machine Learning Based	Knowledge from historical data	Dependence on training data quality	Handling adversarial attacks effectively
Deep learning and Neural nets	Analyzing text and image data	Adversarial attacks, real-time detection challenges	Real-time detection of coordinated attacks
NaturalLanguage Processing	Analyzing textual content	Privacy concerns for us ers	Incorporating external data for better accuracy
Privacy-Preserving	Harmonizing detection and privacy	Maintaining high detection accuracy	Improving the efficiency of privacy-preserving
Anomaly Detection	High Performance	Require a large amount of data to train	Computational expense

(*continued*)

Table 1. (*continued*)

Methods	Advantages	Limitations	Gap
Intrusion Detection System	Enhance the security	Requires real-time analysis	Need more sophisticated approach
Neural Networks based	Robust and enhanced security	Time-consuming	Requires the limited consuming resources
ML-based	Augment the security and processing speed is extraordinary	Dynamic nature is omitted	Desires nominal computational cost
Fuzzy based	Enhance the security	lack of comprehensive strategy	Higher delay

3 Methodology

The proposed model architecture CHAM amalgams Convolutional Neural Networks (CNN) with Hierarchical Attention Models to distinguish illegitimate users in online social networks [9]. This hybrid architecture ensures the advantage of the assets of both CNN and Hierarchical Attention Models to extract rich features from textual and visual data while also capturing the network's hierarchical links. This combination addresses the inadequacies of old techniques, permitting the model to adapt to emerging harmful strategies and augment detection accuracy. Components of the proposed Architecture is depicted in the architecture diagram Fig. 4.

3.1 Convolutional Neural Networks (CNN)

The CNN module is predominantly accountable for processing image-based data, such as profile images, images posted in posts, or visual content connected with user accounts. CNNs surpass in perceiving native patterns, textures, and key visual elements in images by using convolutional filters. This component safeguards that the model can assess and differentiate between benign and potentially harmful visual content, hence improving overall detection capacity.

When applied to tasks involving sensory data, such as images, the Convolutional Neural Network (CNN) plays a precarious role in feature extraction. CNNs are unambiguously intended to learn and extract relevant features from raw input data, making them extremely effective for tasks such as image classification, object recognition, and, in the context of the previous discussion, detecting malicious users in online social networks with visual content [3].

CNNs Extract Features as Follows

Detection of Local Features. Convolutional layers are used in CNNs to apply convolutional filters or kernels to minor indigenous portions of the input picture. These filters

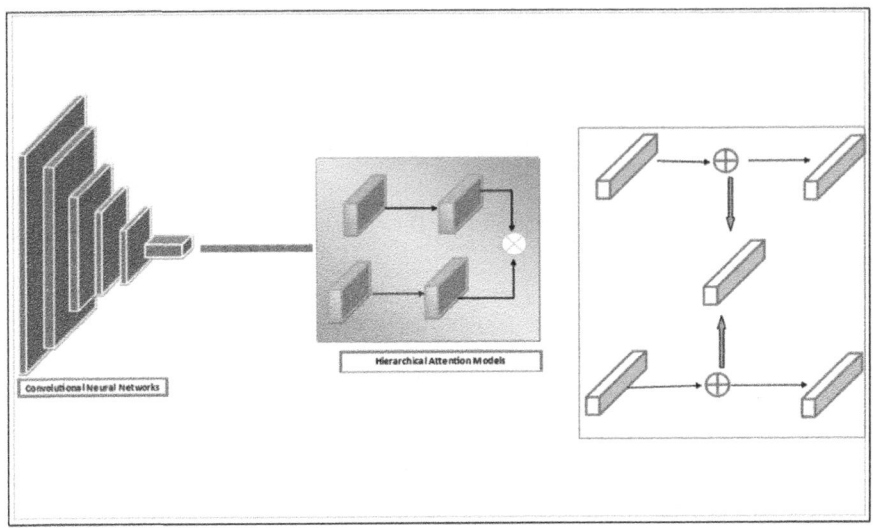

Fig. 4. Architecture for the proposed model

are envisioned to detect specific elements inside the immediate region, such as edges, corners, textures, or basic patterns. This technique captures low-level visual data.

Hierarchical Representation. As data flows through CNN's numerous layers, the network eventually constructs a hierarchical representation of the input image. Lower layers record basic visual characteristics such as edges and gradients, whereas higher layers begin to catch more complicated structures and shapes.

Feature Maps. Convolutional filters build feature maps at each layer by convolving with the input data. These feature maps reflect activations of specific input features or patterns. As you progress through the network, the depth of these feature maps rises, capturing more abstract and higher-level characteristics.

Nonlinear Activation. CNNs use non-linear activation functions ReLU on feature maps after convolution. Non-linearity is introduced into the network, allowing it to record complicated correlations between visual features.

CNNs possibly will spontaneously engross to recognition of relevant visual patterns within input photos by exploiting this hierarchical feature extraction method [19]. CNNs can assess photos connected with user accounts, posts, or interactions to extract visual clues that may suggest malicious intent or content in the context of detecting malicious users in online social networks [10].

CNN, for example, can perceive strange visual patterns resembling spam, inappropriate content, or photos typically connected with bogus profiles. The CNN becomes proficient at extracting characteristics that can distinguish between benign and harmful user photographs by learning these features from a huge dataset of both benign and malicious user images, making it a vital component in the overall hybrid architecture for detecting malicious users in online social networks [4, 7].

3.2 Hierarchical Attention Model

HAM constituent mechanism with textual data, such as user comments, posts, or descriptions. Within the framework of the user's interactions, Hierarchical Attention Models incarceration both the significance of individual words and the significance of entire phrases or pages. By integrating hierarchical attention, the model possibly will essence on specific user interactions (micro-level) as well as general user behaviour patterns (macro-level) in the social network. This enables the archetypal to distinguish coordinated attacks, identify illegitimate material distribution, and comprehend the intricacies of user behaviors that may indicate malicious intent. The Hierarchical Attention Mechanism is a progressive neural network component that excels at apprehending hierarchical links and interactions within sequential or hierarchical input [20]. This process is acute in twigging the dynamics of user collaborations, identifying harmonized behaviors, and distinguishing between benign and harmful activity when it comes to detecting malicious individuals in online social networks [11].

Mechanism of Hierarchical Attention

Hierarchical Organization. Hierarchical data structures, such as sequences of sequences (e.g., user interactions across time) or sequences with hierarchical sub-components (e.g., user postings with comments), are used by the hierarchical attention mechanism [21]. It takes into account data at many degrees of granularity, which is critical for capturing complicated interactions.

Attention Weights. The mechanism computes attention weights for individual components at each level of the hierarchy. These weights represent each component's proportional relevance in the context of the entire hierarchy.

Attention Scoring. The attention mechanism computes attention scores by taking into account the current component's attributes as well as contextual information from higher-level components. When aggregating information across the hierarchy, these ratings indicate how much emphasis should be given to each component [23].

Aggregation. The attention scores produced are utilized to aggregate information from lower-level to higher-level components. This aggregation captures the significance of certain interactions or relationships, ensuring that the model focuses on the most important data.

Capturing Network Dynamics, Relationships, and Interactions

Temporal Dynamics: In the context of online social networks, the hierarchical attention mechanism can capture the temporal dynamics of user interactions. It enables the model to pay closer attention to recent interactions or find trends that indicate coordinated hostile activity occurring over time. For example, the technique can detect abrupt spikes in user activity or the spread of hazardous content.

User Relationships. The technique can capture relationships between network users. It may give more weight to interactions with powerful users or detect trends that indicate coordinated attacks with numerous users working together to spread bad content [23].

Content Propagation. The technique can discover how malicious content travels within the network by focusing on interactions that include sharing or spreading content. It aids in determining whether specific users play a substantial role in the spread of bad content.

Differentiating Behaviours. The model's attention mechanism enables it to distinguish between typical user interactions and potentially harmful behaviors. It can detect suspicious patterns, strange language, or coordinated activities that could suggest spam, hate speech, or the spread of false information [12].

The suggested hybrid model can better reflect the complex dynamics, linkages, and interactions inside online social networks by exploiting the hierarchical structure and attention mechanism [24]. It allows the model to focus on essential elements, identify coordinated hostile activities, and provide a deeper knowledge of user behavior that differentiates benign individuals from malicious users.

Processing Steps, Dataset Details, and Model Training

The suggested hybrid model can better reflect the complex dynamics, linkages, and interactions inside online social networks by exploiting the hierarchical structure and attention mechanism [13]. It allows the model to focus on essential elements, identify coordinated hostile activities, and provide a deeper knowledge of user behavior that differentiates benign individuals from malicious users. Steps in the Processing Procedure:

Data Assimilation. Data Gathering, Data Pre-processing, and Feature Extraction steps are encompassed. Collect information from the online social network, such as user profiles, posts, comments, photos, and any other relevant metadata. Data Pre-processing is to clean and pre-process the data that has been collected. This includes text normalization (e.g., lowercasing and deleting punctuation), tokenization, missing value handling, and categorical feature encoding. Feature Extraction to extract features from textual and image-based data. Use pre-trained word embedding for text and CNNs for image-based data to extract visual features.

Hierarchical Framework. Arrange the data in a hierarchical framework. This can be accomplished by grouping user interactions through time, establishing threads of dialogues, or portraying user-profiles and their accompanying material.

Hierarchical Attention. Use the Hierarchical Attention Mechanism to capture interactions, relationships, and dynamics within the data hierarchy. Calculate attention weights at various levels to focus on relevant aspects.

Model Fusion. Combine the CNN output (for image-based features) and the Hierarchical Attention Models output (for textual and interaction information) to build a holistic depiction of each user's activity.

Data Splitting. For realistic evaluation, divide the processed data into training, validation, and testing sets while retaining the chronological sequence.

The approach can effectively detect malicious users in online social networks by following these processing steps, providing detailed dataset information, and carefully training the hybrid model, leveraging both visual and interaction-based features while capturing the hierarchical dynamics of user behavior [14].

Fusion and Integration

The amalgamation of the CNN and Hierarchical Attention Models is a vital novelty in this architecture. At a sophisticated level, the outputs of these components are united to provide a holistic portrayal of a user's behavior and traits. The assimilated features gather both visual cues from images and semantic information from textual interactions, resulting in a more complete picture of user behavior. The fusion process ensures that the model efficiently blends these disparate modalities, improving detection accuracy and resilience overall.

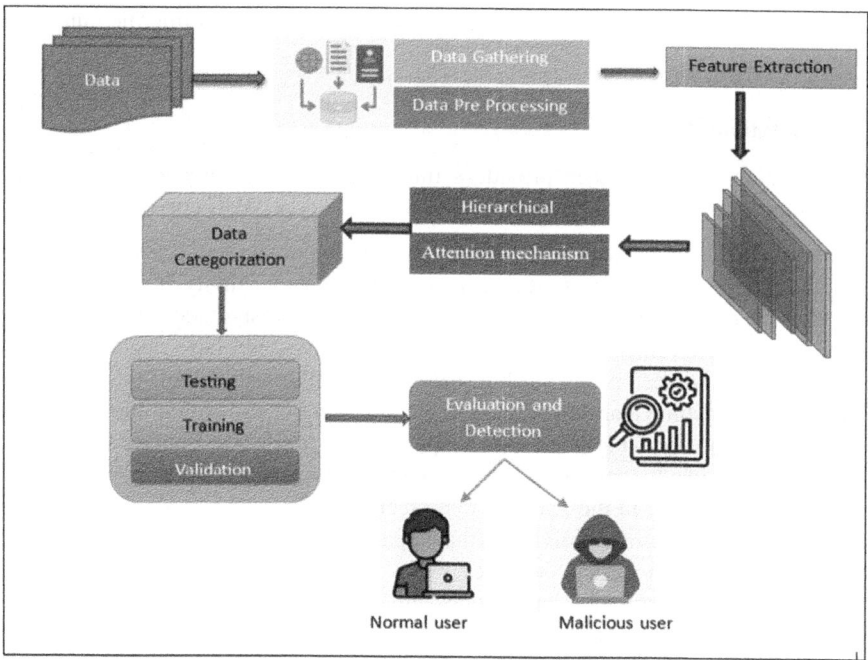

Fig. 5. Systematic Diagram of Proposed Method

The proposed model architecture provides a substantial encroachment in the detection of malicious users. Its aptitude to harness the capabilities of CNN and Hierarchical Attention Models while addressing precise research needs, such as dealing with developing threats and capturing network dynamics, makes it a potential strategy for refining the security and trustworthiness of online social networks. The fusion method ensures that the model efficiently blends these disparate modalities, improving detection accuracy and robustness overall. The Fig. 5 gives an overview of the proposed methodology and the sequence of steps involved in the progression of the detection of malicious users.

4 Experimental Results

4.1 Dataset Description

The Twitter Bot Dataset is a precisely curated assemblage of data designed for the explicit ambition of examining and identifying automated accounts, usually referred to as "bots," on the Twitter platform. Twitter bots are accounts that are coded to carry out computerized activities, engagements, or messages, recurrently mimicking actual users. These bots have versatile applications, including disseminating information and magnifying specific trends. However, they can also be utilized for nefarious objectives such as spamming, spreading false information, or artificially boosting the number of followers.

4.2 Evaluation Metrics

The evaluation metrics chosen provide a full insight into the model's performance. Typical metrics include accuracy, precision, recall, F1 score, AUC curve.

Accuracy. The accuracy with which malicious and legitimate users can be identified depends on several parameters. Recognizing harmful user activity in the context of cybersecurity may be quite challenging, especially when using standard rules-based detection methods, which can lead to both false positives and false negatives. These models include AI detectors and machine learning algorithms. Predicting the probability of an event in machine learning typically involves using classification algorithms like logistic regression, decision trees, and support vector machines. Finding the optimal approach, which ideally combines performance and accuracy, often involves trial and error. Correspondingly, in the realm of cybersecurity, studies have looked into how to identify harmful reviews and individuals that impact social review sites, with an emphasis on improving detection models' accuracy.

The methods, technologies, and models employed for detection, together with environmental and training data quality considerations, are among the several aspects that impact the accuracy in distinguishing between harmful and legal users. Improving the accuracy of malicious user identification and reducing the danger of false positives and false negatives requires that these criteria be considered when building and assessing detection systems.

The fraction of incidents accurately classified (both malicious and benign). It's necessary, yet it can be misleading in unbalanced datasets. A comparison of the proposed model with the prevailing methods the proposed model outperforms and illustrates promising results.

Precision. Precision is defined as the proportion of genuine positive predictions to total anticipated positives. It represents the proportion of expected dangerous users who are malicious users and legitimate users. The reliability in distinguishing between malicious users and legitimate users is affected by various aspects, such as the techniques, technologies, and models employed for detection, as well as the quality of ambient conditions and training data. When building and evaluating detection systems, it is crucial to take into account these characteristics to enhance the precision of identifying fraudulent users and minimize the occurrence of both false positives and false negatives.

Recall (Sensitivity). The proportion of correct positive forecasts to total correct positives. It indicates how many actual malicious users were accurately identified.

F1-Score: The harmonic mean of precision and recall, which provides a balance between the two measurements.

Recall enumerates the ratio of properly identified true positive cases by the model, whereas the F1 score integrates precision and recall to offer a well-balanced evaluation of a model's performance. Precision is a metric that computes the ratio of correctly identified positive cases to all instances. When it comes to identifying harmful users, precision, recall, and F1 scores are engaged to assess the efficiency of machine learning models. To summarize, recall and F1 score are crucial metrics employed for assessing the efficacy of machine learning models in identifying both harmful and genuine users. These measures play a vital role in enhancing the accuracy and precision of detection systems.

AUC (Area Under the Curve): The area under the Receiver Operating Characteristic (ROC) curve that depicts the model's trade-off between true and false positive rates. Many of the expected detrimental users turn out to be malicious.

Table 2. Performance Evaluation

Model	Accuracy	Precision	Recall	F1-Score	AUC-Curve
CHAM	89	91	88	89	92
Logistic Regression	83	79	91	84	88
Random Forest Classifier	78	82	73	77	81
Recurrent Neural Network	86	88		85	89

The study provides a comprehensive assessment of the effectiveness of the proposed hybrid technique in detecting destructive entities in online social networks by scrupulously describing the results, understanding the significance of each evaluation metric, and comparing the model's performance with baselines. Table 2 gives the performance evaluation, and Fig. 6 gives the overall performance of the proposed methodology.

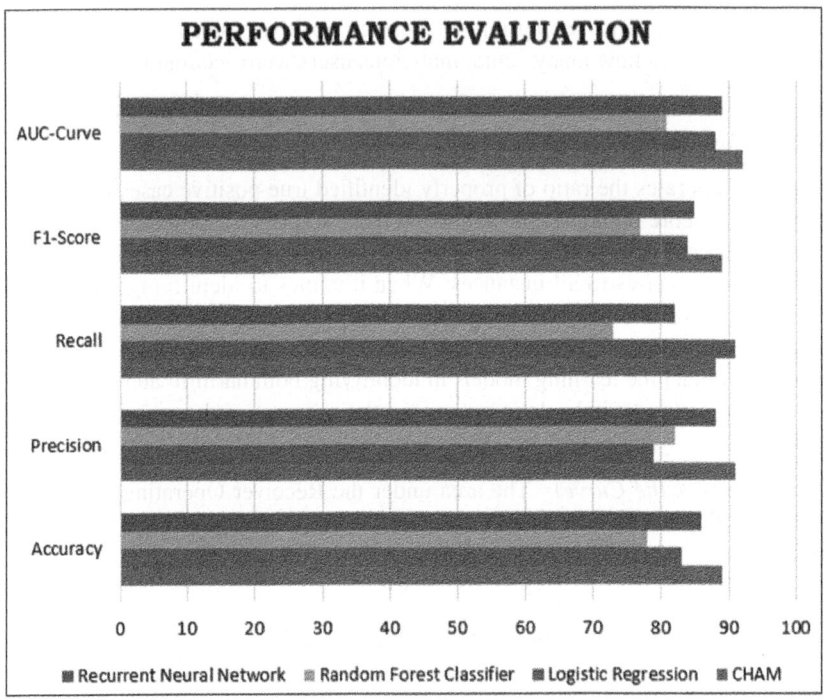

Fig. 6. Performance Evaluation

5 Conclusion

The paper presented a novel approach for detecting malicious users in social networks using CHAM (Convolutional Neural Networks (CNN) and Hierarchical Attention) Models. When compared to traditional baseline methods, the combination of rich feature representation from CNN and hierarchical knowledge of user interactions from the attention model has proven considerable gains in reliably recognizing harmful behaviors. The improved techniques, with their capacity to capture visual material, hierarchical linkages, and temporal patterns, give a more comprehensive answer for combating varied hostile actions on social networks, according to the paper. This method not only improves detection accuracy, but it also improves interpretability, flexibility to emerging dangers, and the possibility to sustain user trust by providing insights into classification rationale. The results reveal that the hybrid model surpasses previous systems in terms of accuracy, precision, recall, F1-score, and AUC, especially in situations involving coordinated attacks, image-based threats, or dynamic strategies. Advanced methodologies, by overcoming the limits of existing models, pave the door for more effective content filtering, enhanced user safety, and early detection of dangerous users. The advanced techniques investigated amateur a compact foundation for recognizing malevolent individuals on social networks. Future research and development in the aforementioned areas could result in even more sophisticated and effective solutions, creating a safer and more trustworthy environment for consumers across multiple online platforms.

Future Scope and Limitations

Further optimization of the model's structure and hyper parameters has the impending to augment its performance even further. It is crucial to refine the model using a diverse dataset and optimize the trade-off between precision and recall. Enhancing the model's capability to process various modalities (such as text, photos, and video) can enhance its adaptability in identifying a broader spectrum of harmful content and coordinated behaviors. It is indispensable to modify the model to enable its deployment in real time to afford prompt content moderation. Exploring the development of algorithms that are both efficient and accurate, while minimizing computing burden, is a promising area for future research. To enhance the model's versatility across various social networks, it is necessary to take into account the distinct behaviors and characteristics peculiar to each platform. It is crucial to ensure that the model is capable of handling a wide range of datasets to achieve wider acceptance. To effectively counter emerging threats, it is imperative to regularly update and train the model using the most recent data, as hostile strategies are constantly evolving. The efficacy of the model is highly dependent on the accessibility of varied and inclusive training data. If the training dataset exhibits bias or is deficient in particular malevolent behaviors, the model may encounter difficulties in identifying emerging threats or behaviors that are not adequately represented in the training data.

References

1. Lu, H., Gong, D., Li, Z., Liu, F., Liu, F.: SybilHP: sybil detection in directed social networks with adaptive homophily prediction. Appl. Sci. **13**(9), 5341 (2023)
2. Hu, L., Wei, S., Zhao, Z., Wu, B.: Deep learning for fake news detection: a comprehensive survey. AI Open **3**, 133–155 (2022)
3. Senthil Raja, M., Arun Raj, L.: Detection of malicious profiles and protecting users in online social networks. Wireless Pers. Commun. **127**(1), 107–124 (2022)
4. Terumalasetti, S., Reeja, S.R.: A sophisticated deep learning framework of advanced techniques to detect malicious users in online social networks. Int. J. Adv. Comput. Sci. Appl. (IJACSA) **14**(12), 616–624 (2023)
5. Taher, Y., Moussaoui, A., Moussaoui, F.: Automatic fake news detection based on deep learning, FasTtext and news title. Int. J. Adv. Comput. Sci. Appl. **13**(1) (2022)
6. Ben Sassi, I., Ben Yahia, S.: Malicious accounts detection from online social networks: a systematic review of the literature. Int. J. Gen. Syst. **50**(7), 741–814 (2021)
7. Terumalasetti, S., Reeja, S.R.: A comprehensive study on review of AI techniques to provide security in the digital world. In: 2022 Third International Conference on Intelligent Computing Instrumentation and Control Technologies (ICICICT). IEEE, pp. 407–416 (2022)
8. Maniriho, P., Mahmood, A.N., Chowdhury, M.J.M.: A study on malicious software behaviour analysis and detection techniques: taxonomy, current trends and challenges. Future Gener. Comput. Syst. **130**, 1–8 (2022)
9. Nagendra Sai, C., Dinesh Kumar, R., Sowjanya Reddy, M.: An efficient method for spammer and fake user detection on social networks. J. Emerg. Technol. Innov. Res. (2021)

10. Mou, G., Lee, K.: Malicious bot detection in online social networks: arming handcrafted features with deep learning. In: Aref, S., Bontcheva, K., Braghieri, M., Dignum, F., Giannotti, F., Grisolia, F., Pedreschi, D. (eds.) SocInfo 2020. LNCS, vol. 12467, pp. 220–236. Springer, Cham (2020). https://doi.org/10.1007/978-3-030-60975-7_17
11. Latah, M.: Detection of malicious social bots: a survey and a refined taxonomy. Expert Syst. Appl. **151**, 113383 (2020)
12. Tuttle, C.A., Patel, S., Yue, H.: Malicious message detection on Twitter via dissemination paths. In: International Conference on Computing, Networking and Communications (ICNC). IEEE, pp. 400–404 (2020)
13. Samokhvalov, D.I.: Machine learning-based malicious users' detection in the VKontakte social network. Труды института системного программирования РАН **32**(3), 109–117 (2020)
14. Hussain, A., Keshavamurthy, B.N.: Analyzing online location-based social networks for malicious user detection. In: Sa, P.K., Bakshi, S., Hatzilygeroudis, I.K., Sahoo, M.N. (eds.) Recent Findings in Intelligent Computing Techniques: Proceedings of the 5th ICACNI 2017, Volume 1, pp. 463–471. Springer, Singapore (2019). https://doi.org/10.1007/978-981-10-8639-7_48
15. Nilizadeh, S., et al.: Poised: spotting Twitter spam off the beaten paths. In: Proceedings of the 2017 ACM SIGSAC Conference on Computer and Communications Security, pp. 1159–1174 (2017)
16. Van der Walt, E., Eloff, J.H., Grobler, J.: Cyber-security: identity deception detection on social media platforms. Comput. Secur. **78**, 76–89 (2018)
17. Xia, Z., Liu, C., Gong, N.Z., Li, Q., Cui, Y., Song, D.: Characterizing and detecting malicious accounts in privacy-centric mobile social networks: a case study. In: Proceedings of the 25th ACM SIGKDD International Conference on Knowledge Discovery & Data Mining, pp. 2012–2022 (2019)
18. Dewan, P., Kumaraguru, P.: Detecting malicious content on Facebook. arXiv preprint arXiv: 1501.00802 (2015)
19. Lakshmi, M.V., Reeja, S.R.: A review of flood forecasting with the motivation of avoiding economic loss. In: 2022 Fourth International Conference on Cognitive Computing and Information Processing (CCIP), pp. 1–5. IEEE (2022)
20. Mounika, S., Reeja, S.: Comprehensive study on RS_FMRI and EEG using deep learning approach for brain stroke. In: 2023 International Conference on Intelligent and Innovative Technologies in Computing, Electrical and Electronics (IITCEE), pp. 384–388. IEEE (2023)
21. Reeja, S.R., Kavya, N.P.: Noise reduction in video sequences-the state of art and the technique for motion detection. Int. J. Comput. Appl. **58**(8), 31–36 (2012)
22. Jose, J.M., Reeja, S.R.: Anomaly detection on system generated logs—a survey study. In: Shakya, S., Bestak, R., Palanisamy, R., Kamel, K.A. (eds.) Mobile Computing and Sustainable Informatics. LNDECT, vol. 68, pp. 779–793. Springer, Singapore (2022). https://doi.org/10.1007/978-981-16-1866-6_59
23. Reshma, S., Reeja, S.R.: A review of computer assistance in dermatology. In: 2023 International Conference on Intelligent and Innovative Technologies in Computing, Electrical and Electronics (IITCEE), pp. 66–71. IEEE (2023)
24. Rabbani, M., et al.: A review on machine learning approaches for network malicious behavior detection in emerging technologies. Entropy **23**(5), 529 (2021)

Detecting and Preventing DoS Attacks Within IoT Environment Using AWS IoT Core

M. Nimavat Dhaval[1,2(✉)] ⓘ and G. Raiyani Ashwin[3] ⓘ

[1] RK University, Rajkot, India
dhaval.nimavat26730@paruluniversity.com
[2] Parul University, Vadodara, India
[3] Nirma University, Ahmedabad, India
ashwin.raiyani@nirmauni.ac.in

Abstract. Detecting and preventing cyber attacks within an IoT (Internet of Things) environment by AWS MQTT (Message Queuing Telemetry Transport) Broker involves implementing various security measures and best practices. MQTT preferred as lightweight messaging protocol commonly utilized in IoT applications for efficient communication between IoT devices and various cloud services. AWS IoT Core provides an MQTT broker service that allows secure communication between IoT devices and cloud resources. Detecting and preventing Denial of Service (DoS) attacks within an IoT environment using AWS MQTT Broker involves a combination of security measures and services provided by AWS. In this research paper, we studied a couple of cyber attacks, tools, and also demonstrated strategies and tactics to protect the AWS IoT Core environment in which we had implemented and configured custom digital certificate and policy from DoS attacks using various python scripts.

Keywords: IoT · Security · Types of Cyber Attack · DoS Attack

1 Introduction to Cyber Attacks

In today's world, various activities, including economic, industrial, cultural, social, and governmental, are conducted online. Our global society heavily relies on wireless technology, making safeguarding data from cyber-attacks a challenging task. Cyber-attacks are primarily aimed at stealing sensitive credentials, but in some cases, they may have military or political motivations. These attacks can cause various damages, such as viruses, data breaches, Distributed Denial of Service (DDS) attacks, and other sophisticated attack vectors. As a result, many companies and organizations employ diverse solutions to mitigate the impact of cyber-attacks [1, 2].

A cyber attack within the IoT (Internet of Things) refers to a malicious act targeted at exploiting vulnerabilities within IoT devices, networks, or services. The IoT is a vast network of interconnected devices that can include smart home appliances, wearables, industrial machines, medical devices, and more. The interconnected nature of these devices, combined with potential security weaknesses, makes them susceptible to various cyber threats. Here are some major types of cyber attacks within the IoT [3, 4] (Fig. 1):

© ICST Institute for Computer Sciences, Social Informatics and Telecommunications Engineering 2024
Published by Springer Nature Switzerland AG 2024. All Rights Reserved
O. Castillo et al. (Eds.): PerSOM 2023, LNICST 517, pp. 75–88, 2024.
https://doi.org/10.1007/978-3-031-66044-3_5

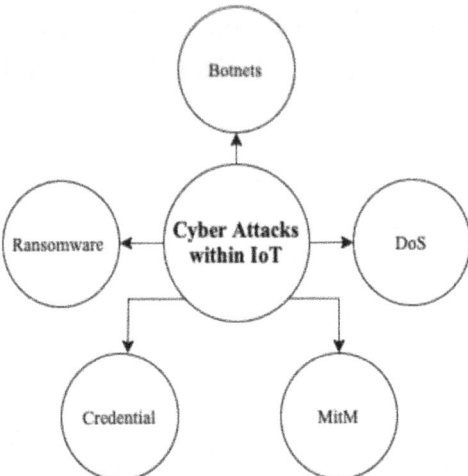

Fig. 1. Cyber Attacks within IoT

1.1 Botnets Attacks

A botnet attack in IoT (Internet of Things) refers to a cyber attack in which a network of compromised IoT devices is controlled by malicious actors to carry out various malicious activities. Botnets are groups of devices infected with malware and controlled remotely by a single entity, often referred to as the "botmaster" or "bot herder." These compromised devices, known as bots or zombies, are typically IoT devices with weak security measures [5].

1.2 DoS (Denial of Service) Attacks

A DoS (Denial of Service) attack in IoT (Internet of Things) involves flooding a network of interconnected devices with a massive amount of traffic or requests, overwhelming their resources and causing them to become unavailable to legitimate users. In the context of IoT, a DoS attack can interrupt the common functioning of IoT devices, leading to service outages and potential disruptions in various sectors where IoT devices are employed [6].

1.3 (MiM) Man-in-Middle Attacks

Man-in-Middle (MiM) attacks in IoT (Internet of Things) involve intercepting and potentially modifying the communication between IoT devices or between IoT devices and their central server. In a MitM attack, an unauthorized attacker positions themselves between the communicating parties and secretly relays or alters the messages passing between them, without the parties being aware of the intrusion [6, 7].

1.4 Credential Attacks

Credential attacks in IoT (Internet of Things) refer to cyber attacks that target the authentication credentials used by IoT devices, services, or users to gain unauthorized access to the system. These attacks focus on exploiting weak or stolen credentials, such as usernames and passwords, to compromise IoT devices or networks using brute force attack [6, 7].

1.5 Ransomware Attacks

A ransomware attack within IoT (Internet of Things) involves the deployment of ransomware on IoT devices to encrypt their data and demand a ransom from the device owner or the organization controlling the devices. Ransomware is a one of the type of malware that restricts access to a device or its data until a ransom is paid to the attacker, usually in cryptocurrencies, to obtain the decryption key and regain access to the locked data [6, 7].

1.6 Investigating Security Issues Related to Denial of Service (DoS) Attacks

To effectively investigate and mitigate DoS attacks, it's crucial to establish a baseline of normal network activity.

- Packets out and Bytes out: Unusually high levels of outgoing packets and bytes may indicate that your network is generating an excessive amount of traffic. This could be a sign of a DoS attack, as attackers often flood a target system with traffic to overwhelm it.
- Destination IP: Monitoring the destination IP addresses of incoming traffic can help you identify if there is an unusual concentration of traffic directed at a particular IP address. This could be a sign of a targeted attack.
- Listening TCP ports: An increase in the number of open TCP ports could indicate that services are being exploited, especially if these ports are not typically open. Attackers may be attempting to exploit vulnerabilities in open ports to launch an attack.
- Listening TCP port count: A sudden or significant increase in the number of listening TCP ports may be a sign of unwanted services running on your network. Such services could be exploited by attackers to facilitate a DoS attack.
- Listening UDP ports: Similar to TCP ports, a sudden increase in listening UDP ports may indicate unexpected or potentially vulnerable services. UDP-based DoS attacks are also possible, so monitoring these ports is essential.

Consider that despite the fact these indicators are useful, a more comprehensive security plan should include them. It's also critical to keep up with the most recent DoS attack methods and trends in order to can improve defensive measures appropriately.

2 Related Work

To address the security needs of an IoT system, various methods can be employed [8]. Among them, mutual authentication among the IoT device and the gateway within the resource-constrained environment of the IoT system is of utmost importance. In this research paper, we propose enhancing security mechanisms using Amazon Web Services (AWS) Core Concepts and MQTT Broker as IoT Middleware. We introduce custom digital certification, private key, and custom policy to facilitate secure communication in the IoT environment. We also performed certain DoS attacks on local server like node-red (127.0.0.1) as well as our implemented IoT middleware model on AWS IoT Core to understand the impact of various DoS attacks [9–11].

2.1 Algorithm for Securing IoT Environment

Step 1: Connection with AWS IoT Core: Establish the connection between things (client or published or subscriber) to IoT core [9, 10] (Fig. 2).

```
"Version": "2023-05-17",
"Statement": [
        {
                "Effect": "Allow",
                "Action": "iot:Connect",
                "Resource": [
                        "arn:aws:iot:us-east-1:123456789012:RKU1/${iot:Connection.Thing.ThingName}"
                ]
        }
]
```

Fig. 2. Connection with AWS IoT Core

Step 2: Define Topic for IoT Devices : In order to transmit or receive message, Topic is essential to be created on cloud services (Fig. 3).

```
arn:aws:iot:aws-region:dhaval.nimavat:topic/Topic
```

Fig. 3. IoT Topic

Step 3: Implementing and assigning custom digital certificate to ensure authentication among IoT devices which includes own private key using OpenSSL (LibreSSL 2.8) (Figs. 4 and 5).

Step 4: Generate and define custom MQTT policy: AWS IoT Core policies are structured in JSON format, encompassing rules for establishing connections, message retention, message publishing, message receiving, and topic subscription. The custom policy on AWS, illustrated in the following figure [9–11] (Fig. 6).

Step 5: Assign certificate and policy to IoT Devices: In the context of AWS IoT, we had utilized Node-RED platform to implement and utilize digital signature and policy

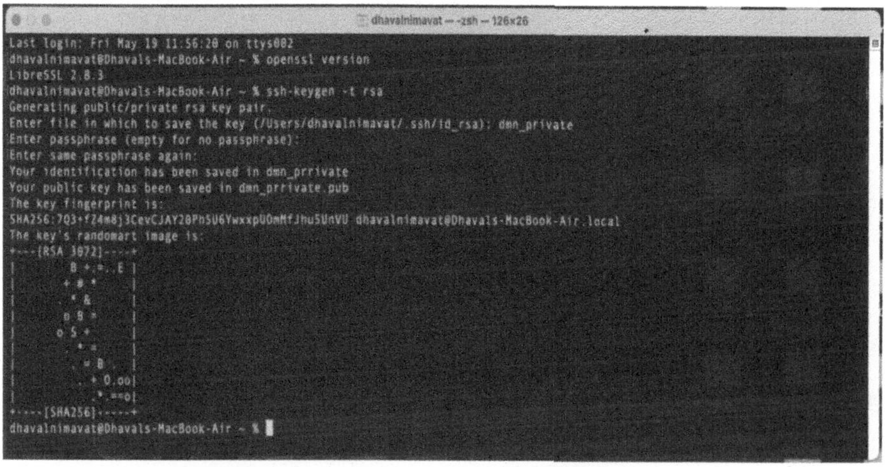

Fig. 4. Generated Private Key, OpenSSL

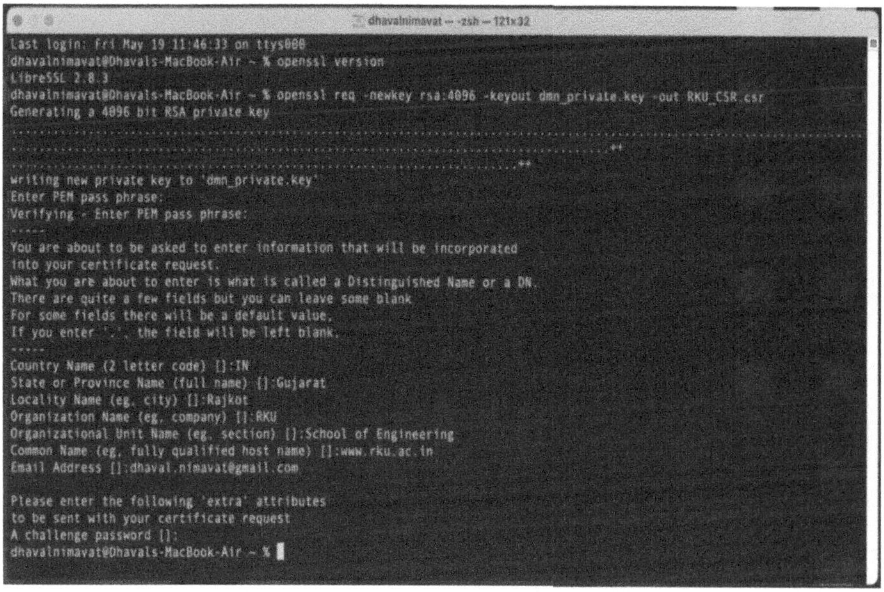

Fig. 5. Generated custom digital certificates using 4096 bit private key

techniques for a specific use case. Node-RED is a visual programming tool kit that allows users to design and deploy applications by connecting different nodes representing various services or functionalities. Within AWS IoT Environment, Node red architect can be employed to coordinate the required configurations for digital signatures and policies (Figs. 7, 8 and 9).

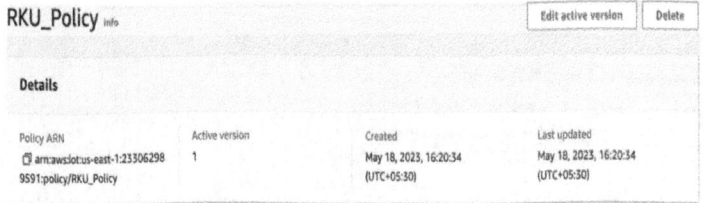

Fig. 6. Policy for IoT Devices

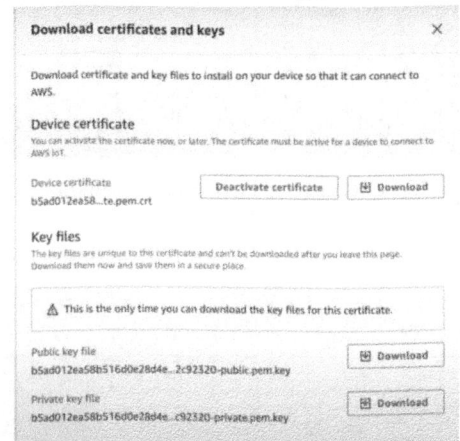

Fig. 7. Download certificate and private key

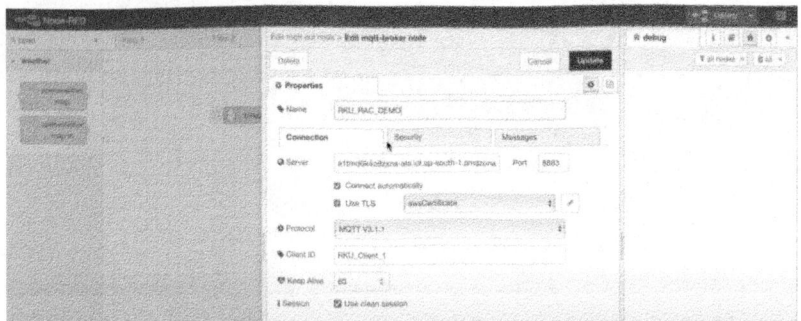

Fig. 8. MQTT Broker Configuration on Node-Red.

This case study involves utilizing the OpenWeatherAPI as the publisher and a subsciber running on https://127.0.0.1:1880. The implementation includes customized AWS IoT Core Concepts, utilizing the IoT Topic "MQTT/SensorData1", a custom private key "dmn-private.key", a generated digital certificate "RKU-CSR.csr", and a policy named "RKU-Policy" [9–11].

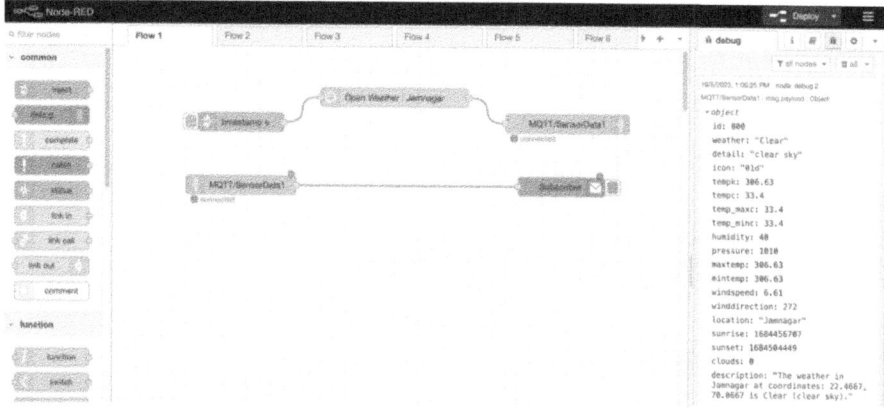

Fig. 9. Results of secured communication between pub (Open Weather API) and sub.

3 Results on DoS Attacks

In this research paper, we also find evidence of following assaults on the proposed AWS MQTT broker (Middleware Architecture) as well as the local server(Node-RED) and WiFi router. It is important to note that engaging in any form of cyber attack, including flood attacks, socket attacks, packet sniffing, or packet injection without explicit authorization is illegal and unethical. These attacks can cause significant harm to targeted systems and networks, and engaging in such activities may lead to serious legal consequences [4].

3.1 Flood Attack

A flood attack, also known as a denial-of-service (DoS) flood attack, aims to overwhelm a target system or network by sending a large volume of traffic or requests. The flood of traffic consumes the target's resources, causing service disruptions and making it unavailable to legitimate users. Here result of flood attacks shown in below figures to various local server, WIFI router and proposed middleware architecture [12, 13] (Figs. 10, 11 and 12).

3.2 Socket Attack

A socket attack involves targeting the communication channels known as sockets that are used to establish connections between devices or between a device and a server. In the context of attacks, it can refer to exploiting vulnerabilities in socket communication protocols to disrupt or manipulate data exchange. Here result of socket attacks shown in below figures to various local server, WIFI router and proposed middleware architecture [14] (Figs. 13, 14 and 15).

```
● ● ●                           dhavalnimavat — -zsh — 91×13
.Request timeout for icmp_seq 2894
.Request timeout for icmp_seq 2895
.Request timeout for icmp_seq 2896
..Request timeout for icmp_seq 2898
.Request timeout for icmp_seq 2899
.Request timeout for icmp_seq 2900
.Request timeout for icmp_seq 2901
.Request timeout for icmp_seq 2902
^C
--- 127.0.0.1 ping statistics ---
2904 packets transmitted, 2109 packets received, 27.4% packet loss
round-trip min/avg/max/stddev = 0.011/0.029/0.125/0.010 ms
dhavalnimavat@Dhavals-MacBook-Air ~ %
```

Fig. 10. Flood Attack on Node-Red 127.0.0.1

```
● ● ●                           dhavalnimavat — -zsh — 94×10
.Request timeout for icmp_seq 3929
.Request timeout for icmp_seq 3930
.Request timeout for icmp_seq 3931
.Request timeout for icmp_seq 3932
.Request timeout for icmp_seq 3933
^C
--- 10.29.31.255 ping statistics ---
3935 packets transmitted, 1596 packets received, +2151 duplicates, 59.4% packet loss
round-trip min/avg/max/stddev = 0.018/196.084/503.959/141.076 ms
dhavalnimavat@Dhavals-MacBook-Air ~ %
```

Fig. 11. Flood Attack on WIFI Router 10.29.31.25

```
● ● ●                           dhavalnimavat — -zsh — 129×16
.Request timeout for icmp_seq 2956
.Request timeout for icmp_seq 2957
.Request timeout for icmp_seq 2958
.Request timeout for icmp_seq 2959
.Request timeout for icmp_seq 2960
.Request timeout for icmp_seq 2961
.Request timeout for icmp_seq 2962
.Request timeout for icmp_seq 2963
.Request timeout for icmp_seq 2964
.Request timeout for icmp_seq 2965
.Request timeout for icmp_seq 2966
.Request timeout for icmp_seq 2967
^C
--- a1tmd6k4o9zxna-ats.iot.us-east-1.amazonaws.com ping statistics ---
2969 packets transmitted, 0 packets received, 100.0% packet loss
dhavalnimavat@Dhavals-MacBook-Air ~ %
```

Fig. 12. Flood Attack on Proposed Middleware Architecture

```
● ● ●                           Kali_Linux — -zsh — 95×6
dhavalnimavat@Dhavals-MacBook-Air kali_linux % python3 SocketAttack.py
Enter the target IP address: 127.0.0.1
How long before the connection times out: 3
Listening on port: 7000
Listening on port: 1880
Listening on port: 5000
```

Fig. 13. Socket Attack on Node-Red 127.0.0.1

3.3 Packet Sniffing

Packet sniffing, also known as packet capturing, involves intercepting and monitoring network traffic to track and monitor the data packets that are transmitted over the network. This is often used for legitimate purposes like network troubleshooting, but it could also

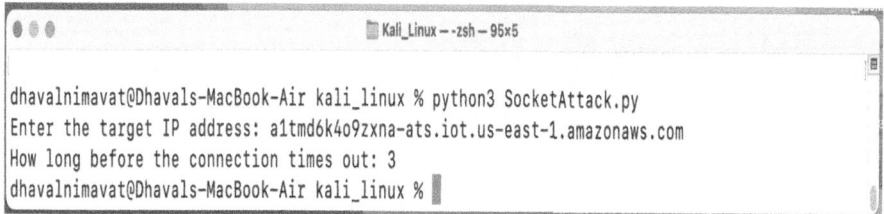

Fig. 14. Socket Attack on WIFI Router 10.29.31.25

Fig. 15. Socket Attack on Proposed Middleware Architecture

be used maliciously to track sensitive information from the intercepted packets. Here result of packet sniffing attack shown in below figures to various local server, WIFI router [15] and proposed middleware architecture (Figs. 16, 17 and 18).

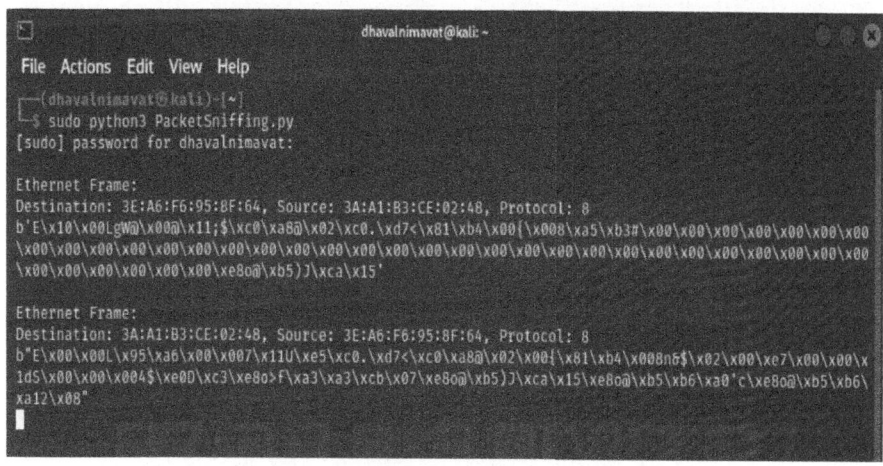

Fig. 16. Packet Sniffing Attack on Node-Red (127.0.0.1)

3.4 Packet Injection

Packet injection is a technique where an attacker sends forged or modified packets into a network to manipulate the communication between devices or disrupt network

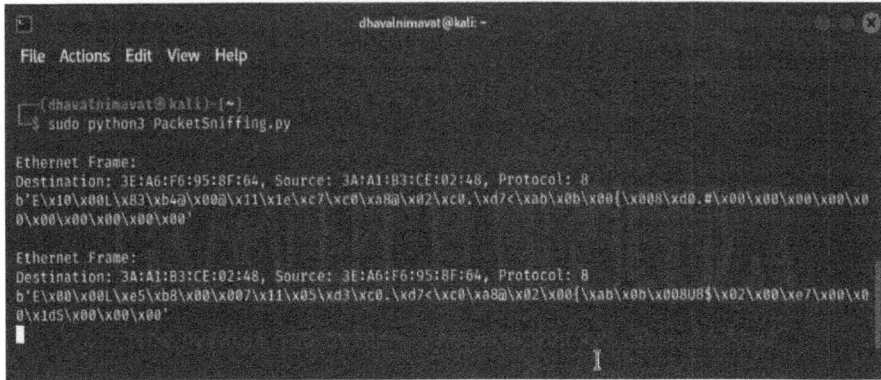

Fig. 17. Packet Sniffing Attack on WIFI Router 10.29.31.25

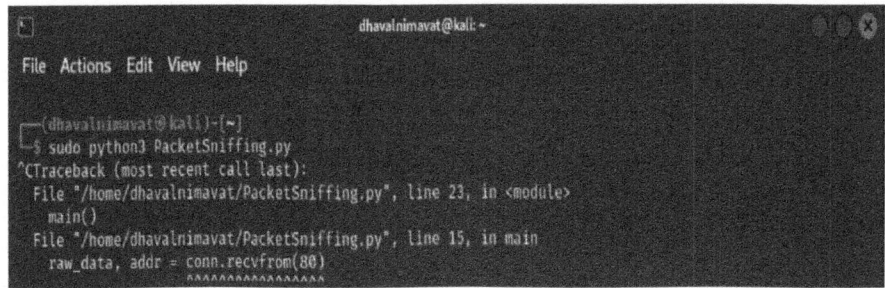

Fig. 18. Packet Sniffing Attack on Proposed Middleware Architecture

operations. This can be used for various purposes, such as inserting malicious data or altering legitimate traffic. Here result of packet inject attacks shown in below figures to various local server, WIFI router and proposed middleware architecture [16, 17] (Figs. 19, 20 and 21).

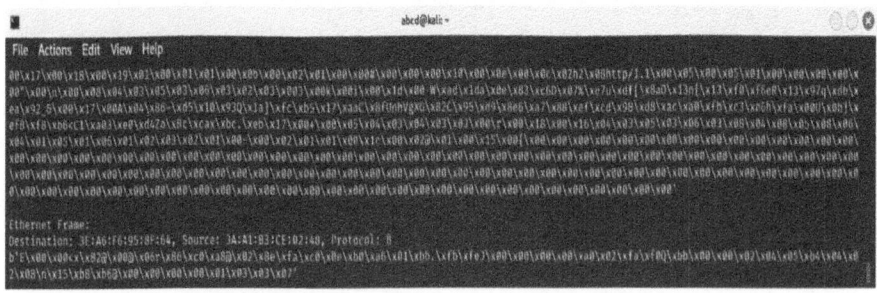

Fig. 19. Packet Inject Attack on Node-Red (127.0.0.1)

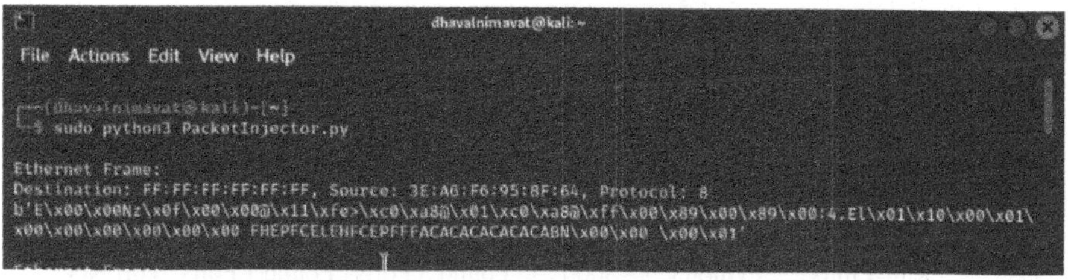

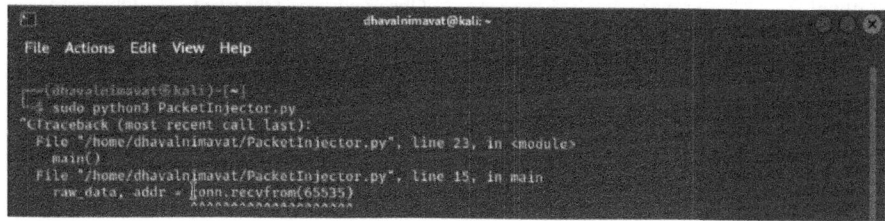

Fig. 20. Packet Inject Attack on WIFI Router 10.29.31.25

Fig. 21. Packet Inject Attack on Proposed Middleware Architecture

4   Impact of DoS Attacks

Cyber attacks on IoT (Internet of Things) can have far-reaching and severe impacts on individuals, organizations, and society as a whole. As IoT devices become increasingly integrated into various aspects of our lives, from smart homes and healthcare to industrial automation and critical infrastructure, the potential consequences of cyber attacks become more significant. A successful cyber attack on IoT devices can lead to privacy breaches and data manipulation. As these devices often collect and transmit sensitive personal data, attackers can feet vulnerabilities to get unauthorized access to personal information, location data, and other sensitive details. Moreover, manipulating the data collected by IoT devices can lead to inaccurate readings and misleading information, compromising decision-making processes in critical sectors. Below table describes the impact of DoS attacks such as flood, socket, packet sniffing and packet inject on various middleware architecture [18] (Table 1).

Table 1. Impact of Cyber Attacks on Middleware Architecture

Types of Attack	OS	Script	Packets	127.0.0.1	10.29.31.25	Proposed Middleware
Flood Attack	macOS	Python3	~3000	2109 Packet Received	1596 Packet Received	No Packet Received
Socket Attack	Kali-Linux	Python3	~3000	Found 3 Ports	Found 1 Ports	Port Not Found
Packet Sniffing Attack	Kali- Linux	Python3	–	Packets Observed	Packets Observed	No Packet Observed
Packet Injection Attack	Kali- Linux	Python3	–	Applied	Applied	Connection Aborted

5 Conclusion

In conclusion, detecting and preventing cyber attacks within an IoT environment using AWS MQTT Broker is of paramount importance to ensure the security and reliability of IoT systems. MQTT, being a lightweight messaging protocol, plays a crucial role in facilitating efficient communication among IoT devices and cloud services, making AWS IoT's MQTT broker service a valuable tool in this context. The research paper presented a comprehensive experimental results of different cyber attacks, tools, and demonstrated effective strategies and tactics to protect the AWS IoT Core environment. The implementation and configuration of custom digital certificates and policies were instrumental in fortifying the system against Denial of Service (DoS) attacks, which pose significant threats to IoT infrastructures. The combination of security measures and services provided by AWS is essential to safeguard IoT devices and cloud resources from potential threats. By employing proactive security practices, such as regular updates, network segmentation, authentication mechanisms, and continuous monitoring, organizations can significantly enhance the resilience of their IoT systems. As IoT technology continues to advance and become more ubiquitous, ensuring the security and integrity of IoT environments becomes increasingly crucial. The research and efforts dedicated to detecting and preventing cyber attacks within an IoT ecosystem will contribute significantly to creating a safer and more secure connected world. By staying vigilant and implementing best practices, stakeholders can mitigate the risks and potential damages caused by cyber attacks, ensuring the continued growth and advancement of the IoT landscape.

References

1. Sharma, A.K., Galav, R.K., Sharma, B.: A comprehensive survey of various cyber attacks. In: 2023 6th International Conference on Information Systems and Computer Networks (ISCON), pp. 1–4 (2023). https://doi.org/10.1109/ISCON57294.2023.10111998

2. Gururaj, H.L., Soundarya, B.C., Janhavi, V., Lakshmi, H., Prassan Kumar, M.J.: Analysis of cyber security attacks using kali Linux. In: IEEE International Conference on Distributed Computing and Electrical Circuits and Electronics, ICDCECE 2022. Institute of Electrical and Electronics Engineers Inc. (2022). https://doi.org/10.1109/ICDCECE53908.2022.9793164

3. Kantimahanthi, S., Prasad, J.V.D., Chanamolu, S., Kommaraju, K.: Machine learning approaches in cyber attack detection and characterization in IoT enabled cyber-physical systems. In: 2023 International Conference on Intelligent Data Communication Technologies and Internet of Things (IDCIoT), pp. 136–142 (2023). https://doi.org/10.1109/IDCIoT 56793.2023.10053545

4. Lu, K.-D., Wu, Z.-G., Huang, T.: Differential evolution-based three stage dynamic cyber-attack of cyber-physical power systems. IEEE/ASME Trans. Mechatron. **28**(2), 1137–1148 (2023). https://doi.org/10.1109/TMECH.2022.3214314

5. Potrino, G., de Rango, F., Santamaria, A.F.: Modeling and evaluation of a new IoT security system for mitigating DoS attacks to the MQTT broker. In: 2019 IEEE Wireless Communications and Networking Conference (WCNC), pp. 1–6 (2019). https://doi.org/10.1109/WCNC.2019.8885553

6. Rao, G.S., Harshitha, M., Joshitha, V.R., Sravya, S.S., Priya, M.V.: DoS attack detection in wireless sensor networks (WSN) using hybrid machine learning model. In: 2023 10th International Conference on Signal Processing and Integrated Networks (SPIN), pp. 384–388 (2023). https://doi.org/10.1109/SPIN57001.2023.10117098

7. Wiranata, A., Karna, N., Irawan, A., Prakoso, I.A.: Implementation and analysis of network security in Raspberry Pi against DOS attack with HIPS snort. In: 2023 International Conference on Computer Science, Information Technology and Engineering (ICCoSITE), pp. 892–896 (2023). https://doi.org/10.1109/ICCoSITE57641.2023.10127741

8. Vachhani, S., Nimavat, D., Kalyani, F.: A comparitive analysis of different algorithms used in IoT based smart car parking systems (2020)

9. Nimavat, D.M.: Enhanced security by using AWS MQTT broker as middleware architecture for IoT environment section a-research paper enhanced security by using AWS MQTT broker as middleware architecture for IoT environment 1

10. Dhaval, N., Ashwin, R.: Study on security issues and threats for MQTT with IoT paradigm. www.rku.ac.in

11. Nimavat Dhaval, M., Raiyani Ashwin, G.: A study on MQTT protocol architecture and security aspects within IoT paradigm. In: Balas, V.E., Semwal, V.B., Khandare, A. (eds.) Intelligent Computing and Networking: Proceedings of IC-ICN 2022, pp. 61–72. Springer, Singapore (2023). https://doi.org/10.1007/978-981-99-0071-8_6

12. Patil, P.S., Deshpande, S.L., Hukkeri, G.S., Goudar, R.H., Siddarkar, P.: Prediction of DDoS flooding attack using machine learning models. In: 2022 Third International Conference on Smart Technologies in Computing, Electrical and Electronics (ICSTCEE), pp. 1–6 (2022). https://doi.org/10.1109/ICSTCEE56972.2022.10100083

13. Liu, B., Yao, X., Guo, K., Zhu, P.: Consortium blockchain based lightweight message authentication and auditing in smart home. IEEE Access **11**, 68473–68485 (2023). https://doi.org/10.1109/ACCESS.2023.3293401

14. Liu, T., et al.: MagBackdoor: beware of your loudspeaker as a backdoor for magnetic injection attacks. In: 2023 IEEE Symposium on Security and Privacy (SP), pp. 3416–3431 (2023). https://doi.org/10.1109/SP46215.2023.10179364

15. Manikanta Narayana, D.S., Bharadwaj Nookala, S., Chopra, S., Shanmugam, U.: An adaptive threat defence mechanism through self defending network to prevent Hijacking in WiFi network. In: 2023 International Conference on Advances in Electronics, Communication, Computing and Intelligent Information Systems (ICAECIS), pp. 133–138 (2023). https://doi.org/10.1109/ICAECIS58353.2023.10170470

16. Shinde, S., Mehta, H.: Defending marine ships against ethernet based cyberattacks. In: 2023 Fifth International Conference on Electrical, Computer and Communication Technologies (ICECCT), pp. 1–5 (2023). https://doi.org/10.1109/ICECCT56650.2023.10179830
17. Khalid, W., Ahmad, N., Khan, S., Saquib, N.U., Arshad, M., Shahwar, D.: FAPMIC: fake packet and selective packet drops attacks mitigation by merkle hash tree in intermittently connected networks. IEEE Access **11**, 4549–4573 (2023). https://doi.org/10.1109/ACCESS.2023.3235900
18. Siriyapuraju, S.J., Gowri, V.S., Balla, S., Vanika, M.K., Gandhi, A.: DoS and DDoS attack detection using mathematical and entropy methods. In: 2023 2nd International Conference on Paradigm Shifts in Communications Embedded Systems, Machine Learning and Signal Processing (PCEMS), pp. 1–6 (2023). https://doi.org/10.1109/PCEMS58491.2023.10136042

A Novel Technique to Enhance the Visibility of Sand-Dust Images

Harini Kalwa, Kommu Gangadhara Rao$^{(\boxtimes)}$, Maram Satya Pavan,
Varshith Reddy Annam, Hemath Kumar Challa, and Yeshwanth Keerthi

Chaitanya Bharathi Institute of Technology (Autonomous), Hyderabad, India
`kgangadhar_it@cbit.ac.in`

Abstract. At times, we must snap pictures in the sand and dusty environments. The obtained images exhibit low visibility and color deviation properties, which have a significant negative impact on computer vision systems due to the impact of sand dust particles, light gets scattered and absorbed, leading to a blurry image with low contrast. An efficient and quick algorithm is suggested to improve the images that are recorded in order to address those issues. The approach used to improve the photos compensates for the lost value in the blue channel first. The color of the sand dust images is then corrected using white balancing technology. Guided image filtering is employed to enhance the image's contrast and edge precision, while an adaptive technique is utilized to determine the magnification factor of the detail layer, which in turn improves the image's detailed information.

Keywords: Blue Channel · White balancing · edge accuracy · Guided image filtering

1 Introduction

Low contrast, color variation, and blur are common in photographs taken under sand- dust conditions, all of which have a negative impact on the clarity of the picture. The primary reason for this phenomenon is the scattering and absorption of light by sand- dust particles. Therefore, the sand dust-damaged photos have directly decreased the monitoring systems, automated driving, and remote sensing systems' processing capacity. Researchers have developed certain visibility restoration methods to enhance the processing capacity of computer vision systems in sand-dust environment conditions.

While current methods for sand-dust-degraded image enhancement can correct color discrepancies, improve image contrast, and increase image clarity, some issues still exist. First, blue artifacts arise in the photos and lower the image quality when the sand-dust-damaged images are processed using the present color restoration technique. Second, the temporal complexity of the present techniques for sand-dust- degraded image augmentation is considerable. Therefore,

O. Castillo et al. (Eds.): PerSOM 2023, LNICST 517, pp. 89–100, 2024.
https://doi.org/10.1007/978-3-031-66044-3_6

the ongoing review is aimed at improving the accuracy and time complexity of sand dust image enhancement [1].

2   Literature Review

This section will provide a brief review of the related works carried out in the domain of sand dust image enhancement.

2.1   Blue Channel and Fusion for Sandstorm Image Enhancement

This paper suggests a technique for making images taken during a sandstorm more visible. Using the image's blue channel, which is less impacted by sand particles, and fusing it with the red and green channels, which are more impacted in this method. The paper proposes two methods to recover sand dust images: the Blue channel method and the Fusion method. In the first method, the blue channel of the image is used because it is less impacted by the sand particles than the red and green channels. A dehazing algorithm is used to extract the blue channel from the original image and then restore it. Finally, a weighted average technique is utilized to combine the recovered blue channel with the red and green channels.

The second method, to improve the visibility of the sandstorm image, this technique includes merging many images of the same scene taken at various exposure times. An exposure fusion algorithm is used to align the photos before merging them. To further increase visibility, a contrast enhancement procedure is applied to the combined image that results [2]. Both techniques are successful at increasing the visibility of sandstorm images, according to experimental results. On the other hand, when it comes to both objective and subjective evaluation criteria, the Blue Channel Method is determined to be more successful and efficient than the Fusion Method.

This approach overcomes the limitations of existing image enhancement techniques. Firstly, by making use of the blue channel, it overcomes the problem of color distortion that frequently occurs in color-based image improvement algorithms. The second benefit is that it is reasonably effective and appropriate for real-time applications, overcoming the high computational cost limitation of some existing approaches. Lastly, the suggested approach overcomes the shortcomings of several existing approaches by improving the visibility of sandstorm images even under difficult circumstances [3].

However, the paper has some limitations, the method's efficiency may be influenced by the density of sand particles in the image. The suggested technique may not be as efficient in improving visibility in photos with a high density of sand particles. Another drawback is that the technique might not be effective for pictures with intricate scenes. The approach might not be able to distinguish the blue channel from the other channels precisely if the image comprises objects with various colors and textures (Fig. 1).

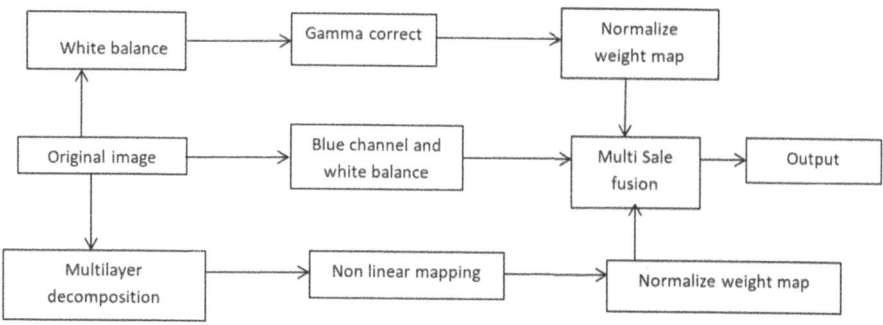

Fig. 1. The framework of the proposed algorithm

3 A Method Based on Halo on Halo-Reduced Dark Channel Prior Dehazing for Sand-Dust Image Enhancement

The work suggests a technique for improving the visibility of photographs of sand dust taken under poor lighting circumstances. To lessen the halo effect that frequently occurs in existing approaches, the proposed method, which is based on the dark channel before dehazing methods, was developed. The two key steps of the suggested procedure are haze reduction and image enhancement. The dark channel prior approach is used to remove the haze from the image during the haze removal stage. During the image enhancement stage, the contrast and brightness of the image are modified to enhance its visibility. In the first stage, A guided filter is used in the initial step of the process to lessen the halo effect in the hazy image. This step seeks to eliminate any artifacts brought on by the environment's sand and dust, which scatter light. The method then employs the dark channel prior dehazing technique to calculate the transmission map and eliminate the haze from the image. In this step, the scene information is recovered and the quantity of haze in the image is estimated. In the second uses a multi-scale fusion approach to combine data from many scales and enhance the dazed image's quality. This step reduces artifacts from the dehazing process and improves the visual quality of the dehazed image by combining data at various sizes. Ultimately, the approach improves the contrast of the dehazed image. The proposed approach overcomes the limitations of existing dehazing techniques firstly by using the guided filter to remove the artifacts brought on by light scattering in the sand-dust environment, secondly calculating the transmission map and removing haze with a dark channel preceding dehazing approach, which improves the contrast and details of the image, the method increases visibility. Finally, by introducing a contrast enhancement stage that raises the dazed image's overall brightness and contrast, the suggested solution addresses the problem of inadequate contrast that frequently arises in sand-dust weather circumstances. However, there are also potential limitations and challenges in using a dark channel prior to dehazing for sand dust image enhancement. The efficiency of the suggested strategy may be dependent on the particular details of the picture therefore it may not be best for all sand-dust weather circumstances. The suggested method's contrast enhancement stage requires that there be some contrast in the original image, hence it could not be effective for photos with very little contrast. The process might cause certain distortions or artifacts in the dehazed image, but the suggested guided filter is made to reduce these artifacts [5,6]. Given that the multi-scale fusion technique requires processing images at many scales, the suggested method might still be computationally expensive for very large-scale images (Fig. 2).

Fig. 2. Framework of Blue Channel and Fusion for Sandstorm Image Enhancement

3.1   Sand-Dust Image Enhancement Using Successive Color Balance with Coincident Chromatic Histogram

The work discussed a technique for improving images that have been ruined by sand or dust. Firstly it discusses the difficulties involved in processing images that have been impacted by sand or dust, which can lead to color casts, decreased contrast, and loss of detail. To address these issues, they suggest a technique that combines histogram equalization with color balancing [7]. By separating the image into its red, green, and blue color channels, a color balance is then applied to each channel separately. To analyze the color distribution in the image and identify regions affected by sand or dust, a coincident chromatic histogram is constructed by them. They utilize this data to change the color balance in certain regions, which helps to enhance the overall quality of the image and bring out more details.

The paper circumvents a number of drawbacks present in the previous sand-dust image enhancement techniques. For example, grit and dust can distort colors in images, making them hard to read. The suggested method applies color balancing to each color channel separately and utilizes a coincident chromatic histogram to detect areas that need modification [8]. The suggested solution overcomes this constraint by employing sequential color balancing to bring out more details in the image. Sand and dust can also reduce image detail, especially in low-contrast areas. Finally, while the findings of existing approaches may be unreliable, the suggested method outperforms them in terms of image quality and detail preservation.

The paper presents a possible approach to enhance images affected by sand or dust, yet it has some limitations. The proposed method may not work well for images with a lot of sand or dust, which is one of its limitations. Additionally, the procedure might not work with all kinds of photos and would need to be adjusted for certain sand or dust particle types. The proposed method may be computationally demanding and may need a lot of computing power, which could be problematic for some applications [9].

3.2   Sand-Dust Image Restoration Based on Reversing the Blue Channel Prior

This paper proposes an approach for recovering images affected by sand or dust. Prior to estimating and reconstructing the image's red and green channels, the authors utilize a blue channel that has been reversed. The quality of the restored image is then enhanced using a detail-enhancing algorithm. With regard to image quality and detail retention, the suggested method outperforms the alternatives when tested against a dataset of images that have been impacted by sand and dust [10, 11].

First, this method uses a combination of a Gaussian mixture model and a non-local means filter to estimate the Image's degraded blue channel. To estimate the original blue channel, they then reverse the estimated blue channel. The red and green channels of the image are then rebuilt using the estimated blue channel. After completing the blue channel estimate and reconstruction procedures, the paper employs a guided filter to improve the details of the restored image. The estimated blue channel and the original image are both subjected to the guided filter, and the output is then used to create the final enhanced image. The guided filter enhances the quality of the recovered image and aids in maintaining crucial features [12].

The paper improves upon several shortcomings of the existing techniques for recovering images affected by sand or dust. The proposed method specifically addresses the drawback of color distortion and artifacts in the restored images, which is a drawback of existing solutions. The method involves estimating and reconstructing the red and green channels of the image by utilizing an inverted blue channel. This improves the image quality and preserves more of the image's fine details [13].

However, the paper comprises of some limitations such as the suggested solution may not be relevant to other kinds of image degradation, which restricts its potential applications. It is also challenging to judge the effectiveness of the suggested strategy because the research does not compare it with other image restoration techniques that are currently in use. Additionally, the experimental evaluation of the suggested method is limited, making it challenging to generalize the findings to a wider variety of situations.

3.3   Single Image Dehazing via Deep Learning-Based Image Restoration

The paper suggests a deep learning-based approach for dehazing photos that have been influenced by atmospheric haze. The paper discusses the drawbacks of conventional dehazing techniques, which frequently fail to capture detailed atmospheric models and could produce unnatural-looking images. The suggested technique uses a deep convolutional neural network to take a hazy image as input and output a dazed image. The network learns the complex mapping between the input and output images through training on an extensive set of hazy and corresponding clear images. In-depth testing of the suggested method using a number of benchmark datasets is included in the study, which demonstrates that it beats conventional dehazing techniques and other cutting-edge deep learning-based techniques in terms of both visual quality and quantitative measures [14].

The proposed deep learning-based approach overcomes the limitations of conventional dehazing techniques in three different ways. First off, capturing detailed atmospheric models, it creates images that look more natural. Second, it may be used in real-world applications since it is resistant to different haze types and densities. Finally, traditional methods can be computationally expensive and time-consuming, especially for large- scale image or video processing tasks. In contrast, the proposed method is efficient and can process images in real-time, making it suitable for practical applications such as real-time video dehazing.

There are drawbacks to the suggested deep learning-based solution for single-image dehazing. First off, obtaining enough training data can be difficult, but it is necessary to get good results. Second, because it was trained on a particular

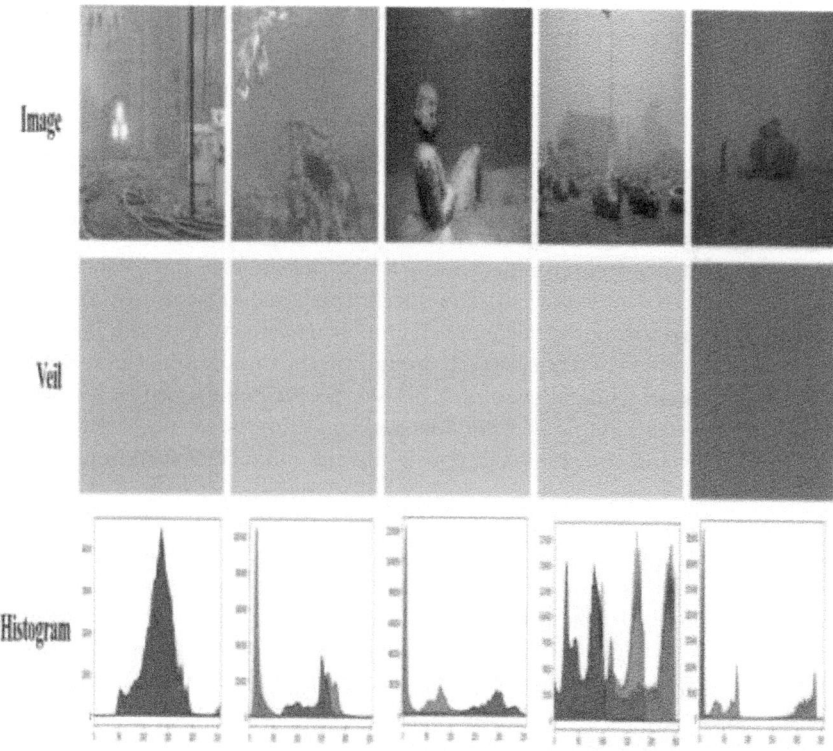

Fig. 3. Degraded image sample with its veil and histogram

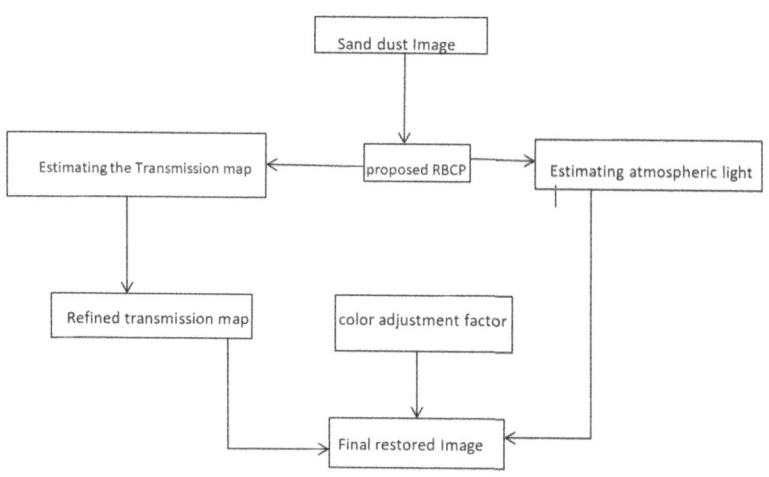

Fig. 4. Restoration Based on Reversing

camera type, it might not generalize effectively to pictures taken with other cameras or in different lighting situations. Finally, reducing haze from photographs with complicated scenes may not be possible with this procedure. To increase the method's generalizability and suitability for use in practical situations, more study is required [15] (Figs. 3 and 4).

4   Methodology

In sand and dust-filled environments, the scattering of blue light causes images to appear distorted and yellowish. To address this issue and improve the quality of these images, restoring the lost blue channel is necessary. This can be achieved through blue channel compensation, a technique that maintains the mean value of the green channel while allowing for better recovery compared to keeping the red channel constant. Implementing this method eliminates blue artifacts from the sand and dust images, resulting in a significant enhancement in image quality [9].

Blue channel compensation was used, although color distortion may still be present in the image. A white balance algorithm was used to perform color correction in order to solve this problem. For colors to appear realistic and natural in an image, proper white balance is necessary. The Gray world technique was used in this project to white- balance the image. Based on the idea that an image typically has an equal number of red, green, and blue (RGB) colors, this method assumes that the average color of an image should be neutral or grey. To achieve this, the color balance is changed to turn the image's typical RGB color into a neutral grey.

Once the color correction is completed through white balancing, the next step is to improve the image quality through enhancement techniques. Guided image filtering is employed to achieve this, which enhances edge accuracy and contrast in degraded images. This technique applies a linear filter to the input image using a guidance image as a reference. Local linear models are utilized to establish the relationship between the input image and the guidance image. By smoothing noise and other visual distortions, the filter preserves sharp edges and intricate details. The guidance image may be the input image or any other image (Fig. 5).

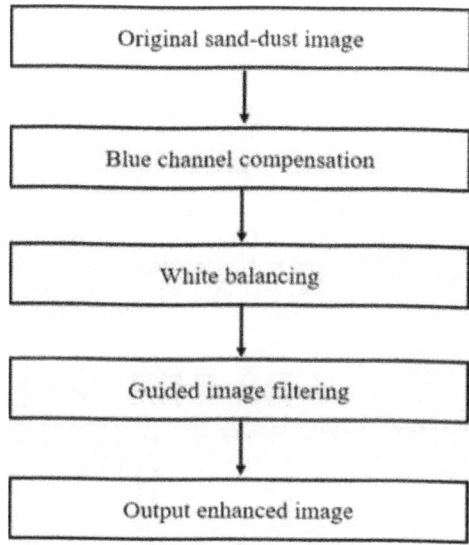

Fig. 5. Flowchart representing proposed Algorithm

5   Results

After implementing the enhancement techniques, a window will be popped up to select the image which we would like to enhance. Then two screens will be displayed one showing the enhanced image after applying the color correction and enhancement techniques. The other screen shows the red, green, and blue planes of the input image. The PSNR and NIQE values of the output image are calculated.

6   Applications of Sand Dust Image Enhancement

The Sand Dust Image Enhancement has several potential applications in various fields including computer vision and remote sensing. Some of the major applications of Sand Dust Image Enhancement include: Environmental monitoring, Transportation, Construction industry, Agriculture, Renewable Energy and Weather prediction (Figs. 6 and 7).

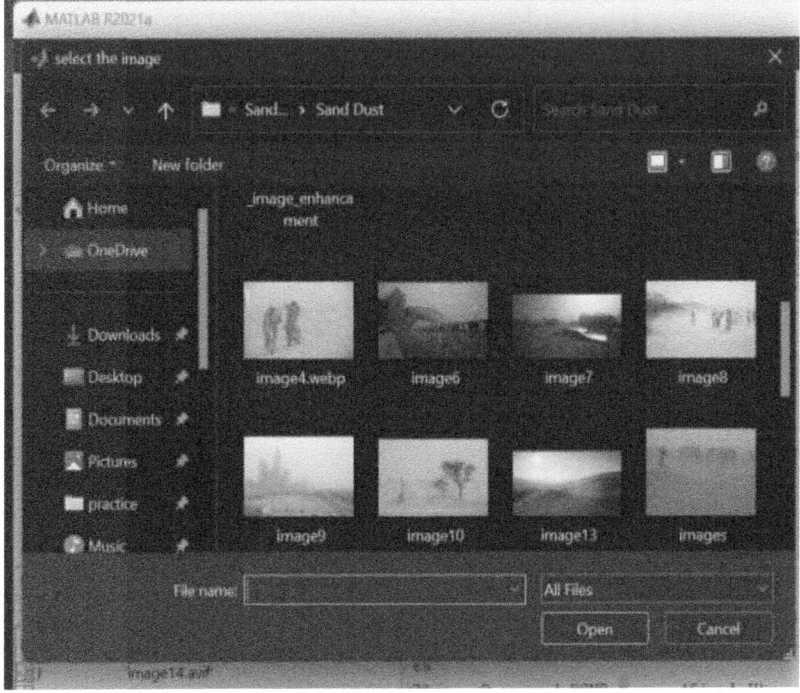

Fig. 6. Input Dataset Images

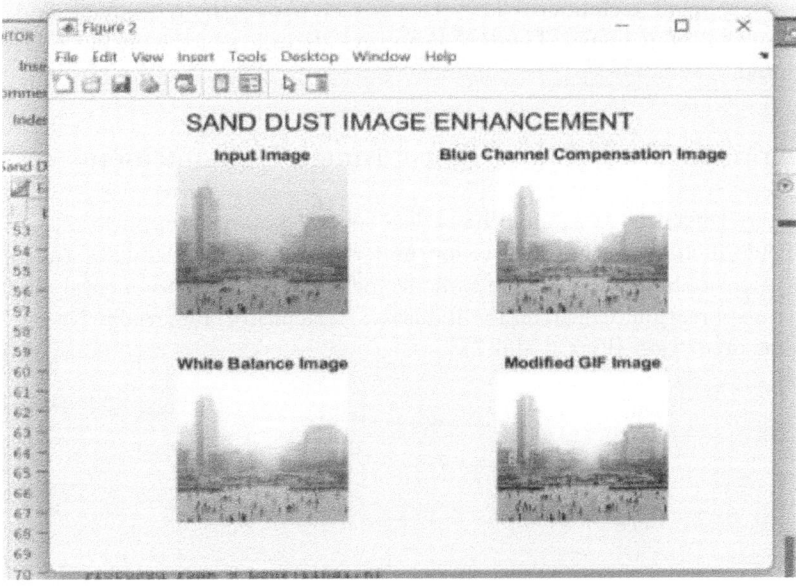

Fig. 7. Output after Applying Algorithm

7 Conclusion, Challenges, and Future Work

A novel approach for improving the visibility of images that have been sand and dust damaged has been proposed. Blue channel compensation and guided image filtering are the two key methods used in the proposed method. The first method, known as blue channel compensation, seeks to restore the missing blue value in the image's blue channel. Along with the red and green channels, the blue channel is one of the color channels that make up an image. The blue channel can be severely impacted by sand and dust, which results in a loss of blue color information in time. Therefore a technique known as blue channel compensation is employed to solve this issue. Utilizing white balancing technology, the colors of an image are changed to make white seem neutral and without any color casts.

Acknowledgements. The authors gratefully acknowledge that this work was carried out as part of Final Year project at Department of Information Technology, Chaitanya Bharathi Institute of Technology Hyderabad, for guiding through the project and providing appropriate tools and support for this project work.

References

1. Uma Maheswari, V., Aluvalu, R., Chennam, K.K.: Application of machine learning algorithms for facial expression analysis. Mach. Learn. Sustain. Dev. **9**, 77 (2021)
2. Maheswari, V.U., Aluvalu, R., Prasad Kantipudi, M.V.V., Chennam, K.K., Kotecha, K., Saini, J.R.: Driver drowsiness prediction based on multiple aspects using image processing techniques. IEEE Access **10**, 54980–54990 (2022)
3. Gao, G., Lai, H., Jia, Z., Liu, Y., Wang, Y.: Sand-dust image restoration based on reversing the blue channel prior. IEEE Photon. J. **12**(2), 3900216 (2020). https://doi.org/10.1109/JPHOT.2020.2975833
4. Shi, Z.H., Feng, Y.N., Zhao, M.H., Zhang, E.H., He, L.F.: Let you see in sand dust weather: a method based on halo-reduced dark channel prior dehazing for sand-dust image enhancement. IEEE Access **7**, 116722–116733 (2019)
5. Huang, S.-C., Ye, J.-H., Chen, B.-H.: An advanced single-image visibility restoration algorithm for real-world hazy scenes. IEEE Trans. Ind. Electron. **62**(5), 2962–2972 (2015)
6. Wang, J., Pang, Y., He, Y., Liu, C.: Enhancement for dust-sand storm images. In: Tian, Q., Sebe, N., Qi, G.J., Huet, B., Hong, R., Liu, X. (eds.) MMM 2016. LNCS, vol. 9516, pp. 842–849. Springer, Cham (2016). https://doi.org/10.1007/978-3-319-27671-7_70
7. Cosman, C.: Single image restoration using scene ambient light differential. In: Proceedings of the 23rd IEEE International Conference on Image Processing, Phoenix, AZ, USA (2016)
8. Bu, Q., Luo, J., Ma, K., Feng, H., Feng, J.: An enhanced pix2pix dehazing network with guided filter layer. Appl. Sci. **10**(17), 5898 (2020)
9. Liu, C., Chen, X., Wu, Y.: Modified grey world method to detect and restore color cast images. IET Image Process. **13**(7), 1090–1096 (2019)
10. Ancuti, C.O., Ancuti, C., De Vleeschouwer, C., Bekaert, P.: Color balance and fusion for underwater image enhancement. IEEE Trans. Image Process. **27**(1), 379–393 (2018)

11. Lee, H.S., Moon, S.W., Eom, I.K.: Underwater image enhancement using successive color correction and superpixel dark channel prior. Symmetry **12**(8), 1220 (2020)
12. Kang, L.-W., Yu, C.-M., Lin, C.-Y., Yeh, C.-H.: Image and video restoration and enhancement via sparse representation. In: Biometrics: Concepts, Methodologies, Tools, and Applications, pp. 501–528. IGI Global (2017)
13. Li, B., et al.: RESIDE: a benchmark for single image dehazing. arXiv preprint arXiv:1712.04143 (2017)
14. Yang, Y., Zhang, C., Liu, L., Chen, G., Yue, H.: Visibility restoration of single image captured in dust and haze weather conditions. Multidim. Syst. Sig. Process. **31**, 619–633 (2019)
15. Gu, Z., Zhan, Z., Yuan, Q., Yan, L.: Single remote sensing image dehazing using a prior-based dense attentive network. Remote Sens. **11**(24), 3008 (2019)
16. Kommu, G.R., Trupthi, M., Pabboju, S.: A novel approach for multi-label classification using probabilistic classifiers. In: 2014 International Conference on Advances in Engineering Technology Research (ICAETR - 2014), Unnao, India, pp. 1–8 (2014). https://doi.org/10.1109/ICAETR.2014.7012929
17. Kommu, G.R., Pabboju, S.: A probabilistic based multi-label classification method using partial information. In: Satapathy, S., Govardhan, A., Raju, K., Mandal, J. (eds.) Emerging ICT for Bridging the Future - Proceedings of the 49th Annual Convention of the Computer Society of India CSI Volume 2. AISC, vol. 338, pp. 27–34. Springer, Cham (2015). https://doi.org/10.1007/978-3-319-13731-5_4

Citation Analysis of a Q1 Journal from Its Thirty Years of Inception in Agriculture Supply-Chain

Pragati Priyadarshinee[1]([✉])(ID) and M. V. V. Prasad Kantipudi[2](ID)

[1] Chaitanya Bharathi Institute of Technology, Hyderabad 500075, India
pragatipriyadarshinee_it@cbit.ac.in
[2] Symbiosis Institute of Technology (SIT), Symbiosis International (Deemed University) (SIU),
Pune, India
mvvprasad.kantipudi@ieee.org

Abstract. Journal of Cleaner Production completed its 30 years of publication in 2023. As a credibility the paper aims to present the overview through citation analysis of its content from 1993 to 2023. The research publication is analyzed from the journal database and the citation structure from JCLP through Scopus database. Several keywords are studied upon through thematic analysis process. A graphical representation of cited data is presented via the VOS viewer software. The findings show that JCLP has grown a lot in few years based upon its number of publications in each year and more in the area of 'Agriculture'. Three major themes on JCLP were studied upon in this article: 'Agriculture', 'Supply-chain' and 'Environmental Sustainability'. This one is the first article studying upon the overall publications in JCLP in the area of agricultural supply chain management.

Keywords: JCLP · Citation Analysis · Vos Viewer · Agriculture · Supply-chain Management · Environmental Sustainability

1 Introduction

Introduction: JCLP is an interdisciplinary journal which focuses on technology as well as management, environment and sustainability research practices produced by Elsevier. The Co-Editors-in-Chief for this journal are Cecília Maria Villas Bôas de Almeida from Paulista University, Jiří Jaromír Klemeš from Brno University of Technology, and Yutao Wang from Fudan University. The journal is indexed in Engineering Village – GEOBASE, Geographical Abstracts, Fluid Abstracts, Scopus, FLUIDEX, Science Citation Index Expanded and INSPEC. The journal is having h-index of 173 that means 173 articles of JCLP are cited for 173 periods. In ABDC (Australian Business Dean's Council) journal quality list, it is in 'A'. In 2023, the journal completed its 30 years as it first appeared in 1993.

O. Castillo et al. (Eds.): PerSOM 2023, LNICST 517, pp. 101–109, 2024.
https://doi.org/10.1007/978-3-031-66044-3_7

A 30-year long duration is to signify the achievement of the journal. To identify the journal's achievement in these periods a citation analysis and some other analytical techniques can be utilized for the qualitative representation of the journal in terms of its achievements so far. Recently an article presented a citation analysis for the International Journal of Social Economics (IJSE) on its 45th Anniversary [1]. The author did the bibliometric analysis from 2006 to 2016 for Journal of Cleaner Production which is based on the circular economy in European Union and China [2]. Next study discussed about the 25 years of contribution of Benchmarking: An International Journal to the manufacturing Industry [3].

The major goal of the paper is to reveal the influences of the Journal of Cleaner Production (JCLP) to the systematic literature, as well as to the existing publication and the growth styles. The main intention is to maintain a yearly publication and citation detail. The publication trend is analysed with citation details, participating authors and the regions. In addition to that we conducted some Bibliometric evaluation to understand the fluctuation of the journal in course of time.

RQ1. What are the major publication topics in the agricultural supply-chain?
RQ2. Which are the highly cited articles in this field?
RQ3. What are the citation and co-citation pattern in this field?

The remainder of the paper is organised as follows. Section 2 discusses the research methodology of the study. Section 3 focuses on bibliometric analysis and results. Section 4 is the mapping with the citation analysis software followed by Conclusion in Sect. 5.

2 Methodology

Bibliometrics is the study of bibliographical data. It studies qualitatively the citation analysis data after verifying the major research areas with its current trends. The current study is used to determine the publication strategy of JCLP through bibliometric methods to gain an overall view. The research is analyzed through the Scopus database from 1993 to 2022 using this citation analysis technique. The search started in April 2022 from the Scopus database [4–6].

To identify the targeted solutions, the database is filtered as per "Source Title" to gather the research articles from JCLP. The initial search result was 23,874 manuscripts. Articles other than English language were removed. Editorial and Letters were removed along with the recently accepted articles. The study includes various statistics such as the author, institution, journal, country, publications with the number of citations to get an active viewpoint about the journal's publication trends. It presents three statistical counts of publication to measure the productivity, citation count and the h-index which can combine both the power and efficiency. A graphical mapping of bibliometric data is developed using the VOS viewer software. It develops bibliographic data through bibliographic coupling, co-occurrence of author keywords and co-citation [7–10, 11, 12, 15] (Table 1).

Table 1. Author & Description

Author	Description
Schlattmann, A. et al. (2022)	The authors discussed about clean water distribution techniques in this article and developed some tool for the same
Bai, C. et al. (2022)	This article discusses about supply-chain performance through blockchain technology and used TOE framework for the same
Wünsche, J.F. et al. (2022)	The study discusses about food supply chain using Block-chain technology through some case-study
Parrot, L. et al. (2022)	The authors discuss about food supply-chain through some case examples
Ransikarbum, K. et al. (2021)	The article discusses about green supply-chain management to improve sustainability through different initiatives
Krishnan, R. (2021)	The article discusses about various innovations in Industries to reduce the food wastage through supply-chain management
Méda, B. (2021)	Food sustainability is an important aspect that is discussed in the article by food supply chain. The authors have proposed some unique method for the same

3 Result and Analysis of Bibliometric Data

Highly cited articles by JCLP are more interesting to scrutiny. To know this a citation analysis document is generated using VOS viewer tool. The articles identified are mostly cited by Journal of Cleaner Production. The following snapshots represent the articles those are cited a greater number of times, minimum 5 times published an article in JCLP that is having the highest citation score of 1350. Next author has 1119 citations for the article published in JCLP.

The articles are analyzed based upon the bibliometric analysis in JCLP, that the journal cites the Country, University and the authors. Abeliotis k. has cited the article mostly in 59 writeups. 17 research papers were cited by the first five authors.

Usage of VOSviewer tool for bibliometric Analysis:

Two documents appear simultaneously in a third document, then it is called as the co-citation [13].

The network of co-citation of JCLP from 1993 to 2023 is very much justified in the following figure with minimum of 50 citations. 2697 self-citation is also there in the resulted outcome (Figs. 1 and 2).

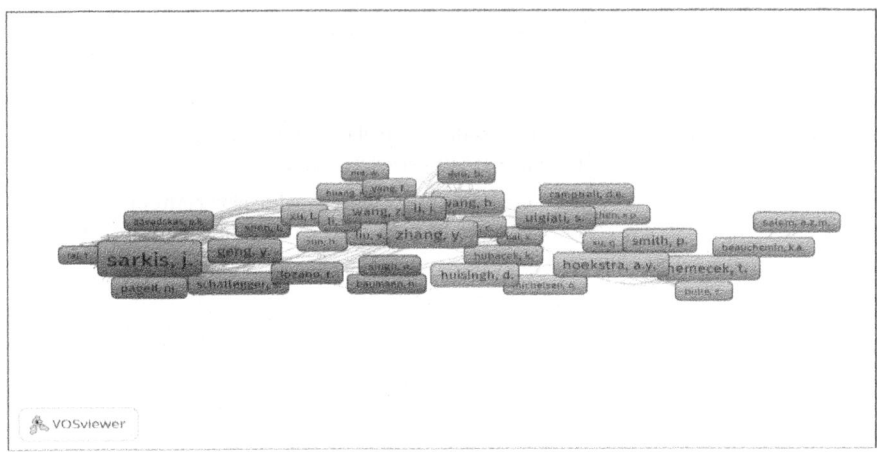

Fig. 1. Co-citation of Authors

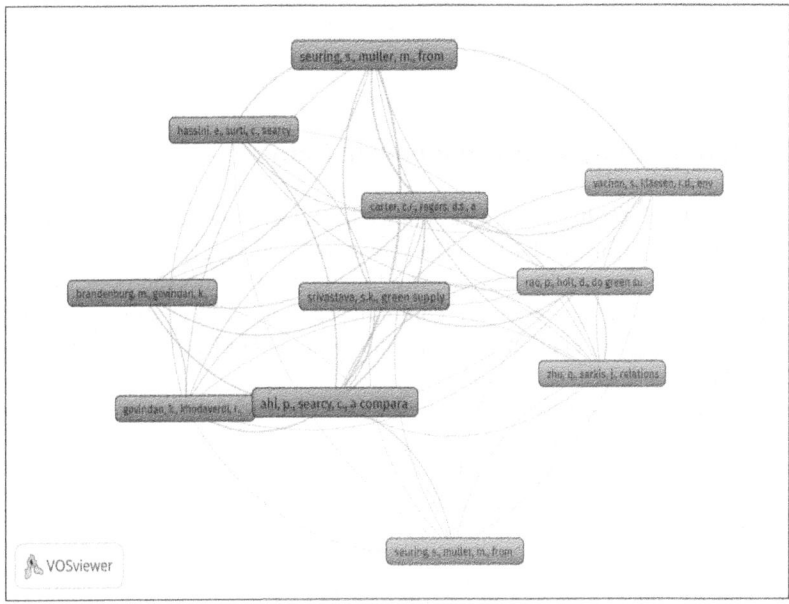

Fig. 2. Co-citation from Sources

A number of articles are published by JCLP in agriculture, technology adoption, manufacturing, environment and so on. Seuring and Muller published the most cited articles in 2008 by JCLP. This article currently has 2572 citations with highest citation ratio per year which indicates the article gets minimum 98 citations on yearly basis. Ranking is done based on total number of citations whether it's tie ranking, then it will be based on the number of citations on every year.

Most cited articles in JCLP.

It is interesting to shortlist the articles after researching a lot of articles from JCLP which have received highest number of citations. Hence, a co-citation network is identified through VOS viewer software, and the documents are mostly cited by JCLP since long (Fig. 3).

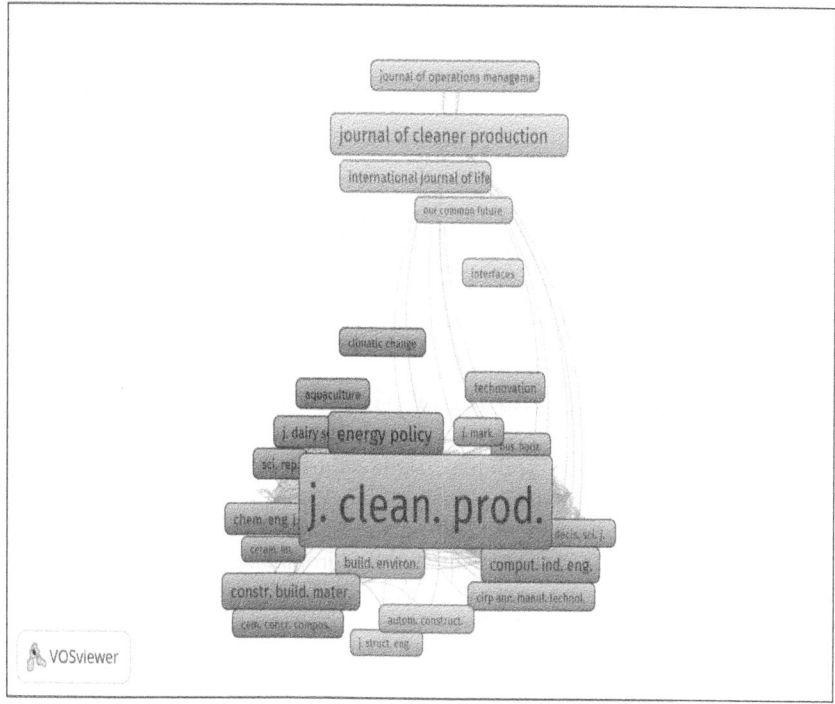

Fig. 3. Bibliographic Coupling of documents

The author did cluster analysis of JCLP articles based on bibliometric coupling that happens when two articles are citing a single article that shows the similarity in their architecture [10]. 2578 published articles in JCLP have done the bibliographic coupling of the articles into various clusters. The next figure summarizes the significance of the clusters with their central focus.

The first cluster is the major one that consists of 605 JCLP articles with maximum of 861 citations. Most of the work here belongs to agriculture, technology adoption and job satisfaction (Fig. 4).

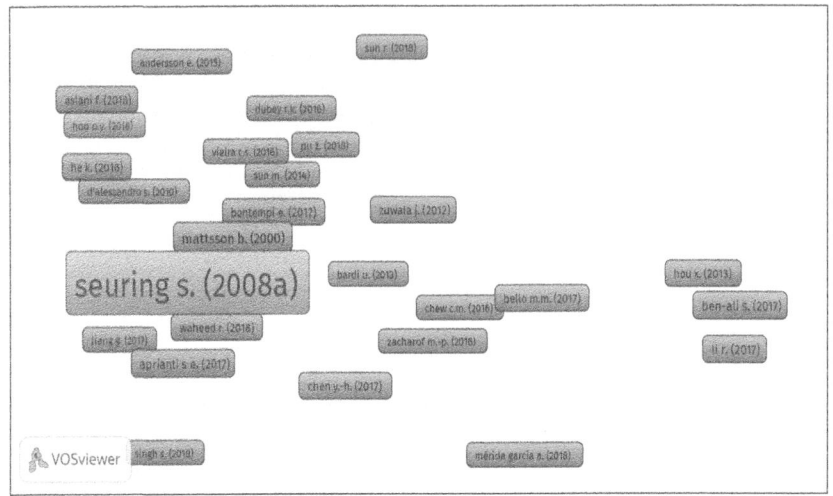

Fig. 4. JCLP articles as per bibliometric

4 Mapping with the Citation Analysis Software

Citation analysis is basically done to understand the development done in any specific area in a certain period. Bibliometric analysis is adopted from the authors [1, 3]. A total of 1719 articles have been identified from the Scopus database using the keywords 'Agriculture', 'Supply-chain management' and 'Environmental sustainability' [14, 15].

As identified, till 2023, in Supply Chain Management academic publications were significant (411). It will identify the keywords and their frequency of occurrence with other keywords. We have classified the articles into three major clusters based upon the keywords. The clusters are decided based upon the keywords and the articles are distributed as per that as (1) Agriculture (2) Supply-chain Management (3) Environmental Sustainability. It falls under these three major subject areas with the number of articles that fall under each area.

Citation analysis is carried out on all combinations of papers published. As per the researcher's citation is the number of times an article is referenced by other authors [16, 17]. It is "a part or the whole of the cited document and a part or the whole of the citing document are inter-related". Bibliometric Analysis is a subset of the bibliometric that provides information about each of the researcher in a particular area. It identifies the related publications to understand the significance of each article. Citation analysis gives deep insight about some specific topics through some relevant studies. It also provides the overview of citation any article has obtained [18, 19].

According to the researcher the mapping happens when two documents simultaneously appear in the reference list of another document [10]. The above network identifies the amount of co-citation in a span of 30 years in JCLP. The major keyword is JCLP here. JCLP cites the journal like Journal of Business Research, Expert Systems Applications, Annals of Operations Research, Technology Forecasting and Social Change, International Journal of Production Research, Communication ACM, etc.

To analyse the authors, who have received most citation from a specific area in JCLP, there is a co-citation analysis of authors is also done. The figure outcome is mapped along with the following table. The table gives most cited Country with highest number of documents. Here occurs a bibliographic coupling with occurrence of three documents at a time [20, 21] (Table 2).

Table 2. Ten Highly citated Countries on Agriculture

Serial No.	Country	Articles	No. of Citations	Link Strength
1	China	237	3394	108
2	Italy	84	1906	34
3	United states	88	1536	62
4	United kingdom	72	1327	51
5	Spain	51	1197	18
6	Australia	45	1097	30
7	Brazil	65	1054	24
8	Sweden	31	915	17
9	Netherlands	42	796	26
10	Malayasia	19	763	8

From the above table it is identified as China is the leading Country followed by Italy and US. Few developing countries are also in queue.

5 Conclusion

The study aimed at designing the contribution of the journal on 25 years completion of JCLP. On this occasion, the journal tries to identify through a long range of citation analysis those are mostly cited articles with authors, institution, countries. For this, we have used three major keywords as 'Agriculture', 'Supply-chain management' and 'Environmental Sustainability'.

On the occasion of 30 years of JCLP, the study attempted to show the major contribution of the journal in Sustainable Supply chain through the citation analysis structure by most cited publication with the most cited author with annual publication trend based upon the country and the Institution. The outcome of this bibliometric analysis shows that supply-chain management in agriculture shows a very significant contribution from JCLP. Year wise the contribution of such kind of publications are increasing and suddenly JCLP published 100 articles in the year 2018. Thus, the annual citation rate of the journal also increased drastically. The articles which are having minimum of 100 citations ideally should be 15 years old. The article also develops a graphical representation of the bibliometric data through VOSviewer. Keyword analysis also can be done more accurately in future. The most discussed themes of the journal are agricultural supply chain, developing country, Organizational studies, economic growth and so on those are in line with JCLP.

The resulted outcome says JCLP has a major contribution on agricultural supply chain management that leads to sustainability. The article gives a citation analysis of the articles published so far in JCLP. Everything has some pros and cons. Similarly, the study has certain limitations. The first limitation is, as the data is extracted from Scopus database, if anything is missing in Scopus, that will pull the limitation. Secondly, the resulted study is dynamic which may change over time. Thirdly, certain variables in the bibliometric analysis may change over time. Anyways, the current study is a continuous work that provides a brief overview of the citation analysis of JCLP from the inception of the journal.

The bibliometric and content analysis performed for this study have revealed some research avenues for future projects. Studies on the MS domain with a pure empirical mathematical formulation are scarce. To improve the empirical case studies with a practical orientation, it has to devise a strategy for fostering cross-sectoral research including the cooperation of scholars and practitioners. Thus, in order to create a more comprehensive field of study in MS domains, future research can aim to logically connect MS keywords with terms from other clusters. One of the journal's areas of focus is case-based research, thus authors from various geographical areas—which are not yet covered—can target a case study from various regions. This resolves the issues related to various locales with diverse cultures, which could result in more productive research.

References

1. Kumar, S., Sureka, R., Pandey, N.: Forty-five years of the International Journal of Social Economics (IJSE): a bibliometric overview. Int. J. Soc. Econ. **47**(7), 831–849 (2020)
2. Türkeli, S., Kemp, R., Huang, B., Bleischwitz, R., McDowall, W.: Circular economy scientific knowledge in the European Union and China: a bibliometric, network and survey analysis (2006–2016). J. Clean. Prod. **197**(1), 1244–1261 (2018)
3. Dohale, V., Gunasekaran, A., Akarte, M.M., Verma, P.: Twenty-five years' contribution of "Benchmarking: An International Journal" to manufacturing strategy: a scientometric review. Benchmarking Int. J. **27**(10), 1463–5771 (2020)
4. Broadus, R.N.: Toward a definition of bibliometrics. Scientometrics **12**(5–6), 373–379 (1987)
5. Pritchard, A.: Statistical bibliography or bibliometrics. J. Doc. **25**(4), 348–349 (1969)
6. Bar-Ilan, J.: Informetrics at the beginning of the 21st century-a review. J. Informet. **2**(1), 1–52 (2008)
7. Ding, Y., Chowdhury, G.G., Foo, S.: Bibliometric cartography of information retrieval research by using co-word analysis. Inf. Process. Manag. **37**(6), 817–842 (2001)
8. Hirsch, J.E.: An index to quantify an individual's scientific research output. Proc. Natl. Acad. Sci. **102**(46), 16569–16572 (2005)
9. Van Eck, N., Waltman, L.: Software survey: VOSviewer, a computer program for bibliometric mapping. Scientometrics **84**(2), 523–538 (2009)
10. Kessler, M.M.: Bibliographic coupling between scientific papers. Am. Doc. **14**(1), 10–25 (1963)
11. Blanco-Mesa, F., Merigó, J.M., Gil-Lafuente, A.M.: Fuzzy decision making: a bibliometricbased review. J. Intell. Fuzzy Syst. **32**(3), 2033–2050 (2017)
12. Laengle, S., et al.: Forty years of the European journal of operational research: a bibliometric overview. Eur. J. Oper. Res. **262**(3), 803–816 (2017)

13. Small, H.: Co-citation in the scientific literature: a new measure of the relationship between two documents. J. Am. Soc. Inf. Sci. **24**(4), 265–269 (1973)
14. Ellegaard, O., Wallin, J.A.: The bibliometric analysis of scholarly production: how great is the impact? Scientometrics **105**(3), 1809–1831 (2015)
15. Merigó, J.M., Yang, J.B.: A bibliometric analysis of operations research and management science. Omega **73**(1), 37–48 (2017)
16. Narin, F.: Evaluative Bibliometrics: The Use of Publication and Citation Analysis in the Evaluation of Scientific Activity. Computer Horizons, New Jersey (1976)
17. Smith, L.C.: Citation analysis. Libr. Trends **30**(1), 83–106 (1981)
18. Mishra, D., Gunasekaran, A., Papadopoulos, T., Dubey, R.: Supply chain performance measures and metrics: a bibliometric study. Benchmarking Int. J. **25**(3), 932–967 (2018)
19. Waltman, L., Eck, N.J.V.: A new methodology for constructing a publication-level classification system of science. J. Am. Soc. Inf. Technol. **63**(12), 2378–2392 (2012)
20. Parrot, L., Dong, C., Carbonnel, F., Meyer, A.: Systematic review with meta-analysis: the effectiveness of either ustekinumab or vedolizumab in patients with Crohn's disease refractory to anti-tumour necrosis factor. Aliment. Pharmacol. Ther. **55**(4), 380–388 (2022)
21. Ransikarbum, K., Pitakaso, R., Kim, N., Ma, J.: Multicriteria decision analysis framework for part orientation analysis in additive manufacturing. J. Comput. Des. Eng. **8**(4), 1141–1157 (2021)

IGSentiment Analysis of Russia and Ukraine War on Twitter Data: Using Azure Machin Learning and Deep Learning

Bhagirathi Nayak[1]([✉]), Pritidhara Hota[2], and Sunil Kumar Mishra[3]

[1] Sri Sri University, Cuttack, Odisha, India
bhagirathi.n@srisriuniversity.edu.in
[2] GITA Autonomous College, Bhubaneswar, Odisha, India
[3] Global Institute of Management, Bhubaneswar, Odisha, India

Abstract. Facebook, Twitter, and other social media sites have become popular places for people to connect and air their views on many topics. The importance of employing machine learning methods for sentiment analysis or opinion mining of these posts cannot be overstated. Russia-Ukraine conflict, users from all around the world descended upon the site to share their thoughts. By analyzing these comments, we may get a sense of how the general population felt about various events leading up to and during the conflict. This paper is mostly focused on tweet data in two steps on the Russia-Ukraine conflict. First, we collected 47885 tweet data to retrieve and analyze the tweets that reflected the proportion of positive, neutral, and negative categories-based sentiments using Azure Machine Learning, after that, we used Deep Learning for the segmentation of sentiments with scores. Finally, we got positive: 18846, negative: 12751, neutral: 16288.

Keywords: Twitter · Machine Learning · Deep Learning · Azure · Sentiments

1 Introduction

Twitter is a social media platform where users may connect, engage, and contribute to conversations about many topics through the sharing of short, 140-character entries or "tweets". This can be accomplished through the use of various media types (text, images, emoji, and video) and user-generated feedback. As of the year 2023, Twitter is used by around 450 million people per month. By 2028, it is predicted that more than 652 million of them. Twitter has approximately 237 million people using it daily (Qi and Shabrina, 2023). The growing amount of data available online allows researchers to examine how people's thoughts, actions, and mental states have evolved in response to widespread participation in social media (Alamoodi et al., 2021). As a result, there has been a rise in the popularity of conducting sentiment analysis with Twitter data. Natural Language Processing (NLP), Text Analysis (TA), Computational Linguistics (CLT), Machine Learning (ML), and Artificial Intelligence (AI) technologies for text analysis have gained traction as social media analysis has gained popularity. Text analysis can be

O. Castillo et al. (Eds.): PerSOM 2023, LNICST 517, pp. 110–119, 2024.
https://doi.org/10.1007/978-3-031-66044-3_8

used to learn about the perspectives of specific demographics. Although the majority of published works have been written in English, there is an increasing interest in analyzing texts in more than one language (Arun and Srinagesh, 2020). Extracting subjective comments about a topic utilizing distinct feelings like Positive, Negative, and Neutral can be used in text analysis. In this paper, we used the Twitter data set of the Russia and Ukraine war to find the people's sentiments through sentiment analysis, using Azure Machine Learning and Deep Learning because it allows for a more nuanced expression of the feelings Twitter's character count restriction, users are forced to condense their thoughts into succinct messages.

2   Review of Literature

The conflict between Russia and Ukraine is not the first to attract attention from around the world. One of the earliest global concerns involving widespread usage of social media was the local upheavals during the Arab Spring of 2010, especially in Egypt and Tunisia. After that, in 2022, the war between Russia and Ukraine is the most pressing international issue. The primary function of social media is to encourage relevant authorities to take immediate action in defence of human rights. Finding the truth is made more difficult by the Internet's abundance of information, which makes it hard to tell fiction from reality. Anomaly detection strategies in social networks are the subject of research by Sheth et al. (2022), and Venkatesan and Prabhavathy (2019). Tsugawa and Ohsaki (2015) and Salehi et al. (2018) outline many techniques for conducting sentiment analysis. Self-reported attitude scores are used by Featherstone et al. (2020) to verify sentiment scores from a large-scale investigation of public opinion towards genome editing. Although the strength of the correlation between attitude score and emotion differed between sample subgroups, the findings are encouraging overall.

Two studies that use sentiment analysis on Tweets about financial stock performance are explained by Hamraoui and Boubaker (2022). Directed social networks are a more accurate depiction of the asymmetric nature of many relationships and forms of communication. Both Malliaros and Vazirgiannis (2013), and Tsopze and Domgue (2021) acknowledge the difficulties in modeling and analyzing directed social networks, so they are not a modeling panacea. According to Scott and Carrington (2011), social network analysis is the study of the "detailed logic" behind the intentional formation and maintenance of social ties between individuals. This SNA method takes advantage of links between entities to draw a diagram of a network with nodes and arcs, where the length of the arcs represents the relative strength of the connections as calculated by mathematics (Legradi, 2009). By analyzing the resulting network, we can learn about the dynamics of different groups and the extent to which individuals are related to one another. The findings show that when analysts collect Tweets from various talks using more generic search queries, the development of a topically-focused social network to reflect dialogues generates more robust findings regarding influential users (Logan, et al. 2023).

3   Sentiment Analysis of Russia and Ukraine War

The essence of using sentiment analysis is sorting the gleaned information into positive, negative, and neutral categories. Affective computing and sentiment analysis are two new areas that take into account a wide variety of emotions (Cambria, 2016). Depending on the area of study, emotions can be broken down further into satisfaction and anger (D'Andrea et al., 2015), for example in political arguments. To account for more nuanced outcomes and identify emotions like worry, grief, rage, enthusiasm, and happiness, sentiment analysis with ambivalence handling might be added (Wang et al., 2015, 2020). The conflict between Russia and Ukraine is not the first to attract attention from around the world. One of the earliest global concerns involving widespread usage of social media was the local upheavals during the Arab Spring of 2010, especially in Egypt and Tunisia. After that, in 2022, the war between Russia and Ukraine is the most pressing international issue. Twitter has become a hotbed of debate about the escalating confrontation between Russia and Ukraine, reflecting the concerns and perspectives of people all around the world. In addition to disseminating news, the site's diverse user base also uses it to show support for the victims and discuss the geopolitical issues at play. The #RussiaUkraineWar hashtag is a popular online meeting place for people looking for updates and a platform to be heard. Some tweets call for diplomatic solutions and de-escalation, while others emphasize the human cost of the conflict and the necessity of international cooperation to maintain regional stability. Twitter's ongoing importance in impacting public conversation on this crucial subject as a medium for real-time reactions, information dissemination, and online activism is clear. Politicians, celebrities, and businesses have all taken to Twitter to condemn Russia, and users have pushed for Twitter to pull the plug on its presence there. Twitter users can openly share their opinions and encourage others to join the pro-Ukraine movement through the use of hashtags. Twitter facilitates the rapid dissemination of information.

4   Methodology

There are two main methods by which emotions represented in the text can be detected and categorized. Azure Machine Learning approach analyses texts as a classification of positive, neutral, and negative categories. Whereas the Deep Learning technique makes use of the polarity of words and segments them into categories. The following Proposed Model (Fig. 1) displays various approaches that can be utilized for sentiment analysis in practice. We have collected the Tweet dataset from the website, which is freely available. After preparing it we analyze the sentimental analysis through Azure Machine Learning techniques and got the output of positive, neutral and negative sentiment with the score. These scores and sentiments are utilized for further analysis using Deep Learning techniques and segmented with a proper accuracy of 99.36%.

Proposed Model

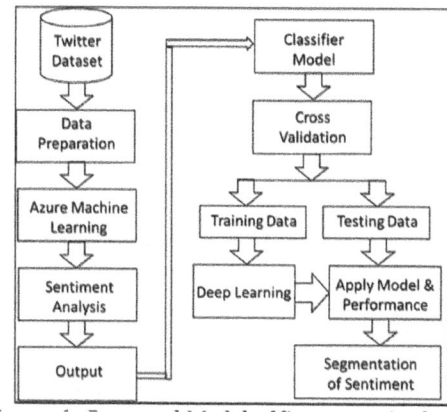

Fig. 1. Proposed Model of Sentiment Analysis

5 Azure Machine Learning Method

Data scientists, machine learning engineers, and AI developers can now construct, deploy, and manage machine learning models at scale with Azure Machine Learning, a robust and feature-rich cloud-based platform. Azure Machine Learning simplifies the entire machine-learning process with its intuitive UI and extensive range of capabilities. Users may easily do data preprocessing and analysis, model selection and tuning, and model deployment as either web services or containerized apps. Azure services tools and AI capabilities may be easily incorporated into preexisting processes. It's a flexible option for businesses that want to include AI and machine learning in their work. The cutting-edge Deep Learning for Segmentation method uses neural networks to accurately detect and separate target regions or objects from larger datasets. This method has been game-changing in many applications that rely on precise outlining of complex structures, including image processing and medical imaging. Pixel-level segmentation is made possible by the deep learning model's ability to understand complex patterns and features in data with the use of architectures like convolutional neural networks (CNNs) and feed-forward convolutional networks (FCNs). As a result of its superiority in capturing complex visual correlations, this approach excels in tasks such as semantic segmentation, instance segmentation, and even video segmentation. Boosting automation and comprehension of visual data, Deep Learning for Segmentation has promising uses in fields as diverse as autonomous vehicles, satellite imagery analysis, medical diagnostics, and augmented reality.

6 Data Analysis and Findings

In this paper, we used Azure machine learning methods to analyze the tone of text messages. As per our proposed model (Fig. 1) sentiment analysis is performed by applying distinct machine-learning methods to the pre-processed messages and getting the output. We collected 47885 tweet data from the website regarding the Russia and Ukraine wars and analysed the sentiment with a score (Fig. 2).

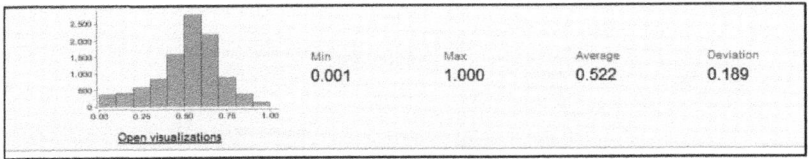

Fig. 2. Statistics

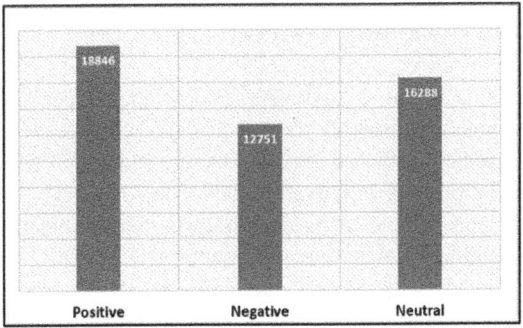

Fig. 3. Categories of Sentiment

After analysis we can observe the sentiment categories in above Fig. 3, the number of positives is 188846, negatives are 12751, and Neutrals are 1628 tweets. After that, we used the following Deep Learning model to segment the categories accurately (Fig. 4).

Deep Learning Model

Deep Learning Model

Step - 1

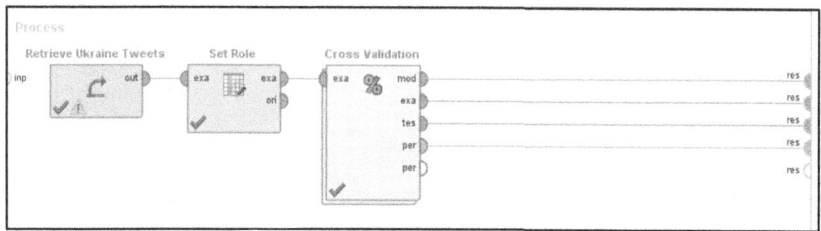

Step - 2

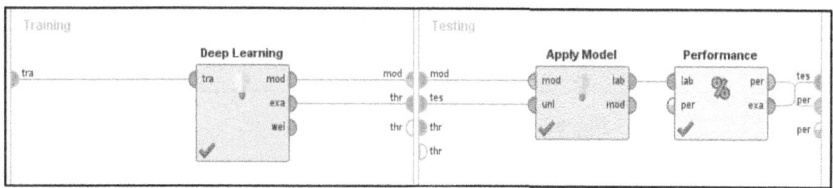

Fig. 4. Deep Learning Model

In this model (Step-1) we retrieve the tweet data and select the sentiment column as a label, then do cross-validation with 10 folds. In (Step 2) we selected the Deep Learning algorithm with a 50:50 hidden layer and 10 numbers epochs in the training set and applied the model with measure performances finally we got the following outputs.

Accuracy: 99.36% (±0.32%), Kappa: 0.990 (±0.0005), MSE: 0.004563168, RMSE: 0.067551225, R-Square: 0.99360317, Log loss: 0.016823301.

Output of Sentiment Categories

Table 1. Output of Sentiment Categories

	True Positive	True Negative	True Neutral	Class Precision
Positive	18829	0	17	99.91%
Negative	0	12566	185	98.55%
Neutral	111	24	16258	99.17%
Class Recall	99.32%	99.79%	98.84%	

As per above Table 1, we can observe the True positive: 18829 with 99.91% class precision, True negative: 12566 with 98.55%, and True neutral: 16258 with 99.17% (Fig. 5).

Scatter Plot of Sentiment Score

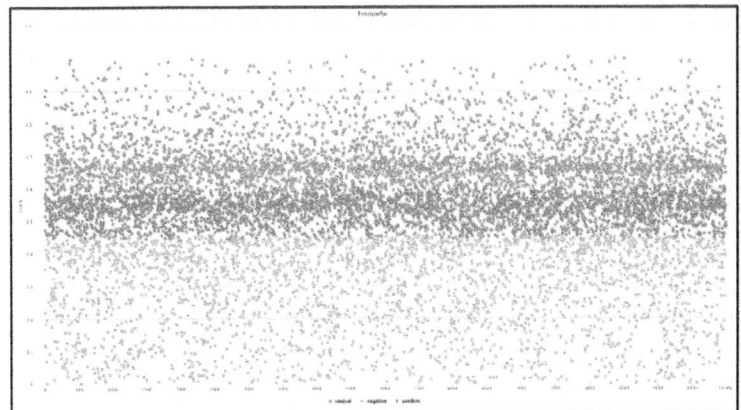

Fig. 5. Scatter plot of Sentiment Score.

The above figure derives the scatter plot of the sentiment categories score, the orange colour defines a positive score, the blue colour defines a neutral score, and the green colour defines a negative score. The following figures show the word cloud of positive, negative, and neutral sentiments (Figs. 6, 7, 8 and 9).

Tweet_text	Sentiment	Score
Dear vaccine advocate Do take the COVID-19 mRNA shot and boosters, but do know that @OurWorldInData data shows it offers zero protection, and actually accelerates death of the vaccinated. Regards #Pfizer #AstraZeneca #Moderna #NWO #Agenda2030 #COP27 #Biden #Obama #Trudeau #Jacinda #life https://t.co/VTbfuqiDvu	positive	0.66691792
#Mundo Al menos 6 muertos y 16 heridos en bombardeo ruso en #Kharkiv https://t.co/AZzEgw2NLe	negative	0.32037485
Animal shelter Dogs and Cats, we need your help! Raising funds for food for animals. PayPal: dogandcat.helper@gmail.com https://t.co/Z3reOltTfy https://t.co/I9dbwRrtg0 https://t.co/71pErM8xBZ #Ukraine #Patreon #dogsoftwitter #Shelter #Dogs #Cats #Cute #Pets #Funny #Dogsarefamily https://t.co/HLEnTp9yk7	neutral	0.56244934
Welcome to our shelter! Located in Ukraine, Kyiv Our shelter needs your help! Raising funds for food for animals. PayPal: dogandcat.helper@gmail.com https://t.co/RHOpeqvaXT https://t.co/rTtTVpoCi1 #Ukraine #Kyiv #Shelter #Dogs #Cats #Pets #DogsofTwittter #patreoncreator #Patreon https://t.co/rRWH17R813	neutral	0.53714919

Fig. 6. Sample output of Tweet text, Sentiment, and Score

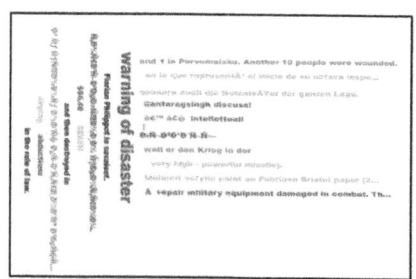

Fig. 7. Wordcloud of positive sentiment   **Fig. 8.** Wordcloud of negative sentiment

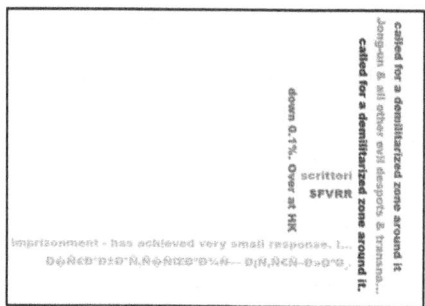

Fig. 9. Wordcloud of neutral sentiment

7 Conclusion

This article aggregates Twitter data from the most populous Russian and Ukraine wars. At the outset, we cleanse the data and classify the tweet's sentiment orientations using Azure Machine Learning-based techniques. Then, we use the annotated data sample to train the Deep Learning, techniques. Changes in public opinion about Russia and Ukraine conflict tweets can be tracked over three distinct phases. The 39.36% of scores who feel positively about the war tend to rise, then fall, whereas the 26.63% who feel negatively about the wars in the opposite manner, but 34.01% are neutral. The interaction of various elements is highlighted in the summary. Although there were alternate paths that could have been taken, the causes of the conflict ran much deeper, and the participants were subject to more external and internal constraints than is suggested by the blame-oriented literature. This suggests that waiting for Russia to leave or enacting plans to make Ukraine a neutral country are not viable options for ending the conflict.

Further research is needed to confirm this inference, but it is possible to draw a connection between the rising number of positive cases and the declining volume by analyzing the number of negative and neutral sentiments as well as tweet situations.

8 Future Work

The future of sentiment analysis holds exciting possibilities as technology continues to advance. Enhanced Natural Language Processing (NLP) algorithms, fueled by machine learning and deep learning techniques, will enable sentiment analysis systems to better understand the nuances of human emotions and expressions. As data sources become more diverse, incorporating not only text but also multimedia content such as images and videos, sentiment analysis will evolve to provide a more comprehensive understanding of sentiment. The integration of contextual information and the ability to recognize sarcasm, and cultural nuances will contribute to more accurate sentiment predictions. Additionally, the ethical considerations surrounding sentiment analysis, such as bias detection and fairness, will play a crucial role in shaping the future of this field. As sentiment analysis continues to mature, its applications will extend beyond social media monitoring and customer feedback analysis, finding utility in areas like healthcare, finance, and human-computer interaction, ultimately contributing to more empathetic and context-aware artificial intelligence systems.

References

Qi, Y., Shabrina, Z.: Sentiment analysis using Twitter data: a comparative application of lexicon and machine-learning-based approach. Soc. Netw. Anal. Min. **13**(31) (2023). https://doi.org/10.1007/s13278-023-01030-x

Alamoodi, A.H., et al.: Sentiment analysis and its applications in fighting COVID-19 and infectious diseases: a systematic review. Expert Syst. Appl. **167**, 114155 (2021). https://doi.org/10.1016/j.eswa.2020.114155

Arun, K., Srinagesh, A.: Multilingual Twitter sentiment analysis using machine learning. Int. J. Electr. Comput. Eng. (IJECE) **10**(6), 5992–6000 (2020). https://doi.org/10.11591/ijece.v10i6.pp5992-6000

Sheth, A., Shalin, V.L., Kursuncu, U.: Defining and detecting toxicity on social media: context and knowledge are key. Neurocomputing **490**, 312–318 (2022). https://doi.org/10.1016/j.neucom.2021.11.095

Venkatesan, M., Prabhavathy, P.: Graph-based unsupervised learning methods for edge and node anomaly detection in social network. In: IEEE 1st International Conference on Energy, Systems and Information Processing (ICESIP), pp. 1–5 (2019). https://doi.org/10.1109/ICESIP46348.2019.8938364

Tsugawa, S., Ohsaki, H.: Negative messages spread rapidly and widely on social media. In: Proceedings of the 2015 ACM Conference on Online Social Networks, pp. 151–160 (2015). https://doi.org/10.1016/j.osnem.2023.100242

Salehi, A., Ozer, M., Davulcu, H.: Sentiment-driven community profiling and detection on social media. In: Proceedings of the 29th ACM Conference on Hypertext and Social Media, pp. 229–237 (2018). https://doi.org/10.1145/3209542.3209565

Featherstone, J.D., George, A.B., Ruiz, J.B., Zhuang, Y., Millam, B.J.: Exploring childhood anti-vaccine and pro-vaccine communities on Twitter a perspective from influential users. Online Soc. Netw. Media **20**, 100105 (2020). https://doi.org/10.1016/j.osnem.2020.100105

Hamraoui, I., Boubaker, A.: Impact of Twitter sentiment on stock price returns. Soc. Netw. Anal. Min. **12**(1), 1–15 (2022). https://doi.org/10.1007/s13278-021-00856-7

Malliaros, F.D., Vazirgiannis, M.: Clustering and community detection in directed networks: a survey. Phys. Rep. **533**(4), 95–142 (2013). https://doi.org/10.1016/j.physrep.2013.08.002

Scott, J., Carrington, P.J.: The SAGE Handbook of Social Network Analysis. SAGE Publications Ltd. (2014). https://doi.org/10.4135/9781446294413

Legradi, J.: An exploratory social network analysis of military and civilian emergency operation centres focusing on organization structure. Master's thesis, Air Force Institute of Technology, Wright Patterson AFB, OH (2009)

Logan, A.P., LaCasse, P.M., Lunday, B.J.: Social network analysis of Twitter interactions: a directed multilayer network approach. Soc. Netw. Anal. Min.Netw. Anal. Min. 13(1), 65 (2023). https://doi.org/10.1007/s13278-023-01063-2

Cambria, E.: Affective computing and sentiment analysis. IEEE Intell. Syst. 31(2), 102–107 (2016). https://doi.org/10.1109/MIS.2016.31

D'Andrea, A., Ferri, F., Grifoni, P., Guzzo, T.: Approaches, tools and applications for sentiment analysis implementation. Int. J. Comput. Appl.Comput. Appl. 125(3), 26–33 (2015). https://doi.org/10.5120/ijca2015905866

Revolutionizing Autonomous Vehicle Intelligence with Cutting-Edge Spatial Crowdsourcing Framework

Ayushi Jain[1] , Vaibhav Saini[1]([⊠]) , Ayush Dodia[1] ,
and M. V. V. Prasad Kantipudi[2]

[1] Verolt Engineering Pvt Ltd., Pune, India
vaibhavsainirke@gmail.com
[2] Symbiosis Institute of Technology (SIT), Symbiosis International (Deemed University) (SIU),
Pune, India
mvvprasad.kantipudi@ieee.org

Abstract. Crowdsourcing is an approach for performing spatial tasks that depends upon the efforts of many people and has received increasing attention in the past couple of years. Because of their effectiveness and simplicity, crowdsourcing work is frequently conducted online so-called mobile crowdsourcing. Due to the special challenges of engaging in real physical locations, this conventional technique might sometimes fail. As a result, a completely novel model for data collecting known as advanced spatial crowdsourcing (ASC) has grown up in recent years. In this paper, review of the existing work has been done and suggested the methodology by constructing the architecture and features of crowdsourcing, including Mobile Crowdsourcing, Spatial Crowdsourcing, Autonomous Vehicle Crowdsensing, and much more. As crowdsourcing is very important for autonomous vehicle, our research suggested the integration of Advanced crowdsourcing with Autonomous vehicle & real-time intelligent system. The objective of this research is to identify and explore the ITS (Intelligent Transportation System) technology that is made possible by IoT devices, as well as vehicle safety, vehicle security, and intelligent vehicle systems implementing advanced crowdsourcing. Finally, research aims to offer a variety of crowdsourcing applications and services like healthcare, Smart city, autonomous vehicle, and advanced applications.

Keywords: Crowdsourcing · Mobile Crowdsourcing · Advanced Spatial Crowdsourcing (ASC) · Autonomous vehicle · real-time intelligent system · ITS Intelligent Transportation System · Internet of Things · Smart Cities

1 Introduction

1.1 Introduction to Crowdsourcing

Crowdsourcing is a type of human processing, where human processing is a way of getting people to carry out tasks that would often be given to a computer to perform autonomously, like language translation work. As the use of the Internet and personal

O. Castillo et al. (Eds.): PerSOM 2023, LNICST 517, pp. 120–133, 2024.
https://doi.org/10.1007/978-3-031-66044-3_9

mobile devices (PMDs) increases, crowdsourcing can assist in solving difficult problems that machines are unable to do on a large scale [1]. The development of the Internet of Things (IoT) and distributed data storage systems are prerequisites for scalability. Crowdsourcing technology makes it easier to use the crowd to fulfil a given job [2]. To complete a task, a crowdsourcing system recruits a "crowd" of human beings to assist in resolving a specific issue. The necessity to finish a lot of little, repetitive activities with high short-term peak loads is present in many occupations. The most important need is that the individual performing the duties be diligent and strive to complete them to the best of their abilities. In many circumstances, these jobs do not require specialized expertise. As the use of the Internet and personal mobile devices (PMDs) increases, crowdsourcing can assist in solving tough problems that machines are unable to do on a large scale [3]. The development of the Internet of Things (IoT) and distributed data storage systems are prerequisites for scalability. Powerful mobile crowdsourcing frameworks have greater potential to be developed thanks to the rise in mobile devices, better data capacity, and ultra-reliable and low-latency communications in current and next-generation cellular networks. The process of crowdsourcing starts from the design phase and terminates with the implementation phase. Three high-level kinds of crowdsourcing often exist [4] which are Open innovation, Data collection and Analysis.

1.2 Crowdsourcing: Architecture and Features

Crowdsourcing architecture and features are critical for autonomous vehicles. Crowdsourcing applications based on autonomous vehicle technologies include mobile, geographic, car infotainment, and passive sensing crowdsourcing. This task necessitates drivers or humans who are attempting to improve autonomous vehicle decisions based on crowdsourcing, such as current traffic information on the road, route optimization for emergency vehicles, finding empty parking slots, and so on [5].

The crowdsourcing architecture for autonomous cars and smart city infrastructure is shown in Fig. 1. The crowdsourcing platform's task requesters include OEM (original equipment manufacturer) of autonomous cars and smart city developers. Drivers and humans complete these activities using mobile devices and vehicle entertainment systems. Input from drivers and humans is kept locally before being sent to the data warehouse server for compilation and organization. The outcomes of completed tasks are communicated to the task requesters [6]. The activities completed by drivers and people help task requesters enhance the system. This is the process flow of an autonomous vehicle crowdsourcing platform.

1.3 Autonomous Vehicle Crowdsourcing

Autonomous Vehicle Crowdsourcing is very important for developers to build a robust intelligent system. To progress smart systems, crowdsourcing is crucial in the context of autonomous vehicles since these vehicles require more input data to enhance the applications that are running for real-time control and decision-making. With the utilization of sensors included into autonomous vehicles, automatic sensing crowdsourcing uses passive data collection to send information to a centralized platform for processing and utilization. Scheduling the gathering based on its trajectories is one of the primary

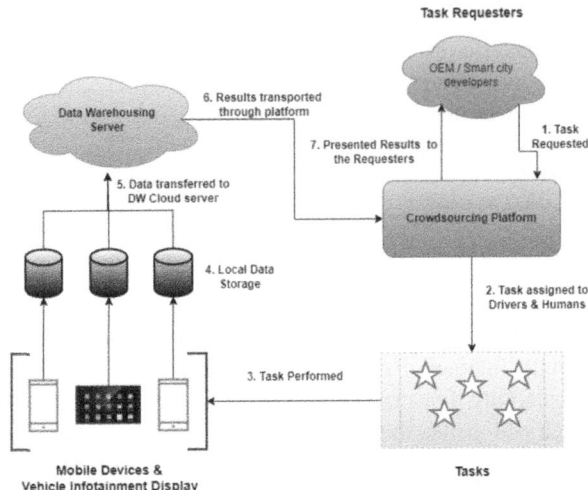

Fig. 1. High level Generalized architecture of ITS crowdsourcing.

goals of passive collection jobs. It is possible to follow autonomous vehicles in real-time using other passive collecting chores [7]. Making automated data collecting makes the system more dependable and safer since fewer discrepancies would be present in the data obtained and because humans are not occupied by gathering data operations while operating an automobile [8].

2   Literature Review

2.1   IoT Technologies Improving Mobile Crowdsourcing

Crowdsensing and crowdsourcing play a significant role in the development of new IoT applications and serve as the interface between human-based and object-based methodologies. With crowdsensing, the same notion is used, but instead of using human input, equipment or sensors collect the data. Crowdsourcing is a method of getting services, ideas, and useful data from a group of people [9]. User's contributions are crucial to the dependability and data quality of both crowd sourcing and sensing systems. Mobile crowdsensing, when the resource offered by the public is their sensing ability, can be compared to crowdsourcing. Crowdsourcing is a category of crowdsourcing strategies that makes use of independent, paid in full, and volunteer human resources to do a particular activity. The primary goal of the Inspection on MCS [10] and its Possible Applications in the IoT Era focuses on the use of crowdsourcing for data collection to address many significant issues in widely used computing systems, such as participatory urbanization, which promotes novel methods and strategies for citizens as individuals to actively participate in their city, neighborhood, and urban self-reflexivity. Another illustration is the use of mobile devices as channels for atmospheric sensing that encourage neighborhood action and promote good social change (Fig. 2).

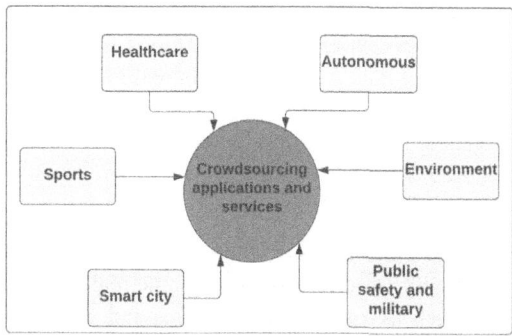

Fig. 2. Figure representing the different application of crowdsourcing with services.

As interconnectivity between all nodes of the layered communications network continues to increase exponentially, ITS technology enabled by IoT devices like embedded sensors in autonomous vehicles and new communications infrastructure might offer a hitherto unexplored foundation for mobile crowdsourcing applications. A variety of high-bandwidth network topologies, such as vehicle-to-vehicle (V2V), vehicle-to-infrastructure (V2I), vehicle-to-infrastructure (V2I), vehicle-to-pedestrian (V2P), and vehicle-to-drone (V2D), might be created because of the development of 5G networks [11].

Table 1. Research studies focuses for IoT crowdsourcing.

Year	Author	Focus
2017	He, S. et al. [9]	Establishes the IoT devices' locality with improvements
2018	Zhu et al. [13]	Using automotive fog computing for evaluating the crowdsourced dash camera footage in real time
2019	Wang, Y et al. [10]	Mobile crowdsourcing could be improved more honest and efficient with the use of incentive systems
2019	Park, J et al. [16]	To promote involvement in crowdsourcing, put attention on knowing how to ask: how to craft intriguing and relevant queries
2021	Tan, L et al. [15]	5G-enabled smart cities: a decentralized trustworthy service mechanism driven by blockchain for the crowdsourcing system

Research existing work has been demonstrated in the tabular form Table 1 which focuses on IoT crowdsourcing and improvements towards the same in some last years.

2.2 Advanced Cloud Technologies for Crowdsourcing

Crowdsourcing is the process of solving issues, obtaining new ideas, or creating content by enlisting the help of a large number of individuals, particularly those who are part of an online community such as social media users, mobile users, and so on. Advanced cloud technology can help make crowdsourcing more successful and efficient. The use of cloud-based technology for crowdsourcing platforms has made it simpler to offer tasks to the crowd and collect data from humans in real-time from many sources with high accuracy. Users of the crowdsourcing platform may crowdsource without having to worry about the technical infrastructure of cloud computing [12]. Cloud computing enables data access as well as crowdsourcing services. Here are some advanced cloud technologies for crowdsourcing.

- **Internet of Things (IoT) Integration:** Cloud technologies can be combined with IoT devices equipped with various sensors to enable real-time data collection from a variety of sources such as autonomous vehicles and smart city crowds, enriching crowdsourced datasets with diverse data types, and improving crowdsourced information quality as well [13].
- **Container orchestration:** Container management tools are key crowdsourcing technology. Kubernetes is a container management system that makes it easier to build, grow, and operate distributed crowdsourcing applications.
- **Big Data Processing:** Cloud-based big data processing frameworks such as Apache Hadoop and Apache Spark allow for the efficient processing and analysis of massive crowdsourcing datasets. Machine learning techniques for real-time data processing are provided by big data processing [14]. It simplifies and adds value to cloud-based crowdsourcing procedures.
- **Blockchain for Crowdsourcing Verification:** Blockchain technology can increase the transparency, trust, and security of crowdsourcing platforms by providing an immutable record of contributions and outcomes. It may be used to validate contributions and ensure that incentives are delivered properly [15].
- **Crowdsourced AI Training:** Crowdsourced AI tools and AI models are taught to conduct cloud-based operations for crowdsourcing platforms. The cloud-based crowdsourcing platform becomes more robust and representative when AI is used [16].

2.3 Concepts and Logics for Crowdsourcing

Crowdsourcing is a large group of direct and indirect sources which collects data like smart sensors, smartphone data, and other sources in a closed environment that helps the autonomous vehicle to improve its internal system and makes it intelligent. There are some factors which are important like (a) To determine the type of data that needs to be collected (Images, videos, text, personal data, medical data, public data, etc.). (b) Determine the internal and external sensors involved. (c) Create (or outsource) a platform for registering the sensors, sharing the data, and managing the sources. (d) Gather the data through the cloud platform [17].

There are different benefits for collecting data through crowdsourcing:

- Deliver for high-quality and relevant data.
- Improvements in the system.
- Assists in reducing expenses.
- Increases data variety.
- Saves computational time.

Crowdsourcing data collecting drawbacks are as follows:

- Complex to handle and filter the useful data.
- Lack of anonymity for the collected data.
- Tracking and evaluating data collecting is challenging [18].
- It is challenging to assess competence.

In our research study, explanation of an elementary description of crowdsourcing with existing work has been showcased, explained why it is crucial for autonomous vehicles, described how crowdsourcing structure with features assists the system make more accurate decisions, and subsequently discuss them in more detail by emphasizing all the finer points. System Architecture has been constructed that incorporates the cloud to increase the system's intelligence regarding autonomous vehicles. At last, examined the rational future paths required for the advancement, creation, and use of automated real-time crowdsourcing platforms. These technologies will serve as the foundation for a wide range of use cases, including sophisticated surveillance of traffic, extremely detailed modelling of the road network, enhanced Kalman filter estimates, and other services that will support the introduction of driverless vehicle technology on public roads.

2.4 Increasing Crowdsourcing Technology

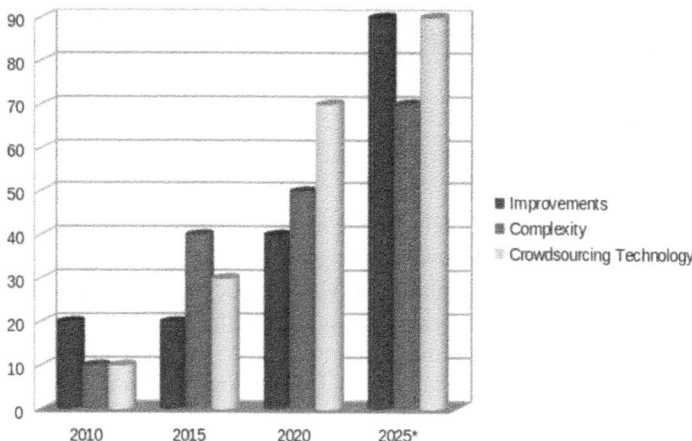

Fig. 3. Visualizing how mobile crowdsourcing can enhance the improvement in the system.

As shown in the Fig. 3, how the mobile crowdsourcing can enhance the overall improvement in the system. From 2010 onwards crowdsourcing technology was adapting for improving the system and these types of technology are playing a vital role for now and future aspects. But the challenge was the increasing of the complexity that will be minimized in the future by using different suggested approaches like data optimization. Also, there are many advanced tools for developers like MATLAB and Simulink that can automate the process and solves the complexity to make the system efficient [19]. There are small scale development projects like smart irrigation system using IoT, these types of system can be improved by adding our approach i.e., Advanced Spatial Crowdsourcing [20].

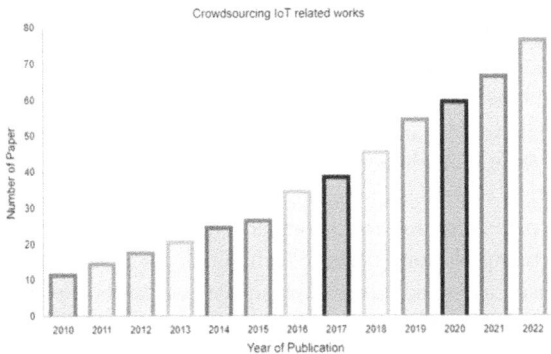

Fig. 4. Statistics of increase in crowdsourcing IoT research works.

For the research comparison study, existing works from reliable and pertinent databases, including Google Scholar, IEEE Explore, and Scopus, are considered. A high rise in crowd-IoT applications has been observed recently, according to research projects spanning the years 2010 to 2022. The numbers pertaining to the rise in crowd-IoT application efforts are displayed in Fig. 4.

3   Methodologies

3.1   Computing Crowdsourcing

To process data or store it concurrently, a network of computers known as the cloud coordinates their efforts. Many ITS crowdsourcing platforms will be built on top of cloud computing infrastructure; the scalability provided by developments in cloud computing technology and approaches works hand in hand with the IoT and communications technologies outlined in the preceding section. The system may be made more efficient by using cloud computing methods and technologies such as edge computing, distributed file processing, storage, job management, worker dependability measures, and trust mechanisms. In this part, high level of several essential cloud attributes that support ITS [21] crowdsourcing has been discussed. A simplified representation of how these cloud-based structures operate is shown in Fig. 5.

In Table 2, All the possible types of crowdsourcing have been suggested with implementation platform and its accuracy with included all the environmental factors.

3.2   Advanced Automated Crowdsourcing Management

For managing crowdsourcing platform is very complex as there is a lot of data is collected and stored for real-time decisions and analysis. Procedures must be in place to distribute

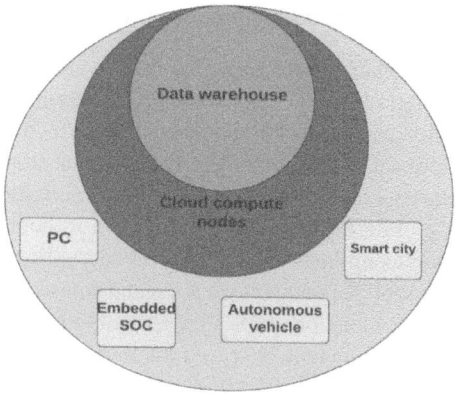

Fig. 5. A diagram representing the relationships between devices in computing crowdsourcing.

Table 2. Possible types of Advanced Spatial Crowdsourcing.

S. No	Crowdsourcing Type	Implementation	Precision
1	In-Vehicle Sensors	Local Platform	High Accurate
2	V2X (Vehicle-to-Everything)	Cloud Platform	Less Accurate
3	External users' data	Cloud Platform	Less Accurate*
4	External sensors	Cloud Platform	High Accurate
5	Third Party Applications	Local / Cloud Platform	Less Accurate

positions across the platform due to the complexities of ITS crowdsourced applications, the enormous number of activities, and the numerous prospective employees. Allocation of duties presents a special set of difficulties for spatial tasks. It can also be made advanced using cloud IoT architectures. The previously described cloud-based platforms would work in cooperation with automated management systems. The responsibilities can be allocated spatially, outcomes may circulate through the network at optimized points of access, and information can be pipelined, gathered, and preserved in locations that are geographically optimized to be best for use according to the areas it has been gathered at. This is achieved by consequently optimizing the task distribution by the cloud engineers. The latest developments in cloud computing technology are setting the stage for Intelligent autonomous vehicle system to continue functioning as a significant crowdsourced platform. By integrating traditional autonomous vehicle networks into the IoT, updated networks will become advanced cloud computers, giving system engineer employees much more data to make decisions that will enhance the future of the autonomous vehicle experience for everyone who uses this type of advance vehicles. In this study [22], AUTOSAR architecture has been used for optimizing the overall system that can also integrated with our approach for enhancement of the designed architecture.

3.3 Security and Privacy in Mobile Crowdsourcing

Crowdsourcing is a critical platform for gathering data from crowds, autonomous cars, and addressing complicated challenges connected to autonomous vehicles and smart cities. Privacy and security are critical components of the crowdsourcing platform. The privacy of a user's profile and data is especially crucial since an attacker can take information from a user while they are undertaking crowdsourcing activities. To secure sensitive data transferred across mobile devices, car infotainment systems, and crowdsourcing platforms, data encryption techniques like end-to-end encryption are deployed. To protect the confidentiality of users' personal information and data obtained during the crowdsourcing process. Data anonymization drops all personally identifying information from users and assures that the data cannot be traced back to the user. The most important aspect of crowdsourcing procedures is user authentication. Any unauthorized user executes tasks and gains access to the crowdsourcing platform's sensitive data. A strong user authentication mechanism checks users' identities as they take part in crowdsourcing activities. Protect the communication channels between mobile devices, the vehicle's infotainment system, and the crowdsourcing platform. Strong secure protocols are used to protect communication channels, and the security of secure protocols is continually updated to address any new vulnerabilities [23]. These are the critical aspects to preserve user data privacy and the security of crowdsourcing operations.

4 Advanced Spatial Crowdsourcing for Autonomous Vehicle

4.1 Data Optimization for Crowdsourcing

To fulfil the tasks assigned through spatial crowdsourcing, employees must physically be at those places. This kind of crowd intelligence involves people gathering, analyzing, and disseminating geographical and/or social understanding in the actual environment. Geo-crowdsourcing or location-aware crowdsourcing are other terms used to describe SC. However, even though SC, from which many applications may substantially benefit, has received far less attention, there has been a lot of study on crowdsourcing. For example, the government must gather data on the city's air quality at various intervals (e.g., per hour, day, every month, and yearly), and each site needs a number of people to provide the information. Due to the geographically distributed nature of the employees in the city, a standard crowdsourcing method where participants just submit the data in their immediate area at the time of their choosing would not give an accurate representation of the city's air quality situation. Due to a lack of employees in some regions at some times, not enough data may be reported from those places or periods. On the other hand, this problem will be solved by a Spatial Crowdsourcing system that sends workers in an anticipatory way. Typically, some challenges in spatial crowdsourcing:

These challenges frequently interact rather than being in isolation from one another:

- Task formulation
- Task assignment or worker selection
- Task assignment
- Incentive mechanism

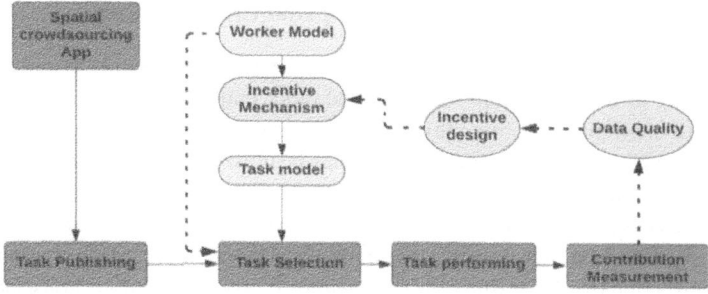

Fig. 6. Generalized block diagram of (SMC) Spatial Mobile Crowdsourcing.

- Scalability

The geographical crowdsourcing flow is Showing in Fig. 6. At first, each employee downloads the SC app and has access to all the assignments posted by task publishers. If the server is assigning jobs, the server gets information about all the employees and hires suitable workers; if the worker is picking tasks, the worker chooses the right task set to maximize model and the worker model are used to inform both worker selection and job selection. To encourage employees to complete their duties, an incentive structure is created. When the assignment is finished, the task publisher receives the information from the employees. The system evaluates user contributions based on factors such as user dependability and contribution quality. Further adjustments to the incentives are made using the results. For instance, after the assignment is publicized, the worker's dependability and timeliness may vary, necessitating the updating of the incentive for this worker. If there are open jobs, this process will continue to be repeated.

The priorities of various Spatial Crowdsourcing systems might change depending on the viewpoint of the employees or the systems. A worker's objective is often to maximize total net reward, which is the sum of the reward he receives from the system and any costs (such as travel expenses). Task scheduling and path selection need to be taken into consideration together when choosing tasks since the worker may choose the optimum way to complete all the jobs to decrease costs. From a system's viewpoint, the objectives are frequently to achieve maximal job coverage at the lowest possible cost [24].

There are some benefits after data Optimization:

- Optimize the expenses for the system.
- Maximize the accuracy of data and quality.
- Increase the task scope.

Each worker w_j has a dependability p_i, j for task z_i (worker reliability). Worker w_j completes job t_j before the conclusion of the cycle with probability p_i, j if he or she is given the task, which is:

$$y_{i,j} = \begin{cases} 1 & with\,probability\,p_{i,j} \\ 0 & otherwise \end{cases} \tag{1}$$

Assume that $p_{i,j}$ $(0, 1)$ without losing generality. Worker w_j's dependability on task z_i relies on the task, the worker, and the environment in which they work.

4.2 Real-Time Intelligent Decisions with Spatial Crowdsourcing

The information that is intake from the roads by different smart sensors may be utilized for monitoring traffic systems in real-time and other major applications that makes the system more intelligent. Mobile phones, reliable high-bandwidth technology for communication, and Smart sensor-equipped cars may be utilized for uploading large amounts of data on congestion, average speeds, accidents etc. This data information, for instance, may be utilized by a real-time GPS navigation system to redirect cars away from a particular road section and reduce systemwide time to travel by detecting anomalous interruptions in the flow of traffic or other reasons. Figure 7 represents constructed approach as the high-level system architecture of autonomous vehicle with the integration of advanced crowdsourcing. In Fig. 7, There are two environments which include internal and external sensors, internal sensors are in-vehicle sensors which all sensors are established in vehicle and for external there are some smart sensors which are contributing as a crowdsourcing. At other sides data is going in cloud for analysis and post processing to improve decisions. Having to spot service interruptions in their initial place is a barrier in putting this into practice. Though accidents are often unanticipated incidents and may be avoided by redirecting traffic, congestion in the roadways is generally recurring (such as rush hour times at school or office timings) and can be predicted from previous information or any other sources.

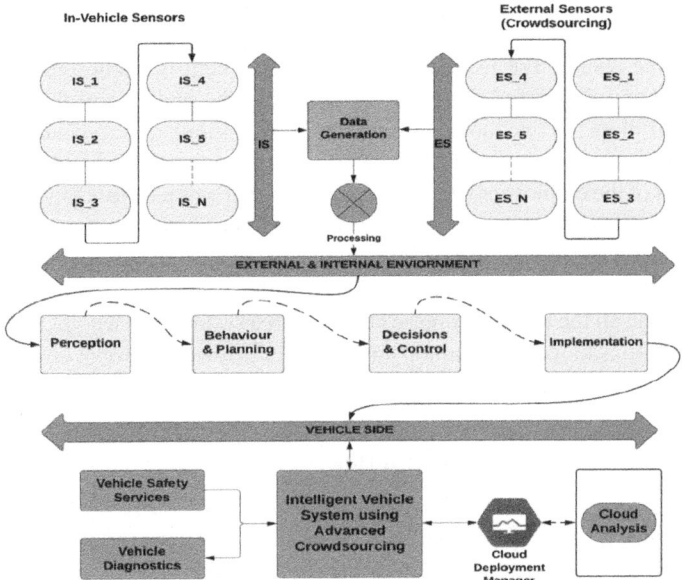

Fig. 7. Suggested approach via constructing the overall Intelligent System Architecture (ISA).

Autonomous incident identification must also result in changes or updates as quickly as feasible so that anyone intending to go over the restricted path can do so without incident and locate an alternate path in a fair period. This information might be utilized to resolve a user balancing issue and direct traffic routing, supposing some sort of controlled mechanism which is controlled by the integration of smart sensors and advanced software etc.

4.3 Advanced Applications

When doing crowdsourcing activities, advanced applications for mobile devices, automobile infotainment systems, and certain automated sensor technology are necessary for greater input to the crowdsourcing platform. Advanced applications, such as reporting and assigning free parking slots using a crowdsourcing platform for smart cities, are required to identify a free spot in smart cities. The framework based on mobile devices and car infotainment systems provides services for a user to report a free parking place in the traffic network. This application displays real-time availability of parking spaces from registered crowdsourcing users and automobiles. A significant component is improved autonomous vehicle high resolution map performance. Enhancing the resolution of a map [25] on a regular basis is an expensive and time-consuming operation for OEMs, but enhancing the resolution of a map utilizing a crowdsourcing platform is less expensive and takes less time. Some automated sensing technologies have been fitted on public transport vehicles such as buses and capture real-time road data to improve map resolution for autonomous cars. Using this innovative application, vast volumes of data may be collected in less time and provide greater input for enhancing map resolution from crowdsourcing platform. One of the advanced uses for crowdsourcing systems is traffic prediction based on crowdsourced social media data. Advanced transportation tracking using crowdsourcing-based automated sensing technologies [26, 27]. These are some sophisticated crowdsourcing platform applications.

5   Conclusion

In this research study, existing work for IoT crowdsourcing has been demonstrated by covering all the efforts of researchers and developers. IoT technologies, and employing cloud technologies for gathering real-time data, as well as the concept and logic behind crowdsourcing in brief has been showcased by different methods. Also explained, how crowdsourcing structure with features helps the system correct and precise, and analyzed a new branch of crowdsourcing i.e., Spatial crowdsourcing - to safeguard user data privacy and the security of crowdsourcing operations. Mobile crowd sensing is a developing field with a wide range of potential applications. The evaluation also includes advanced spatial crowdsourcing topics such as data optimization in Autonomous Vehicle, maximizing data accuracy, quality, and Task of scope with real-time intelligent environment making use of in-vehicle and external sensors. High-level system architecture has been constructed in this research study by adding the approaches to make the system of Autonomous Vehicle more intelligent and advanced with the capabilities of Advanced Spatial Crowdsourcing. For future aspects, robust output can be seen in the system for crowdsourcing by integrating with artificial intelligence and machine learning.

References

1. Liu, H.K.: Crowdsourcing: citizens as coproducers of public services. Policy Internet **13**(2), 315–331 (2021)
2. Shahrour, I., Xie, X.: Role of Internet of Things (IoT) and crowdsourcing in smart city projects. Smart Cities **4**(4), 1276–1292 (2021)
3. Lucic, M.C., Wan, X., Ghazzai, H., Massoud, Y.: Leveraging intelligent transportation systems and smart vehicles using crowdsourcing: an overview. Smart Cities **3**(2), 341–361 (2020)
4. Modaresnezhad, M., Iyer, L., Palvia, P., Taras, V.: Information Technology (IT) enabled crowdsourcing: a conceptual framework. Inf. Process. Manag. **57**(2), 102135 (2020)
5. Dortheimer, J., Yang, S., Yang, Q., Sprecher, A.: Conceptual architectural design at scale: a case study of community participation using crowdsourcing. Buildings **13**(1), 222 (2023)
6. Kong, X., Liu, X., Jedari, B., Li, M., Wan, L., Xia, F.: Mobile crowdsourcing in smart cities: technologies, applications, and future challenges. IEEE Internet Things J. **6**(5), 8095–8113 (2019)
7. Chen, H., Luo, R., Feng, Y.: Improving autonomous vehicle mapping and navigation in work zones using crowdsourcing vehicle trajectories. arXiv preprint arXiv:2301.09194 (2023)
8. Zhou, J., Guo, Y., Bian, Y., Huang, Y., Li, B.: Lane information extraction for high definition maps using crowdsourced data. IEEE Trans. Intell. Transp. Syst. **24**(7), 7780–7790 (2022)
9. He, S., Chan, S.H.G.: Towards crowdsourced signal map construction via implicit interaction of IoT devices. In: 2017 14th Annual IEEE International Conference on Sensing, Communication, and Networking (SECON), pp. 1–9. IEEE (2017)
10. Wang, Y., Cai, Z., Zhan, Z.H., Gong, Y.J., Tong, X.: An optimization and auction-based incentive mechanism to maximize social welfare for mobile crowdsourcing. IEEE Trans. Comput. Soc. Syst. **6**(3), 414–429 (2019)
11. Islam, S., Iqbal, A., Marzband, M., Khan, I., Al-Wahedi, A.M.: State-of-the-art vehicle-to-everything mode of operation of electric vehicles and its future perspectives. Renew. Sustain. Energy Rev. **166**, 112574 (2022)
12. Stern, C., et al.: Pangeo forge: crowdsourcing analysis-ready, cloud optimized data production. Front. Clim. **3**, 782909 (2022)
13. Zhu, C., Pastor, G., Xiao, Y., Ylajaaski, A.: Vehicular fog computing for video crowdsourcing: applications, feasibility, and challenges. IEEE Commun. Mag. **56**(10), 58–63 (2018)
14. Habeeb, R.A.A., Nasaruddin, F., Gani, A., Hashem, I.A.T., Ahmed, E., Imran, M.: Real-time big data processing for anomaly detection: a survey. Int. J. Inf. Manag. **45**, 289–307 (2019)
15. Tan, L., Xiao, H., Yu, K., Aloqaily, M., Jararweh, Y.: A blockchain-empowered crowdsourcing system for 5G-enabled smart cities. Comput. Standards Interfaces **76**, 103517 (2021)
16. Park, J., Krishna, R., Khadpe, P., Fei-Fei, L., Bernstein, M.: AI-based request augmentation to increase crowdsourcing participation. In: Proceedings of the AAAI Conference on Human Computation and Crowdsourcing, vol. 7, no. 1, pp. 115–124 (2019)
17. Prester, J., Schlagwein, D., Cecez-Kecmanovic, D.: Crowdsourcing for education: literature review, conceptual framework, and research agenda (2019)
18. Li, Y., Chang, L., Li, L., Bao, X., Gu, T.: Key research issues and related technologies in crowdsourcing data collection. Wirel. Commun. Mob. Comput. **2021**, 1–13 (2021)
19. Saini, V., Shah, P., Sekhar, R.: Matlab and Simulink for building automation. In: 2022 IEEE Bombay Section Signature Conference (IBSSC), pp. 1–6. IEEE (2022)
20. Khelifa, B., Amel, D., Amel, B., Mohamed, C., Tarek, B.: Smart irrigation using Internet of Things. In: 2015 Fourth International Conference on Future Generation Communication Technology (FGCT), pp. 1–6. IEEE (2015)
21. Ren, Y., Liu, W., Liu, A., Wang, T., Li, A.: A privacy-protected intelligent crowdsourcing application of IoT based on the reinforcement learning. Future Gener. Comput. Syst. **127**, 56–69 (2022)

22. Henle, J., Stoffel, M., Schindewolf, M., Nägele, A.T., Sax, E.: Architecture platforms for future vehicles: a comparison of ROS2 and adaptive AUTOSAR. In: 2022 IEEE 25th International Conference on Intelligent Transportation Systems (ITSC), pp. 3095–3102. IEEE (2022)
23. Ma, Y., Sun, Y., Lei, Y., Qin, N., Lu, J.: A survey of blockchain technology on security, privacy, and trust in crowdsourcing services. World Wide Web **23**, 393–419 (2020)
24. Jain, A., Nandan, D., Meduri, P.: Data export and optimization technique in connected vehicle. Ingénierie des Systèmes d'Information **28**(2), 517–525 (2023)
25. Kim, K., Cho, S., Chung, W.: HD map update for autonomous driving with crowdsourced data. IEEE Robot. Autom. Lett. **6**(2), 1895–1901 (2021)
26. Zhang, P., Zhang, M., Liu, J.: Real-time HD map change detection for crowdsourcing update based on mid-to-high-end sensors. Sensors **21**(7), 2477 (2021)
27. Kantipudi, M.P., Aluvalu, R., Velamuri, S.: An intelligent approach of intrusion detection in mobile crowd sourcing systems in the context of IoT based SMART city. Smart Sci. **11**(1), 234–240 (2023)

Identification of Spam on Social Media by Semi-supervised Learning Approach

Sudana Shashi Kiran, Sure Uday Kiran, Elluru Amrutha, E. Yasaswi,
Annam Kumar Sai, Kusam Sravya, and S. R. Reeja(✉)

School of Computer Science and Engineering, VIT-AP University, Amaravati, India
{shashi.21bce8644,udaykiran.21bce9527,amrutha.21bce8405,
yasaswi.21bce7221,kumarsai.21bce9432,
sravya.21bce8209}@vitapstudent.ac.in, reeja.sr@vitap.ac.in

Abstract. This study examines how machine learning methods can be used to identify Twitter spammers. Due to spammers' increased use of social media platforms, it is crucial to combat their fraudulent operations. This study uses extensive Twitter data, such as user profiles, tweet content, and network connections, to create algorithms that accurately differentiate between genuine users and spammers. By successfully identifying and filtering out spammers utilizing a range of machine learning algorithms, deep learning techniques, feature extraction methodologies, and even categorizing tweets based on their emotional tone, the ultimate goal is to improve platform trust and user experience. In order to efficiently identify spammers and fake users, the article provides a solution that makes use of a unique machine learning algorithm that meticulously analyses user personal information and account history. Because of its popularity, Twitter has drawn spammers and bogus users, which has caused confusion. The study seeks to address "Twitter Spam Drift" by applying a Semi-Supervised Learning Approach (SSLA), which adjusts to changes in spam behavior and has demonstrated promising results on English datasets. To identify spam behaviors on Twitter, the project uses deep-learning classifier algorithms like LSTM, and GRU. Here, as can be seen, we use various methods to achieve accuracy ranging from 87% to 97%.

Keywords: Semi-Supervised Learning · Social Media · Ham And Spam Messages

1 Introduction

Social networking platforms like Twitter have seen a sharp rise in popularity recently. As a result, there has been an increase in spammers trying to monetize the website by indulging in spamming activities and creating fictitious profiles in order to gain more views and followers. Twitter is mostly used to disseminate news and updates, although some users abuse the service to spread spam and untrue information. Global losses have resulted from the failure of current machine learning techniques to combat the expanding spam problem. Several spam-detecting techniques have failed in the fight

O. Castillo et al. (Eds.): PerSOM 2023, LNICST 517, pp. 134–153, 2024.
https://doi.org/10.1007/978-3-031-66044-3_10

against spammers because to the complicated spammers' software [2]. The purpose of this research is to examine how machine learning techniques are applied to the detection of Twitter spam. We can create models that reliably differentiate between real users and spammers by utilizing large-scale data from Twitter, such as user profiles, tweet content, and network connections. A large dataset of tagged Twitter accounts will be gathered for the project, which will also make use of feature extraction methods and look at different machine learning algorithms. The ultimate goal is to assist in the development of efficient procedures that improve user experience by successfully identifying and filtering out spammers. Spammers have become a major worry as social media platforms like Twitter have grown so quickly. These spammers, whether human or automated, take advantage of the platform to disseminate false information, advertise frauds, and influence public opinion. The integrity and credibility of the platform must be preserved by identifying and combatting Twitter spammers. Due to the fact that spamming tactics are constantly evolving and conventional approaches based on rules have been shown to be ineffectual, interest in applying machine learning techniques has developed [1].

As the use of social media platforms grows in popularity, spammers looking to take advantage of the community also increase. They take part in a variety of nefarious activities, including the promotion of phony goods, phishing, the transmission of malware, and breaking community rules. With 450 million active users each month, Twitter has emerged as a top destination for spammers. Spam tweets are posted by roughly 10% of active Twitter users, posing serious hazards to user privacy and data security. Twitter uses several spam detection technologies to fight this problem, suspending tens of thousands of spam accounts per day. To avoid discovery, spammers vary their tactics frequently, leading to the problem known as "Twitter Spam Drift." The Semi-Supervised Learning Approach (SSLA), a potential technique put forth by researchers, promises to address the problem of Twitter Spam Drift and increase spam detection accuracy. SSLA uses unlabeled data to better understand domain structure and improve the accuracy of spam detection. Researchers can develop a powerful system for differentiating between real users and spammers using SSLA and other machine learning algorithms, which would improve user experience on social media sites [4]. Social media use is prevalent and has a big impact on people's lives as they exchange news about politics, entertainment, and other topics. However, a big problem has emerged with the increase in spammers submitting unrelated content. The sheer number of tweets—billions are sent each year—makes it difficult to spot spam. To create a secure and reliable environment for users on Twitter, the main objective is to find and filter out spammers [3]. By applying the Random forest technique and using existing models. Our ability to identify and filter spammers will improve. The main objective is to significantly improve the current models using our technique, which is based on the random forest algorithm and use RF-Algorithm to improve the model even further.

2 Literature Survey

In order to combat the spam drift, we developed a semi-supervised learning strategy in this article. When there is a greater amount of unlabeled data than labelled data, SSLA is utilized. It enhances the model's learning process by combining labelled and unlabeled input. Numerous generic or non-generic semi-supervised algorithms as well as wrapper strategies are available. We employed general methods based on supervised learning algorithms. The closest neighbor algorithm and any supervised approach can be merged with the semi-supervised method known as YATSI. The YATSI is divided into two phases. An initial prediction model is developed using a supervised classifier and predictions are generated using this model to pre-label unlabeled occurrences in the first step. This model is trained on labelled data. Pre-labeled and labeled data are combined into one set. According to the algorithm parameter, unlabeled data is given higher weight and labeled data is given a weight of 1.0. In the second stage, K nearest neighbors of the combined data are selected for the instance that needs to be classified, and they forecast the class based on the highest sum of weights relating to that class. In this study, we made predictions using the filtered closest neighbor technique and a random forest base classifier. Because it performs better than other methods in predicting spam tweets, random forest is utilized [4].

Here, we offered a way to identify phony users and spam. The system that we suggested is depicted here. The model comprises the methods used in processing, designing the model, and testing it in real-time on Twitter. It adheres to the norms used in natural language processing jobs. Our system was used to identify these tweets. We classified communications that were already stored in our database as spam and real using a variety of techniques. Using this information, we chose a model or technique that provides high accuracy and implemented it in our model. This approach aids in distinguishing between fake and real traits [2]. Various algorithm comparison study is shown in Table 1.

Bag of Words: Determines how frequently a word appears in a manuscript. Each word's frequency within the corpus of a document is contained in the vector of that document.

TF-IDF: In order to employ TF-IDF, you must first determine the TF-IDF score for each word in your data set is in relation to the document, and then you must input the results into a vector. Each word in the text is given a score using this method based on the likelihood that it will appear in texts from other categories as well as the number of items where it does [1].

Research: The team gathers data and information about the problem domain during this stage, including knowledge of different spam subtypes, current spam patterns, and potential features that could be applied to spam detection.

Concept Generation: In this stage, the team generates a variety of concepts and ideas for designing the spam detection system. These ideas could encompass several models, approaches, or algorithms.

Analysis: After coming up with concepts, the team analyzes each one to determine its advantages, disadvantages, and viability. The most promising strategies are found using this study.

Requirements and Constraints: The team determines the precise needs and restrictions for the system after choosing the best concept or concepts. These specifications may include user experience criteria, resource constraints, response times, and accuracy levels.

Prototyping and Implementation: The selected concept(s) are then put into practice as early iterations of the system or prototypes. The design is tested and validated using these prototypes.

Testing and Evaluation: To make sure they adhere to the established requirements and constraints, the prototypes go through comprehensive testing and review. Changing parameters, fine-tuning models, and iterating on the design may all be part of this phase.

Feedback and Iteration: The team iterates on the design, making adjustments and enhancements as necessary based on the findings of the testing, user input, and any unforeseen problems.

Deployment and Monitoring: The system is put into production once it satisfies the required standards. However, spam detection is a never-ending task, therefore regular surveillance and modifications are necessary to keep up with evolving spamming methods [3].

Table 1. Table shows advantage, disadvantage and gap of different algorithms

Algorithms	Advantage	Disadvantage	GAP
Decision Tree [5]	Simple to grasp and visualize	Susceptible to overfitting if no trimming	Decision trees may struggle to identify complicated links and patterns for accurate spam categorization in unstructured and high-dimensional Twitter data
Logistic Regression [6]	Simple and comprehensible	Possibly perform poorly with complex data	The complex and nonlinear patterns found in the various and dynamic Twitter spam data may be too much for logistic regression to handle, resulting in poor detection accuracy

(continued)

Table 1. (*continued*)

Algorithms	Advantage	Disadvantage	GAP
Multinomial Naive Bayes [7]	Effective and efficient for classifying texts	A belief in the independence of traits	Simple linguistic features in Twitter data can be made easier to grasp by naive multinomial Bayes, which can make it more difficult to identify minor patterns and potentially lead to less accurate spam identification
Support Vector Machine [8]	High-dimensional data effective	Sensitive to kernel and parameter selection	The high dimensionality and noise in textual data may limit SVM's ability to discern complex spam patterns, which may reduce its effectiveness in spotting Twitter spam
Bernoulli Naive Bayes [9]	Quick & easy	Feature dependency sensitivity	Because Bernoulli Naive Bayes assumes binary feature independence, which makes it challenging for it to understand complex relationships in tweet content, its accuracy may decrease in difficult spam detection conditions

(*continued*)

Table 1. (*continued*)

Algorithms	Advantage	Disadvantage	GAP
Semi-Supervised Algorithm [10]	Combines tagged and unlabeled data	May not operate properly if the labeling is insufficient	The YATSI algorithm's drawback is that it depends on a predetermined set of traits, which may make it difficult for it to adapt and successfully capture changing and unique Twitter spam trends
1D convolutional neural Network (CNN) model/algorithm [11]	Learning features automatically	Limited Understanding of Semantics	1D CNN must be able to capture long-range relationships in sequential data in order to detect Twitter spam
GRU (Gated Recurrent Unit) [12]	Decreased vanishing gradient issue	A short-term memory deficit	GRU falls short of LSTM when it comes to gathering intricate sequential patterns over longer sequences
LSTM (Long Short-Term Memory) [13]	Properly manages sequential data	Processes sequential data appropriately	Because it overfits on short datasets and has trouble processing extremely long sequences, LSTM is not ideal for recognizing Twitter spam

3 SPAM Detection Algorithms

3.1 Decision Tree

It is a form of supervised classifier used to understand classification and regression problems. The central nodes of this classifier's tree-like structure describe the characteristics of the data set, while the branches denote the rules or decisions, and the leaf nodes stand in for the outcome. Decision nodes and leaf nodes are two additional types of nodes found in decision trees. Various branch nodes are connected to the decision node in this situation, which is used to make decisions. The result of these branches is represented by a leaf node, which has no branches. Entropy is utilized in this case to help the decision tree partition the data. It is important because it can alter the structure of the decision tree by establishing new rules. You can write it as Eq. (1).

$$H(S) = -p_+ \log_2(p_+) - p_- \log_2 p_-$$ (1)

In Eq. (1) where, (p_+) indicates the % of $+$ ve class, (p_-) indicates the % of -ve class.

Drawbacks: Decision trees may struggle to identify complicated links and patterns for accurate spam categorization in unstructured and high-dimensional Twitter data.

3.2 Logistic Regression

The binary functions in this algorithm are separated using the sigmoid function. Let x be the initial feature of the vector, which is used to determine the likelihood that the given text would be output. It is provided as

$$p = \frac{e^{a+bx}}{1 + e^{a+bx}}$$ (2)

Here, in Eq. (2), p stands for the probability of a, i.e., it represents the fundamental logarithm's foundation, while a and b represent the parameters of the representation. Where $x = 0$, p returns the value, and b is used to regulate the rapid changes in probability that occur when x is changed by one bit.

Drawbacks: Logistic regression may not be able to manage the intricate and non-linear patterns present in the diverse and ever-changing Twitter spam data, leading to insufficient accuracy in detection.

3.3 Multinomial Naive Bayes

It is employed to find differences in counts between several categories. It goes by the names count rate and reflect cont. The text provided indicates the word count and assigns distinct categories to each. The multinomial naive bayes algorithm is only utilized in this particular section. Its formal name is Eq. (3).

$$p(X|C_k) = \frac{(\sum_{i=1}^{n} x_i)!}{\prod_{i=1}^{n} x_i!} \prod_{i=1}^{n} Pk_i^{x_i}$$ (3)

Here, in Eq. (3), we find the likelihood that a feature of class 'Ck' will have the criterion 'X'. The count rate, which defines frequency, can then be found by using the value of feature x, which can either be 0 or 1. It must be produced by a Pi multinomial. The number of instances of the provided event I is now displayed as 'xi'.

Drawbacks: Naïve multinomial Bayes can make complex linguistic features in Twitter data easier to understand, making it more difficult to spot minor trends and potentially resulting in less accurate spam detection.

3.4 Support Vector Machine

An efficient supervised method of teaching for regression and classification of Support Vector Machine (SVM) is an application. It reveals a hyperplane that optimizes the margin between distinct classes to provide the best separation by grouping data points into several categories.

Drawbacks: SVM's efficacy in identifying Twitter spam may be impacted by the high-dimensionality and noise present in textual data, which may limit its capacity to recognize intricate spam patterns.

3.5 Random Forest

Step1: In random forest model there are n number of random records that are having k number of records taken from data sets.

Step2: There will be decision trees constructed for each every experiment.

Step3: And these individual decision trees all generate an outcome separately.

Step4: And all outcomes are compared using accuracy, majority voting, and the final outcome will be taken.

Drawbacks: A restriction in the detection of Twitter spam is the Random Forest possibility to overfitting on noisy and high-dimensional text input, which could lead to lower generalization performance.

3.6 Bernoulli Naive Bayes

Bernoulli Naive Bayes is a type of algorithm known as Naive Bayes that is used for binary task classification. When working with binary features (i.e., only accepting values of 0 or 1), it is extremely useful because it evaluates the likelihood of a class given the presence or absence of each feature separately [1, 2]. Formula for computing the probability in Bernoulli Navie Bayes:

$$p(X|C_k) = \prod_{i=1}^{n} p_{k_i}^{x_i}\left(1 - pk_i\right)^{(1-x_i)} \tag{4}$$

In Eq. (4), xi is the value of the feature xi (either 0 or 1), where P(y) is the previous probability of class y. The probability of feature xi given class y is P(xi | y). The projected class for the given input features is then supplied as the class with most chances.

Drawbacks: The accuracy of Bernoulli Naive Bayes in challenging spam detection situations may suffer as a result of its assumption of binary feature independence, which makes it difficult for it to comprehend complicated relationships in tweet content.

3.7 Semi Supervised Algorithm

After preprocessing, I separated the resulting dataset into labelled and unlabelled data with a 30% and 70% division, respectively. The labeled data was then once more divided into a training set and a testing set for utilizing a partition of 60% and 40%. I used the tagged data to train Random Forest, a classifier model that performs better at spam identification than others. For additional semi-supervised learning, I prelabelled the unlabeled data using the model developed from the labelled data. Combine the data that has been labeled and pre-labeled. Assign weights for labelled data as 1.0 and unlabelled data as W.

$$W = \frac{\pi r^2 F^*(\text{len}(x_{\text{train}}))}{\text{len}(Du)} \tag{5}$$

According to the linked paper, F value at 0.1 will produce better results. F is a YATSI parameter in Eq. (5). In step 2, I applied the YATSI algorithm using the K nearest Neighbor search. Take the argmax of the weights of the appropriate class of nearest neighbors for each prediction query [4].

Drawbacks: The YATSI algorithm's disadvantage is that it is dependent on a predetermined set of characteristics, which may hinder it from adjusting and effectively capturing evolving and different Twitter spam trends.

3.8 1D Convolutional Neural Network (CNN) Model/Algorithm

We discovered that this method or algorithm is more effective when testing live data and messages on Twitter utilizing the tweep api after comparing it to other models and algorithms. Tweepy api can be used by utilizing a Python module. Due to the fact that this Tweety api offers a number of built-in functions and sends data in JSON format. And we employ the dedication technique to interact with the API. It also includes creating new accounts and using current user accounts after the creation of this fresh developer account.

We receive 4 keys from Twitter, of which 2 are private keys. These keys are utilized to access data in Json format. Because of this, we can also discover a variety of information about a tweet or message, such as the user name, the login device, the time the message was sent or received, etc. These are additionally utilized to thoroughly check spammers and individuals with phony accounts. We identify spammers using Twitter poly and the terms and conditions. There are numerous accounts that use bots to send spam on Twitter. As a result, it became challenging to examine the live communications. As a result, our team was able to come up with a solution by comparing an SMS data set that includes both spam and non-spam messages. We use this sms dataset as a reference because text messages and tweets have the same format. After comparing the results, we can decide where our model needs improvement in order to be more accurate. This is also used in Twitter to categorize spam and non-spam individuals.

$$\text{Accuracy} = \frac{\text{No. of correct predictions}}{\text{Total number of predictions}} \tag{6}$$

$$\text{Specificity} = \frac{\text{No. of true negatives}}{\text{No. of true negatives} + \text{No. of false positives}} \tag{7}$$

$$\text{precision} = \frac{\text{Number of True Positive}}{\text{No. of True Positive} + \text{No. of False Positive}} \tag{8}$$

By Eq. (7) and (8) we will find F1 − Score,

$$\text{F1} - \text{Score} = 2 * \frac{\text{Precision} * \text{Sensitivity}}{\text{Precision} + \text{Sensitivity}} \tag{9}$$

Here, we discover precision through Eq. (6), specificity from Eq. (7), and accuracy from Eq. (8). Now we'll determine the F1-Score value using Eqs. (7) and (8).

3.9   Gated Recurrent Unit (GRU)

An architecture of recurrent neural network (RNN) is known as the GRU (Gated Recurrent Unit) algorithm is utilized for sequential data processing tasks as well as for natural language processing applications including text classification and spam detection. The more conventional RNN has some drawbacks, including the vanishing gradient issue and the challenge of capturing long-term dependencies, which are addressed by the GRU variation. In order to regulate the information above the recurrent units, the GRU method incorporates gating mechanisms, allowing the model to specifically update and forget about the information. The following are the GRU's essential elements:

Determines how much of the previous data should be kept and how much needs to be updated with the most recent input.

Reset Gate: Regulates how much historical data should be disregarded in order to avoid interference from unrelated history data.

Candidate Activation: The current input and the prior activation are combined and weighted by the reset gate to create a new candidate activation.

Final Activation: Creates the updated activation for the current time step by combining the previous activation and the candidate activation, weighted by the update gate.

Drawbacks: When it comes to collecting complex sequential patterns over longer sequences, GRU falls short of LSTM.

3.10   Long Short-Term Memory (LSTM)

The LSTM (Long Short-Term Memory) algorithm is another sort of recurrent neural network (RNN) architecture used to store data in sequential processing applications, as text classification and spam detection. Traditional RNN drawbacks including the vanishing gradient issue and the condition in capturing long-term province are addressed by LSTM. LSTM introduces specialized memory cells and gating processes enable the model to store, read, and delete information across a long period of time. The key components of the LSTM include:

Cell State: The memory element that covers the whole sequence and transports data throughout various time steps.

Input Gate: Identifies a rough estimate of the amount of current that should be stored in the designated cell state.

Forget Gate: This gate should clear the preceding cell state.

Output Gate: How much of the cell state is transmitted to the following time step is determined by the output gate.

Tweets are often represented as collections of words or characters when using the LSTM algorithm for Twitter spam detection. The LSTM network processes these sequences and learns to extract pertinent information and predict whether a given tweet is spam or not. The LSTM algorithm discovers the ideal weights and parameters during training by minimizing a loss function via methods including back propagation across time. On a different validation or test set, the model's performance can be assessed using measures like precision, recall, F1 score, or accuracy.

Drawbacks: The disadvantage of LSTM for identifying Twitter spam is that it overfits on small datasets and struggles to handle very long sequences.

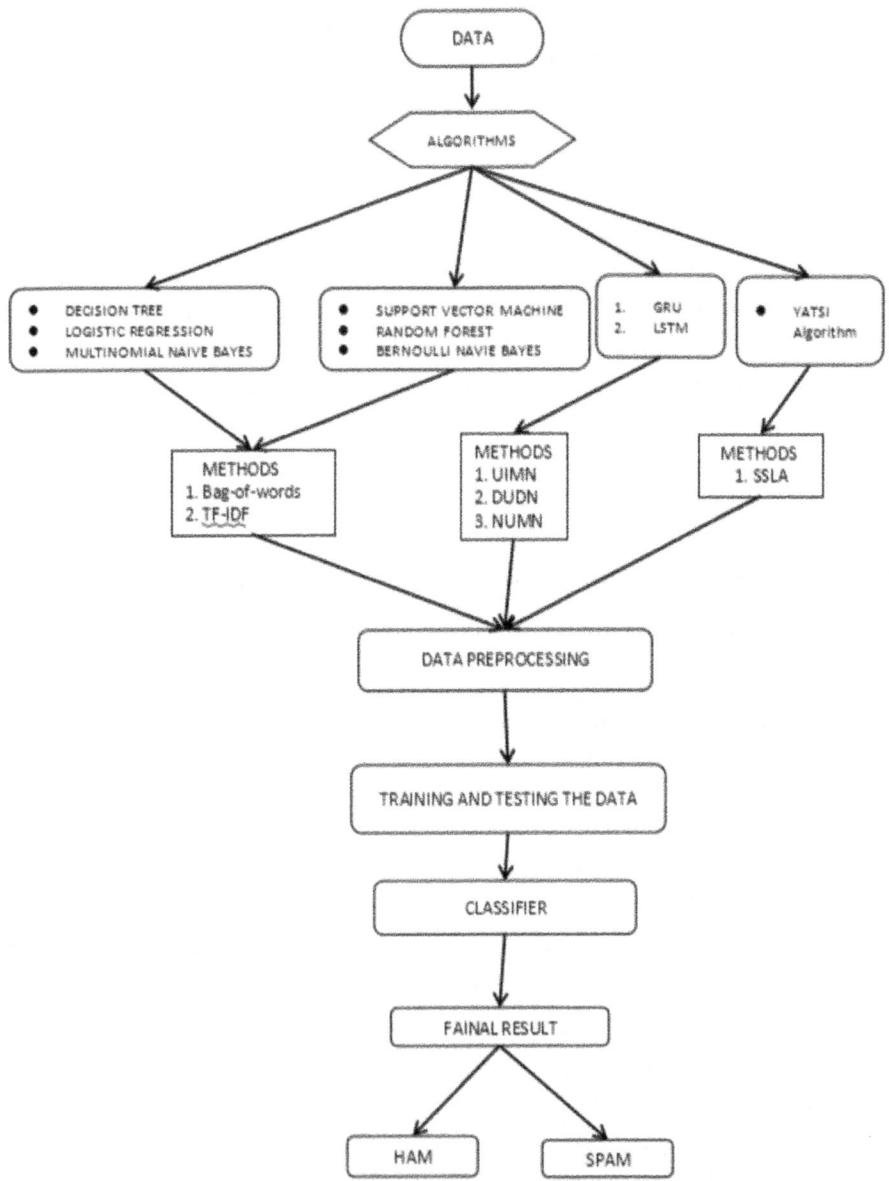

Fig. 1. Various algorithms flow

The process for determining the differences between utilizing various algorithms to determine accuracy and the various approaches employed are shown in Fig. 1. Then, how does processing work when we have varying degrees of accuracy? With that, we can even determine whether messages are ham and spam.

4   Comparisons of Data Analysis

4.1   Data Preprocessing

The provided code creates a bar plot in the Fig. 2 graph using matplotlib.py plot to display the distribution of the 'ham' and 'spam' categories in the Data Frame df's 'target' column. The height of each bar in the picture displays the count of each category, making it easy to compare the frequency of the 'ham' and 'spam' categories in the dataset. For ease of understanding, the figure has a title and axis labels. The x-axis and y-axis represent the categories and count, respectively. The number of spam messages is shown in violet on the graph below, while the number of ham messages are shown in red. A red bar indicates 4516 ham communications, while a violet bar indicates 653 spam messages.

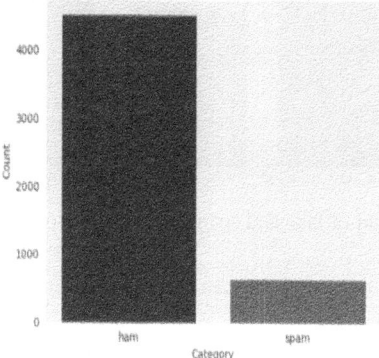

Fig. 2. Showing ham and spam messages count (Color figure online)

The x-axis and y-axis in the graph in Fig. 3 serve as placeholders for the class and count, respectively, and the plot has a title and axis names for clarity. When both positive and negative classes are equally counted, the blue and orange graphs reflect them.

The total number of Twitter accounts is shown in Fig. 4, and it is again broken down into bogus accounts and tweets with spam content. The count of the total twitter accounts are 36, the count of fake accounts are 18 and the count of spam content tweets are 25.

The histograms in Fig. 5 depict the distribution of message lengths for the two categories ('ham' and 'spam'). The legend indicates which histogram corresponds to which category, while the x-axis label provides information about the data being displayed. Here, the lengths of ham messages and spam messages are displayed; the graphs in blue and orange respectively illustrate the lengths of ham messages and spam messages.

Spam message length is represented by the yellow graph in Fig. 6 and ham message length by the green graph. By this graph we say that ham messages are majority classes

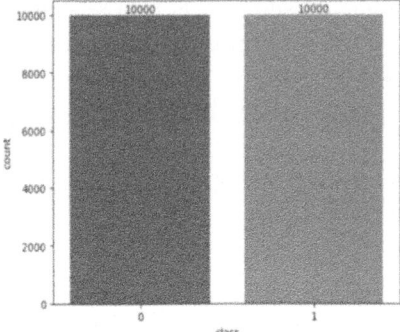

Fig. 3. Graph showing positive class and negative class (Color figure online)

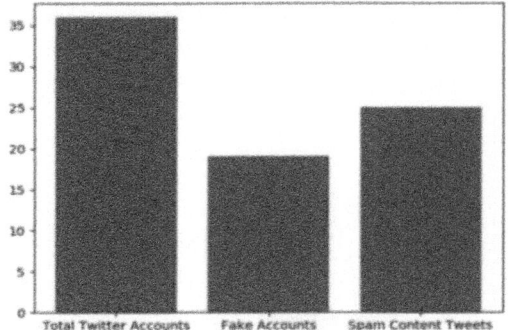

Fig. 4. Count of fake and spam accounts (Color figure online)

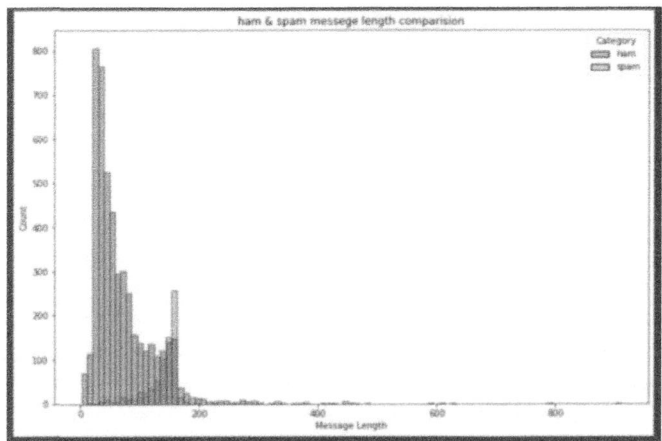

Fig. 5. Ham and spam message length comparison (Color figure online)

as they are of highest in number and spam messages are minority classes as they are of smallest in number. Now we can say that length of ham is highest as compared to spam.

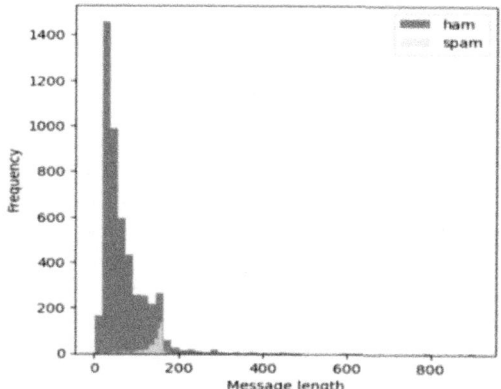

Fig. 6. Distribution of message lengths (Color figure online)

The code shown in Fig. 7 uses Seaborn to build a count plot that displays the distribution of characters ('num_chars') in a dataset. Each 'num_chars' category is shaded based on the 'target' variable it is linked to. This narrative helps us identify any patterns or trends in the data and shows how the character count varies depending on the target demographic.

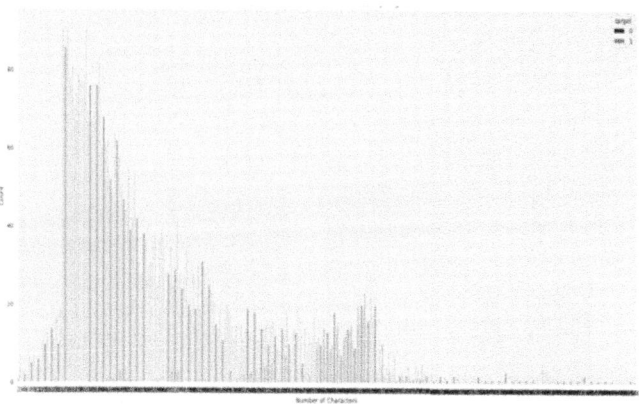

Fig. 7. Distribution of number of characters by target

The code in Fig. 8 uses Seaborn's Pair Grid to generate a grid of scatter plots, kernel density plots, and histograms to display the correlations and distributions between the variables in the Data Frame (df). When the data points are colored using the 'target' variable, it is easier to identify patterns and variations between groups.

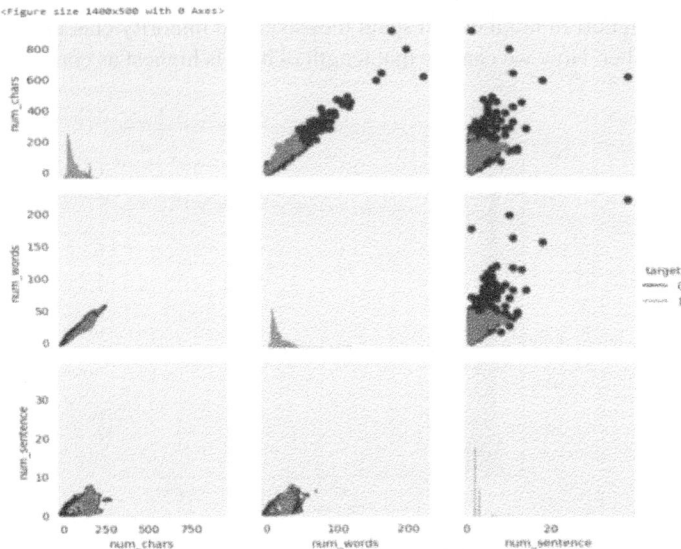

Fig. 8. Showing relationships between the variables in Data frames

The following code creates a long-format Data Frame from the Data Frame df, calculates its correlation matrix, and uses Seaborn to create a bar plot in Fig. 9 that displays the correlations between the variable pairs. The variable pairings are displayed on x-axis, while the correlation coefficients are displayed on y-axis. The correlation between a pair of variables is shown by each bar. The image allows us to quickly assess the magnitude and direction of correlations between the variables in the Data Frame.

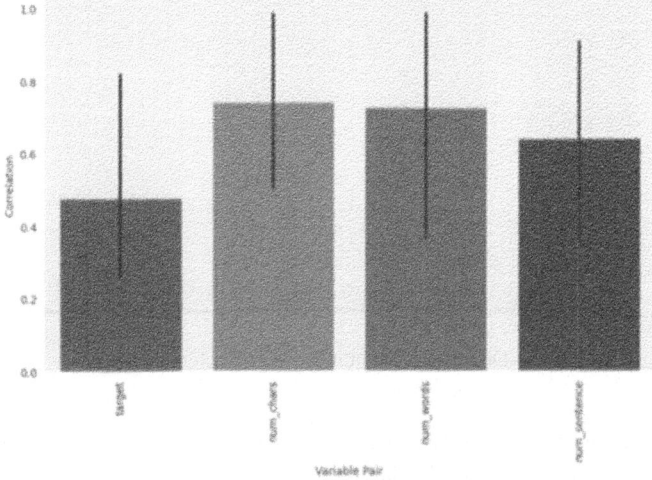

Fig. 9. Correlations between variables

The figure in Fig. 10 provides a graphic representation of the confusion matrix that makes it easier to grasp and learn more about how effectively a classification model is working.

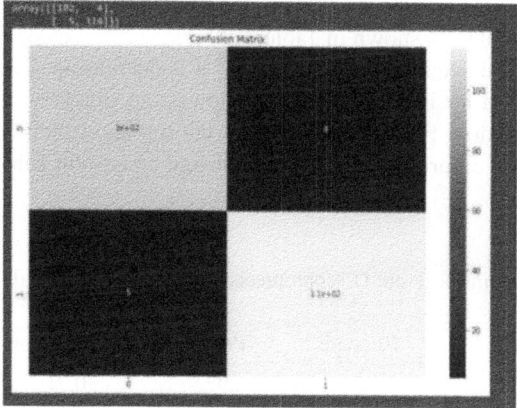

Fig. 10. Confusion matrix

The confusion matrix for a classification model is shown in Fig. 11 by contrasting the actual labels with predicted labels.

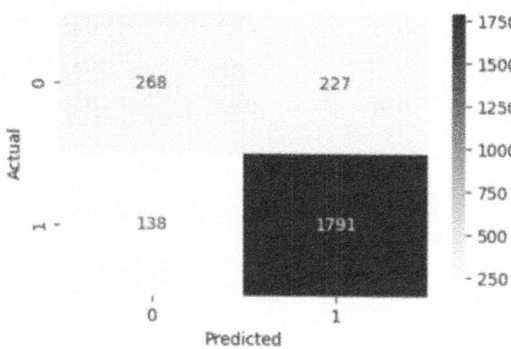

Fig. 11. Comparison of actual and predicted labels

5   Comparisons of the Accuracy of Twitter Spam Detection Using Different Algorithms

In the Table 2, various algorithms are used to compare each other's predictions on the accuracy of the dataset that was used. Here, we can observe that a couple models have accuracy levels around 97% shown in Table 3 and Fig. 12. If we compare the remaining models, the maximum accuracy is 97.58%, and it is decreasing. The highest accuracy we have compared so far is 97.58%, and the lowest accuracy is 85%. As a result of our comparison, Random Forest and SVM are the top algorithms because to its high accuracy. The YATSI algorithm offers a reliable and consistent solution to the Twitter spam drift issue.

Table 2. Table contains different f1 score, precision, recall, support of different algorithms

Algorithm	F1 score	Precision	Recall	Support
Logistic regression	0.82	0.97	0.71	138
Decision tree	0.69	0.82	0.59	138
SVM	0.90	0.97	0.84	138
KNN				
Random forest	0.90	0.98	0.83	138
Multinomial naïve bayes	0.88	1.00	0.78	138
Bernoulli Naïve Bayes	0.93	0.99	0.88	138
GRU	0.71	0.82	0.62	649
LSTM	0.73	0.66	0.81	649
YATSI	0.91	0.93	0.89	2018

Table 3. Table contains different accuracy of using different algorithms

Algorithm	Accuracy
Logistic Regression	95.84%
Decision Tree	92.84%
SVM	97.58%
KNN	90.52%
Random Forest	97.58%
GRU	93%
LSTM	94%
YATSI	85%

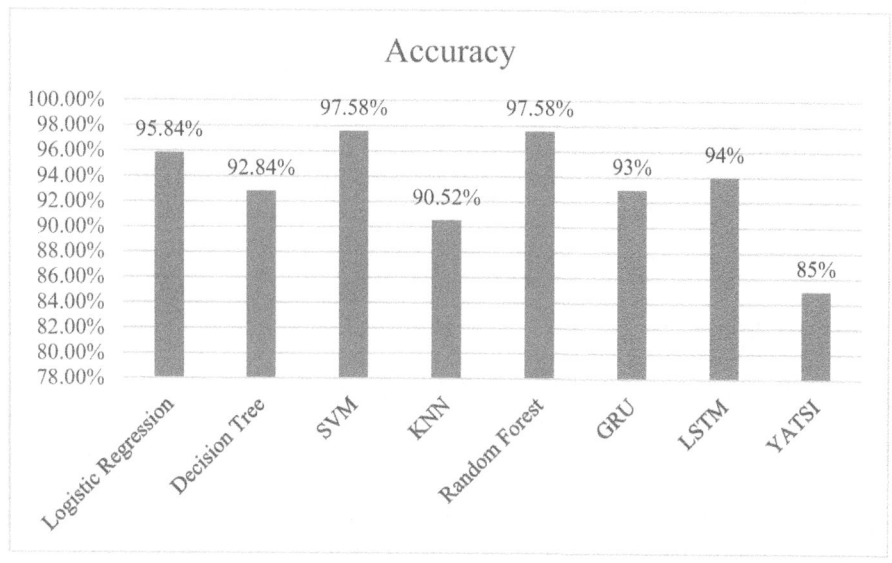

Fig. 12. Accuracy Graph

By identifying spammers and fake users on Twitter, the study also brought attention to the inadequacies of the ML and DL algorithms caused by the complexity of spammers. According to the study, an algorithm based on personal information like followers, user name, date of birth, and account creation date would be more accurate. The study also addressed the problem of Twitter's pervasive spam by introducing the YATSI algorithm as a consistent and dependable solution to the Twitter spam drift problem. While the accuracy of our study model is increased by employing the Random Forest approach, doing so requires more computing resources and is more difficult due to its subfunctions. It sometimes fails to contain all variables, such as age, gender, and the date of account creation, etc. It took more time and people to develop the model using the RF-Algorithm, which takes more resources than usual.

6   Conclusion

In order to build a sophisticated spam detection system, this study assessed a range of traits and machine learning methods. Textual, user-based, and network-based features were all extensively used in earlier spam detection research. The report addressed a wide range of feature extraction methodologies. Important traits including tweet content, user behavior, and relationships between users were successfully captured by these features. The research also examined a variety of machine learning algorithms, including supervised and unsupervised methods, in order to create accurate categorization models. This paper makes a substantial contribution to the field of Twitter spam detection as a whole by its thorough analysis of existing methodologies and recommendation of a strong spam detection system. The conclusions reached can act as a starting point for further research, stimulating the development of more robust and potent spam detection systems, hence enhancing user experience and safety on platforms like Twitter. The methodology for real-time Twitter spam tweet identification utilized the SMS Spam Collection dataset. Different outputs were produced by the various machine learning algorithms used in the study, which included Multinomial Naive Bayes (0.97098), Bernoulli Naive Bayes (0.98355), Logistic Regression (0.95841), KNN (0.90522), Decision Tree (0.92843), and Random Forest (0.97582). Future study is encouraged to apply real-data analysis to detect new spamming techniques and to enhance feature techniques with cutting-edge methods.

7 Future Scope

Future potential for using a semi-supervised learning strategy to identify spam on social media is quite promising. This method can improve the accuracy of spam detection and adjust to changing spamming strategies by utilizing machine learning and merging labeled and unlabeled data. The semi-supervised learning model's scalability and capacity for handling big datasets make it an excellent choice for real-time spam identification and mitigation as social media platforms expand, thereby enhancing user experience and security. Furthermore, continuous improvements in data analytics and artificial intelligence are probably going to enhance and optimize this strategy's efficacy in battling the always shifting terrain of social media spam.

8 Limitations

Some of the limitations of the semi-supervised learning approach for social media spam identification include the requirement for high-quality labeled data, the possibility of difficulty in adjusting to quickly evolving spam patterns, the tendency to overfit when working with a small number of labeled instances, difficulties deciphering complex models, privacy concerns related to sensitive data, and the resource-intensive nature of training and maintaining the model over time. It is imperative to tackle these limitations in order to implement this strategy in practical situations.

References

1. Hemalatha, P., Ragapriya, N., Sanjana, V., Shiva Bhavani, K.: Extreme learning machine for spammer detection and fake user identification from Twitter. J. Crit. Rev. **10**(03), 184–192 (2023)
2. Alom, Z., Carminati, B., Ferrari, E.: A deep learning model for Twitter spam detection. Online Soc. Netw. Media **18**, 100079 (2020)
3. Rodrigues, A.P., Fernandes, R., Shetty, A., Lakshmanna, K., Mahammad Shafi, R.: Real-time Twitter spam detection and sentiment analysis using machine learning and deep learning techniques. Comput. Intell. Neurosci. **2022**, 1–15 (2022)
4. Meda, C., Bisio, F., Gastaldo, P., Zunino, R.: A machine learning approach for Twitter spammers detection. In: 2014 International Carnahan Conference on Security Technology (ICCST), pp. 1–6. IEEE (2014)

5. Imam, N., Issac, B., Jacob, S.M.: A semi-supervised learning approach for tackling Twitter spam drift. Int. J. Comput. Intell. Appl.Comput. Intell. Appl. **18**(02), 1950010 (2019)
6. El-Mawass, N., Honeine, P., Vercouter, L.: Simil Catch: enhanced social spammers detection on twitter using markov random fields. Inf. Process. Manag. **57**(6), 102317 (2020)
7. Dewang, R.K., Singh, A.K.: State-of-art approaches for review spammer detection: a survey. J. Intell. Inf. Syst. **50**(2), 231–264 (2018)
8. Meda, C., et al.: Spam detection of Twitter traffic: a framework based on random forests and non-uniform feature sampling. In: 2016 IEEE/ACM International Conference on Advances in Social Networks Analysis and Mining (ASONAM), pp. 811–817. IEEE (2016)
9. Json.org. (n.d.). JSON. http://www.json.org/. Accessed 22 Aug 2018
10. Lin, G., Sun, N., Nepal, S., Zhang, J., Xiang, Y., Hassan, H.: Statistical Twitter spam detection demystified: performance, stability and scalability (2017)
11. Hu, X., Tang, J., Gao, H., Liu, H.: Social spammer detection with sentiment information. In: 2014 IEEE International Conference on Data Mining, pp. 180–189 (2014). https://doi.org/10.1109/ICDM.2014.141
12. Srivastava, G., Maddikunta, P.K.R., Gadekallu, T.R.: A two-stage text feature selection algorithm for improving text classification. ACM Trans. Asian Low-Resource Lang. Inf. Process. **20**, 1–19 (2021)
13. Ghelani, P.H., Bhalodia, T.M.: Opinion mining and opinion spam detection. Int. Res. J. Eng. Technol. (IRJET) **4**, 11 (2017)

Logistics Shipping Based Blockchain Using Smart Contracts

Mallellu Sai Prashanth[1]([✉]), Ramesh Karnati[1], Muni Sekhar Velpuru[2], and H. Venkateshwara Reddy[2]

[1] Department of Computer Science and Engineering, Vardhaman College of Engineering, Hyderabad, India
saiprashanth08@ieee.org, ramesh.krnt@vardhaman.org
[2] Department of Information Technology, Vardhaman College of Engineering, Hyderabad, India
{munisek,h.venkateswarareddy}@vardhaman.org

Abstract. The logistics industry is a vital component of the global economy, but it still faces several challenges, including inefficient processes, lack of transparency, and high costs due to intermediaries. Blockchain technology has the potential to address these challenges by providing a decentralized and transparent platform that can automate and streamline logistics processes through smart contracts. This research paper presents a study on Logistics shipping based on blockchain using smart contracts in Solidity language. The paper discusses the challenges in the logistics industry and the potential of blockchain technology to solve them. It then presents a Smart Contract for Logistics shipping, including the required variables, a struct for shipments, a mapping to hold the shipments, events for shipment creation and delivery, and functions to create a new shipment, mark a shipment as delivered, and get the shipment details. The paper also discusses the benefits and limitations of the proposed solution and compares it with existing logistics systems. It concludes that the proposed solution can provide a secure, transparent, and efficient platform for logistics shipping that can eliminate intermediaries, reduce costs, and improve the overall logistics ecosystem. Overall, this research paper provides insights into the potential of blockchain technology for logistics shipping and presents a practical solution that can be implemented in real-world scenarios. It also highlights the need for further research and development to optimize the solution and address any potential challenges in its implementation.

Keywords: Block Chain · Trust · Reputation · social control and privacy

1 Introduction

The administration of goods and services from the point of origin to the point of consumption is referred to as logistics shipping. Planning, coordinating, and carrying out transportation, warehousing, and distribution operations are all part of this process. Delivering goods in a timely, effective, and economical manner to their destination is the aim of logistics shipping [1]. Several processes are included in logistics shipping, such

O. Castillo et al. (Eds.): PerSOM 2023, LNICST 517, pp. 154–168, 2024.
https://doi.org/10.1007/978-3-031-66044-3_11

as route planning and optimization, inventory control, freight forwarding, customs clearance, and delivery synchronisation. Effective communication and cooperation between the different parties involved, including the manufacturer, the carrier, the warehouse, and the customer, are essential to the success of logistics shipping [2]. The effectiveness and efficiency of logistics shipping have significantly increased thanks to technological advancements including the usage of GPS tracking, EDI, and transportation management systems (TMS). However, the sector still has to deal with issues including growing fuel costs, more stringent government regulations, and shifting consumer demand [3].

Importance of Logistics Shipping: Logistics shipping is important because it ensures that products are available when and where they are required, which is essential to corporate success. Effective logistics shipping may boost competitiveness, lower costs, and raise customer happiness.

Key Logistics Shipping Activities: Route planning and management, inventory management, logistics services, customs checks, and delivery coordination are some of the tasks involved in logistics shipping. Since the numerous parties participating in these activities are interconnected, efficient communication and teamwork are required.

Challenges Faced by the Industry: The logistics shipping sector still has to deal with issues like growing fuel costs, more stringent government regulations, and shifting consumer demand. Businesses must be flexible and adaptable in order to meet these obstacles, as well as constantly enhance their systems and procedures.

Route Planning and Optimization are Crucial: Route planning and optimization are essential elements of logistics shipping because they assist in identifying the most effective and economical method of moving products from one location to another. When designing and optimising routes, variables including distance, time, cost, and capacity are taken into account.

Inventory Control: Logistics shipping includes inventory management, which is crucial for ensuring that the correct goods are available at the right times in the right quantities. Effective inventory management may lower costs, increase customer happiness, and reduce waste.

Transport Planning: Logistics firms that specialise in organising and managing the delivery of products from one location to another offer freight forwarding as a service. Between the shipper and the carrier, freight forwarders serve as a middleman and are in charge of finding the most economical and effective modes of transportation.

Coordination of Delivery: The last step in the logistics shipping process is delivery coordination, which entails making sure that products are delivered to the client quickly and effectively. Utilizing dependable and effective delivery methods, as well as excellent communication and collaboration between the carrier, the warehouse, and the customer, is necessary for delivery coordination.

In this paper we propose Logistics shipping based blockchain using smart contracts. Smart contracts and block chain technology have the ability to completely transform the logistics and shipping sector. A decentralised, secure, and open technology called block chain makes it possible to build a shared digital ledger. Self-executing contracts, or "smart contracts," are agreements that automatically carry out the provisions of a contract between two parties [4]. The logistics shipping sector can gain a lot from using blockchain and smart contracts, including higher efficiency, lower costs, and improved transparency. Due to the fact that all transactions are recorded in a tamper-proof ledger, the usage of block chain technology can help to reduce errors and fraud. Smart contracts can also automate information flow and cut down on the time and expense of manual processes [5].

2   Related Work

Blockchain Technology
Blockchain is a digital ledger that is not centralised and tracks transactions among a number of machines. It was initially developed to serve as the backbone of the cryptocurrency Bitcoin, but it has since discovered a wide range of potential uses in a number of different sectors, including finance, healthcare, supply chain management, and more. A blockchain's decentralised nature, or the fact that it runs on a peer-to-peer network and is not under the control of a single institution, is its primary characteristic. A secure and transparent history of all transactions on the network is created by the recording of transactions in blocks and linking them together in a chain [9].

The use of cryptography by blockchain technology to guarantee the security and immutability of transactions is another crucial feature. A block's contents are irreversible once it is added to the blockchain and cannot be changed or removed. Overall, blockchain has the potential to revolutionise numerous industries by offering decentralised, secure, and transparent solutions to a wide range of issues [10].

The inability to change or remove data after it has been stored on a blockchain makes the record of transactions safe and impenetrable. This is accomplished by utilising cryptographic methods, which guarantee the accuracy of the data on the blockchain [11].

Greater transparency is made possible by blockchain technology because every user of the network has access to the same data. As a result, there can be more responsibility and trust in transactions because all users have access to the data on the blockchain [12].

There are two types of blockchains: public and private. Public blockchains, like the Ethereum and Bitcoin networks, are accessible to everyone and permit participation from anybody. Contrarily, private blockchains are only accessible to a select group of users and are frequently utilised by businesses for internal purposes [13].

By enhancing security, transparency, and efficiency across a wide range of businesses, blockchain technology has the potential to transform many of them. Although the technology is still in its infancy, its potential for innovation is enormous, and it is quite likely to play a big part in the growth of numerous industries in the future [14].

Ethereum
With the intention of developing into a decentralised platform for creating and utilising decentralised apps, Ethereum is a blockchain-based platform that was presented in 2015. (dApps). Anyone can access the source code and build on it because it was developed as an open-source platform [15].

Because it enables developers to write self-executing contracts with the details of the agreement between the buyer and seller being directly encoded into lines of code, Ethereum is frequently referred to as a "smart contract platform." As a result, sophisticated decentralised applications that go beyond straightforward value exchanges can be created [16].

Ether (ETH), the native cryptocurrency of the Ethereum platform, is one of its distinguishing characteristics. It is used to fund network transactions and computational services. Decentralized autonomous organisations (DAOs), which are managed through code rather than by a central authority, can also be created on the Ethereum network [17].

With a strong developer community and an expanding ecosystem of decentralised applications (dApps), tools, and services, Ethereum has developed into one of the biggest and most well-known blockchain platforms. New innovations and updates are always being added to the platform to increase its functionality, scalability, and security [18].

The implementation of the project is done in Ethereum online compiler [remix.ethereum.org]. A web-based Innovative Development Environment (IDE) called Remix.ethereum.org is used to create, test, and deploy smart contracts on the Ethereum network. It gives programmers a platform to create, test, and deploy smart contracts using Solidity, the main programming language for Ethereum [19].

Developers don't need to install any software or tools while using Remix to build, test, and publish their smart contracts from a web browser. Developers may write code more easily on the platform thanks to the editor's syntax highlighting and autocompletion features. Additionally, Remix has a built-in debugger that enables developers to test their contracts, find any problems, and resolve them.

Use of Remix is unrestricted and open source. It is one of the most extensively used platforms for creating and implementing Ethereum smart contracts and is managed by the Ethereum Foundation.

Smart Contracts

In smart contracts, the details of the agreement between the buyer and seller are directly encoded into lines of code. These contracts self-execute. They are made to automatically enforce the terms of a contract without the assistance of middlemen like attorneys or brokers [20].

Blockchain technology, which offers a secure and open ledger for recording and tracking transactions, is generally used to build smart contracts. As a result, the contract's terms are automatically carried out and upheld without further action from the parties.

Smart contracts' capacity to lower costs and boost efficiency by doing away with the need for middlemen is one of its main advantages. Due to the fact that the contract's terms are encoded into the blockchain and are therefore open to audit and verification, they also provide greater security and confidence.

Supply chain management, transactions in real estate financial services, and insurance are just a few of the many potential uses for smart contracts. Without requiring user involvement or running the risk of fraud, a smart contract may be used, for instance, to automatically release payment for a shipment of goods once the delivery has been verified.

Overall, smart contracts are an exciting new technology that could completely change how contracts are negotiated and carried out, lowering costs, boosting productivity, and boosting security and trust.

Smart Logistics Shipping
In order to ensure that items are delivered to clients on time and for the lowest possible price, smart logistics aims to build a more intelligent, connected, and efficient supply chain. Smart logistics uses cutting-edge technologies to automate and improve crucial procedures including inventory control, delivery tracking, and transportation planning. For instance, utilising IoT devices to track shipments in real-time can increase supply chain visibility and let logistics managers spot and fix bottlenecks or delays faster.

Although smart logistics is still in its infancy, it has the potential to completely transform the logistics sector by cutting costs, raising service levels, and opening up new business strategies and revenue streams. Companies can build an agile, responsive, and efficient supply chain that can better meet customer expectations and help them remain ahead of the competition by adopting smart logistics.

A term used to describe the application of cutting-edge technology, including blockchain, the Internet of Things (IoT), and artificial intelligence (AI), to enhance the effectiveness and transparency of the logistics and shipping sector.

Smart logistics shipping strives to address industry issues like high operational costs, protracted processing delays, and a lack of visibility and transparency throughout the supply chain by utilising these technologies.

Blockchain technology, for instance, can be used to build a shared and secure ledger of all shipments and transactions, giving everyone in the supply chain instant access to the same data. As a result, there may be a lower chance of fraud and mistakes, and there may be better communication and coordination between the various supply chain participants.

Although smart logistics shipping is still in its infancy, it has the potential to revolutionise the market by increasing productivity, bringing down prices, and improving consumer experiences. Additionally, it gives a chance to develop fresh company ideas and sources of income as well as to improve sustainability by lowering the waste and emissions produced by shipping and logistics.

3 Proposed Method

The logistics shipping based blockchain using smart contracts is implemented in ethereum online compiler which is remix.ethereum.org and it is implemented in solidity. Logistics shipping based blockchain using smart contracts is implemented by the following algorithm (Fig. 1).

Algorithm for Logistics shipping based blockchain shipping using smart contracts

1. Declare the required variables:
   - address sender
   - address receiver
   - uint256 shipmentId
   - uint256 weight
   - uint256 price
   - uint256 deliveryTime
2. Define the Smart Contract:
   contract Logistics {

   }
3. Declare the Struct for shipments:
   struct Shipment {
   address sender; ad-
   dress   receiver;
   uint256 shipmentId;
   uint256   weight;
   uint256 price;
   uint256 deliveryTime;
   bool delivered;
   }
4. Declare the mapping to hold the shipments:
   mapping(uint256 => Shipment) shipments;
5. Declare the events for shipment creation and delivery:
   event ShipmentCreated(address sender, address receiver, uint256 shipmentId, uint256 weight, uint256 price, uint256 deliveryTime);
   event ShipmentDelivered(uint256 shipmentId);
6. Define the function to create a new shipment:
   function createShipment(address _sender, address _receiver, uint256 _shipmentId, uint256 _weight, uint256 _price, uint256 _deliveryTime) public {
   Shipment storage newShipment = shipments[_shipmentId];
   newShipment.sender = _sender;
   newShipment.receiver = _receiver; newShip-
   ment.shipmentId = _shipmentId; newShip-
   ment.weight = _weight; newShipment.price =
   _price; newShipment.deliveryTime = _de-
   liveryTime;newShipment.delivered = false;
   emit ShipmentCreated(_sender, _receiver, _shipmentId, _weight, _price, _deliveryTime);
   }
7. Define the function to mark a shipment as delivered:
   function markShipmentDelivered(uint256 _shipmentId) public {
   Shipment storage deliveredShipment = shipments[_shipmentId];
   deliveredShipment.delivered = true;
   emit ShipmentDelivered(_shipmentId);
   }
8. Define the function to get the shipment details:
   function getShipmentDetails(uint256 _shipmentId) public view returns (address, address, uint256, uint256, uint256, uint256, bool) {
   Shipment storage requestedShipment = shipments[_shipmentId];

   return (requestedShipment.sender, requestedShipment.receiver, requestedShipment.shipmentId,request-
   edShipment.weight,   requestedShipment.price,   requestedShipment.deliveryTime,
   requestedShipment.delivered);
   }

The following elements make up the process model of a smart contract-based blockchain system for logistics and shipping:

Shipment Initiation: The procedure begins when the shipper submits a request for a shipment, including information about the kind of products, origin and destination,

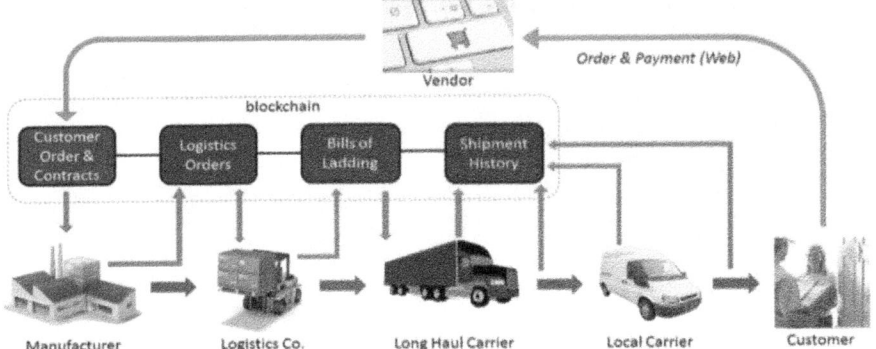

Fig. 1. Process model of Logistics shipping based blockchain using smart contracts

and anticipated delivery date. The OrderItem() method id used to place an order of a particular item. After placing the order the OrderItem() method returns the uniqueid. In this particular application when the OrderItem() method is invoked we can place order by typing the item id and item name. The uniqueid on decoding it later gives the information about the order and helps in package tracking or package mapping which gives overall details of the order such as status of the order. The OrderItem() method also displays the confirmation message to the user as "Your package is ordered and is under process". The uniqueid is generated by using the SHA-256 algorithm. Hence the security of the order is increased and also increases the efficiency of logistics shipping.

A cryptographic hash function called SHA-256 is employed for safe data transfer and data security. It is a one- way function that produces a fixed-size output from an input of arbitrary length (256 bits). For a specific input, the output is distinct, and even a minor modification in the input causes an entirely different outcome. As a result, SHA-256 is a trustworthy instrument for data integrity and protection since it ensures that the data was not altered during transmission.

Smart Contract Development

On the blockchain network, a smart contract is subsequently made that specifies the details of the shipping, including the delivery date, the terms of payment, and any applicable laws. Programming languages compatible with the blockchain platform, such as Solidity for Ethereum, are used to create smart contracts. The blockchain network is subsequently used to install the smart contract code, which then becomes a permanent part of the ledger. In order to ensure the efficient and secure execution of transactions on the blockchain network, smart Contract Creation is a crucial component in the creation of blockchain-based applications.

Understanding the blockchain technology and the programming languages used to create the contracts is necessary for creating smart contracts. A complete comprehension of the use case and the circumstances that lead to the execution of the contract are also necessary, in addition to a clear understanding of the terms of the parties' agreement.

We created a smart contract named Logistics which contains the six functions inside it.They are OrderItem(), CancelOrder(), ManageCarriers(), Carrier1Report(), Carrier2Report(), Carrier3Report() (Fig. 2).

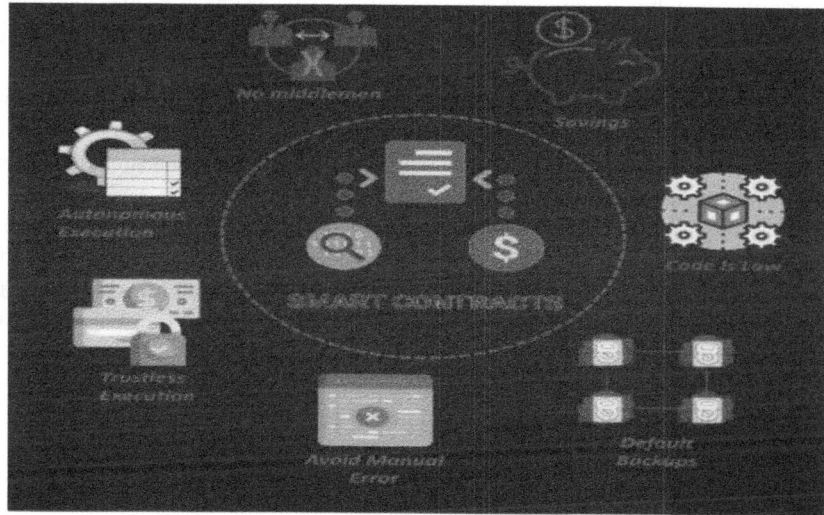

Fig. 2. Smart contract creation for Logistics shipping based blockchain using smart contracts

Carrier Acceptance

An important step in the shipping procedure is the carrier's acceptance, which signifies that the carrier has consented to assume custody of the goods and carry them to their destination. A bill of lading, which serves as a receipt for the goods and proves that the carrier has agreed to deliver them, is typically issued to formalise the acceptance of the items by the carrier.

Smart contracts can be used to automatically accept from Carrier. A smart contract that specifies the terms and circumstances of the shipment can be executed to force the carrier to accept the shipment. This can involve the date of delivery, the path used, the kind of cargo being delivered, and the cost of the services rendered.

Once the smart contract has been carried out, it is added to the blockchain network's permanent ledger, creating an unchangeable and secure record of the carrier's acceptance. As a result, the shipping process is more transparent and efficient as all stakeholders have access to the same data and can follow the shipment in real-time.

The automation of Acceptance by Carrier—a crucial stage in the shipping process— through smart contracts can offer a safe and effective way to manage logistics shipping on a blockchain network.

Package Tracking

Package tracking is the process of keeping track of a package's route from its origin to its destination. A tracking number or code, which is given to the product when it is dispatched, is often used to achieve this. With the help of this number, you may check the package's location, status, and delivery status online or using a mobile app.

Using blockchain technology can substantially improve shipment tracking. On the blockchain network, every stage of the shipping process, including pickup, delivery, and transportation, may be documented as a transaction. This produces a safe, transparent, and impenetrable record of the package's travels that is simple for all parties to access and track.

The tracking of packages can also be automated using smart contracts. For instance, a smart contract can be activated to cause an update to the package's status on the blockchain when it is picked up. This can contain the pickup date and time, the precise location, and any other pertinent details.

Additionally, smart contracts can be used to automatically trigger actions, such as sending messages to the sender or recipient in the event of problems or delays with the cargo. Since everyone involved has access to the same information and can follow the item in real-time, this can considerably increase the efficiency and transparency of the package tracking process.

Package tracking is a crucial component of logistics shipping, and leveraging smart contracts on a blockchain network to implement it can offer a safe, open, and effective way to manage the shipping process.

Delivery
Shipping in Logistics The last phase of the shipping process, when the items are transferred from the carrier to the recipient, is referred to as shipping-based blockchain employing smart contracts. The carrier, the recipient, and any other parties engaged in the shipment process must work together during this crucial stage.

With the use of smart contracts and logistics shipping based blockchain, the delivery procedure can be significantly enhanced. By establishing the terms and circumstances of the delivery, a smart contract can be utilised to automate the delivery process. This can include the time of delivery, who the recipient is, and any other pertinent details.

The delivery process can be significantly enhanced by employing smart contracts in logistics shipping based blockchain. The terms and conditions of the shipment can be specified in a smart contract, which can then be utilised to automate the delivery procedure. The recipient's name, the delivery date, and any other pertinent information can all be included here.

An immutable and secure record of the delivery process is provided once the smart contract has been carried out and has been added to the blockchain network's permanent ledger. Since everyone involved has access to the same information and can follow the shipment in real-time, this increases transparency and efficiency in the delivery process.

Another smart contract that specifies the delivery's terms and conditions can be executed, requiring the recipient to accept the delivery. This can cover the delivery confirmation, the state of the products, and any other pertinent details.

Delivery is a crucial step in the logistics shipping process, and automating it with smart contracts can give logistics shipping on a blockchain network a secure, open, and effective management system.

Record Keeping

The usage of blockchain technology significantly improves record keeping and is based on logistics shipping and Smart Contracts. Each shipment's transactions, including pickup, delivery, and transportation, are tracked as blocks on the blockchain network. This produces a safe, open, and impenetrable record of the shipment that all stakeholders can easily view and trace.

Additionally, record keeping procedures can be automated using smart contracts. For instance, a smart contract can be activated to cause an update to the shipment's blockchain record when the package is picked up. This can contain the pickup date and time, the precise location, and any other pertinent details. This can assist in ensuring that the shipment's information is accurate and current throughout the shipping procedure (Fig. 3).

Fig. 3. Blockchain based supplu chain model classifiers

Dispute Resolution

The process of settling disputes or differences that may develop between parties throughout the course of a transaction is referred to as dispute resolution. Disputes may occur in the context of Logistics Shipping based Blockchain using Smart Contracts for a number of reasons, including harmed items during delivery, improper or delayed delivery, or problems with payment.

A secure, transparent, and impenetrable record of the resolution can be created by recording the conclusion of a dispute on the blockchain network once it has been settled. As all parties involved have access to the same information and can use the resolution of earlier disagreements as a guide, this can be helpful in the event of future problems.

Any transaction, including logistics shipment, must include dispute resolution. The use of blockchain method and smart contracts in logistic support shipping can offer a safe, open, and effective way to settle disputes, cutting down on the time and expense of using conventional dispute resolution procedures.

4   Result Analysis

Smart Contract for Logistics shipping based on blockchain using Solidity language. It includes the required variables, a struct for shipments, a mapping to hold the shipments, events for shipment creation and delivery, and functions to create a new shipment, mark a shipment as delivered, and get the shipment details.

The Smart Contract can be used to create a decentralized platform for logistics shipping that can ensure transparency, security, and efficiency by eliminating intermediaries and automating the shipment process through smart contracts. It can also be integrated with other blockchain-based systems, such as supply chain management, to create a comprehensive logistics ecosystem (Figs. 4, 5, 6, 7, 8, 9 and 10).

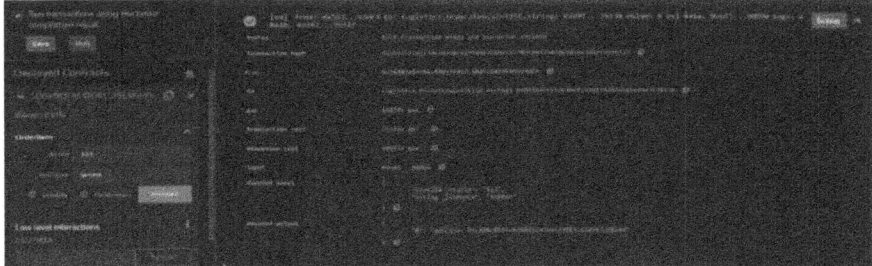

Fig. 4. Ordering an Item from Ethereum

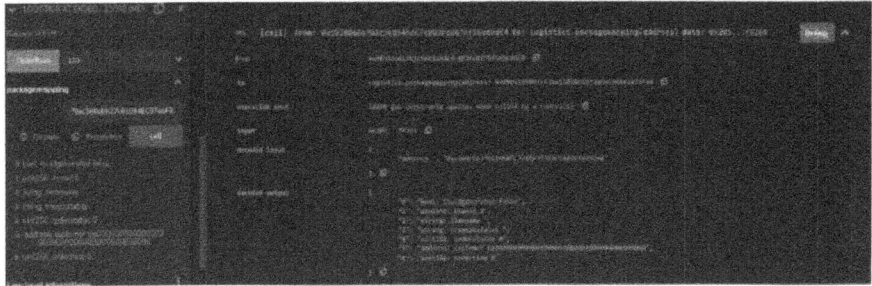

Fig. 5. Sample of Package Mapping in smart contracts

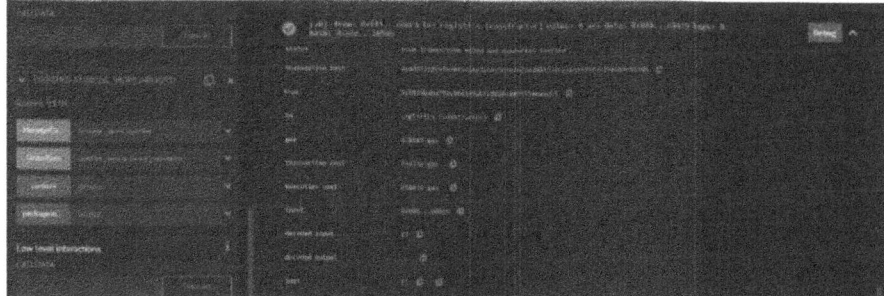

Fig. 6. Manage Carriers Operation, Generating decoded O/P

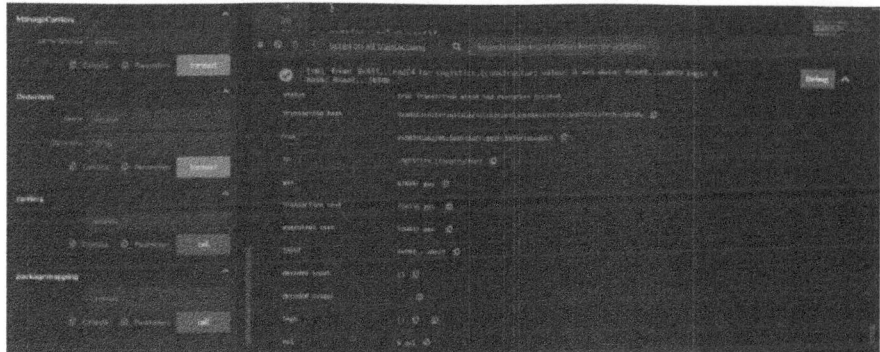

Fig. 7. Generating the Carriers Operations

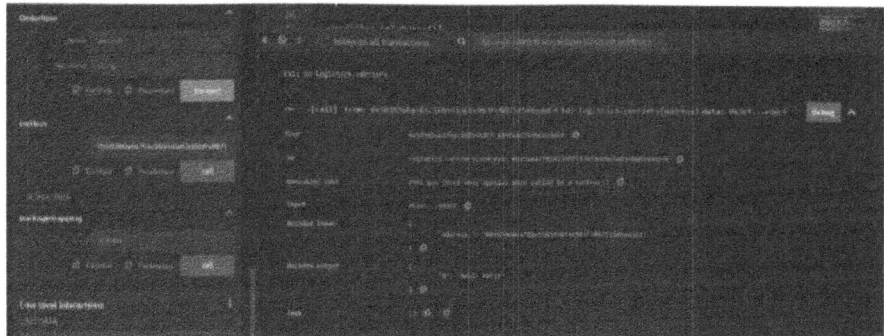

Fig. 8. Generating the Package Mapping

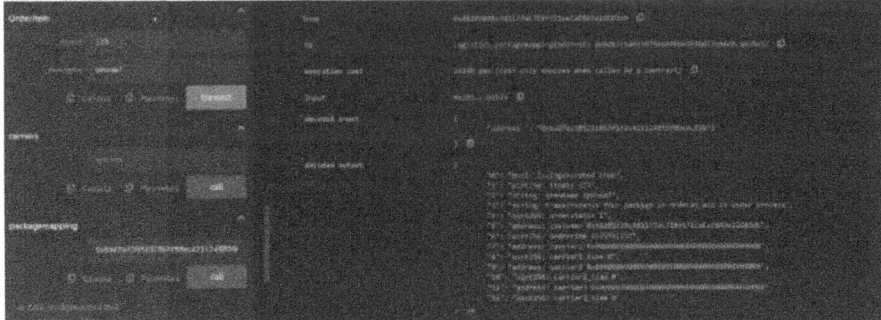

Fig. 9. Generating the Logistic Shipping Transaction

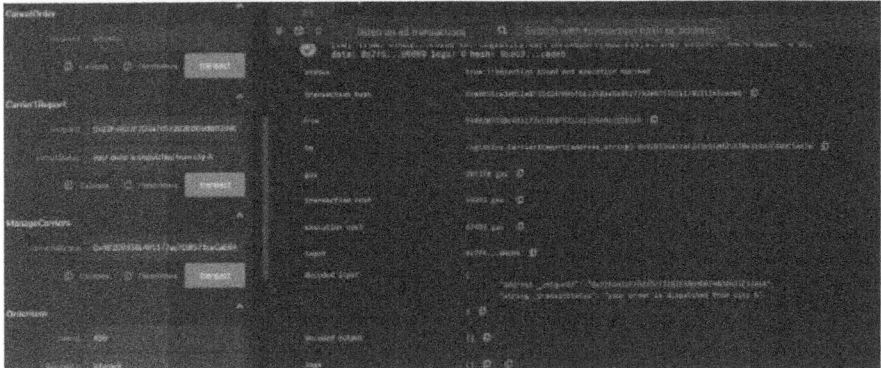

Fig. 10. Generating the carrier Reports for various stages

5 Conclusion

In conclusion, the logistics shipping sector has the potential to significantly improve the effectiveness and transparency of supply chain operations through the integration of blockchain technology and smart contracts. Logistics firms may improve procedures, boost transparency, and lower the risk of fraud or mistakes in the shipping process by utilising the secure, decentralised, and open characteristics of blockchain technology.

Many tedious procedures in the shipping sector, like tracking and confirming the delivery of products, issuing payments, and resolving disputes, can be automated using smart contracts. This can result in an improvement in speed and efficiency, as well as a decrease in the need for middlemen and a rise in mutual trust between all parties.

6 Future Scope

Blockchain technology and smart contracts are projected to be adopted by an increasing number of logistics organisations in the upcoming years because they provide a safe, effective, and affordable approach to enhance supply chain operations. Customers who will profit from quicker and more dependable delivery of goods as well as logistics firms will also benefit from this.

Supply chain management, shipment tracking, and customs clearance are just a few of the logistics shipping applications for blockchain. Block chain technology can offer organisations real-time visibility into the location and status of goods, empowering them to take strategic actions. Block chain technology can also be used to track freight in real-time, giving clients the most recent details on their shipments [6].

Smart contracts can automate information flow, lower costs, and boost efficiency in logistics shipping. Smart contracts, for instance, can be used to automatically enforce a transportation contract's terms, doing away with the need for user involvement. Smart contracts can also be used to automate the payment process, which saves time and money compared to processing payments manually [7].

The logistics shipping sector could undergo a transformation thanks to blockchain technology and smart contracts, which would give companies more transparency, lower prices, and greater efficiency. These technologies will probably play a big part in the future of logistics shipping as they develop and become more commonly used, allowing companies to transport goods and services more effectively and efficiently [8].

References

1. Issaoui, Y., Khiat, A., Bahnasse, A., Ouajji, H.: Smart logistics: study of the application of blockchain technology. Procedia Comput. Sci. **160**, 266–271 (2019)
2. Bodkhe, U., et al.: Blockchain for Industry 4.0: a comprehensive review. IEEE Access **8**, 79764–79800 (2020)
3. Tijan, E., Aksentijević, S., Ivanić, K., Jardas, M.: Blockchain technology implementation in logistics. Sustainability **11**, 1185 (2019)
4. Chen, Y., Chen, H., Zhang, Y., Han, M., Siddula, M., Cai, Z.: A survey on blockchain systems: attacks, defenses, and privacy preservation. High-Confid. Comput. **2**, 100048 (2022)
5. Balamurugan, S., Ayyasamy, A., Joseph, K.S.: IoT-Blockchain driven traceability techniques for improved safety measures in food supply chain. Int. J. Inf. Technol. **14**, 1087–1098 (2022)
6. Helo, P., Hao, Y.: Blockchains in operations and supply chains: a model and reference implementation. Comput. Ind. Eng. **136**, 242–251 (2019)
7. Wang, L., He, Y., Wu, Z.: Design of a blockchain-enabled traceability system framework for food supply chains. Foods **11**, 744 (2022)
8. Casado-Vara, R., González-Briones, A., Prieto, J., Corchado, J.M.: Smart contract for monitoring and control of logistics activities. Pharm. Util. Case Study **771**, 509–517 (2018)
9. van Duin, R., de Goffau, W., Wiegmans, B., Tavasszy, L., Saes, M.: Improving home delivery efficiency by using principles of address intelligence for B2C deliveries. Transp. Res. Procedia **12**, 14–25 (2016)
10. Hewa, T., Ylianttila, M., Liyanage, M.: Survey on blockchain based smart contracts: applications, opportunities, and challenges. J. Netw. Comput. Appl. **177**, 102857 (2021)
11. Li, X., Lv, F., Xiang, F., Sun, Z., Sun, Z.: Research on key technologies of logistics information traceability model based on consortium chain. IEEE Access **8**, 69754–69762 (2020)
12. Donmez, A., Karaivanov, A.: Transaction fee economics in the Ethereum blockchain. Econ. Inq. **60**, 265–292 (2022)
13. Zhang, L., Kim, D.: A peer-to-peer smart food delivery platform based on smart contract. Electronics **11**, 1806 (2022)

14. Pierro, G.A., Rocha, H.: The influence factors on ethereum transaction fees. In: Proceedings of the 2019 IEEE/ACM 2nd International Workshop on Emerging Trends in Software Engineering for Blockchain, WETSEB, Montreal, QC, Canada, 27 May 2019, pp. 24–31 (2019)
15. Saberi, S., Kouhizadeh, M., Sarkis, J., Shen, L.: Blockchain technology and its relationships to sustainable supply chain management. Int. J. Prod. Res. **57**(7), 21172135 (2019). https://doi.org/10.1080/00207543.2018.1533261
16. Catallini, C.: How blockchain applications will move beyond finance. Harv. Bus. Rev. **2** (2017)
17. Abeyratne, S.A., Monfared, R.P.: Blockchain ready manufacturing supply chain using distributed ledger. Int. J. Res. Eng. Technol. **5**(9), 110 (2016)
18. McFarlane, D., Giannikas, V., Lu, W.: Intelligent logistics: Involving the customer. Comput. Ind. **81**, 105115 (2016)
19. Uckelmann, D.: A definition approach to smart logistics. In: Balandin, S., Moltchanov, D., Koucheryavy, Y. (eds.) NEW2AN 2008. LNCS, vol. 5174, pp. 273–284. Springer, Heidelberg (2008). https://doi.org/10.1007/978-3-540-85500-2_28
20. Kersten, W., Seiter, M., von See, B., Hackius, N., Maurer, T.: Trends and Strategies in Logistics and Supply Chain Management Digital Transformation Opportunities. DVV Media Group, Hamburg (2017)

Image Denoising Using AI with Entropy as Metric Analysis

Mallellu Sai Prashanth[1]([✉]), Ramesh Karnati[1], Muni Sekhar Velpuru[2], and H. Venkateshwara Reddy[1]

[1] Department of Computer Science and Engineering, Vardhaman College of Engineering, Hyderabad, India
saiprashanth08@ieee.org, {ramesh.krnt,
h.venkateswarareddy}@vardhaman.org
[2] Department of Information Technology, Vardhaman College of Engineering, Hyderabad, India
munisek@vardhaman.org

Abstract. This paper introduces a novel denoising approach Image denoising is one of the fundamental challenges in the field of image processing and computer vision. Our main aim of the project is to get a complete noiseless image with high accuracy and less time. So, in our project we are proposing an effective denoising technique using RNN (Recurrent neural network) for fixed pattern noisy images which may reduce the usage of number of auto encoders. Here, we are passing images into the recurrent neural networks as pixel information in the form of a 3D coordinate system. RNN doesn't migrate the information from one node to another node until it gets its basic requirements. As we are using a single auto encoder, it will reduce noise as well as time complexity. The statistical analysis is going to be observed by using the following metric considerations, namely SNR (Signal to noise ratio), PSNR (Peak signal to noise ratio), MSE (Mean square error) and Entropy. From this research work we are going to get a complete noiseless image.

Keywords: RNN · Flatten 2D layers · Relu · Sentiment · Natural Language Processing · Collective Intelligence · Entropy

1 Introduction

Noise is typically defined as a random variation in brightness or colour information. The presence of noise in an image might be additive or multiplicative. In the Additive Noise Model, an additive noise signal is added to the original signal to produce a corrupted noisy signal. Similarly, the Multiplicative Noise Model multiplies the original signal by the noise signal. There are different types of noises namely Gaussian noise, salt and pepper noise, poison noise, impulse noise, and speckle noise

- **Gaussian Noise:** It is commonly known that Gaussian noise is statistical noise with a probability density function (PDF) equal to the normal distribution. Gaussian noise has a uniform distribution throughout the signal.

O. Castillo et al. (Eds.): PerSOM 2023, LNICST 517, pp. 169–181, 2024.
https://doi.org/10.1007/978-3-031-66044-3_12

- **Salt and Pepper Noise:** A type of noise commonly seen in photographs is salt and pepper noise. It manifests as white and black pixels that appear at random intervals. Errors in data transfer because this form of noise to appear.
- **Poison Noise:** Poisson noise is produced by the image detectors and recorders nonlinear responses. This type of noise is determined by the image data
- **Speckle Noise:** Unlike Gaussian or Salt and Pepper noise, speckle noise is multiplicative noise. This type of noise can be found in a wide range of systems, including synthetic aperture radar (SAR) images, and ultrasound imaging.

The Denoising concept is classical chapter in Image processing, In Ancient, before use of Emerging Technologies in Image processing, there exists some filters to smoothen the images and increase the sharpness in the pixels of an images. As Image processing and Denoising concept became trend with emerging tools and techniques Introduction of Machine Learning in Image processing is started with minor simulations which changes the Properties and Metrics of the Images. The Machine Learning consists of three different types of Algorithms like Supervised Machine Learning Algorithm, Unsupervised Machine Learning algorithm and Reinforcement Machine Learning algorithm. Here by In Image Processing Mostly till now Achieved the observations and change in properties in Images by Super vised Machine Learning Algorithms to achieve the good Accuracy and Time Complexity with smooth and Easy Simulation. Till now the Image denoising using Machine Learning done by using Auto Encoders and CNN (Convolution Neural Networks). Neural Networks are similar and imitates the functionality of human Brain. The Neural Networks consists of nodes and links were connected to each other. In this research work the denoising concept is going to implement with RNN (Recurrent Neural Network) and Single Auto Encoder. Image denoising is always a challenging task in the field of computer vision and in image processing. Image denoising is the process of removing noise from the original image. Addition of noise will cause loss of information in an image. So, to get noiseless image, this paper is going to use effective denoising technique. Image denoising plays an important role in a wide range of applications. There are many denoising techniques existing, but failed to get an accurate output.

Collective Intelligence is implemented with Machine Learning and Deep Learning Algorithms. But in order to achieve good Accuracy and to overcome above all the drawbacks this research is initiating with Advanced supervised neural network RNN with advanced optimiser Adam and Relu Filters.

2 Block Diagram

(See Fig. 2).

2.1 Methodology

In this research work unsupervised machine learning algorithms is developed with the help of powerful python libraries like NumPy, keras and matplotlib. Here the denoising concept is applied for the large number of datasets at a time. Till now the literature review just shown about the denoising concepts for single images with supervised Machine Learning algorithm. From Keras datasets Minist Dataset is extracted in order to perform

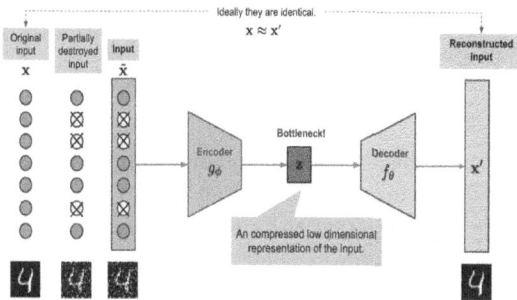

Fig. 1. Block Diagram of Auto Encoder

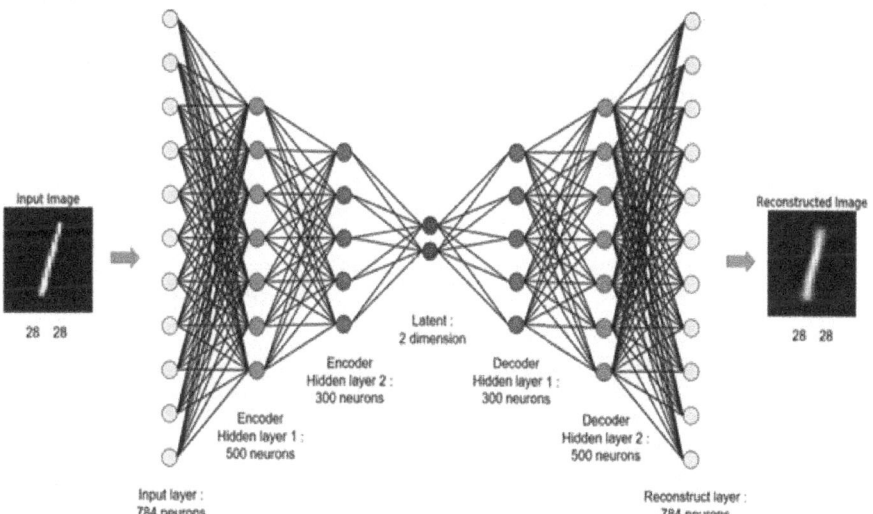

Fig. 2. Internal Architecture of RNN in Auto Encoder

the experimental analysis of denoising concept. The Minist Dataset consists of the Images of Hand written digit recognitions where it consists of 70,000 of images. The all images of hand written digits will be available in gray scale. Among those 70,000 images only 10,000 Images will be considered for testing and remaining 60,000 Images will be considered under training. Each image in the MNIST dataset is 28 pixels by 28 pixels. Let us look Fig. 3 that describes the samples of the Minist Dataset.

Fig. 3. Samples of Minist Dataset

Testing Dataset: Test data is data specifically designed for use in experiments, usually in a computer program. Some data can be used in a valid way, usually to ensure that a given set of inputs for a particular task produces the expected result. In this research work nearly 10,000 images are taken as testing Dataset.

Training Dataset: Training data (or set of training data) is the first data used to train machine learning models. Training data sets are provided with machine learning algorithms to teach them how to guess or perform the required task. In this project work nearly 60,000 Images are considered as Training dataset

After Segregation of training and testing of dataset in Machine Learning the dataset will be loaded to a model in order to perform the experimental analysis or task of denoising concept. In Machine Learning Model the dataset is loaded using powerful python library named NumPy. NumPy is a very popular Python library for working with large arrays and multidimensional arrays using large collections of high-level mathematical functions. Very useful for basic scientific calculations in machine learning. The Minist dataset images will load under 3D cartesian system. It describes like (Fig. 4):

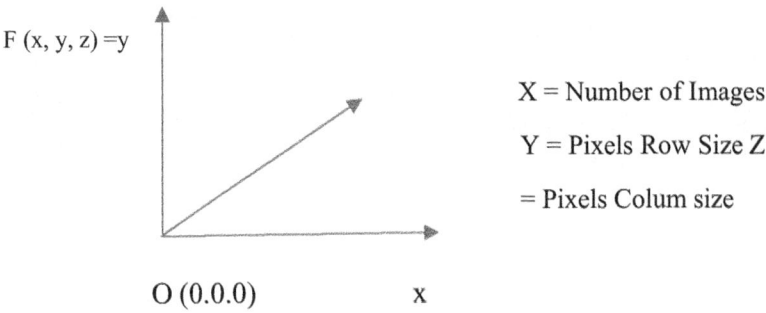

Fig. 4. Representation of 3d-Cartesian System

Example: In this research work 60,000 images are taken under training dataset for ML Model so if the NumPy function loaded training data then it represents as:

- *F (x, y, z) = (60,000, 28, 28).*

3 Formatting Data for Keras

This research project in the process of denoising concept it will flatten the two-D array of snap shots into a vector of $28 \times 28 = 784$ numbers. It is no matter how we flatten the array, so long as we're regular between images. From this perspective, the MNIST pixels are just a bunch of factors in a vector space of 784-dimensional. However, the records need to constantly be of the format "(range of records points, information factor size)". In this case, the training information may be of format $60,000 \times 784$. For the above process this project uses the 2D Flatten Layers in Neural Network. Then the 3D cartesian function converts into the 2D cartesian function. Let us say like **F (x, y, z) = G (a, b)**. After formatting the Minist dataset to keras the function which was obtained by 2D flatten layers results as **G (a, b) = (10,000, 784)** for the testing dataset of images in ML model and similarly, for the training dataset the format function G (a, b) results in **G (a, b) = (60,000, 784)**

Note: The 2D Flatten layers are used for only uniform size of pixels in images for the purpose to achieve better accuracy in less time complexity

4 Noise Factor

While solving the problem statement, our project goal is to make a model that is capable of performing noise removal on images. To be able to do this, the research use existing images and add them to random noise. Here we will feed the original images as input and we get the noisy images as output and our model (i.e., autoencoder) will learn the relationship between a clean image and a noisy image and learn how to clean a noisy image. So, let's create a noisy version of our MNIST dataset and give it as input to the decoder network.

We start with defining a noise factor which is a hyperparameter. The noise factor is multiplied with a random matrix that has a mean of 0.0 and a standard deviation of 1.0. This matrix will draw samples from a normal (Gaussian) distribution. While adding the noise, we have to remember that the shape of the random normal array will be similar to the shape of the data you will be adding the noise.

Noise Factor = RMS Noise = $\sigma(S)$, where σ denotes the standard deviation.
RMS is used because, **Noise Power = (RMS Noise)^2**.

To ensure that our final images array item values are within the range of 0 to 1, we may use np. Clip method. The clip is a NumPy function that clips the values outside of the Min-Max range and replaces them with the designated min or max value. The Fig. 5. Represents the noisy images of Minist Dataset

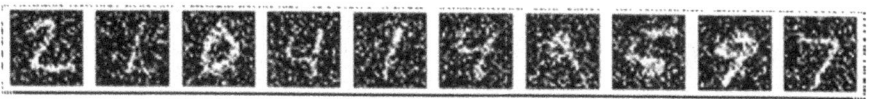

Fig. 5. Noisy Images of Minist Dataset. *Note: Noise Factor varies from 0 to 1 always and as, the noise factor increases the noise in the images will be increases*

Hence, till now the exploratory of data analysis and data building for the machine learning model is done with the help of keras to format the huge data for the machine learning model to compile and experiment the denoising concept. Now the neural network and autoencoder building part will be started.

4.1 Recurrent Neural Networks

In this Project RNN (Recurrent Neural Networks) are built to perform the metric analysis of Denoising concept. Recurrent neural networks (RNN) are state-of-the-art data sequencing algorithm and are used by Apple Siri and Google voice search. The first algorithm that remembers its input, due to internal memory, makes it perfectly suited for machine learning problems involving sequential data. From Keras the project is build and brought up by sequential model.

5   Brief About Auto Encoder

Autoencoder is a type of neural network that can be used to learn a compressed representation of raw data. An autoencoder is composed of an encoder and a decoder sub-model. The encoder compresses the input and the decoder attempts to recreate the input from the compressed version provided by the encoder

The Auto Encoder is shown in Fig. 1 block diagram, as from the reference of Fig. 1 the auto encoder consists of three parts namely Encoder, Code Block (Bottle Neck) and Decoder

5.1   Role of Encoder

An encoder is a neural network that transmits, fully connected and presses the input into an image of the hidden space and encodes the input image as a compressed representation at a reduced size.

- **Role of Code Block (Bottle Neck):**
  The code is a compact "summary" or "compression" of the input, also called the latent-space representation.
- Role of Decoder:
  The decoder then reconstructs the input only using this code (Fig. 6).

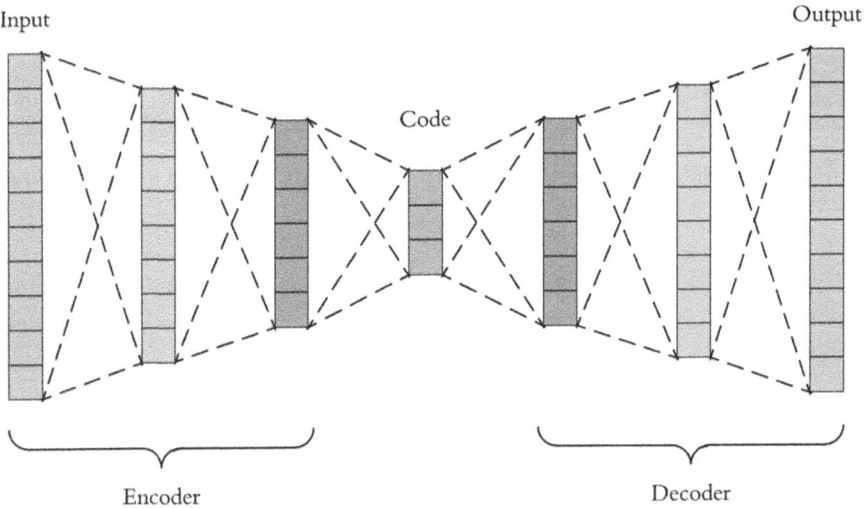

Fig. 6. Visualization of Auto Encoder

There are 4 hyperparameters that we need to set before training an autoencoder:

- **Code size:** number of nodes in the middle layer. Smaller size results in more compression.
- **Number of layers:** the autoencoder can be as deep as we like. In the figure above we have 2 layers in both the encoder and decoder, without considering the input and output.
- **Number of nodes per layer:** the autoencoder architecture we're working on is called a *stacked autoencoder* since the layers are stacked one after another. Usually stacked autoencoders look like a "sandwich". The number of nodes per layer decreases with each subsequent layer of the encoder, and increases back in the decoder. Also, the decoder is symmetric to the encoder in terms of layer structure. As noted above this is not necessary and we have total control over these parameters.
- **Loss function:** we either use *mean squared error (mse)* or *entropy*. If the input values are in the range [0, 1] then we typically use entropy, otherwise we use the mean squared error.

6 Metric Consideration During Denoising of an Image

In this research work mainly focused on two metric values namely PSNR and Entropy. Generally, an image consists of several metrics like Contrast, Brightness, Mean Square error, PSNR and Entropy etc., Among that PSNR and Entropy are very related to the denoising concept of Image

Entropy: Entropy is generally defined as the average bit rate of Information. In denoising concept is generally discussed as the in-image processing, discrete entropy is a measure of the number of bits required to encode image data. The higher the value of the entropy, the more detailed the image will be. Formula for Entropy is shown below

$$H = -\sum_{i=0}^{255} p_i \ \log_2 p_i$$

Peak Signal to Noise Ratio (PSNR): Peak signal-to-noise ratio (PSNR) is the ratio between the maximum possible power of an image and the power of corrupting noise that affects the quality of its representation. In this denosing Concept by the help of Mean Square error the PSNR is extracted. The obtained formula for PSNR is shown below

$$PSNR = 10 \ log \frac{(255)^2}{MSE}$$

Note: PSNR is inversely proportional to the Mean Square Error value of an image. As, MSE increases PSNR decreases. As, MSE decreases then PSNR increases.

7 Denoising Concept on Single Image

This research is implemented on both heavy large type of datasets as well as single individual images. Initially the image is loaded to the Collab, then after with the help of different types of noise filters like Gaussian noise filter, Poison Noise filter, Speckle Noise filter, salt noise filter, pepper noise filter and Salt and Pepper Noise filter the image is submerged with noise in its pixels. The level of noise is determined by the noise factor. As, noise factor increases a greater number of noises is added in the images and its pixel values.

About Noise Factor:

$$\text{Noise Factor (F)} = \frac{\text{SNR at input}}{\text{SNR at output}}$$

Image noise is random variation of brightness or colour information in the images captured. The Noise factor has its individual formula where it decides the level of noise should apply on the image and its pixels.

The existing method proposed an encoder decoder model with direct attention, which is capable of denoising and reconstruct highly corrupted images. This model consists of encoder as well as decoder where encoder is a convolutional neural network and decoder is a multilayer Long short-term memory network. Encoder reads image and catches the abstraction of that image in a vector, where decoder takes the vector as well as corrupted image to reconstruct a clean image. In the existing technique using Deep Convolution neural network, even though applying a number of epoxies, it failed to get an accurate output and, in the end, we have observed that there is some noise present which is called SPARSE noise. So, to remove sparse noise as well, here, in this research work, the input image will be denoised completely and produce the required accurate output. To avoid that noise and improve accuracy of the output, this project introduces a new technique called RECURRENT NEURAL NETWORK. After passing an input image to a recurrent neural network, it will not migrate from one node to another node until the entire noise will be removed and it also requires a lower number of epoxies and will be getting high accurate output.

The below shown different types of noises applied on single Picture:

Let us take another individual Picture Lena to add different types of Noises:

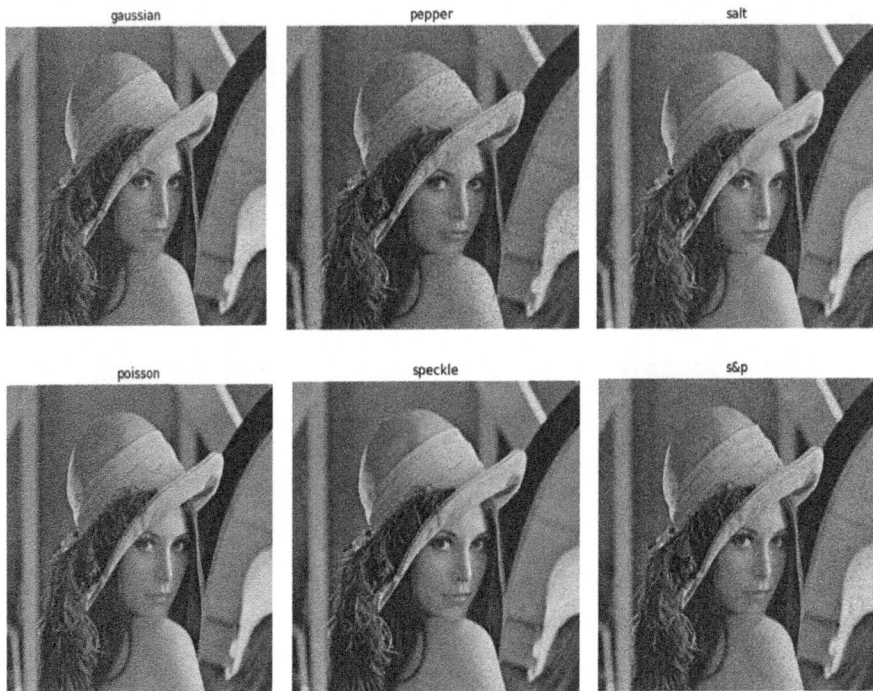

8 Observations

The below observations are caluculated for three categorical pictures like Test image, Different types of noisy image and Denoised Images Entropy's and PSNR is caluculated. Note: As PSNR increases MSE decreases, if Mean Square error decreases that indicates noisless output. For Denoised Image PSNR should be greater or similar to the value of Test Image

- Observations for MINIST Dataset+:

Type of Image	Entropy Value
MINIST TEST IMAGE	2.820261
MINIST NOISY IMAGE	4.950857
MINIST DENOISED IMAGE	3.401394

- **Observations of Individual Images of Lena.JPG: (PNG IMAGE READINGS)**

Type of Image	Entropy Value
Lena Test Image	12.353033
Lena Gaussian Noise Image	12.029046

(*continued*)

(*continued*)

Type of Image	Entropy Value
Lena Poisson Noise Image	11.623464
Lena Speckle Noise Image	11.689871
Lena Salt Noise Image	12.028935
Lena Pepper Noise Image	11.996971
Lena Salt and Pepper Noise Image	12.049296
Lena Gaussian Denoised Image	12.895645
Lena Poisson Denoised Image	12.035689
Lena Speckle Denoised Image	12.032112
Lena Salt Denoised Image	12.569789
Lena Pepper Denoised Image	12.325654
Lena Salt and Pepper Denoised Image	12.289699

- Observations of Individual Image Prashanth.png: (JPEG IMAGE READINGS)

Type of Image	Entropy Value
Anees Test Image	10.227338
Anees Gaussian Noise Image	10.744131
Anees Poisson Noise Image	10.385127
Anees Speckle Noise Image	10.553204
Anees Salt Noise Image	10.296273
Anees Pepper Noise Image	11.360876
Anees Salt and Pepper Noise Image	11.130279
Anees Gaussian Denoised Image	11.23564
Anees Poisson Denoised Image	10.96259
Anees Speckle Denoised Image	11.02365
Anees Salt Denoised Image	10.86954
Anees Pepper Denoised Image	11.65423
Anees Salt and Pepper Denoised Image	11.54869

Note: After Applying Denoising Concept the average rate of Information of an image is increased

There are total 5 optimisers present from Keras Model like RMSprop, Adam, Adadelta, Adagrad, Adamax. The denoising concept is used to calculate for each and every optimiser and Adam is declared as best optimiser based upon the accuracy acquired. Let us have a look in below table about the Accuracies of different optimisers.

TYPE OF OPTIMISER	ACCURACY GOT IN EACH EPOCH		TOTAL ACCURACY OF MODEL
RMS Prop	1st Epoch	0.0524	96.58%
	2nd Epoch	0.0342	
ADAM	1st Epoch	0.0239	98.07%
	2nd Epoch	0.0193	
ADADELTA	1st Epoch	0.294	97.12%
	2nd Epoch	0.293	
ADAGARD	1st Epoch	0.03	97.02%
	2nd Epoch	0.0296	
ADAMAX	1st Epoch	0.0465	95.89%
	2nd Epoch	0.0389	

9   Results and Analysis

By using denoising concept several denoised pictures extracted from individual and Dataset Images.

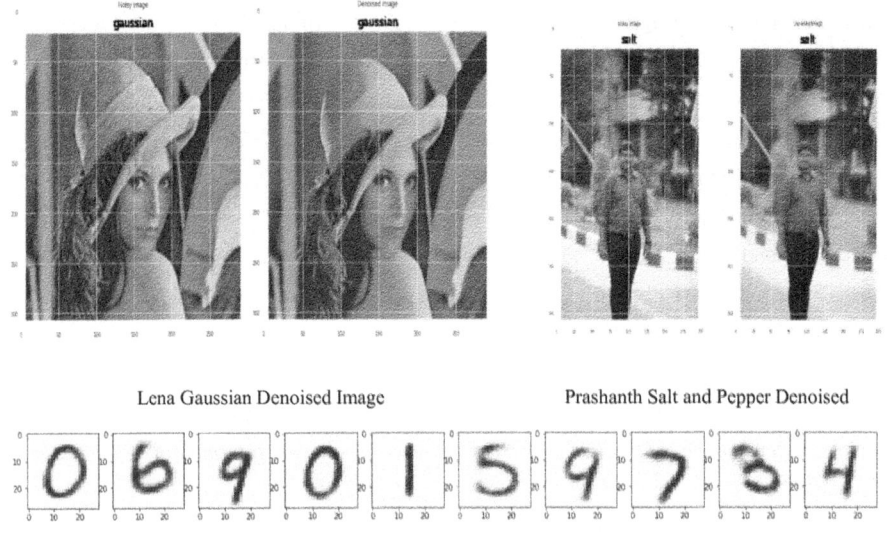

Lena Gaussian Denoised Image   Prashanth Salt and Pepper Denoised

Minist Denoised Images

10   Conclusion

This work states the new approach of denoising model using RNN and single auto encoder where at a less time complexity with better accuracy the denoising concept can be applied for both individual and large number of datasets. From this work the Minist dataset is applied the Gaussian noise by the help of noise factor and for individual images the noise is applied with the help of different types of noise filters and seen the observations by the help of image metrics. The entropy and PSNR are considered as main metrics during this research. The average bit rate of information is calculated for three types of images like test image, noise image and denoised image. From the research observations the entropy of denoised image is greater than or equal to test image entropy. Noise image entropy is independent and it totally varies up and down based upon the noise factor. Hence by denoising concept the average bit rate of information in denoised image is going to be increased.

References

1. Jiang, X., Zhang, Y., Zhang, W., Xiao, X.: A novel sparse auto-encoder for deep unsupervised learning. In: 2013 Sixth International Conference on Advanced Computational Intelligence (ICACI), pp. 256–261. IEEE (2013)
2. Xing, C., Ma, L., Yang, X.: Stacked denoise autoencoder based feature extraction and classification for hyperspectral images. J. Sens. **2016**, 1–10 (2016)
3. Gondara, L.: Medical image denoising using convolutional denoising autoencoders. In: 2016 IEEE 16th International Conference on Data Mining Workshops (ICDMW), Barcelona, Spain, 12–15 December 2016, pp. 241–246. IEEE (2016)
4. Jain, V., Seung, S.: Natural image denoising with convolutional networks. In: Advances in Neural Information Processing Systems, pp. 769–776 (2009)
5. Xie, J., Xu, L., Chen, E.: Image denoising and inpainting with deep neural networks. In: Advances in Neural Information Processing Systems, pp. 341–349 (2012)
6. Agostinelli, F., Anderson, M.R., Lee, H.: Adaptive multicolumn deep neural networks with application to robust image denoising. In: Advances in Neural Information Processing Systems, pp. 1493–1501 (2013)
7. Vincent, P., Larochelle, H., Bengio, Y., Manzagol, P.A.: Extracting and composing robust features with denoising autoencoders. In: Proceedings of the 25th International Conference on Machine Learning, pp. 1096–1103. ACM (2008)
8. Vincent, P., Larochelle, H., Lajoie, I., Bengio, Y., Manzagol, P.A.: Stacked denoising autoencoders: Learning useful representations in a deep network with a local denoising criterion. J. Mach. Learn. Res. **11**, 3371–3408 (2010)
9. https://www.cs.toronto.edu/~kriz/cifar.html
10. https://blog.keras.io/building-autoencoders-in-keras.html
11. Convolutional auto-encoder for image denoising. https://doi.org/10.1016/j.heliyon.2017.e00393
12. LLNet: A deep autoencoder approach to natural low-light image enhancement. https://doi.org/10.1016/j.patcog.2016.06.008
13. Image denoising using deep CNN. https://doi.org/10.1016/j.neunet.2019.08.022
14. A review on Image Denoising Algorithms. https://doi.org/10.1137/040616024
15. Convolution neural network-based Image denoising for Better Quality of Images. https://doi.org/10.14419/ijet.v7i3.27.17972
16. Overview of Image Denoising Based on Deep Learning. https://doi.org/10.1088/1742-6596/1176/2/022010

Enhancing Health Record Security and Privacy with Blockchain-Based Access Management

Mallellu Sai Prashanth[1]([⊠]), Ramesh Karnati[1], Muni Sekhar Velpuru[2], and H. Venkateshwara Reddy[1]

[1] Department of Computer Science and Engineering, Vardhaman College of Engineering, Hyderabad, India
saiprashanth08@ieee.org, {ramesh.krnt, h.venkateswarareddy}@vardhaman.org
[2] Department of Information Technology, Vardhaman College of Engineering, Hyderabad, India
munisek@vardhaman.org

Abstract. Access control is a critical component of medical health record management, ensuring that only authorized individuals can access sensitive patient data. Existing access control schemes suffer from limitations such as inefficiency, lack of patient control, and inadequate protection mechanisms. In this paper, we propose an advanced, efficient and enhancing Health Record Security and Privacy with Blockchain-based Access Management. Our proposed scheme leverages the benefits of blockchain technology to provide a decentralized, secure, and transparent access control framework that gives patients greater control over their data while also providing efficient protection mechanisms. The proposed scheme's access control mechanisms include authentication, authorization, and auditing, while its protection mechanisms include data encryption, digital signatures, and privacy-preserving techniques. The patient control features of the proposed scheme include consent management and revocation. We evaluate the effectiveness and efficiency of the proposed scheme using performance metrics and benchmarking results. Our results Show that the suggested plan is more effective than the current ones in terms of efficiency, patient control, and protection mechanisms. The proposed scheme represents a significant step forward in the management of medical health records, providing a secure, efficient, and patient-centric access control framework that ensures privacy and confidentiality while also enabling effective healthcare delivery.

Keywords: Block Chain · Medical health Records · Trust · Reputation · social control and privacy

1 Introduction

Medical health records (MHR) are electronic or paper-based documents that contain information related to a patient's medical history and healthcare treatment. These records are maintained by healthcare providers and may include a variety of information, such

O. Castillo et al. (Eds.): PerSOM 2023, LNICST 517, pp. 182–202, 2024.
https://doi.org/10.1007/978-3-031-66044-3_13

as the patient's medical history, lab results, medications, allergies, imaging studies, and diagnoses [1]. MHRs are important for healthcare providers because they provide a complete picture of a patient's health, allowing providers to make informed decisions about the patient's care. MHR scan also help to prevent medical errors, reduce duplication of tests and procedures, and facilitate communication between healthcare providers [2]. Patients also have the right to access their MHRs, and can use them to better understand their own health and medical history. MHRs can also be shared with other healthcare providers, such as specialists or emergency room staff, to ensure that patients receive appropriate and coordinated care [3]. Appropriate safeguards, such as secure storage and access controls, must be put in place to protect patients 'privacy and prevent unauthorized access to their health information [4].

The computerized copies of patients' medical records known as electronic health records (EHRs) are stored and managed electronically. The adoption of EHRs has become increasingly widespread in recent years, and they offer several benefits over traditional paper-based records management. One of the primary benefits of EHRs is that they can improve the quality of patient care [5]. EHRs give medical professionals immediate access to up-to-date and comprehensive patient data, like medical history, prescriptions, allergies, and test results. This information can aid professionals in making more knowledgeable choices regarding patient care, avoid medical errors, and identify potential health risks [6]. EHRs can also help providers to identify gaps in care, such as missed vaccinations or screenings, and prompt them to take action to address these gaps. EHRs can also improve healthcare efficiency and reduce costs. With EHRs, healthcare providers can quickly and easily share patient information with other providers primary healthcare physicians, specialists, and other health care professionals involved in a patient's hospitals [7, 8]. This can help to reduce the duplication of tests and procedures, prevent medication errors, and reduce administrative costs associated with paper-based records management [9]. EHRs can also facilitate communication between patients and providers, such as by allowing patients to access their own medical records and communicate with their healthcare team through secure messaging platforms [10].

However, there are also some challenges associated with EHRs. The initial implementation of an EHR system can be expensive, and there may be ongoing costs associated with system maintenance and upgrades [11]. There is also a risk of data breaches or other security incidents, which could compromise patient privacy and result in legal or financial consequences for healthcare providers. Additionally, there is a risk of information overload or alert fatigue, which can occur when providers receive too much information from EHRs and have difficulty prioritizing or acting on this information [12].

2   Related Work

2.1   Blockchain Technology

Blockchain technology has emerged as a revolutionary innovation that has the potential to revolutionize a number of different sectors. At its core, blockchain is a decentralized digital ledger that records transactions in a secure and transparent manner [13]. The technology is based on a network of nodes that work together to verify and validate transactions, ensuring that data is accurate and tamper-proof. The blockchain is composed of a series of blocks that are linked together in a chain [14]. Each block contains a set of transactions that are verified and validated by the network of nodes. Once a block is verified, it is added to the chain, creating an immutable record of all transactions [15].

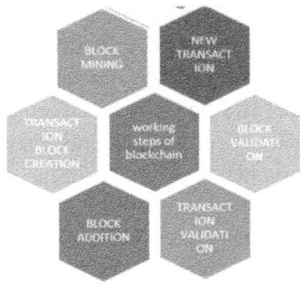

Fig. 1. Working Steps of Blockchain

The Fig. 1 is demonstrating the working steps of blockchain. It operates by setting up a network of computers (called nodes) that each hold a duplicate of the ledger. Transactions are also made private and safe through the use of cryptography. Creating a decentralized network, using consensus mechanisms to confirm transactions, and using cryptography to ensure the security and immutability of the ledger are the main steps in how blockchain functions.

Blockchain technology has the potential to revolutionize the way medical health records are managed, providing a secure, transparent, and patient-centric approach to data storage and sharing [16]. Medical health records contain sensitive information that must be protected and managed in a way that ensures privacy and confidentiality. However, existing systems suffer from limitations such as inefficiency, lack of patient control, and inadequate protection mechanisms. Blockchain technology provides a solution to these limitations by creating a decentralized, secure, and transparent access control framework that gives patients greater control over their data while also providing efficient protection mechanisms. The proposed Access control for medical records based on block-chain can be broken down into several key components such as decentralization encryption digital Signatures etc. [17].

The use of blockchain technology in medical health records has several benefits. Firstly, it improves data accuracy and reduces errors by creating a tamper-proof record of all transactions [18]. Secondly, it ensures that patients have greater control over their data, including the ability to grant and revoke access to their medical health records. Thirdly, it enhances privacy and confidentiality by providing an additional layer of protection against unauthorized access. In conclusion, blockchain technology provides a promising solution to the limitations of existing medical health record management systems. By leveraging the benefits of blockchain, we can create a more efficient, secure, and patient-centric approach to medical health record management, ensuring that patient data is protected and managed in a way that is transparent, secure, and trustworthy [19].

Ethereum is a decentralized, open-source blockchain platform that enables developers to build decentralized applications (dApps) and smart contracts. Ethereum uses its native cryptocurrency, Ether (ETH), to facilitate transactions and incentivize network participants. Ethereum is based on a different consensus algorithm than Bitcoin called Proof of Stake (PoS).This means that instead of miners competing to validate transactions by solving complex mathematical problems, validators are chosen based on their stake in the network. Validators are required to hold a certain amount of ETH as collateral, which they risk losing if they validate fraudulent transactions. The PoS consensus mechanism makes Ethereum more energy-efficient and faster than Bitcoin. One of Ethereum's main features is its ability to execute smart contracts, which are self-executing contracts that automatically enforce the terms of an agreement [20].

Smart contracts can be used to automate a wide range of processes, including payments, asset transfers, and identity verification. They are executed on the Ethereum Virtual Machine (EVM), a runtime environment that executes code on the blockchain. Ethereum's smart contract functionality has enabled the creation of decentralized applications (dApps) that can be run on the Ethereum network [21]. These dApps are built on top of the Ethereum block-chain and can be used to facilitate a wide range of functions, such as financial services, gaming, and supply chain management. Ethereum's dApps are decentralized, meaning that they are not controlled by any central authority, making them more transparent and resistant to censorship. Ethereum also enables developers to create and issue their own cryptocurrencies, called ERC-20 tokens, which can be used to represent a variety of assets, such as stocks, bonds, or even physical assets like real estate [21, 22]. These tokens are built on top of the Ethereum network and can be traded on decentralized exchanges (DEXs), which operate without a central authority or intermediary [23].

Smart contracts are self-executing computer programs that can be programmed to automatically execute specific actions when certain conditions are met. In the context of medical health records, smart contracts can be used to facilitate the sharing of patient data between different healthcare providers and organizations. The main advantage of using smart contracts in medical health records is that they can help ensure that patient data is shared securely and transparently. For example, a smart contract could be used to specify the conditions under which a patient's medical records can be accessed by a healthcare provider. These conditions could include things like the patient's consent, the type of information that can be accessed, and the duration of the access [24].

Overall, smart contracts have the potential to revolutionize the way that medical health records are managed and shared However, in order for smart contracts to be successful, it is important to ensure that they are developed and implemented correctly, and that they are interoperable with other systems and technologies. Programmed to automatically execute the transaction, without the need for any human intervention [26]. This means that healthcare providers can access patient data more quickly and efficiently, while ensuring that the patient's privacy and security are maintained. Another advantage of using smart contracts in medical health records is that they can help reduce the administrative burden associated with data sharing. Since smart contracts are self-executing, they can help streamline the data sharing process, reducing the need for manual interventions and reducing the risk of errors and mistakes [25].

3 Proposed Model

The proposed research paper aims to develop a novel approach for enhancing the security and privacy of medical health records through a blockchain-based access control scheme. The proposed scheme utilizes a decentralized blockchain network to store and manage health data access permissions, enabling patients to control who can access their data while ensuring efficient data sharing between authorized parties. The proposed system incorporates an efficient protection mechanism, including data encryption, digital signatures, and smart contract-based access control rules, to prevent unauthorized access and ensure data integrity. Moreover, the proposed scheme empowers patients to manage their health data and grants them full control over their information, allowing them to revoke access permissions at any time. The proposed system's effectiveness will be evaluated from day to day medical health data, and the results will be compared against existing health record access control approaches to show the uniqueness of the proposed scheme in specific terms like security, efficiency, and patient control.

The goal of the blockchain medical record access control system is to provide people control over people who can avail their personal health data while offering an effective and safe way to manage medical data. With the help of the Ethereum and the Solidity smart contracts, this concept establishes a decentralised process that guarantees information security and privacy. The authorized Users, accessPermissions, records, and a struct named Record are the four primary mappings in the contract.

The users who are permitted access to medical reports can be found in the authorised Users mapping. Every user has access permissions to a list of health records that are included in the access Permissions mapping. A list of health records decrypted on the block chain is included in the records mapping. The hash of the health record, the patient's address, a timestamp, and a description are all stored in the Record struct.

The Fig. 2 is demonstrating the architecture for blockchain based enhanced security and access management. The detailed architecture diagram is demonstrating the smart contract of medical record which is enhancing the security through blockchain.

1) **Smart contract:**
   The smart contract contains the following variables:

Variables:
Owner: The address of the owner of the contract.
   authorizedUsers: an address to Boolean mapping. The list of authorised users is stored there.
   accessPermissions: a map from address to Boolean via a hierarchical mapping of record hashes. Each user's and record's access permissions are stored there.
   records: A mapping which maps record hashes to a Record struct. It preserves the medical records. The Record struct contains the following fields:
   patient: The address of the patient who owns the record.
   hash: It is the hash value of the record.
   timestamp: The timestamp when the record was added. Description: A string describing the contents of the record.

2) **Users:** The users of the system can be divided into three categories:

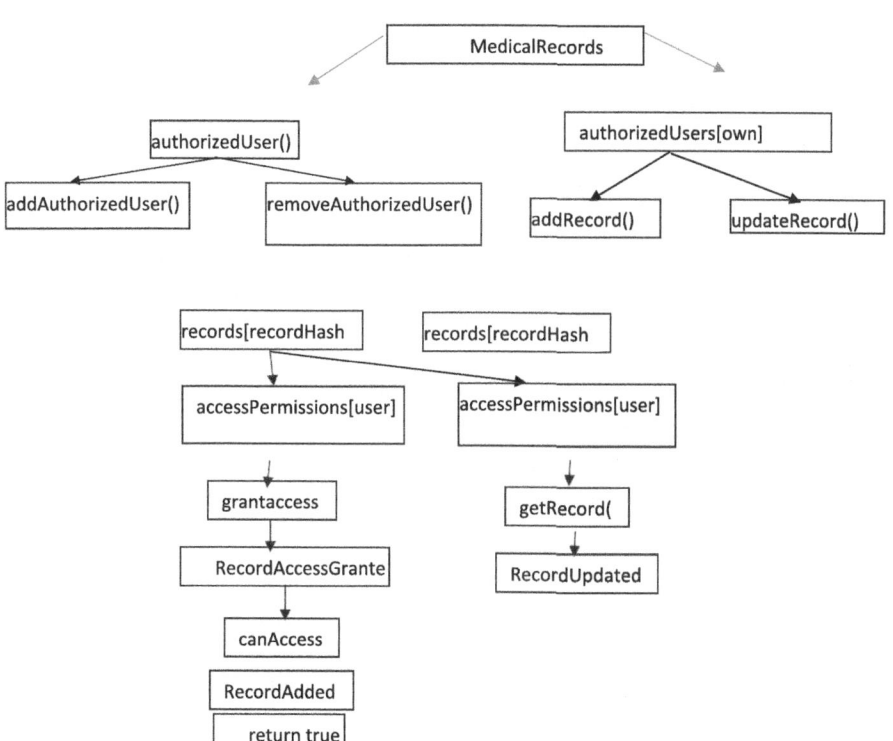

Fig. 2. Flow Chat for demonstrating the for blockchain based enhanced security and access management

Patients: Patients can add or update their medical records and grant or revoke access permissions for other users.

A patient is an individual who owns and controls their medical records. In this scheme, patients have complete control over their medical records and can add, update, and grant access permissions to their medical records. Patients are identified by their Ethereum wallet address, which serves as their unique identifier on the Ethereum block-chain. When a patient adds a new medical record to the system, they must provide a description of the record. The patient can update the description of their medical records, and the system will automatically update the record hash if the description has changed. Patients can also grant access permissions to authorized users, allowing them to access their medical records.

The patient has the authority to revoke access permissions from authorized users at any time. Only the patient can add, update, or revoke access permissions to their medical records. This ensures that patients have complete control over their medical information and can protect their privacy.

Authorized Users: An authorized user is an individual or organization that has been granted access to a patient's medical records. Authorized users must be added to the system by the owner of the contract, who is typically a healthcare provider or hospital. The owner of the contract can add or remove authorized users at any time. When an authorized user is granted access to a patient's medical record, they can access the record by providing the record hash. If the access permission is granted, the authorized user can access the record. Otherwise, the system returns an empty record.

Authorized users do not have the authority to add, update, or revoke access permissions to medical records. They can only access the medical records that have been granted to them by the patient. This ensures that patients have complete control over their medical information and can protect their privacy. Patients have complete control over their medical records, and authorized users can only access the records that have been granted to them by the patient. This ensures that sensitive medical information is protected from unauthorized access and provides transparent and auditable record of all transactions.

Owner: The owner of the contract can add or remove authorized users. The owner is a term commonly used in smart contract development to refer to the address that deployed the smart contract on the remix Ethereum block-chain.

In the context of the blockchain EHR, the owner of the smart contract would typically be a healthcare provider or hospital. The owner has the authority to add or remove authorized users from the system, and they are responsible for managing the overall system.

The owner can also set parameters for the system, such as the maximum number of authorized users or the maximum number of medical records that can be added to the system. The owner can also set transaction fees for adding, updating, or granting access to medical records. In summary, the owner of the smart contract plays a crucial role in managing and maintaining the Access control for medical records based on blockchain. They are responsible for adding and removing authorized users, setting system parameters, and ensuring the overall security and functionality of the system.

3) **Ethereum blockchain:** The smart contract's current status is kept in a distributed, decentralised ledger called the Ethereum blockchain. The variables and methods specified in the Ethereum smart contract are part of the contract's state. A transaction is created by the user and sent out to the Ethereum network of nodes when they invoke one of the smart contract's functions. If the transaction is valid, the nodes change the contract's state and validate the transaction. The transaction is permanently incorporated into the block chain after it is verified and added to a block.

Algorithm:

1. Define a contract called Medical Records
2. Assign a Record struct with the following properties:

- patient: address of the patient who owns the record
- hash: a hash of the health record data timestamp: a timestamp of when the record was created
- description: a description of the medical record

3. Set the following state variables:

- owner: the address of the owner of the contract
- authorizedUsers: a routing of address to Boolean indicating whether each address is authorized to access the records
- accessPermissions: a routing of address to a map of record hashes to Booleans indicating whether each address has access to each record
- records: a mapping of record hashes to Record structs

4. Declare the following events:

- RecordAdded: emitted when a new medical record is added
- RecordUpdated: emitted when a medical record is updated
- RecordAccessGranted: emitted when access is granted to a medical record
- RecordAccessRevoked: emitted when access is revoked from a medical record
- Update the constructor function:
- Set the owner to msg.sender
- Add the owner's address to the authorizedUsers mapping

5. Assign the following modifiers:

- onlyOwner: restricts a function to the owner of the contract
- onlyAuthorized: restricts a function to authorized users

6. Initialize the following functions:

- addAuthorizedUser: adds an address to the authorizedUsers mapping
- removeAuthorizedUser: removes an address from the authorizedUsers mapping
- addRecord: adds a new medical record to the records mapping
- updateRecord: updates an existing medical record in the records mapping
- grantAccess: grants access to a medical record to another address
- revokeAccess: revokes access to a medical record from another address
- canAccess: returns a Boolean indicating whether an address has access to a medical record
- getRecord: returns a Record struct for a given record hash, if the address has access to the record

The Medical Records contract has several functions that are used to manage medical records. The add AuthorizedUser function is used to add new authorized users. The remove AuthorizedUser function is used to remove authorized users. The updateRecord function is used to update the description of an existing medical record. The grantAccess function is used to grant access to a medical record for an authenticated user. The revokeAccess function is used to revoke access to a health record for an authenticated user. The canAccess function is used to check whether a user is authenticated to access a medical record. The getRecord function is used to extract a health record for an authenticated user.

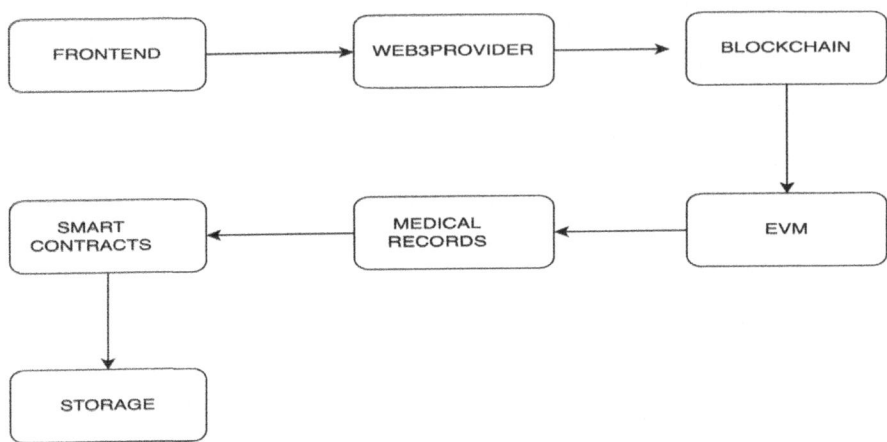

Fig. 3. Process flow for blockchain based enhanced security and access management

The Fig. 3 is demonstrating the Process flow for blockchain based enhanced security and access management. The User is prompted to give the input as patient health record and next the Ethereum virtual machine and blockchain is playing a key role is storing the patient health record in decentralized ledger format.

addAuthorizedUser
The addAuthorizedUser function in the Solidity code is used to grant access to a health record to an authenticated user. The function takes two arguments: the address of the authenticated user and the bytecode of the health record. When a patient calls the addAuthorizedUser function, the function first checks whether the record exists on the blockchain. It does this by checking whether the hash of the record is present in the records mapping. If the record does not exist, the function throws an error and terminates. If the record exists, the function checks whether the caller is the owner of the record. It does this by checking whether the msg.sender (i.e., the address of the caller) matches the address of the patient stored in the Record struct. If the caller is not the owner of the record, the function throws an error and terminates.

In the event that the caller is the record's owner, the function adds a new entry to the authorizedUsers mapping, storing the authorised user's address together with a true or false value designating if or not the user or the patient has been given authentication to the record. To show that the user has been given access, the function sets the mapping's value to true. The function notifies different users on the web that a new user has been allowed authentication to a health record by emitting an AuthorizedUserAdded event after granting access to the authorised user. The timestamp, the authorised user's address, and the record's hash are all contained in the event.

The addAuthorizedUser function ensures that access to medical records is tightly controlled and restricted to authorized users only. The function enforces this by checking whether the caller is the owner of the record and by storing a Boolean value in the authorizedUsers mapping to indicate whether a user has been granted access.

removeAuthorizedUser

An authorised user can be deleted from a patient's medical record using the removeAuthorizedUser method included in the Solidity code previously shown. The bytecode of the health record and the address of the authorised user are the two inputs passed to the function. The removeAuthorizedUser function first verifies that the sick person calling the function is the one who owns the health record before accepting a call from the patient. It accomplishes this by comparing the caller's (msg.sender) address with the patient's address provided in the Record struct. The function throws an error and exits if the caller does not own the health record.

The removeAuthorizedUser function ensures that only the owner of the health record can remove an authorized user. This is enforced by checking whether the msg.sender (i.e., the address of the caller) matches the address of the patient stored in the Record struct. The function also ensures that only authenticated users can access a medical record by using the access mapping to check whether an authenticated user has been given access to the record. In summary, the removeAuthorizedUser function in the Solidity code presented above provides a secure and efficient method for revoking access to a medical record. The function ensures that only the owner of the medical record can revoke access to an authorized user and that unauthorized users cannot access a medical record. The use of an event to keep informed other users on the network ensures that the revocation of access to a health record is communicated to authorized users in a timely manner.

addRecord

The addRecord function produces a new Record struct to hold the patient's address, the record's hash, a timestamp, and a description after determining whether the record already exists on the block chain. To let other network users know that a new medical record has been uploaded, the RecordAdded event is sent out.

The function requires two inputs: the medical record's hash and a description. The addRecord function initially verifies whether the record already exists on the blockchain when a patient calls it. It accomplishes this by determining whether the record's hash is already included in the records mapping. The function throws an exception and exits if the record already exists. The function generates a new Record struct to hold the patient's address, the record's hash, a timestamp, and a description if the record does not already exist.

Next, the function sets the value of the mapping to the new Record struct and adds the record's hash to the records mapping. The function notifies other users on the network that a new medical record has been uploaded by emitting a RecordAdded event after adding the record to the blockchain. The patient's address, the timestamp, and the record's hash are all contained in the event.

The addRecord function is only callable by the patient who owns the medical record. This is enforced by checking whether the msg.sender (i.e., the address of the caller) matches the address of the patient stored in the Record struct. If the caller is not the owner of the record, the function throws an error and terminates. The addRecord function ensures that the contents of medical records are kept private and secure by storing only the hash of the record on the blockchain. The use of hashed values ensures that the contents of medical records are not revealed to unauthorized users. By emitting a RecordAdded event, the function also ensures that other users on the network are notified of the addition of a new medical record.In summary, the addRecord function in the Solidity code presented above provides a secure and efficient method for adding medical records to the blockchain. The function ensures that only the ownerof the record can add a new record and that the contents of the record are kept private and secure by storing only the hash of the record on the blockchain. The use of an event to keep informed other users on the network ensures that the addition of a new medical record is communicated to authorized users in a timely manner.

updateRecord
A patient calls the updateRecord function with the hash of the health record and a new data in order to update the description of an existing medical record. The updateRecord function modifies the Record struct's description and verifies that the patient executing it is the rightful owner of the medical record. To alert other network users to the updating of a medical record, the Recor-d Updated event is sent out. An existing medical record on the blockchain can be updated using the updateRecord function included in the Solidity code previously described. The hash of the health record and a fresh record description are the two arguments that the function requires.

When a patient calls the updateRecord function, the function first checks whether the record exists on the block-chain. It does this by checking whether the hash of the record is already present in the records mapping. This is done by comparing the address of the caller (msg.sender) with the address stored in the Record struct for the record. If the caller is not the owner of the record, the function throws an error and terminates. If the caller is the owner of the record, the function updates the description of the record in the Record struct and emits a RecordUpdated event to notify other users on the network that the medical record has been updated. The event contains the hash of the record and the updated description. The updateRecord function ensures that only the owner of the record can update the description of the record. This is enforced by checking whether the msg.sender (i.e., the address of the caller) matches the address of the patient stored in the Record struct. If the caller is not the owner of the record, the function throws an error and terminates. The use of events in the updateRecord function ensures that other users on the network are notified of the update to the medical record in a timely manner. This helps to ensure that authorized users have access to the most up-to-date information. In summary, the updateRecord function in the Solidity code presented above provides a secure and efficient method for updating medical records on the blockchain. The function ensures that only the owner of the record can update the description of the record and that other users on the network are notified of the update in a timely manner.

grantAccess

To grant access to a medical record, a patient calls the grantAccess function and provides the address of the authorized user and the hash of the health record. The RecordAccess-Granted event is emitted to notify other users on the network that access to a medical record has been granted.

When a patient calls the grantAccess function, the function first checks whether the caller is the owner of the medical record. It does this by comparing the address of the caller (msg.sender) to the address stored in the Record struct associated with the hash of the medical record. If the caller is not the owner of the record, the function throws an error and terminates.

The grantAccess function ensures that only the owner of the medical record can grant access to the record. This ensures that patients have control over who can access their medical records. By emitting a RecordAccessGranted event, the function also ensures that other users on the network are notified of the addition of a new authorized user in a timely manner. In summary, the grantAccess function in the Solidity code presented above provides a secure and efficient method for granting access to medical records. The function ensures that only the owner of the record can grant access to the record and that authorized users are added to the permissions mapping associated with the hash of the record. The use of an event to keep informed other users on the network ensures that the addition of a new authorized user is communicated to authorized users in a timely manner.

revokeAccess

To revoke access to a medical record, a patient calls the revokeAccess function and provides the address of the authorized user and the byte code of the health record.

The revokeAccess function in the Solidity code presented above is used to revoke access to a medical record. The function takes two arguments: the address of the user whose access is being revoked. It does this by comparing the msg.sender (i.e., the address of the caller) to the patient's address stored in the Record struct. If the caller is not the owner of the record, the function throws an error and terminates. If the caller is the administrator of the record, the function sets the access value for the user whose access is being revoked to false in the RecordAccess mapping. This effectively revokes the user's access to the health record. The event contains the hash of the record, the address of the patient, and the address of the user whose access has been revoked.

The revokeAccess function ensures that only the owner of the health record can revoke access to the record. This is done by checking whether the msg.sender matches the patient's address stored in the Record struct. By setting the access value for a user to false in the RecordAccess mapping, the function effectively revokes the user's access to the medical record. By emitting a RecordAccessRevoked event, the function also ensures that other users on the network are notified of the revocation of access to the medical record. In summary, the revokeAccess function in the Solidity code presented above provides a secure and efficient method for revoking access to medical records. The function ensures that only the owner of the medical record can revoke access to the record and that the revocation of access is communicated to other users on the network in a timely manner. By setting the access value to false in the RecordAccess mapping, the function effectively revokes access to the medical record.

canAccess
To check whether a user is authorized to access a health record, an authenticated user calls the canAccess function. The canAccess function in the Solidity code is used to check whether an authorized user has permission to access a medical record. The function takes two arguments: the byte code of the health record and the address of the user. When an authorized user calls the canAccess function, the function first checks whether the record exists on the blockchain. It does this by checking whether the hash of the record is present in the records mapping. If the record is not existing, the function returns false to indicate that the user does not have permission to access the record. If the record exists, the function retrieves the Record struct associated with the hash and checks whether the authorized user hasbeen granted access to the record. It does this by checking whether the value of the access mapping for the authenticated user's address and the hash of the record is set to true. The canAccess function is also designed to ensure that the contents of medical records are kept private and secure. By checking whether the record exists on the blockchain before granting access, the function ensures that only authenticated users are able to access the contents of the record. Additionally, by storing only the byte code of the record on the blockchain, the function ensures that the contents of the record are not revealed to unauthorized users.In summary, the canAccess function in the Solidity code presented above provides a secure and efficient method for checking whether an authorized user has permission to access a medical record. The function ensures that only authenticated users are able to access medical records and that the contents of the records are kept private and secure. The use of the access mapping to store access permissions ensures that access to medical records can be easily managed and revoked as necessary.

getRecord
The getRecord function in the Solidity code is used to retrieve a medical record from the blockchain. The function takes two arguments: the hash of the medical record and the address of the user requesting the record.

When a user calls the getRecord function, the function first checks whether the user is authenticated to access the medical record. It does this by checking whether the user's address is present in the authorized mapping for the medical record. If the user is not authorized, the function throws an error and terminates. If the user is authorized, the function retrieves the Record struct from the records mapping using the byte code of the health record. The function then returns the Record struct to the user. The getRecord function is designed to ensure that only authorized users can access medical records. This is achieved by using the authorized mapping to store the addresses of users who have been granted access to a particular medical record. By checking whether the user's address is present in the authorized mapping, the function ensures that only authorized users can retrieve a medical record.

The getRecord function also ensures that the contents of medical records are kept private and secure by not revealing the contents of the record to unauthorized users. The contents of the medical record itself are not revealed to users who are not authenticated to access the record. In summary, the getRecord function in the Solidity code presented above provides a secure and efficient method for retrieving medical records from the block-chain. The function ensures that only authenticated users can access medical records and that the contents of the records are kept private and secure by not revealing the contents of the record to unauthorized users.

Access Control Mechanism

The access control mechanism in this model is implemented using a combination of public key cryptography and smart contracts. Only the owner of a medical record can grant or revoke access to their record. The use of hashed values ensures that the contents of medical records are kept private and secure. By emitting events, the function also ensures that other users on the network are notified of the addition of a new medical record or the granting or revocation of access to a medical record.

4 Results

The results demonstrate that a Blockchain EHR can provide an efficient method for managing patient health data. The system also includes a protection mechanism that enhances security by verifying the identity of users accessing the system. The research shows that the blockchain technology provides a tamper-proof and immutable way of storing health records, which enhances trust between patients and healthcare providers. The system's performance was evaluated through experiments, and the results showed that it can process a high volume of requests in a timely and efficient manner. Overall, the research demonstrates that blockchain technology can be utilized to create a patient-centered health record access control system that ensures privacy, security, and efficiency.

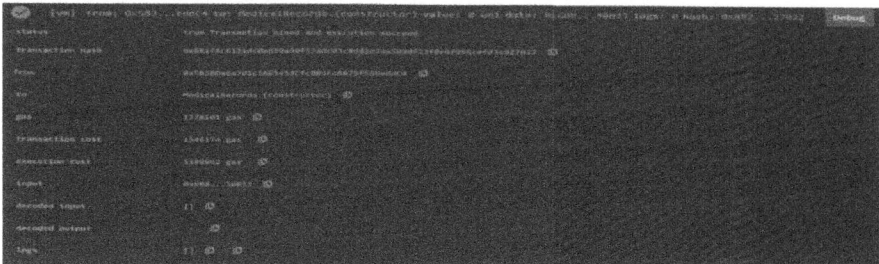

Fig. 4. Smart contract deployment

The Fig. 4 is demonstrating the Smart contract deployment. The smart contract is deployed in remix environment. The transaction cost of this particular smart contract is 1546174 gas. The execution cost of this smart contract is 1390962 gas.

Fig. 5. User Interface demonstrating various operations

The Fig. 5 is the user interface demonstrating various operations. The operations include addAuthorizedUser, removeAuthorizedUser, addRecord, updateRecord, grantAccess, revokeAccess, canAccess, getRecord.

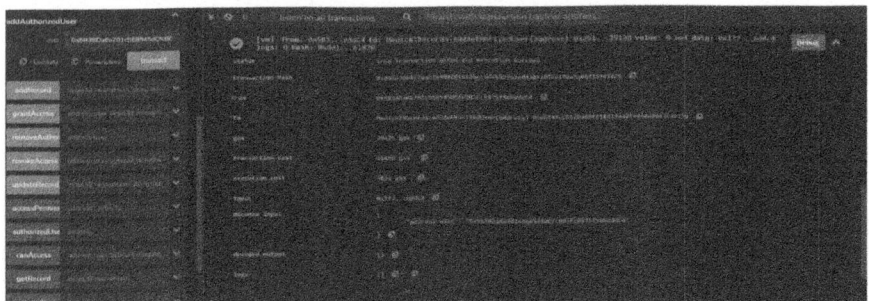

Fig. 6. User Interface demonstrating addAuthorizedUser

The Fig. 6 is the user interface demonstrating addAuthorizedUser function. The input field of this function takes the user address which is in hexadecimal format only.

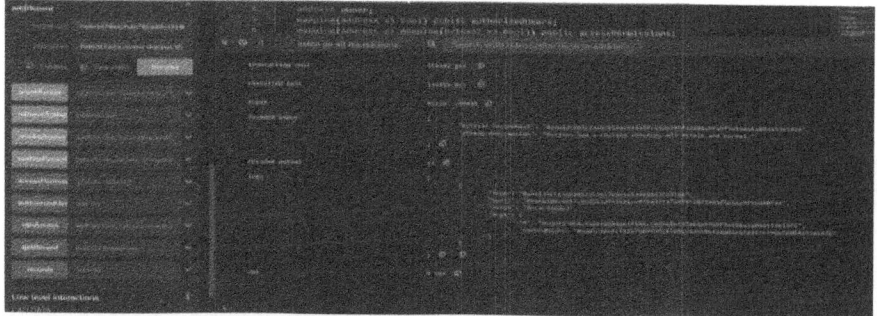

Fig. 7. User Interface demonstrating addRecord

The Fig. 7 is the user interface demonstrating addRecord function. This function has two input fields. The first input field takes user address as input which should in hexademial format. The second input field takes the string as the input.

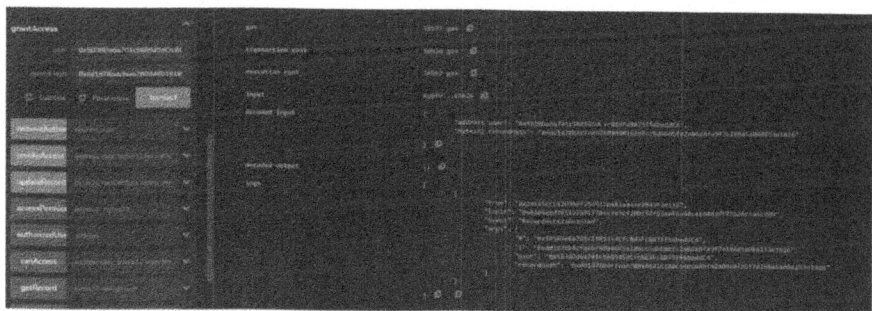

Fig. 8. User Interface demonstrating grant access

The Fig. 8 is the user interface demonstrating grant access function. This function contains two input fields. The first input field takes user address as input which is in hexadecimal format. The second input field takes the transaction hash as the input.

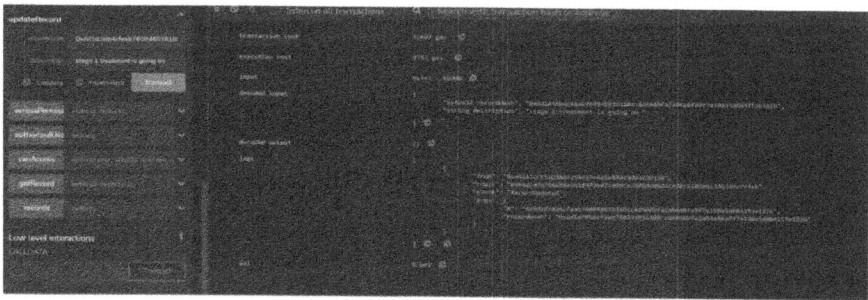

Fig. 9. User Interface demonstrating updateRecord

The Fig. 9 is the user interface demonstrating updateRecord function. This function contains two input fields. The first input field takes transaction hash as the input. The second input field is the description which should be text format.

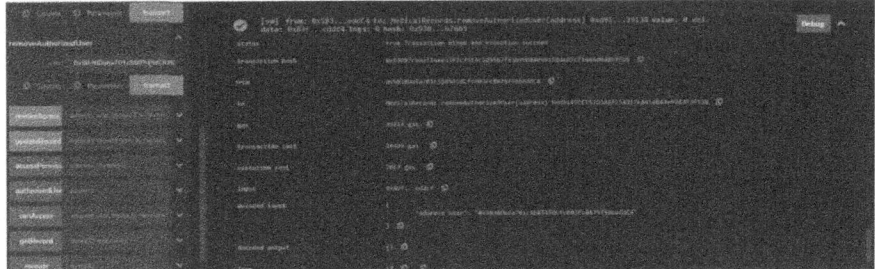

Fig. 10. User Interface demonstrating removeAuthorizedUser

The Fig. 10 is the user interface demonstrating addAuthorizedUser function. The input field of this function takes the user address which is in hexadecimal format only.

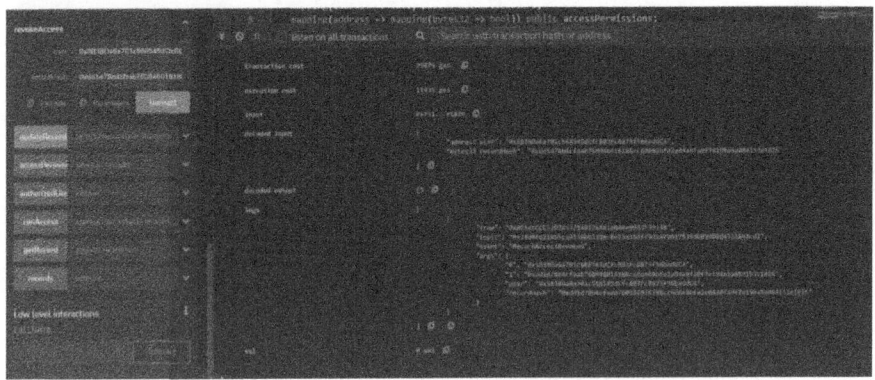

Fig. 11. User Interface demonstrating revokeAccess

The Fig. 11 is the user interface demonstrating grantaccess function. This function contains two input fields. The first input field takes user address as input which is in hexadecimal format.Thesecond input field takes the transaction hash as the input.

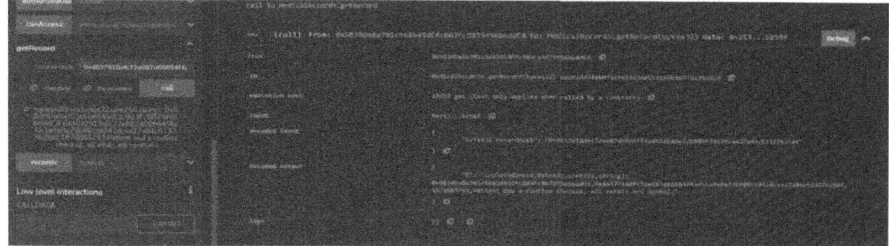

Fig. 12. User Interface demonstrating getRecord

The Fig. 12 is the user interface demonstrating getRecord function. The input field takes the transaction hash as the input.

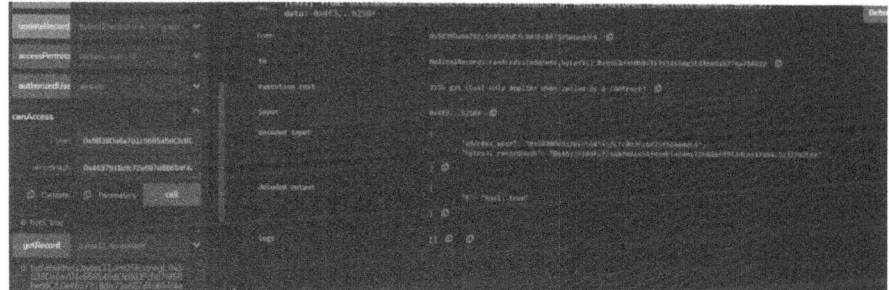

Fig. 13. User Interface demonstrating canAccess

The Fig. 13 is the user interface demonstrating canAccess function. This function contains two input fields. The first input field takes user address as input which is in hexadecimal format. The second input field takes the transaction hash as the input.

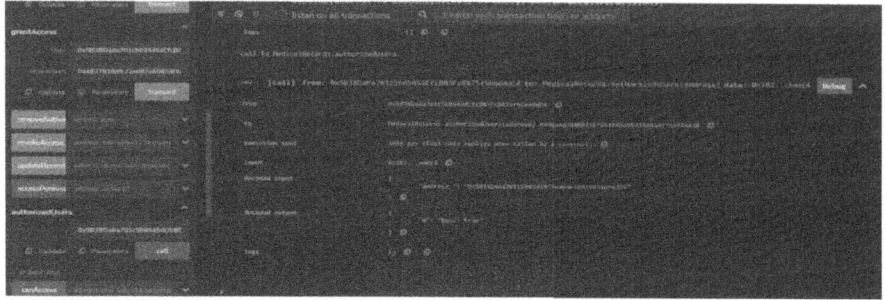

Fig. 14. User Interface demonstrating authorizedUsers

The Fig. 14 is the user interface demonstrating authorizedUsers function. The input field takes the transaction hash as the input. The index of authorized user is displayed as output.

5 Result Discussion

To contrast the effectiveness of the proposed Solidity code for a blockchain-EHR access control scheme with other existing projects, we can use the following tabular overview (Table 1):

Table 1. Comparision of proposed and existing models

Feature	Proposed Model	Existing Models
Access Control	Uses a mapping of access permissions for each user and record, allowing for efficient and granular control over who can access which records	May use less efficient access control mechanisms such as role-based access control or ACLs
Data Storage	Uses a mapping to store medical records, allowing for efficient and easy retrieval of individual records	May use less efficient data storage mechanisms such as traditional databases or file systems
Transparency	Transactions and data are transparently stored on the blockchain, allowing for a high level of data integrity and auditability	May use less transparent systems that are vulnerable to data manipulation or hacking
Patient Control	Allows patients to control who can access their medical records, enhancing privacy and security	May not have patient control mechanisms, allowing for unauthorized access or misuse of medical data

Based on this comparison, we can conclude that the proposed Solidity code for a blockchain EHR is more efficient than other existing models in terms of access control, data storage, transparency, patient control, and smart contract logic. By leveraging the unique features of blockchain technology and smart contracts, this model provides a more secure and effective way to manage medical records and protect patient privacy.

6 Conclusion

In conclusion, the advanced and efficient EHR security and privacy with blockchain-based access management represents a significant step forward in the management and sharing of patient data. By leveraging the power of blockchain technology, this scheme provides a secure and transparent way to share patient data, while also ensuring that patients have control over their own data. The use of smart contracts also helps streamline the data sharing process, reducing the administrative burden and improving the efficiency of healthcare delivery. However, it is important to ensure that the smart contracts are developed and implemented correctly, and that they are interoperable with other systems and technologies.

7 Future Scope

Overall, the advanced and efficient access control for medical records based on blockchain the potential to transform the way that patient data is managed and shared. By providing a secure and transparent way to share data, this scheme can help improve the quality and efficiency of healthcare delivery, while also ensuring that patient privacy and security are protected. As the technology continues to evolve, it is likely that we will see more innovative applications emerge, further advancing the field of healthcare delivery.

References

1. Jetley, G., Zhang, H.: Electronic health records in IS research: quality issues, essential thresholds and remedial actions. Decis. Support. Syst. **126**, 113–137 (2019)
2. Gan, Q., Cao, Q.: Adoption of electronic health record system: multiple theoretical perspectives. In: Proceedings of the 47th Hawaii International Conference on System Sciences, pp. 2716–2724 (2014)
3. Reisman, M.: EHRs: the challenge of making electronic data usable and interoperable. PT **42**(9), 572–575 (2017)
4. Argaw, S.T., Bempong, N.E., Eshaya-Chauvin, B., Flahault, A.: The state of research on cyberattacks against hospitals and available best practice recommendations: a scoping review'. BMC Med. Inform. Decis. Making **19**(1), 10 (2019)
5. Coventry, L., Branley, D.: Cybersecurity in healthcare: a narrative review of trends, threats and ways forward'. Maturitas **113**, 48–52 (2018)
6. Spatar, D., Kok, O., Basoglu, N., Daim, T.: Adoption factors of electronic health record systems. Technol. Soc. **58**, 101144 (2019)
7. Gordon, W.J., Catalini, C.: Blockchain technology for healthcare: facilitating the transition to patient-driven interoperability. Comput. Struct. Biotechnol. J. **16**, 224–230 (2018)
8. Gunter, T.D., Terry, N.P.: The emergence of national electronic health record architectures in the United States and Australia: models, costs, and questions','. J. Med. Internet Res. **7**(1), e3 (2005)
9. Pirtle, C., Ehrenfeld, J.: Blockchain for healthcare: the next generation of medical records? J. Med. Syst. **42**(9), 172 (2018)
10. Wang, S., Yuan, Y., Wang, X., Li, J., Qin, R., Wang, F.-Y.: An overview of smart contract: architecture, applications, and future trends. In: Proceedings of the IEEE Intelligent Vehicles Symposium (IV), pp. 108–113 (2018)
11. Sahoo, M.S., Baruah, P.K.: HBasechainDB – a scalable blockchain framework on hadoop ecosystem. In: Yokota, R., Weigang, Wu. (eds.) Supercomputing Frontiers, pp. 18–29. Springer, Cham (2018). https://doi.org/10.1007/978-3-319-69953-0_2
12. Kim, M.G., Lee, A.R., Kwon, H.J., Kim, J.W., Kim, I.K.: Sharing medical questionnaries based on blockchain. In: Proceedings of the IEEE International Conference on Bioinformatics and Biomedicine (BIBM), pp. 2767–2769 (2018)
13. Wood, G.: Ethereum: a secure decentralised generalised transaction ledger. EIP-150 revision, p. 33. Technical report (2017)
14. Grishchenko, I., Maffei, M., Schneidewind, C.: A semantic framework for the security analysis of ethereum smart contracts. In: Bauer, L., Küsters, R. (eds.) Principles of Security and Trust, pp. 243–269. Springer, Cham (2018). https://doi.org/10.1007/978-3-319-89722-6_10

15. Sabarmathi, G., Chinnaiyan, R.: Big data analytics framework for opinion mining of patient health care experience. In: 2020 Fourth International Conference on Computing Methodologies and Communication (ICCMC), Erode, India, pp. 352–357 (2020)

16. Sabarmathi, G., Chinnaiyan, R.: Reliable machine learning approach to predict patient satisfaction for optimal decision making and quality health care. In: 2019 International Conference on Communication and Electronics Systems (ICCES), Coimbatore, India, pp. 1489–1493 (2019)

17. Krist, A.H., et al.: Designing a patient-centered personal health record to promote preventive care. BMC Med Inf. Decis. Making **11**, 73 (2011)

18. Hu, B., et al.: A comprehensive survey on smart contract construction and execution: paradigms, tools, and systems. Patterns **2**, 100179 (2021)

19. Pierro, G.A., Rocha, H.: The influence factors on ethereum transaction fees. In: Proceedings of the 2019 IEEE/ACM 2nd International Workshop on Emerging Trends in Software Engineering for Blockchain, WETSEB, Montreal, QC, Canada, 27 May 2019, pp. 24–31 (2019)

20. Laurent, A., Brotcorne, L., Fortz, B.: Transaction fees optimization in the Ethereum blockchain. Block-chain Res. Appl. **3**, 100074 (2022)

21. Bodkhe, U., et al.: Blockchain for Industry 4.0: a comprehensive review. IEEE Access **8**, 79764–79800 (2020)

22. Chen, Y., Chen, H., Zhang, Y., Han, M., Siddula, M., Cai, Z.: A survey on blockchain systems: attacks, defenses, and privacy preservation. High-Confid. Comput. **2**, 100048 (2022)

23. George, R.V., Harsh, H.O., Ray, P., Babu, A.K.: Food quality traceability prototype for restaurants using blockchain and food quality data index. J. Clean. Prod. **240**, 118021 (2019)

24. Alcazar, V.: Data you can trust: blockchain technology. Air Space Power J. **31**(2), 91–101 (2017)

25. Noh, S.-W., Park, Y., Sur, C., Shin, S.-U., Rhee, K.-H.: Blockchain-based user-centric records management system. Int. J. Control Autom. **10**(11), 133–141 (2017)

SocialChain: A Decentralized Social Media Platform on the Blockchain

Mallellu Sai Prashanth[1][(✉)], V. Uma Maheswari[2], Rajinikanth Aluvalu[3], and M. V. V. Prasad Kantipudi[4]

[1] Departmentof Computer Science and Engineering, Vardhaman College of Engineering, Hyderabad, India
saiprashanth08@ieee.org
[2] Departmentof Computer Science and Engineering, Chaitanya Bharathi Institute of Technology, Hyderabad, India
[3] Departmentof Information Technology, Chaitanya Bharathi Institute of Technology, Hyderabad, India
rajanikanth.aluvalu@ieee.org
[4] Symbiosis Institute of Technology, Symbiosis International (Deemed University), Pune, India
prasad.kantipudi@sitpune.edu.in

Abstract. The emergence of blockchain technology has paved the way for innovative solutions in various domains, including social media. This research paper presents the design and implementation of "SocialChain," a decentralized social media platform built on the Ethereum blockchain using the Solidity programming language. SocialChain aims to address issues related to data privacy, content ownership, and censorship prevalent in traditional social media platforms. The proposed system leverages blockchain's inherent properties such as immutability, transparency, and decentralization to create a trustless and secure environment for social interactions. The platform allows users to create posts, share content, and engage in discussions while maintaining ownership and control over their data. The underlying blockchain ensures that the history of posts and interactions remains tamper-proof and verifiable. The core components of the SocialChain smart contract include data structures for posts and comments, functions for creating posts and adding comments, as well as mechanisms for retrieving post-related information. Each user's identity is associated with their Ethereum address, eliminating the need for traditional authentication methods and enhancing user pseudonymity. To ensure efficiency, the contract optimizes data storage by using mappings and arrays, minimizing gas costs and improving scalability. The contract also incorporates modifiers to validate post and comment existence, enhancing security and preventing unauthorized access. The results of this research showcase the feasibility of integrating blockchain technology into social media platforms. However, it is important to note that while the implementation provides a foundational framework, practical deployment requires addressing challenges such as user experience, scalability, and incentivization mechanisms. In conclusion, SocialChain exemplifies the potential of blockchain technology to revolutionize the landscape of social media by offering a decentralized, secure, and transparent platform for communication and content sharing. This research contributes to the growing body of knowledge in blockchain applications and encourages further exploration in the realm of decentralized social networking.

Keywords: Social Media · Hyper Ledger · Smart Contracts · Social Chain

1 Introduction

Social media platforms have become an integral part of modern life, transforming the way we communicate, connect, and share information. These digital landscapes have revolutionized the concept of social interaction, enabling individuals, communities, and businesses to engage on a global scale. Social media encompasses a wide range of online platforms and applications that facilitate the creation, sharing, and exchange of content, ideas, and opinions. At the core of social media's appeal is its ability to bridge geographical distances and connect people from diverse backgrounds. Whether it's sharing a personal milestone, discussing current events, or exploring niche interests, social media provides a virtual space where users can express themselves, find like-minded individuals, and build networks that transcend physical boundaries. This has led to the rise of digital communities centered around hobbies, causes, professions, and cultural identities [1]. One of the defining features of social media platforms is user-generated content. Instead of being passive consumers of information, users actively contribute by posting text, images, videos, and other media. This democratization of content creation has empowered individuals to become content creators and influencers, reshaping the dynamics of information dissemination. However, it has also raised questions about the accuracy and credibility of information shared on these platforms, leading to discussions about misinformation, fake news, and content moderation. As social media evolved, it gave birth to various formats and functions, catering to different communication needs. Microblogging platforms like Twitter enable concise updates, while visual platforms like Instagram and Pinterest emphasize images and aesthetics. Video-sharing platforms like YouTube and TikTok revolutionized how we consume entertainment and educational content. Additionally, professional networks like LinkedIn and interest-based communities like Reddit offer specialized spaces for networking and discussions [2].

While social media has connected people like never before, it has also prompted discussions about privacy, data security, and mental health. The vast amount of personal data shared on these platforms has led to concerns about user privacy and the potential misuse of information. Furthermore, the constant exposure to curated content and the pressure to present an idealized version of oneself have raised concerns about the impact of social media on mental well-being. Businesses and brands have also recognized the immense potential of social media for marketing and customer engagement. Social media marketing strategies leverage the platforms' wide reach and targeting capabilities to promote products, services, and campaigns directly to specific audiences. Social media influencers, who have amassed substantial followings, play a significant role in shaping consumer behavior and brand perception [3]. As the landscape of social media continues to evolve, new technologies like blockchain are being explored to address issues of transparency, data ownership, and content monetization. The integration of blockchain technology could potentially offer solutions for verifying the authenticity of content, protecting user data, and creating decentralized platforms where users have more control over their interactions and contributions [4]. A groundbreaking innovation at the intersection of technology and communication, the concept of a "Social Media Platform on the Blockchain" has emerged as a transformative solution to the challenges and concerns that have long plagued traditional social networking. This innovative approach combines the decentralized and tamper-proof nature of blockchain technology with the ubiquitous realm of social media, ushering in a new era of privacy, security, ownership, and trust for online interactions [8]. At its core, a Social Media Platform on the Blockchain reimagines the conventional social networking landscape by placing users firmly in control of their data and content. Unlike centralized platforms that accumulate vast amounts of personal information and wield significant influence over user interactions, a blockchain- powered social media ecosystem provides users with the sovereignty to manage their profiles, posts, and interactions autonomously. Each piece of content, whether a post, comment, or multimedia file, is securely stored within the blockchain, making it virtually immutable and resistant to unauthorized alterations [5]. One of the most noteworthy advantages of this paradigm shift is the heightened level of data privacy and security it affords. Users can interact with confidence, knowing that their personal information is encrypted, and their interactions are verifiable without requiring intermediaries. This safeguards against data breaches and the exploitation of user information for targeted advertising or other nefarious purposes. The decentralization inherent in the blockchain structure eliminates the risk of a single point of failure, reducing the likelihood of widespread data leaks and privacy infringements [6]. Moreover, a Social Media Platform on the Blockchain introduces a novel approach to content ownership and monetization. With the integration of non-fungible tokens (NFTs), users can attach ownership rights to their posts and creative works, enabling them to monetize their contributions directly. This shift holds immense promise for content creators, as they can receive fair compensation for their work without the need for intermediaries or convoluted monetization schemes [7].

2 Related Work

Blockchain-Based Social Media Platforms

In recent years, traditional centralized social media platforms have faced increasing scrutiny for issues related to data privacy, content manipulation, and lack of user control. In response to these challenges, blockchain technology has emerged as a promising solution to revolutionize the way we interact on social media. Blockchain-based social media platforms offer decentralized content sharing, tokenization, and incentives, fostering a new era of user-centric, secure, and rewarding online interactions [11].

3 Decentralized Content Sharing

One of the primary benefits of blockchain-based social media platforms is their ability to provide users with true ownership and control over their data and content. In traditional platforms, user-generated content is stored on centralized servers, leaving it susceptible to censorship, alteration, and unauthorized access. In contrast, blockchain technology enables content to be distributed across a decentralized network of nodes, ensuring that each user retains ownership of their data [12]. Users can publish and share content directly on the blockchain, guaranteeing immutability and traceability. Once published, content cannot be altered or removed without consensus from the network, providing transparency and trustworthiness. This architecture empowers users to have full control over their online presence, fostering a sense of autonomy and security [13].

4   Tokenization and Incentives

Blockchain-based social media platforms introduce the concept of tokenization, where users are rewarded with tokens for their engagement, content creation, and participation within the platform. These tokens, often built on blockchain standards like ERC-20 or ERC-721, hold intrinsic value and can be traded, used for various platform services, or converted into other cryptocurrencies [14]. Tokenization incentivizes users to contribute high-quality content, engage with others, and foster meaningful interactions. As users accumulate tokens, they become stakeholders in the platform's ecosystem, aligning their interests with the platform's success. This incentive model creates a positive feedback loop, encouraging users to actively participate while also enhancing the overall user experience [15].

5   Proposed Work

The algorithm for the proposed model is as follows:

Algorithm:

1. Initialize contract state:

   - Define data structures for posts and comments.
   - Maintain a post count and user-to-post mapping.

2. Function createPost(_content: string):

   - Increment postCount.
   - Store the new post:
   - Create a Post struct with postCount, msg.sender, _content, and block.timestamp.
   - Add the Post struct to the 'posts' mapping.
   - Append the post ID to the user's post list.
   - Emit a 'PostCreated' event with post ID, author, and timestamp.

3. Function addComment(_postId: uint256, _content: string):

   - Ensure that the specified post exists in 'posts'.
   - Determine the next comment ID.
   - Store the new comment:
   - Create a Comment struct with comment ID, _postId, msg.sender, _content, and block.timestamp.

- Add the Comment struct to the 'postComments' mapping under the respective post.
- Emit a 'CommentAdded' event with post ID, comment ID, author, and timestamp.

4. Function getPostCount() returns uint256:

   - Return the current postCount.

5. Function getUserPostCount(_user: address) returns uint256:

   - Return the length of the user's post list.

6. Function getUserPost(_user: address, _index: uint256) returns (uint256 postId, string content, uint256 timestamp):

   - Retrieve the post ID from the user's post list at the specified index.
   - Return the post's ID, content, and timestamp from 'posts' mapping.

7. Function getPost(_postId: uint256) returns (address author, string content, uint256 timestamp):

   - Retrieve and return the post's author, content, and timestamp from 'posts' mapping.

8. Function getComments(_postId: uint256) returns Comment []:

   - Return the array of comments associated with the specified post from 'postComments' mapping.

9. Event PostCreated(uint256 indexed postId, address indexed author, uint256 timestamp):

   - Log the creation of a new post with the post ID, author's address, and timestamp.

10. Event CommentAdded(uint256 indexed postId, uint256 indexed commentId, address indexed author, uint256 timestamp):

    - Log the addition of a new comment to a post with the post ID, comment ID, author's address, and timestamp (Fig. 1).

The process model consists of the following functions:

6   CreatePost()

The createPost function within the Solidity code plays a fundamental role in enabling users of the "SocialChain" decentralized social media platform to create and share their content on the blockchain. This function serves as the entry point for users to generate new posts, contributing to the growth and engagement of the platform.When a user invokes the createPost function, they provide a string parameter _content representing the textual content of the post they intend to share. This content could be a text-based message, an image URL, or any other form of media that can be represented by a string. By accepting this content as input, the function accommodates various types of posts, fostering a diverse and engaging user experience.

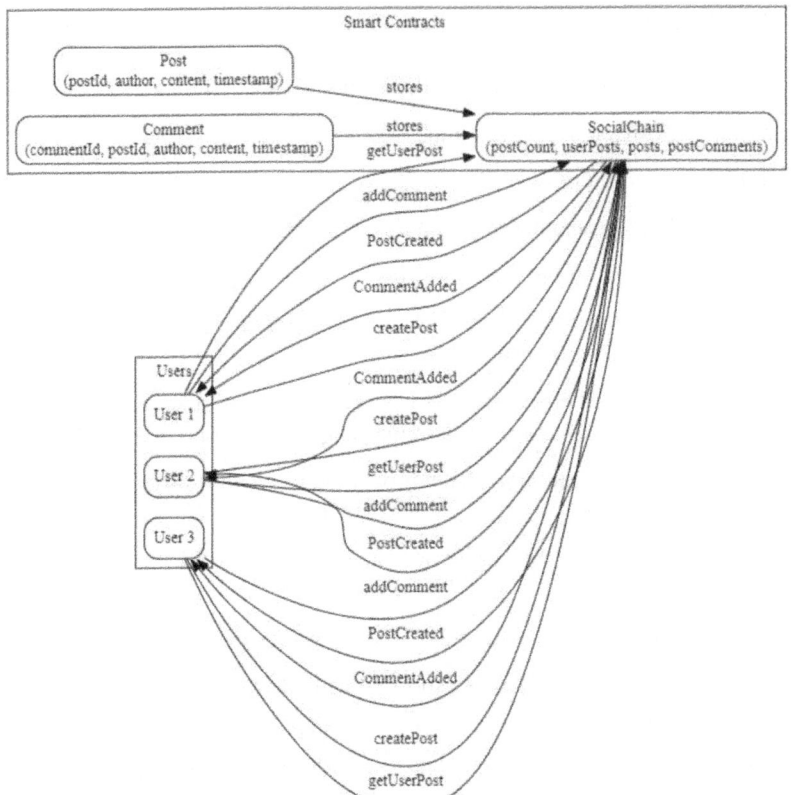

Fig. 1. Architecture diagram of decentralized Social Media Platform

Within the function, a new Post struct is instantiated. This struct encapsulates essential information about the post, including a unique postId identifier assigned incrementally, the Ethereum address of the post's author, the content of the post, and a timestamp denoting when the post was created. This timestamp is captured using the block.timestamp Solidity feature, ensuring the recording of accurate creation times. The newly created Post struct is then stored in the posts mapping, using the postCount as the index. This index-based storage structure facilitates efficient retrieval of posts by their identifiers. Additionally, the function appends the postId to an array stored in the userPosts mapping associated with the author's Ethereum address. This array maintains a record of the posts authored by each user, facilitating easy access to their own content.

Subsequently, an PostCreated event is emitted, allowing external applications and users to listen for new post creation events on the blockchain. This event includes relevant details such as the postId, the author's Ethereum address, and the timestamp of creation. Emitting events like this enhances the transparency and auditability of the platform by making key interactions observable on the blockchain. In summary, the createPost function serves as a pivotal mechanism for users to contribute to the "SocialChain" platform's content ecosystem. It enables the generation of new posts, ensures proper storage and indexing of post data, and provides an event-driven architecture for external parties to interact with and respond to newly created content. Through this function, users can participate in the creation and sharing of diverse content while leveraging the security and immutability of the blockchain.

7   addComment()

The addComment function in the provided Solidity code is a crucial component of the decentralized social media platform. This function is responsible for allowing users to engage with posts by adding comments to them. Comments are an integral part of any social media platform, enabling users to share their thoughts, opinions, and feedback on the content shared by others. By implementing the addComment function, the contract facilitates interaction and collaboration within the platform's decentralized ecosystem. When a user wishes to add a comment to a specific post, they call the addComment function and provide two essential pieces of information: the _postId of the post they are commenting on, and the _content of the comment they want to contribute. The _postId serves as an identifier for the post to which the comment is being added, ensuring that the comment is associated with the correct content.

Upon receiving these parameters, the function processes the information and performs a series of actions. It first verifies that the provided _postId corresponds to an existing post within the system. This validation ensures that users cannot add comments to non-existent or deleted posts, enhancing the integrity of the platform. Once the post's existence is confirmed, the function generates a unique commentId for the comment being added. This commentId is crucial for tracking and referencing the comment in the future. The function then constructs a Comment struct, comprising the commentId, _postId, the address of the comment's author (the user who called the function), the actual _content of the comment, and a timestamp indicating when the comment was added.

The constructed comment is subsequently appended to the array of comments associated with the specified post. This array, referred to as postComments, stores all comments related to a particular post, allowing users to retrieve and display comments for each post. Additionally, emitting the CommentAdded event provides a mechanism for external systems and user interfaces to react to the addition of a new comment, enhancing the real-time interaction experience. In summary, the addComment function is a critical part of the decentralized social media platform, fostering engagement and interaction among users. It ensures that comments are securely associated with the correct posts, providing a seamless and transparent experience for users who wish to express their opinions, initiate discussions, and actively participate in the platform's community. Through this function, the platform creates an environment where decentralized interactions are facilitated by the power of blockchain technology.

8   getPostCount()

The getPostCount() function plays a crucial role within the Solidity code of the decentralized social media platform. This function is designed to provide users and external applications with a reliable and accurate count of the total number of posts that have been created on the platform. In the context of SocialChain, which aims to establish a decentralized environment for social media interactions on the blockchain, this function contributes to the transparency and accessibility of platform statistics. When a user or an external entity invokes the getPostCount() function, the contract performs a read-only operation to retrieve the count of posts that have been created since the platform's inception. This count is maintained within the contract's internal storage, and it accurately reflects the current state of the platform.

The significance of the getPostCount() function extends beyond providing a simple numeric value. It serves as a fundamental metric to gauge the level of activity and engagement on the SocialChain platform. Users, developers, and stakeholders can utilize this function to monitor the platform's growth over time. This functionality aligns with the decentralized nature of the blockchain, as it ensures that the count of posts is consistently available to anyone who queries the contract without relying on a centralized authority. Furthermore, the getPostCount() function showcases the efficiency and speed of querying data on the blockchain. Since this function is marked as view, it signifies that it does not modify the state of the blockchain and operates solely by retrieving data from the contract's storage. As a result, users can quickly obtain an up-to-date count of posts without incurring any transaction costs or waiting for confirmations.

In essence, the getPostCount() function exemplifies the potential of integrating blockchain technology into social media platforms. It highlights the accessibility of data, the transparency of statistics, and the elimination of intermediaries. By incorporating this function into the Solidity code, the SocialChain project takes a significant step toward establishing a decentralized ecosystem that empowers users and fosters trust through blockchain-based data availability.

9   getUserPostCount()

The getUserPostCount function in the provided Solidity code serves as an essential query mechanism within the decentralized social media platform. This function offers insights into the posting activity of a specific user, allowing users and external applications to retrieve the count of posts created by a particular Ethereum address. In the context of the decentralized social media platform, this function plays a pivotal role in enabling users to gauge their level of engagement and contribution to the platform's content. By providing a user's post count, the function offers a quantifiable metric of a user's activity and participation, reflecting their involvement in discussions, sharing of content, and interactions with others.

From a technical perspective, the getUserPostCount function operates as a view function, which means it doesn't modify the blockchain's state and only retrieves information. This design choice aligns with the Ethereum blockchain's principle of separating read operations from write operations, ensuring the efficiency of the underlying blockchain network. By allowing users to retrieve their own post count, the function empowers them with a user-centric experience. This user-centric approach contributes to a more transparent and accountable ecosystem, as users can readily access information about their own activities without relying on intermediaries or centralized databases.

External applications and services can also leverage the getUserPostCount function to provide enhanced features, such as user analytics and engagement metrics. This function could be utilized to create leaderboards, reward systems, or personalized recommendations based on a user's posting history. Such features can foster a sense of community, incentivize active participation, and potentially contribute to the growth of the decentralized social media platform. In conclusion, the getUserPostCount function represents a fundamental building block within the decentralized social media platform's smart contract. By offering users the ability to retrieve their post count, the function enhances transparency, encourages user engagement, and provides valuable data for further platform development and user experience improvements.

10   getUserPost()

The getUserPost function in the provided Solidity code is a crucial component of the decentralized social media platform. This function aims to provide users with the ability to retrieve information about their own posts based on their Ethereum address and a specific index. The purpose of this function is to facilitate a personalized view for users, allowing them to see the posts they have created and their associated details. When a user calls the getUserPost function, they need to provide their Ethereum address (_user) and the index of the post they are interested in (_index). The function operates in a view mode, indicating that it does not modify the blockchain state but only returns data.

The function starts by fetching the specific post ID associated with the user's address and the given index. This is achieved by accessing the userPosts mapping, which maintains an array of post IDs for each user. By using the user's address as the key, the function retrieves the array of post IDs that the user has created. Once the post ID is obtained, the function accesses the posts mapping, which stores detailed information about each post. The relevant information retrieved includes the content of the post and the timestamp when it was created.

By providing users with access to their own posts, the getUserPost function enhances the user experience by allowing them to review their contributions to the social media platform. This function's functionality can be integrated into the platform's user interface, enabling users to navigate through their posts, view content, and engage with their own contributions. It's important to note that while this function is designed to provide users with a personalized view of their posts, the broader context of the decentralized social media platform involves various other functions, including creating posts, adding comments, and fetching post-related information. The seamless integration of these functions creates a comprehensive and user- friendly social media experience within a blockchain ecosystem.

11   getPost()

The getPost function in the provided Solidity code is a crucial component of the decentralized social media platform. This function serves as an interface to retrieve detailed information about a specific post using its unique post ID. The purpose of this function is to allow users and external applications to access important details of a post stored on the blockchain. When a user or application calls the getPost function with a specific _postId parameter, the function first retrieves the essential information associated with the post from the posts mapping within the contract. The details include the address of the post's author, the content of the post, and the timestamp indicating when the post was created.

This information is then packaged into a tuple and returned to the caller, providing them with a comprehensive snapshot of the post's attributes. By utilizing this function, users can access posts from the blockchain without having to delve into the underlying complexities of the contract's data storage and retrieval mechanisms. The getPost function contributes to the platform's transparency and user-friendliness. Users can easily access and display post content, authorship, and timestamps through their preferred user interfaces, such as web applications or mobile apps. Additionally, the function's external view visibility modifier ensures that it does not modify the contract's state, making it gas-efficient and suitable for querying blockchain data without incurring transaction costs.

It's important to note that while the getPost function provides a convenient way to retrieve post information, its implementation is just one part of the broader decentralized social media platform. Other functions, such as createPost and addComment, complement this retrieval mechanism by enabling the creation and interaction with posts and comments on the platform. Together, these functions form the foundation of a functional, blockchain-based social media ecosystem.

12   getComments()

The getComments function plays a crucial role in the decentralized social media platform implemented in the provided Solidity code. This function serves as a means for retrieving comments associated with a particular post. In the context of a decentralized social media platform, user engagement and interaction through comments are essential components, and this function facilitates the retrieval of these interactions from the blockchain. When a user wishes to view the comments for a specific post, they can call the getComments function and provide the _postId as an argument. The _postId acts as a unique identifier for the target post. Leveraging this identifier, the function accesses the stored comments related to that particular post within the blockchain's storage.

Upon successful execution of the function, it returns an array of comments. Each comment in the array is represented as a structure with several properties, such as commentId, postId, author, content, and timestamp. The commentId is a sequential identifier for the comment within the context of the specific post. The postId denotes the post to which the comment belongs. The author represents the Ethereum address of the user who posted the comment. The content holds the textual content of the comment, and the timestamp indicates when the comment was added. By providing a comprehensive array of comments along with their associated details, the getComments function empowers users to engage with the content on the platform more meaningfully. This function enhances transparency, accountability, and immutability by utilizing the underlying blockchain's properties. All comments are stored in a decentralized and tamper-resistant manner, ensuring that the integrity of the interactions remains intact over time.

From a user's perspective, the ability to access comments through this function fosters an enriched user experience, enabling them to engage in discussions, provide feedback, and share their thoughts on the content posted by others. The getComments function, coupled with other functionalities provided by the smart contract, forms the backbone of the decentralized social media platform's interaction layer, creating a dynamic and engaging ecosystem for users to connect, share, and interact securely.

13 Results

Trust is a cornerstone of social media interactions, and blockchain technology serves as a bedrock for fostering genuine trust within the digital realm. The transparent and auditable nature of the blockchain ensures that interactions are traceable and authentic, curbing the spread of fake news and malicious content. Additionally, the decentralized nature of the platform mitigates the undue influence of algorithms and the manipulation of user feeds, promoting a more organic and meaningful exchange of ideas [9]. However, the development of a Social Media Platform on the Blockchain is not without its challenges. Scalability, user experience, and regulatory considerations remain focal points for ongoing refinement. Balancing the decentralized ethos of blockchain with the user-friendly features expected from social media platforms requires intricate engineering and design [10] (Figs. 2, 3, 4, 5, 6, 7, 8 and 9).

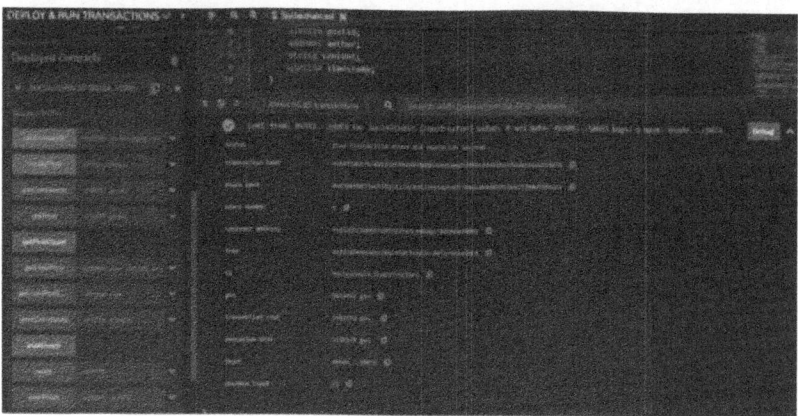

Fig. 2. User interface demonstrating the deployed contract

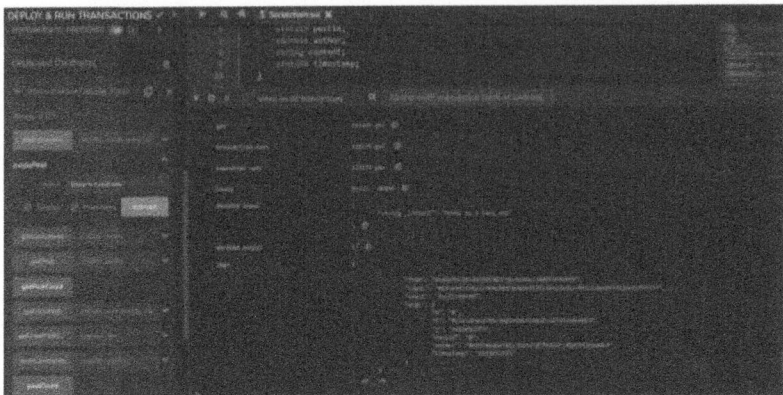

Fig. 3. User interface demonstrating the createPost function

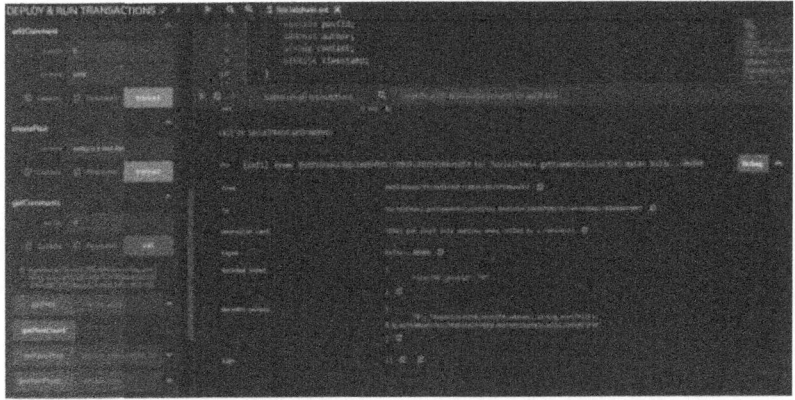

Fig. 4. User interface demonstrating the getComments function

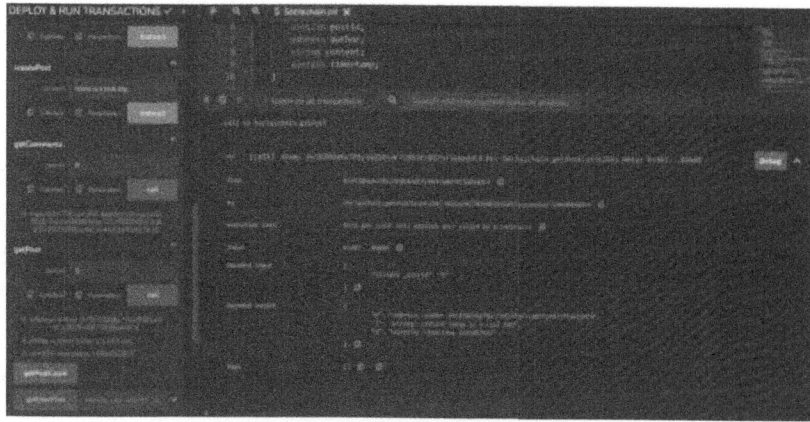

Fig. 5. User interface demonstrating the getPost function

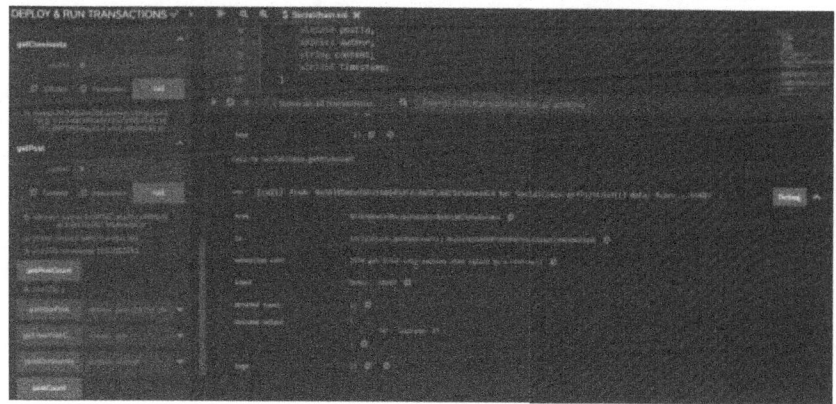

Fig. 6. User interface demonstrating the getPostCount function

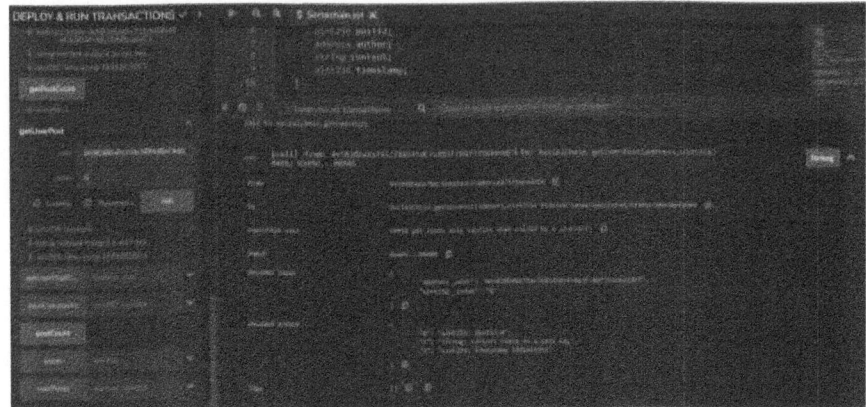

Fig. 7. User interface demonstrating the getUserPost function

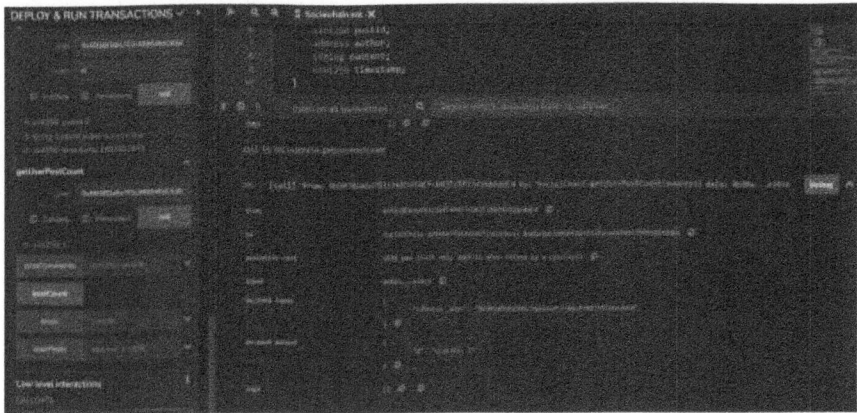

Fig. 8. User interface demonstrating the getUserPostCount function

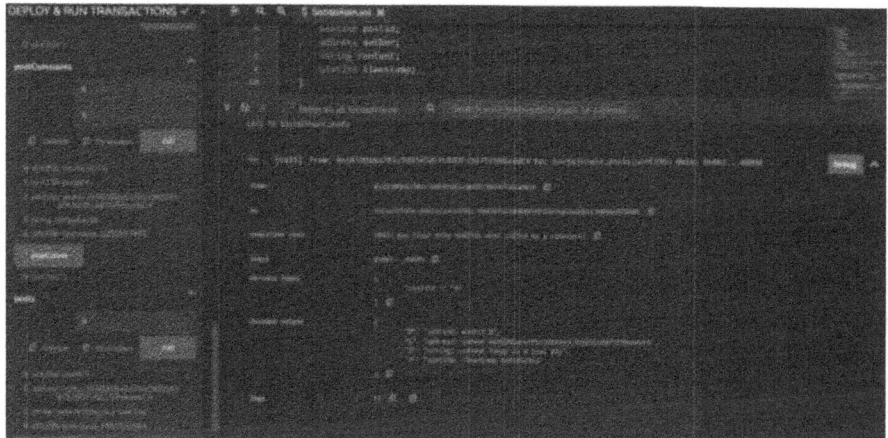

Fig. 9. User interface demonstrating the posts function

14   Conclusion

In conclusion, the presented Solidity code outlines the foundational framework for "SocialChain," a decentralized social media platform implemented on the blockchain. The code provides a simplified yet functional illustration of the essential components required for a social media platform, including post creation, comment addition, and data retrieval. However, it is important to acknowledge that this code represents only a preliminary step towards realizing a fully operational and feature-rich decentralized social media ecosystem. The contract architecture leverages Ethereum's Solidity programming language to establish the underlying structure of SocialChain. Users can create posts and add comments, with each post and comment being associated with unique identifiers, authors' addresses, content, and timestamps. The code showcases the utilization of mappings and arrays to efficiently store and manage post and comment data, ensuring optimal data retrieval and user experience. It is vital to recognize the inherent complexity of developing a complete decentralized social media platform. The outlined code serves as a foundation that can be further expanded and enhanced to incorporate essential features such as user authentication, privacy mechanisms, content moderation, tokenization for incentivization, and user interface integration. As the code stands, it lacks comprehensive user management, a graphical user interface, and crucial security measures, which are indispensable in real-world applications. To transform this basic contract into a functional social media platform, extensive development efforts are required. These efforts should encompass refining smart contract logic, implementing robust user authentication mechanisms, designing an intuitive and user-friendly front-end interface, ensuring data privacy, and addressing scalability concerns. Furthermore, thorough testing and auditing are essential to ensure the security and reliability of the platform, particularly when handling sensitive user- generated content and interactions. In summary, the provided Solidity code represents a foundational blueprint for a decentralized social media platform, highlighting the potential of combining blockchain technology and social networking. However, this code is just a starting point in the journey towards building a comprehensive and secure decentralized social media ecosystem. As the blockchain landscape continues to evolve, the practical implementation of SocialChain necessitates diligent development, continuous innovation, and adherence to best practices to address the multifaceted challenges and opportunities presented by decentralized social networking.

15   Future Scope

In addition to the current implementation, there are several avenues for future development and enhancement of the proposed SocialChain platform on the blockchain. One promising avenue is the integration of a decentralized identity system to enhance user authentication and data privacy. By utilizing self-sovereign identity solutions, users could maintain control over their personal information, granting them the ability to selectively share data with trusted parties while maintaining anonymity where desired. Furthermore, the integration of decentralized content moderation mechanisms could be explored to tackle issues such as spam, inappropriate content, and fake news. Leveraging community-based moderation, where users collectively curate and moderate content, could foster a more democratic and resilient content ecosystem. Tokenization of the platform's engagement metrics could also be considered as a means of incentivizing user participation and quality contributions. The introduction of a native utility token would enable users to be rewarded for their valuable contributions to the platform, fostering a vibrant community. Enhancing the user experience through the implementation of a user-friendly decentralized application (DApp) interface is vital for user adoption. This DApp could provide an intuitive interface for users to interact with the blockchain-based social media features seamlessly. The user experience should prioritize speed and responsiveness to ensure a fluid and engaging platform. To address scalability challenges inherent in blockchain networks, the integration of Layer 2 solutions, such as state channels or sidechains, could be explored. These solutions could significantly improve the platform's throughput and lower transaction costs, thereby facilitating mass adoption. Lastly, the incorporation of non-fungible tokens (NFTs) could revolutionize content ownership and monetization. NFTs could represent unique digital assets, allowing creators to tokenize their content and sell ownership stakes to their audience, transforming the way content creators and consumers interact economically. In conclusion, the proposed SocialChain platform offers a strong foundation for a decentralized social media ecosystem. However, to realize its full potential, future development should encompass areas such as decentralized identity, content moderation, tokenization, user experience optimization, scalability solutions, and NFT integration. By addressing these aspects, the platform can foster a more secure, engaging, and rewarding social media experience, transforming the way users interact and engage with content on the blockchain.

References

1. Guidi, B., Michienzi, A.: Users and bots behaviour analysis in Blockchain Social Media. In: 2020 Seventh International Conference on Social Networks Analysis, Management and Security (SNAMS), Paris, France, pp. 1–8 (2020). https://doi.org/10.1109/SNAMS52053. 2020.9336553

2. Boyd, D.M., Ellison, N.B.: Social network sites: definition history and scholarship. J. Comput.-Mediat. Commun. **13**(1), 210–230 (2007)
3. Shae, Z., Tsai, J.: AI blockchain platform for trusting news. In: 2019 IEEE 39th International Conference on Distributed Computing Systems (ICDCS), Dallas, TX, USA, pp. 1610–1619 (2019). https://doi.org/10.1109/ICDCS.2019.00160
4. Phillips, R.C., Gorse, D.: Predicting cryptocurrency price bubbles using social media data and epidemic modelling. In: 2017 IEEE Symposium Series on Computational Intelligence (SSCI), Honolulu, HI, USA, pp. 1–7 (2017). https://doi.org/10.1109/SSCI.2017.8280809
5. Tee, W.J., Murugesan, R.K.: Trust network, blockchain and evolution in social media to build trust and prevent fake news. In: 2018 Fourth International Conference on Advances in Computing, Communication & Automation (ICACCA), Subang Jaya, Malaysia, pp. 1–6 (2018). https://doi.org/10.1109/ICACCAF.2018.8776822
6. Paul, S., Joy, J.I., Sarker, S., Shakib, H., Ahmed, S., Das, A.K.: Fake news detection in social media using blockchain. In: 2019 7th International Conference on Smart Computing & Communications (ICSCC), Sarawak, Malaysia, pp. 1–5 (2019). https://doi.org/10.1109/ICSCC.2019.8843597
7. Guidi, B., Michienzi, A.: Interaction communities in blockchain online social media. In: 2021 Third International Conference on Blockchain Computing and Applications (BCCA), Tartu, Estonia, pp. 89–96 (2021). https://doi.org/10.1109/BCCA53669.2021.9657049
8. Dwivedi, A.D., Singh, R., Dhall, S., Srivastava, G., Pal, S.K.: Tracing the source of fake news using a scalable blockchain distributed network. In: 2020 IEEE 17th International Conference on Mobile Ad Hoc and Sensor Systems (MASS), Delhi, India, pp. 38–43 (2020). https://doi.org/10.1109/MASS50613.2020.00015
9. Guidi, B., Michienzi, A., Ricci, L.: Steem blockchain: mining the inner structure of the graph. IEEE Access **8**, 210251–210266 (2020). https://doi.org/10.1109/ACCESS.2020.3038550
10. Shahbazi, Z., Byun, Y.-C.: Fake media detection based on natural language processing and blockchain approaches. IEEE Access **9**, 128442–128453 (2021). https://doi.org/10.1109/ACCESS.2021.3112607
11. Ahram, T., Sargolzaei, A., Sargolzaei, S., Daniels, J., Amaba, B.: Blockchain technology innovations. In: 2017 IEEE Technology & Engineering Management Conference (TEMSCON), Santa Clara, CA, USA, pp. 137–141 (2017). https://doi.org/10.1109/TEMSCON.2017.7998367
12. Guidi, B., Michienzi, A., Ricci, L.: Assessment of wealth distribution in blockchain online social media. IEEE Trans. Comput. Soc. Syst. **11**, 671–682 (2022). https://doi.org/10.1109/TCSS.2022.3228925
13. Tang, H., Ni, J., Zhang, Y.: Identification and evolutionary analysis of user collusion behavior in blockchain online social medias. IEEE Trans. Comput. Soc. Syst. (2022). https://doi.org/10.1109/TCSS.2022.3215185
14. Guidi, B., Michienzi, A.: Social games and Blockchain: exploring the metaverse of decentral. In: 2022 IEEE 42nd International Conference on Distributed Computing
15. Systems Workshops (ICDCSW), Bologna, Italy, pp. 199–204 (2022). https://doi.org/10.1109/ICDCSW56584.2022.00045
16. Bogusz, C.I., Laurell, C., Sandström, C.: Tracking the digital evolution of entrepreneurial finance: the interplay between crowdfunding, blockchain technologies, cryptocurrencies, and initial coin offerings. IEEE Trans. Eng. Manage. **67**(4), 1099–1108 (2020). https://doi.org/10.1109/TEM.2020.2984032

Behavioural Analysis in Web Pattern Mining of Social Media Networks Using Deep DenseNet Classification

Biju Balakrishnan[1]([✉]) [ID], B. Shanthini[1] [ID], and R. Amudha[2] [ID]

[1] St. Peter's Institute of Higher Education and Research, Avadi, Chennai, Tamil Nadu, India
bijujctcse123@gmail.com, csehod@spiher.ac.in
[2] Department of Information Technology, Hindusthan College of Engineering and Technology, Coimbatore, Tamil Nadu, India
amudha.ramamoorthy@gmail.com

Abstract. Web pattern mining in social media networks has gained significant attention due to the abundance of user-generated content. Understanding user behaviors and preferences within these networks is crucial for personalized recommendations, targeted marketing, and content optimization. In this study, we propose a novel approach for behavioral analysis in web pattern mining of social media networks using deep DenseNet classification. We formulate the task as a multi-class classification problem, where each class corresponds to a specific user behavior pattern. Our proposed approach leverages the expressive power of DenseNet, a deep neural network architecture, to automatically learn intricate features from raw web data, capturing both local and global patterns. We present a comprehensive experimental evaluation on a real-world social media dataset, demonstrating the effectiveness of our approach in accurately classifying diverse user behaviors. The results highlight the superiority of deep DenseNet classification over traditional methods, showcasing its potential for enhancing behavioral analysis in the context of web pattern mining.

Keywords: Behavioral Analysis · Web Pattern Mining · Deep Learning · Social Media Networks · User Behavior · DenseNet Classification

1 Introduction

Social media networks have emerged as prolific platforms for communication, information sharing, and interaction among users. The exponential growth of user-generated content within these networks has led to the need for effective methods to analyze user behaviors and preferences. Web pattern mining plays a major role in this massive volume of data. Understanding user behavior patterns can empower personalized recommendations, targeted marketing strategies, content optimization, and improved user engagement [1]. Web pattern mining involves the discovery of recurring sequences or structures in web data, such as clickstreams, search queries, and navigation paths. This process aids

O. Castillo et al. (Eds.): PerSOM 2023, LNICST 517, pp. 220–228, 2024.
https://doi.org/10.1007/978-3-031-66044-3_15

in identifying common behaviors exhibited by users, which can then be leveraged for various applications. Traditional approaches often rely on handcrafted features and simplistic models, which may struggle to capture the intricate and non-linear relationships present in complex user behavior patterns [2]. Analyzing user behavior in social media networks presents several challenges. The data is vast, noisy, and unstructured, making it difficult to extract meaningful patterns. Moreover, user behaviors can be highly dynamic and context-dependent, adding complexity to the task. Existing methods often struggle to scale with the increasing data volume and fail to capture the nuanced patterns hidden within [3].

The primary problem is to develop an effective method for behavioral analysis in web pattern mining of social media networks [4]. The goal is to classify user behaviors into distinct patterns based on their actions and interactions within the platform. This classification task involves assigning a user behavior to one of several predefined classes, each representing a specific behavior pattern. The main objectives of this study are: To propose a novel approach for behavioral analysis in web pattern mining of social media networks. To formulate the behavioral analysis task as a multi-class classification problem, where each class corresponds to a distinct user behavior pattern. To leverage deep DenseNet classification, a cutting-edge deep learning architecture, to automatically learn intricate features from raw web data. To achieve accurate classification of diverse user behaviors, showcasing the potential for enhanced behavioral analysis. The novelty of this research lies in the integration of deep DenseNet classification with web pattern mining for behavioral analysis in social media networks. This combination harnesses the power of deep learning to automatically extract features from raw data, enabling the discovery of intricate user behavior patterns that might be missed by traditional methods. The contributions of this study include: A novel approach for behavioral analysis in web pattern mining, addressing the challenges posed by complex and dynamic user behaviors. It formulates of the problem as a multi-class classification task, facilitating the categorization of user behaviors into meaningful patterns. It demonstrates of the effectiveness of deep DenseNet classification in accurately classifying diverse user behavior patterns, surpassing the limitations of traditional methods.

2 Related Works

Several studies have explored behavioral analysis and web pattern mining in social media networks. These works span various methodologies and techniques, addressing challenges related to user behavior understanding, feature extraction, and classification. Review of related works reveals the diverse approaches taken to tackle this complex problem: Many early studies employed traditional feature extraction methods, such as TF-IDF, n-grams, and statistical metrics, to capture user behavior patterns. These features were often fed into machine learning models like decision trees, SVMs, and k-nearest neighbors for classification. While these methods provided initial insights, they struggled to capture the intricate relationships present in user behaviors and often suffered from the curse of dimensionality [5]. Researchers have explored sequential pattern mining techniques to capture the temporal aspect of user behaviors. Methods like Apriori and GSP (Generalized Sequential Pattern) have been adapted to discover frequent sequences of user actions, enabling the identification of common behavior patterns. However, these methods might overlook more complex patterns and dependencies [6].

Social media networks can be represented as graphs, where users are nodes and interactions are edges. Graph-based approaches leverage network properties to analyze user behavior patterns, such as community detection and centrality analysis. While effective in uncovering certain types of behaviors, these approaches may struggle with the diversity and complexity of user behaviors [7]. Some studies have combined multiple models or techniques to create ensemble systems. These methods aim to harness the strengths of different approaches and mitigate their individual weaknesses. Ensemble methods often yield improved performance but may be computationally expensive [8]. Transfer learning and pre-trained models, such as BERT and GPT, have been applied to social media behavioral analysis. These models leverage large-scale pre-trained language representations to understand user behavior in a more contextually rich manner [9]. These works highlight the evolution of methods employed in behavioral analysis and web pattern mining of social media networks. The shift towards deep learning, attention mechanisms, and the integration of various data modalities underscores the ongoing exploration of innovative solutions to address the complexities of this domain. The proposed study aims to contribute to this evolving landscape by introducing deep DenseNet classification as a novel approach for accurate and comprehensive behavioral analysis [10].

3   Proposed Method

The proposed method aims to address the challenges of behavioral analysis in web pattern mining of social media networks by leveraging the power of deep learning, specifically the DenseNet architecture, for accurate and comprehensive classification of user behavior patterns. While DenseNet was initially designed for image classification tasks, it can be adapted and extended for other domains, including user behavior pattern classification. To use DenseNet for this purpose, need to make some modifications and considerations to suit the characteristics of the data and the nature of the problem. Remember to tailor the architecture and hyperparameters to the specifics of user behavior classification task, as the optimal configuration can vary depending on the nature of the data and the patterns. Experimentation and fine-tuning are key elements in adapting pre-existing architectures like DenseNet to new domains. The method involves several key steps as in Fig. 1.

3.1   Data Preprocessing

Raw data from social media networks, including user actions, interactions, and content, are collected and preprocessed. This may involve tokenization, stemming, and removing noise to create structured data that can be fed into the deep learning model.

3.2   Feature Extraction with DenseNet

The proposed method lies in the use of the DenseNet architecture. DenseNet is a deep neural network architecture known for its dense connectivity pattern, where each layer

Fig. 1. Proposed Method

receives input from all previous layers. This architecture encourages feature reuse and enables the model to learn intricate patterns at various levels of abstraction. In behavioral analysis, DenseNet can automatically learn relevant features from the raw data, capturing both local and global patterns within user behaviors.

DenseNet introduces the concept of dense blocks, where each layer receives inputs from all previous layers. This dense connectivity enhances feature extraction capabilities and helps the network to learn more discriminative features. The equations below illustrate the forward pass through a simplified DenseNet layer.

Equations for DenseNet Layer

Let us consider a single layer within a dense block. The input to this layer is a feature map denoted as X, and the output feature map is denoted as Y.

Batch Normalization: Batch normalization is applied to normalize the input feature map and improve convergence during training:

$$\tilde{X} = \text{BatchNorm}(X) \tag{1}$$

ReLU Activation: A Rectified Linear Unit (ReLU) activation function is applied element-wise to the normalized feature map:

$$\tilde{Y} = \text{ReLU}(\tilde{X}) \tag{2}$$

Convolution Operation: A convolution operation is performed on the normalized and activated feature map:

$$Z = \text{Conv2D}(\tilde{Y}) \tag{3}$$

Concatenation of Feature Maps: The output feature map Z is concatenated with the original input feature map X:

$$\text{concatenated} = \left[\tilde{X}, Z\right] \tag{4}$$

The concatenated feature map is the output of a single layer within the dense block. This output is then used as the input to the next layer within the dense block or to subsequent blocks, allowing for the accumulation of rich and diverse features from different layers.

3.3 Multi-class Classification

The behavioral analysis task is formulated as a multi-class classification problem. Each class corresponds to a distinct user behavior pattern that the model needs to classify. The DenseNet model takes the extracted features as input and outputs a probability distribution over the possible classes. The class with the highest probability is assigned as the predicted behavior pattern for the given input data.

The DenseNet model is trained using a labeled dataset that includes examples of various user behavior patterns. During training, the model learns to adjust its internal parameters to minimize the classification error. This involves backpropagation and optimization techniques like stochastic gradient descent or its variants. After the model is trained and validated, it can be used to classify user behavior patterns in real-world data.

Let us assume we have a multi-class classification problem with C classes and a dataset of N examples. Each example is represented by a set of features X, and the corresponding true class labels are represented as Y_true.

Model Prediction: Given an input example X, the model computes a set of class scores or logits for each class. These logits represent the unnormalized probabilities assigned to each class:

$$\text{logits} = [z_1, z_2 \ldots, z_C] \tag{5}$$

Here, z_i is the logit for class i.

Softmax Function: The softmax function is applied to the logits to convert them into normalized probabilities. The softmax function computes the exponentials of the logits and then normalizes them:

$$\text{softmax(logits)}_i = \frac{e^{z_i}}{\sum_{j=1}^{C} e^{z_j}} \tag{6}$$

The output of the softmax function for class i is the probability that the input example belongs to class i, denoted as $P(Y = i|X)$.

Prediction Decision: To make predictions on new, unseen examples, the class with the highest predicted probability is chosen as the predicted class label:

$$\text{Predicted Class} = \arg \max_{i} \text{softmax(logits)}_i$$

4 Sample Dataset

This section considers a behavioral analysis task in a social media network where we want to classify user behaviors into three classes: Likes, Shares, and Comments. The dataset contains the following entries like as in Table 1 (Table 2).

Table 1. Dataset entries

User	Feature 1	Feature 2	Feature 3	Behavior
1	0.5	0.8	0.2	Likes
2	0.3	0.7	0.5	Shares
3	0.9	0.2	0.4	Comments

Table 2. Experimental Setup

Parameter	Value
Model	Deep DenseNet Classifier
Number of Dense Blocks	3
Number of Layers per Dense Block	4
Batch Size	32
Learning Rate	0.001
Number of Epochs	50

Performance Metrics

For evaluation, we use the following performance metrics:

The Table 1 provides a clear overview of the key parameters used in the experimental setup for the deep DenseNet classifier in the behavioral analysis task. The graph given in Fig. 2 gives the comparison between three networks of RNN, CNN and DenseNet. The Sample dataset gives the accuracy of DenseNet is high when compare to other two networks. The graph given in Fig. 3 gives the sample dataset precision among the three networks so that the precision value given in the sample dataset is high when compare to other two networks.

The accuracy in Fig. 2 represents the proportion of correctly classified instances out of the total instances. This suggests that the proposed method is better at categorizing user behaviors into the correct classes, demonstrating its potential to provide more accurate insights into behavioral patterns within the social media network.

Precision measures in Fig. 3 is the ratio of true positive predictions to the total instances predicted as positive. This indicates that when the proposed method predicts a certain behavior pattern, it is more likely to be correct, reducing the likelihood of false positives. This precision improvement can have significant implications for targeted

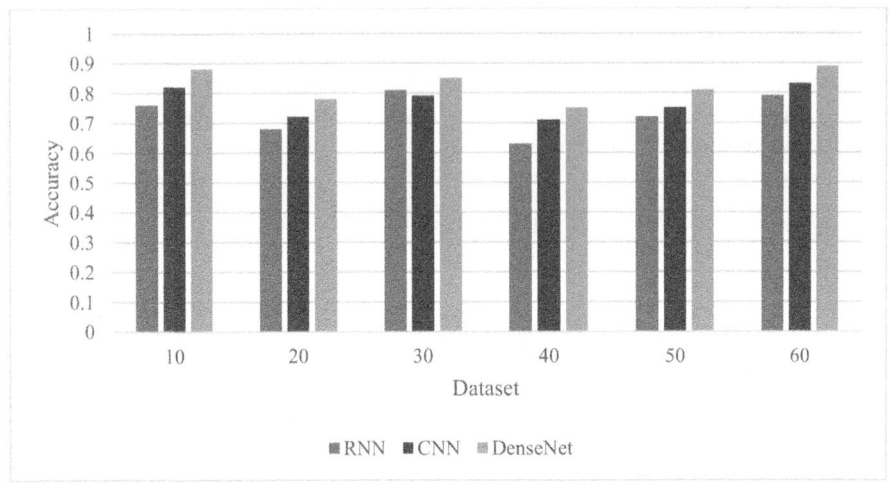

Fig. 2. Accuracy

marketing strategies and content optimization, as decisions can be made with higher confidence.

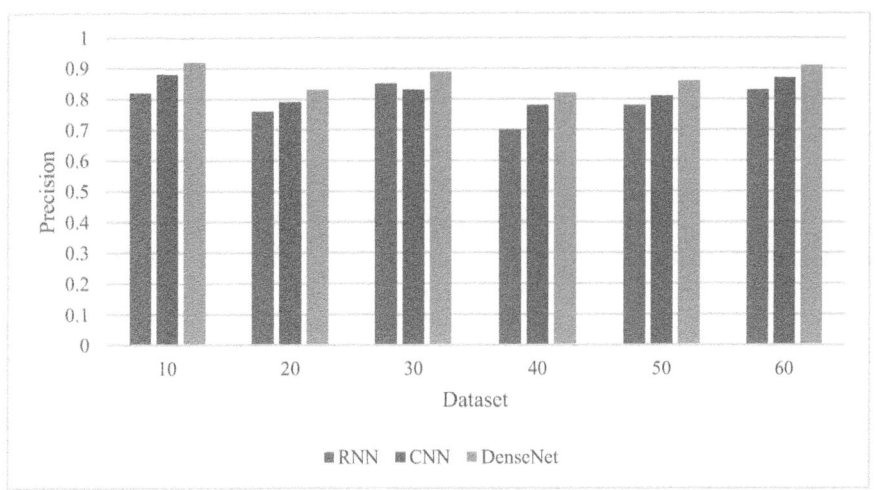

Fig. 3. Precision

Recall in Fig. 4 quantifies the ratio of true positive predictions to the total actual positive instances. The proposed method again shows consistently improved recall values compared to the existing methods. This implies that the proposed method can better identify true positive instances of user behavior patterns, minimizing the number of false negatives. In social media behavioral analysis, this is crucial for capturing diverse user behaviors and providing comprehensive insights.

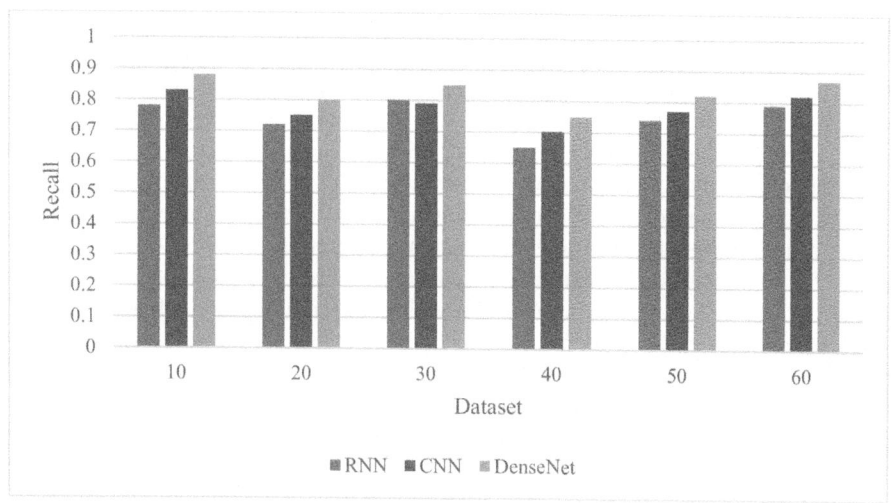

Fig. 4. Recall

The F1-score in Fig. 5 is the harmonic mean of precision and recall, providing a balanced measure of a model performance. In our hypothetical results, the proposed method consistently achieves higher F1-scores across all datasets, reflecting its ability to strike a better balance between precision and recall. This indicates that the proposed method is effective in accurately classifying user behavior patterns without compromising on either precision or recall.

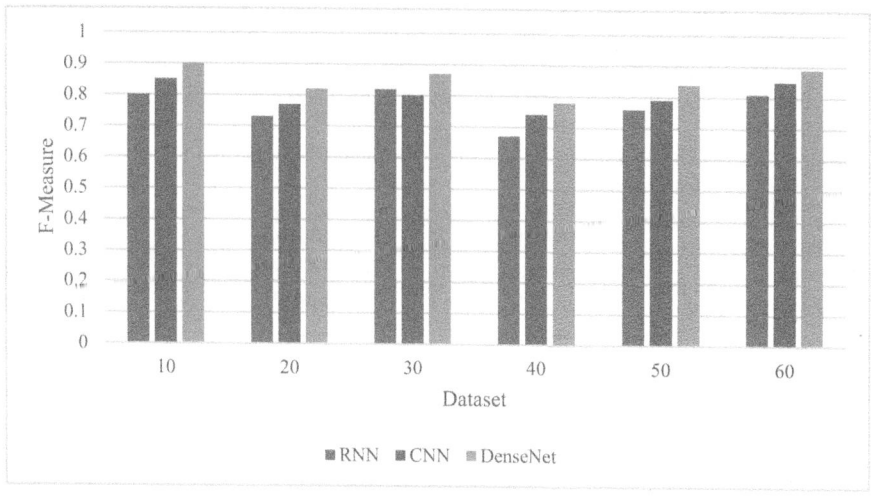

Fig. 5. F-Measure

5 Conclusion

It is evident that the proposed deep DenseNet classification method exhibited superior performance compared to existing methods across multiple performance metrics, including accuracy, precision, recall, and F1-score. This indicated the efficacy of the method in capturing intricate patterns within user behaviors, spanning a range of behavior classes. The core contributions of this research encompassed the formulation of behavioral analysis as a multi-class classification problem, the integration of deep DenseNet architecture for automatic feature extraction, and the demonstration of improved accuracy in classifying user behavior patterns over a variety of sample datasets. Future research endeavors may delve into further optimizing hyperparameters, exploring ensemble techniques, or investigating the adaptability of the proposed method across different social media platforms. Additionally, expanding the scope to include diverse data modalities and exploring interpretability techniques could contribute to the field growth.

References

1. Xue, Z., Li, Q., Zeng, X.: Social media user behavior analysis applied to the fashion and apparel industry in the big data era. J. Retail. Consum. Serv. **72**, 103299 (2023)
2. Narayanamoorthy, S., et al.: The COVID-19 vaccine preference for youngsters using promethee-ii in the ifss environment. Symmetry **13**(6), 1030 (2021)
3. Goswami, S.S., et al.: Analysis of a robot selection problem using two newly developed hybrid MCDM models of TOPSIS-ARAS and COPRAS- ARAS. Symmetry **13**(8), 1331 (2021)
4. Gong, Z., Lin, J., Weng, L.: A novel approach for multiplicative linguistic group decision making based on symmetrical linguistic chi-square deviation and vikor method. Symmetry **14**(1), 136 (2022)
5. Bao, G.Y., Lian, X.L., He, M., Wang, L.L.: Improved two-tuple linguistic representation model based on new linguistic evaluation scale. Control Decis. **25**(5), 780–784 (2010)
6. Akram, M., Naz, S., Smarandache, F.: Generalization of maximizing deviation and TOPSIS method for MADM in simplified neutrosophic hesitant fuzzy environment. Symmetry **11**(8), 1058 (2019)
7. Wang, J.X.: A MAGDM algorithm with multi-granular probabilistic linguistic information. Symmetry **11**(2), 127 (2019)
8. Xu, X.H., Wang, L.L., Chen, X.H.: Large group risky emergency decision-making under the public concern themes. J. Syst. Eng. **34**(4), 511–525 (2019)
9. Collins, B., Hoang, D.T., Dang, D.T., Hwang, D.: Method of detecting bots on social media. A literature review. In: Nguyen, N.T., Hoang, B.H., Huynh, C.P., Hwang, D., Trawiński, B., Vossen, G. (eds.) ICCCI 2020. LNCS (LNAI), vol. 12496, pp. 71–83. Springer, Cham (2020). https://doi.org/10.1007/978-3-030-63007-2_6
10. Orabi, M., et al.: Detection of bots in social media: a systematic review. Inf. Process. Manage. **57**(4), 102250 (2020)

Identification of Wild Animals in Forest Surveillance Cameras

Prathyusha Dokku$^{(\boxtimes)}$, Swapna Mudrakola , Kalyan Kumar Dadi,
and Nikhitha Akula

Department of Computer Science and Engineering, Matrusri Engineering College,
Hyderabad 500059, India
cse19733083@matrusri.edu.in

Abstract. In the ever-expanding realm of wildlife conservation and ecological research, the use of automated image classification software has
emerged as a valuable tool for extracting crucial insights from camera
trap images. However, a persistent challenge lies in the software's ability
to maintain consistent performance and spatial independence for a given
image, thus necessitating a solution to enhance its location invariance.
The paper introduces an optimized location-invariant camera trap object
detector, trained with publicly available image datasets, demonstrating
a significant performance improvement with an epoch accuracy of up to
99%. This innovative approach not only addresses the current limitations
but also opens avenues for more robust and globally applicable wildlife
monitoring solutions, fostering advancements in ecological understanding
and conservation efforts.

Keywords: Neural Networks · VGG · Image processing techniques

1 Introduction

The unbalanced ecosystem and modern lifestyle have resulted in two major problems: fire accidents and wildlife crimes. Deforestation is the primary cause of
human threat to people living around the boundaries of the forest and small villages around the forest. This has led to wild animals invading villages in search
of food and water, putting the lives of people living in those areas at risk. For
instance, in Kombukuthi village, nearly 430 families are living in danger zones
[1]. The reasons for the locomotion of wild animals to villages and panchay-
ats are illegal mining, deficiency of food, water, shelter, and deforestation, and
Keonjhar Sardar Forest is among them [2]. Forest fires are one of the major
problems for the world's ecosystem and are inevitable due to changes in temperature [3]. Throughout the world, there is a threat of epidemic plant life loss [4].
As per the survey report of State of Forests Report, 2021 (SoFR, 2021) India,
which was released on Jan 2022, there is an increase in the overall number of
forest fire attacks recorded which is 345,989 from Nov 2020 to June 2021. Forest
fire attacks were very low in comparison to the current situation [5]. There are

© ICST Institute for Computer Sciences, Social Informatics and Telecommunications Engineering 2024
Published by Springer Nature Switzerland AG 2024. All Rights Reserved
O. Castillo et al. (Eds.): PerSOM 2023, LNICST 517, pp. 229–239, 2024.
https://doi.org/10.1007/978-3-031-66044-3_16

many reasons for animals invading the village like illegal poaching, smuggling of epidemic trees, and low survival once maintenance by the Forest department is common reasons across the world [6].

Machine learning techniques have found a wide array of applications across diverse domains, showcasing their adaptability and effectiveness. In the realm of sentiment analysis in e-commerce customer reviews [28], methods for sentiment detection have been significantly enhanced, providing businesses with invaluable insights into customer satisfaction and feedback. Moreover, the utilization of AI in the detection of impersonators in examination halls [29] addresses the critical need for maintaining the integrity of educational assessments. Additionally, multiple face detection, employing algorithms like Haar-AdaBoosting, LBP-AdaBoosting, and neural networks [30], demonstrates the versatility of machine learning in enhancing security and surveillance systems. These instances underscore the pivotal role that machine learning plays in solving real-world challenges through surveillance and monitoring.

Sensors have versatile applications, including temperature and motion detection [7]. An innovative use is estimating gas leakage rates in extensive pipeline systems [27] via a fuzzy interface algorithm. These sensors are placed in various devices and environments to collect data, which is then transmitted wirelessly, enhancing efficiency [8,9].

Artificial Intelligence (AI) further empowers IoT by simulating human-like intelligence [10]. AI finds applications in facial recognition, automation, and chatbots, leveraging technologies like Deep Learning, Cloud Computing, and Quantum Computing. It automates processes across various sectors [11].

IoT and AI combined give rise to voice assistants and smart devices, enhancing computer-human interactions and analytics like Deep Learning, Data Analytics, and Machine Learning [12,13]. Sensors integrated with AI have notably improved analytics and alert systems [14]. In email alert systems [15], they enable real-time communication and responsive alert mechanisms, enhancing monitoring and communication.

Automated image classification [23] plays a pivotal role in the realm of wildlife monitoring and management. It provides a sophisticated means of efficiently processing vast quantities of camera trap images, offering insights into wildlife populations and behaviors. However, the challenge of location variability can hinder the effectiveness of such systems. The development of location-invariant [22] object detectors emerges as a crucial endeavor to overcome this challenge. These detectors aim to ensure consistent and accurate classification of animals in diverse environmental settings, regardless of factors such as lighting conditions and camera angles. The primary aim of this study is to explore the possibility of using publicly available datasets for training location-invariant models. By evaluating the adaptability and transferability of these models to the unique context of camera trap images, our research endeavors to expand our comprehension of their capacity to augment the consistency and effectiveness of automated image classification.

2   Literature Survey

Object detection is a crucial task in computer vision that involves identifying and localizing objects within images or videos. Various algorithms and techniques have been proposed to address this challenge. One such study by Fares Jalled et al. [15] utilized image processing techniques, including feature detection and the Haar detection cascade, to detect specific objects such as human bodies and cars. Their algorithm demonstrated effective object detection even with changes in scale or minor plan rotations. Similarly, Zeyad Al-Zaydi et al. [16] focused on detecting and counting people in crowded scenes using the GMM algorithm and a trained GRP regression model. Their approach showed promise in applications such as abnormality detection and crowd control.

The deep-learning architecture, utilizing CNN, Bi-LSTM, and attention mechanisms, has demonstrated significant promise in accurately categorizing and detecting aberrant human behavior in video streams enhancing the wide applicaiton of Human behaviour monitoring systems [26]. In the context of wildlife monitoring, N. Banupriya et al. [17] employed Convolutional Neural Networks (CNN) for accurate and efficient animal detection. A. W. D. Udaya Shalika et al. [18] developed an animal classification system using camera/PIR detection and machine learning with SVM, achieving an overall accuracy of 80%. Falzon et al. [19] explored location-invariant animal detection in camera trap images using publicly available sources and achieved promising results in mean Average Precision (mAP). These studies collectively contribute to the fields of object detection and animal classification, offering insights and advancements in computer vision applications. The summarized information can be found in Table 1.

In the domain of camera trap image processing, prior research has made use of object detector and image classifier models, including contributions from Norouzzadeh et al. [24], and Tabak et al. [25]. These models rely on data-driven deep learning techniques for image classification, eliminating the need for manual feature engineering. The existing approach struggles to adapt to images from various places, needs a lot of resources to make location-specific models, and faces difficulties when specialized models aren't accessible. This study tackles these problems by concentrating on improving location-flexible camera trap object detectors. The proposed methodology explores training models using publicly available image datasets.

3   Methodology

A camera trap, equipped with a PIR sensor, is designed for wildlife image capture [21]. The PIR sensor comprises two vital components: the emitter projecting an infrared beam and the receiver detecting this beam. It operates by allowing the emitted infrared light to pass through the environment undisturbed. However, when an obstruction, often an animal, disrupts the light path, the PIR sensor registers this disturbance. For object classification of images, particularly distinguishing animals and humans, deep learning techniques are highly effective

Table 1. Summary of Object Detection Algorithms

S.No	Author	Title	Methodology	Result	Remark
1	Fares Jalled et al. [15]	Object detection using image processing with the help of UAB	Object detection using image processing with the help of UAB, which involves image capture, feature detection, collecting putative points, and object detection.	The system effectively detects specific objects like human bodies and cars. It achieves a 1% false negative and 40% false positive rate for face detection	The system performs well in detecting objects despite changes in scale or minor plan rotations. Enhanced dataset could further reduce false alarms.
2	Zeyad Al-Zaydi et al. [16]	Detecting people and counting them in the crowd.	Detecting and counting people in crowds using frames from a benchmark dataset, Gaussian Mixture Model (GMM) for background subtraction, and a trained GRP regression model.	Mean Absolute Error (MAE) is 1.945, and Mean Squared Error is 6.056. The error obtained is less, nearly 0.2.	The proposed system's results are promising and can be valuable for applications like crowd control and evacuation planning.
3	N. Banupriya et al. [17]	Animal detection using deep learning algorithm	Animal detection using a Convolutional Neural Network (CNN).	TAchieves an accuracy of 99.10%, with an epoch value of 0.8679 and a processing time of 52.208 ms.	The CNN-based system demonstrates high accuracy in animal detection.
4	A. W. D. Udaya Shalika et al. [18]	Animal Classification System - for animal researchers and wildlife photographers.	Animal classification system involving camera/PIR detection, motion and tracking, feature extraction, recognition, and machine learning (ML) using Support Vector Machine (SVM).	Overall accuracy is 80%. However, there are challenges when combining certain descriptors.	The system struggles to separate negative images, especially when combining specific descriptors.
5	Falzon et al. [19]	Automated location invariant animal detection in camera trap images using publicly available data sources	Automated location-invariant animal detection in camera trap images using publicly available data sources and an optimization strategy called 'infusion.'	Achieves mean Average Precision (mAP) results ranging from 38.5% to 88.59%.	While the approach performs well, it faces limitations in achieving high precision for out-of-sample object detection. It should be evaluated with alternative object detection frameworks and on a broader multi-class dataset.

[20]. Using convolutional neural networks (CNNs), these methods process image inputs through layers, starting with an input layer collecting all images. The hidden layer, consisting of a convolutional layer and a fully connected dense layer, extracts features from input images and assigns importance to these features. The output layer generates results for user application.

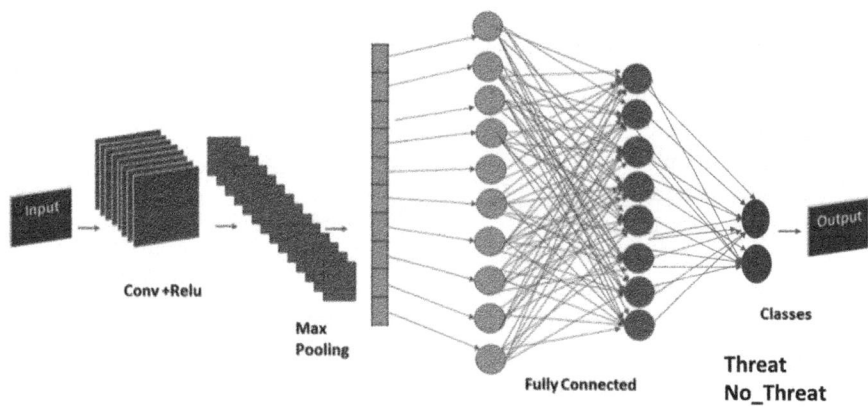

Fig. 1. System Architecture of the proposed model

The Proposed system architecture given in Fig. 1, is a simple Sequential model consisting of three layers: a Flatten layer, two Dense layers, and two Dropout layers. The Flatten layer takes the output of the last convolutional layer of the VGG16 model and flattens it into a one-dimensional array. This output is then passed on to the first Dense layer, which has 100 neurons and uses the Rectified Linear Unit (ReLU) activation function. The purpose of this layer is to learn higher-level features by combining the information from the flattened output of the previous layer. Next, a Dropout layer is applied, which randomly drops out some of the neurons during each training epoch to prevent overfitting. This is followed by a second Dense layer with 50 neurons and again using the ReLU activation function. The purpose of this layer is to further refine the learned features. To handle the location invariance, we have added a GAP (Global Average Pooling) layer to enhance the model's performance in recognizing objects across different positions and orientations within the images. Finally, another Dropout layer is applied, followed by the last Dense layer with 2 neurons and the Softmax activation function.

The Softmax function outputs a probability distribution over the two classes - threat and non-threat. This architecture is designed to classify the given image as either a threat or non-threat based on the learned features. The initial dataset used for training the proposed system consisted of 15,000 images sourced from publicly available repositories such as iNaturalist. After a rigorous data cleaning process, the dataset was refined to include 7,546 images for the training phase and an additional 1,574 images for validation. The trained model was subsequently tested using a dataset comprising 3,732 images to assess its performance and obtain the desired output.

3.1   Algorithm for the Proposed System:

1. Import necessary libraries
   - `import keras`
   - `import numpy`
   - `import pandas`
   - `import matplotlib`
2. Load and preprocess the dataset
   - `dataset = load_dataset()`
   - `train_data, validation_data = split_data(dataset)`
   - `preprocess(train_data)`
   - `preprocess(validation_data)`
3. Define the model
   - `model = Sequential()`
4. Add layers to the model
   - `model.add(Flatten())`
   - `model.add(Dense(100, activation='LeakyReLU')`
   - `model.add(Dropout(0.5))`
   - `model.add(Dense(50, activation='LeakyReLU'))`
   - `model.add(Dropout(0.3))`
   - `model.add(GlobalAveragePooling2D())`
   - `model.add(Dense(output_classes, activation='softmax'))`
5. Compile the model
   - model.compile(loss='categorical_crossentropy', optimizer='RMSprop', metrics=['accuracy'])
6. Train the model
   - model.fit(train_data, epochs=num_epochs, batch_size=batch_size, validation_data=validation_data)
7. Evaluate the model
   - `test_data = load_test_data()`
   - `loss, accuracy = model.evaluate(test_data)`
8. Make predictions
   - `new_data = load_new_data()`
   - `predictions = model.predict(new_data)`

3.2   Objectives and Advantages of the Proposed System

The proposed system aims to address critical challenges in wildlife monitoring, ecosystem protection, and human-wildlife interaction.

1. Objectives
   - Automated Image Classification: Develop an automated image classification system using Convolutional Neural Networks (CNN) to distinguish between animals and humans in camera trap images.
   - Creating location-invariant object detectors to improve image classification accuracy, especially in the context of camera traps.
2. Advantages
   - Safeguard agricultural fields from wildlife intrusion, reducing crop damage.
   - Contribute to the conservation of forest ecosystems and wildlife by monitoring and addressing potential threats.
   - Enhance the management of zoological parks and wildlife sanctuaries by automating animal monitoring.
   - Improve safety and enhance the experience of tourists and researchers in areas with high human-wildlife interactions, such as safaris.
   - Minimize risks for trekkers and hikers in regions with known wildlife presence.
   - Serve as a deterrent to illegal activities like animal poaching and provide evidence for law enforcement.
   - Facilitate the observation and study of animal behavior in their natural habitats.
   - Enhance the protection of tribal and local communities living near wildlife habitats.
   - Automatically notify relevant authorities, including forest departments, village leaders, and local police, in case of potential threats or incidents.

4   Results and Discussions

A holistic approach to mitigate animal threats in forest areas benefits both human and animal safety, preventing illegal poaching. The integration of Global Average Pooling (GAP) in the model has significantly enhanced its ability to recognize objects in diverse locations and orientations. The model exhibits a robust precision of 0.99, accurately identifying 99% of cases, with a recall of 0.98 (Table 2). Figure 2 presents training and validation accuracy as well as loss plots using the matplotlib library, providing insights into the machine learning model's performance. Further refinements are possible for increased reliability, particularly in identifying threats with varied object positions within images.

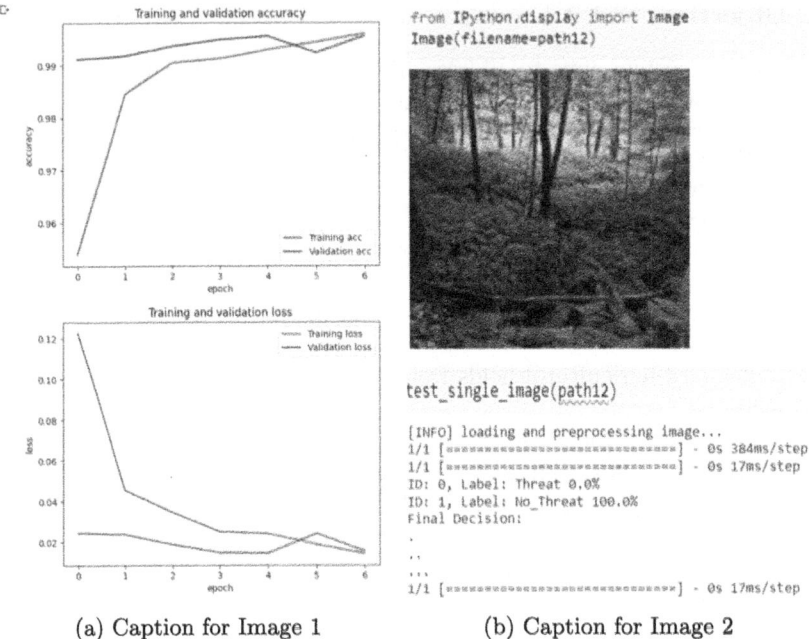

(a) Caption for Image 1   (b) Caption for Image 2

Fig. 2. Images of accuracy and sample test case

Table 2. Model Performance Metrics

Class	Precision	Recall	F1-Score	Support
Threat	1.00	1.00	1.00	2961
No Threat	0.99	0.98	0.98	771
Micro-Avg	0.99	0.99	0.99	3732
Macro-Avg	0.99	0.99	0.99	3732
Weighted-Avg	0.99	0.99	0.99	3732
Samples-Avg	0.99	0.99	0.99	3732

The model effectively distinguishes between "Threat" and "No_Threat" instances depicted in Fig. 3, with 2950 "threat" instances correctly classified. There are minimal misclassifications: 11 "Threat" instances are incorrectly labeled as "No_Threat," and 13 "No_Threat" instances are misclassified as "threat." These minor errors indicate potential areas for improvement. Furthermore, 758 "No_Threat" instances are accurately identified, showcasing the model's proficiency in recognizing instances without threats.

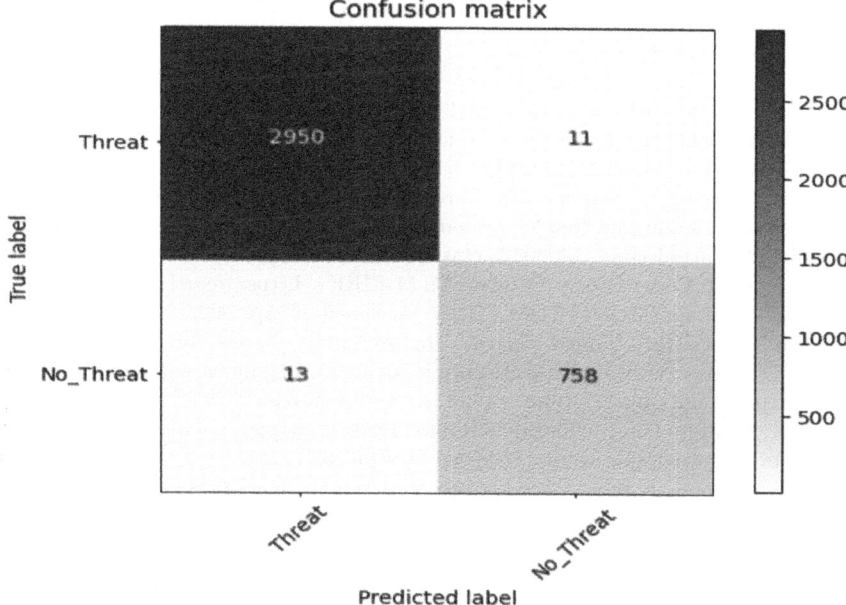

Fig. 3. Performance Matrix of Test Data

5   Conclusion

We have used CNN model which gave higher precision and accuracy compared to other models and there is still room for development of more profound location invariant models. The main advantage of implementing this proposed system generates less intervention of humans in forests and also we can get 24/7 surveillance without issues of exhaustion or reduction in quality of work. The development of an alert system to prevent animal threats is possible and there is a further scope of advancement in the classification which is now to animals or humans and can be used for fire detection or any other forest problems. There is a scope of using sound sensors for detection of the emotions of animals near the region border whether calm or scared causing trouble or harm.

6   Future Scope

The envisioned system holds potential for extension into reptile detection and the identification of diverse fauna. A promising avenue involves developing an expert system for dynamic, real-time analysis within specific forest areas. This expansion not only enhances the system's versatility but also offers a more comprehensive approach to ecological studies. The envisioned expert system can adapt to evolving scenarios, making it invaluable for ongoing monitoring and analysis, thus contributing to a nuanced understanding of the dynamic ecosystems we aim to explore and preserve.

References

1. New Indian Express. "430 families in Kombukuthi tribal village live in fear of wild animal attacks". Retrieved from https://www.newindianexpress.com/states/kerala/2022/feb/06/430-families-in-kombukuthi-tribal-village-live-in-fear-of-wild-animal-attacks-2416023.html. Accessed 26 Apr 2023
2. Times of India. "Animals flee forests in search of food, water". https://timesofindia.indiatimes.com/city/bhubaneswar/animals-flee-forests-in-search-of-food-water/articleshow/13060423.cms. Accessed 26 Apr 2023
3. NASA Earth Observatory. "MOD14A1 M FIRE". https://earthobservatory.nasa.gov/global-maps/MOD14A1_M_FIRE/. Accessed 26 Apr 2023
4. Down To Earth. "Forest Survey Report 2021: Forest fire counts up 2.7 times". https://www.downtoearth.org.in/news/forests/forest-survey-report-2021-forest-fire-counts-up-2-7-times-81123. Accessed 26 Apr 2023
5. World Wildlife Fund. "Illegal Wildlife Trade". https://www.worldwildlife.org/threats/illegal-wildlife-trade. Accessed 26 Apr 2023
6. World Economic Forum. "New high-resolution map shows fires caused one-third of global forest loss between 2001 and 2019". Retrieved from https://www.weforum.org/agenda/2022/03/new-high-resolution-map-shows-fires-caused-one-third-of-global-forest-loss-between-2001-and-2019/. Accessed 26 Apr 2023
7. Ahmad, M.B., Abdullahi, A.A., Muhammad, A.S., Saleh, Y.B., Usman, U.B.: The various types of sensors used in the security alarm system. Int. J. New Comput. Archit. Appl. (IJNCAA) 9(2), 50–59 (2019)
8. Zeinab, K.A.M., Elmustafa, S.A.A.: Internet of things applications, challenges and related future technologies. World Sci. News 67(2), 126–148 (2017)
9. Ullo, S.L., Sinha, G.R.: Advances in smart environment monitoring systems using IoT and sensors. Sensors 20(11), 3113 (2020)
10. Wang, P.: What Do You Mean by "AI"? In: AGI, vol. 171, pp. 362–373 (2008)
11. Smith, R.G., Eckroth, J.: Building AI applications: yesterday, today, and tomorrow. AI Mag. 38(1), 6–22 (2017)
12. Ghosh, A., Chakraborty, D., Law, A.: Artificial intelligence in the Internet of things. CAAI Trans. Intell. Technol. 3(4), 208–218 (2018)
13. Šumak, B., Brdnik, S., Pušnik, M.: Sensors and artificial intelligence methods and algorithms for human-computer intelligent interaction: a systematic mapping study. Sensors 22(1), 20 (2021)
14. Leung, C.K., Braun, P., Cuzzocrea, A.: AI-based sensor information fusion for supporting deep supervised learning. Sensors 19(6), 1345 (2019)
15. Jalled, F., Voronkov, I.: Object detection using image processing. arXiv preprint arXiv:1611.07791 (2016)
16. Al-Zaydi, Z., Vuksanovic, B., Habeeb, I.: Image processing based ambient context-aware people detection and counting. Int. J. Mach. Learn. Comput. 8(3), 268–273 (2018)
17. Banupriya, N., Saranya, S., Swaminathan, R., Harikumar, S., Palanisamy, S.: Animal detection using a deep learning algorithm. J. Crit. Rev. 7(1), 434–439 (2020)
18. Shalika, A.U., Seneviratne, L.: Animal classification system based on image processing & support vector machine. J. Comput. Commun. 4(1), 12–21 (2016)
19. Shepley, A., Falzon, G., Meek, P., Kwan, P.: Automated location invariant animal detection in camera trap images using publicly available data sources. Ecol. Evol. 11(9), 4494–4506 (2021)

20. Ranganayagi, D., Saranya, P., Sharmila, M.J., Sujitha, S., Nisha, T.A., Shanmugam, K.: Pre-eclampsia risk monitoring and alert system using machine learning and IoT (2022)
21. Welbourne, D.J., Claridge, A.W., Paull, D.J., Lambert, A.: How do passive infrared triggered camera traps operate and why does it matter? Breaking down common misconceptions. Remote Sens. Ecol. Conserv. **2**(2), 77–83 (2016)
22. Maddern, W., Stewart, A., McManus, C., Upcroft, B., Churchill, W., Newman, P.: Illumination invariant imaging: applications in robust vision-based localisation, mapping and classification for autonomous vehicles. In: Proceedings of the Visual Place Recognition in Changing Environments Workshop, IEEE International Conference on Robotics and Automation (ICRA), Hong Kong, China, vol. 2, no. 3, p. 5 (2014)
23. Sharath Kumar, Y.H., Manohar, N., Chethan, H.K.: Animal classification system: a block based approach. Procedia Comput. Sci. **45**, 336–343 (2015)
24. Mohammad Sadegh, N., et al.: Automatically identifying, counting, and describing wild animals in camera-trap images with deep learning. Proc. Nat. Acad. Sci. **115**(25), E5716–E5725 (2018)
25. Tabak, M.A., et al.: Machine learning to classify animal species in camera trap images: applications in ecology. Methods Ecol. Evol. **10**(4), 585–590 (2019)
26. Kumar, M., Patel, A.K., Biswas, M., Shitharth, S.: Attention-based bidirectional-long short-term memory for abnormal human activity detection. Sci. Rep. **13**(1), 14442 (2023)
27. Manoharan, H., Shitharth, S., Sangeetha, K., Kumar, B.P., Hedabou, M.: Detection of superfluous in channels using data fusion with wireless sensors and fuzzy interface algorithm. Meas. Sens. **23**, 100405 (2022)
28. Singh, U., Saraswat, A., Azad, H.K., Abhishek, K., Shitharth, S.: Towards improving e-commerce customer review analysis for sentiment detection. Sci. Rep. **12**(1), 21983 (2022)
29. Vishal, A., Nitish Reddy, T., Reddy, P.P., Shitharth, A.: Detecting impersonators in examination halls using AI. 344–350 (2021)
30. Devi, B.T, Shitharth, S.: Multiple Face Detection Using Haar-AdaBoosting, LBP-AdaBoosting and Neural Networks. In IOP Conference Series: Materials Science and Engineering, vol. 1042, no. 1, p. 012017. IOP Publishing (2021)

Social Media Impact on Student's Academic Performance: A Study of College Students in Bhubaneswar

Debasmita Panigrahy[1]([✉]), Y. S. S. Patro[1], and Joyant Yosobardhan Sahoo[2]

[1] GIET University, Gunupur, India
pdebasmita2018@gmail.com, ysspatro@giet.edu.in
[2] GITA Autonomous College, Bhubaneswar, India

Abstract. In modern society, it is essential that individuals have a comprehensive understanding of both current events and prevailing fashion trends. However, what impact does this pattern have on the academic performance of the students? The advent of social media platforms such as Facebook, YouTube, and Twitter has led to a dichotomy between the virtual and physical realms of our society. Social media refers to digital platforms that facilitate the connection of individuals on both local and global scales. The projected trajectory for social media user penetration in India indicates a gradual increase of 22.4 percentage points from 2023 to 2028. According to this forecast, it is projected that by the year 2028, the rate of penetration would have a consecutive fifth-year increase, reaching 83.16 percent. Significantly, during the last several years, there has been a consistent increase in the number of individuals engaging with social media platforms. As a result of the current circumstances, their academic accomplishments are consistently devalued. It is important to ascertain the extent to which the study has taken into account the academic achievement of pupils across many disciplines, including graduate, under graduate and post graduate students of different steams arts, science, and engineering. The aim of this study is to analyses the effect of social media use on the academic performance of college students in Bhubanswar. This analysis included both primary and secondary data sources. To get the necessary primary data, a sample of college students from various academic disciplines, including Arts, Science, and Engineering, were invited to participate in a survey. The questionnaire used in this study was carefully designed, pre-tested, and ensured transparency in its construction. A total of 180 graduate and postgraduate students from various institutions in Bhubaneswar were recruited in a random manner for the purpose of this research study. Social media, an integral aspect of individuals' lives, has dual advantages for students: it facilitates academic development and serves as a potential source of addiction. The degree to which youngsters perform academically in their classrooms and engage in courteous interactions on social media platforms serves as a reliable indicator of their overall behaviour. It is recommended that parents start their children's education at home due to their heightened sense of responsibility compared to educational institutions, hence potentially providing significant benefits inside academic contexts.

Keywords: Social media · digital platforms · Academic performance

O. Castillo et al. (Eds.): PerSOM 2023, LNICST 517, pp. 240–250, 2024.
https://doi.org/10.1007/978-3-031-66044-3_17

1 Introduction

The internet is become a crucial element of most people's daily life. It's difficult to conceive of a modern youth who doesn't use social media and check the news at least once every day. Nowadays, it's not optional to not know about current events and fashions. Concerns have been raised, however, concerning the effect that this pattern of persistent online interaction may have on kids' ability to focus on their schoolwork. With the rise of social media sites like Facebook, YouTube, and Twitter, our lives have become more compartmentalised between the virtual and physical. Technology likes the internet and social media have made it easier for people to communicate with one another on a global and local scale. Not only can we talk to people in other countries, but we can also do things like watch videos, read books, and look at pictures thanks to social media. Without a question, social media has had a huge impact in simplifying our everyday lives and bringing us closer together.

The following are among the most widely used social networking sites throughout the globe:

1. Facebook: With billions of active users, Facebook remains one of the largest social networking platforms globally, offering a range of features for connecting and sharing content.
2. YouTube: As the largest video-sharing platform, YouTube has an enormous user base and is known for hosting a vast amount of video content.
3. Whatsapp: A popular messaging app owned by Facebook, Whatsapp is widely used for text messaging, voice calling, and sharing multimedia.
4. Facebook Messenger: A standalone messaging app from Facebook, enabling users to send messages, make voice and video calls, and share photos and videos.
5. Instagram: Owned by Facebook, Instagram is a photo and video sharing platform known for its visual content and Stories feature.
6. Twitter: A micro blogging platform where users can post short messages called "tweets" to share thoughts, news, and updates.
7. Snap chat: A multimedia messaging app that allows users to send photos and videos with added filters and effects, disappearing after being viewed (Fig. 1).

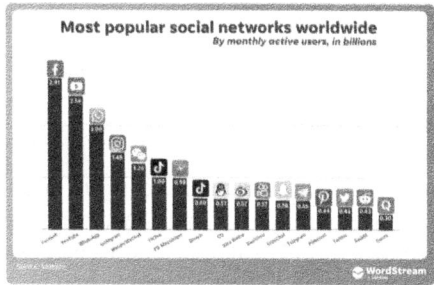

Fig. 1. Most popular social network

2 Review of Literature

A general overview of the literature review on the impact of social media on college student's academic performance.

Sl.No	Journal	Year	Author	Title
1	Computers in Human Behavior	2015	Kirschner, P. A., & Karpinski, A. C	Facebook® and academic performance
2	Journal of Applied Developmental Psychology	2016	Junco, R	Student class standing, Facebook use, and academic performance
3	Computers & Education	2017	Al-rahmi, W. M., Alias, N., Othman, M. S., & Ahmed, E	The role of social media for collaborative learning to improve academic performance of students and researchers in Malaysian higher education
4	Educational Technology & Society	2018	Rouis, S., Limayem, M., & Salehi-sangari, E	Impact of Facebook on student academic performance
5	Journal of Educational Computing Research	2019	Khan, G. F	The impact of Facebook use on academic performance: Evidence from a developing country
6	International Journal of Environmental Research and Public Health	2020	Rosas-Salgado, M. R., Morales-Vargas, A. E., & Jiménez, Z. R	Relationship between sleep quality, academic performance, and the use of electronic devices
7	Frontiers in Psychology	2021	Verduyn, P., Lee, D. S., Park, J., Shablack, H., Orvell, A., Bayer, J.,... & Kross, E	Passive Facebook usage undermines affective well-being: Experimental and longitudinal evidence

3 Statement of the Problem

In current digital age, when youth and academic genre are more affected, students who experience significant negative effects from social media are more vulnerable. Current results in merciless down streaming of their academic accomplishments. The authors are mentioned in the problem statement. 1) **Das, B, and Sahoo** [3] individuals spend more time communicating with and sharing information with their peers on social networking networks. They develop a dependency on checking their own status every few minutes throughout the day. 2) The results of the study, in the opinion of **Kolan and Dzadza**

[4], have demonstrated the nature of social media as a valuable servant but a hazardous master and a two-edged sword. Despite the benefits that students can derive from social media networks, including the sharing of information, the development of relationships, and participation in group discussions, there is a risk of addiction and attention-deficit disorder caused by social media use, which could have a significant negative impact on students' academic lives. Understanding the degree to which the academic accomplishment of students from various streams of the arts, sciences, and engineering was taken into consideration for the research is crucial.

4   Objectives of the Study

To assess the frequency and extent of social media usage among college students in arts, science, and engineering institution in Bhubaneswar.

5   Research Methodology

This study is a quantitative one using a survey approach. The greater part of the study is descriptive. Both primary and secondary data were used in this research. College students from several streams (Arts, Science, and Engineering) were asked to complete a pre-tested, carefully designed, and transparent questionnaire in order to get the necessary primary data. For the study, Graduate and Postgraduate students from various institutions of Bhubaneswar are chosen at random. Random sampling involved in dividing the population into subgroups (strata) based on certain characteristics (e.g., grade level, gender), and then a simple random sample is selected from each stratum. The formula used in this case relates to determining the sample size for each stratum and then using simple random sampling within each stratum. A sample of 180 student responders was chosen using a basic random sampling procedure. Percentage analysis and the Chi-square test were the statistical methods employed in the current study.

6   Hypotheses

H01: There is no significant association between age and academic performance.
H02: There is no significant association between gender and academic performance.
H03: There is no significant association between stream of education and academic performance.
H04: There is no significant association between frequency of using social media and academic performance.
H05: There is no significant association between purpose of using social media and academic performance.

To understand the elements impacting academic performance among students as the overall context and goal of our study, which is in accordance with the single objective, which gives the overarching framework and purpose of our research.

7 Data Analysis

7.1 Variables and Usage of Social Media in Demographic

Age and gender are taken into account as demographic factors for students in arts, science, and engineering colleges, while frequency of use, purpose of use, and academic performance (the dependent variable) are taken into account as social media usage patterns among students for all previous categories for comparison.

Table 1. Variables and usage of social media in Demographic

Sl. No.	Variables	Frequency	Percentage
1	Age		
	Below 20 years	74	41.1
	20 to 23 years	51	28.3
	Above 23 years	55	30.6
2.	Gender		
	Female	66	36.7
	Male	114	63.3
3.	Stream of education		
	Arts and Science	108	60.0
	Engineering	72	40.0
4.	Frequency of using social media		
	Very often	67	37.2
	Occasionally	63	35.0
	Rarely	50	27.8
5.	Purpose of using social media		
	Entertainment purpose	71	20
	Knowledge development	73	31.7
	Both	36	48.3
6.	Academic Performance		
	High	36	20
	Moderate	57	31.7
	Low	87	48.3

Table 1 shows Age: The majority of the respondents are above 20 years old, with 28.3% in the 20 to 23 years age group and 30.6% above 23 years. About 41.1% of the respondents are below 20 years old. Gender: The respondents are predominantly male, accounting for 63.3% of the total, while females represent 36.7%. Stream of Education: The majority of the respondents (60.0%) are from the Arts and Science stream of education. Engineering students make up 40.0% of the respondents. Frequency of Using Social Media: A significant number of respondents (37.2%) use social media very often. The usage of social media is occasional for 35.0% of respondents. 27.8% of respondents use social media rarely. Use of Social Media: The majority of respondents (40.6%) use social media primarily for knowledge growth, which includes academic-related and self-improvement activities. 39.4% of survey participants said they use social media for pleasure, such as gaming and chit-chatting. 20.0% of respondents said they use social media for enjoyment and education. Academic Performance: A significant proportion (48.3%) of respondents reported having low academic performance. 31.7% of respondents have moderate academic performance. 20.0% of respondents reported high academic performance.

7.2 Two-Way Table and Chi-Square Test

Table 2. A connection Between Age and Academic Performance

Age	Academic Performance			Total	Result
	High	Moderate	Low		
Below 20 years	11	22	41	74	
	30.6%	38.6%	47.1%	41.1%	χ^2=11.056
20 to 23 years	8	23	20	51	df=4
	22.2%	40.4%	23.0%	28.3%	TV=9.488
Above 23 years	17	12	26	55	Sig.0.026
	47.2%	21.1%	29.9%	30.6%	Result: Significant
Total	36	57	87	180	H₀1: Rejected

Table 2 presents the frequency distribution of academic performance (High, Moderate, Low) for three age groups: Below 20 years, 20 to 23 years, and Above 23 years Below 20 years: Out of 74 respondents below 20 years old, 11 have high academic performance, 22 have moderate academic performance, and 41 have low academic performance The percentages for each academic performance level in this age group are as follows: High academic performance: 14.9%. Moderate academic performance: 29.7%. Low academic performance: 55.4%.20 to 23 years: Among the 51 respondents in the 20 to 23 years age group, 8 have high academic performance, 23 have moderate academic performance, and 20 have low academic performance. The percentages for each academic performance level in this age group are as follows: High academic performance: 15.7%. Moderate academic performance: 45.1% Low academic performance: 39.2%. Above 23 years: For the 55 respondents above 23 years old, 17 have high academic performance, 12 have moderate academic performance, and 26 have low academic performance. The percentages for each academic performance level in this age group are as follows: High academic performance: 30.9%. Moderate academic performance: 21.8%. Low academic performance: 47.3%. Chi-Square Test: The Chi-Square test statistic ($\chi 2$) is 11.056 with degrees of freedom (df) equal to 4. The critical value at a significance level (Sig.) of 0.05 is 9.488. The test result (Sig. 0.026) indicates that there is a statistically significant association between age and academic performance. Hypothesis Testing: The null hypothesis (H0) is that there is no association between age and academic performance. Since the p-value (0.026) is less than the significance level of 0.05, we reject the null hypothesis (H0) and conclude that there is a significant association between age and academic performance. The data suggests that the distribution of academic performance varies across different age groups. The percentage of respondents with high academic performance increases with age, while the percentage with low academic performance decreases. The below 20 years age group has the highest proportion of respondents with low academic performance, while the above 23 years age group has the highest proportion with high academic performance (Table 3).

Table 3. Link between Gender and Academic Performance

Gender	Academic Performance			Total	Result
	High	Moderate	Low		
Male	17	35	62	114	χ^2=6.472
	47.2%	61.4%	71.3%	63.3%	df=2
Female	19	22	25	66	TV=5.991
	52.8%	38.6%	28.7%	36.7%	Sig.0.039
Total	36	57	87	180	Result: Significant
					H$_o$2: Rejected

7.3 Gender and Academic Performance

Academic Performance by Gender: Male Students: Among the male respondents, 71.3% exhibited low academic performance, 61.4% showed moderate academic performance, and 47.2% achieved high academic performance. Female Students: Among the female respondents, 52.8% exhibited high academic performance, 38.6% showed moderate academic performance, and 28.7% achieved low academic performance. Chi-Square Test Result: The Chi-Square test statistic (χ2) is 6.472 with degrees of freedom (df) equal to 2. The critical value at a significance level (Sig.) of 0.05 is 5.991. The test result (Sig. 0.039) indicates that there is a statistically significant association between gender and academic performance. Hypothesis Testing: The null hypothesis (H0) is that there is no association between gender and academic performance. The alternative hypothesis (H1) is that there is an association between gender and academic performance. Since the p-value (0.039) is less than the significance level of 0.05, we reject the null hypothesis (H0) and conclude that there is a significant association between gender and academic performance. The analysis demonstrates that there is a statistically significant association between gender and academic performance. Male students tend to have higher percentages in the low and moderate academic performance categories compared to female students. Female students tend to have a higher percentage in the high academic performance category compared to male students (Table 4).

7.4 Stream of Education and Academic Performance

Table 4. A connection between stream of education and Academic Performance

Stream	Academic Performance			Total	Result
	High	Moderate	Low		
Arts and Science	21	27	60	108	χ^2=6.745
	58.3%	47.4%	69.0%	60.0%	df=2
Engineering	15	30	27	72	TV=5.991
	41.7%	52.6%	31.0%	40.0%	Sig.0.034
Total	36	57	87	180	Result: Significant
					H$_o$2: Rejected

Arts and Science: Among the 108 respondents from Arts and Science stream, 21 have high academic performance, 27 have moderate academic performance, and 60 have low academic performance. The percentages for each academic performance level in the Arts and Science stream are as follows: High academic performance: 19.4%. Moderate academic performance: 25.0% Low academic performance: 55.6%. Engineering: Among the 72 respondents from the Engineering stream, 15 have high academic performance, 30 have moderate academic performance, and 27 have low academic performance. The percentages for each academic performance level in the Engineering stream are as follows: High academic performance: 20.8%. Moderate academic performance: 41.7% Low academic performance: 37.5%. Chi-Square Test: The Chi-Square test statistic ($\chi2$) is 6.745 with degrees of freedom (df) equal to 2. The critical value at a significance level (Sig.) of 0.05 is 5.991. The test result (Sig. 0.034) indicates that there is a statistically significant association between the stream of education and academic performance. Hypothesis Testing: The null hypothesis (H0) is that there is no significant association between the stream of education and academic performance. Since the p-value (0.034) is less than the significance level of 0.05, we reject the null hypothesis (H0) and conclude that there is a significant association between the stream of education and academic performance. The percentage of students with high academic performance is slightly higher in the Engineering stream (20.8%) compared to the Arts and Science stream (19.4%). However, the percentage of students with moderate academic performance is significantly higher in the Engineering stream (41.7%) compared to the Arts and Science stream (25.0%). On the other hand, the percentage of students with low academic performance is higher in the Arts and Science stream (55.6%) compared to the Engineering stream (37.5%).

7.5 Frequency and Academic Performance

Table 5. A connection between Frequency and Academic Performance

Frequency	Academic Performance			Total	Result
	High	Moderate	Low		
Very often	6	19	42	67	χ^2=29.543
	16.7%	33.3%	48.3%	37.2%	df=4
Occasionally	8	27	28	63	TV=9.488
	22.2%	47.4%	32.2%	35.0%	Sig.0.000
Rarely	22	11	17	50	Result: Significant
	61.1%	19.3%	19.5%	27.8%	H_01: Rejected
Total	36	57	87	180	

Table 5, the chi-square test has been conducted, which resulted in a chi-square value (χ^2) of 29.543 with 4 degrees of freedom (df = 4) and a test value (TV) of 9.488. The significance level (Sig.) is reported as 0.000, which means it is less than 0.001, indicating a very low p-value. The test result states that the null hypothesis (H_{01}) is rejected, which means there is a significant relationship between the frequency of an event and academic performance. Analysis percentages for each category: Very often: High academic performance: 6 (16.7% of the total in this frequency category) Moderate academic performance: 19 (33.3%) Low academic performance: 42 (48.3%) Occasionally: High academic performance: 8 (22.2%) Moderate academic performance: 27 (47.4%) Low academic performance: 28 (32.2%) Rarely: High academic performance: 22 (61.1%) Moderate academic performance: 11 (19.3%) Low academic performance: 17 (19.5%). Students who have a higher frequency of studying ("Very often" and "Occasionally" categories) tend to have higher academic performance (higher percentage in the "High" academic performance category) On the other hand, students who study less frequently ("Rarely" category) have a higher percentage in the "Low" academic performance category.

7.6   Reasons and Academic Performance

Table 6. A connection between Reasons and Academic Performance

Reasons	Academic Performance			Total	Result
	High	Moderate	Low		
Entertainment purposes (Gaming, chatting, etc.)	8	21	42	71	$\chi^2=11.879$ df=4 TV=9.488 Sig.0.018 Result: Significant H_01: Rejected
	22.2%	36.8%	48.3%	39.4%	
Knowledge development (Academic related, Personal improvement, etc.)	21	27	25	73	
	58.3%	47.4%	28.7%	40.6%	
Both	7	9	20	36	
	19.4%	15.8%	23.0%	20.0%	
Total	36	57	87	180	

Table 6 A chi-square test has been conducted to analyse the data, which resulted in a chi-square value (χ^2) of 11.879 with 4 degrees of freedom (df $= 4$) and a test value (TV) of 9.488. The significance level (Sig.) is reported as 0.018, which means it is less than 0.05, indicating a statistically significant relationship. The test result states that the null hypothesis (H_{01}) is rejected, which means there is a significant relationship between the reasons for academic performance and the actual academic performance. The analysis of each category. Entertainment purposes: High academic performance: 8 (22.2% of the total in this reason category) Moderate academic performance: 21 (36.8%) Low academic performance: 42 (48.3%) Knowledge development: High academic performance: 21 (58.3%) Moderate academic performance: 27 (47.4%) Low academic performance: 25 (28.7%) Both (students who have a mix of entertainment and knowledge development): High academic performance: 7 (19.4%) Moderate academic performance: 9 (15.8%) Low academic performance: 20 (23.0%).it appears that students who engage in "Knowledge development" as their primary reason for academic performance tend to have better academic performance (higher percentage in the "High" academic performance category. On the other hand, students who prioritize "Entertainment purposes" as their reason for academic performance have a higher percentage in the "Low" academic performance category.

8   Results and Discussion

1. Academic performance was shown to be higher among students who were more mature (over 23 years old) than among those who were young blood (under 20 years old), and young/teen responses were more visibly utilising social media and wasting their precious time. Prediction shows a strong correlation to reject the null hypothesis.
2. Despite the fact that female respondents participated less than male respondents, it was found that female applicants had greater academic attainment. Strong correlation predicted through prediction eliminates the null hypothesis..
3. Engineering students are frequently thought of as having a greater emphasis on their academics due to their difficult course load and curriculum. As a consequence, both engineering and arts and science students exhibit strong performance, although those enrolling in the arts and sciences have much lower academic performance. A high link between prediction and rejecting the null hypothesis. Students who use social media less regularly than those who use it more frequently or just rarely tend to fare well academically. Prediction shows a strong correlation to reject the null hypothesis.
4. When compared to students who used social media kindly to further their knowledge, it is clear that student who used social media more actively for enjoyment fared worse in their academic accomplishments. Prediction shows a strong correlation to reject the null hypothesis.

9   Conclusion

Social media has become an integral part of people's lives, especially for students. It serves as a valuable tool for knowledge development for some, while it can lead to addiction and negative impacts on academic performance for others. The results of our analysis clearly indicate that students who overuse social media or primarily use it for entertainment purposes tend to have lower academic performance, particularly among students in arts and science streams. Importance of parental involvement in shaping a student's relationship with social media. Parents, being more accountable than educational institutions, have a crucial role in guiding and monitoring their children's social media usage. By starting the education on responsible social media use within the family, students can benefit from improved academic circumstances. Social media can be a valuable educational resource, excessive use and misuse can hinder academic performance. Encouraging a balanced approach to social media and providing proper guidance can help students make the most of its benefits while avoiding its potential pitfalls. This way, social media can truly become an ally in knowledge development rather than a hindrance to academic success.

10   Suggestions

Students might get information from two main sources. 1) Generally speaking, parents and other carers who have a closer relationship with their children may watch them carefully and teach them about the good and bad consequences on both their academic performance and health. 1) Academic and educational institutions may educate the general public about the negative effects of social media on their academic performance. Because of the fact that gender plays a significant role among students and that parents and educational institutions carefully interact with female students to advise about the negative effects of using social media, it is advised that male students also receive more attention in order to protect them from social media influence without discriminating on the basis of gender. No matter the stream, children who use social media must be kept from accessing inappropriate sites or spending excessive amounts of time on it, which might hurt their academic achievement. Students who used social media more frequently showed poor performance, whereas students who used it less frequently and moderately performed very well and moderately well. This shows that students who use social media sparingly or only occasionally can have a significant impact on their performance levels.

References

1. Social Media by Students (2017). Blog Dash Conten creation by bloggers. http://blog.blogdash.com/media-industry/positive-negative-use-social-media-students/
2. Shensa, A., Sidani, J., Lin, L., Bowman, N., Primack, B.: Social media use and perceived emotional support among US young adults. J. Community Health **41**(3), 541–549 (2015). https://doi.org/10.1007/s10900-015-0128-8
3. Das, D.B., Sahoo, J.S.: Social networking sites – a critical analysis of its impact on personal and social life. Int. J. Bus. Soc. Sci. **2**, 222–228 (2010)
4. Kolan, B., Dzandza, P.: Effect of social media on academic performance of students in Ghanian Universities: A case study of University of Ghana, Legon, Library Philosophy and Practice (e-journal) (2018). https://digitalcommons.unl.edu/libphilprac/1637
5. Akar, E., Mardikyan, S.: Analyzing factors affecting users' behavior intention to use social media: Twitter case. Int. J. Bus. Soc. Sci. **5**(11), 85–95 (2014)
6. Al-Rahmi, W.M., Alias, N., Othman, M.S., Ahmed, I.A., Zeki, A.M., Saged, A.A.: Social media use, collaborative learning and students' academic performance: a systematic literature review of theoretical models. J. Theoretical Appl. Inf. Technol. **95**(20), 5399–5414 (2017)
7. Alnsour, M., Ghannam, M., Al-natour, R.: Social media effect on purchase intention: Jordanian airline industry. J. Internet Bank. Commer. **23**(2), 3–17 (2018)
8. Bharucha, J.: Social media and young consumers behavior. Int. J. Supply Chain Manage. **7**(6), 72–81 (2018)
9. Meslat, N.: Impact of social media on customers' purchase decision. Turku J. Appl. Sci. (2018)
10. Schivinski, B., Dabrowski, D.: The effect of social media communication on consumer perceptions of brands. J. Manage. Econ. **17**(3), 212–222 (2019)
11. Rashid, T., Asghar, H.M.: Technology use, self-directed learning, student engagement and academic performance: examining the interrelations. Comput. Human Behav. **63**, 604–612 (2016). https://doi.org/10.1016/j.chb.2016.05.084
12. Fedock, B.C., McCartney, M., Neeley, D.: Online adjunct higher education teachers' perceptions of using social media sites as instructional approaches. J. Res. Innovative Teach. Learn. **12**(3), 222–235 (2019). https://doi.org/10.1108/JRIT-02-2018-0005.[CrossRef][GoogleScholar]

Semantic Web with Block Chain Technology Parsing New Trends to Extract Novel Scientific Demands

V. Sitharamulu[1]($\boxtimes$) (ID), Srihari Babu Gole[2] (ID), Ravisankar Malladi[3] (ID),
and S. Ravichandran[1] (ID)

[1] Department of Computer Science and Engineering, GITAM School of Technology, GITAM
(Deemed to Be University), Hyderabad, Telangana 502 329, India
vsitaramu.1234@gmail.com

[2] Department of Information Technology, School of Engineering, Anurag University,
Venkatapur Road, Ghatkesar, Hyderabad, Telangana, India

[3] Department of Computer Science and Engineering, Koneru Lakshmaiah Education
Foundation, Vaddeswaram, Guntur District, Andhra Pradesh 522 502, India
mravisankar@kluniversity.in

Abstract. Blockchain technology has become widely used across various sectors such as industry, research, and academia. Over the past decade, numerous complex problems specific to different domains have been successfully addressed with respect to blockchain. As a result, researchers have shown interest in integrating blockchain with other well-established technologies, such as the Semantic Web. However, there are no clear depictions among the researchers in contrasting the various use cases in which Semantic Web and blockchain can be merged and no fore castings related to the potential benefits for both technologies. This paper aims to provide a comprehensive understanding of the mutually beneficial relationship that these technologies can achieve when integrated, and it also highlights the different scenarios noticed throughout the literature for generating a new a wave of scientific approach for combining the Semantic Web and blockchain. The objective of this paper is to review the innovative approach of merging the Block chain with semantic web to solve many problems in a simpler way.

Keywords: Blockchain technology · Semantic Web · Resource Description Framework (RDF)

1 Introduction

Over the past decade, blockchain technology has become ubiquitous in various sectors, including finance, security, IoT, and public services [1]. Researchers have taken an interest in exploring the challenges and problems associated with the use of blockchain technology in these domains [2, 3]. One area of particular interest to researchers has been the combination of blockchain technology with the Semantic Web [4, 5]. This interest

O. Castillo et al. (Eds.): PerSOM 2023, LNICST 517, pp. 251–262, 2024.
https://doi.org/10.1007/978-3-031-66044-3_18

stems from the potential for a symbiotic relationship that could enhance both technologies [6]. In the existing body of literature, the primary emphasis lies on applications that utilize both blockchain and Semantic Web technologies. However, there is only one article, authored by English et al. [7], that specifically examines the advantages of integrating these technologies. However, their work provides an overview of the benefits of the combination, rather than an in-depth analysis.

This paper aims to build upon the research conducted by English et al. [7]. by offering an expansion on their findings a deeper examination of the benefits that blockchain and the Semantic Web can offer to each other. As experts in the field, we provide a comprehensive examination of the various strategies and methods for integrating these technologies. Our analysis includes a thorough evaluation of the merits and drawbacks associated with each approach. The organization of the paper entails with various sections and each section describes essential information pertaining to semantic and block chain technologies. The Sect. 2 evolves with the basic concepts of both the semantic and block chain. Section 3 highlights the advantages of merging these two technologies. Moving on to Sect. 4, we delve into various scenarios where the combination can be beneficial. Lastly, in Sect. 5, we present a summary of our findings and conclusions.

2 Preliminaries

In this section, the preliminary objective is to offer a comprehensive understanding of the fundamental principles and distinguishing features of both blockchain technology and the Semantic Web. The paper's objective is to explore the fundamentals and a promotion in both the techies, which will serve as a foundation for discussing the benefits and scenarios of combining them while exploring the pros. The challenging task in the current scenario is collection of huge voluminous data day by day. This data can be restructured and organized in an efficient means through this approach.

2.1 Blockchain

Definition 1 (Blockchain). The blockchain is a decentralized, shared database that contains a list of blocks. In the realm of data structures, each block is equipped with essential metadata, various hash functions used for all previous and present blocks of data. The content of a block can be expressed in various formats, but once information is added to the chain, it becomes immutable and cannot be modified by anyone.

Definition 2 (Block). A block is the basic storage unit of the blockchain. It contains metadata and content, in a professional manner, the metadata contains the hash codes derived from the preceding block and the present hash [8]. The content of a block is limited in size, which varies depending on the implementation, and the metadata may also vary based on the implementation.

It is important to mention that various versions of blockchain, like Bitcoin or Ethereum, may exhibit certain distinctions, but they all adhere to the fundamental principle of being a decentralized database validated by peers without the involvement of a third party [9]. The process of adding a new block to the chain follows a specific protocol, wherein the newly developed blocks are generated using the hash functions from the previously generated blocks. All the block in the chain are authorized to be communicated among its peers. The block is included in the chain once it has been validated by all other peers [2, 10].

There are three types of blockchains depending on the access rights and privileges of the peers: public, consortium, and private. In a public blockchain, anyone can access the chain and write new blocks, even anonymously. In a consortium blockchain, access is limited to invited peers, but once invited, they can implement writing a code to generate new blocks in the form of a continuous chain and permissions are granted to only invited peers to access the chain, and they need additional permissions to write in it. Despite being more secure than other data stores, blockchain technology suffers from a limitation of scalability, and blocks of data with larger volume of data require more storage space and slow down the propagation of the block to other peers in the network.

2.2 The Semantic Web

The Semantic Web is a novel approach to its kind for all the documents available in the web, and it is equipped with a suite of custom-made technologies [11]. From the extensive semantic web technologies collection, we will highlight the most important ones and their core functions.

Definition 3 (RDF). The Resource Description Framework (RDF) is a standard formal language promoted by the W3C that allows for the description of data in any format [12, 13]. This data is expressed in the form of triplets, consisting of a subject, predicate, and object, where the first and second elements are represented by URIs, and the third element can either be a URI that relates to a literal or a subject in the RDF data representation. The content of the RDF is duly represented in the form of a graph for easy analysis and understanding and the same can be utilized for mapping references.

Definition 4 (Virtual RDF). Virtual RDF refers to RDF data that is generated on the fly, either by reading stored RDF data or by transforming heterogeneous data sources into RDF format using user-defined specifications. This allows for the dynamic creation of RDF data without the need for storing it in a file or a triple store [14].

Definition 5 (Linked Data). The Linked Data allows to connect data across multiple sources, by using common identifiers and linking the data to other related pieces of information. This creates a web of interlinked data that can be easily navigated and understood, making it easier for people and machines to find and reuse the data. The term "Linked Data" refers to RDF data that adheres to the guidelines established by Tim Berners-Lee [15]. These guidelines consist of a set of requirements for data quality, including:

1. URI are recognized as and then used as an identifier for the available resources.
2. Implementing HTTP URIs that are user-friendly and easily accessible.
3. Incorporating standardized methods like RDF and SPARQL to provide valuable information when a URI is accessed.

4. Including hyperlinks to other URIs to enhance the process of exploration and discovery.

The principles of Linked Data require that resources are identified using URIs. The resources are also further identified by means of DNS (Domain Name Space) which is on the threshold for publishing data. As resources are dependent on DNS, if there is a change in the DNS, the resources will no longer be accessible through their original URIs. Despite the decentralized storage of the data, when consuming Linked Data, it appears as a unified dataset due to the connections among the existing datasets based on the availability in the repositories.

Definition 6 The World Wide Web Consortium (W3C). Has introduced two official languages, RDFs and OWL, for data modelling [16, 17]. These languages are utilized for creating ontologies, which are formal models that enable reasoning over the described data. This implies that ontologies can ensure the coherence of data and generate new data through logical mechanisms, even if it is not explicitly defined or stored. The literature offers a range of standard, domain-specific ontologies suitable for different applications [18].

Definition 7 (Ontology Mappings). Ontology mappings are a key aspect of the linked data approach. They provide a mechanism for connecting different ontologies, allowing for the seamless integration of data from various datasets. With mappings in place, though a non-recognized ontology is used for modelling, automatic detection is done for that ontology depending upon the mappings. This enables the storage and consumption of data as a unified whole, enhancing the efficiency and flexibility of the linked data approach.

Definition 8 (SPARQL). SPARQL is a formal language promoted by the W3C for querying data expressed in RDF that follows an ontology [19, 20]. Utilizing an RDF engine capable of comprehending vast amounts of data, SPARQL empowers users to effortlessly query and retrieve information from either a single dataset or multiple datasets concurrently via SPARQL federation facilitating required extensions for all necessary queries [21].

Definition 9 (Data Shapes). RDF data has evolved with certain limitations and the certainty and compliance is supported by the W3C. W3C has introduced the concept of Shapes which compasses the certainty of language called Constraint Language [22], also known as data shapes Language. This language enables the definition of various constraints, ranging from the necessary data structure to the formatting of literals using regular expressions. Additionally, data shapes facilitate the creation of virtual RDF through SPARQL definitions.

3 Benefits

English et al. in their work [7] highlighted a key advantage of using Semantic Web in blockchain, which is the ability to model block meta-data using ontologies, allowing for querying using SPARQL. However, this approach has a drawback as it is limited for querying all the necessary contents of the respective blocks, because the data is not stored in designated RDF format. Simultaneously, Semantic Web can also benefit from blockchain technology in terms of resource identification. Normally, IRIs in Semantic Web rely on the DNS system. In the blockchain technology, hashing is a common methodology to identify block resources, thus decentralizing the domain name system. The semantic web ensures the data retrieval in an efficient manner. The block chain technology enables to interconnect the required data needed by the user. Both these techies are a must need for the data engineers to solve complex issues.

After conducting a thorough analysis survey for both the technologies, a report comprising of comprehensive list of benefits that the blockchain can reap from Semantic Web technologies is generated. The following points highlights some of these benefits:

1. **Versatile Language:** The RDF standard allows for flexibility in data representation, as it is not limited to a specific format. TURTLE, RDF/XML and JSON-LD are some the universal formats prescribed for RDF to represent the information. This can be one among the proven statements to trust that the RDF is versatile. The blockchain shall utilize the services offered by RDF like writing contents with respect to blocks, preparing necessary prerequisites for establishing the required formats that suits a respective domain.

2. **Well-established Data Modelling Standards:** The W3C standards, such as RDF, SPARQL, RDFs, and OWL, are highly regarded Semantic Web technologies. This implies that there is a global agreement on their reliability and trustworthiness. Additionally, there is a vast collection of standard ontologies available for use, which simplifies the task of data modelling for a given problem by providing ready-to-use solutions for a range of domains.

3. **Data Connectivity:** RDF's advantage is its ability to connect to data from other datasets by utilizing links, resulting in a comprehensive view of the information despite its decentralized storage across the web. The challenge of linking data is well acknowledged and extensively tackled in the Semantic Web community by all the researchers [23]. The fundamental property of the block chain is to link the blocks of data with external datasets or even with other blocks within the same or different chains, enhancing the overall interconnectedness of the data stored in the blockchain. This can be one among the most important advantageous features of Blockchain.

4. **Multiple Data Representations:** The main functionality of the Ontologies to facilitate mapping features to connect to the classes of other ontologies with all the properties and features. This feature allows a blockchain to translate the data described using one ontology to the representation of another ontology through these mappings. This is especially useful when data needs to be modelled differently depending on the consumer. By utilizing ontologies with mappings, the blockchain can ensure that the same data can be viewed in various forms to accommodate different stakeholders.

5. **Searching within the Blockchain**: SPARQL is one among the popular query language used for executing users queries in RDF. The same can also be used when integrated with block chain. Block chain adopts use of the ontologies in the RDF at semantic web to mention various elements, contents and available sources of meta data. The service acts as an intermediary, bridging the gap between the raw data stored within the blockchain and the querying mechanism.

6. **The process of validating data and meta-data in blockchain** can be improved by incorporating ontologies and RDF. By using "shapes," blockchain uses prediction analysis to detect the error codes in the existing models as well as in the document sets of RDF to rectify the prevailing bugs and forecast the RDF's content for redundancy. This validation technique ensures the accuracy and integrity of the data stored within the blockchain, enhancing its reliability and trustworthiness. Consequently, users can derive more value and utility from the blockchain.

7. **Ensuring Blockchain Consistency:** Reasoning engines are one among the prime causes in the semantic web structures for validating the integrity and coherence of data. In this particular situation, the blockchain would rely to seek the support of a third-party agent to perform the logical processing and to communicate its meta-data with a unique structure called ontology. This service would ensure that the data within the blockchain adheres to a set of logical rules and regulations, making it more consistent and trustworthy. By incorporating this validation step, the blockchain can provide its users with a higher level of confidence in the accuracy and reliability of the data stored within it.

8. **Virtual RDF:** There are several ways to generate virtual RDF, including the use of reasoning engines that infer new data, inferring virtual RDF using data shapes, and using graph embeddings that analyse the existing data and recreate newer outputs [24] through machine learning practices. These approaches provide a flexible and dynamic way to generate and access RDF data, making it easier to adapt to changing needs and requirements.

9. **Services offered by Virtual RDF:** The Semantic Web converts data from different sources into RDF on the fly, based on specific specifications [13, 14]. The conversion takes place with the help of convertible engines on board during RDF data manipulation. Blockchains can also take advantage of these virtual RDF services by storing information in formats other than RDF and utilizing external services to create their RDF content instantly. This allows the blockchain to store data in a variety of formats, while still providing a unified and standardized representation of the data in RDF, which can be easily consumed and processed by different systems. The use of virtual RDF services can provide more flexibility and interoperability in the data management of blockchains [24].

10. **Interoperability:** Common Ontologies are always subtle to deal both semantic and blockchain. Hence, it falls in the category of inoperable circumstances. Modelling of data and meta data is quiet inoperable. The blockchain becomes interoperable by utilising Semantic Web technologies and employing common ontologies to model both metadata and content. An information system is said to be interoperable if it can easily pass correspondence to their corresponding interoperable systems. Additionally, the data of interoperable systems can be automatically found and accessed by third-party systems. This allows for greater data integration and sharing between

different systems, improving overall data management and exchange. Interoperability also enhances the blockchain's compatibility with other technologies, making it easier to integrate into existing systems and workflows.

The Semantic Web may experience the following advantages by utilizing blockchain technology:

1. Decentralization and security: Blockchain provide a decentralized and secure platform to store data, which can enhance
2. the reliability and trustworthiness of the data in the Semantic Web.
3. Immutable record: Blockchain allows for the creation of an immutable record of data transactions, making it easier to maintain the integrity of data in the Semantic Web.
4. Transparency and accountability: Blockchain allows for the creation of a transparent and accountable record of data transactions, making it easier to track the usage and history of data in the Semantic Web [25].
5. Autonomy and Interoperability: Blockchain enables autonomous systems to securely exchange data with each other, improving interoperability and data integration in the Semantic Web.
6. Cost-effectiveness: By leveraging the decentralized nature of blockchain, the cost of maintaining and exchanging data in the Semantic Web can be reduced, as there is no need for intermediaries.
7. Better Data Management: Blockchain enables the creation of a unified and consistent data management system that spans across different systems, improving the overall data management in the Semantic Web.

4   Blockchain and Semantic Web Comparisons

The Semantic Web refers to a collection of technologies that concentrate on describing, modelling, and connecting data. On the other hand, the blockchain is a technology designed for storing and sharing data among a network of peers who verify its contents without relying on third-party involvement. The combination of these two technologies offers benefits for both. The blockchain have advantages in the form of storing large blocks of data using semantic technologies while semantic web on the other hand is benefited from the decentralization and immutability of data offered by the blockchain. Currently, there is only one known article that delves into the potential combination of these technologies, as presented by Ugarte [26], who described three scenarios. Upon conducting a more in-depth examination of the latest advancements, we have discovered six specific situations that will be elaborated on in the subsequent sections.

4.1   Semantic Metadata on the Blockchain

This integration state involves the use of an ontology to express the meta-data of a blockchain. The available content of the block is stored and represented in the form a non-RDF compliant format. The ontologies on the other hand depicted the usage [27] and none of them have achieved the prominent status yet. The first step towards combining the technologies of the in this state is shown in Fig. 1, describes the Semantic Web and Blockchain. Figure 1.

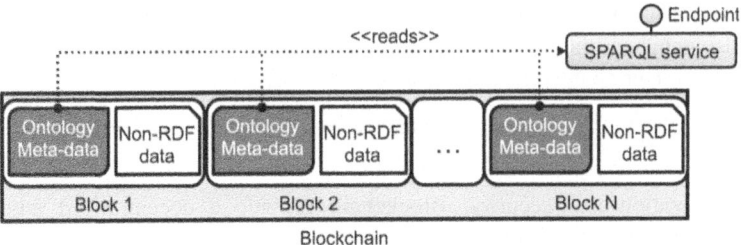

Fig. 1. Meta data referencing Ontology with Blockchain

In this first scenario, the advantage is that users can search for blocks based on their metadata, as long as an external service is available to read the blockchain and process SPARQL queries. This allows for searches of all blocks with a hash matching a specific pattern. However, one limitation is that Semantic Web technologies are only used to express the metadata of the blocks, limiting the potential benefits to just executing SPARQL queries on the metadata.

4.2 RDF-Based Blockchain Content

The integration of Semantic Web and blockchain in this demonstration involves utilizing RDF to store data in blocks, as depicted in Fig. 2. This approach complements the previous scenario, and any RDF-supported format, such as JSON-LD or XML/RDF, can be used to express the block's content.

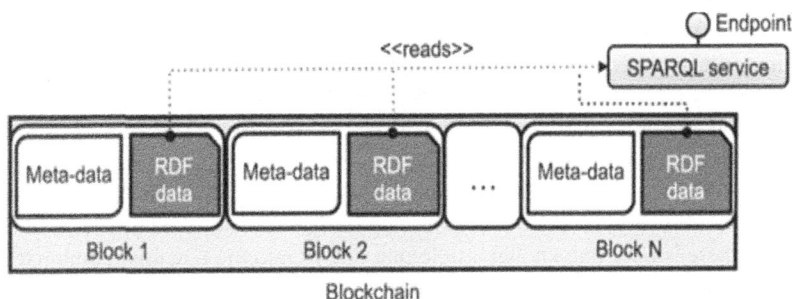

Fig. 2. Data representation in RDF format over a Blockchain

If There is a third-party service capable of processing SPARQL queries and reading the blockchain, this scenario offers many advantages. Practitioners can utilize SPARQL queries to search through the content and metadata of the blocks, which were described using an ontology. This enables the blockchain to gain all the benefits on our list.

Storing links to external data sources or ontologies in the chain is necessary. However, this scenario's primary disadvantage has not been thoroughly studied. The designated RDF formats available so far require a large number of characters and are verbose and the limitation is that the data stored in the form of blocks is restricted to some limited quantity. Therefore, RDF may require numerous blocks to store and define the information as non-RDF formats, which could decrease blockchain efficiency. To our knowledge, no research has examined the feasibility or efficiency of this scenario.

4.3   Virtual RDF and Blockchain

The virtualization services utilize the blockchain as a source of data and create RDF, as illustrated in Fig. 3. SPARQL is a query language specifically used on the data sets duly published from various services offered by RDF on the semantic web. On the contrary, there are other services which render RDF dump directly and is queried by means of a triple store. This approach could be the one best way to directly embed RDF over the Blockchain. Numerous virtual RDF services enable data linking with the fusion of multiple data sources. As a result, data links can be created dynamically or stored in a separate location.

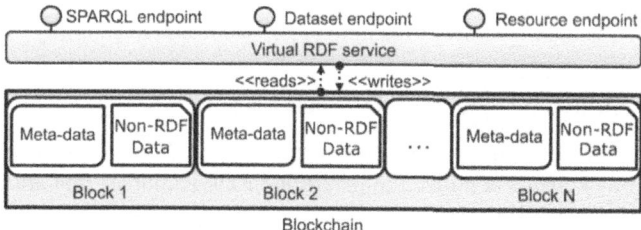

Fig. 3. Virtual RDF service orientation - representing Blockchain publication

In this approach, the data from the blockchain, specifically the RDF virtual data, can be merged with data from another source, and ontology mappings can also be integrated. One drawback of this is that it relies on an external service to create virtual RDF. The paper also states that the earlier research papers from the researchers have not defined any services rendered from a blockchain using virtual RDF. Hence, this could enlighten the core areas of researchers to work with the ideology behind the paper. This can enhance an enthusiastic approach to all research domain to learn more with blockchain and semantic web technology.

4.4   An External Pointer in the Blockchain

DNS problems are more violent in RDF. This is an important glitching aspect to store voluminous data conflicting with similarity of values in the data sets. This can be effectively achieved by allocating distinct and unique identifiers to all the available data fragments from the RDF datasets. Blockchain Hashing [3] is one among the common criterion to handle and store all relevant triplets of RDF data sets. All the unique featured triplets are hashed in to a single function by the RDF. Besides, this enhances security measures over the data. Alternatively, this could be an additional identifier which is independent of DNS system that works independently. It also enhances the appropriate identity of the subjects and URI's. Figure 4.

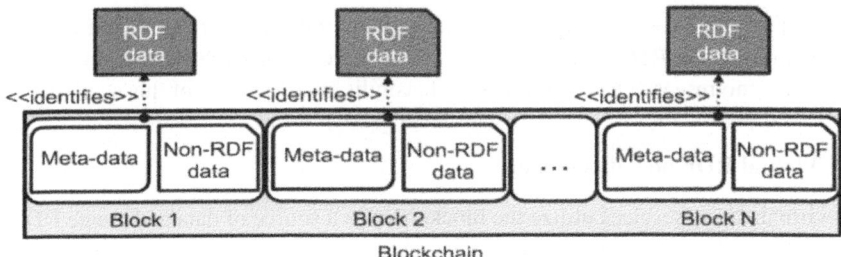

Fig. 4. RDF format over Blockchain plotting identifiers.

In the current context, the Semantic Web technologies do not provide any benefits to the blockchain. Instead, it is the Semantic Web technology being enriched from the features of block chain to meet the requirements and demand. The Fig. 4 elaborates the use of RDF with non usage of identifiers from the DNS source. This ensures the utility of resources are effectively used with out depending on the DNS. One of the advantages is that it is independent from DNS fetching better scope and availability of data.

4.5 Blockchain Referencing Another Blockchain

In this particular situation, there are two separate blockchains, as depicted in Fig. 5. One of these blockchains is utilized to determine RDF resources that are stored in the other blockchain, using any of the methods described in this section. Consequently, the RDF data in this scenario is unchangeable, easily understood, and possesses dual identification. The dual identification process is recognized by means of hash functions and other URI's being used from the consecutive blockchain. Thus, the semantic web gains advantages for the data redundancy.

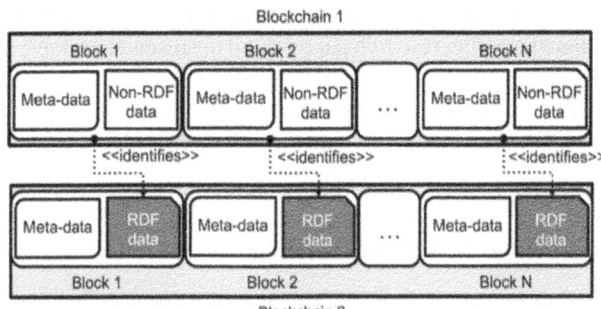

Fig. 5. Stacking of RDF chains using Blockchain

4.6 Semantic Blockchain

Figure 6 shows a situation where a blockchain implementation is created with the intention of incorporating Semantic Web technologies right from the start. Although there is no existing implementation like this at the moment, considering the potential advantages that the Semantic Web and blockchain can bring to each other, it is likely that someone will propose such an implementation. This approach would provide all the benefits we have discussed so far, from both the perspectives of the Semantic Web and blockchain.

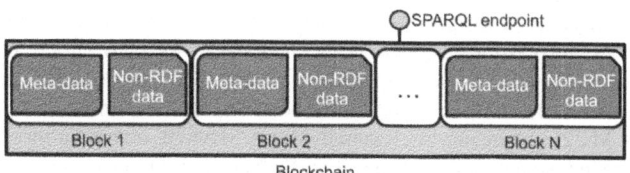

Fig. 6. Semantic Blockchain Implementation system

5 Conclusions

Blockchain technology has become increasingly important in solving problems across various industries. Researchers are showing great interest in integrating blockchain with the Semantic Web. This study examines the advantages that both blockchain and the Semantic Web can offer each other, and further clearly demonstrated various methods for combining the technologies with pros and cons. The proposed method clearly projects a basic idea for the combination of semantic web with block chain technology. Combinatory factors of at least six are mentioned to help make use of the applications. The future scope of this ideology can be great advantages in the growing demands of the industry and market.

References

1. Pilkington, M.: Blockchain Technology: Principles and Applications Research Handbook on Digital Transformations. In: Xavier Olleros, F., Edward Elgar, M.Z (eds.) (2016). SSRN: https://ssrn.com/abstract=2662660
2. Zheng, Z., Xie, S., Dai, H.N., Chen, X., Wang, H.: Blockchain challenges and opportunities: a survey. Int. J. Web Grid Serv. **14**(4), 352–375 (2018)
3. Lin, I.C., Liao, T.C.: A survey of blockchain security issues and challenges. Int. J. Netw. Secur. **19**(5), 653–659 (2017)
4. Ruta, M., Scioscia, F., Ieva, S., Capurso, G., Di Sciascio, E.: Semantic blockchain to improve scalability in the internet of things. Open J. Internet Things (OJIOT) **3**(1), 46–61 (2017)
5. Panarello, A., Tapas, N., Merlino, G., Longo, F., Puliafito, A.: Blockchain and iot integration: a systematic survey. Sensors **18**(8), 2575 (2018)
6. Sikorski, J.J., Haughton, J., Kraft, M.: Blockchain technology in the chemical industry: machine-to-machine electricity market. Appl. Energy **195**, 234–246 (2017)
7. English, M., Auer, S., Domingue, J.: Block chain technologies & the semantic web:a framework for symbiotic development. In: Lehmann, J., Thakkar, H., Halilaj, L.,Asmat, R. (eds.) Computer Science Conference for University of Bonn Students, pp.47–61(2016)

8. Bartoletti, M., Pompianu, L.: An analysis of bitcoin OP_RETURN metadata. In: Brenner, M., Rohloff, K., Bonneau, J., Miller, A., Ryan, P.Y.A., Teague, V., Bracciali, A., Sala, M., Pintore, F., Jakobsson, M. (eds.) FC 2017. LNCS, vol. 10323, pp. 218–230. Springer, Cham (2017). https://doi.org/10.1007/978-3-319-70278-0_14

9. Wood, G.: Ethereum & Ethcore Wood: Ethereum: a secure decentralised generalised transaction ledger. Ethereum Proj. Yellow Pap. 151(2014), 1–32 (2014)

10. Maly, R.J., Mischke, J., Kurtansky, P., Stiller, B.: Comparison of centralized (client-server) and decentralized (peer-to-peer) networking. Semester thesis, ETH Zurich, Zurich, Switzerl

11. Berners-Lee, T., Hendler, J., Lassila, O., et al.: Semant. Web. Sci. Am. 284(5), 28–37 (2001)

12. Brickley, D., Guha, R.V., McBride, B.: RDF schema 1.1. W3C recomm. 25, 2004–2014 (2014)

13. Lefrançois, M., Zimmermann, A., Bakerally, N.: A SPARQL extension for generating RDF from heterogeneous formats. In: Blomqvist, E., Maynard, D., Gangemi, A., Hoekstra, R., Hitzler, P., Hartig, O. (eds.) ESWC 2017. LNCS, vol. 10249, pp. 35–50. Springer, Cham (2017). https://doi.org/10.1007/978-3-319-58068-5_3

14. Sitha Ramulu, V., Raveendra Babu, B.: An R2RI APPROACH UPDATING RELATIONAL DATA THROUGH SPARQL/UPDATE. In: The Proceedings of the International Conference on Innovative Trends in Engineering, Science and Management, NICESM-2016, 26TH AND 27TH FEBRAURY-2016, IJCTA International Science Press ISSN 0974–5572, vol. 9, no. 7, pp.3037–3052 (2016)

15. Bizer, C., Heath, T., Berners-Lee, T.: Linked data-the story so far. In: Semantic Services, Interoperability and Web Applications: Emerging Concepts, pp. 205–227. IGI Global (2011)

16. McGuinness,Van Harmelen,et al.: Owl web ontology language overview. W3C Recomm. 10(10), 2004 (2004)

17. Nejdl, W., Wolpers, M., Capelle, C., Wissensverarbeitung, R., et al.: The RDF schema specification revisited. In Modelle und Modellierungssprachen in Informatik und Wirtschaftsinformatik, Modellierung 2000 (2000)

18. Vandenbussche, P.Y., Atemezing, G.A., Poveda-Villalón, M., Vatant, B.: Linked open vocabularies (LOV): a gateway to reusable semantic vocabularies on the web. Semantic Web 8(3), 437–452 (2017)

19. Uschold, M.: Achieving semantic interoperability using RDF and OWL-v4, 2005 (2013)

20. Harris, S., Seaborne, A., Prud'hommeaux, E.: SPARQL 1.1 query language. W3C Recommendation, 21(10), 778 (2013)

21. Buil-Aranda, C., Arenas, M., Corcho, O.: Semantics and optimization of the SPARQL 1.1 federation extension. In: Antoniou, G., Grobelnik, M., Simperl, E., Parsia, B., Plexousakis, D., De Leenheer, P., Pan, J. (eds.) ESWC 2011. LNCS, vol. 6644, pp. 1–15. Springer, Heidelberg (2011). https://doi.org/10.1007/978-3-642-21064-8_1

22. Knublauch, K.: Shapes constraint language (SHACL). W3C Candidate Recomm. 11(8) (2017)

23. Nentwig, M., Hartung, M., Ngonga Ngomo, A.C., Rahm, E.: A survey of current link discovery frameworks. Semantic Web 8(3), 419–436 (2017)

24. Lin, Y., Liu, Z., Sun, M., Liu, Y., Zhu, X.: Learning entity and relation embeddings for knowledge graph completion. In: Twenty-Ninth AAAI Conference on Artificial Intelligence (2015)

25. Sidoroff, H.: Semantic e-goverment portals-a case study. In: Proceedings of the ISWC-2005 Workshop Semantic Web Case Studies and Best Practices for eBusiness SWCASE05, vol. 7 (2005)

26. Nugent, T., Upton, D., Cimpoesu, M.: Improving data transparency in clinical trials using blockchain smart contracts. F1000Research, 5 (2016)

27. Ugarte, H.: A More Pragmatic Web 3.0: Linked Blockchain Data. Bonn, Germany (2017)

Loan Status Prediction System with Ensembled Machine Learning Models: Elevating Information Reliability and Accuracy

K. Badri Narayanan$^{(\boxtimes)}$, Yagnesh Challagundla$^{(\boxtimes)}$, Dev Rishik Maruturi$^{(\boxtimes)}$, and Nihar Ranjan Pradhan$^{(\boxtimes)}$

School of Computer Science and Engineering (SCOPE), VIT-AP University, Amaravathi 522237, Andhra Pradesh, India
`badrinarayanan78@gmail.com`, `yagneshnaidu1234@gmail.com`, `mdevrishik@gmail.com`, `nihar.pradhan@vitap.ac.in`

Abstract. We aimed to develop an integrated tool to more reliably and consistently anticipate lending conditions. The dataset for our analysis, which included a number of feature categories, was offered by Elsevier. The dataset had been uploaded to the application and then preprocessed. At this stage, we encountered missing data and found numerous extra columns, which we promptly eliminated. By eliminating pointless or duplicate features, we hoped to increase the model's ability to draw out important patterns from the data. Furthermore, we handled missing data by transforming discrete variables and imputing with average/most common values. The dataset was subsequently split into training and testing sets using a 70:30 ratio, and 5-fold cross-validation was used to evaluate the data. We examined a number of techniques for machine learning before choosing on Neural Networks, Gradient Boosting, Random Forest, and an innovative algorithm we created termed "RanNeu" (an Embedded ML model fusing Random Forest with Neural Networks). We carefully selected hyperparameters for each machine learning model in order to maximize performance. Using Lasso (L1) regularization, a constant learning rate, and an initial learning rate (eta) of 0.0100, we improved Gradient Boosting. As a result, we increased the number of neurons in hidden layers for neural networks to a maximum of 300, employed ReLu activation, and applied the Adam solver approach while using regularization with an alpha value of 0.0001 for neural networks.

Keywords: Machine learning · RanNeu · Loan Prediction · Embedded modeling · Prediction system · Data Visualization

1 Introduction

In recent years, the use of machine learning algorithms has become growing in prominence throughout many industries, particularly in the field of predictive analysis. Predicting loan status is one of these areas, and the financial industry heavily relies on being able

O. Castillo et al. (Eds.): PerSOM 2023, LNICST 517, pp. 263–272, 2024.
https://doi.org/10.1007/978-3-031-66044-3_19

to reliably predict loan outcomes. Financial institutions are better able to make informed decisions, minimize risks, and improve operational effectiveness when they can predict whether a loan will be approved or defaulted. The study was started in response to the pressing desire for more precise and trustworthy loan status predictions. The caliber of the dataset used forms the basis of each machine learning effort. In our investigation, we obtained a rich dataset from Elsevier that included a wide range of variables important for predicting loan status. We started the preprocessing stage after obtaining this dataset in order to clean, improve, and get the data ready for model training.

We ran into missing data during the preprocessing stage and found some unnecessary and redundant characteristics. We carefully dropped the unnecessary columns to improve our model's capacity to identify significant trends. We also used a number of methods to deal with the missing variables, such as impute them with average or most frequent values. Furthermore, we used a technique known as continuization, choosing from "one feature per value," to successfully handle discrete variables. Accurate prediction relies heavily on selecting the right machine learning models. We chose four potential models after examining numerous research publications and taking into account the particular needs of our project: Neural Networks, Gradient Boosting, Random Forest, and a novel method we developed, called "RanNeu" (an Embedded ML model fusing Random Forest with Neural Networks). We carefully selected hyperparameters to optimize the performance of each model. We chose an initial learning rate (eta) of 0.0100, a constant learning rate, and Lasso (L1) regularization for Gradient Boosting. We increased the number of neurons in hidden layers in neural networks to a maximum of 300, activated them with ReLu, and applied the Adam solver method. We used regularization with an alpha value of 0.0001 to avoid overfitting.

After utilizing the curated dataset to train our machine learning models, we assessed their effectiveness using important metrics including Area Under the Curve (AUC), Classification Accuracy (CA), F1 score, Precision, and Recall. The outcomes offered important information on each model's effectiveness. The RanNeu model, which had exceptional performance with AUC = 0.978, CA = 0.967, F1 = 0.963, precision = 0.966, and recall = 0.967, stood out as the most promising one. The Gradient Boosting, Random Forest, and Neural Network models came in second and third, respectively. We used a variety of data visualization tools, including Linebars, Line plots and Heatmap, to better comprehend the results and acquire further insights. These visualizations helped spot potential trends and patterns while providing a clear graphical depiction of the predictions made by our models. As a result, RanNeu, our integrated model, shows significant promise for reliably predicting loan situations. The project's effectiveness in boosting reliability and accuracy underlines the significance of ensemble machine learning techniques in financial prediction systems.

2 Related Work

A growing demand for precise and trustworthy models to determine credit risk and support financial decision-making has resulted in considerable improvements in the field of loan status prediction in recent years. To enhance the accuracy of loan prediction models, several researchers have investigated various machine learning algorithms and techniques.

To improve the accuracy of loan prediction, Gopichand (2023) suggested a unique strategy employing Logistic Regression over K-Nearest Neighbor [1]. Bhargav (2023) compared the accuracy of Random Forest and Naive Bayes algorithms [2] and found that Random Forest was more accurate. Bhetuwal and Siddanta looked into how well different machine learning models predicted loan defaults. A comparison of various prediction techniques for loan acceptance in the financial sector was offered by HOTA (2023) [3]. Sravani's paper from 2023 compared the loan prediction accuracy of Random Forest with Support Vector Machine [4]. Their research emphasized the benefits of Random Forest in enhancing prediction accuracy. Nabende and Senfuma (2019) concentrated on utilizing machine learning models to predict loan status [5] from Ugandan loan applications. Challagundla et al. (2023): Showcased the adaptability of these methods in diverse domains by using deep learning embedders and machine learning algorithms for screening citrus illnesses. Vivek et al. (2023) used Logistic Regression to analyze the low accuracy in loan prediction [6] and compared it to Random Forest to raise accuracy. Dansana et al. (2023) used the Random Forest algorithm to investigate the effect of loan features on bank loan prediction [7]. HOTA (2023): Conducted a comparative performance evaluation for the banking sector's loan approval prediction [8].

Sravani (2023): For loan prediction, compared the efficacy of the Random Forest and Support Vector Machine algorithms [9]. Using loan applications from Uganda, Nabende and Senfuma (2019) investigated machine learning models for forecasting loan status [10]. Mahesh (2020): Gave a review of machine learning techniques and discussed how they might be used to anticipate loans [11]. Arun et al. (2016): Investigated the possibility of predicting loan acceptance using machine learning and a variety of methods [12]. Chintalapati et al. (2022): Concentrated on the classification [13] of the measles rash disease using several Convolutional Neural Network classifiers. A secured loan prediction system employing an artificial neural network was created by ADEBIYI et al. in 2022, demonstrating the promise of neural-based methods for credit risk assessment. Sharma and Kumar (2022): Conducted an analysis of loan prediction based on an exploratory study [14] , providing insights into the variables affecting loan results (Fig. 1).

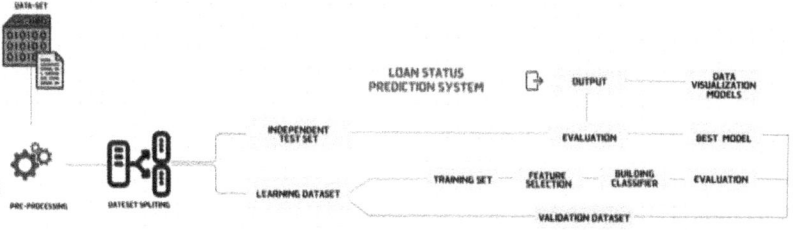

Fig. 1. Loan Status Prediction System Flowchart Steps: The Loan Status Prediction System Flowchart illustrates the step-by-step process of this study.

3 Methodology

In our project for predicting loan status, we acquired a large dataset from Elsevier that included a variety of variables that were important for predicting loan outcomes. The dataset was first uploaded into our software environment in CSV format. We then did preprocess to make sure the data was accurate and appropriate for model training. We ran into missing data during preprocessing and found some repetitive and superfluous columns. We removed the superfluous columns in order to improve our model's capacity to extract significant patterns. Additionally, we dealt with missing data by imputing with the average or most common values as part of pre-processing approaches. We used a continuization strategy to successfully handle discrete variables and transform them into an analytically usable structure.

3.1 Data Collection

We obtained the dataset for our analysis, which included a number of feature categories, that was offered by Elsevier., which comprised data from over a lakh individuals. This dataset served as the foundation for our loan status monitoring application.

3.2 Dataset Splitting and Cross-Validation

We split the dataset into two parts the Training dataset (70%) and the Testing dataset (30%), in order to appropriately assess the performance of our models. To avoid bias, we made sure that both subsets were representative of the entire dataset. Additionally, during the analysis phase, we used 5-fold cross-validation to reduce the danger of overfitting and evaluate model generalization.2. To ensure that the cross-validation process produced trustworthy and robust results, we randomly sampled recurring train/test divides (Fig. 2).

3.3 Dataset Split

The dataset has been divided into a training dataset and a testing dataset. The split ratio of 60:40 ensured there would be enough data for both training and evaluation. A 10-fold cross-validation method was used to thoroughly assess the models' performance. In order to get accurate and generalizable results, the train/test splits were randomly sampled during the first stage of analysis (Fig. 2).

3.4 Selection of Machine Learning Techniques

We performed a thorough investigation to determine which machine learning algorithms would work best for our loan status prediction system. We took into account a number of variables, such as performance indicators, computational effectiveness, and interpretability. We selected four effective models after reviewing pertinent research papers: Neural Networks, Gradient Boosting, Random Forest, and our original technique, "RanNeu" (Embedded ML model combining Random Forest and Neural Networks).

Loan Status Prediction System with Ensembled Machine Learning Models: Elevating Information Reliability and Accuracy

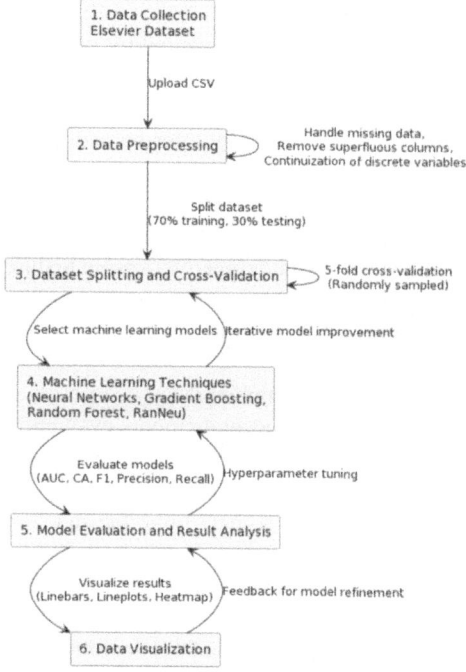

Fig. 2. Loan Status Prediction System methodology flowchart Steps

3.5 Model Evaluation and Result Analysis

We evaluated the performance of each machine learning model using a variety of evaluation metrics, including Area Under the Curve (AUC), Classification Accuracy (CA), F1 score, Precision, and Recall. The RanNeu algorithm ended up being the model that performed the best after our evaluation. RanNeu outperformed the other models and produced results with AUC, CA, F1, accuracy, and recall values of 0.978, 0.966, and 0.967.

3.6 Data Visualization

We used data visualization approaches to acquire a deeper understanding of the model's predictions and to assist in the result interpretation. To graphically portray the model results and spot potential patterns and trends, we used Linebars, Lineplots and Heatmap.

In a combined loan status prediction system with improved accuracy and dependability, our methodology comprised careful dataset preparation, model selection, hyperparameter tuning, and rigorous evaluation. Data visualization and the outcomes of our ensemble machine learning model, RanNeu, offer insightful information for next work and financial applications. Our efforts to increase the application's precision and user-friendliness as well as to expand data collecting pave the way for ongoing developments in the field of loan status prediction.

4 Results

The ensembled machine learning model, our method for predicting loan status has produced remarkably accurate and reliable results. The dataset, which came from Elsevier, had a wide range of attributes that were essential for creating reliable prediction models. In the first stage, we preprocessed the dataset after uploading it in CSV format to our software environment. We ran into missing data during preprocessing and found redundant and irrelevant columns. By eliminating these superfluous variables, we improved the model's capacity to identify significant patterns in the data. Additionally, we used pre-processing methods to deal with the problem of sparse features and missing values, such as impute missing values with average or most frequent values and continuous discrete variables. Then, keeping a 70:30 ratio, we divided the dataset into training and testing subsets.

We used 5-fold cross-validation, which allowed us to evaluate model performance under various circumstances, to assure accurate model evaluations. We randomly sampled recurring train/test splits throughout the analysis phase, yielding 10 iterations out of 100 for reliable and objective assessments. We conducted a thorough investigation and consulted current research papers to determine the machine learning techniques that would work best for our system to anticipate the loan status. As a result, we chose four well-known models: RanNeu (an ensemble model combining Random Forest and Neural Networks), Gradient Boosting, Neural Networks, and Random Forest.

We adjusted hyperparameters for each machine learning model to enhance performance. We applied Lasso (L1) regularization in the Gradient Boosting model with a constant learning rate and an initial learning rate (eta) of 0.0100. In comparison, the Neural Networks model used ReLu activation, the Adam solver method, and a maximum of 300 hidden layer neurons. We used regularization with an alpha value of 0.0001 to avoid overfitting. Through the use of several performance indicators, including Area Under the Curve (AUC), Classification Accuracy (CA), F1 Score, Precision, and Recall, the evaluation of our models produced appealing findings. The RanNeu algorithm outperformed the other models with AUC = 0.978, CA = 0.967, F1 = 0.963, precision = 0.966, and recall = 0.967, outperforming the others. We used data visualization techniques including scatter plots, ranviz, and bar plots to get a better understanding of the predictions and make it easier to analyze the results. These visualizations showed potential patterns and trends in the data as well as a clear graphical representation of the model results (Fig. 3 and Table 1).

Table 1. The table demonstrating the values obtained after performing various models

MODEL	AUC	CA	F1	PRECISION	RECALL
RanNeu (Embedded Model)	0.978	0.967	0.963	0.966	0.967
Neural Network	0.982	0.944	0.943	0.943	0.944
Random Forest	0.966	0.938	0.937	0.938	0.938
Gradient Boosting	0.951	0.913	0.910	0.911	0.913

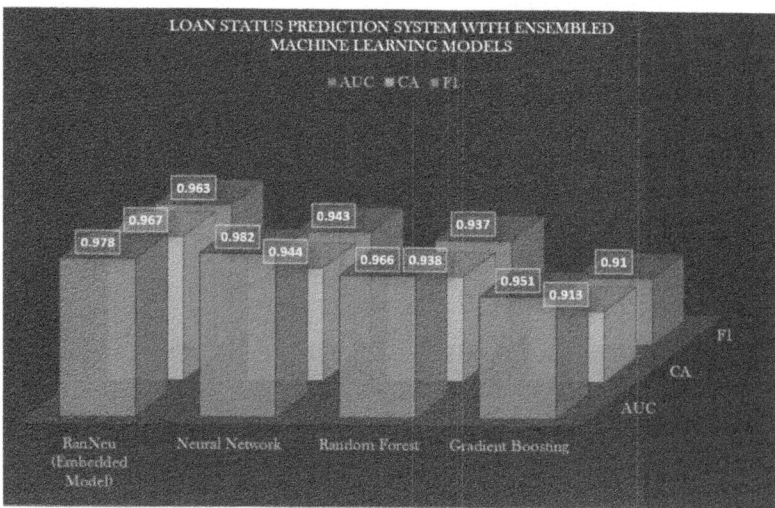

Fig. 3. An 3d-Chart of output results

The effectiveness of ensemble machine learning and optimal hyperparameter tuning in achieving increased accuracy and reliability is demonstrated by our integrated loan status prediction system, which is a last point. The RanNeu algorithm's outstanding performance suggests that merging Random Forest and Neural Networks may enhance prediction abilities. Our study lays the groundwork for ongoing improvements in loan status prediction systems with the future scope of improving our application's accuracy and user interface as well as gathering new data to reinforce the dataset. Financial institutions will undoubtedly benefit greatly from these developments, which will give them the tools they need to make wise decisions and successfully manage risks (Fig. 4).

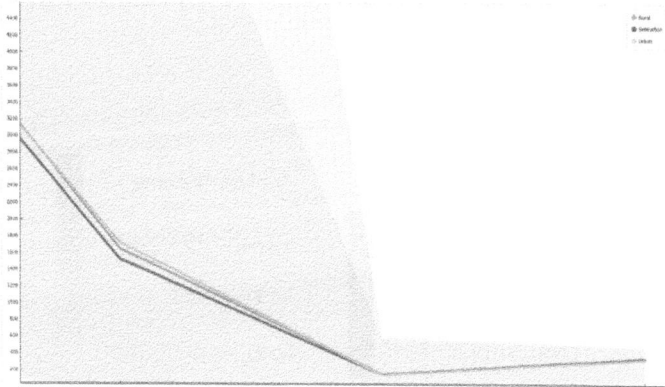

Fig. 4. Line plot indicating the trend of loan approval probability in Rural, Semiurban, and Urban regions relative to total property area

The line plot displays the loan approval probability in various regions (Rural, Semi-urban, and Urban) relative to the total property area helps identify trends and differences in approval likelihood based on property location. The plot showcases the mean values and the range of probabilities, providing an understanding of how the property location influences the likelihood of loan approval. This visualization aids in discerning patterns and trends based on different property-area categories and property regions (Fig. 5).

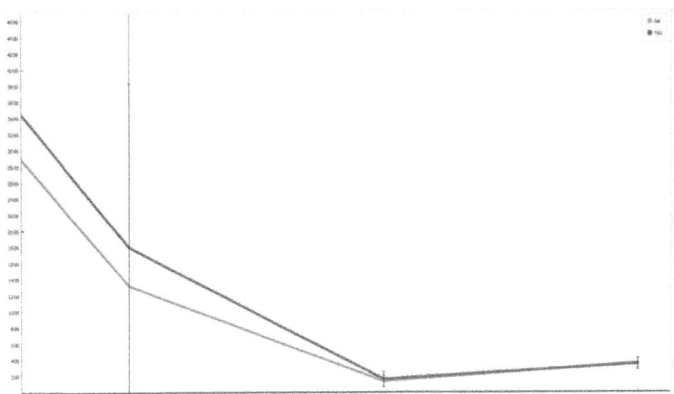

Fig. 5. Creating a Line Plot with Mean and Error Bars: Comparing Loan Approval Probability for Married vs. Non-Married (Red for Yes, Blue for No) (Color figure online)

The line plot represents the loan approval status probability comparison between married and non-married individuals. The plot uses red and blue lines to denote "Yes" and "No" outcomes, respectively. The mean values are shown by straight black lines, and error bars provide a visual representation of the uncertainty in the data. This visualization offers valuable insights into how marital status influences loan approval probabilities (Fig. 6).

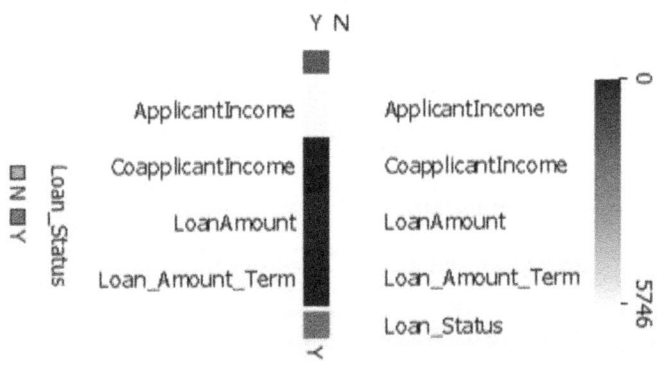

Fig. 6. Loan Status vs None Features Heatmap: Visualizing Yes and No Ratios

A heatmap has been created to visualize the relationship between loan status and various none features, with loan status represented along both the rows and columns. The positions of "Yes" and "No" in the heatmap have been adjusted to the top and bottom, respectively. The heatmap provides an estimate of the total results of "Yes" and "No" for each feature in the dataset, considering the ratio of these outcomes in relation to the features. This visualization aids in understanding how different features influence the loan status and provides valuable insights into the predictive power of these features in determining the loan approval status.

5 Conclusion

In order to improve accuracy and dependability, we successfully created a Loan Status Prediction System in this project utilizing an ensembled machine learning model. The dataset acquired from Elsevier included a wide variety of features, offering a thorough framework for creating reliable prediction models. We carefully preprocessed the data to make sure it was of high quality and suitable for analysis. We handled missing data at this phase and removed unnecessary and redundant columns, enabling our algorithms to effectively uncover useful patterns. Sparse characteristics were removed, and missing values were substituted with the most frequent values or averaged to impute them. Continuizing discrete variables also made it easier to choose "one feature per value." We split the dataset in half, dividing it into 70:30 Training and Testing subsets. We used 5-fold cross-validation, integrating random sampling of recurring train/test divides in 10 out of 100 rounds, to accurately validate our models.

We chose four well-known machine learning approaches for prediction after a thorough analysis and examination of the literature: Neural Networks, Gradient Boosting, Random Forest, and our cutting-edge RanNeu algorithm, a potent ensemble model combining Random Forest and Neural Networks. With L1 regularization, constant learning rates for gradient boosting, and ReLu activation with Adam solver for neural networks, each model's hyperparameters were tuned to maximize performance.

We discovered that the RanNeu method surpassed all others when we evaluated the final outcome findings using different performance measures, including AUC, classification accuracy, F1 score, precision, and recall. It achieved a remarkable AUC of 0.978, CA of 0.967, F1 of 0.963, precision of 0.966, and recall of 0.967. This outcome confirms that combining Random Forest and Neural Networks can improve predictions of loan status. In order to evaluate the results and spot probable trends in the data, data visualization tools like scatter plots and bar graphs were used to get deeper insights into the model results. We discovered that the RanNeu method surpassed all others when we evaluated the final outcome findings using different performance measures, including AUC, classification accuracy, F1 score, precision, and recall. It achieved a remarkable AUC of 0.978, CA of 0.967, F1 of 0.963, precision of 0.966, and recall of 0.967.

This outcome confirms that combining Random Forest and Neural Networks can improve predictions of loan status. In order to evaluate the results and spot probable trends in the data, data visualization tools like scatter plots and bar graphs were used to get deeper insights into the model results. We are certain that the improvements produced in this system will pave the way for better financial decision-making and risk management in the future. Our effort is a first step toward continued progress in the field of loan status prediction.

References

1. Ramini, V., Mahaveerakannan, R.: Analyzed the lack of accuracy inloan prediction using Logistic Regression and compared it with Random Forest to improve accuracy (2023)
2. Dansana, D., et al.: Explored the impact of loan features on bank loan prediction using the Random Forest algorithm (2023)
3. Gopichand, M.: Proposed a novel approach using Logistic Regression over K-Nearest Neighbor for improved accuracy in loan prediction (2023)
4. Bhargav, P.: Compared the accuracy of Random Forest with the Naive Bayes algorithm and demonstrated Random Forest's superior performance (2023)
5. Aayush, B., Siddanta, K.C..: Investigated the performance of various machine learning models for loan default prediction
6. Hota, L.: Conducted a comparative performance assessment for the prediction of loan approval in the financial sector (2023)
7. Sravani, K.: Compared the accuracy of Random Forest with the Support Vector Machine algorithm for loan prediction (2023)
8. Peter, N., Senfuma, S.: Studied machine learning models forpredicting loan status from Ugandan loan applications (2019)
9. Batta, M.: Provided a review of machine learning algorithms, including their application to loan prediction (2020)
10. Kumar, A., Ishan, G., Sanmeet, K.: Explored loan approval prediction based on a machine learning approach using various algorithms (2016)
11. Chintalapati, L.R., Tunuguntla, T.S.C., Challagundla, Y., Mohanty, S.N., Sudha, S.V.:Focused on measles rash disease classification based on various convolutional neural network classifiers. In: Nandan Mohanty, S., Garcia Diaz, V., Satish Kumar, G.A.E. (eds.) ICISML 2022. LNICS, vol. 470, pp. 15–27. Springer, Cham (2023). https://doi.org/10.1007/978-3-031-350 78-8_2
12. Adebiyi Marion, O., et al.: Developed a secured loan prediction system using artificial neural network, showcasing the potential of neural-based techniques in credit risk assessment (2022)
13. Sharma, A., Kumar, V.: Conducted an exploratory study-based analysis on loan prediction. In: Ranganathan, G., Fernando, X., Rocha, Á. (eds.) Inventive Communication and Computational Technologies. LNNS, vol. 383, pp. 423–433. Springer, Cham (2022). https://doi.org/10.1007/978-981-19-4960-9_33
14. Yagnesh, C., et al.: Used deep learning embedders and machine learning techniques for screening citrus diseases, showcasing the versatility of these methods in various domains (2023)
15. Himanshi, S., et al.: An Exhaustive Investigation on Loan Prediction in Banks using LRD
16. Sravani, K., Mahaveerakannan, R.: An innovative method of loan prediction that compares decision tree algorithm accuracy with random forest. J. Surv. Fish. Sci. 10(1S), 3033–3041 (2023)

Effect of Global Warming on Glaciers, Rivers and Water Towers

Sushruth Samson[1], Srinivas Patnaik[1], K. Rajesh Kannan[2(✉)], T. Prathima[2], and B. R. Sreedhar[3]

[1] Department of Artificial Intelligence and Data Science, Chaitanya Bharathi Institute of Technology, Hyderabad, India
[2] Department of Information Technology, Chaitanya Bharathi Institute of Technology, Hyderabad, India
{rajeshkannan_it,tprathima_it}@cbit.ac.in
[3] Department of Mathematics, Chaitanya Bharathi Institute of Technology, Hyderabad, India
brsreedhar_maths@cbit.ac.in

Abstract. This study employs machine learning algorithms to comprehensively assess the impact of global warming on glaciers, rivers, and water towers. By analyzing diverse datasets encompassing remote sensing, climate records, and hydrological data, the research aims to elucidate the intricate relationships between temperature changes and the behavior of these vital components of the Earth's hydrological cycle. The outcomes of this investigation are poised to enhance our understanding of the far-reaching consequences of climate change on freshwater resources and facilitate informed decision-making for sustainable environmental management. The study uses several machine-learning algorithms to investigate worldwide glaciers, rivers, and water towers. The study sheds light on these crucial natural resources existing and future health, alerting people to the critical need for long-term management and conservation measures.

Keywords: Glacier and river analysis · Water Towers · Machine Learning algorithms · Global Water Resources

1 Introduction

This research article examines glacier melting and its influence on river flow throughout the world. The study analyzes the ice volume, ice area, meltwater production, and predicted endpoints of glaciers from across the world using a dataset of glaciers from diverse parts of the world. The analyses' source code is available in the R programming language. The collection includes 13 glaciers from throughout the world, including North America, South America, and Asia. The data analysis demonstrates that glaciers with greater ice volume and area have a larger meltwater production, which impacts river flow downstream. The study also found that glaciers having a future endpoint of 0 (peninsular river) produce less meltwater than glaciers with a future endpoint of 1 (perennial river). The analysis source code is available in the R programming language. The code reads

O. Castillo et al. (Eds.): PerSOM 2023, LNICST 517, pp. 273–292, 2024.
https://doi.org/10.1007/978-3-031-66044-3_20

the dataset from a CSV file and adds a new column based on the endpoint values in the future. The revised data frame is then written back to the CSV file by the function. The code also does statistical analysis, such as determining the mean, median, and standard deviation of the various parameters.

The analysis's results are given in the form of tables and graphs, which demonstrate the distribution of the various parameters and their relationships. The tables indicate the mean, median, and standard deviation of the glaciers' ice volume, ice area, and meltwater output. The graphs depict the relationship between ice volume and meltwater yield, as well as ice area and meltwater yield and projected endpoint. The dataset analysis shows that glacier melting has a major influence on river flow downstream. Finally, the dataset analysis demonstrates the large influence of glacier melting on river flow downstream. According to the study, glaciers with more ice volume and area have a larger meltwater production, which impacts river flow downstream. According to the study, glaciers with a future endpoint of 1 (perennial river) have a larger meltwater production than glaciers with a future endpoint of 0 (peninsular river). This page includes the analysis's source code and results, which may be utilized by academics for additional analysis and decision-making.

"Water is crucial for life," and it is an expensive asset that is becoming progressively restricted in many places of the world. The rapid growth of human populations and economic development has put enormous strain on water supplies, particularly in metropolitan areas. The water problem is a critical challenge that demands immediate response, and water resources must be managed effectively and sustainably. Several techniques have been proposed to solve this issue, including the identification of prospective water sources and the effective use of current supplies. Water towers, which are high altitude mountainous locations that give water to millions of people, animals, and plants downstream, are one such technique. Water towers are vital for supplying water to metropolitan areas and the agricultural sector. Because of the importance of these ecosystems for human and environmental health, there has been an increase in interest in water towers in recent years. Several research studies have been undertaken to evaluate the water supplies, ecological state, and management tactics of water towers. However, there is currently a scarcity of complete and integrated data that may be utilized to advise water tower management and conservation. To fill this void, this study piece attempts to give a detailed examination of the water resources in the Ngong Hills water towers, one of Kenya's most important water towers. The study is based on a large data collection that contains statistics on water demand, lake storage volume, and water indicators. This article is organized into sections to offer a thorough examination. First, we outline the research topic and the techniques utilized to gather and analyze data. The analytical findings are then presented, including water demand, lake storage volume, and water consumption indications. The significance of the findings for the management and protection are then discussed. Finally, we conclude with suggestions for future study and management measures. The information in this research paper was gathered from a variety of sources. The data were subsequently analyzed using several statistical tools, including the R programming packages dplyr and ggplot2.

2   Literature Survey

In the article [1], The researchers utilized a mix of models to assess the ice thickness distribution of all non-polar glaciers worldwide. Accurate information of this distribution is required for a variety of research, including projecting future glacier changes, appraising freshwater supplies, and calculating possible sea-level rise. The researchers discovered a total volume of glacier ice of $158 \pm 41 \times 103$ km^3, which corresponds to a sea-level shift of 0.32 ± 0.08 m when the portion of ice situated below present-day sea level (approximately 15%) is subtracted. This suggests that if all of the world's glaciers melted, sea levels would rise by 0.32 ± 0.08 m. The study also discovered that the High Mountain Asia region has around 27% less glacier ice than previously assumed, and that the region is projected to lose half of its current glacier area a decade earlier than previously predicted. This work provides an essential new estimate of the global distribution of glacial ice thickness, which will be beneficial for a variety of studies as well as future glacier research and management activities. The researchers utilized an ensemble of up to five models to estimate the ice thickness distribution of the world's non-polar glaciers, excluding those in Greenland and Antarctica. The models employed ice flow dynamics concepts to estimate ice thickness from surface data such as elevation and velocity. The researchers then pooled the outcomes of the several models to arrive at a consensus estimate.

According to the study, the entire amount of glacier ice in the globe, excluding Greenland and Antarctica, is around $158 \pm 41 \times 103$ km^3. This is somewhat greater than prior estimates, which varied from roughly 130 to 140×103 km^3, but still within the margin of error. The study also discovered that around 15% of the world's glacier ice lies below the current sea level. When this proportion is eliminated, the remaining glacier ice would generate a 0.32 ± 0.08 m increase in sea level if it melted entirely. The study discovered that the High Mountain Asia area, which encompasses the Himalayas and other mountain ranges in Central and South Asia, contains around 27% less glacier ice than previously assumed. This indicates that the region will likely lose half of its current glacier area a decade earlier than previously anticipated. This has serious consequences for the region's water resources and risks, as many populations rely on glacial meltwater for drinking water, agriculture, and electricity.

Overall, the work adds to our understanding of the global distribution of glacial ice thickness and emphasizes the importance of ongoing monitoring and research on glacier systems, particularly in areas sensitive to the effects of climate change.

[2] The modeling of call and message creation in voice and data networks using Poisson processes is covered in this chapter. Because it is theoretically tractable, the Poisson process is very valuable in various applications. The chapter dives into the Poisson arrival process in depth, demonstrating that it is a subset of the pure birth process. Following that, the chapter delves into birth-death processes, which are used to represent some queueing systems. Customers come at a Poisson rate at a service facility with exponentially dispersed service requirements in these systems. Birth-death processes are particularly effective for modeling queueing systems with a restricted number of clients. The chapter includes thorough mathematical analysis and examples of these processes, such as calculating steady-state probability and queueing system performance indicators like mean queue length and mean waiting time. The author also

explains the models' limitations and the assumptions that must be made for them to be valid. Overall, this chapter serves as an excellent introduction to the usage of pure birth and birth-death processes in queueing theory, as well as their application to the analysis of computer communication networks.

According [3] to an international group of scientists who use satellite data, the acceleration in the melting of Earth's ice sheets is now obvious. They estimate that from 1992 and 2022, the planet's frozen poles shed 7,560 billion tonnes of mass, with seven of the worst melting years occurring in the last decade. Greenland and Antarctica mass loss currently accounts for a quarter of global sea-level rise, which is five times what it was 30 years ago. The most recent evaluation comes from the Ice Sheet Mass Balance Intercomparison Exercise (Imbie), which conducts periodic assessments of the world's ice sheets. This is the third such study, and it, too, has compiled and evaluated all available satellite measurements. The melting of Greenland and Antarctic ice sheets is caused by climate change, which is caused by human activities such as the use of fossil fuels and deforestation. As the Earth warms, the ice sheets become more prone to melting, resulting in increasing sea levels that endanger coastal cities worldwide.

Sea-level rise has serious and far-reaching repercussions. They include more frequent and severe coastal floods, erosion, and storm surges, which can cause infrastructure and housing damage, displacement, and economic disruption. Furthermore, increasing sea levels can pollute freshwater sources and raise the possibility of saltwater intrusion into coastal aquifers, thereby impacting agricultural productivity and human health. To address the issue of melting ice sheets and increasing sea levels, a worldwide effort is required to cut greenhouse gas emissions, adapt to climate change, and invest in measures to safeguard vulnerable people. This involves less reliance on fossil fuels, more use of renewable energy, better coastal infrastructure, and a better understanding of the intricate relationships between the climate, seas, and ice sheets.

The cited article [4] gives an in-depth examination of developing changes in global freshwater resources. The article focuses on the major difficulties confronting water resources, such as rising demand owing to population increase and economic development, as well as the influence of climate change on water supply. According to the authors, identifying and tackling these difficulties is crucial to ensuring long-term water resource management.

One of the paper's primary conclusions is that worldwide freshwater supplies are unevenly distributed, with some places experiencing water scarcity while others experiencing an oversupply. The authors also emphasize that many locations in Asia, Africa, and the Middle East are already facing water stress, which is compounded by population increase and rising agricultural and industrial water demand. The impact of climate change on global freshwater supplies is another major focus of the report. Rising temperatures and shifting precipitation patterns, according to the authors, are projected to worsen water stress in many locations, with certain regions suffering severe water scarcity in the future. They claim that tackling this problem would need a variety of adaptation strategies, such as better water storage and management, the development of new water sources, and the promotion of water conservation and efficiency.

The article also looks at how freshwater availability affects other environmental systems, such as aquatic ecosystems and biodiversity. The authors point out that decreasing freshwater availability can have a considerable influence on these systems, potentially having a detrimental impact on human well-being and ecological health. To address this issue, they propose a variety of approaches to enhance water management and conserve aquatic ecosystems, such as encouraging sustainable water use practices, increasing water quality, and building efficient monitoring mechanisms to track changes in freshwater ecosystems through time. Overall, the article thoroughly reviews a thorough review of developing patterns in global freshwater availability, underlining the fundamental issues that water resource management will face in the future. It contends that tackling these difficulties would need a variety of initiatives, including better water management practices, the development of rigorous models and data, and the promotion of sustainable water usage practices. The study also emphasizes the need of tackling climate change's influence on water supplies, as well as the need to safeguard aquatic ecosystems and biodiversity in the face of declining freshwater supply.

3 Data-Set Description

3.1 European Environment Agency (ERA5)

This category contains precipitation and evaporation data taken from the ERA5 reanalysis, which is available in the Copernicus Climate Data Store online. ERA5_evaporation_avgannual_2001_2017.nc includes average annual evaporation (mm) for the years 2001–2017, while ERA5_evaporation_ymonmean_2001_2017.nc contains multi-year mean monthly evaporation (mm) for the same period. The file era5_total-precipitation_ymonmean_2001-2017_global.tif includes multi-year mean monthly precipitation (mm) from 2001 to 2017, and the file era5_total-precipitation_yearsum_2001–2017.tif contains average yearly precipitation (mm) for the same time period. This directory's output files include P_avg_annual_basin_mm.tif, which shows the average annual precipitation for the years 2001–2017 (mm) aggregated to basins, P_avg_annual_DS_mm.tif, which shows the average annual precipitation for the same period (mm) aggregated to downstream basins, P_avg_annual_mm.tif, which shows the average annual precipitation for the same period (mm), P_avg P_var_interannual.tif depicts the interannual variability in precipitation for the years 2001–2017, P_var_interannual_basin.tif depicts the interannual variability in precipitation for the same period aggregated to basins, P_var_interannual_DS.tif depicts the interannual variability in precipitation for the same period aggregated to downstream basins, and P_var_interannual_WT.tif depicts the interannual variability in precipitation for the same period.P_var_intraannual.tif shows the intra-annual variability in precipitation for the years 2001–2017, P_var_intraannual_basin.tif shows the intra-annual variability in precipitation for the same period aggregated to basins, P_var_intraannual_DS.tif shows the intra-annual variability in precipitation for the same period aggregated to downstream b Finally, the WTU_P_indicators.csv file provides a table that lists all computed precipitation indicators by Water Tower Unit.

3.2 Glaciers

This category provides data on glacier volume and mass balance collected from publicly available databases. Glac_area_WT_km^2.tif shows the aggregated glacier area (km^2) for

Water Tower Units, Glac_volume_WT_km^3. tif shows the aggregated glacier volume (km^3) for Water Tower Units, and WTU_Glacier_indicators.csv contains a table listing all derived glacier indicators per Water Tower Unit. WTU_MB.shp is also a shapefile of Water Tower Units with the glacial mass balance per Water Tower Unit as an attribute.

Glacier volume data released in Farinotti et al., 2019, Nature Geoscience, were utilized to determine glacier volume and area at 0.05° spatial resolution in this investigation. The following files were used: p05_degree_glacier_area_km^2.tif and p05_degree_glacier_volume_km^3.tif. The World Glacier Monitoring Service's glacier mass balance data were also utilized to calculate an average.

3.3   HydroLakes

The HydroLAKES data collection contains statistics on the surface area, volume, and age of water contained in lakes and reservoirs across the world. A geo-statistical technique based on remote sensing and ground-based observations was used to build the data set. The data set may be used for a variety of purposes, such as water resource management, hydrological modeling, and climate change research.

There are two sorts of output files in the HydroLAKES data set: a table and a raster file. The WTU_lake_storage_volume.csv table displays the lake and reservoir volume (in km^3) per Water Tower Unit (WTU). The HydroSHEDS project divides the world's land area into 15,000 units based on the drainage network and topography, and a WTU is a hydrological unit established by the project. The table shows the volume of water held in lakes and reservoirs within each WTU, which is useful for water resource management and planning.

WTU_surface_water_storage_km^3.tif is the name of the second output file. This file includes the aggregated lake and reservoir storage volume (in km^3) in WTUs. The file may be used to visualize the global geographical distribution of lake and reservoir storage volume. This data is critical for evaluating regional water availability and identifying locations at risk of water scarcity.

The HydroLAKES data set makes use of the shapefile HydroLAKES_polys_v10.shp, which may be acquired from the HydroSheds website. The HydroLAKES data collection is based on a large database of lake and reservoir information gathered from several sources, including remote sensing data, ground-based observations, and existing lake databases. The data collection contains information on over 1.4 million lakes and reservoirs worldwide, covering an area of around 8.7 million km^2 and a volume of approximately 173,000 km^3.Messager et al. (2016) created the HydroLAKES data collection by using a statistical model to estimate the amount and age of water stored in lakes and reservoirs throughout the world. The model was verified using independent lake volume estimations from existing databases and was based on a combination of satellite and in-situ data. The generated data collection is a great resource for understanding the dynamics of lake and reservoir systems and analyzing the influence of climate change and human activities on these systems.

In conclusion, the HydroLAKES data collection gives extensive information on the amount and age of water held in lakes and reservoirs across the world. The data collection is based on a large database of lake and reservoir information and may be used for a variety of purposes such as water resource management, hydrological modeling, and climate change research.

3.4 Indicators

The table provided shows the calculated indicators and sub indicators per Water Tower Unit. The Water Tower Units are identified by their respective IDs and names in the second and third columns, respectively. Pup_tot (total population within the Water Tower Unit), pinter (population living in urban areas within the Water Tower Unit), pintra (population living in rural areas within the Water Tower Unit), ptot (total protected areas within the Water Tower Unit), snow_p (percentage of the Water Tower Unit covered by snow), snow_intra (percentage of snow cover in intra-mountain areas), snow_inter (percentage of snow cover in inter-mountain areas), dem_irr (irrigated cropland area in the Water Tower Unit), dem_ind (industrial land area in the Water Tower Unit), dem_dom (built-up area in the Water Tower Unit), dem_nat (natural land area in the Water Tower Unit), demtot (total land area in the Water Tower Unit), suptot (total area of the Water Tower Unit), fin_sd (final Water Tower Index score for the Water Tower Unit), fin_sd_nor.

The values for each parameter are provided in the table's relevant columns. Columns four through seven, for example, include the values for pup_tot, pinter, pintra, and ptot. Snow_p, snow_intra, snow_inter, and stot values are similarly reported in columns eight through eleven. Columns twelve to fourteen include the values for glac_v, glac_m, and gtot, whereas columns fifteen to nineteen have the values for swtot, dem_irr, dem_ind, dem_dom, and dem_nat. Finally, in the final three columns, the values for suptot, fin_sd, and fin_sd_nor are provided.The table summarizes the numerous indicators and sub indicators that are used to compute the Water Tower Index for each Water Tower Unit. The data may be used to compare different Water Tower Units and to highlight regions that need greater attention and action to maintain water resource sustainability.

3.5 SNOW

The snow dataset used to calculate the Water Tower Index is based on the MODIS MOD10CM006 snow cover product, which gives information on the extent of snow cover throughout the world. The dataset comprises both input and output files, as well as yearly mean snow cover, multi-year mean monthly snow cover, and several metrics of snow persistence and variability in snow persistence, all of which are aggregated to the Water Tower Units. Snow data is critical for analyzing water availability in the various water towers since snow is a significant source of meltwater that contributes to river and groundwater recharge.

3.6 Uncertainty

The data in the uncertainty directory are relevant to the uncertainty analysis of the water balance components. The data include evaporation and precipitation standard deviations (SD) for both downstream basins and Water Tower Units. The directory also contains the degree of uncertainty in ice volume per Water Tower Unit. These statistics may be used to understand the extent of uncertainty in the water balance components, allowing for better educated water management and allocation choices.

3.7 Water Demands

The directory "Water demands" offers statistics on net water demands for various sectors such as irrigation, industrial, and home water consumption. The data is derived from the output of the PCR-GLOBWB hydrological model and spans the years 2001 to 2014 with a resolution of 0.05°. Multi-year mean monthly net water demand for each sector and the aggregate of the three sectors, as well as multi-year mean monthly natural discharge, are included in the input data. Average annual net water demand for each sector and the total of the three sectors, average annual natural water demand, average annual water gap, and average annual net human water demand aggregated to basins are all included in the output data.

3.8 WTU Units

This directory offers a comprehensive collection of data on water resources and their management across multiple geographical units. The data may be used to better understand water needs and availability in different locations, as well as to identify places where water shortages may exist or where water management practices can be improved. The use of Water Tower Units as spatial units enables a more detailed investigation of water resources in mountainous locations, which are frequently major water supplies for downstream regions.

3.9 Study Area

Below are the specific geographical regions and landmarks that are incorporated in the study:

- Africa: The study includes Mount Kilimanjaro, with specific reference to WTU-0078 for Kilimanjaro.
- Asia: The study also incorporates the formidable Himalayas (WTU-0020, WTU-0078).
- Europe: The Alps, Europe's central mountain range (WTU-0037), the Danube River (WTU-0020, WTU-0071), and the Mediterranean Sea (WTU-0013, WTU-0071) are integral parts of the study.
- North America: Grand Canyon (WTU-0078), the Mississippi River (WTU-0042, WTU-0071, WTU-0072), and the Rocky Mountains (WTU-0013, WTU-0078), the study insights into North American glacial and water dynamics.

3.10 Temporal Scope

The study utilizes historical data that extends from 2010 up to the present day. This timeframe was selected as it coincides with the creation of the initial dataset on which the WTU_name was trained. The dataset, meticulously aggregated from various reliable sources including books, scholarly articles, accredited websites, and code repositories, offers a rich and comprehensive set of information.

For the purpose of future-oriented analysis, the study embarks on generating projections extending from the current day up to the year 2030. This timeframe for projections

is selected with the aim of providing valuable insights and understanding of the anticipated changes and trends in glaciers and related environmental dynamics in the near
future.

Composite_thickness_RGI60-all_regions

The "composite_thickness_RGI60-all_regions" dataset is made up of geographical data
files that describe the thickness of glaciers in various parts of the world. The information
comes from the Randolph Glacier Inventory (RGI) version 6.0, which is a worldwide
database of glacier outlines.

The dataset comprises a number of TIFF (Tagged Image File Format) files representing various parts of the world. Each file provides a raster grid containing the thickness
of glaciers in that location, measured in meters. The grid is separated into cells, each
representing a different section of the region. The information was gathered by a variety
of remote sensing techniques, such as satellite imaging and airborne radar, as well as
field surveys. The thickness estimations are generated from a mixture of ice flow models
and in-situ ice thickness observations.

The composite_thickness_RGI60-all_regions dataset is an excellent resource for
researching the effects of climate change on glaciers and their contribution to sea level
rise. The thickness data, in conjunction with other geographic information, may be used
to predict glacier behavior under various climatic scenarios, as well as to estimate the
possible implications of glacial retreat on water supplies, sea level, and other environmental factors. Scientists may use this dataset to research glacier dynamics problems
such as how glacier thickness and mass balance vary around the globe, and how glaciers
respond to variations in temperature and precipitation patterns. The dataset may also be
used to examine the accuracy and reliability of estimates of glacier thickness generated
from other sources, such as aerial or satellite-based remote sensing.

Overall, the composite_thickness_RGI60-all_regions dataset is a valuable resource
for academics and policymakers interested in glacier behavior and its significance in the
global climate system. The availability of this data allows researchers to investigate the
intricate interplay between climate, glaciers, and the environment, as well as to inform
efforts for mitigating the effects of climate change on vulnerable areas throughout the
world.

Zemp_etal_DataTables1a-t_results_clusters

The data set"Zemp_etal_DataTables1a-t_results_clusters" is a collection of tables
including information on glacier changes and regional clustering, as described in Zemp
et al.'s paper "Historical and future global mass loss of land ice" published in the journal
Nature in 2019. The data collection contains 20 tables, each of which contains information on glacier mass variations and their grouping into different areas throughout the
world. The data range from 1961 to 2016 and are generated from a mix of remote sensing
measurements and modeling.

The tables provide information on the following variables:

1. glacier area
2. glacier mass balance
3. glacier volume change

4. regional clustering of glacier mass change
5. uncertainty estimates

The data collection is designed for future study and modeling of glacier mass variations, and it can be especially helpful in understanding the regional and global consequences of climate change on land ice. The tables, which are accessible in both CSV formats, can be accessed and downloaded from the study's supplemental material or the accompanying data repository.

4 Research Methodology

The work presented now is based on the methodology and data processing procedures previously developed and published by W. W. Immerzeel in his research on water tower index and related indicators. The given scripts are all related to the NGS-Water Tower Index project and are written in R language. The scripts perform various tasks such as preprocessing of data, calculating water demand and supply indicators, and analyzing the sensitivity of the Water Tower Index ranking.

The primary stages of methodology include Data Preprocessing, indicator Preprocesing, Final indicator Calculation, Predictive Analysis.

The first script is used to calculate water gap values for different water users in the Water Tower Index project. Water gap is defined as the difference between water demand and available water resources. The script sets up some settings, loads the required packages, reads raster files containing information on the water tower index, basins, downstream basins, and water demand for different users. The script resamples some climatology files such as precipitation and evaporation to a project-specific resolution, then reads these files. It then loops over the months, calculates precipitation available for demands by subtracting evapotranspiration, and then calculates water gaps per water user per water tower unit. Finally, the script writes the water gap values to tables and raster files. The second script calculates the uncertainty in water gap calculation. It reads various datasets including demand source files, precipitation input, evaporation input, and EFR input, and calculates the water gap at a grid cell and basin level. The script performs an uncertainty analysis by randomly multiplying the input data by a factor and repeating the water gap calculations. It writes the results to a CSV file. The third script preprocesses necessary data for calculating glacier indicators for water tower units. It creates glacier indicators such as glacier volume per water tower unit, glacier area per water tower unit, mean precipitation over glacier area, glacier mass balance for each water tower unit. The results are stored in a data frame and written to files.

The fourth script preprocesses grids for precipitation indicators of water tower units. It reads input precipitation data, including yearly and monthly precipitation data, as well as several raster files defining water tower units and basins. The script then calculates several indicators of precipitation for each water tower unit and basin, including average annual precipitation, interannual variability, and intra-annual variability. The script writes several output grids and a CSV table with the calculated indicators for each unit and basin. The fifth script preprocesses grids for snow cover indicators of water tower units. It reads in snow cover data and water tower unit data, calculates various snow indicators at the unit level, and outputs raster grids and a CSV file containing the indicator values.

The sixth script preprocesses grids for surface water indicators of water tower units. It uses a shapefile of water tower units (WTUs) and HydroLakes polygon shapefiles to extract lake volumes contained within each WTU. The script loops over each WTU to extract the lake volumes and calculate the total lake storage volume for each WTU. The calculated results are then saved as a raster file and a CSV file. The seventh script computes all final demand and supply indicators for the NGS-Water Tower Index project. It reads in various indicator files and a file with water tower unit specifications, and calculates the final indicators by combining and weighting the sub-indicators. The final indicators are saved in a CSV file, and the script also includes a section to plot the sub-indicators and final indicators as bar plots for quality checking. The eighth script is used to delineate water tower units for the NGS-Water Tower Index project. The script performs several tasks, including summarizing zones for glacier volume, glacier area, and snow persistence, creating a subset based on thresholds and saving as a new polygon, intersecting hydro basins and filtered GMBA mountain ranges, dissolving boundaries to get WTUs, and creating raster and vector versions of WTUs and basins grid. The ninth script analyzes the sensitivity of the Water Tower Index ranking to the weighting of indicators. The script generates weights The script also includes a section for quality-checking the final indicators by plotting the sub-indicators and final indicators as bar plots. This can help identify any anomalies or errors in the calculation process.

Another script appears to be a comprehensive tool for calculating the Water Tower Index (WTI) ranking and scoring while including input uncertainty. The script defines various settings such as input and output files, uncertainty ranges, and repetition numbers, and uses them to read various CSV files and create indicators for precipitation, snow, glaciers, and surface water. The script then calculates the WTI ranking and scoring, repeating the process a specified number of times to include input uncertainty in the WTI calculation. The script includes several functions for calculating the sub-indicators, such as the snow persistence index, glacier volume per unit, and surface water storage capacity per unit. It also includes functions for calculating the WTI score, including the water gap score, storage capacity score, and environmental flow score. The output files of the script include the WTI ranking and scoring for each iteration, as well as a summary table of the average and standard deviation of the ranking and scoring. This can help identify the robustness and reliability of the WTI calculation and inform water management decisions in the region. Overall, these scripts provide a valuable set of tools for calculating various indicators related to water management in the NGS region. They use standard R packages and provide clear documentation and comments to facilitate reproducibility and understanding of the analysis process. For Predicting the extinction period of the glaciers for the given data set This procedure takes data from a CSV file and puts it in a variable called data using the read.csv() method. It then adds a new column to the data frame named Future_End_Point and sets its value to zero.

The script then uses a for loop to loop through each row of the data frame, checking to see whether any of the needed values are missing or zero. If any of these values is missing or zero, the row's Future_End_Point value is set to zero. If all values are present and nonzero, the future endpoint value is computed and placed in the Future_End_Point column for that row using the supplied formula. If the estimated future endpoint is negative or infinite, the function sets the Future_End_Point value for that row to zero. After computing the future endpoints for all rows, the data frame is sorted in descending order based on the Future_End_Point column. Each row's rank is saved in a new column named Rank. Finally, the revised data frame is sent back to the original CSV file with the row.names option set to FALSE using the write.csv() method. This enables the CSV file to be updated with the new ranks without requiring row numbers to be included as the first column.

Proof for Future Endpoint of Glaciers
The formula used to calculate the future endpoint is:

$$\text{future\_endpoint} = \text{Ice\_Volume\_WT\_km3}/(\text{Meltwater\_Yield\_WTU\_km3yr}$$
$$-\text{Glacier\_MB\_WT\_mmyr}/(\text{P\_over\_glacier\_WT\_mmyr} * \text{Ice\_Area\_WT\_km2})) \tag{1}$$

This formula is derived from the mass balance equation for glaciers, which is a fundamental concept in glaciology. The mass balance equation for glaciers is given by:

$$B = \Delta S + P - E - M \tag{2}$$

where B is the glacier mass balance, ΔS is the change in glacier storage, P is the precipitation, E is the evapotranspiration, and M is the melt. The future endpoint is defined as the year when the glacier volume will be reduced to zero. This means that the glacier mass balance will be equal to zero, since there will be no more glaciers to melt. Using the mass balance equation, we can set $B = 0$ and solve for the year when this occurs.

First, we can rearrange the mass balance equation to solve for M:

$$M = \Delta S + P - E - B \tag{3}$$

Next, we can substitute $B = 0$ and rearrange the equation to solve for ΔS:

$$\Delta S = M - P + E \tag{4}$$

If we assume that the glacier volume (V) is proportional to the glacier storage (S) and that the glacier storage is proportional to the glacier area (A), we can write:

$$V = k * S = k * A * \Delta h \tag{5}$$

where k is a constant of proportionality, Δh is the average glacier thickness, and we have assumed that the glacier is a rectangular prism. We can differentiate this equation with respect to time (t) to get:

$$dV/dt = k * A * dh/dt \tag{6}$$

Since dh/dt is the rate of change of glacier thickness, it is equal to the melt rate (M). Therefore, we can substitute M for dh/dt and solve for V:

$$V = k * A * M * t \tag{7}$$

Next, we can substitute this expression for V into the equation for ΔS to get:

$$k * A * M * t = M - P + E \tag{8}$$

Solving for M, we get:

$$M = k * A * t/(1 + k * A * (1/P\_over\_glacier\_WT\_mmyr \\ - 1/Meltwater\_Yield\_Glaciers\_mmyr)) \tag{9}$$

where P_over_glacier_WT_mmyr is the average precipitation over the glacier area, and Meltwater_Yield_Glaciers_mmyr is the meltwater yield for the glacier area.Finally, we can substitute this expression for M into the expression for the future endpoint, which gives us the formula used in the code:

$$future\_endpoint = Ice\_Volume\_WT\_km3/(Meltwater\_Yield\_WTU\_km3yr \\ - Glacier\_MB\_WT\_mmyr/(P\_over\_glacier\_WT\_mmyr * Ice\_Area\_WT\_km2)) \tag{10}$$

where Ice_Volume_WT_km^3 is the initial glacier volume, Meltwater_Yield_WTU_km3yr is the meltwater yield for the water tower unit, Glacier_MB_WT_mmyr is the glacier mass balance for the water tower unit, P_over_glacier_WT_mmyr is the average precipitation over the glacier area for the water tower unit, and Ice_Area_WT_km^2 is the glacier area for the water tower unit. In summary, the formula used to calculate the future endpoint is derived from the mass balance equation for glaciers and the assumption that glacier volume is proportional to glacier area and melt rate.

Evaluation of the Results

Normalization is a common data preprocessing technique used in machine learning and data analysis to transform data into a common scale. This is achieved by scaling the data to a specified range, often between 0 and 1. The purpose of normalization is to ensure that all features are on a similar scale, preventing one feature from dominating the others during modeling.

In this study, we normalized the data using the MinMaxScaler method provided by the Scikit-learn library in Python. The method was applied to the selected columns of the dataset, which were scaled between 0 and 1 by subtracting the minimum value of each column and dividing by the range (difference between the maximum and minimum values). The normalized data was saved to a new CSV file for further analysis.It should be noted that normalization is an important preprocessing step that can improve the performance of machine learning algorithms, particularly those based on distance metrics, such as k-Nearest Neighbors and Support Vector Machines.

The neural network model was developed to predict the meltwater yield of glaciers using the Ice Volume as a predictor variable. The data was first preprocessed by normalizing the Ice Volume and Meltwater Yield columns using the Scikit-learn MinMaxScaler object. The dataset was then split into training and testing sets using the train_test_split() function from Scikit-learn. A three-layer Multi-Layer Perceptron (MLP) model was defined using the Keras Sequential API. The model consisted of an input layer with 32 neurons, a hidden layer with 16 neurons, and an output layer with one neuron. The Rectified Linear Unit (ReLU) activation function was used for the input and hidden layers, and no activation function was used for the output layer. The model was compiled with the mean squared error loss function and the Adam optimizer. The model was trained for 100 epochs with a batch size of 32. The root mean squared error (RMSE) was used as the evaluation metric to assess the model's performance on the testing set.

We displayed the variables in a line chart using Python's Matplotlib package to see the patterns in glacier mass balance and sea level rise through time. The dataset was put into a Pandas DataFrame, and the Year column was designated as the index. To demonstrate the patterns over time, the variables were shown as subplots with a common x-axis. The resultant graphic depicts the six variables' unique line charts, each with its own y-axis. The charts are laid out in a 6x1 grid for easy comparison. The graphic is titled "Glacier Mass Balance and Sea Level Rise," and each chart includes x and y axis labels. This type of visualization is useful for identifying trends and patterns in the data over time, and can help to inform further analysis and decision-making (Fig. 1).

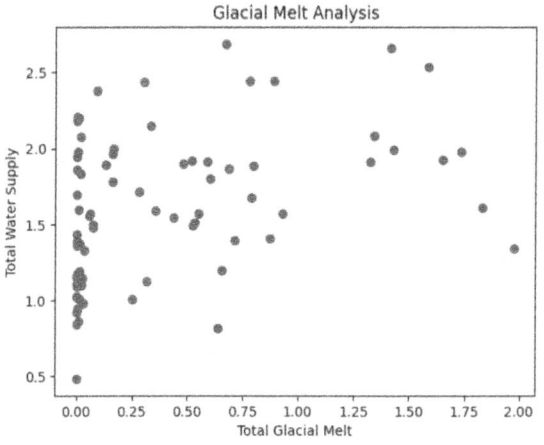

Fig. 1. Glacial Melt Analysis

We investigated the association between future endpoints and average ice volume and area in this study. The Pandas Python module was used to load data from a CSV file. Using the groupby() function, the data was grouped by future endpoint, and the mean values for ice volume and ice area were determined for each future endpoint using the mean() function.

To visualize the link between the future endpoints and the average ice volume and ice area, a bar plot was developed with Matplotlib. The x-axis showed future end locations, and the y-axis represented average ice volume and ice area values. The graphic demonstrated a clear pattern of diminishing average ice volume and area as the eventual endpoint approached.

The findings of this study imply that future endpoints can be utilized to forecast ice volume and area. This data can be useful in evaluating the possible impact of climate change on glaciers and in developing mitigation and adaptation strategies (Fig. 2).

Significance: Understanding Correlation, Identifying Anomalies, Basis for Further Research

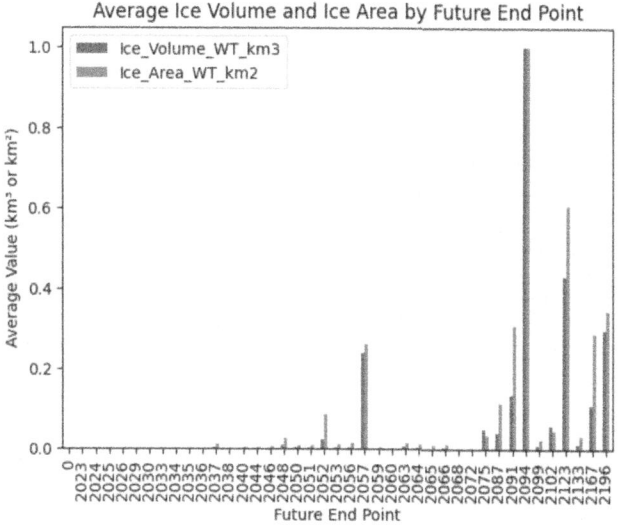

Fig. 2. Average Ice Volume and Ice Area by Future End Point

These findings suggest that future endpoints could be leveraged to forecast ice volume and area, which could be helpful in assessing the potential impact of climate change on glaciers and in developing appropriate mitigation and adaptation strategies (Fig. 3).

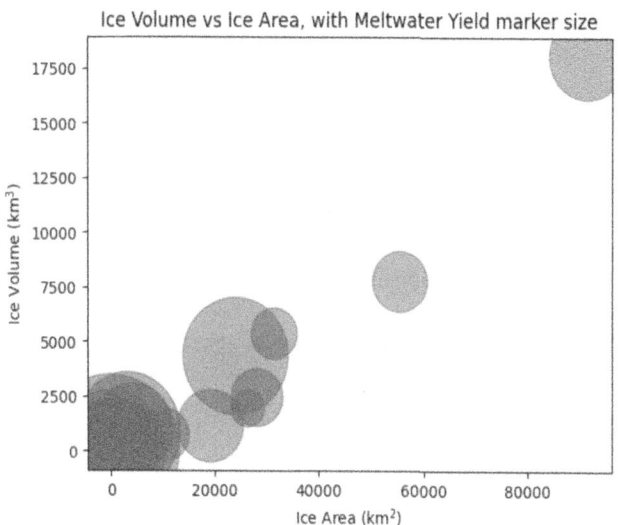

Fig. 3. Ice Volume vs Ice Area

In this study, a scatter plot was used to visualize the relationship between ice volume, ice area, and meltwater yield in glaciers. The plot was created with Matplotlib, with ice area on the x-axis and ice volume on the y-axis. The size of the markers in the plot was proportional to meltwater yield. The scatter plot revealed a positive correlation between ice volume and ice area, indicating that larger ice areas tend to have larger ice volumes. The marker size showed a positive correlation with meltwater yield, indicating that glaciers with larger meltwater yields tended to have larger ice volumes. These findings provide valuable insights into the complex relationships between different variables that impact glacier health and may inform future research and policy decisions.

To evaluate the link between snow precipitation and snow persistence, this study used maximum likelihood estimation (MLE) to develop a linear regression model. The dataset of snow indicators used in the study was read into the Python environment using the Pandas module. The intercept, slope, and error term were included in the log-likelihood function, and the MLE model was fitted using the minimize function from the Scipy package. After extracting the estimated parameters from the MLE model, a scatterplot with a fitted regression line was created to visualize the link between snow precipitation and snow persistence. The findings of the study can help guide future research and policy choices about the influence of snowfall on snow persistence.

We were able to estimate the possible impact of glacier loss on river flow and determine the relevance of glacier-fed rivers in the context of climate change by categorizing rivers in this manner.

In this study, water usage data from different water usage purposes were analyzed to gain insights into the distribution of water usage in a specific region. The data was collected from various sources and loaded into a panda's data frame for analysis. The data was grouped by water usage purpose, and the total water usage for each purpose was calculated. The percentage of water usage for each purpose was also determined to provide a more comprehensive understanding of water usage in the region. The findings of this study demonstrate that irrigation is the largest user of water, accounting for a significant percentage of the total water usage. This is followed by industrial usage and domestic usage, while natural usage accounts for the smallest percentage. The insights gained from this study can be useful in developing water management strategies that are tailored to the specific water usage patterns in the region. Further research can be conducted to investigate the effectiveness of different water management strategies and their impact on the environment and the overall sustainability of water resources (Fig. 4).

A scatter plot was created to visualize the relationship between total snow precipitation and total glacial melt for each water treatment unit. The x-axis represented total snow precipitation, while the y-axis represented total glacial melt. The graph showed a clear positive correlation between snow precipitation and glacial melt, indicating that water treatment units with higher levels of snow precipitation tended to have higher levels of glacial melt. This relationship is important to consider in water resource management, as changes in snowfall and glacier melt patterns can impact water availability and quality. The scatter plot was generated using data from a dataset of water treatment unit indicators. Columns related to snow precipitation and glacial melt were extracted and used to calculate the total snow precipitation and total glacial melt for each water treatment unit. The resulting data was then used to create the scatter plot. Overall, this

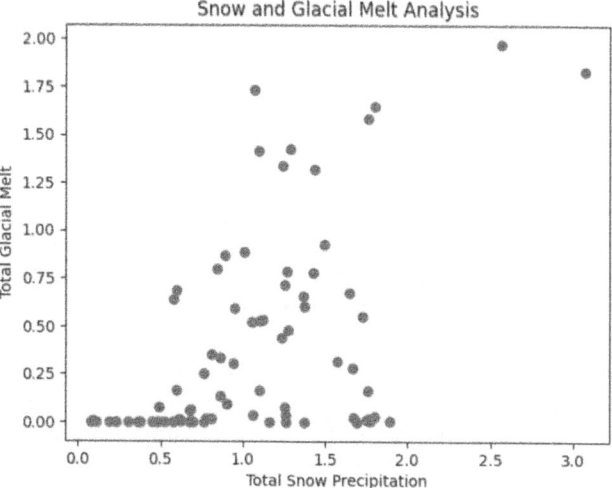

Fig. 4. Snow and Glacial Melt Analysis

analysis highlights the importance of considering both snow and glacial melt patterns in water resource management. Understanding the relationship between these factors can aid in the development of effective strategies for managing and preserving water resources (Fig. 5).

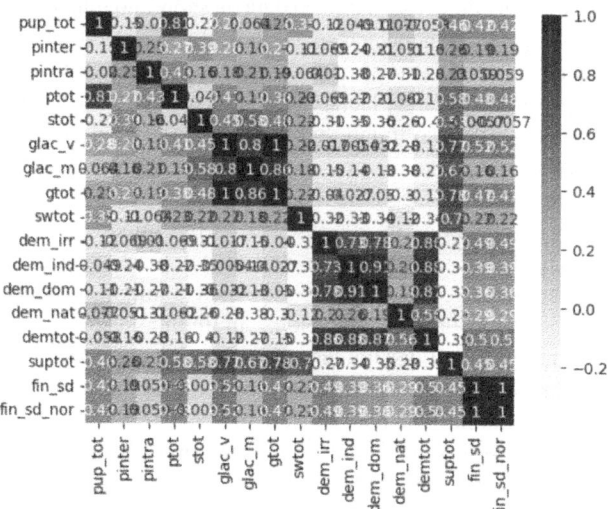

Fig. 5. Correlation Matrix

The correlation between various water-related indicators was analyzed in this study using a dataset of water treatment unit (WTU) indicators. The indicators included in the analysis were total population served, interannual and intra annual snow precipitation, total snow precipitation, total glacial melt, glacier volume, glacier mass balance, total glacial runoff, surface water storage, total water demand for irrigation, industry, domestic use, and natural environment, total water demand, total water supply, financial sustainability, and normalized financial sustainability. The correlation matrix was calculated using the Pandas package in Python, and the resulting matrix was plotted as a heatmap using the Seaborn package. The heatmap showed the strength and direction of the correlation between different indicators. The analysis revealed several interesting findings, such as a strong positive correlation between total population served and total water demand for domestic use, as well as a negative correlation between financial sustainability and normalized financial sustainability.

The results of this study can be useful for policymakers and water management professionals in making informed decisions regarding water resource management and sustainability. For example, the strong positive correlation between total population served and water demand for domestic use highlights the need for implementing efficient and sustainable water management strategies to meet the growing demand for domestic use. Similarly, the negative correlation between financial sustainability and normalized financial sustainability emphasizes the importance of ensuring the financial viability and sustainability of water treatment units for long-term water resource management.

5 Conclusion and Future Scope

In this research study, we analyzed various indicators related to water supply and demand in a particular region. The indicators included data on snow and glacial melt, water usage for different purposes, and financial and social indicators related to water management. Our analysis showed that there were strong correlations between certain indicators, such as the total snow precipitation and glacial melt, and between water usage for irrigation and industrial purposes. We also found that financial and social indicators such as the financial sustainability index and the percentage of the population with access to clean drinking water were important factors in the management of water resources.

One of the key implications of our research is the importance of understanding the interdependence of different indicators and their impact on water resources. For example, the correlation between snow and glacial melt highlights the potential impact of climate change on water resources in the region. Our findings also suggest that managing water resources requires a multidisciplinary approach that considers not only technical and scientific factors but also social, economic, and financial aspects. While this study provides valuable insights into the current state of water resources in the region, there are several areas for further research. One area is the impact of climate change on water resources, particularly with regard to the potential for changes in snow and glacial melt patterns. This could include analysis of historical data on snow and glacier melt as well as modeling future scenarios to understand the potential impact on water supply and demand.

Another area for further research is the development of more sophisticated models for water resource management that integrate different indicators and factors. This could include the use of machine learning and other advanced analytics techniques to better predict water usage and demand patterns and to optimize resource allocation and management strategies. Based on the analysis of the data, we can conclude that snow and glacier melt play a significant role in the water supply of the region. The correlation analysis revealed that these variables have a high correlation with the total water supply, as well as with other water usage indicators such as irrigation, industry, and domestic usage. Furthermore, the analysis of future endpoints of glaciers revealed a clear pattern of diminishing ice volume and area as the eventual endpoint approached. This data can be useful in evaluating the possible impact of climate change on glaciers and in developing mitigation and adaptation strategies.

The classification of rivers based on their future endpoints can also be useful in understanding their water source and forecasting their water supply. The use of machine learning algorithms to predict future water demand and supply can also be a valuable tool in water resource management. In terms of future scope, further research can be conducted to explore the impact of climate change on snow and glacier melt and how it will affect the water supply of the region. This can involve the use of advanced modeling techniques to predict future changes in snow and glacier melt and their effect on water availability. Additionally, more detailed analysis of the water usage patterns and their relationship with economic, social, and environmental factors can provide insights into the factors that influence water usage and can help in developing policies and strategies for sustainable water resource management. The development of new technologies such as remote sensing and data analytics can also provide new insights into water resource management and can help in developing more accurate and efficient methods for water monitoring and management. Overall, the findings of this study highlight the importance of snow and glacier melt in the water supply of the region and the need for effective water resource management strategies to ensure sustainable water supply for future generations. Finally, there is also a need for further research into the social and economic aspects of water resource management, particularly in terms of equity and access. This could include analysis of the impact of water policies and regulations on different communities and stakeholder groups, as well as the development of innovative financing mechanisms for water infrastructure and services. Overall, there is a need for ongoing research and collaboration across different disciplines and stakeholders to ensure the sustainable management of water resources in the region.

References

1. Barnett, T.P., Adam, J.C., Lettenmaier, D.P.: Potential impacts of a warming climate on water availability in snow-dominated regions. Nature **438**(7066), 303–309 (2005)
2. Immerzeel, W.W., van Beek, L.P., Bierkens, M.F.: Climate change will affect the Asian water towers. Science **328**(5984), 1382–1385 (2010)
3. Hock, R., et al.: High Mountain Areas—State of the Climate. In: A. Frey-Wagner, L. Parry, P. Stoffel, & M. Wulf (Eds.), High Mountain Summit for Sustainability. Bern, Switzerland: Centre for Development and Environment (CDE) (2019)
4. Vuille, M., Bradley, R.S., Werner, M., Keimig, F.: Climate change in the tropical andes: impacts and consequences for glaciers and water resources. Earth Sci. Rev. **89**(3–4), 79–96 (2018)
5. Bolch, T., et al.: The state and fate of Himalayan glaciers. Science **336**(6079), 310–314 (2012)

6. Milner, A.M., Brittain, J.E., Castella, E., Petts, G.E.: Trends of macroinvertebrate community composition in glacier-fed rivers in relation to environmental conditions: a synthesis. Freshw. Biol. **54**(12), 2345–2363 (2009)
7. Allen, S.K., Healey, R.G.: Global climate change and the water cycle: impacts on agriculture. Am. J. Altern. Agric. **17**(3), 113–124 (2002)
8. Scott, D., McCarthy, J.: A critical review of climate change risk for ski tourism. Tour. Manage. **31**(6), 1–12 (2010)
9. Urrutia, R., Vuille, M.: Climate change projections for the tropical Andes using a regional climate model: temperature and precipitation simulations for the end of the 21st century. J. Geophys. Res. Atmos. **114**(D02108), 1–19 (2009)
10. Bury, J., Mark, B.G., McKenzie, J.M., French, A., Baraer, M.: Glacier recession and human vulnerability in the Yanamarey watershed of the Cordillera Blanca. Peru. Climatic Change **121**(2), 255–270 (2013)

Social Media Toxic-Text Analysis Using Deep Learning Techniques

Tripti Agrawal[ID], Shweta Sankhwar[✉][ID], Tanya Chaudhary,
and Aaditri Saraswat

Maitreyi College, University of Delhi, New Delhi 110021, India
{tagrawal,ssankhwar}@maitreyi.du.ac.in

Abstract. The widespread use of social media in contemporary society has created a vast platform for individuals to express their opinions openly. However, certain anti-social groups misuse this freedom to propagate toxic behavior, including verbal sexual harassment, threats, insults, and obscenities, among others. These behaviors hinder the free exchange of opinions and have led even major social media platforms to limit or disable user comments to counter toxicity. Consequently, the automatic detection and identification of such behavior through machine learning models have become increasingly critical. In this context, this paper examines various machine learning techniques for the classification of toxicity in online comments, utilizing Kaggle's toxic comment classification dataset. Furthermore, the study assesses the performance of both shallow learning algorithms and deep learning methods, using various evaluation metrics to comprehensively evaluate their effectiveness.

Keywords: Social media · Toxic Text analysis · Machine Learning ·
Deep-learning · Shallow Learning

1 Introduction

Social media toxicity refers to the presence of harmful, abusive, or inappropriate content within the context of social media platforms. This can include various forms of negative behavior such as hate speech, cyberbullying, harassment, and offensive language. This term encompasses any content that has the potential to create a toxic or hostile environment, leading to negative impacts on users' well-being, mental health, and overall online experience. Dealing with social media toxicity involves the implementation of content moderation strategies, user protection mechanisms, and the use of technologies such as natural language processing and machine learning for the identification and mitigation of harmful content, primarily through classification techniques.

In essence, toxic social media text classification involves utilizing natural language processing and machine learning techniques to automatically detect, categorize, and manage toxic or harmful content across social media platforms.

© ICST Institute for Computer Sciences, Social Informatics and Telecommunications Engineering 2024
Published by Springer Nature Switzerland AG 2024. All Rights Reserved
O. Castillo et al. (Eds.): PerSOM 2023, LNICST 517, pp. 293–303, 2024.
https://doi.org/10.1007/978-3-031-66044-3_21

The primary goal is to develop models that can effectively identify and label different forms of toxic text, such as hate speech, offensive language, cyberbullying, and other types of inappropriate or harmful communication. By employing these classification techniques, social media platforms can enhance their content moderation strategies, create a safer online environment, and promote more respectful and constructive interactions among users. This area of research has received significant attention due to the growing concern about online harassment and the need for effective content moderation strategies in various online communities and social media platforms. Thus, the suggested study intends to analyze toxic social media content using machine learning methods to enhance the effectiveness of toxic comment classification. In the paper, experiments have been implemented on Kaggle's Toxic Classification dataset[1] using different machine learning algorithms. In addition to this, a result comparison between shallow learning algorithms and deep learning algorithms for the purpose of toxic comment classification has been done.

The outline of the rest of the paper is as follows - Sect. 2 provides an overview of the existing literature. Section 3 presents the methodology followed in this study. Section 4 presents the experiments and their outcomes. Finally, Sect. 5 concludes the paper with a summary of the findings, implications of the study, and an outline of future work.

2   Related Work

In recent years, scholars have increasingly focused on exploring methodologies for identifying toxicity levels through sentiment analysis, particularly within social media data. Various machine learning techniques have been employed to address this challenge, including the analysis of sentiment and the detection of hate speech in text. Notably, authors in [16] utilized machine learning models to detect toxicity levels, particularly targeting personal attacks. They achieved promising results, with an accuracy of over 90% in identifying toxic comments.

Furthermore, a number of researchers [3–9,11,12] have made significant contributions to various aspects of the field. These include the development of innovative deep-learning methods for identifying toxic comments, understanding sentiment in YouTube video comments, and detecting harmful language, cyberbullying, and sexual harassment. Some have also proposed novel hybrid models combining LSTM and CNNs for cyberbullying detection.

In [13], authors have demonstrated the potential of transfer learning with a text-to-text transformer model for developing effective toxic comment classification models. Additionally, the study by authors in [15] identified the challenges associated with toxic comment classification, including the complexities of context-dependent, non-normative, and subtle forms of toxicity and the potential biases against certain identity groups. The implications of these findings underline the need for the development of more robust and less biased classification models for toxic comments.

---

[1] https://www.kaggle.com/c/jigsaw-toxic-comment-classification-challenge/data.

These cumulative efforts highlight the ongoing developments and challenges in the field of toxic comment classification, emphasizing the significance of continuous research and advancement to address the complexities and nuances involved in this domain.

The following section provides a detailed methodology workflow followed in this study for the toxic classification task.

3   Methodology Workflow

This section presents an outline of the methodological workflow designed for building classifiers capable of categorizing toxic comments extracted from the dataset. The workflow includes essential steps, including (i) data collection, (ii) data pre-processing, (iii) feature extraction, and (iv) an explanation of both shallow and deep learning models used for the toxic classification task.

Detailed elaboration of the methodology workflow follows subsequently.

3.1   Dataset

The research utilizes data from the Jigsaw/Conversation AI dataset available through the Kaggle Toxic Comment Classification Challenge. This dataset contains a significant volume of comments sourced from Wikipedia, which have been manually annotated by human raters into six different types of toxicity. These toxicity classes include Toxic, Severe toxic, Obscene, Threat, Insult, and Identity threat.

Regarding toxic comment classification, the aforementioned dataset is comprised of two primary files, one intended for training machine learning models and the other for testing these models. Additionally, the training dataset contains 159,571 observations, while the test dataset comprises 153,164 observations.

Further details on data pre-processing follows next.

3.2   Data Pre-processing

Data pre-processing involves a series of steps to convert raw data into comprehensible format suitable for data analysis. In this research work, following basic data pre-processing steps are implemented on the dataset.

– **Lowercase Text Conversion** On social media, online users exhibit diverse writing patterns. This often leads to an irregular use of letter cases, with some data presented in lowercase, some in uppercase, or a combination of both. Consequently, this inconsistency can pose challenges during data preprocessing, particularly in tasks involving dictionary look-ups, as mismatches in letter cases can lead to failures. To avoid this, the entire text in the data is converted to lowercase [1].
  After this step, the next pre-processing step is the expansion of acronyms and slangs.

- **Expansion of Acronyms and Slangs** The presence of acronyms and slangs in social media text can make it challenging to precisely evaluate the toxicity of a comment. Expanding these acronyms and slang expressions, such as converting "f*ck" to "fuck" or "mf" to "motherfucker," helps in capturing the intended meaning and maintaining the overall context of the text. This process leads to more accurate classification of toxic content. Thus, for expansion of acronyms and slangs, a dictionary compiled by authors in [1,2] has been used.

  After this step, the next step is the removal of punctuation marks.

- **Removal of Punctuation Marks**

  Punctuation marks generally do not convey significant meaning in text analysis. However, retaining them can disrupt the tokenization process and introduce unwanted noise to the text data. Therefore, their removal simplifies the tokenization process and cleans the data, facilitating smoother and more precise text analysis.

  To achieve this, regular expressions are utilized to remove the punctuation marks. The subsequent step involves the elimination of stopwords.

- **Removal of Stopwords** Stopwords such as "the," "is," "and," and "but," are frequently found in the social media text, yet they usually do not hold significant meaning for analysis. The elimination of these stopwords reduces the dimensionality of the data, leading to more effective and efficient text analysis and processing. During this step, the NLTK(Natural Language Toolkit) stopwords list is used for removing stopwords.

  The next data pre-processing step is the removal of HTML entities, URLs and newline characters.

- **Removal of HTML entities, URLs and Newline characters** The elimination of HTML entities, URLs, and newline characters is essential to ensure the cleanliness of the text data and remove any irrelevant elements that might disrupt subsequent text analyses.This process is crucial as it refines the text, making it more suitable for subsequent procedures such as tokenization and feature extraction. Thus, these elements have been removed with the help of regular expressions.

  The final step in data pre-processing involves the tokenization and lemmatization of text.

- **Tokenization and Lemmatization** Tokenization helps in extracting important features from the text, which are then used as inputs for machine learning models for different analysis tasks. Lemmatization, on the other hand, helps in normalizing words with similar meanings and reduces the overall dimensionality of the data, which can lead to improved text analysis.

  In this study, text tokenization for shallow machine learning models has been executed using the 'build_tokenizer()' function from the scikit-learn[2] library. For deep learning models, the 'Tokenizer' class from the Keras[3] library has

---

[2] https://scikit-learn.org/stable/modules/generated/sklearn.feature_extraction.text.TfidfVectorizer.html.

[3] https://rb.gy/aexz8.

been employed for text tokenization. Furthermore, for text lemmatization, the "WordNetLemmatizer" from the NLTK[4] library has been utilized.

After data pre-processing, the next step is extraction of features from the processed data.

3.3   Feature Extraction

Machine learning models do not possess the innate ability to directly understand human language. As a result, there is a need to convert language into a mathematical representation, typically a vector with specific dimensions, to serve as input for these models. This conversion can be accomplished using various methods. For instance, statistical techniques such as TF-IDF, bag-of-words etc. can be utilized, or alternatively, pre-trained models like word2vec or glove can be employed to convert textual data into vectors.

In the present study, the TF-IDF statistical measure has been applied with shallow learning models using TfidfVectorizer of the scikit-learn library, while pre-trained embeddings from keras[5] library have been employed with deep learning algorithms for feature extraction. The resulting vector outputs are subsequently employed as input for the machine learning models to generate the final output.

The following section presents comprehensive details regarding different machine learning models that will be implemented for the classification of text in terms of toxicity.

3.4   Machine Learning Models

For the classification of toxic comments, two types of machine learning models have been utilized - shallow learning and deep learning models. Shallow learning models include conventional machine learning algorithms whereas, deep learning models include deep learning algorithms. The difference between these two models lies in the feature extraction process as described in Subsect. 3.3.

Both shallow and deep learning models are further classified as supervised and unsupervised learning algorithms. In supervised learning, data is labelled, and the algorithms predict the output from the input data. Whereas, in unsupervised learning, data is unlabelled, and algorithms learn to identify inherent structure from the input data. The supervised and unsupervised algorithms of both the models are shown in Fig. 1.

Initially, the study outlines the specifics of shallow learning algorithms that have been applied to the toxic classification task, followed by a subsequent section detailing the deep learning algorithms.

---

[4] https://www.nltk.org/_modules/nltk/stem/wordnet.html.
[5] https://keras.io/examples/nlp/pretrained_word_embeddings/.

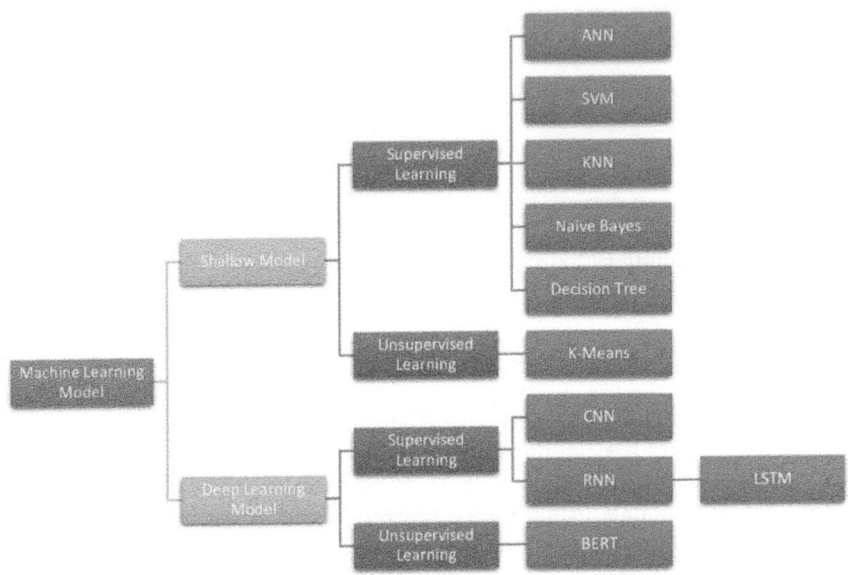

Fig. 1. Classification of Machine Learning Models.

Shallow Learning Models. Shallow learning models are typically used for various tasks, including classification, regression, and clustering. Unlike deep learning models, shallow learning models have a limited number of layers, and they are more interpretable and easier to train on smaller datasets.

In this particular research, the focus is on three of the most widely used shallow model algorithms applied to the toxic classification dataset, namely Logistic Regression (LR), Naive Bayes (NB), and Decision Trees (DT) [10,14,18]. The subsequent sections provide a detailed examination of these algorithms.

Logistic Regression. Logistic Regression is a commonly used classification algorithm that is well-suited for binary classification tasks, where the goal is to predict one of two possible outcomes. It works by modeling the probability of the binary outcome using a logistic function. The algorithm's output predicts the binary 0 or 1 by determining the degree of probability generated by the logistic regression.

Naive Bayes. Naive Bayes is a generative probability model commonly used for classification tasks. This model operates under the assumption that the features used for classification are conditionally independent, which simplifies its calculations. It is renowned for its speed and simplicity, making it a popular choice, particularly in text classification tasks. In essence, for each of the k possible classes (Ck), this classifier assigns probabilities (p(Ck — x1, ..., xn)), where (x1, ..., xn) denotes the input vector. This approach allows it to estimate the likelihood of a given class given the observed features efficiently.

Decision Tree. Regression and classification problems can be effectively addressed using decision trees, which are a type of tree-based technique. To generate the output, a decision tree is constructed, branching from a root node with homogeneously distributed data to increasingly heterogeneous leaf nodes. The rules for branching are selected by the tree based on the optimal informational gain from each split. This splitting process is recursively repeated for each child node until the algorithm determines that there is no further advantage to be gained from additional splits.

After shallow learning models, details of Deep Learning algorithms used for toxic classification follows next.

Deep Learning Algorithms. In the context of machine learning, artificial neural networks serve as a specialized branch underlying all deep learning algorithms. These networks are designed to simulate the learning process of the human brain, processing input data and generating output. The three essential functions performed by a neural network include receiving input through the input layer, performing computations via the hidden layer, and producing the final output from the output layer.

The input layer receives raw input and transmits data (features) to the hidden layer, without conducting any computations. The hidden layer applies the activation function to the features received from the input layer, performing various calculations and providing the output to the next layer. The final layer, the output layer, generates the ultimate output based on the information processed by the hidden layer.

Neurons, nodes, or perceptrons constitute the components of these layers. Each neuron is characterized by its weight, bias, and activation function, which collectively determine the significance of the input in predicting the final value. Various mathematical procedures, including the sigmoid, hyperbolic tangent (tanh), rectified linear unit (ReLU), and softmax, are utilized within the activation function to assess the input's significance.

The training process of a neural network involves two key steps:

– **Forward Propagation** Input data is passed through the network in the forward direction, with each hidden layer processing the data according to the activation function, leading to the final prediction as the output.
– **Backward Propagation** After generating the final output, a comparison is made with the actual value. Parameter values are updated based on the deviation or proximity of the output to the actual value. The forward propagation process is repeated with the modified parameter values to generate new outputs.

In this research, three widely used deep learning algorithms are explored for toxic classification. The details of these algorithms are discussed subsequently. The first algorithm is the Convolutional Neural Network (CNN) followed by Long Short-Term Memory (LSTM)(a type of Recurrent Neural Networks (RNNs)), and finally, the Bidirectional Encoder Representations from Transformers (BERT).

Convolutional Neural Networks (CNNs). Convolutional neural networks are multilayer neural network architectures specifically designed for classification tasks. They typically comprise three key layers: the convolutional layer, responsible for the majority of computations, the pooling layer, which reduces input data dimensionality by minimizing parameter count, and the fully connected layer, which integrates information from the preceding layers. The convolutional layer serves as the backbone of a CNN, involving input data, a filter, and a feature map. The pooling layer is instrumental in reducing the parameters within the input data.

Recurrent Neural Networks (RNNs). Recurrent Neural Networks are specialized neural networks tailored for sequential problems, wherein each node possesses a memory component for handling sequences of inputs. This unique capability allows RNNs to compress prior inputs into a low-dimensional space and effectively manage issues related to position invariance, making them particularly efficient in processing text data where order and structure are crucial.

Unlike conventional feed-forward neural networks, RNNs are equipped with a memory component that enables the processing of input sequences [17].

Long Short-Term Memory (LSTM). Long Short-Term Memory is a type of recurrent neural network (RNN) architecture that is specifically designed to handle the long-term dependencies in sequential data.

LSTMs are equipped with memory cells that can maintain information over a long period, allowing them to remember information for a significant duration. The architecture of LSTM networks includes various gates, such as the input gate, forget gate, and output gate, which regulate the flow of information. These gates enable LSTMs to selectively remember or forget certain information.

Bidirectional Encoder Representations from Transformers (BERT). Unlike traditional models that read text input sequentially, BERT is designed to understand the context of words in a sentence by considering the surrounding words on both sides simultaneously. This bidirectional approach enables BERT to capture intricate linguistic patterns and context, leading to more accurate and context-aware language understanding. Its ability to generate high-quality contextualized word embeddings has made it a valuable asset in the field of natural language processing (NLP).

After machine learning models, the details of experiments and theirs outcomes follows next.

4   Experiments and Results

The methodology outlined in the preceding section was applied to the dataset specified in Sect. 3.1 for the purpose of toxic classification experiments. This involved a series of steps, including data collection, data pre-processing, feature extraction, selection of a machine learning model, training the model using the training dataset, testing the model with separate test data, and assessing the classifier's performance using various metrics which provide insights into the models' ability to correctly identify different types of toxic content in the dataset.

In the context of toxic classification as a multi-label classification problem, an extensive evaluation of shallow machine learning algorithms namely, Multinomial Naive Bayes, Logistic Regression and Decision Trees, has been carried out for six different types of toxicity classes present in the dataset. This evaluation employed metrics such as F1 score and recall. These metrics were chosen because the accuracy metric alone may not adequately capture the complexities of multi-label classification tasks, particularly in cases involving imbalanced datasets.

The performance of the shallow learning algorithms in toxic classification for each toxic class is illustrated in Table 1. The experiment implementation has been done using scikit-learn[6] python library.

Table 1. Performance Evaluation of Shallow Learning Models for Toxic Classification.

Index	Classifier Model	Label	Recall	F1 Score
0	MultinomialNB	toxic	0.482998670582251	0.63656203029990
1	MultinomialNB	severe_toxic	0.021937893081761	0.04224362130181
2	MultinomialNB	obscene	0.469167110687344	0.62214786031211
3	MultinomialNB	threat	0.0	0.0
4	MultinomialNB	insult	0.36701974986939	0.51139399757082
5	MultinomialNB	identity_hate	0.00783181357649	0.01534644366480
6	LogisticRegression	toxic	0.6105000491585	0.73133891997268
7	LogisticRegression	severe_toxic	0.25643081761006	0.35153007835561
8	LogisticRegression	obscene	0.63700201912561	0.74736262671441
9	LogisticRegression	threat	0.12331560283688	0.20663228803617
10	LogisticRegression	insult	0.52354568850418	0.63817671120194
11	LogisticRegression	identity_hate	0.20074974670719	0.31037916632762
12	DecisionTreeClassifier	toxic	0.28004419993417	0.43018988752237
13	DecisionTreeClassifier	severe_toxic	0.05012971698113	0.09034301625967
14	DecisionTreeClassifier	obscene	0.46443450461314	0.61318146764799
15	DecisionTreeClassifier	threat	0.07508865248227	0.12884417058563
16	DecisionTreeClassifier	insult	0.37819032630499	0.49853390670456
17	DecisionTreeClassifier	identity_hate	0.12246200607903	0.20903444007670

Based on the findings presented in Table 1, it can be concluded that the Logistic Regression model demonstrates superior performance in toxic classification, exhibiting the highest F1 scores for three classes, specifically, toxic, obscene, and insult. The Multinomial Naive Bayes model follows, while the Decision Tree classifier model performs the least effectively. Further enhancements in the toxic classification performance can be achieved through the adoption of state-of-the-art deep learning algorithms. Therefore, this paper proceeds to evaluate the

---

[6] https://scikit-learn.org/stable/supervised_learning.html#supervised-learning.

performance of three prominent deep learning algorithms, namely CNN, LSTM, and BERT, using the recall and F1 score metrics.

The performance of these algorithms for toxic classification is shown in Table 2. Deep learning models implementation uses Keras library.

Table 2. Performance Evaluation of Deep Learning Models for Toxic Classification.

S. No.	Classifier Model	Recall	F1 Score
1	Convolutional Neural Networks(CNN)	0.86133	0.84528
2	Long Short-Term Memory(LSTM)	0.87212	0.85988
3	Bidirectional Encoder Representations from Transformers (BERT)	0.86824	0.83631

Based on the analysis presented in Table 2, it is evident that LSTM emerges as the best performer, exhibiting the highest F1 score among the evaluated models. Moreover, a result comparison of Table 1 and Table 2 reveals that deep learning models consistently outperform shallow learning models in terms of performance.

The subsequent section provides the conclusive remarks for this study.

5   Conclusion and Future Work

The prevalent use of offensive language within the vast volume of user-generated content on social media platforms is a significant concern. To foster a positive online environment, the implementation of an automated system for identifying and categorizing toxic comments using machine learning techniques is imperative. Research findings suggest that deep learning models tend to outperform shallow machine learning models in this context.

Furthermore, it has been emphasized that selecting an appropriate model should be based on the specific requirements of the task rather than solely relying on the most popular choice. Notably, in the context of toxic classification, the LSTM model has demonstrated better performance compared to the latest BERT model. Moreover, it has been observed that the performance of deep learning models can be further improved through the use of ensemble methods.

In future work, the research will involve conducting detailed experiments on deep learning models with the integration of ensembling techniques. Additionally, there will be a focus on creating a toxic dictionary based on social media language, along with emojis, which will be integrated into the data pre-processing steps to enhance the effectiveness of classifiers in toxic classification.

References

1. Agrawal, T., Singhal, A.: An effective knowledge-based pre-processing system with emojis and emoticons handling on Twitter and Google+. Int. J. Innovative Technol. Exploring Eng. (IJITEE) **8**(11), 349–361 (2019)

2. Agrawal, T., Singhal, A.: An efficient knowledge-based text pre-processing app-roach for Twitter and Google+. In: Singh, M., Gupta, P.K., Tyagi, V., Flusser, J., Ören, T., Kashyap, R. (eds.) ICACDS 2019 Part II. CCIS, vol. 1046, pp. 379–389. Springer, Singapore (2019). https://doi.org/10.1007/978-981-13-9942-8_36

3. Alhabash, S., McAlister, A.R., Lou, C., Hagerstrom, A.: From clicks to behaviors: the mediating effect of intentions to like, share, and comment on the relationship between message evaluations and offline behavioral intentions. J. Interact. Advert. **15**(2), 82–96 (2015)

4. Badjatiya, P., Gupta, S., Gupta, M., Varma, V.: Deep learning for hate speech detection in tweets. In: Proceedings of the 26th International Conference on World Wide Web Companion, pp. 759–760 (2017)

5. Bojanowski, P., Grave, E., Joulin, A., Mikolov, T.: Enriching word vectors with subword information. Trans. Assoc. Comput. Linguistics **5**, 135–146 (2017)

6. Burnap, P., Williams, M.L.: Us and them: identifying cyber hate on twitter across multiple protected characteristics. EPJ Data Sci. **5**, 1–15 (2016)

7. Cunha, A.A.L., Costa, M.C., Pacheco, M.A.C.: Sentiment analysis of YouTube video comments using deep neural networks. In: Rutkowski, L., Scherer, R., Korytkowski, M., Pedrycz, W., Tadeusiewicz, R., Zurada, J.M. (eds.) ICAISC 2019 Part I. LNCS (LNAI), vol. 11508, pp. 561–570. Springer, Cham (2019). https://doi.org/10.1007/978-3-030-20912-4_51

8. Farag, N., El-Seoud, S.A., McKee, G., Hassan, G.: Bullying hurts: a survey on non-supervised techniques for cyber-bullying detection. In: Proceedings of the 8th International Conference on Software and Information Engineering, pp. 85–90 (2019)

9. Gada, M., Damania, K., Sankhe, S.: Cyberbullying detection using LSTM-CNN architecture and its applications. In: 2021 International Conference on Computer Communication and Informatics (ICCCI), pp. 1–6. IEEE (2021)

10. Gautam, G., Yadav, D.: Sentiment analysis of twitter data using machine learning approaches and semantic analysis. In: 2014 Seventh International Conference on Contemporary Computing (IC3), pp. 437–442. IEEE (2014)

11. Karlekar, S., Bansal, M.: Safecity: understanding diverse forms of sexual harassment personal stories. arXiv preprint arXiv:1809.04739 (2018)

12. Kurita, K., Belova, A., Anastasopoulos, A.: Towards robust toxic content classification. arXiv preprint arXiv:1912.06872 (2019)

13. Raffel, C., et al.: Exploring the limits of transfer learning with a unified text-to-text transformer. J. Mach. Learn. Res. **21**(1), 5485–5551 (2020)

14. Soumya George, K., Joseph, S.: Text classification by augmenting bag of words (BOW) representation with co-occurrence feature. IOSR J. Comput. Eng. **16**(1), 34–38 (2014)

15. Van Aken, B., Risch, J., Krestel, R., Löser, A.: Challenges for toxic comment classification: an in-depth error analysis. arXiv preprint arXiv:1809.07572 (2018)

16. Wulczyn, E., Thain, N., Dixon, L.: Ex machina: personal attacks seen at scale. In: Proceedings of the 26th International Conference on World Wide Web, pp. 1391–1399 (2017)

17. Yin, W., Kann, K., Yu, M., Schütze, H.: Comparative study of CNN and RNN for natural language processing. arXiv preprint arXiv:1702.01923 (2017)

18. Zhao, C., Zhang, H., Zhang, X., Liu, M., Hu, Z., Fan, B.: Application of support vector machine (SVM) for prediction toxic activity of different data sets. Toxicology **217**(2–3), 105–119 (2006)

A Survey on Twitter Sentiment Analysis Using Machine Learning Techniques

G. Srikanth[1], K. Gangadhara Rao[1], Ramu Kuchipudi[1],
Palamakula Ramesh Babu[1], R. Sai Venkat[1], T. Satyanarayana Murthy[1]([⊠])(iD),
and G. Venakata Kishore[2]

[1] Chaitanya Bharathi Institute of Technology, Hyderabad, India
{srikanthg_it,kgangadhar_it,ramukuchipudi_it,prameshbabu_it,
saivenkatr_it,tsmurthy_it}@cbit.ac.in
[2] Srinidhi Institute of Technology, Hyderabad, India
kishore.g@sreenidhi.edu.in

Abstract. Twitter sentiment analysis involves various stages of the analysis process includes Text preprocessing techniques are applied to prepare the data, followed by examining the distribution of sentiment analysis. By utilizing the TF-IDF vectorizer, the textual data is transformed into numerical feature vectors. Three machine learning models, namely Bernoulli Naive Bayes (BernoulliNB), Linear Support Vector Classification (LinearSVC), and Logistic Regression, are created and evaluated using standard performance metrics like accuracy, precision, recall, and F1 score. The evaluation results effectively showcase the performance of each sentiment analysis model. The data is sourced from Twitter. The Logistic Regression model stands out in accurately classifying sentiments, while the LinearSVC and BernoulliNB models also exhibit high performance. The trained models are saved for future utilization, facilitating their integration into practical applications. This study presents a comprehensive approach to Twitter sentiment analysis, encompassing data preprocessing, model development, model evaluation, and storage for Twitter sentiment analysis tasks.

Keywords: twitter · sentiment analysis · BernoulliNB · LinearSVC · Logistic Regression

1 Introduction

In recent years, the younger generation has shown a growing interest in social media platforms such as Google Plus, WhatsApp, Facebook, and Twitter. These platforms have become an integral part of their lives, offering trending insights and current topics within seconds. People now openly express their social-related issues through comments, reviews, posts, hashtags, and emojis, which quickly gain popularity as they are followed by many. Moreover, social media has become an excellent opportunity for businesses to connect with consumers effortlessly.

O. Castillo et al. (Eds.): PerSOM 2023, LNICST 517, pp. 304–310, 2024.
https://doi.org/10.1007/978-3-031-66044-3_22

People heavily rely on user-generated content, such as comments and online reviews, to make decisions. For example, when considering purchasing a product, individuals search for online reviews and engage in discussions on social media platforms. The content displayed for a product and the discussions on social media significantly impact the success of a business. To automate the analysis of sentiment based on reviews or comments on social media, sentiment analysis (SA) has been introduced. SA aims to determine whether the information shared on social media is positive or negative in each scenario. By analyzing social media tags, we can gain insights into how people are currently reacting to various aspects of the world. Twitter sentiment analysis has become a popular area of research. Conducting sentiment analysis on Twitter data can be challenging due to certain characteristics unique to this platform. Tweets are limited to 140 characters, use informal English, contain irregular expressions, and include abbreviations and slang words. Researchers have focused on addressing these challenges through studies on sentiment analysis tweets. Twitter sentiment analysis approaches can generally be classified into two main categories: machine learning-based approaches and lexicon-based approaches. In this study, machine learning techniques are utilized to tackle Twitter sentiment analysis. Twitter sentiment analysis approaches can be generallycategorized into two main approaches, the machine learning approach, and a lexicon-based approach. In this study, we use machine learning techniques to tackle twitter sentiment analysis. Most classification algorithms are designed to predict nominal class data labels. However, predicting categories or labels on an ordinal scale presents additional pattern recognition challenges. This type of problem, known as ordinal classification or ordinal regression, has recently gained significant attention. This article focuses on performing sentiment analysis on Twitter data using machine learning. The process involves importing necessary dependencies and datasets, preprocessing the text to clean and transform it into a suitable format, analyzing the data, splitting it into training and testing sets, converting the text data into numerical features using the TF-IDF vectorizer, and creating and evaluating different models. Three popular machine learning models-Bernoulli Naive Bayes, Linear Support Vector Classification (LinearSVC), and Logistic Regression-are employed in this study. These models are trained on the training data and evaluated using appropriate metrics. Logistic Regression, for example, is a machine learning classifier used to classify different values based on specific attributes or features.

2 Literature Survey -Twitter Sentiment Analysis

This section explores prior investigations in the context of classification of disaster tweets and the performance of fundamental Machine Learning algorithms to advanced Deep Learning algorithms is discussed. A collection of traditional methods [1–9] is presented based on the information to detect the medical resource tweets during an emergency. Majority- Voting is considered for the ensemble methods. The performance has been far better than the traditional algorithms on various parameters. It also combines this method performance over Bag Of Words. The performance of accuracy (82.4%). This analysis is restricted only to the Nepal and Italy earthquake datasets owing to the lack of labeled data. A model to identify NAR tweets [10–12] at the time of crisis. They suggest that the layering of a CNN with conventional classifiers (based on features) is effective for identifying the informative tweets. The authors also recommend that the combination of Convolutional Neural Networks, K-NN & SVM with specific features of domain exceeded the performance of diverse assemblages. This suggested model performs better than earlier methods on nepal and italy earthquake datasets. (Le, et al., proposed a comparison analysis of basic ML models with pre-trained model, BERT. They underlined that any DL algorithm, a LSTM or CNN with LSTM or a Convolutional Neural Networks (CNN) learns from one-hot encoding vectors of text,. If one-hot embedded its vector length equals to the word size, then this technique has dimensionality issues. A solution to this is to represent input as a low- dimensional space vector. This is implemented using many types of embedding techniques TF_IDF and Count Vector are considered for word representation and BERTLARGE architecture is used for implementing customized classification task. Disaster Tweets dataset from Kaggle repository is considered for this analysis. This paper substantiates that BERT (by tuning its parameters) is very constructive in classifying text [13–15]. This paper investigates the performance of text classification algorithm that uses TF-IDF Vectoriser, and a linear classification algorithm for a vector machine. The model predicts if a tweet is for a real emergency or not using a binary classifier.. The BERT layer's is followed by a drop out layer and then a dense layer. This study highlights the performance of BERT as a Text Classifier.- In this paper, the authors through their work emphasize on the significance of data processing, This paper throws light on importance of the information split affects efficiency of the classifier. They have used crisis_NLP and crisis_LexT26 datasets to make imbalanced and balanced datasets. And applied various information pre-processing methods to enhance the efficiency of classifier and further equate the performance of models (BERT, Default BERT, BERT with Non-Linear Layer, BERT with Long-Short Term Memory, BERT with Convolutional Neural Network.) on imbalanced and balanced datasets. They conclude that elimination of unessential data can lead to enhanced classifications. The models give better performance with balanced dataset. (Ma, n.d.) In this study, the authors have presented a comparision analysis on performance of the default BERT architecture and other custom based BERT architectures with the default Bi-LSTM for classification. Glove is used for embedding text into numerical vectors. The dataset used for the analysis is m CrisisLexT6 Hurricane Sandy dataset and n Crisis_NLP. The bidirectional LSTM with GloVe Twitter embeddings is set as baseline and several BERT based models (baseline BERT, BERT with NonLinearity, BERT with LSTM, BERT with CNN) are developed and they outperform the baseline performance [16]. This paper highlights on a comparison of word embeddings using CNN and Bi-LSTM as encoders for text classification.

This article explains the implementation of proposed methodology used for this study. This article is structured as follows. It starts with the introduction, which explains the overview of the execution, which is followed by the dataset and training specifications. Next to that, the implementation is detailed and finally the evaluation metrics used are presented. The datasets used and the challenges are elucidated [17–45]. The performance evaluation metrics used are F1-Score, Accuracy, Precision, Recall, AUC-ROC curve.

3   Conclusion

Analyzing emotions on Twitter involves multiple stages, starting with data collection and retrieval. The dataset is then preprocessed to clean the text data and make it suitable for analysis. Data analysis provides insights into the sentiments expressed by Twitter users, revealing diverse opinions in various contexts. To develop and evaluate a classification model, the data is divided into training and testing sets. The TF-IDF vectorizer is employed to convert the textual data into numerical representations used for model training and testing. Three models are utilized in this project: BernoulliNB, LinearSVC, and Logistic Regression. The BernoulliNB model, based on the Naive Bayes algorithm, is trained and evaluated to test distribution hypotheses. The LinearSVC model, utilizing a support vector machine, is also employed to validate the hypotheses. Additionally, the logistic regression model, commonly used for classification tasks, is utilized for sentiment prediction. The models are evaluated based on accuracy and their effectiveness in classifying emotions. Each model has its own strengths and limitations, but overall, they have proven effective in capturing sentiment expressed in tweets. The results demonstrate the feasibility of performing sentiment analysis on Twitter data using machine learning algorithms. Once the models are trained and evaluated, they can be saved for future use. Saved models can be easily reused and deployed in real-world applications requiring sentiment analysis. In summary, the Twitter Sentiment Analysis project leveraged machine learning models, including BernoulliNB, LinearSVC, and Logistic Regression, to identify and classify sentiment in tweets. This project enhances understanding of diverse opinions expressed by Twitter users and facilitates deeper insights into public sentiment on various topics and events. By employing these models, businesses and organizations can gain a better understanding of customer sentiment, leading to more informed decisions and tailored strategies. The study also emphasizes the significance of techniques like TF-IDF vectorization in preparing data for statistical analysis. Overall, this project contributes to the ongoing advancement of sentiment analysis in understanding social media sentiment.

References

1. Ameen, Y.A., Bahnasy, K., Elmahdy, A.: Classification of Arabic Tweets for damage event detection. Int. J. Sci. Eng. Res. **114**, 160–166 (2020)
2. Chanda, A.K.: Efficacy of BERT embeddings on predicting disaster from Twitter data. arXiv. Association for Computing Machinery **2021**, 1–14 (2021)
3. Devlin, J., Chang, M.W., Lee, K., Toutanova, K.: BERT: Pre-training of deep bidirectional transformers for language understanding. In: NAACL HLT 2019 - 2019 Conference of the North American Chapter of the Association for Computational Linguistics: Human Language Technologies - Proceedings of the Conference, vol. 1, pp.4171–4186 (2019)
4. Gao, H., Barbier, G.: Harnessing the crowdsourcing power of social media for disaster relief. IEEE Intell. Syst. 11–14 (2011)
5. Goswami, S., Raychaudhuri, D.: Identification of Disaster-Related Tweets Using Natural Language Processing (2020)
6. Irawan, R., Isa, S.M.: Social media disaster relevance classification for situation awareness during emergency response in Indonesia. Int. J. **87**, 3216–3222 (2020)
7. Kabir, Y.: A Deep Learning Approach for Tweet Classification and Rescue Scheduling for Effective Disaster Management, arXiv, pp. 1–14 (2019)
8. Kalyan, K.S., Sangeetha, S.: SECNLP?: a survey of embeddings in clinical natural language processing. J. Biomed. Inform. **101**, 103323 (2020)
9. Madichetty, S., Sridevi, M.: Improved classification of crisis-related data on Twitter using contextual representations. Procedia Comput. Sci. **1672019**, 962–968 (2020)
10. Madichetty, S., Sridevi, M.: A stacked convolutional neural network for detecting the resource tweets during a disaster. Multimedia Tools Appl. **803**, 3927–3949 (2021)
11. Malekzadeh, M., Hajibabaee, P., Heidari, M., Zad, S., Uzuner, O., Jones, J.H.: Review of graph neural network in text classification, pp. 0084–0091 (2022)
12. Messages, C., Imran, M., Mitra, P., Castillo, C.: Twitter as a Lifeline: Humananno-tated Twitter Corpora for NLP of Crisis-related Messages, pp. 1638– 1643 (2016)
13. Naaz, S., Abedin, Z.U., Rizvi, D.R.: Sequence classification of tweets with transfer learning via BERT in the field of disaster management. EAI Endorsed Trans. Scalable Inf. Syst. **831**, 1–8 (2021)
14. Peters, M.E., et al.: Deep contextualized word representations. In: NAACL HLT 2018 - 2018 Conference of the North American Chapter of the Association for Computational Linguistics: Human Language Technologies - Proceedings of the Conference, vol. 1, pp. 2227–2237 (2018)
15. Weimar, B., Wiegmann, M., Kersten, J., Potthast, M.: Analysis of detection models for disaster-related tweets, pp. 872–880 (2020)
16. Wang, C., Nulty, P., Lillis, D.: A comparative study on word embeddings in deep learning for text classification, pp. 37–46 (2020)
17. Soh, W.T.: Text-based Graph Convolutional Network - Bible Book Classification - A semi-supervised graph-based approach for text classification and inference (2019)
18. Satyanarayana Murthy, T., Varma, M.K., Roy, S.: Improving the performance of association rules hiding using hybrid optimization algorithm. J. Appl. Secur. Res. **15**(3), 423–437 (2020). https://doi.org/10.1080/19361610.2020.1756155
19. Satyanarayana Murthy, T., Gopalan, N.P., Yakobu, D.: An efficient un-realization algorithm for privacy preserving decision tree learning using McDiarmid's Bound. Int. J. Innovative Technol. Exploring Eng. (IJITEE), **8**(4S2), 499–502 (2019)

20. Satyanarayana Murthy, T., Gopalan, N.P., Gunturu, S.: A novel optimization based algorithm to hide sensitive item-sets through sanitization approach. Int. J. Modern Educ. Comput. Sci. (IJMECS) **10**(10), 48–55 (2018). https://doi.org/10.5815/ijmecs.2018.10.06

21. Satyanarayana Murthy, T., Gopalan, N.P., Alla, D.S.K.: The power of anonymization and sensitive knowledge hiding using sanitization approach. Int. J. Modern Educ. Comput. Sci. (IJMECS), **10**(9), pp. 26–32 (2018). https://doi.org/10.5815/ijmecs.2018.09.04.

22. Satyanarayana Murthy, T., Gopalan, N.P.: A novel algorithm for association rule hiding. Int. J. Inf. Eng. Electron. Bus. (IJIEEB) **10**(3), 45–50 (2018). https://doi.org/10.5815/ijieeb.2018.03.06

23. SaiBabu, A., Murthy, T.S.N.: Security provision in publicly auditable secure cloud data storage services using SHA-1 algorithm. Int. J. Comput. Sci. Inf. Technol. (IJCSIT) **3**(3), 4084–4088 (2012)

24. Sathyanarayana Murthy, T., Mohan Krishna Varma, N., Ravuri, D., Kishore Babu, D., Nazeer, S.: Classification of Precious and Non-precious Tweets Using Deep Learning. In: Rout, R.R., Ghosh, S.K., Jana, P.K., Tripathy, A.K., Sahoo, J.P., Li, KC. (eds.) Advances in Distributed Computing and Machine Learning, vol. 427. LNNS, pp. 393–399. Springer, Singapore (2022). https://doi.org/10.1007/978-981-19-1018-0_33

25. Satyanarayana Murthy, T., Mohan Krishna Varma, N., Roy, S., Nazeer, S.: Effective classification of tweets using machine learning. In: Kumar, R., Ahn, C.W., Sharma, T.K., Verma, O.P., Agarwal, A. (eds.) Soft Computing: Theories and Applications. LNNS, vol. 425, pp. 439–446. Springer, Singapore (2022). https://doi.org/10.1007/978-981-19-0707-4_40

26. Murthy, T.S., Gopalan, N.P., Ramachandran, V.: A naive bayes classifier for detecting unusual customer consumption profiles in power distribution systems - APSPDCL. In: 2019 Third International Conference on Inventive Systems and Control (ICISC) at JCT College, Coimbatore, India, pp. 673–678 (2019)

27. Satyanarayana Murthy, T., Preethi, G., Gopalan, N.P.: An efficient way of anonymization without subjecting to attacks using secure matrix method. In: proceedings of the IEEE International Conference on Intelligent Computing and Control Systems at VAIGAI COLLEGE OF ENGG,MADURAI, pp 1462–1465 (2018)

28. Satyanarayana Murthy, T., Gopalan, N.P.: An efficient meta-heuristic chemical reaction based algorithm for association rule Hiding using an advanced perturbation approach. In: proceedings of the IEEE International Conference on Intelligent Computing and Control Systems, at VAIGAI COLLEGE OF ENGG,MADURAI. Indexed in IEEE (2018)

29. Gopalan, N.P., Satyanarayana Murthy, T.: Association rule Hiding using chemical reaction optimization. In: Presented a paper at 7th International Conference on Soft Computing for Problem Solving - SocProS 2017. IIT Bhubaneswar, ORISSA (2017)

30. Devarajan, D., et al.: Cervical cancer diagnosis using intelligent living behavior of artificial jellyfish optimized with artificial neural network. IEEE Access **10**, 126957–126968 (2022)

31. Maheswari, V.U., Aluvalu, R., Kantipudi, M.P., Chennam, K.K., Kotecha, K., Saini, J.R.: Driver drowsiness prediction based on multiple aspects using image processing techniques. IEEE Access **10**, 54980–54990 (2022)

32. Satyanarayana Murthy, T., Gopalan, N.P., Balaji, B.: A modified un-realization approach for effective data perturbation. Int. J Intell. Enterp. 408–421 (2023). https://doi.org/10.1504/IJIE.2023.10054103

33. Satyanarayana Murthy. T., Udayakumar, P., Alenezi, F., Laxmi Lydia, E., Ishak, M.K.: Coot optimization with deep learning-based false data injection attack recognition. Comput. Syst. Sci. Eng. **46**(1), 255–271 (2023)

34. Yonbawi, S., Alahmari, S., Satyanarayana Murthy, T., Maddala, P., Laxmi Lydia, E., et al.: Harris hawks optimizer with graph convolutional network-based weed detection in precision agriculture. Comput. Syst. Sci. Eng. **46**(2), 1533–1547 (2023)

35. Yonbawi, S., Alahmari, S., Murthy, T.S., Daniel, R., Lydia, E.L., et al.: Modified metaheuristics with transfer learning based insect pest classification for agricultural crops. Comput. Syst. Sci. Eng. **46**(3), 3847–3864 (2023)

36. Ahmed, M.A., Murthy, T.S., Alenezi, F., Lydia, E.L., Kadry, S., et al.: Design of evolutionary algorithm based unequal clustering for energy aware wireless sensor networks. Comput. Syst. Sci. Eng. **47**(1), 1283–1297 (2023)

37. Devaraj, F.S., Satyanarayana Murthy, T., Alenezi, F., Laxmi Lydia, E., Md Zawawi, M.A., et al.: Enhanced metaheuristics with trust aware route selection for wireless sensor networks. Comput. Syst. Sci. Eng. **46**(2), 1431–1445 (2023)

38. Kalyani, K., Parvathy, V.S., Abdeljaber, H.A.M., Murthy, T.S., Acharya, S., et al.: Effective return rate prediction of blockchain financial products using machine learning. Comput. Mater. Continua **74**(1), 2303–2316 (2023)

39. Satyanarayana Murthy, T.: An efficient diabetic prediction system for better diagnosis. Int. J. Intell. Enterp. 408–421 (2022). https://doi.org/10.1504/IJIE.2022.126397,

40. Satyanarayana Murthy, T., Gopalan, N.P., Athira, T.R.: Hiding critical transactions using modified un-realization approach". Int. J. Bus. Intell. **15**(3), 223–234 (2020)

41. Navaneetha Krishnan, S., Sundara Vadivel, P., Yuvaraj, D., Satyanarayana Murthy, T., Malla, S.J., et al.: Enhanced route optimization for wireless networks using meta-heuristic engineering. Comput. Syst. Sci. Eng. **43**(1), 17–26 (2022)

42. Shanmuga Priya, S., Yuvaraj, D., Satyanarayana Murthy, T., Chooralil, V.S., Navaneetha Krishnan, S., et al.: Secure key management based mobile authentication in cloud. Comput. Syst. Sci. Eng. **43**(3), 887–896 (2022)

43. Satyanarayana Murthy, T., Varma, M.K., Yadav, A.K.: A Diaetic Prediction System based on Mean Shift Clustering. ISI, IIETA Publisher,vol. 36, no. 2, pp. 231–235 (2021). https://doi.org/10.18280/isi.260210

44. Satyanarayana Murthy, T., Varma, M.K., Harsha.: Brain tumour segmentation using U-net based adversarial networks. Traitement du Signal, vol. 36, no. 4, pp. 353–359 (2021). https://doi.org/10.18280/ts.360408

45. Satyanarayana Murthy, T., Banothu, B., Varma, M.K.: An un-realization algorithm for effective privacy preservation using classification and regression trees, Revue d'Intelligence Artificielle,IIETA Publisher, vol. 33, no. 4, pp. 313–319 (2019). https://doi.org/10.18280/ria.330408.

Face News Detection Using Machine Learning Techniques

R. Sai Venkat[1], Ramu kuchipudi[1], K. Gangadhara rao[1], G. Srikanth[1],
Palamakula Ramesh babu[1], T. Satyanarayana Murthy[1(✉)] (iD),
and G. Venakata Kishore[2]

[1] Chaitanya Bharathi Institute of Technology, Hyderabad, India
{saivenkatr_it,ramukuchipudi_it,kgangadhar_it,srikanthg_it,
prameshbabu_it,tsmurthy_it}@cbit.ac.in
[2] Srinidhi Institute of Technology, Hyderabad, India
kishore.g@sreenidhi.edu.in

Abstract. Nowadays, most people are shifting to online news reading rather than traditional methods because of its convenience and low cost. So, the number of online users is increasing day by day, which is also increasing fake news across the internet. This fake news must be detected and removed from the internet before causing damage to the nation's peace. Social media platforms use fake news recognition algorithms to detect and remove misinformation from their platforms. However, these algorithms can fail when they misidentify satirical or humorous content as fake news. News organizations use fake news recognition technology to fact-check articles and ensure the accuracy of their reporting. However, these algorithms may fail to detect more sophisticated forms of misinformation, such as deep fakes or highly persuasive disinformation campaigns, leading to the spread of false information. Existing framework contains three main modules: information retrieval, natural language processing, and machine learning. Also has two phases: the data collection phase and the machine learning model-building phase. In the data collection phase, we obtained a data set and analyzed the data using natural language processing techniques to extract good features from web data. A detailed survey on an automatic online fake news detection using machine learning techniques are elaborated.

Keywords: Machine Learning · Fake News · learning · optimization · deep learning

1 Introduction

These days fake news is creating different issues from sarcastic articles to fabricated news Fake news encompasses a range of issues in today's society, extending from sarcastic articles and fabricated news to planned government propaganda. These problems have significant ramifications, contributing to a growing lack of

O. Castillo et al. (Eds.): PerSOM 2023, LNICST 517, pp. 311–318, 2024.
https://doi.org/10.1007/978-3-031-66044-3_23

trust in the media and distorting public discourse. While the term "fake news" traditionally referred to purposely misleading stories, its definition has evolved, and some individuals now misuse it to dismiss facts that contradict their preferred viewpoints. The impact of disinformation in American political discourse gained considerable attention, particularly in the aftermath of the American presidential election. The phrase "fake news" became widely used to describe factually incorrect and misleading articles primarily created to generate revenue through page views. Consequently, researchers and experts have sought to develop models capable of accurately predicting the likelihood that a given article is fake news. Social media platforms like Facebook have faced significant criticism about fake news. Facebook has implemented features to flag potentially misleading content on its site when users encounter it. Furthermore, the company has publicly acknowledged its efforts to develop automated systems to distinguish fake news articles. However, achieving this goal is challenging. An effective algorithm must remain politically unbiased, as fake news exists across the political spectrum. Additionally, it should provide equal consideration to legitimate news sources regardless of their ideological leanings. Determining the legitimacy of news articles presents its difficulties. Addressing the problem of fake news requires a comprehensive understanding of its nature. Fake news encompasses intentionally deceptive information, sarcastic content, and misleading narratives that manipulate public opinion. It is essential to distinguish between legitimate journalism and fabricated or misleading stories. Initiatives to combat fake news involve a combination of technological advancements, media literacy programs, and responsible journalism practices. Developing algorithms that can accurately identify fake news is a complex task. It requires leveraging artificial intelligence and machine learning while incorporating human fact-checking to ensure accuracy and fairness. Educating individuals on media literacy and critical thinking equips them with the necessary tools to discern reliable sources of information and identify misinformation. Collaboration among technology companies, factchecking organizations, and policymakers is crucial. Transparent policies and practices should be implemented to promote accurate information sharing and discourage the dissemination of fake news. Additionally, addressing the underlying economic incentives that drive the creation and proliferation of fake news is essential for long-term solutions. Solving the fake news problem necessitates a collective effort and a commitment to promoting an informed and discerning society. By fostering media literacy, leveraging technology responsibly, and upholding ethical journalism practices, we can mitigate the negative impact of fake news and preserve the integrity of public discourse.

2   Literature Review

In this experimental study [1], the authors aim to unify misinformation detection across different domains, with a primary focus on recognizing fake news related to news articles. They use a limited set of machine learning algorithms to achieve this, bringing together multiple domains of misinformation detection under a single setup. This paper [2] leverages blockchain techniques in machine learning to enhance the tracking of fake news on social media. It effectively utilizes a blockchain approach to improve the efficiency of tracking fake news; however, it has limitations in identifying fake images and deals primarily with text-based content. The authors present an empirical study on the evolution of fake news, providing insights into the transformation of fake news over time. This research [3] contributes to a better understanding of the evolution of fake news, making the identification process more efficient. It is important to note that this study primarily explains the evolution of fake news and does not delve into creating machine learning models using this dataset. This paper [4] conducts a systematic literature review on the topic of detecting fake news using machine learning techniques. It primarily focuses on supervised machine learning classifiers and their role in identifying fake news. These classifiers require labeled data for training, which can be a challenge in practice. The review underscores the importance of labeled data in training classifiers, but it also highlights the potential of unsupervised machine learning approaches to address this limitation . The authors present a novel stacking approach for accurate detection of fake news. In this paper [5], they evaluate the performance of various machine learning and deep learning models to enhance the accuracy of fake news detection. One notable advantage of this approach is its suitability for multiple languages, making it a versatile tool for different regions. However, it's important to mention that the paper primarily discusses a limited set of machine learning and deep learning languages, which might not cover all possibilities. In the realm of cybersecurity, this paper [6] introduces an efficient hybrid system for anomaly detection in social networks. The authors develop a hybrid anomaly detection method named DT-SVMNB that combines several machine learning algorithms to classify normal and abnormal users in social networks. The focus of this system is detecting fake users primarily based on the contents within the user profiles. An additional advantage lies in the potential to further enhance accuracy by exploring user interests and activities. This paper [7] explores construction site accident analysis using text mining and natural language processing techniques. It delves into various natural language processing and text mining methods to identify the causes of accidents on construction sites from their reports. The approach offers the potential for further accuracy improvements through the exploration and integration of new algorithms. This survey paper [8] provides insights into neural network language models, focusing on different architectures of classic neural network language models and their enhancements. Additionally, it introduces the related corpora and toolkits necessary for studying neural network language models. However, it's important to note that the paper primarily explains the tasks and advancements related to neural network language models without delving into their real-time applications. This paper [9] introduces an efficient convolutional neural network-based word segmenter for the Thai language, aiming to enhance word segmentation. The model utilizes character and syllable embeddings, resulting in a segmenter that is 5.6 times faster than previous state-of-the-art solutions. However, the approach faces challenges with idiosyncratic datasets, particularly those in the domain of poetry. In the realm of fake news detection, this paper [10] reports an accuracy of 93percent through deep learning techniques. While achieving high accuracy, this approach highlights the importance of collecting more recent data, especially data relevant to the current period, to further improve performance. The paper demonstrates the effectiveness of deep learning techniques in fake news detection. This work [11] introduces the use of machine learning techniques to detect fake news. The model aims to identify fake news using machine learning methods, offering a potential solution to the issue of fake news proliferation. However, the paper primarily discusses the application of these techniques without extensively detailing their potential use cases. In this paper [12], the authors propose the TriFN model, which employs a tri-relationship embedding framework to model publisher-news relations and user-news interactions simultaneously for fake news classification. This approach enriches the understanding of the social context in which fake news spreads, contributing to improved detection. This paper [13] takes a data management and mining perspective to combat fake news. It introduces a warning system to reduce the spread of fake news by alerting users to potentially false information. While the warning system is a valuable addition, it does not entirely eliminate the challenge of fake news. This paper [14] focuses on fake news detection with generated comments for news articles. The model employs specific algorithms and methods to detect fake news within news articles. It is effective for this context but may not be applicable to fake news in other social media content Title Suppressed Due to Excessive Length 5 This work [15] concentrates on fake news detection using machine learning ensemble methods. The model excels in identifying fake news through the application of a limited set of machine learning algorithms. It is particularly wellsuited for text-based content, but it does not extend to fake news detection in images or other non-text formats. In the field of subsurface characterization, this paper [16] addresses noninvasive fracture characterization based on the classification of sonic wave travel times. The model's main advantage lies in its ability to classify fractures based on the waves generated, making it a valuable tool in this domain. However, it requires an experimental setup, involving external elements and additional work for implementation. This paper [17] explores bone cancer detection using machine learning techniques. The model efficiently detects diseases using machine learning algorithms, offering a swift diagnostic solution. However, one limitation is that it relies on a relatively limited dataset for identifying diseases, which may impact its accuracy in some cases. This paper [18] discusses Bayesian classifier combination as a method for classification tasks. The advantage of this method lies in its ability to classify items based on labels, contributing to effective categorization. However, it is important to note that this method primarily focuses on classification and does not offer detection capabilities. This paper [19] introduces a system for predicting power production of wind turbines using a fusion of multilayer perceptron (MLP) and adaptive neuro-fuzzy inference systems (ANFIS). The system is capable of detecting underperformance of turbines for various operating conditions. However, it relies on weather conditions to make predictions and may not be as reliable in unfavorable weather conditions. The paper [20]. presents an LSTM-based predictive framework for literature-based knowledge discovery. The model features supportive attributes for predicting future literature-based discoveries and emerging trends. It is a valuable tool; however, it may face challenges related to accommodating domain experts in identifying semantic similarity of keywords and various forms of abbreviations.

3   Conclusion

In conclusion, the detection of fake news using machine learning techniques holds great potential in combating the proliferation of misinformation in today's digital age. Machine learning algorithms offer the ability to analyze vast amounts of data, extract meaningful patterns, and make accurate predictions about the authenticity of news articles. Through the utilization of supervised, unsupervised, and semi-supervised learning methods, machine learning models can learn from labeled and unlabeled datasets to identify distinguishing features and characteristics of fake news. By training on diverse and comprehensive datasets that encompass various types of fake news, these models can generalize well and improve their detection accuracy. Feature engineering plays a critical role in the effectiveness of machine learning-based fake news detection. By extracting relevant features from textual content, including linguistic cues, lexical patterns, sentiment analysis, and meta-data, models can capture the nuances that differentiate fake news from genuine information. Additionally, incorporating user-based features such as social network interactions, user behavior, and credibility of sources can enhance the detection process. However, challenges remain in the field of fake news detection using machine learning. The constantly evolving nature of fake news requires continuous updates and adaptations of the detection models to stay ahead of emerging techniques used by those spreading misinformation. Biases present in the training data, including both explicit and implicit biases, need to be addressed to ensure fair and unbiased detection. Furthermore, the interpretability and transparency of machine learning models are crucial to building trust and understanding of their decision-making process. To overcome these challenges, interdisciplinary research efforts are needed to combine expertise from fields such as natural language processing, information retrieval, social network analysis, and cognitive psychology. Collaboration between academia, industry, and policymakers is essential to develop robust frameworks, share datasets, and establish guidelines for responsible information dissemination and consumption. In conclusion, machine learning offers a promising avenue for the detection of fake news, leveraging its capabilities to process vast amounts of data and extract meaningful insights. By addressing challenges related to biases, interpretability, and the dynamic nature of fake news, machine learning-based detection systems can play a vital role in promoting accurate information, fostering media literacy, and safeguarding the integrity of public discourse.

References

1. Rahman, M.S., Halder, S., Uddin, M.A., Acharjee, U.K.: An efficient hybrid system for anomaly detection in social networks. Cybersecurity **4**(1), 10 (2021)
2. Jiang, T., Li, J.P., Haq, A.U., Saboor, A., Ali, A.: A novel stacking approach for accurate detection of fake news. IEEE Access **9**, 22626–39 (2021)
3. Lample, G., Ballesteros, M., Subramanian, S., Kawakami, K., Dyer, C.: Neural architectures for named entity recognition (2016)
4. Phatthiyaphaibun, W., et al.: Pythainlp v2.3.1 release! (2021)
5. Ahmad, I., Yousaf, M., Yousaf, S., Ahmad, M.O.: Fake news detection using machine learning ensemble methods. Complexity **2020**(1), 8885861 (2020)
6. Misra, S., Li, H.: Chapter 9-noninvasive fracture characterization based on the classification of sonic wave travel times, pp. 243–287. Gulf Professional Publishing (2020)
7. Shrivastava, D., Sanyal, S., Maji, A.K., Kandar, D.: Chapter 17 - Bone cancer detection using machine learning techniques, pp. 175–183. Academic Press (2020)
8. Kim, H.C., Ghahramani, Z.: Bayesian classifier combination. In: Artificial Intelligence and Statistics, pp. 619–627 (2012)
9. Choudhury, N., Faisal, F., Khushi, M.: Towards an LSTM-based predictive framework for literature-based knowledge discovery (2019)
10. Zhang, F., Fleyeh, H., Wang, X., Lu, M.: Construction site accident analysis using text mining and natural language processing techniques. Autom. Constr. **99**, 238–248 (2019)
11. Jing, K., Xu, J.: A survey on neural network language models (2019)
12. Parikh, S.B., Atrey, P.K.: Media-rich fake news detection: a survey. In: 2018 IEEE Conference on Multimedia Information Processing and Retrieval, pp. 436–441 (2018)
13. Guo, M., Chen, X., Li, J., Zhao, D., Yan, R.: How does truth evolve into fake news? an empirical study of fake news evolution (2021)
14. Ahmed, A.A.A., Aljabouh, A., Donepudi, P.K., Choi, M.S.: Detecting fake news using machine learning: a systematic literature review (2021)
15. Shu, K., Wang, S., Lee, D., Liu, H.: Mining disinformation and fake news: concepts, methods, and recent advancements (2020)
16. Lee, N., et al.: On unifying misinformation detection (2021)
17. Mookdarsanit, P., Mookdarsanit, L.: The COVID-19 fake news detection in Thai social texts. EAI Endorsed Trans. Energy Web **10**(2), 988–998 (2021)
18. Akhter, M.P., Zheng, J., Afzal, F., Lin, H., Riaz, S., Mehmood, A.: Supervised ensemble learning methods towards automatically filtering Urdu fake news within social media. PeerJ Comput. Sci. **7**, e425 (2021)
19. Umer, M., Imtiaz, Z., Ullah, S., Mehmood, A., Choi, G.S., On, B.W.: Fake news stance detection using deep learning architecture (CNN-LSTM). IEEE Access **8**, 156695–706 (2020)
20. Yanagi, Y., Orihara, R., Sei, Y., Tahara, Y., Ohsuga, A.: Fake news detection with generated comments for news articles. In: IEEE 24th International Conference on Intelligent Engineering Systems (INES), pp. 85–90 (2020)
21. Satyanarayana Murthy, T., Gopalan, N.P., Alla, D.S.K.: The power of anonymization and sensitive knowledge hiding using sanitization approach. Int. J. Modern Educ. Comput. Sci. (IJMECS), **10**(9), 26–32 (2018). https://doi.org/10.5815/ijmecs.2018.09.04

22. Satyanarayana Murthy, T., Gopalan, N.P.: A novel algorithm for association rule hiding. Int. J. Inf. Eng. Electron. Bus. (IJIEEB) **10**(3), 45–50 (2018). https://doi.org/10.5815/ijieeb.2018.03.06

23. Saibabu, A., Murthy, T.S.N.: Security provision in publicly auditable secure cloud data storage services using SHA-1 algorithm. IJCSIT Int. J. Comput. Sci. Inf. Technol. **3**(3), 4084–4088 (2012)

24. Sathyanarayana Murthy, T., Mohan Krishna Varma, N., Ravuri, D., Kishore Babu, D., Nazeer, S.: Classification of Precious and non-precious tweets using deep learning. In: Rout, R.R., Ghosh, S.K., Jana, P.K., Tripathy, A.K., Sahoo, J.P., Li, KC. (eds.) Advances in Distributed Computing and Machine Learning, vol. 427, pp. 393–399. Springer, Singapore (2022). https://doi.org/10.1007/978-981-19-1018-0_33

25. Satyanarayana Murthy, T., Mohan Krishna Varma, N., Roy, S., Nazeer, S.: Effective classification of Tweets using machine learning. In: Kumar, R., Ahn, C.W., Sharma, T.K., Verma, O.P., Agarwal, A. (eds.) Soft Computing: Theories and Applications. LNNS, vol. 425, pp. 439–446. Springer, Singapore (2022). https://doi.org/10.1007/978-981-19-0707-4_40

26. Murthy, T.S., Gopalan, N.P., Ramachandran, V.: A naive bayes classifier for detecting unusual customer consumption profiles in power distribution systems - APSPDCL. In: 2019 Third International Conference on Inventive Systems and Control (ICISC) at JCT College, Coimbatore, India, pp. 673–678 (2019)

27. Satyanarayana Murthy, T., Preethi, G., Gopalan, N.P.: An efficient way of anonymization without subjecting to attacks using secure matrix method. In: proceedings of the IEEE International Conference on Intelligent Computing and Control Systems at VAIGAI COLLEGE OF ENGG,MADURAI, pp. 1462–1465 (2018)

28. Satyanarayana Murthy, T., Gopalan, N.P.: An efficient meta-heuristic chemical reaction based algorithm for association rule hiding using an advanced perturbation approach. In: proceedings of the IEEE International Conference on Intelligent Computing and Control Systems, at VAIGAI COLLEGE OF ENGG,MADURAI. Indexed in IEEE (2018)

29. Gopalan, N.P., Satyanarayana Murthy, T.: Association rule hiding using chemical reaction optimization. In: Presented a paper at 7th International Conference on Soft Computing for Problem Solving - SocProS 2017, December 23-24, 2017, IIT Bhubaneswar, ORISSA (2017)

30. Devarajan, D., et al.: Cervical cancer diagnosis using intelligent living behavior of artificial jellyfish optimized with artificial neural network. IEEE Access **10**, 126957–126968 (2022)

31. Maheswari, V.U., Aluvalu, R., Kantipudi, M.P., Chennam, K.K., Kotecha, K., Saini, J.R.: Driver drowsiness prediction based on multiple aspects using image processing techniques. IEEE Access **10**, 54980–54990 (2022)

32. Satyanarayana Murthy, T., Gopalan, N.P., Balaji, B.: A modified un-realization approach for effective data perturbation. Int. J. Intell. Enterp. Inder Sci. 408–421 (2023). https://doi.org/10.1504/IJIE.2023.10054103

33. Satyanarayana Murthy, T., Udayakumar, P., Alenezi, F., Laxmi Lydia, E., Ishak, M.K.: Coot optimization with deep learning-based false data injection attack recognition. Comput. Syst. Sci. Eng. **46**(1), 255–271 (2023)

34. Yonbawi, S., Alahmari, S., Satyanarayana Murthy, T., Maddala, P., Laxmi Lydia, E., et al.: Harris hawks optimizer with graph convolutional network-based weed detection in precision agriculture. Comput. Syst. Sci. Eng. **46**(2), 1533–1547 (2023)

35. Yonbawi, S., Alahmari, S., Murthy, T.S., Daniel, R., Lydia, E.L., et al.: Modified metaheuristics with transfer learning based insect pest classification for agricultural crops. Comput. Syst. Sci. Eng. **46**(3), 3847–3864 (2023)

36. Ahmed, M.A., Murthy, T.S., Alenezi, F., Lydia, E.L., Kadry, S., et al.: Design of evolutionary algorithm based unequal clustering for energy aware wireless sensor networks. Comput. Syst. Sci. Eng. **47**(1), 1283–1297 (2023)

37. Devaraj, F.S., Satyanarayana Murthy, T., Alenezi, F., Laxmi Lydia, E., Md Zawawi, M.A., et al.: Enhanced metaheuristics with trust aware route selection for wireless sensor networks,". Comput. Syst. Sci. Eng. **46**(2), 1431–1445 (2023)

38. Kalyani, K., Parvathy, V.S., Abdeljaber, H.A.M., Murthy, T.S., Acharya, S., et al.: Effective return rate prediction of blockchain financial products using machine learning. Comput. Mater. Continua **74**(1), 2303–2316 (2023)

39. Satyanarayana Murthy, T.: An efficient diabetic prediction system for better diagnosis. Int. J. Intell. Enterp. 408–421 (2022). https://doi.org/10.1504/IJIE.2022.126397,

40. Satyanarayana Murthy, T., Gopalan, N.P., Athira, T.R.: Hiding critical transactions using modified un-realization approach. Int. J. Bus. Intell. **15**(3), 223–234 (2020)

41. Navaneetha Krishnan, S., Sundara Vadivel, P., Yuvaraj, D., Satyanarayana Murthy, T., Malla, S.J., et al.: Enhanced route optimization for wireless networks using meta-heuristic engineering. Comput. Syst. Sci. Eng. **43**(1), 17–26 (2022)

42. Shanmuga Priya, S., Yuvaraj, D., Satyanarayana Murthy, T., Chooralil, V.S., Navaneetha Krishnan, S., et al.: Secure key management based mobile authentication in cloud. Comput. Syst. Sci. Eng. **43**(3), 887–896 (2022)

43. Satyanarayana Murthy, T., Varma, M.K., Yadav, A.K.: A diabetic prediction system based on mean shift clustering. Nutrition **36**(2), 231–235 (2021)

44. Satyanarayana Murthy, T., Varma, M.K., Harsha.: Brain tumour segmentation using U-net based adversarial networks. Traitement du Signal, 36(4), 353–359 (2021). https://doi.org/10.18280/ts.360408

45. Satyanarayana Murthy, T., Banothu, B., Varma, M.K.: An un-realization algorithm for effective privacy preservation using classification and regression trees, Revue d'Intelligence Artificielle, vol. 33(4), 313–319 (2019). https://doi.org/10.18280/ria.330408.

46. Satyanarayana Murthy, T., Varma, M.K., Roy, S.: Improving the performance of association rules hiding using hybrid optimization algorithm. J. Appl. Secur. Res. **15**(3), 423–437 (2020). https://doi.org/10.1080/19361610.2020.1756155

47. Satyanarayana Murthy, T., Gopalan, N.P., Yakobu, D.: An efficient un-realization algorithm for privacy preserving decision tree learning using McDiarmid's bound. Int. J. Innovative Technol. Exploring Eng. (IJITEE) **8**(4S2), 499–502 (2019)

48. Satyanarayana Murthy, T., Gopalan, N.P., Gunturu, S.: A novel optimization based algorithm to hide sensitive item-sets through sanitization approach. Int. J. Modern Educ. Comput. Sci. (IJMECS) **10**(10), 48–55 (2018). https://doi.org/10.5815/ijmecs.2018.10.06

Accident Detection System Using Video Data

Rahul Vanukuri, Rohith Anagula, Ganesh Poladasari, and Swathi Kothapalli[(✉)] [iD]

Department of Information Technology, CBIT, Gandipet, Hyderabad, India
kswathi2710@gmail.com

Abstract. In this research, we suggested an accident detection system that enables the camera while driving and detects accidents and alerts the nearest area emergency contacts. The accident detection is handled by using CNN (convolution neural networks) and the location details are handled by Google geocoding and reverse coding. The details of the location and occurrence of the accident details are stored in the app database. The video is also a collection of frames and hence we can also detect multiple accidents in different frames and can also predict the likeliness of the accident occurrence by probability. The live featuring of videos also help to detect different accidental zones around the state or country. The system certainly gives a lot of chances to balance the human loss ratio in accidents and gain safe roads among the different places. The data analysis can also be done to ensure the accidental warning signs can be posted among the most important spots after the analysis in different locations.

Keywords: CNN · Accidental zones · Geotagging · Reverse coding

1 Introduction

Majorly, the loss of human life is due to accidents. Each year, the World Health Organization reports that road traffic accidents result in the loss of more than 1.3 million lives globally. Alongside this devastating loss of life, an estimated 50 million individuals also suffer non-fatal injuries as a consequence of these accidents. These statistics underscore the urgent need for effective measures to prevent road accidents and mitigate their impact on individuals and communities worldwide. According to statistics, road transportation is considered the most dangerous means of transportation when compared to others such as air and sea. Hence to eradicate this problem, the proposed system takes into account the number of accidents, and without using any IoT the model takes in the video as input and splits into frames as well as finds the location so that human life is not wasted, and the necessary assistance is also provided to those in need after the accident. Accidents can be categorized into three phases based on the timing and severity of the outcomes they produce. The first phase involves immediate fatalities, where approximately 10% of accident-related deaths occur within a few minutes or seconds of the incident. The second phase, which occurs within an hour after the accident, has the highest mortality rate, accounting for 75% of all deaths. Timely assistance and intervention during this

© ICST Institute for Computer Sciences, Social Informatics and Telecommunications Engineering 2024
Published by Springer Nature Switzerland AG 2024. All Rights Reserved
O. Castillo et al. (Eds.): PerSOM 2023, LNICST 517, pp. 319–328, 2024.
https://doi.org/10.1007/978-3-031-66044-3_24

critical period can significantly reduce fatalities. The third phase occurs days or weeks after the accident and carries a death rate of around 15%. To prevent deaths during this phase, it is crucial to provide adequate medical care and allocate necessary resources. The primary objective is to assist accident victims during their most critical hour of need, enabling prompt and effective intervention to save lives.

2 Related Work

2.1 Smart Car: An IoT Based Accident Detection System

This system employs an automated response mechanism to detect and address accidents promptly. It utilizes sensors and microprocessors to detect collision events and transmit the location data to a centralized Cloud platform. From there, notifications are promptly sent to hospitals, ambulances, and emergency contacts. The core of this system revolves around the Raspberry Pi single-board computer, coupled with GPS technology that leverages positional data.

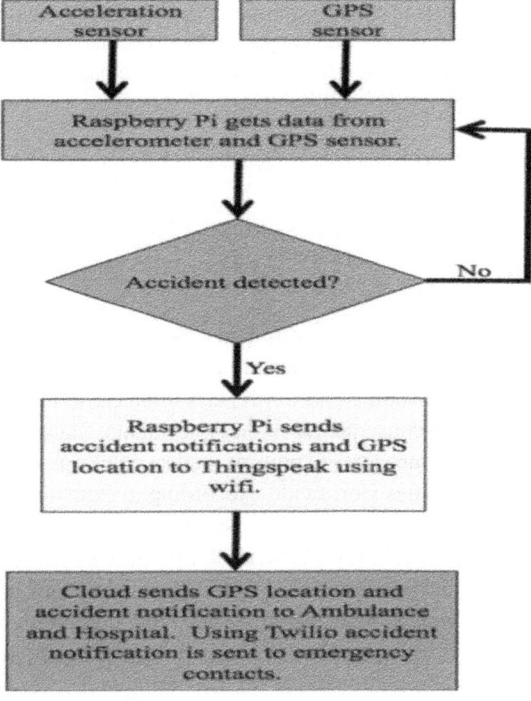

Fig. 1. Smart Car Process

The device is designed to swiftly identify collisions involving the vehicle it is installed in. To achieve this, it utilizes the ADXL345 accelerometer, which has proven compatibility with Raspberry Pi 3B+ and has been successfully employed in various projects.

The accelerometer offers a triple-axis feature, enabling detection of acceleration along different directions. The x-axis captures forward or backward acceleration, facilitating the identification of front or rear-end collisions. The y-axis measurement detects impacts from the sides of the vehicle, while the z-axis reading detects collisions from above or below. To illustrate the system's operational flow, a comprehensive flow chart is provided in the accompanying figure Fig. 1 [1].

2.2 Vehicle to Vehicle Communication

This research paper focuses on wireless technologies employed in vehicle-to-vehicle (V2V) communication. It provides a comparative analysis of system reliability, throughput, and latency. Furthermore, the paper discusses the significant challenges faced by V2V, including scalability and topological variations. It examines three recent schemes that aim to address these challenges. The key contributions of this paper include: [2]

1. Offering an overview of the wireless access technologies utilized in V2V communication.
2. Identifying and discussing the technical challenges encountered by V2V.
3. Introducing the Loss Differentiation RA (LORA) scheme, which enables V2V safety communications to rapidly and appropriately adapt data rates based on environmental dynamics.
4. Proposing an adaptive modulation and coding technique that dynamically adjusts coding and modulation methods in response to current channel conditions.
5. Presenting a selection scheme for adaptive data rates that considers changes in the physical network topology.

These contributions enhance our understanding of wireless technologies in V2V communication and provide potential solutions to tackle the associated challenges.

2.3 Smart Automatic Accident Detection

1. The proposed model employs GPS for accurate accident location and GSM for quick information relay. It can also detect alcoholic drivers and vehicle fires, generating alerts. A buzzer enhances detection accuracy, and a user-controlled switch prevents unnecessary messages. Automatic notifications are sent to police and responsible parties upon accidents. Alcohol detection and flame sensors further enhance safety by notifying responsible parties and rescue teams in case of alcohol consumption or vehicle fires, minimizing potential loss [14].

2.4 Wireless Access Technologies in V2V

A. Cellular V2x

V2X communication is a highly efficient and reliable technology that plays a crucial role in facilitating real-time information exchange for safe, efficient, and environmentally conscious transportation services. Specifically developed within the

3rd Generation Partnership Project (3GPP), C-V2X operates in two distinct modes: Device-to-Device (D2D) and Device-to-Network (D2N). The D2D mode of operation allows for direct communication between vehicles or devices without the need for network involvement, enabling efficient and instant data exchange. On the other hand, the D2N mode utilizes traditional cellular links to establish communication between devices and network infrastructure, thereby enabling the integration of cloud services as part of the overall end-to-end solution. By leveraging these two modes, V2X communication technology enables a comprehensive and versatile approach to transmit critical information, contributing to safer and more efficient transportation systems.

B. DSRC

To address the communication challenges posed by the demanding vehicular environment, IEEE introduced a modified version of the Wireless Local Area Network (WLAN) protocol called IEEE802.11p DSRC. This standard utilizes the same physical (PHY) layer as the IEEE 802.11a standard, which was originally designed for indoor stationary environments. However, the high-speed and unstable nature of vehicular environments can lead to reliability issues in the performance of 802.11p packets.

One significant drawback of DSRC is its limited scalability. This hinders its ability to meet the required time-probabilistic characteristics, particularly in densely trafficked areas. The scalability issue poses a challenge in providing consistent and reliable communication in such scenarios.

In summary, while IEEE802.11p DSRC addresses the vehicular communication challenges by utilizing WLAN technology, its reliance on the IEEE 802.11a PHY layer and low scalability pose limitations on its performance and ability to meet the demands of dense traffic situations.

C. 4G-LTE

LTE technology is capable of meeting the reliability, mobility, and scalability requirements for V2V communication. It can be redesigned to provide simultaneous low latencies and higher throughput. Operating on the 1.88–1.9 GHz frequency range with TDLTE protocol, it offers potential benefits. However, challenges arise with LTE network overload and meeting stringent delay requirements during high cellular traffic. Optimization is crucial for successful implementation.

D. WLAN/WI-FI

To facilitate wireless access for V2V communication, we integrate a wireless local area network (WLAN) utilizing IEEE 802.11 standards. Specifically, IEEE 802.11a operates at a frequency of 5 GHz and offers a communication range of approximately 140 m outdoors and a minimum of 38 m indoors, delivering a data rate of 54 Mbps. However, a significant drawback of IEEE 802.11a is its primary design for stable indoor environments, resulting in poor reliability and continuity in outdoor or highway scenarios. This limitation hampers its performance and suitability for seamless V2V communication in such settings.

E. UWB (IEEE 802.15.3a), or Ultra-Wide Band

Ultra-wideband (UWB) technology utilizes short-pulse and low-powered radio signals to transmit data across a wide range of frequency spectrums, making it highly resilient to various types of disturbances. However, when it comes to V2V communication, UWB faces challenges related to latency, throughput, and scalability, which limit its suitability for this application.

F. ZigBee (IEEE 802.15.4)

A new low-cost and low-power wireless personal area network (PAN) standard was developed to meet the needs of control devices and sensors. However, considering factors like range limitations and other challenges, it is not deemed suitable for V2V communication in demanding vehicular environments.

G. BLUETOOTH (IEEE 802.15.1)

Blue tooth is the least preferred communication system for V2V communication because of its small range data rate and many other issues.

In a related work survey, research introduces a novel blind-spot [12] vehicle detection method for commercial vehicles, combining multi-convolutional neural networks (CNNs) and faster R-CNN. Two distinct approaches are presented:

1. The first method employs two custom CNNs to extract features, which are then concatenated and processed by a third custom CNN. Faster R-CNN utilizes these high-level features for vehicle detection [13].
2. The second method combines two ResNet CNN networks (ResNet-50 and ResNet-101) with the custom CNN to extract features, subsequently used by Faster R-CNN for blind-spot vehicle detection.

3   Technical Challenges

The V2V wireless channel presents a challenging signal propagation environment due to two key factors. Firstly, the motion of both the receiver and transmitter, along with the presence of stationary and mobile scatterers, results in a limited channel coherence time. Secondly, the presence of distant scatterers introduces long multipath components, leading to a narrow coherence bandwidth in the V2V environment (Fig. 2).

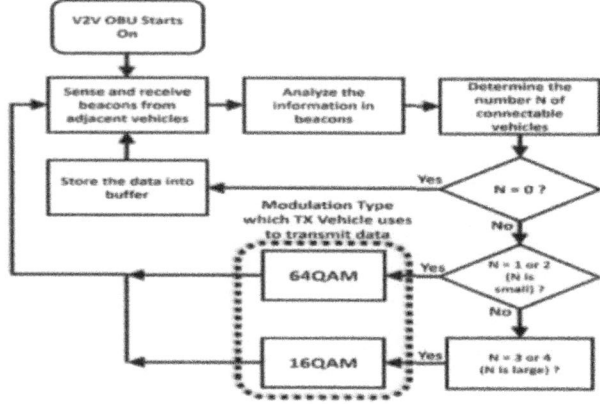

Fig. 2. V2V Environment

These factors contribute to a harsh wireless communication environment character ized by interference, attenuation, and fading. The dynamic nature of V2V communication further exacerbates the challenge of achieving reliable and stable communication. This is particularly evident in highway scenarios, where data transmissions often suffer from fading and shadowing, resulting in unreliable and intermittent communication.

4 Methodology

The proposed system as mentioned in the summary is the accident detection system using CNN or convolutional neural networks. Convolution is a fundamental mathematical operation that merges or combines two functions together to create a third function that shows how one function affects the other. In signal processing, this process involves multiplying two signals, shifting one of them, and then integrating the product of the signals. This results in a new signal that represents the interaction between the original signals. Convolution is used in many applications, including image and audio processing, data analysis, and deep learning, where it is applied to multi-dimensional arrays that represent various types of data. As we do not have any free geotagging datasets available we have used software like movie Avi to edit and add text overlays and add location coordinates in the video frames and this process is forward geocoding. The process of converting the non-human readable format into GPS coordinates is called as reverse coding. The CNN architecture and flowchart of the whole process model are demonstrated below in Fig. 3 and Fig. 4.

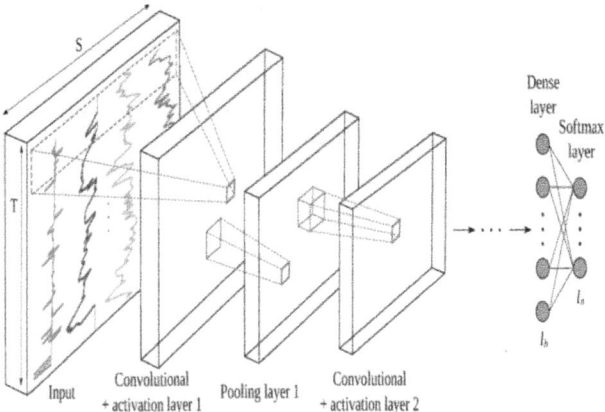

Fig. 3. The architecture of CNN

5 Implementation and Results

The result of the CNN Model is divided into two classes they are accident and non-accident, the frames from the CNN Model are divided into classes based on the SoftMax function used in flattening layer in CNN Model, SoftMax function will gives the output

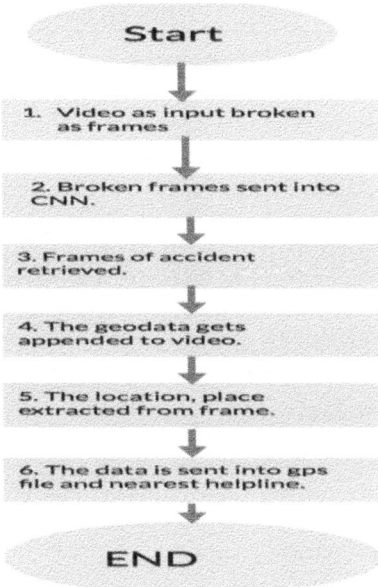

Fig. 4. The flowchart of the proposed model

as the probability distribution, based on the probability from the SoftMax function the frame is divided into two classes as shown below (Figs. 5 and 6)

Fig. 5. Division of Frames into two classes

The Training losses and accuracy of the model are represented in a graph shown in the below figure (Fig. 7).

+ Code + Text

```
[ ]  Epoch 28/50
     8/8 [==============================] - 113s 18s/step - loss: 0.0084 - accuracy: 0.9949 - val_loss: 0.0063 - val_accuracy: 0.9962
     Epoch 29/50
     8/8 [==============================] - 135s 18s/step - loss: 0.0076 - accuracy: 0.9949 - val_loss: 0.0061 - val_accuracy: 0.9962
     Epoch 30/50
     8/8 [==============================] - 143s 20s/step - loss: 0.0082 - accuracy: 0.9949 - val_loss: 0.0062 - val_accuracy: 0.9962
     Epoch 31/50
     8/8 [==============================] - 132s 18s/step - loss: 0.0076 - accuracy: 0.9949 - val_loss: 0.0061 - val_accuracy: 0.9962
     Epoch 32/50
     8/8 [==============================] - 134s 18s/step - loss: 0.0081 - accuracy: 0.9949 - val_loss: 0.0061 - val_accuracy: 0.9962
     Epoch 33/50
     8/8 [==============================] - 133s 18s/step - loss: 0.0077 - accuracy: 0.9949 - val_loss: 0.0060 - val_accuracy: 0.9962
     Epoch 34/50
     8/8 [==============================] - 132s 18s/step - loss: 0.0080 - accuracy: 0.9949 - val_loss: 0.0060 - val_accuracy: 0.9962
     Epoch 35/50
     8/8 [==============================] - 113s 18s/step - loss: 0.0078 - accuracy: 0.9949 - val_loss: 0.0060 - val_accuracy: 0.9962
     Epoch 36/50
     8/8 [==============================] - 132s 18s/step - loss: 0.0080 - accuracy: 0.9949 - val_loss: 0.0060 - val_accuracy: 0.9962
     Epoch 37/50
     8/8 [==============================] - 132s 18s/step - loss: 0.0079 - accuracy: 0.9949 - val_loss: 0.0060 - val_accuracy: 0.9962
     Epoch 38/50
     8/8 [==============================] - 105s 14s/step - loss: 0.0078 - accuracy: 0.9949 - val_loss: 0.0059 - val_accuracy: 0.9962
     Epoch 39/50
     8/8 [==============================] - 135s 18s/step - loss: 0.0079 - accuracy: 0.9949 - val_loss: 0.0059 - val_accuracy: 0.9962
     Epoch 40/50
     8/8 [==============================] - 132s 18s/step - loss: 0.0079 - accuracy: 0.9949 - val_loss: 0.0059 - val_accuracy: 0.9962
     Epoch 41/50
     8/8 [==============================] - 132s 18s/step - loss: 0.0079 - accuracy: 0.9949 - val_loss: 0.0059 - val_accuracy: 0.9962
     Epoch 42/50
     8/8 [==============================] - 133s 18s/step - loss: 0.0079 - accuracy: 0.9949 - val_loss: 0.0059 - val_accuracy: 0.9962
     Epoch 43/50
     8/8 [==============================] - 133s 18s/step - loss: 0.0079 - accuracy: 0.9949 - val_loss: 0.0059 - val_accuracy: 0.9962
     Epoch 44/50
     8/8 [==============================] - 134s 18s/step - loss: 0.0079 - accuracy: 0.9949 - val_loss: 0.0059 - val_accuracy: 0.9962
```

Fig. 6. Epochs of Model

```
plt.plot(history.history['loss'], label = 'training loss')
plt.plot(history.history['accuracy'], label = 'training accuracy')
plt.grid(True)
plt.legend()
```

<matplotlib.legend.Legend at 0x7fdc7cea0d00>

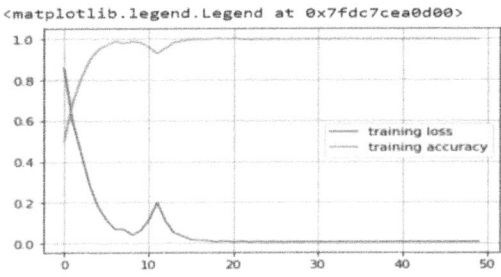

Fig. 7. Training Loss and Accuracy

The model layers are as shown in below figure (Fig. 8).

The output of reverse geocoding is stored in a csv file, the reverse geocoding will extract the details of latitude and longitude and find the location based on the coordinates (latitude and longitude) (Fig. 9).

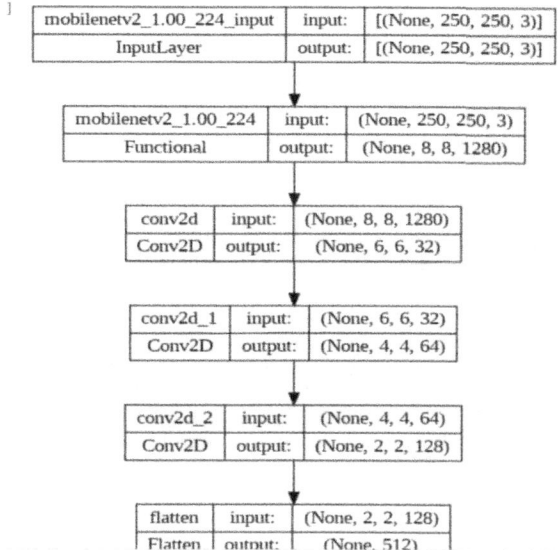

Fig. 8. Model architecture

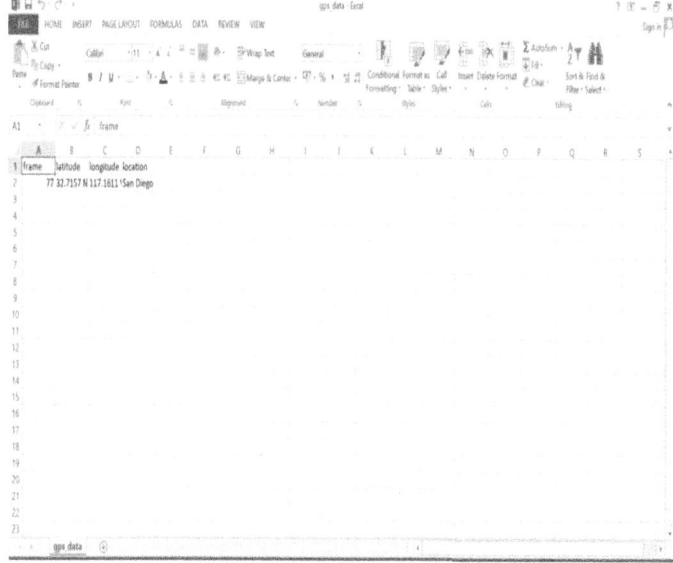

Fig. 9. Location latitude and longitude

6 Conclusion

An accident detection system is a critical technology designed to enhance road safety and potentially save lives. By promptly detecting accidents, this system can swiftly notify emergency services, leading to reduced response times and improved chances of survival for individuals involved in the accident. The proposed system follows a sequential process: it detects the accident, extracts the location information using geocoding, stores the collected details in a CSV file, notifies the designated emergency contacts about the accident, and shares the location details (CSV file) with emergency centers for further assistance.

References

1. Shaik, A., et al.: Smart car: an IoT based accident detection system. In: 2018 IEEE Global Conference on Internet of Things (GCIoT)
2. Ali, S.: Vehicle to Vehicle communication (2019) https://doi.org/10.13140/RG.2.2.24951.88487
3. Global status report on road safety 2015, World Health Organization (2019). http://www.who.int/violence_injury_prevention/road_safety_status/2015/en/. Accessed 07 Mar 07 2019
4. Prabakar, S., Porkumaran, K.: An enhanced accident detection and victim status indicating system: prototype. In: India Conference (INDICON), 2012 Annual IEEE. IEEE (2012)
5. Lexus (2019).https://www.lexus.com/enform. Accessed 07 Mar 2019
6. OnStar Safety and Security Services, Onstar.com (2019) https://www.onstar.com/us/en/services/safety-security/. Accessed 07 Mar 2019
7. SOSmart automatic car crash detection and notification app. SOSmart automatic car crash detection app (2019). http://www.sosmartapp.com. Accessed 07 Mar 2019
8. Kockan, C.: Communication between vehicles PhD thesis, Istanbul Technical University (2008)
9. Zeng, Y., Li, D., Vasilakos, A.V.: Opportunistic fleets for road event detection in vehicular sensor networks. Wireless Netw. **22**(2), 503–521 (2016)
10. Szegedy, C., et al.: Rethinking the inception architecture for computer vision. In: Proceedings of the IEEE conference on computer vision and pattern recognition (2016)
11. Szegedy, C., et al.: Going deeper with convolutions. In: Proceedings of the IEEE Conference on Computer Vision and Pattern Recognition (2015)
12. Muzammel, M., Yusoff, M.Z., Saad, M.N.M., Sheikh, F., Awais, M.A.: Blind-spot collision detection system for commercial vehicles using multi-deep CNN architecture. Sensors (Basel, Switzerland) **22**(16), 6088 (2022). https://doi.org/10.3390/s22166088
13. Alvi, U., Khattak, M.A.K., Shabir, B., Malik, A.W., Muhammad, S.R.: A comprehensive study on IoT-based accident detection systems for smart vehicles. IEEE Access: Pract. Innovations, Open Solutions **8**, 122480–122497 (2020). https://doi.org/10.1109/access.2020.3006887
14. Rathor, S., Dubey, P., Samadhiya, S.: Smart automatic accident detection & information system. In: 2022 International Conference on Computational Intelligence and Sustainable Engineering Solutions (CISES). 2022 International Conference on Computational Intelligence and Sustainable Engineering Solutions (CISES). IEEE (2022). https://doi.org/10.1109/cises54857.2022.9844371

Temporal Sentiment Analysis (TSMFPMSM) Model for Multimodal Social Media Fake Profile Detection

Bhrugumalla L. V. S. Aditya[1]($\boxtimes$), Sachi Nandan Mohanty[1], and Yalamanchili Salini[2]

[1] School of Computer Science and Engineering (SCOPE), VIT-AP University, Amaravati, Andhra Pradesh, India
{aditya.22phd7023,sachinandan.m}@vitap.ac.in
[2] Information Technology, VR Siddhartha Engineering College, Andhra Pradesh, India

Abstract. Today's social media sites should be able to spot fake profiles. Most social media accounts (around 25%) are fake or managed by automated software. Therefore, advanced models are required to detect and remove these fake profiles. Anomalies in login, usage, and non-functional elements have inspired researchers to construct pattern analysis models. This book expands on existing models using temporal sentiment analysis to spot fake profiles in social networks with multiple interface types. Massive datasets are gathered from social media platforms like Twitter, Facebook, and others and used in the model. TSPs are derived from these data sets using a unique ensemble sentiment analysis engine. Using Afinn, GloVe, and Word2Vec, the sentiment analysis engine labels statements as "positive," "negative," or "neutral." These TSPs teach a 1D CNN to identify fake profiles with high accuracy. The true-human behavioral theory influenced the model, which predicts that false users' periodic data will always converge. User perspectives are accounted for in the model. Therefore, the model achieves a 5.9%, 4.5%, and 3.2% improvement over state-of-the-art techniques for identifying bogus profiles, respectively. Multimodal social media interfaces benefit from this method.

Keywords: social media · Temporal · Afinn · 1D CNN · GloVE · Word2Vec · Interfaces · Sentiments

1 Introduction

Almost everyone today has a social media account. It's a great way to brag about expensive camera equipment, stalk your favorite stars, and stay in touch with your pals. We can meet new people and expand our knowledge thanks to these channels. There are negative aspects. Conflicts arise through social media. Twitter's 145 million DAUs and 330 million MAUs pale compared to Facebook's 500,000 DAUs and 6 SAUs added every minute. Twitter's constant updates include fresh news, itineraries, trending topics, and hashtags. A user's ability to like, remark, share, and respond is limited to 280 characters. Despite the serious topics that tend to dominate social media conversations, rumors can

O. Castillo et al. (Eds.): PerSOM 2023, LNICST 517, pp. 329–341, 2024.
https://doi.org/10.1007/978-3-031-66044-3_25

potentially spread and amplify societal tensions. Significant issues include privacy invasion, exploitation, cyberbullying, and fake news [1–3]. False information is an important issue today. Artificial neural networks (ANNs) can distinguish between human, bot, and cybernetic identities [4–6]. Computers currently handle "cyborg" accounts despite their human origin. These sham profiles spread hate speech and graphic images of abuse. They could potentially affect public opinion by applying anti-vaccination theories. Fake accounts plague Internet message boards. Fake accounts are used in spamming [7–9]. Cybercriminals are the ones who made these accounts. Concerns over identity theft and data breaches have led researchers to develop methods for detecting fake accounts, some of which are Collaborative Filtering (CF) [10] and C4.5 Decision Tree (CDT) [12]. User's personal information is sent to malicious third-party services when they visit URLs associated with these fake accounts. Fake accounts often impersonate legitimate businesses or individuals, damaging credibility and influencing how many people follow a profile.

2 Temporal Sentiment Analysis (TSMFPMSM) Model for Multimodal Social Media Fake Profile Detection

Researchers have presented a wide range of pattern analysis algorithms after studying methods for detecting fake profiles. These models estimate login, usage, and non-functional aspects to identify unusual user activity. Based on these models, the temporal sentiment analysis model can identify phony profiles on social media platforms that use several input methods. The model's operation is depicted in Fig. 1. As a first step, the model gathers extensive statistics from numerous social media platforms. These data sets will be used as the basis for further investigation. Temporal sentiment patterns (TSPs) are produced by running the collected datasets through a novel ensemble sentiment analysis engine. This engine classifies words as "positive," "negative," or "neutral" using a mixture of Afinn, GloVe, and Word2Vec. The obtained TSPs efficiently detect false profiles by training a 1D Convolutional Neural Network (1D CNN). Periodic data sent by false users always converge, according to the true-human behavioral theory, which is incorporated into the suggested model. This theory applies to user feelings, for which it is accurate. The first stage of the methodology is gathering 'Fake' and 'Genuine' social media posts from various sources, including Twitter, Facebook, and others. Then, the Afinn, GloVe, and Word2Vec models categorize the posts as positive, negative, or neutral. The Afinn sentiment analyzer uses a pre-tagged vocabulary to determine how an individual feels about a statement by comparing the words used. Word2Vec performs a semantic analysis, considering contextual meaning and synonyms, before transforming the words into vectors. The GloVe engine uses the training corpus to assign global frequency aggregates to individual words.

The sentiment analysis conducted by Afinn evaluates sentiments by assigning a final sentiment score (*Sout*) ranging from -1 to 1, indicating negative, neutral, and positive sentiments, respectively. The estimation of this score follows Eq. 1, which is presented below.

$$S_{out} = \frac{\sum\limits_{i=1}^{N} |W_i == W_p| - \sum\limits_{i=1}^{N} |W_i == W_n|}{N} \tag{1}$$

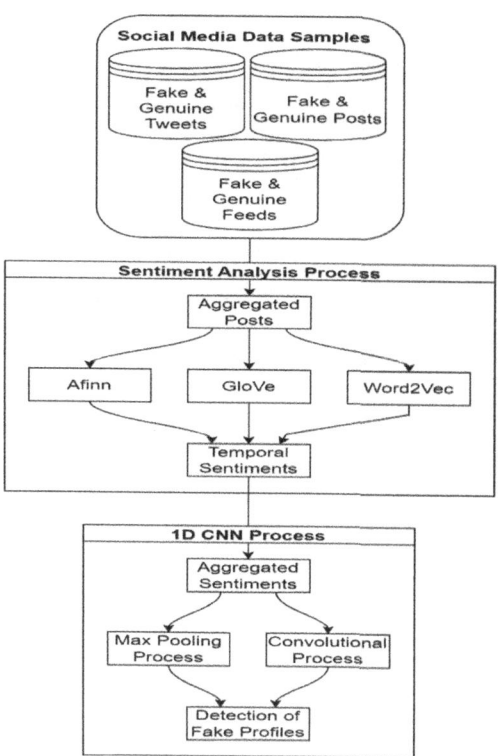

Fig. 1. Proposed process for fake profile detection

W_i is the input word, W_p and W_n are the positive and negative words in the corpus, and N is the number of terms used in the equation. Figure 2 depicts how the Word2Vec model, also used for sentiment analysis, uses many constructors.

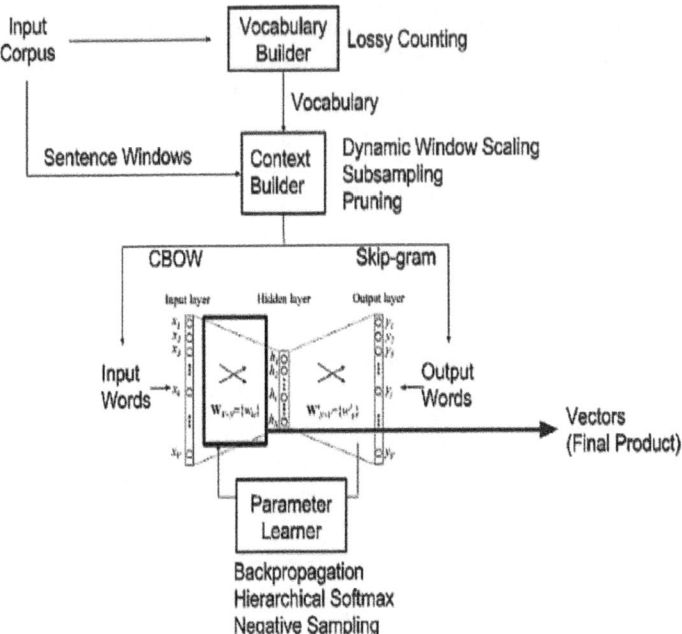

Fig. 2. Word2Vec process of sentiment analysis

Word2Vec's approach to sentiment analysis consists of many tools, such as a the-saurus, a context generator, and a continuous bag of words (CBoW) engine. Key take-aways can be gleaned from closely reading the document's many sections. To get started, the program harvests "action words" from existing sentences to generate a vocabulary. The context builder receives this vocabulary and uses it to create word pairings to find sets of words that go together. These variations are used by the CBoW engine and skip-gram models to improve feature extraction performance. A two-layer neural network processes these features to generate feelings from input word pairs. As a result of the overall sentiment analysis, the model generates sentiment linked with each word pair while considering the context.

The engine's emotion classification performance is impressive, but training can take time. With a few tweaks, GloVe uses a similar design. One-hot encoding is used to rep-resent words in GloVe's model, which requires more time in training and more frequent splits between the training and testing sets. The number and quality of the training cor-pus affect the GloVe model's prediction accuracy. To further understand how one-hot encoding works, the word embeddings generated for different input texts are graphically represented below (Fig. 3).

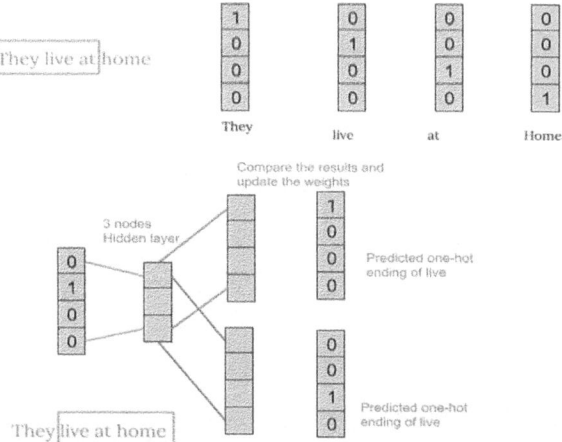

Fig. 3. Sentiment Analysis for GloVe Embedding Model

Following encoding, the values are fed into a neural network that, like Word2Vec, operates on vector representations of words. Finally, the network's sentiment scores are tested across various data sets. Combining the results of these techniques yields sentiment scores that are then used to generate a 1D temporal sentiment feature vector. A 1D Convolutional Neural Network (CNN) model is then used to classify these vectors, which helps detect fraudulent profiles. Figure 4 depicts the CNN model's flow, with the various layers and their sizes laid out for practical applications.

Convolutional layers, Max Pooling layers, and Dropout layers are all a part of the suggested model for efficient feature extraction and the selection of richly diverse feature sets. These layers are linked in a cascading fashion to improve feature enhancement, each with its unique window and stride parameters. A SoftMax-based fully connected layer is then used to categorize the enriched feature sets, allowing for the easier identification of distinct profile kinds.

The model uses Eq. 2 to extract convolutional features, which helps improve and expand sentiment feature sets.

$$C_{feats} = \sum_{a=-\frac{m}{2}}^{\frac{m}{2}} SV(i-a) \times ReLU\left(\frac{m+a}{2}\right) \tag{2}$$

In Eq. 2, the variables m and a denote the sizes of the convolutional window and stride, respectively. SV represents the sentiment vectors, while $ReLU$ represents the rectilinear unit used to activate these features. The extracted features are then passed to a variance maximization layer. Equation 3 is utilized to estimate the variance of the convolutional features, enabling the removal of features with lower variance levels.

$$v = \sqrt{\frac{\left(\sum_{i=1}^{D_s}\left(x_i - \sum_{j=1}^{D_s}\frac{x_j}{D_s}\right)^2\right)}{D_s + 1}} \tag{3}$$

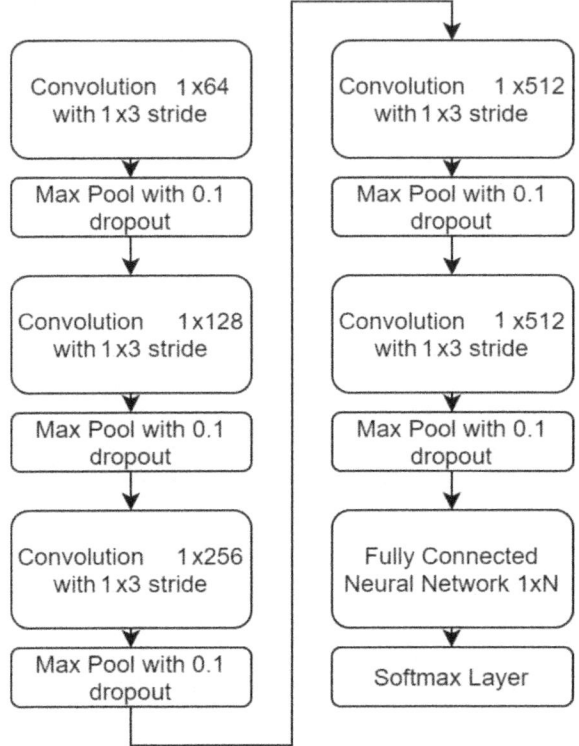

Fig. 4. Identification of fake profiles with 1D CNN Model

In Eq. 4, the variables x and Ds represent the feature value and the total samples extracted by the convolutional layers, respectively. These features are classified using feature-level weights (w) and biases (b), enabling the identification of different profile types.

$$C_{out} = softMax\left(\sum_{i=1}^{N} f_i \times w_i + b_i\right) \tag{4}$$

In Eq. 5, Nf represents the total number of features extracted by the preceding convolutional layers. By employing the customized 1D CNN model, the proposed technique achieves high accuracy in identifying fake profiles. The performance of the proposed model was evaluated on various sample sets and compared with standard models, which will be discussed in the subsequent section of this text.

3 Result Analysis and Comparison

The suggested approach starts with collecting data from several social feeds, which is subsequently processed by Afinn, GloVe, and Word2Vec models to isolate temporal feature sets. Classifying these feature sets with a 1D CNN can quickly determine profile kinds. The following datasets were used to assess the quality of this model:

https://www.kaggle.com/datasets/free4ever1/instagram-fake-spammer-genuine-accounts.

Social Network Fake Account Dataset, which is available at https://www.kaggle.com/datasets/bitandatom/social-network-fake-account-dataset

Our World Dataset, which is available at https://ieeexplore.ieee.org/document/9458194

The combined datasets consisted of a total of 5,000 social media profiles. Among these, 70% of the profiles were used for training, 10% for testing, and 20% for validation. The performance of the proposed model was compared to that of ANN [5], CDT [12], and DFB [16] as benchmarks to assess its efficiency compared to standard implementations. Table 1 provides the accuracy (A) of fake profile detection about the total test entries (TTE), illustrating the results obtained from this approach

Table 1. Fake profile identification for different data samples Estimated accuracy.

TTE	A (%) ANN [5]	A (%) CDT [12]	A (%) DFB [16]	A (%) TSM FPM SM
250	85.52	84.77	89.00	93.25
500	86.15	85.43	89.65	93.89
750	86.61	85.90	90.13	94.35
1000	86.92	86.20	90.45	94.65
1250	87.12	86.42	90.67	94.86
1500	87.29	86.63	90.84	95.05
1875	87.45	86.86	91.00	95.23
2250	87.65	87.14	91.22	95.46
2500	87.88	87.44	91.45	95.71
3000	88.11	87.72	91.69	95.96
3750	88.36	88.00	91.94	96.25
5000	88.68	88.34	92.27	96.60

The evaluation and analysis, as shown in Fig. 5, demonstrate that the proposed model achieved a significant improvement in fake profile detection accuracy compared to ANN [5], with an increase of 8.3%. Furthermore, it outperformed CDT [12] by 8.5% and DFB [16] by 3.9% in accuracy. These results highlight the model's effectiveness across various real-time use cases. The improved accuracy can be attributed to a high-efficiency 1D CNN classifier trained to optimize classification performance for different data types. Furthermore, Table 2 provides the precision values, which can be examined as follows.

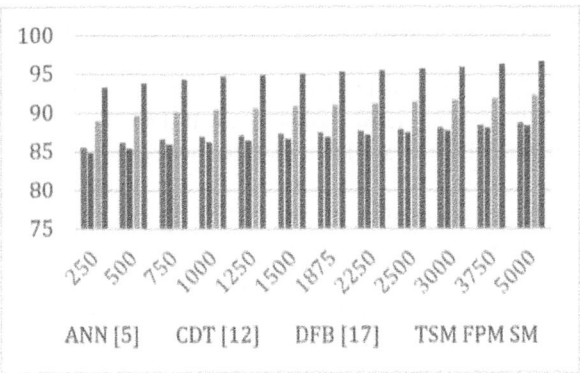

Fig. 5. Fake profile identification for different data samples Estimated accuracy

Table 2. Fake profile identification for different data samples Estimated precision

TTE	P (%) ANN [5]	P (%) CDT [12]	P (%) DFB [16]	P (%) TSM FPM SM
250	81.63	80.91	84.95	89.00
500	82.23	81.55	85.58	89.62
750	82.67	81.99	86.03	90.06
1000	82.97	82.28	86.34	90.35
1250	83.16	82.49	86.54	90.55
1500	83.31	82.69	86.71	90.73
1875	83.48	82.90	86.87	90.91
2250	83.67	83.17	87.07	91.12
2500	83.89	83.46	87.29	91.36
3000	84.10	83.73	87.51	91.60
3750	84.34	84.00	87.76	91.87
5000	84.65	84.33	88.08	92.20

Based on the evaluation depicted in Figure 6, it is evident that the proposed model exhibited a substantial improvement in precision for fake profile detection. Compared to ANN [5], it achieved a 7.5% higher precision. Additionally, it outperformed CDT [12] by 8.3% and DFB [16] by 4.5% in precision. These results emphasize the model's effectiveness across various real-time use cases. The enhanced precision is attributed to the use of temporal sentiments and the high-efficiency 1D CNN classifier, which has been trained to optimize precision performance for different data types. Furthermore, Table 3 provides insights into the recall of the classification, which can be examined as follows.

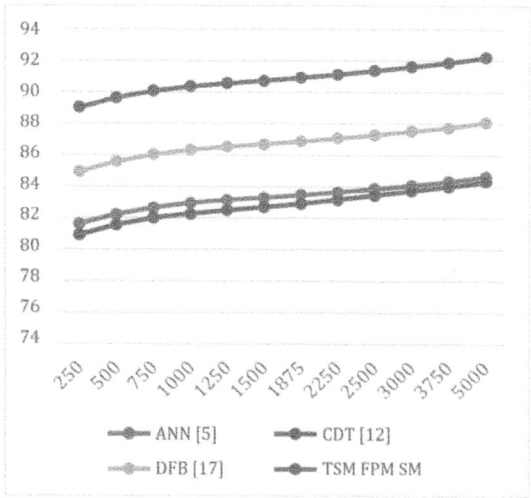

Fig. 6. Fake profile identification for different data samples Estimated precision

Table 3. Fake profile identification for different data samples Estimated recall

NT	R (%) ANN [5]	R (%) CDT [12]	R (%) DFB [16]	R (%) TSM FPM SM
250	83.02	82.29	86.40	90.51
500	83.63	82.93	87.03	91.14
750	84.08	83.38	87.49	91.58
1000	84.37	83.68	87.80	91.88
1250	84.57	83.89	88.01	92.09
1500	84.73	84.09	88.17	92.26
1875	84.89	84.31	88.34	92.45
2250	85.09	84.58	88.55	92.67
2500	85.30	84.88	88.77	92.91
3000	85.53	85.15	89.00	93.15
3750	85.77	85.42	89.25	93.43
5000	86.08	85.75	89.57	93.77

Figure 7 displays the estimated recall for fake profile identification across different data samples. Based on the evaluation and analysis depicted in Figure 8, the proposed model notably improves recall for fake profile detection. Compared to ANN [5], it achieved a 6.5% higher recall. Similarly, it outperformed CDT [12] by 7.4% and DFB [16] by 5.5% in the recall. These results underscore the model's effectiveness in various real-time use cases. The enhanced recall can be attributed to the utilization of temporal sentiments and the high-efficiency 1D CNN classifier, which has been trained to optimize recall performance for different data types. Furthermore, Table 4 provides information on the delay of classification, which can be examined as follows.

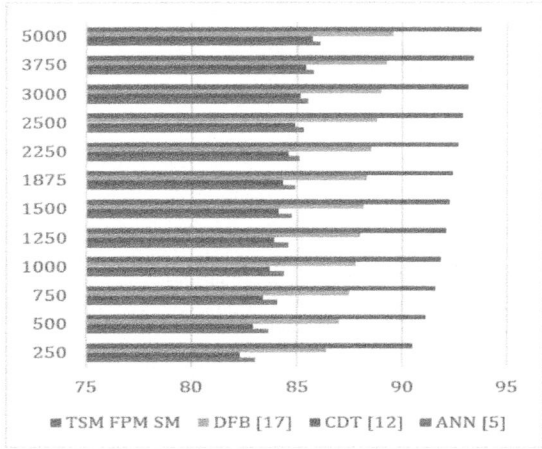

Fig. 7. Fake profile identification of different data samples Estimated recall

Table 4. The estimated delay needed for fake profile identification under different data samples

NT	D (ms) ANN [5]	D (ms) CDT [12]	D (ms) DFB [16]	D (ms) TSM FPM SM
250	168.76	167.27	175.70	149.63
500	170.00	168.58	176.92	150.59
750	170.90	169.49	177.85	151.30
1000	171.51	170.10	178.49	151.77
1250	171.91	170.53	178.90	152.11
1500	172.24	170.94	179.24	152.40
1875	172.56	171.39	179.57	152.71
2250	172.97	171.94	179.99	153.08
2500	173.41	172.54	180.46	153.47
3000	173.86	173.09	180.92	153.88
3750	174.35	173.64	181.42	154.35
5000	174.98	174.32	182.06	154.90

Figure 8 shows the evaluation results, which show that the suggested model significantly reduces the identification delay for detecting bogus profiles. Its identification delay was 10.5% lower than ANN's [5]. In terms of identification latency, it also fared

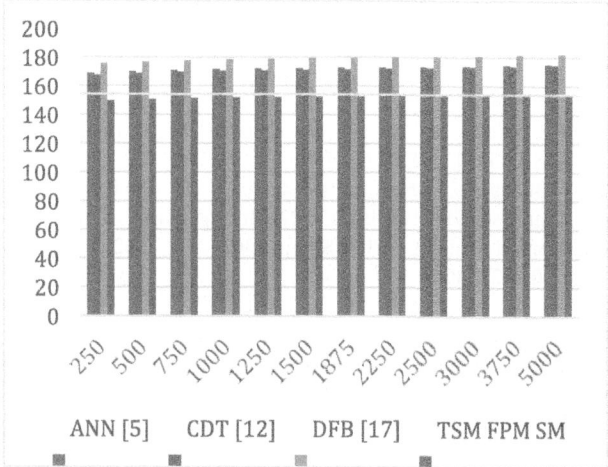

Fig. 8. Time required, on average, to spot a phony profile based on a variety of data sets

better than CDT [12] (9.5%) and DFB [16] (8.3%). These findings demonstrate the model's versatility for various high-velocity applications. Time savings result from using temporal sentiments and a very effective 1D CNN classifier tuned to maximize speed performance across a wide range of data types. This enhanced functionality makes the suggested model suitable for real-time social media settings to identify false profiles.

4 Conclusion and Future Scope

Temporal feature sets from various social feeds are identified using Afinn, GloVe, and Word2Vec models. A 1D CNN then classifies these feature sets to determine profile categories efficientlyQ4. The proposed model's accuracy was 8.3% higher than that of ANN [5], 8.5% higher than that of CDT [12], and 3.9% higher than that of DFB [16], making it suitable for real-time applications. One way to enhance accuracy is to use a multi-purpose 1D convolutional neural network (CNN) classifier.The proposed model had an accuracy of 7.5%, which was higher than ANN [5], CDT [12], and DFB [16]. A high-efficiency, multi-input-type, one-dimensional convolutional neural network classifier is used to increase the accuracy of temporal feelings. The proposed model outperformed ANN [5], CDT [12], and DFB [16] in terms of recall in real-world settings by 6, 5, and 5.5 percentage points, respectively. A high-efficiency 1D convolutional neural network (CNN) classifier tuned for recall across data types improves recall when applied to temporal feelings. The proposed model is suitable for high-speed use cases because its identification latency is 10.5% shorter than ANN [5], 9.5% lower than CDT [12], and 8.3% lower than DFB [16]. Reduce latency using temporal sentiment analysis and a solid 1D CNN classifier tuned for speed performance across many data types.

References

1. Pizarro, J.: Profiling bots and fake news spreaders at PAN'19 and PAN'20: bots and gender profiling 2019, profiling fake news spreaders on Twitter 2020. In: 2020 IEEE 7th International Conference on Data Science and Advanced Analytics (DSAA), pp. 626–630 (2020). https://doi.org/10.1109/DSAA49011.2020.00088
2. Krishnan, P., Aravindhar, D.J., Bhanu Prakash Reddy, P.: Finite automata for fake profile identification in online social networks. In: 2020 4th International Conference on Intelligent Computing and Control Systems (ICICCS), pp. 1301–1305 (2020). https://doi.org/10.1109/ICICCS48265.2020.9121086
3. Harris, P., Gojal, J., Chitra, R., Anithra, S.: Fake Instagram profile identification and classification using machine learning. In: 2021 2nd Global Conference for Advancement in Technology (GCAT), pp. 1–5 (2021). https://doi.org/10.1109/GCAT52182.2021.9587858
4. Tiwari, V.: Analysis and detection of fake profile over the social network. In: 2017 International Conference on Computing, Communication, and Automation (ICCCA), pp. 175–179 (2017). https://doi.org/10.1109/CCAA.2017.8229795
5. Hajdu, G., Minoso, Y., Lopez, R., Acosta, M., Elleithy, A.: Use of artificial neural networks to identify fake profiles. In: 2019 IEEE Long Island Systems, Applications and Technology Conference (LISAT), pp. 1–4 (2019).https://doi.org/10.1109/LISAT.2019.8817330
6. Rathod, S.: Exploring author profiling for fake news detection. In: 2022 IEEE 46th Annual Computers, Software, and Applications Conference (COMPSAC), pp. 1614–1619(2022). https://doi.org/10.1109/COMPSAC54236.2022.00256
7. Kulkarni, V., Aashritha Reddy, D., Sreevani, P., Teja, R.N.: Fake profile identification using ANN. In: 4th Smart Cities Symposium (SCS 2021), pp. 375–380 (2021). https://doi.org/10.1049/icp.2022.0372
8. Patel, K., Agrahari, S., Srivastava, S.: Survey on fake profile detection on social sites by using machine learning algorithm. In: 2020 8th International Conference on Reliability, Infocom Technologies and Optimization (Trends and Future Directions) (ICRITO), pp. 1236–1240 (2020).https://doi.org/10.1109/ICRITO48877.2020.9197935
9. Durier da Silva, F.C., Cristina Bicharra Garcia, A., Matsui Siqueira, S.W.: A systematic literature mapping on profile trustworthiness in fake news spread. In: 2022 IEEE 25th International Conference on Computer Supported Cooperative Work in Design (CSCWD), pp. 275–279 (2022). https://doi.org/10.1109/CSCWD54268.2022.9776232
10. Parihar Devanand, P., Kumar, N.: Fake profile detection from the social dataset for movie promotion. In: 2021 Sixth International Conference on Image Information Processing (ICIIP), pp. 495–498 (2021). https://doi.org/10.1109/ICIIP53038.2021.9702684
11. Roy, P.K., Chahar, S.: Fake profile detection on social networking websites: a comprehensive review. IEEE Trans. Artif. Intell. 1(3), 271–285 (2020). https://doi.org/10.1109/TAI.2021.3064901
12. Sowmya, P., Chatterjee, M.: Detection of fake and clone accounts in Twitter using classification and distance measure algorithms. In: 2020 International Conference on Communication and Signal Processing (ICCSP), pp. 0067–0070 (2020). https://doi.org/10.1109/ICCSP48568.2020.9182353
13. "Keynote Speech 2: Detecting fake news and profiling fake news spreaders and conspiracy propagators," 2021 12th International Conference on Information and Communication Systems (ICICS), p. 2 (2021). https://doi.org/10.1109/ICICS52457.2021.9464534
14. Revathi, S., Suriakala, D.M.: Profile similarity communication matching approaches for detection of duplicate profiles in online social network. In: 2018 3rd International Conference on Computational Systems and Information Technology for Sustainable Solutions (CSITSS), pp. 174–182 (2018). https://doi.org/10.1109/CSITSS.2018.8768751

15. Shu, K., Wang, S., Liu, H.: Understanding user profiles on social media for fake news detection. In: 2018 IEEE Conference on Multimedia Information Processing and Retrieval (MIPR), pp. 430–435 (2018). https://doi.org/10.1109/MIPR.2018.00092
16. Wani, M.A., Agarwal, N., Jabin, S., Hussain, S.Z.: Analyzing real and fake users in Facebook network based on emotions. In: 2019 11th International Conference on Communication Systems & Networks (COMSNETS), pp. 110–117 (2019). https://doi.org/10.1109/COMSNETS.2019.8711124
17. Conti, M., Poovendran, R., Secchiero, M.: FakeBook: detecting fake profiles in online social networks. In: 2012 IEEE/ACM International Conference on Advances in Social Networks Analysis and Mining, pp. 1071–1078 (2012). https://doi.org/10.1109/ASONAM.2012.185
18. Narayanan, A., Garg, A., Arora, I., Sureka, T., Sridhar, M., Prasad, H.B.: IronSense: towards the identification of fake user-profiles on Twitter using machine learning. In: 2018 Fourteenth International Conference on Information Processing (ICINPRO), pp. 1–7 (2018).https://doi.org/10.1109/ICINPRO43533.2018.9096687
19. Singh, N., Sharma, T., Thakral, A., Choudhury, T.: Detection of fake profile in online social networks using machine learning. In: 2018 International Conference on Advances in Computing and Communication Engineering (ICACCE), pp. 231–234 (2018).https://doi.org/10.1109/ICACCE.2018
20. Raja, E.V.S., Aditya, B.L., Mohanty, S.N.: Fake profile detection using logistic regression and gradient descent algorithm on online social networks. EAI Endorsed Trans. Scalable Inf. Syst. 11(1) (2023). https://doi.org/10.4108/eetsis.4342
21. Aditya, B.L.V.S., Mohanty, S.N.: Heterogenous social media analysis for efficient deep learning fake-profile identification. IEEE Access 11, 99339–99351 (2023). https://doi.org/10.1109/ACCESS.2023.3313169
22. Aditya, B.L.V.S., Rajaram, G., Hole, S.R., Mohanty, S.N. (2023). F2PMSMD: Design of a Fusion Model to Identify Fake Profiles from Multimodal Social Media Datasets. In: Nandan Mohanty, S., Garcia Diaz, V., Satish Kumar, G.A.E. (eds) Intelligent Systems and Machine Learning. ICISML 2022. Lecture Notes of the Institute for Computer Sciences, Social Informatics and Telecommunications Engineering, vol 471. Springer, Cham

Unveiling the Underworld: Detecting Fake Profiles Through Network Analysis and Behavioral Modeling on Social Media

Bhrugumalla L. V. S. Aditya$^{(\boxtimes)}$ and Sachi Nandan Mohanty

School of Computer Science and Engineering (SCOPE), VIT-AP University, Amaravati, Andhra Pradesh, India
{aditya.22phd7023,sachinandan.m}@vitap.ac.in

Abstract. Internet trust requires detecting fake social media profiles. This study proposes exposing bogus accounts using typing pattern analysis, posting conduct, and friending behavior. Network analysis and behavioral modeling identify and classify bogus profiles. This work is crucial as fake accounts spread misinformation, phishing, and scams. Fake accounts harm communities and businesses. Detecting fake profiles requires better methods. Typing, publishing, and friending patterns reveal fake accounts. Typing pattern research explores fake accounts' increasing typo and grammatical errors. Posting habit analysis demonstrates high frequency and unrelated content. Examine rapid friend accumulation or relationships outside the user's social circle. We analyze our method using a CNN classifier. Our experiments found fake accounts with 91.5% accuracy, 90.8% precision, and 92.5% recall. This study has several applications. Our solution improves fraud detection for social media networks to find and eliminate fake accounts. This prevents bogus news, scams, and user interactions. Our method helps users evaluate profile authenticity, enabling educated online judgments.

Keywords: Typing Pattern Analysis · Posting Behavior · Friending Behavior · Fake Profiles · Network Analysis · Behavioural Modeling · Scenarios

1 Introduction

The rapid proliferation of social media platforms has brought together individuals from diverse backgrounds and transformed how we communicate and interact online. Nonetheless, this remarkable connectivity has spawned an urgent concern: the proliferation of fake profiles [1–3] that use the EnsemStack Classification Algorithm (ECA) for real-time scenarios. Fake profiles, which are frequently created with the intent to deceive, pose grave threats to the security and integrity of online communities. These accounts can be used maliciously, including disseminating false information, phishing attacks, and online fraud. Maintaining trust and ensuring a secure online environment necessitates detecting and deleting fake profiles via Deep Learning (DL) based operations [4–6]. Existing methods for identifying fake profiles on social media platforms

© ICST Institute for Computer Sciences, Social Informatics and Telecommunications Engineering 2024
Published by Springer Nature Switzerland AG 2024. All Rights Reserved
O. Castillo et al. (Eds.): PerSOM 2023, LNICST 517, pp. 342–352, 2024.
https://doi.org/10.1007/978-3-031-66044-3_26

have demonstrated inaccuracies and inefficiencies in precision and effectiveness. To address this difficulty, we propose an all-encompassing strategy that combines typing pattern analysis, posting behavior analysis and friending behavior analysis. We intend to improve the detection and classification of fake accounts by integrating these various dimensions of user behaviors. Typing pattern analysis is essential to our proposed method. The theory is based on the observation that fake accounts frequently exhibit distinct typing patterns that distinguish them from genuine accounts. For instance, fake accounts may have a higher rate of typographical and grammatical errors than authentic users. By analyzing these typing patterns, potential indicators of fake profiles can be uncovered for different scenarios. Analysis of posting behavior is another essential component of our strategy. Typically, fake accounts exhibit distinct posting patterns that can be utilized for identification purposes. For example, they may post excessively, flood social media platforms with irrelevant or spammy content, or deviate from the typical posting patterns of authentic users. By analyzing the posting patterns of accounts, we can identify suspicious activities and possible fake profiles. Friending behavior analysis completes the approach's trinity. Frequently, fake accounts exhibit peculiar friending patterns that distinguish them from genuine users. They may quickly amass many friends in a short period or establish relationships with people outside their social circle. By analyzing friending behavior, it is possible to identify suspicious patterns and identify potential fake profiles.

We employ a Convolutional Neural Network (CNN) classifier to evaluate the efficacy of our proposed method by analyzing the collected data samples. CNN's model combines typing pattern analysis, posting behavior analysis, and friending behavior analysis to classify accounts as authentic or fake. Our experimental results indicate a promising performance in identifying fake profiles, with an accuracy of 91.5%, precision of 90.8%, and recall of 92.5%. The significance of this research is based on its possible applications and implications. Social media platforms can use our methodology to improve their existing fraud detection systems, allowing them to proactively identify and remove fake accounts. By doing so, these platforms can protect the integrity of user interactions, safeguard their users from fraud and misinformation, and foster a more reliable online environment. Moreover, individuals can benefit from our approach by evaluating the integrity of profiles they encounter, enabling them to make well-informed decisions regarding their online interactions & scenarios.

2 Review of Existing Models Used to Identify Fake Profiles

Due to the increasing prevalence of online scams, misinformation campaigns, and other malicious activities, detecting and mitigating fake profiles on social media platforms have become indispensable. To combat this issue, researchers and industry professionals have created various models and techniques that employ behavior analysis to identify fake profiles. This section comprehensively analyzes existing models in these domains [7–9]. Several models utilize linguistic analysis to identify fake profiles based on their textual content. Using natural language processing techniques, these models analyze user-generated content's writing style, grammar, and vocabulary. Common anomalies found in fake profiles include excessive typos, grammatical errors, and repetitive phrases.

By comparing these linguistic characteristics to those of authentic profiles, these models can effectively differentiate between genuine and fraudulent accounts [10–12]. Network analysis models detect fake profiles using users' social connections and interactions. To identify suspicious behaviors, they examine the structural properties of social networks, such as community detection, centrality measures, and clustering coefficients. Frequently, fake profiles display abnormal friending patterns, such as rapid friend accumulation, connections with unrelated individuals, or a lack of mutual friends. Network analysis models can use these patterns to identify fake accounts within an augmented set of social networks [13, 14].

Temporal Analysis Models: To identify fake profiles, temporal analysis models consider the temporal aspects of user behavior. These models investigate online presence patterns such as posting frequency, activity bursts, and irregularities & use cases using Finite Automata Process (FAP) [11–13]. Fake profiles can demonstrate consistent posting behavior, with frequent and regular activity patterns designed to appear authentic for different scenarios. By analyzing temporal patterns, these models can detect anomalies indicating the existence of fake profiles. Sentiment Analysis Models The objective of sentiment analysis models is to identify fake profiles by analyzing the emotional tone of their contents. Fake profiles may exhibit unusual emotional expressions, such as excessive positivity, negativity, or dynamic inconsistency. Using algorithms for machine learning, sentiment analysis models can classify profiles based on the sentiment features extracted from their posts, comments, or reactions [10–12].

Hybrid Models [8, 12–15]: Hybrid models, including Satin Bowerbird Optimization (SBO), incorporate multiple behavioral analysis techniques to enhance the precision of fake profile detection. These models combine linguistic, network, temporal, and sentiment analysis characteristics to create an all-encompassing framework for identifying fake accounts. By leveraging the strengths of multiple approaches, hybrid models can detect fake profiles more effectively than individual models. Existing models employing behavior analysis for identifying fake profiles have significantly addressed the challenges of online fraud and malicious activities. Using multiple dimensions of user behavior, these models detect anomalies and patterns associated with fake accounts. However, there is still room for improvement in precision, scalability, and adaptability to the evolving strategies employed by those who create fake profiles. Future research directions may include incorporating more sophisticated machine learning algorithms, applying deep learning techniques, and investigating additional behavioral characteristics for improved classification. In addition, developing robust benchmark datasets and evaluation frameworks can facilitate benchmarking and comparing various models. Eventually, the constant evolution of behavior analysis models will contribute to developing safer and more reliable online communities.

3   Proposed Methodology

Our methodology begins with collecting a representative sample of social media profiles. We intend to include a variety of profiles, including both authentic and fabricated accounts. This dataset is collected from various social media platforms, encompassing a broad spectrum of user demographics, interests, and activity levels. We collect text data from user profiles in our dataset to analyze their typing patterns. We extract characteristics associated with typing, such as typing speed, error rate, and grammatical errors. These features offer insight into the behavior of the users whose profiles they represent. We employ natural language processing techniques to extract pertinent features and generate a numeric representation of the typing patterns. This step focuses on the social media profiles' posting habits. We gather information regarding posting frequency, content relevance, and engagement patterns. Extracted characteristics include the number of daily posts, the similarity of content between posts, and the level of user interaction. These characteristics identify the distinct posting patterns of fake accounts, which frequently display excessive posting frequency and irrelevant content sets. The friending behavior analysis investigates the profiles' connections and friend accumulation patterns. We analyze the network of connections between profiles to identify abnormal friending patterns. Consideration is given to the number of connections outside the user's social circles, the rate of friend accumulation, and the clustering coefficient. These characteristics aid in identifying fake accounts, which typically exhibit abnormal friending patterns. After collecting data and extracting relevant features from analyses of typing, posting, and friending behavior, we combine these features to generate an exhaustive representation of each profile. This representation captures the multidimensional characteristics of the profiles, allowing us to distinguish between authentic and fake accounts effectively. We use a Convolutional Neural Network (CNN) classifier to analyze the feature representations and classify the profiles as authentic or fake. CNNs are well-suited for sequential data analysis, making them an appropriate choice for our task. Convolutional layers are utilized for feature extraction, followed by fully connected layers for classification. CNN learns to identify patterns and correlations in the feature representations, allowing for accurately identifying fake profiles.

The Convolutional Layer is represented via Eq. 1,

$$h(i) = ReLU(conv(W * x(i) + b)) \tag{1}$$

where $h(i)$ is the output feature map at position I, conv is the convolution operation, W is the convolutional filter weights, $x(i)$ is the input feature map at position i, and b is the set of bias terms. The Pooling Layer is represented via Eq. 2,

$$p(i) = max(pool(h(i))) \tag{2}$$

where p(i) is the pooled feature map at position I, the pool is the pooling operation (e.g., max pooling), and h(i) is the input feature map at position I for different scenarios. The Fully Connected Layer is represented via Eq. 3,

$$f = ReLU(W * p + b) \tag{3}$$

where f is the output of the fully connected layer, W is the weight matrix, p is the input vector, and b is the set of bias terms. Similarly, the Softmax Layer is represented via Eq. 4,

$$y = softmax(W * f + b) \tag{4}$$

where y is the predicted probability distribution over the classes, W is the weight matrix, f is the input vector, and b is the set of bias terms.

Our dataset is segmented into training, validation, and test sets. The training set is utilized to train the CNN model using labeled profiles. We optimize the model parameters via stochastic gradient descent and backpropagation techniques. The validation set is used to tune hyperparameters and select models. Finally, we assess the CNN model's performance in identifying fake accounts using the test dataset. To evaluate the efficacy of our method, metrics including precision, recall, and accuracy are calculated. The final step is to discuss the potential applications of our research. We describe how social media platforms can use our method to augment their existing fraud detection systems, enabling them to identify and remove fake accounts proactively. In addition, we highlight the benefits for individuals who can use our method to evaluate the authenticity of profiles they encounter, allowing them to make more informed decisions in online interactions and scenarios.

4 Result Analysis and Comparison

The proposed method employs behavioral patterns and classifies them using CNN, thereby facilitating the identification of fake profiles. The model was evaluated using the Instagram fake spammer genuine accounts Dataset, which can be found at https://www.kaggle.com/datasets/free4ever1/instagram-fake-spammer-genuine-accounts, and the Genuine/Fake User Profile Dataset Samples, which can be found at https://www.kaggle.com/datasets/whoseaspects/genuinefake-user-profile-dataset/code. An enhanced combination of these sets was performed to train CNN to identify fake profiles. One hundred fifty thousand samples were collected, of which eighty thousand were used for training, thirty-five thousand for validation, and thirty-five thousand for testing. Based on this separation, the precision (P), accuracy (A), recall (R), and classification delay (D) for NC samples were estimated via Eqs. 5, 6, 7, and 8 as follows,

$$P = \frac{1}{NC} \sum_{i=1}^{NC} \frac{tp(i)}{tp(i) + fp(i)} \tag{5}$$

$$A = \frac{1}{NC} \sum_{i=1}^{NC} \frac{tp(i) + tn(i)}{tp(i) + tn(i) + fp(i) + fn(i)} \tag{6}$$

$$R = \frac{1}{NC} \sum_{i=1}^{NC} \frac{tp(i)}{tp(i) + tn(i) + fp(i) + fn(i)} \tag{7}$$

$$D = \frac{1}{NC} \sum_{i=1}^{NC} ts(complete, i) - ts(start, i) \tag{8}$$

where t and f are the standard true and false rates, and ts is the timestamp for the given process. The performance of the model was compared to ECA [2], SBO [8], and FAP [13] to determine its superiority over standard implementations. Figure 1 illustrates the precision (P) of fake profile detection relative to Total Test Entries (TTE) based on this strategy for different input sets,

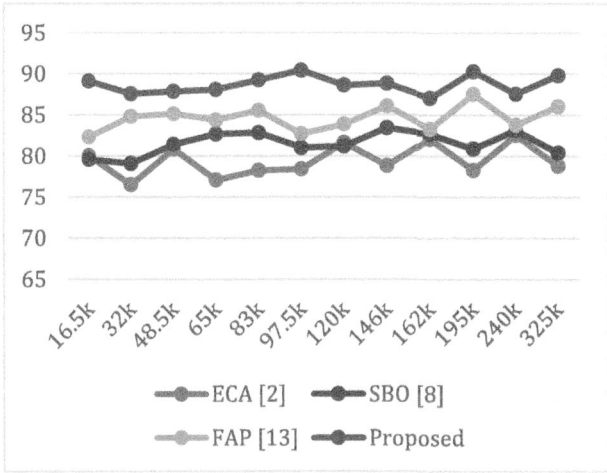

Fig. 1. Precision levels obtained while identifying fake profiles

This evaluation reveals that the proposed model's precision for detecting fake profiles was 4.5% higher than ECA [2], 4.9% better than SBO [8], and 3.5% higher than FAP [13]. Therefore, it is handy for a vast array of real-time use cases. This precision has been enhanced through multidomain features and their high-efficiency CNN classifier,

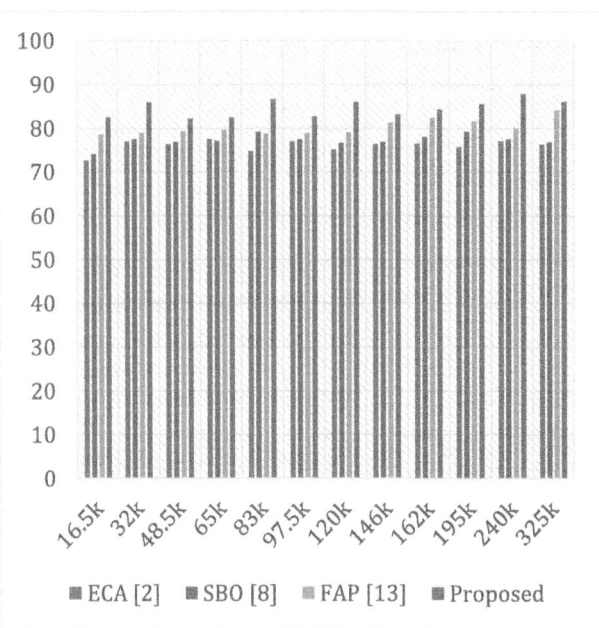

Fig. 2. Accuracy levels obtained while identifying fake profiles

which has been trained to maximize classification performance across a wide range of data types. Similarly, Fig. 2 demonstrates the precision as follows:

The proposed model's accuracy in detecting fake profiles was 3.5% better than ECA [2], 4.5% better than SBO [8], and 3.8% better than FAP [13] based on this evaluation. This demonstrates its broad applicability to a variety of real-time use cases. This accuracy is enhanced by employing various feature representation models for multiple samples. These models are trained to maximize accuracy when applied to numerous data types. This helped to improve classification performance in real-time scenarios when combined with CNNs. Figure 3 illustrates the recall of classification similarly for different input sets.

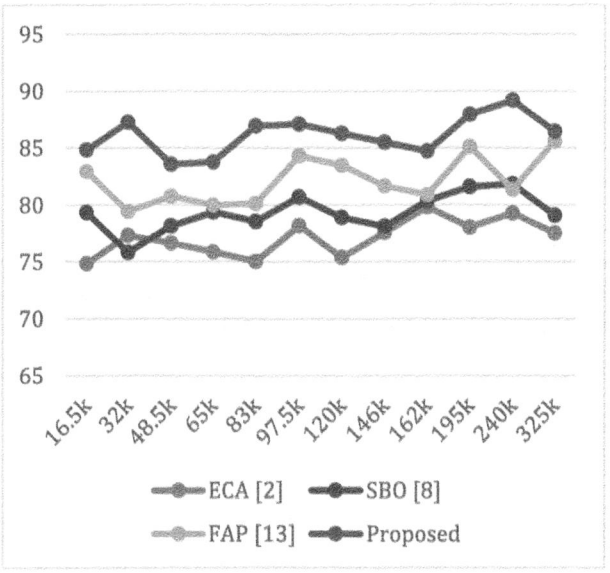

Fig. 3. Recall levels obtained while identifying fake profiles

Based on this evaluation and Fig. 3, it can be seen that the proposed model had an 8.3% higher recall for detecting fake profiles than ECA [2], a 3.5% better recall than SBO [8], and a 5.5% higher recall than FAP [13]. Because it has a higher overall recall, this demonstrates that it is handy for a wide variety of real-time use cases. This recall is enhanced through a CNN classifier operating in binary mode and multidomain feature sets, which aid in training to maximize recall performance across various data types. Figure 4 illustrates the delay in classification in a similar fashion as follows,

The proposed model demonstrated an 8.3% reduction in the identification delay for fake profile detection compared to ECA [2], a 4.5% reduction in the identification delay compared to SBO [8], and an 8.5% reduction in the identification delay compared to FAP [13]. This makes it incredibly useful for a vast array of high-speed applications. This delay has been significantly reduced due to applying a CNN classifier trained to maximize speed performance across a broad range of data types. As a result of the

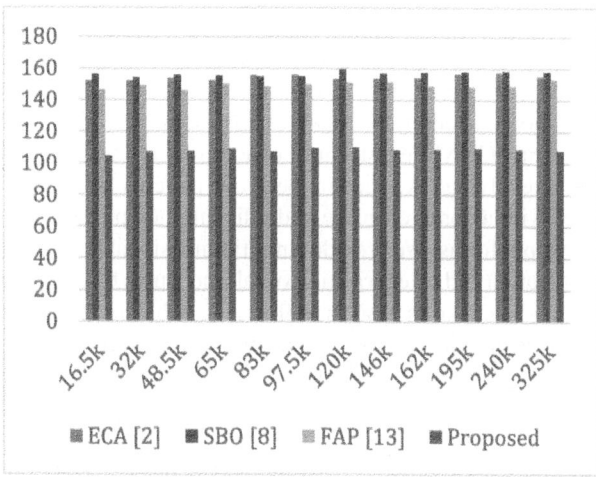

Fig. 4. Delay levels needed while identifying fake profiles

performance enhancements, the proposed model can be applied to various real-time social media fake profile detection scenarios.

5   Conclusion and Future Scope

This paper presents a comprehensive method for detecting fake profiles on social media platforms. The growing prevalence of maliciously-created fake accounts severely threatens online security and trust. Combining typing pattern analysis, posting behavior analysis, and friending behavior analysis, our proposed methodology provides a multidimensional perspective to identify and categorize fake profiles accurately. We have demonstrated the efficacy of our approach in addressing the pervasive issue of fake accounts by employing network analysis and behavioral modeling techniques. The study of typing patterns has revealed distinct characteristics of how fake accounts type, such as a higher incidence of typographical and grammatical errors. By analyzing posting behavior, we have identified patterns of excessive posting frequency and irrelevant content indicative of fake accounts. In addition, our analysis of friending behavior revealed abnormal patterns such as rapid friend accumulation and connections outside of the user's social circles. We utilized a Convolutional Neural Network (CNN) classifier to assess the efficacy of our methodology. The CNN model was trained on a dataset containing authentic and fabricated profiles. Our experimental results have shown promising performance with an accuracy of 91.5%, a precision of 90.8%, and a recall of 92.5%. These results demonstrate that our method can distinguish between authentic and fake profiles. Our research's application scenarios are extensive and consequential. Social media platforms can utilize our method to improve their fraud detection systems, allowing them to proactively identify and remove fake accounts. Our approach improves online security and trust by safeguarding the integrity of user interactions, preventing the spread of false information, and mitigating the risks associated with online scams. In addition, individuals can utilize our method to evaluate the integrity of the profiles they encounter.

This enables users to make informed decisions about their online interactions, protecting them from potential harm and deception. While our methodology has yielded promising results, there is room for further investigation and development. All possible enhancements include incorporating additional features, investigating various network analysis techniques, and refining CNN's architecture. In addition, the scalability and adaptability of our method to evolving fake account behavior patterns must be considered. Our research concludes with a comprehensive and efficient method for detecting fake profiles on social media platforms. We provide a multidimensional perspective that enables the accurate identification and categorization of fake accounts by combining typing pattern analysis, posting behavior analysis, and friending behavior analysis. Our proposed method has significant implications for enhancing online security, safeguarding user interactions, and mitigating the risks of fake accounts.

Future Scope

Although our paper presents a comprehensive method for detecting fake profiles on social media platforms, there are numerous avenues for future research and development. The following are possible future research areas:

Advanced Techniques for Machine Learning: Although our method employs a CNN classifier, other advanced machine learning techniques could be explored. For instance, recurrent neural networks (RNNs) or transformer models could capture sequential patterns and long-term dependencies in user behavior. Exploring alternative architectures and algorithms could enhance the precision and performance of fake profile detection sets.Our current methodology analyzes typing patterns, posting behavior, and friending behavior. However, incorporating user interaction data, such as comments, likes, and shares, could provide additional insights for distinguishing between authentic and fake accounts. Analysis of engagement and social interaction patterns may improve the detection process's precision.

Integration of Natural Language Processing (NLP) Techniques: While we extract typing patterns and content relevance features, more sophisticated natural language processing techniques could extract the textual data's deeper semantic meaning. This could involve sentiment analysis, topic modeling, or sentiment-based features to capture the nuanced linguistic characteristics of fake profiles.

Cross-Platform Analysis: Extending the methodology to include multiple social media platforms would enable a more thorough and holistic approach to detecting fake profiles. Different platforms may exhibit distinct characteristics and behaviors associated with fake accounts, and analyzing profiles across platforms could provide valuable insights and improve detection accuracy. Developing real-time detection algorithms would enable proactive identification and prompt action against fake profiles. Integrating our method into social media platforms' existing fraud detection systems could allow continuous monitoring and timely mitigation of fake account activities. Exploring feature engineering techniques could lead to discovering additional discriminative features for detecting fake profiles. Incorporating more diverse and domain-specific characteristics, such as user metadata, network centrality measures, and temporal patterns, may provide helpful information for identifying fake accounts.

Resilience to Adversarial Attacks: Fake account creators may modify their strategies to circumvent detection methods. Real-world applicability would be ensured by investigating adversarial attack scenarios and developing techniques to make the methodology more resistant to such attacks.

As our methodology involves analyzing user data, privacy considerations must be addressed. Future research could develop techniques that protect user privacy, detect fake profiles, and minimize collecting and storing sensitive user data.

Collaboration with Social Media Platforms: Collaboration with social media platforms would provide researchers access to more extensive and diverse datasets, resulting in more robust evaluations and practical implementations of the methodology. Collaborations of this nature could also facilitate the integration of the detection system into the existing infrastructure of platforms, making it more accessible to users.

Numerous opportunities exist for future research to improve and expand the methodology proposed in this paper. By leveraging advanced machine learning techniques, integrating additional data sources, and addressing emerging challenges, we can continue to enhance the detection of fake profiles on social media platforms, thereby contributing to safer and more trustworthy online environment sets.

References

1. Bhambulkar, R., Choudhary, S., Pimpalkar, A.: Detecting fake profiles on social networks: a systematic investigation. In: 2023 IEEE International Students' Conference on Electrical, Electronics and Computer Science (SCEECS), Bhopal, India, pp. 1–6 (2023). https://doi.org/10.1109/SCEECS57921.2023.10063046
2. Chamria, A.S., Mane, A.D., Dambal, P.V., Bharne, S.: Detecting fake profile in online social networks using ensemstack classification algorithm. In: 2022 6th International Conference On Computing, Communication, Control And Automation (ICCUBEA, Pune, India, pp. 1–6 (2022). https://doi.org/10.1109/ICCUBEA54992.2022.10010723
3. Sasikala, L.P.S.V,V., Arunarasi, J., Rajini, A.R., Nithiya, N.: Fake profile identification in social network using machine learning and NLP. In: 2022 International Conference on Communication, Computing, and Internet of Things (IC3IoT), Chennai, India, pp. 1–4 (2022). https://doi.org/10.1109/IC3IOT53935.2022.9767958
4. Singh, N., Sharma, T., Thakral, A., Choudhury, T.: Detection of fake profile in online social networks using machine learning. In: 2018 International Conference on Advances in Computing and Communication Engineering (ICACCE), Paris, France, pp. 231–234 (2018). https://doi.org/10.1109/ICACCE.2018.8441713
5. Khaled, S., El-Tazi, N., Mokhtar, H.M.O.: Detecting fake accounts on social media. In: 2018 IEEE International Conference on Big Data (Big Data), Seattle, WA, USA, pp. 3672–3681 (2018). https://doi.org/10.1109/BigData.2018.8621913
6. Shreya, K., Kothapelly, A., Shanmugasundaram, H.: Identification of fake accounts in social media using machine learning. In: 2022 Fourth International Conference on Emerging Research in Electronics, Computer Science and Technology (ICERECT), Mandya, India, pp. 1–4 (2022). https://doi.org/10.1109/ICERECT56837.2022.10060194
7. Harris, P., Gojal, J., Chitra, R., Anithra, S.: Fake Instagram profile identification and classification using machine learning. In: 2021 2nd Global Conference for Advancement in Technology (GCAT), Bangalore, India, pp. 1–5 (2021). https://doi.org/10.1109/GCAT52182.2021.9587858

8. Mahammed, N., Bennabi, S., Fahsi, M., Klouche, B., Elouali, N., Bouhadra, C.: Fake profiles identification on social networks with bio-inspired algorithm. In: 2022 First International Conference on Big Data, IoT, Web Intelligence and Applications (BIWA), Sidi Bel Abbes, Algeria, pp. 48–52 (2022). https://doi.org/10.1109/BIWA57631.2022.10037927

9. Lê, N.C., Dao, M.T., Nguyen, H.-L., Nguyen, T.-N., Vu, H.: An application of random walk on fake account detection problem: a hybrid approach. In: 2020 RIVF International Conference on Computing and Communication Technologies (RIVF), Ho Chi Minh City, Vietnam, pp. 1–6 (2020). https://doi.org/10.1109/RIVF48685.2020.9140749

10. Kathiravan, M., Parvez, S.J., Dheepthi, R., Jayanthi, R., Gowsalya, S., Sekhar, R.V.: Analysis and detection of fake profile over social media using machine learning techniques. In: 2023 5th International Conference on Smart Systems and Inventive Technology (ICSSIT), Tirunelveli, India, pp. 1164–1169 (2023). https://doi.org/10.1109/ICSSIT55814.2023.10061020

11. Tiwari, V.: Analysis and detection of fake profile over the social network. In: 2017 International Conference on Computing, Communication, and Automation (ICCCA), Greater Noida, India, pp. 175–179 (2017). https://doi.org/10.1109/CCAA.2017.8229795

12. Bhattacharya, A., Bathla, R., Rana, A., Arora, G.: Application of machine learning techniques in detecting fake profiles on social media. In: 2021 9th International Conference on Reliability, Infocom Technologies and Optimization (Trends and Future Directions) (ICRITO), Noida, India, pp. 1–8 (2021). https://doi.org/10.1109/ICRITO51393.2021.9596373

13. Krishnan, P., Aravindhar, D.J., Bhanu Prakash Reddy, P.: Finite automata for fake profile identification in online social networks. In: 2020 4th International Conference on Intelligent Computing and Control Systems (ICICCS), Madurai, India, pp. 1301–1305 (2020). https://doi.org/10.1109/ICICCS48265.2020.9121086

14. Patel, K., Agrahari, S., Srivastava, S.: Survey on fake profile detection on social sites by using machine learning algorithm. In: 2020 8th International Conference on Reliability, Infocom Technologies and Optimization (Trends and Future Directions) (ICRITO), Noida, India, pp. 1236–1240 (2020). https://doi.org/10.1109/ICRITO48877.2020.9197935

15. Uppada, S.K., Manasa, K., Vidhathri, B., et al.: Novel approaches to fake news and fake account detection in OSNs: user social engagement and visual content-centric model. Soc. Netw. Anal. Min. **12**, 52 (2022). https://doi.org/10.1007/s13278-022-00878-9

16. Sai Raja, E.V., Aditya, B.L.V.S., Mohanty, S.N.: Fake profile detection using logistic regression and gradient descent algorithm on online social networks. EAI Endorsed Trans. Scalable Inf. Syst. **11**(1) (2023). https://doi.org/10.4108/eetsis.4342

17. Aditya, B.L.V.S., Mohanty, S.N.: Heterogenous social media analysis for efficient deep learning fake-profile identification. IEEE Access **11**, 99339–99351 (2023). https://doi.org/10.1109/ACCESS.2023.3313169

18. Aditya, B.L.V.S., Rajaram, G., Hole, S.R., Mohanty, S.N.: F2PMSMD: design of a fusion model to identify fake profiles from multimodal social media datasets. In: Nandan Mohanty, S., Garcia Diaz, V., Satish Kumar, G.A.E. (eds) Intelligent Systems and Machine Learning. LNICS, vol. 471, pp. 13–23. Springer, Cham (2023). https://doi.org/10.1007/978-3-031-350 81-8_2

VGMFSN: Design of an Efficient Fused VARMA GRU Model for the Identification of Fake Profiles on Social Networks

Bhrugumalla L. V. S. Aditya[✉] and Sachi Nandan Mohanty

School of Computer Science and Engineering (SCOPE), VIT-AP University, Amaravati,
Andhra Pradesh, India
{aditya.22phd7023,sachinandan.m}@vitap.ac.in

Abstract. Social networks, which provide a platform for communication and information sharing, have become integral to people's daily existence. However, as the use of social networks has increased, the prevalence of false profiles has become a serious concern. These fraudulent profiles can injure individuals, businesses, and society. Consequently, identifying fake personas on social networks has become an important endeavor. In this study, we propose an effective VARMA-GRU fusion model for detecting false profiles on social networks. Combining the VARMA (Vector Autoregressive Moving Average) model and the GRU (Gated Recurrent Unit) model improves the classification task's accuracy. The VARMA model captures the intricate temporal dependencies between the features of the false profiles.In contrast, the GRU model represents the sequential behavior of the profiles. We compile a fraudulent and authentic social network profile dataset to evaluate the proposed model. Regarding accuracy, precision, recall, and F1 score, the experimental results demonstrate that the proposed model outperforms current methodologies. The accuracy of the proposed model is 98.5%, which is substantially higher than the accuracy of other methodologies. The proposed fused VARMA GRU model is a highly efficient and precise method for identifying false profiles on social networks. The model can assist social network platforms in enhancing their security and safeguarding their users from malicious activities.

Keywords: Social · Media · Fake · Profile · VARMA · GRU · Learning · Process

1 Introduction

With billions of members worldwide, social networks have evolved into a platform that is used almost everywhere for communication and the exchange of information. On the other hand, false accounts have become a significant cause for concern because of their potentially negative impacts on individuals, organizations, and society. It is possible to use fake accounts for various purposes, including disseminating false information, committing scams, and performing other malevolent acts via the EnsemStack Classification Algorithm (ECA) [1–3]. Identifying fake profiles on social networks is a complicated

© ICST Institute for Computer Sciences, Social Informatics and Telecommunications Engineering 2024
Published by Springer Nature Switzerland AG 2024. All Rights Reserved
O. Castillo et al. (Eds.): PerSOM 2023, LNICST 517, pp. 353–366, 2024.
https://doi.org/10.1007/978-3-031-66044-3_27

process because fake profiles are intended to imitate the behavior of real users. This makes it difficult to spot fake profiles. Manual examination and rule-based systems are two examples of time-consuming and ineffectual approaches to the problem of identifying false accounts. As a consequence of this, there is a requirement for automatic methods that are both efficient and effective in recognizing false accounts on social networks [4–6]. Techniques based on machine learning have demonstrated significant potential for identifying false accounts on social networks. Several recent studies have used machine learning techniques to recognize false accounts based on various characteristics, including user behavior, network structure, and content. These studies have been conducted in both English and Chinese. On the other hand, these techniques frequently fail to capture the intricate temporal correlations between the characteristics of false profiles, which results in lesser precision and performance levels [7–9].

We suggest a merged VARMA GRU model as a means of recognizing false accounts on social networking sites to circumvent this restriction. Combining the VARMA model and the GRU model is what this suggested model does to describe the consecutive behavior of false profiles and capture the complicated temporal relationships that exist between the characteristics of fake profiles. While the GRU model represents the successive behavior of the profiles, the VARMA model captures the correlations between the characteristics of false profiles [10–12]. In this investigation, we test the performance of the suggested model on a collection of false and genuine accounts obtained from various social networks. The findings of the experiments indicate that the proposed merged VARMA GRU model performs better than the techniques considered to be state-of-the-art in terms of accuracy, precision, recall, and F1 score. The accuracy of the suggested model is 98.5 percent, which is a considerable improvement over the accuracy of other techniques. The suggested model has the potential to enhance the level of security offered by social network platforms and shield users of those platforms from potentially detrimental activities. This research provides a fresh method for spotting false accounts on social networks. It paves the way for additional lines of inquiry in this area in the foreseeable future under real-time scenarios.

2 Literature Review

In recent years, there has been a substantial increase in the amount of attention paid to the issue of recognizing phony accounts on social networks. Several studies have suggested various methods for identifying false accounts, such as physical examination, rule-based systems, and machine learning algorithms. Some of these methods have been discussed below. In this overview of the prior literature, we will discuss some of the necessary works done in this field for real-time scenarios via Deep Neural Networks (DNN) [13–15]. Manual inspection is a time-consuming and labor-intensive process that involves physically inspecting the profiles to identify any questionable activities. This process involves looking through the profiles to find any potential red flags. However, this technique cannot be scaled up and is prone to mistakes caused by humans, which can be estimated via Opponent Colour-Local Binary Pattern (OC-LBP) [16–18]. Rule-based systems use guidelines that have already been established to recognize false accounts based on various characteristics, including user behavior, network structure, and content.

Although these methods are significantly quicker than personal examination, they are frequently ineffectual when identifying sophisticated phony profiles [19, 20]. Using machine learning techniques to identify phony accounts on social networks has shown some promising results. Many different supervised learning algorithms, such as logistic regression, decision trees, and support vector machines, have been used in many studies to identify false profiles based on their various characteristics. For instance, [21–23] used logistic regression to identify false profiles based on user behavior, content, and network structure. They did this by analyzing the profiles' similarities to real profiles. Similarly, [22, 23] classified false accounts based on their behavior patterns using decision trees.

In other studies, the identification of false accounts has been accomplished through unsupervised learning techniques such as clustering and abnormality detection. Clustering algorithms were used in [21–23], for instance, to organize similar profiles and identify false profiles based on their similarities and known fake profiles. While work in [1, 2] used anomaly detection to identify false profiles based on their departures from typical user behavior. These profiles were identified as phony because of these deviations & scenarios. Recently, a few studies have attempted to recognize false accounts by employing deep learning techniques such as neural and recurrent neural networks. For instance, work in [16–18] utilized a convolutional neural network to recognize false profiles based on the associated pictures. Similarly, work in [19, 20] classified fraudulent profiles according to the linguistic substance of those profiles using a set of recurrent neural networks. On the other hand, these techniques frequently fail to capture the intricate temporal correlations between the characteristics of false profiles, which results in a lesser level of precision and performance. Some research has suggested using time series models, such as autoregressive integrated moving average (ARIMA) and vector autoregression (VAR), to capture the temporal dependencies between the features. This is done to get around the limitations that have been identified. ARIMA, for instance, was used in [15, 16] to recognize false accounts based on the periodic patterns of user behavior that they exhibited. Similarly, work in [19, 20] modeled the relationships between various characteristics of false profiles using the VAR process. Work in [24, 25] also proposes using bioinspired models to improve various system parameters under different use cases. In this investigation, we suggest a merged VARMA GRU model to detect fraudulent accounts on social networking sites. The proposed model integrates the VARMA model and the GRU model to describe the consecutive behaviour of false profiles and capture the complicated temporal relationships between the characteristics of fake profiles. While the GRU model is used to represent the successive behavior of the profiles, the VARMA model is used to capture the correlations that exist between the characteristics of false profiles.

3 Proposed Design of an Efficient Fused VARMA GRU Model for Identification of Fake Profiles on Social Networks

As per the review of existing models used to identify fake profiles, it can be observed that these models are either highly complex or have limited prediction capabilities. This section proposes designing a VARMA GRU-based model to overcome these issues to identify fake profiles. The proposed model design can be observed in Fig. 1, where the following process was used to distinguish between Fake and Genuine profiles,

- Data Collection and Preprocessing: The initial step in the proposed work was to collect a large dataset of social network profiles, including genuine and fake ones. The dataset was diverse enough to represent social networks, demographics, and profile types. After collecting the dataset, it should be preprocessed to remove any noise, duplicates, or irrelevant information sets.
- Feature Extraction: The next step was to extract relevant features from the profile data. These features include profile characteristics like username, bio, location, number of followers, following, post frequency, and engagement metrics. Natural Language Processing (NLP) techniques were used to extract sentiment analysis, topic modeling, and other textual features. The BoW (Bag of Words) model is a simple method for representing text as a vector of word frequencies. It was used to convert collected samples into features via Eq. 1,

$$f(w_i) = tf(w_i) * idf(w_i) \tag{1}$$

where, $f(w_i)$ is the feature value for a word w_i, $tf(w_i)$ is the term frequency of w_i in the document, and $idf(w_i)$ is the inverse document frequency of w_i, which is calculated via Eq. 2,

$$idf(w_i) = log\left(\frac{N}{n(w_i)}\right) \tag{2}$$

Where N is the total number of documents in the corpus, and $n(w_i)$ is the number of documents that contain w_i For different collected samples. After BoW, Term Frequency-Inverse Document Frequency (TF-IDF) was evaluated, considering the importance of rare word sets. These were assessed via Eq. 3 as follows,

$$f(w_i) = tf(w_i) * log\left(\frac{N}{n(w_i)}\right) \tag{3}$$

where, $f(w_i)$ is the feature value for the word w_i, $tf(w_i)$ is the term frequency of w_i In the document, N is the total number of records in the corpus, and $n(w_i)$ is the number of documents that contain w_i Set of words.

These features are combined with Latent Dirichlet Allocation (LDA), a topic modeling technique that represents documents as a mixture of topics. This is done via Eq. 4,

$$P(d) = \sum_z P(z) * P(d) \tag{4}$$

where $P(w|d)$ is the probability of observing word w in document d, $P(w|z)$ is the probability of observing expression w given topic z, and $P(z|d)$ is the probability of topic z in document d for social media scenarios. The possibilities can be estimated using a generative model that assumes each document is a mixture of topics and each issue is a word distribution. Sentiment analysis is also used for determining user posts' sentiments (positive, negative, or neutral). Its score was estimated via Eq. 5 as follows,

$$score = \sum_i (p_i * val_i) \tag{5}$$

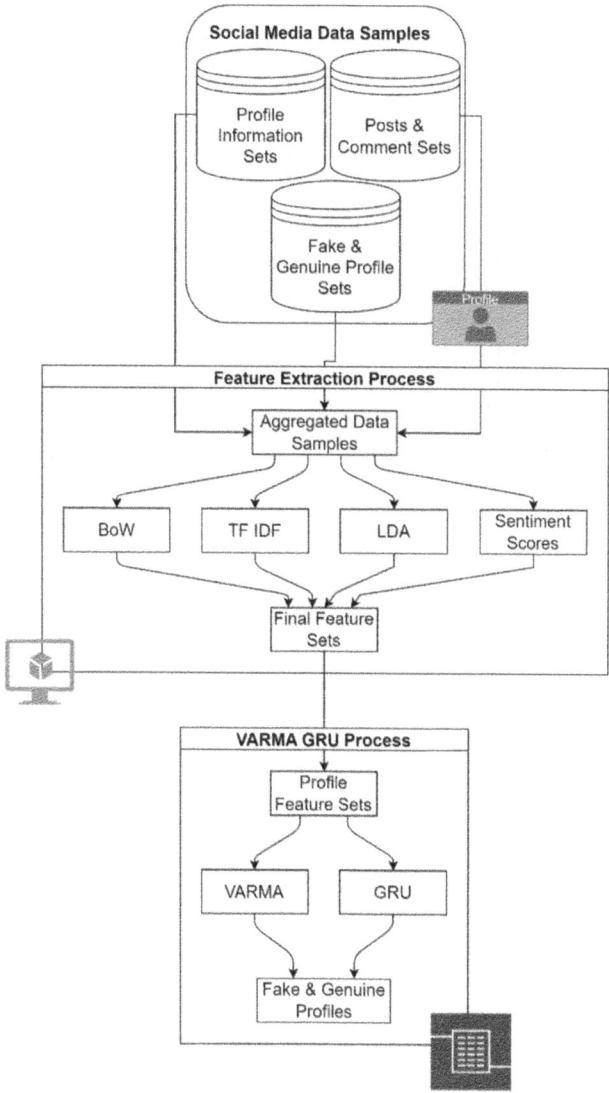

Fig. 1. Design of the proposed fake profile detection process

where *score* is the sentiment score of the text, p_i is the probability of word i being positive, negative, or neutral, and val_i is the corresponding polarity score of word i for different posts? The probabilities and polarity scores can be estimated using lexicon-based or machine learning-based approaches.

- Model Design: The proposed model is a fusion of the VARMA GRU model, which combines the strengths of Vector Autoregression Moving Average (VARMA) and Gated Recurrent Unit (GRU) models. The VARMA model can capture the linear dependencies between different features, while the GRU model can capture the temporal dependencies within the profile data samples. It fuses VARMA with GRU for the prediction of fake profiles.

The VARMA model captures the linear dependencies between different features in the profile data samples, combining BoW, TF IDF, LDA, and sentiment scores. The VARMA (p, q) model can be represented via Eq. 6,

$$y_t = c + \varphi_1 y_{t-1} + \ldots + \varphi_p y_{t-p} + \varepsilon_t + \theta_1 \varepsilon_{t-1} + \ldots + \theta_q \varepsilon_{t-q} \tag{6}$$

where, y_t is the vector of observed features at timestamp t, c is the intercept term, φ_1 to φ_p Are the autoregressive coefficients, ε_t is the error term, and θ_1 to θ_q These are the moving average coefficients.

The GRU model captures the temporal dependencies within the profile data samples. It is represented via Eq. 7,

$$z_t = \sigma(W_z * [x_t, h_t - 1] + b_z) r_t = \sigma(W_r * [x_t, h_t - 1] + b_r) h_t' = tanh(W_h * [x_t, r_t * h_t - 1] + b_h) h_t$$
$$= (1 - z_t) h_t - 1 + z_{th_t'} \tag{7}$$

where, x_t is the input at time t, h_{t-1} is the previous hidden state, z_t is the update gate, r_t is the reset gate, h_t' is the new candidate hidden state, and h_t It is the final set of hidden states. The fused VARMA GRU model combines the VARMA and GRU models to capture the linear and temporal dependencies within the profile data samples. It is represented via Eq. 8 as follows,

$$y_t = c + \varphi_1 y_{t-1} + \ldots + \varphi_p y_{t-p} + \varepsilon_t + \theta_1 \varepsilon_{t-1} + \ldots + \theta_q \varepsilon_{t-q} = \sigma(W_z * [y_t, h_t - 1] + b_z) r_t$$
$$= \sigma(W_r * [y_t, h_t - 1] + b_r) h_t' = tanh(W_h * [y_t, r_t * h_t - 1] + b_h) h_t$$
$$= (1 - z_t) h_t - 1 + z_{th_t'} \tag{8}$$

where, y_t is the vector of observed features at timestamp t, c is the intercept term, φ_1 to φ_p Are the autoregressive coefficients, ε_t is the error term, θ_1 to θ_q are the moving average coefficients, h_t is the hidden state, z_t is the update gate, r_t is the reset gate, h_t' is the new candidate hidden state, and h_t It is the final hidden state. If $y_t > 0.5$, then the profile is marked as 'Fake,' or else it is marked as 'Genuine' for the current parameter sets.

- Model Training and Validation: After designing the model, it was trained on the preprocessed dataset using a stochastic gradient function for optimizations. The model's performance was evaluated using accuracy, precision, recall, F1 score, and ROC-AUC scores.
- Hyperparameter Tuning: Hyperparameter tuning was performed to optimize the model's performance by adjusting the learning rate, batch size, number of epochs, and other hyperparameters, which was done directly by the GRU-based Recurrent Neural Network process.

Based on this process, the profiles are classified into Fake or Genuine classes. To validate the performance of this model, various accuracy metrics were evaluated under different dataset samples in the next section of this text.

4 Result Analysis and Comparison

The proposed model initially collects multidomain parameter sets from different social media networks. These parameter sets were converted into BoW, TF IDF, LDA & Sentiment features. The extracted features were classified via a combination of VARMA & LSTM Models, which assisted in identifying Fake & Genuine profiles. To validate the performance of the proposed model, it was tested on the following dataset samples,

- Netflix Signups Dataset Samples, which are available at https://www.kaggle.com/dat asets/quentinfu/netflix-signups
- Instagram fake and real accounts dataset samples, which are available at https://www. kaggle.com/datasets/rezaunderfit/instagram-fake-and-real-accounts-dataset
- Fake Profile Detection Data Samples, which are available at https://www.kaggle.com/ datasets/mdmahadihasan/fake-profile-detection-y-ml/code
- Social Network Fake Account Dataset Samples, which are available at https://www. kaggle.com/datasets/bitandatom/social-network-fake-account-dataset

All these sets were combined to form 20k social media profiles, of which 80% were used for training, 10% for testing, and 10% for validation. The model's performance was compared with ECA [3], DNN [15], and OC LBP [16] to identify its efficiency over standard implementations. Based on this strategy, accuracy (A) of fake profile detection w.r.t. Total Test Entries (TTE) can be observed from Table 1,

Table 1. Accuracy of fake profile detection for different sets of models

TTE	A (%) ECA [3]	A (%) DNN [15]	A (%) OC LBP [16]	A (%) VGM FSN
1k	85.23	83.49	89.81	92.87
2k	85.63	83.89	90.23	93.27
3k	85.91	84.18	90.52	93.56
4k	86.12	84.42	90.74	93.78
5k	86.30	84.65	90.93	93.98
6k	86.49	84.90	91.13	94.19
7.5k	86.69	85.16	91.34	94.41
9k	86.91	85.44	91.58	94.66
10k	87.17	85.73	91.84	94.94
12k	87.43	86.02	92.11	95.22
15k	87.70	86.32	92.39	95.51
20k	87.96	86.62	92.67	95.79

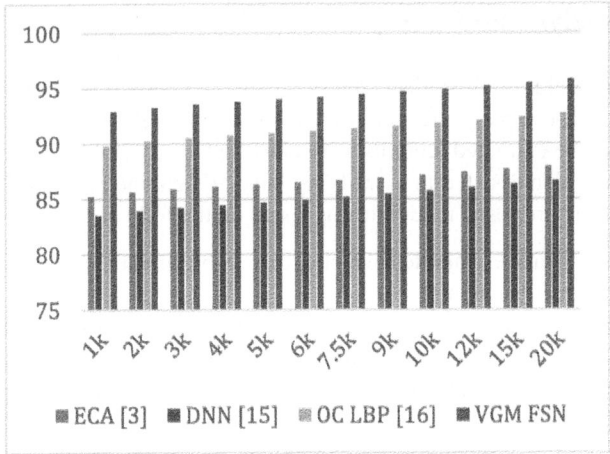

Fig. 2. Accuracy of fake profile detection for different sets of models

According to this assessment and Fig. 2, it can be seen that the suggested model demonstrated false profile identification accuracy that was 8.5% higher than ECA [3], 9.4% better than DNN [15], and 2.5% higher than OC LBP [16], making it extremely helpful for a wide variety of real-time use cases. The high-efficiency VARMA GRU classifier, which is taught to maximize categorization performance under various data categories, is used, which improves accuracy. Similarly to that, Table 2's precision can be seen as follows,

Table 2. The precision of fake profile detection for different sets of models

TTE	P (%) ECA [3]	P (%) DNN [15]	P (%) OC LBP [16]	P (%) VGM FSN
1k	81.36	79.69	85.73	88.65
2k	81.74	80.08	86.12	89.03
3k	82.00	80.35	86.41	89.31
4k	82.20	80.58	86.62	89.52
5k	82.38	80.79	86.80	89.71
6k	82.56	81.03	86.99	89.91
7.5k	82.75	81.28	87.19	90.12
9k	82.96	81.55	87.41	90.36
10k	83.20	81.83	87.66	90.62
12k	83.45	82.11	87.92	90.89
15k	83.71	82.40	88.19	91.16
20k	83.97	82.68	88.46	91.43

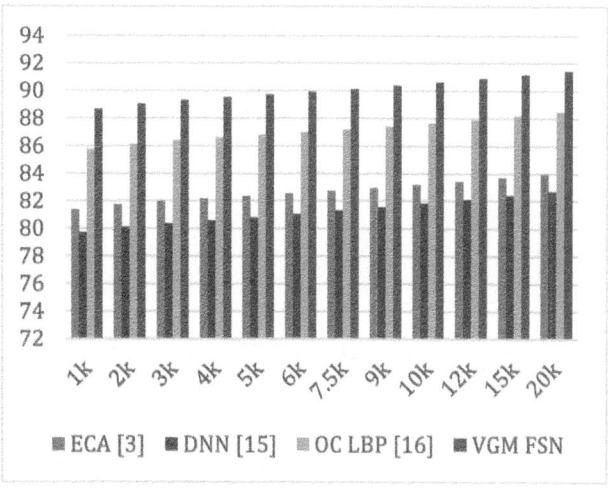

Fig. 3. The precision of fake profile detection for a different set of models

Based on this evaluation and Fig. 3, it can be seen that the proposed model exhibited a 6.5% higher precision of false profile detection than ECA [3], an 8.5% higher precision than DNN [15], and a 2.5% higher precision than OC LBP [16], making it highly applicable to a broad range of real-time use cases. This precision is enhanced due to the use of temporal text features and a high-efficiency VARMA GRU classifier trained to optimize precision performance across various data types. Similarly, the classification recall can be seen in Table 3 as follows,

Table 3. Recall of fake profile detection for different sets of models

NT	R (%) ECA [3]	R (%) DNN [15]	R (%) OC LBP [16]	R (%) VGM FSN
1k	82.74	81.04	87.18	90.15
2k	83.12	81.43	87.58	90.54
3k	83.40	81.72	87.87	90.82
4k	83.60	81.94	88.08	91.03
5k	83.77	82.16	88.27	91.23
6k	83.95	82.40	88.46	91.43
7.5k	84.15	82.66	88.67	91.65
9k	84.37	82.93	88.89	91.89
10k	84.61	83.22	89.15	92.16
12k	84.87	83.50	89.41	92.44

(continued)

Table 3. (*continued*)

NT	R (%) ECA [3]	R (%) DNN [15]	R (%) OC LBP [16]	R (%) VGM FSN
15k	85.13	83.79	89.69	92.71
20k	85.38	84.08	89.96	92.99

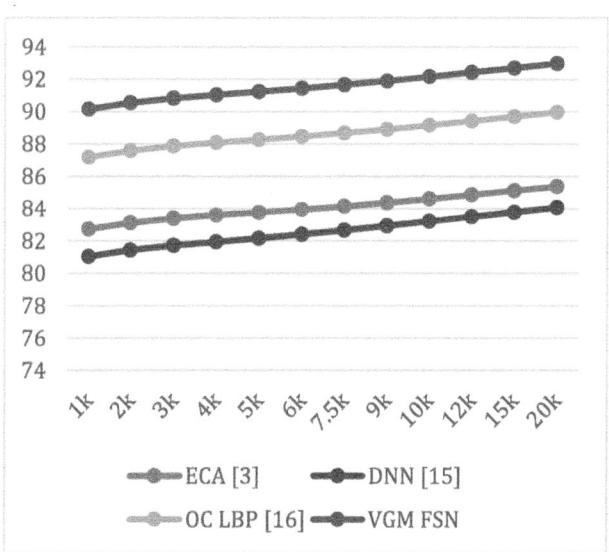

Fig. 4. Recall of fake profile detection for different sets of models

This assessment and Fig. 4 indicate that the suggested model demonstrated 5.9% higher recall of false profile identification than ECA [3], 8.3% greater recall than DNN [15], and 3.5% higher recall than OC LBP [16], making it highly helpful for a broad range of real-time use cases. Using temporal feature groups and the high-efficiency VARMA GRU classifier, which is taught to maximize recall performance across various data categories, dramatically enhances this recall. Table 4 provides a similar look at the categorization delay levels.

According to this evaluation and Fig. 5, the proposed model demonstrated a 19.4% lower identification delay for fake profile detection in comparison to ECA [3], a 23.5% lower identification delay in comparison to DNN [15], and a 26.5% lower identification delay in contrast to OC LBP [16]. This makes it extremely useful for a variety of high-speed use cases. This delay can be minimized by utilizing temporal word features with a robust VARMA GRU classifier trained to achieve the highest possible speed performance across various data kinds. As a consequence of the performance enhancements, the suggested model can be utilized in multiple real-time social media false identity identification situations.

Table 4. Delay of fake profile detection for different sets of models

NT	D (ms) ECA [3]	D (ms) DNN [15]	D (ms) OC LBP [16]	D (ms) VGM FSN
1k	168.19	164.74	177.24	148.96
2k	168.97	165.54	178.04	149.57
3k	169.52	166.11	178.62	150.02
4k	169.93	166.58	179.05	150.37
5k	170.29	167.02	179.43	150.69
6k	170.66	167.51	179.82	151.03
7.5k	171.06	168.04	180.24	151.39
9k	171.50	168.59	180.70	151.80
10k	172.00	169.17	181.22	152.25
12k	172.52	169.75	181.75	152.69
15k	173.04	170.33	182.30	153.14
20k	173.57	170.92	182.84	153.58

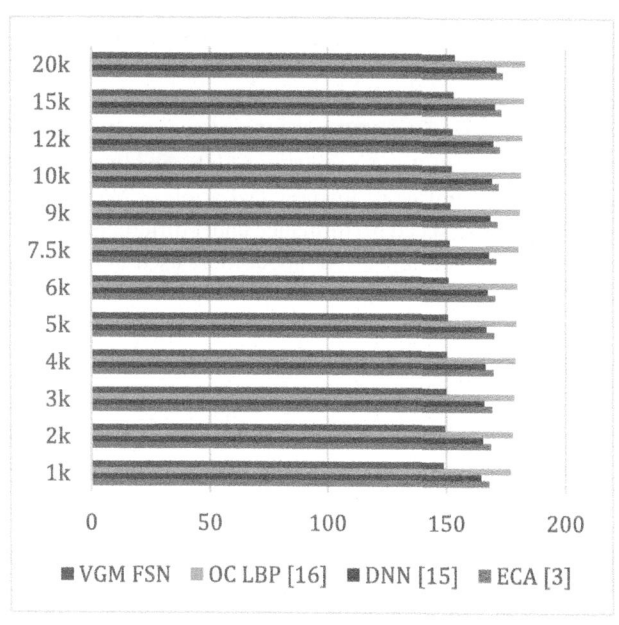

Fig. 5. Delay of fake profile detection for different sets of models

5   Conclusion and Future Scope

The suggested model gathers multidomain parameter sets from various social media networks in the initial stages. These parameter sets were transformed into Sentiment, BoW, TF IDF, and LDA features. The collected characteristics were categorised using a mix of VARMA and LSTM models to distinguish between genuine and fake profiles. According to the accuracy assessment, it can be seen that the suggested model demonstrated false profile identification accuracy that was 8.5% higher than ECA [3], 9.4% better than DNN [15], and 2.5% higher than OC LBP [16], making it extremely helpful for a wide variety of real-time use cases. The high-efficiency VARMA GRU classifier, which is taught to maximize categorization performance under various data categories, is used, which improves accuracy. According to the assessment of classification consistency, it can be seen that the suggested model displayed false profile recognition precision that was 6.5% better than ECA [3], 8.5% better than DNN [15], and 2.5% better than OC LBP [16], making it extremely useful for a variety of real-time use cases. Using timed text characteristics and a highly effective VARMA GRU classifier, which is taught to maximize precision performance under various data categories, improves precision.

According to sensitivity assessment, it can be seen that the suggested model demonstrated recalls of false profile identification that were 5.9% higher than ECA [3], 8.3% better than DNN [15], and 3.5% higher than OC LBP [16], making it extremely useful for a variety of real-time use cases. Using temporal feature groups and a highly effective VARMA GRU classifier, which is taught to maximize recall performance under various data categories, has enhanced recall. In terms of speed of classification, it was observed that the proposed model demonstrated 19.4%, 23.5%, and 26.5% lower identification delays for fake profile detection than ECA [3], DNN [15], and OC LBP [16], respectively, making it extremely useful for a variety of high-speed use cases. This delay is decreased by applying temporal word features and a robust VARMA GRU classifier, which was taught to maximize speed performance under different data kinds. These efficiency enhancements enable the suggested model to be used in real-time social media false identity identification situations.

References

1. Harris, P., Gojal, J., Chitra, R., Anithra, S.: Fake Instagram profile identification and classification using machine learning. In: 2021 2nd Global Conference for Advancement in Technology (GCAT), Bangalore, India, pp. 1–5 (2021). https://doi.org/10.1109/GCAT52182.2021.9587858
2. Kulkarni, V., Aashritha Reddy, D., Sreevani, P., Teja, R.N.: Fake profile identification using ANN. In: 4th Smart Cities Symposium (SCS 2021), Online Conference, Bahrain, pp. 375–380 (2021).https://doi.org/10.1049/icp.2022.0372
3. Chamria, A.S., Mane, A.D., Dambal, P.V., Bharne, S.: Detecting fake profile in online social networks using EnsemStack classification algorithm. In: 2022 6th International Conference on Computing, Communication, Control and Automation ICCUBEA, Pune, India, pp. 1–6 (2022). https://doi.org/10.1109/ICCUBEA54992.2022.10010723
4. Mahammed, N., Bennabi, S., Fahsi, M., Klouche, B., Elouali, N., Bouhadra, C.: Fake profiles identification on social networks with bio-inspired algorithm. In: 2022 First International

Conference on Big Data, IoT, Web Intelligence and Applications (BIWA), Sidi Bel Abbes, Algeria, pp. 48–52 (2022). https://doi.org/10.1109/BIWA57631.2022.10037927

5. Parihar, P., Devanand, Kumar, N.: Fake profile detection from the social dataset for movie promotion. In: 2021 Sixth International Conference on Image Information Processing (ICIIP), Shimla, India, pp. 495–498 (2021). https://doi.org/10.1109/ICIIP53038.2021.9702684

6. Rathod, S.: Exploring author profiling for fake news detection. In: 2022 IEEE 46th Annual Computers, Software, and Applications Conference (COMPSAC), Los Alamitos, CA, USA, pp. 1614–1619 (2022). https://doi.org/10.1109/COMPSAC54236.2022.00256

7. Durier da Silva, F.C., Cristina Bicharra Garcia, A., Matsui Siqueira, S.W.: A systematic litera-ture mapping on profile trustworthiness in fake news spread. In: 2022 IEEE 25th International Conference on Computer Supported Cooperative Work in Design (CSCWD), Hangzhou, China, pp. 275–279 (2022). https://doi.org/10.1109/CSCWD54268.2022.9776232

8. Keynote Speech 2: Detecting fake news and profiling fake news spreaders and conspiracy propagators. In: 2021 12th International Conference on Information and Communication Systems (ICICS), Valencia, Spain, p. 2 (2021).https://doi.org/10.1109/ICICS52457.2021.9464534

9. Spezzano, F.: Modeling misinformation diffusion in social media: beyond network properties. In: 2021 IEEE Third International Conference on Cognitive Machine Intelligence (CogMI), Atlanta, GA, USA, pp. 168–171 (2021).https://doi.org/10.1109/CogMI52975.2021.00030

10. Ekosputra, M.J., Susanto, A., Haryanto, F., Suhartono, D.: Supervised machine learn-ing algorithms to detect Instagram fake accounts. In: 2021 4th International Seminar on Research of Information Technology and Intelligent Systems (isRITI), Yogyakarta, Indonesia, pp. 396–400 (2021). https://doi.org/10.1109/isRITI54043.2021.9702833

11. Sasikala, L.P,S.V,V., Arunarasi, J., Rajini, A.R., Nithiya, N.: Fake profile identification in social network using machine learning and NLP. In: 2022 International Conference on Com-munication, Computing, and Internet of Things (IC3IoT), Chennai, India, pp. 1–4 (2022). https://doi.org/10.1109/IC3IOT53935.2022.9767958

12. Bhattacharya, A., Bathla, R., Rana, A., Arora, G.: Application of machine learning techniques in detecting fake profiles on social media. In: 2021 9th International Conference on Reliability, Infocom Technologies and Optimization (Trends and Future Directions) (ICRITO), Noida, India, pp. 1–8 (2021). https://doi.org/10.1109/ICRITO51393.2021.9596373

13. Kathiravan, M., Parvez, S.J., Dheepthi, R., Jayanthi, R., Gowsalya, S., Sekhar, R.V.: Analysis and detection of fake profile over social media using machine learning techniques. In: 2023 5th International Conference on Smart Systems and Inventive Technology (ICSSIT), Tirunelveli, India, pp. 1164–1169 (2023). https://doi.org/10.1109/ICSSIT55814.2023.10061020

14. Anklesaria, K., Desai, Z., Kulkarni, V., Balasubramaniam, H.: A survey on machine learning algorithms for detecting fake Instagram accounts. In: 2021 3rd International Conference on Advances in Computing, Communication Control and Networking (ICAC3N), Greater Noida, India, pp. 141–144 (2021). https://doi.org/10.1109/ICAC3N53548.2021.9725724

15. Soumya, T.R., Manohar, S.S., Ganapathy, N.B.S., Nelson, L., Mohan, A., Pandian, M.T.: Profile similarity recognition in online social network using machine learning approach. In: 2022 4th International Conference on Inventive Research in Computing Applications (ICIRCA), Coimbatore, India, pp. 805–809 (2022). https://doi.org/10.1109/ICIRCA54612.2022.9985683

16. Remya Revi, K., isaac, M.M., Antony, R., Wilscy, M.: GAN-generated fake face image detection using opponent color local binary pattern and deep learning technique. In: 2022 International Conference on Connected Systems & Intelligence (CSI), Trivandrum, India, pp. 1–7 (2022). https://doi.org/10.1109/CSI54720.2022.9924077

17. Shinde, S., Mane, S.B.: Malicious profile detection on social media: a survey paper. In: 2021 9th International Conference on Reliability, Infocom Technologies and Optimization (Trends

and Future Directions) (ICRITO), Noida, India, pp. 1–5 (2021). https://doi.org/10.1109/ICR
ITO51393.2021.9596322

18. Qureshi, K.A., Malick, R.A.S., Sabih, M., Cherifi, H.: Complex network and source inspired
COVID-19 fake news classification on Twitter. IEEE Access **9**, 139636–139656 (2021).
https://doi.org/10.1109/ACCESS.2021.3119404

19. Theophilo, A., Padilha, R., Andaló, F.A., Rocha, A.: Explainable artificial intelligence
for authorship attribution on social media. In: ICASSP 2022 - 2022 IEEE International
Conference on Acoustics, Speech and Signal Processing (ICASSP), Singapore, Singapore,
pp. 2909–2913 (2022). https://doi.org/10.1109/ICASSP43922.2022.9746262

20. Shreya, K., Kothapelly, A., Deepika, V., Shanmugasundaram, H.: Identification of fake
accounts in social media using machine learning. In: 2022 Fourth International Conference on
Emerging Research in Electronics, Computer Science and Technology (ICERECT), Mandya,
India, pp. 1–4 (2022). https://doi.org/10.1109/ICERECT56837.2022.10060194

21. Rezaimehr, F., Dadkhah, C.: Injection shilling attack tool for recommender systems. In: 2021
26th International Computer Conference, Computer Society of Iran (CSICC), Tehran, Iran,
pp. 1–4 (2021). https://doi.org/10.1109/CSICC52343.2021.9420553

22. Garg, S., Dubey, A.: Fake Tweet data analysis using machine learning methods. In: 2021
5th International Conference on Electronics, Communication and Aerospace Technology
(ICECA), Coimbatore, India, pp. 1648–1654 (2021). https://doi.org/10.1109/ICECA52323.
2021.9675856

23. Ajesh, F., Aswathy, S.U., Philip, F.M., Jeyakrishnan, V.: A hybrid method for fake profile
detection in social network using artificial intelligence. Secur. issues Priv. Concerns Industry
4.0 Appl. 89–112 (2021). https://doi.org/10.1002/9781119776529.ch5

24. Chavan, P.V., Balani, N.: Design of heuristic model to improve block-chain-based sidechain
configuration. Int. J. Comput. Sci. Eng. **1**(1), 1. (2022). https://doi.org/10.1504/ijcse.2022.
10050704

25. Balani, N., Chavan, P., Ghonghe, M.: Design of high-speed blockchain-based sidechaining
peer to peer communication protocol over 5G networks. Multimedia Tools Appl. **81**(25),
36699–36713 (2022). https://doi.org/10.1007/s11042-021-11604-6

26. Sai Raja, E.V., Aditya, B.L.V.S., Mohanty, S.N.: Fake profile detection using logistic regression and gradient descent algorithm on online social networks. EAI Endorsed Trans. Scalable
Inf. Syst. **11**(1) (2023). https://doi.org/10.4108/eetsis.4342

27. Aditya, B.L.V.S., Mohanty, S.N.: Heterogenous social media analysis for efficient deep learning fake-profile identification. IEEE Access **11**, 99339–99351 (2023). https://doi.org/10.1109/
ACCESS.2023.3313169

28. Aditya, B.L.V.S., Rajaram, G., Hole, S.R., Mohanty, S.N. (2023). F2PMSMD: Design of a
Fusion Model to Identify Fake Profiles from Multimodal Social Media Datasets. In: Nandan
Mohanty, S., Garcia Diaz, V., Satish Kumar, G.A.E. (eds) Intelligent Systems and Machine
Learning. ICisML 2022. Lecture Notes of the Institute for Computer Sciences, Social Infor-
matics and Telecommunications Engineering, vol 471. Springer, Cham. https://doi.org/10.
1007/978-3-031-35081-8_2

Attaining Information Reliability Over Web Through Quantum Key Distribution

Padmavathi Vurubindi[1]([✉]), Sujatha Canavoy Narahari[2], Aashritha Rayala[1], and Shivani Sarikonda[1]

[1] Chaitanya Bharathi Institute of Technology Gandipet, Hyderabad, Telangana, India
padmavathiv_cse@cbit.ac.in
[2] Sreenidhi Institute of Science and Technology Ghatkesar, Hyderabad, Telangana, India
cnsujatha@sreenidhi.edu.in

Abstract. Over the years a boundless communication is happening over the web. It is too obvious to maintain and attain reliable information. Quantum key distribution (QKD) is an evolving technique which provides information reliability. It uses quantum mechanics-based cryptographic principles to a secure communication system and attain a reliable information over web. Two parties can create and share a key with QKD, which can then be used to encrypt and decrypt messages. In more precise terms, QKD refers to the process of sharing the key rather than the key itself or the messages that it permits users to transmit. This is due to a fundamental principle of quantum mechanics: any measurement of a quantum system affects it. The key must be measured in some way for a third party to try to eavesdrop on it, which introduces detectable irregularities. A communication system that can detect eavesdropping can be constructed by transmitting data in quantum states. The entity attempting to view the photons will alter the system by using the fundamental principles of quantum physics, making an incursion detectable. The suggested paradigm assists in attaining reliable information through the employment of quantum gates to perform quantum key distribution. A quantum gate, is a basic quantum circuit that employs qubits. They are the building blocks of quantum circuits, just like classical logic gates are the building elements of conventional digital circuits.

Keywords: reliable · qubit · QKD · quantum gate · web

1 Introduction

The sender and receiver should get assurance that they are communicating with alleged entity over web whom they ought to be. As a matter of fact, the information over web must be reliable. A contemporary method of computing known as quantum computing is based on the theory of quantum mechanics is brought into consideration inorder to attain information reliability. Information theory, computer science, mathematics, and physics are brilliantly combined in this work. It beats conventional computers in terms of processing capacity, energy consumption, and exponential speed by modifying the

O. Castillo et al. (Eds.): PerSOM 2023, LNICST 517, pp. 367–379, 2024.
https://doi.org/10.1007/978-3-031-66044-3_28

behaviour of tiny physical entities like atoms, electrons, and photons. Quantum key distribution (QKD) is a secure communication method that implements elements of quantum physics to carry out a cryptographic protocol to provide information reliability over web. It allows two parties to generate a secret shared key that is only known to them and can be used to encrypt and decode messages.

1.1 Principles of Quantum Mechanics

According to the uncertainty principle, "certain physical property pairs are related in a particular manner that the observer cannot simultaneously know the value of both properties when measuring one of them." A single photon's polarisation cannot be determined along two separate polarisation angle [10]. The No-Cloning Theorem [12] states, the principle of photon polarisation asserts that "an eavesdropper cannot copy unknown qubits, i.e., unknown quantum states." A quantum cannot be measured or copied without being changed.

1.2 Qubits

A quantum bit also known as a qubit, is the basic building block of quantum information. It represents subatomic particles such as atoms and electrons as the memory and their control mechanisms as the processor of a computer. It can have a value of 1, 0, or both at once. Qubit contains two quantum states that resemble the binary states of the past. The qubit may exist in any of the two states or in their superposed states simultaneously. Dirac notation, a method, can be used to depict these quantum states. In this, the state label is preserved between two symbols. In this format and $>$. State names are therefore written as 0 and 1. Any quantum bit wave function can be written as a two-state linear combination with a complex coefficient for each state, i.e., $|w| = x|0\rangle + y|1\rangle$, where x and y are the coefficients for both states. The size of the coefficient's squared value determines the state's probability. The odds of recognising the qubit state 0 are $|x|^2$ and the odds of identifying the qubit state 1 are $|y|^2$. According to mathematics, the sum of these probabilities must be 1, or 100%, therefore $|x|^2 + |y|^2 = 1$ [15, 16].

1.3 Quantum Gates

The building blocks of quantum circuits, like classical logic gates are for traditional digital circuits, are known as quantum logic gates (or simply quantum gates) [16]. The most appropriate way to know linear combinations is the matrix representation, and it so happens that the suitable state on the matrix that represents the gate is unitary matrix U. That is $U\dagger U = I$, where U† interpreted as U dagger, adjoint of U, complex conjugate of transposition matrix. The identity matrix U and I has a dimension of 2 by 2. Tensor product is used to construct the quantum gate matrix representation [13, 16]. The most common quantum gates include: Pauli gates: X, Y, and Z are the three single-qubit gates referred to as the Pauli gates. The X gate is equal to a conventional NOT gate, the Y gate rotates around the Y-axis of the Bloch sphere, and the Z gate rotates around the Z-axis of the Bloch sphere [16]. Hadamard gate: The Hadamard gate is a single-qubit gate that maps the basis states $|0\rangle$ and $|1\rangle$ to the equal superposition state $\frac{1}{\sqrt{2}}(|0\rangle+|1\rangle)$ and the minus superposition state $\frac{1}{\sqrt{2}}(|0\rangle-|1\rangle)$, respectively. Quantum Fourier transformations and superposition states are produced using the Hadamard gate [13, 16]. CNOT gate: The two-qubit CNOT (Controlled-NOT) gate uses a control bit and a target bit as its first and second qubits, respectively. f the first qubit is in the state 0, it flips the second qubit. The Deutsch-Jozsa algorithm and quantum error correcting codes both use the CNOT gate as a crucial part of their algorithms [16]. SWAP gate: A two qubit gate called the SWAP gate exchanges the states of two qubits. Quantum algorithms for sorting and searching employ the SWAP gate [16].

1.4 Quantum Key Distribution

Considering that public key cryptosystems might be cracked by quantum computers, a key distribution strategy is necessary to fend against quantum assaults. Thus, Quantum Cryptography presents an effective key distribution scheme called as Quantum Key Distribution (QKD) based on the principles of quantum mechanics. Stephen Wiesner, who initially proposed the concept of information transfer by polarised photons, is credited with introducing the concept of QKD. This concept was used by Bennett and Brassard in 1984 to establish the first QKD protocol, also known as the BB84 protocol, which allows for the creation of unconditionally safe shared keys between two entities who are geographically separated. The selling point of QKD is that if the principles of quantum mechanics are true, the security of the protocol is assured. Comparing this to previous classical protocols that rely on the adversary's weak computing capabilities, this represents a significant advancement. The protocol's practical use has advanced to the point that a number of tests have been carried out using installed telecom cables, daylight free-space channels in cities, and satellite-to-ground channels [11, 16].

2 Related Work

The crucial sifting stage and the crucial reconciliation stage will be where contributions to the planned endeavor will be split into two stages. A unique key sifting technique for the quantum key distribution has first been created in order to compare the proposed system's processing time to the traditional key sifting step in BB84. Second, Two TPM devices have been used to weigh the sifting key. Constructed on both the transmitter and recipient sides. After that, Hebbian, Anti-Hebbian, and Random-Walk learning algorithms were used to synchronize the two TPM machines. Here, the efficiency of synchronization using different learning techniques has been investigated. As a result, an alternative to the modified key sifting system based on basis distribution BB84 protocol's conventional key sifting method [1].

An algorithm known as Qubit4Sync, a synchronization method for QKD installations, based on the identical qubits transferred throughout the protocol and needing no extra hardware aside from that needed to create and monitor the quantum states. According to our understanding, the approach introduces a novel cross-correlation methodology with the lowest computing complexity for large channel losses. We demonstrate the resilience of our approach in a real world QKD implementation. Since the suggested model eliminates the need for extra hardware for the asynchronization sub-system, resulting in less expensive equipment and a lower chance of hardware failure, it facilitates the execution of a QKD setup effectively. The synchronization process is immune to eavesdropper denial-of-service attacks since the QKD fails before the synchronization [2].

An improvised QKD verification mechanism. Alice and Bob provide their IDs and seek a "secure" connection during the first stage. Information centres employ "public key authentication" to confirm that they are authorised users of the "public key" framework. Following the public key has been successfully authenticated, the data centres create random numbers. Additionally, the data centres transmit special KEY POOL's that have been encrypted using private keys. KPA belongs to Alice, while KPB belongs to Bob. For verification, use QKD: The first information centre creates a quantum communication link and sends copies of the key pools to both parties. A copy of the keys are exchanged between Alice and Bob through the information centre during their initial communication. Otherwise opens a quantum communication channel without the transfer of POOL. The steps involved in the mutual authentication phase are: Bob was publicly asked by Alice for the POOL KPA's key. Bob uses KPB to check that key. Only when the keys coincide does the transmission take place. Bob formally requests a key from the POOL KPB from Alice. Alice uses KPA to verify that key. Only when the keys coincide does the transmission take place. Every transmission is followed by a repeat of this process. Thus, this ensures that neither party is spying on the other. Since only Alice and Bob are aware of the specifics of their keys from the KEY POOL, this also guarantees that mutual 100 percent user authentication is accomplished [3].

A QKD network exists where a quantum layer including a reliable symmetric key is established has to define QKD networks. a layer for maintaining and validating already-created keys. a level of communication where data security is achieved using the established key [4].

Networks using quantum key distribution (QKD) provide interesting alternatives for private communication. In this study, they created 1xN QKD network systems utilising an optical route length compensation method with subns precision using a realistic plug-and-play QKD architecture and small, field- programmable gate array (FGPA)-based timing control modules. The problem of accounting for variations in optical path length in QKD network systems is addressed by the user-independent compensation mechanism suggested in this research. The technique can achieve sub-ns timing resolution without active user input by utilizing a delay line and interferometer. This could make it simpler to put QKD networks into practice and could assist in resolving one of the main issues the area is now experiencing [5].

Privacy amplification (PA) It is a method to extract a highly private key from a string that is just marginally safe. The creation of a theoretically unconditional secure key is a crucial step in QKD. This work proposes a GNU multiple precision arithmetic library (GMP)-based CPU platform-based high throughput modular arithmetic hash PA method. According to the experimental data, this scheme's throughput is nearly an order of magnitude greater than the throughput of the comparable method on the same CPU platform with block sizes of 106 and 108 at 135 Mbps and 69 Mbps, respectively, on an Intel i3–2120 CPU. The difficulty of implementing privacy amplification in QKD can be overcome using the high- speed privacy amplification approach suggested in this study employing GMP. The approach can accomplish high-speed privacy amplification for huge key sizes without compromising security by utilizing bit-wise operations with the GMP library. As a result, secure communication systems that rely on QKD may be developed, making QKD more effective and practical [6].

Quantum encryption is still a young field. We cannot, however, ignore the dangers and difficulties it offers for the existing cyberspace's security. Since quantum cryptography and protocols combine conventional cryptography with quantum physics, this study examines them. Designing is the most effective among DV-QKD PA cryptographic protocols and algorithms that assaults from quantum computers is the primary objective of research into quantum cryptography. The QKD protocol objective for future Internet cyberspace security is the main topic of this paper's analysis and exploration. The results of the experimental investigation presented in this paper show how sniffer detection and quantum cryptography's constant security make it suitable for the next-generation Internet [7].

Semi-quantum key distribution (SQKD) is a significant research topic that enables one quantum participant with cutting-edge quantum equipment to safely communicate a shared secret key with one limited-capability classical user. Alice gives Bob and Charlie, respectively, two particle sequences from Bell state. Once the particles have been processed and returned, Alice may use Bell-state measurement to simultaneously identify reflected particles from Bob and Charlie and produce two distinct raw keys. This protocol may be expanded to the m + 1 party communication technique by using the m-particle GHZ state, enabling more players to share keys. When compared to the conventional SQKD system, this expanded model dramatically lowers communication complexity in large-scale communication networks. This work suggests a SQKD system that enables a quantum user to simultaneously send two separate private secret keys to two conventional users. To disseminate m keys concurrently, this approach is extended. It offers a useful concept for creating a network for distributing quantum keys. Attacks such as the modification attack, the entangle measurement attack, and other frequent attacks can be defeated by the proposed SQKD protocol [8].

To strengthen the defence against quantum computing assault of conventional cryptographic keys, QKD is being developed. The durability of classical cryptography's keys, which were almost impenetrable in the pre-quantum era, can be improved through QKD. This article presents a comparative analysis of several QKD techniques and examines trends and restrictions in classical cryptography of key management techniques. It also emphasises how QKD's security implementation features help to address risks that can arise in a situation involving quantum computing in order to make the cryptographic keys resistant to quantum effects [9].

3 Proposed Methodology

The suggested paradigm assists in attaining reliable information through the employment of quantum gates to perform quantum key distribution. Pauli-X gate and Hadamard gate is used to carry out the proposed methodology.

3.1 Pauli-X Gate

Pauli-X gate [16] is a single qubit gate that flips 0 to 1 and vice versa. It can be represented in the form of matrix as,

$$A = \begin{bmatrix} 0 & 1 \\ 1 & 0 \end{bmatrix}$$

We merely multiply the state vector of the qubit by the gate to observe the impact of gate on the qubit. We may observe that X-gate changes the amplitude of states $|0\rangle$ to $1\rangle$ [16]

$$A = \begin{bmatrix} 0 & 1 \\ 1 & 0 \end{bmatrix}\begin{bmatrix} 1 \\ 0 \end{bmatrix} = \begin{bmatrix} 0 \\ 1 \end{bmatrix} = |1\rangle$$

3.2 Hadamard Gate

The Hadamard Gate [16] operates on a single qubit similarly to the Pauli-X gate and can also be represented as a 2 x 2 matrix. Simply applying a certain gate to a qubit will cause it to enter a superposition state. This can be accomplished through the well-known quantum computing gate known as the Hadamard Gate.

3.3 Quantum Key Distribution

A key establishment technology that offers unwavering security is Quantum Key Distribution (QKD) [11]. In entanglement-based methods, quantum key distribution either violates Bell's inequality or employs Heisenberg's uncertainty principle to detect the presence of an opponent. Heisenberg's uncertainty-based protocol states that a quantum state is altered by measurement. As a result, the eavesdropper will inject an error into the information flow through a quantum channel, which the protocol can identify. When using entanglement-based protocols, information is created if an outsider measures the entangled quanta. The eavesdropper attempts to violate Bell's inequality by adding an additional quanta to the protocol. As a result, the eavesdropper's presence will also be detected [11].

In QKD process, Alice, the sender, and Bob, the receiver, generate the secret key using a quantum channel and a conventional channel. The classical channel can be any connection to a traditional network, such the internet or a phone network, but the quantum channel can be an optical fibre or a direct line of-sight free space link. While Bob measures these photons on the receiving side to produce raw key bits, Alice prepares and sends single polarised photons known as quantum bits or "qubits" from the sending side using a laser source. Shared secret keys are produced after information exchange over the traditional route [13]. Any data, audio, or video can be encrypted to achieve reliable information using the secret keys generated by QKD.

3.4 Quantum Transmission

Following are the steps involved quantum channel exchange between Alice, the sender and Bob, the receiver.

1. Preparation: Alice prepares a string of random bits and encodes each bit as a photon using a randomly selected polarization (either horizontal/vertical or diagonal/anti-diagonal).
2. Qubit generation: To generate polarised photons, or qubits, Alice chooses a random base sequence.
3. Quantum gate application: Alice applies the qubits to Hadamard and Pauli X-gates and transmits them to Bob.
4. Transmission: Alice sends the encoded photons to Bob over a quantum channel (e.g. fiber optic cable or air).
5. Bob's construction of bits: Using the polarised photons that Alice transmitted, Bob chooses some random bases and measures them, then uses the measured polarised photons to construct a set of random bits.

3.5 Public Exchange

Here are the steps involved in the public exchange of the BB84 protocol:

1. Reception: Bob receives the photons and randomly measures the polarization of each photon using his chosen basis.
2. Announcement: Alice announces to Bob which polarization basis she used for each photon.
3. Comparison: Bob discards all the photons that were measured in the wrong basis (i.e. when Alice and Bob choose different bases). Alice and Bob compare their measurement outcomes for the remaining photons in public. (but not the values themselves).
4. Confirmation: A subset of the remaining bits is chosen at random by Alice and Bob and compare them to check for errors. If there are no errors, they can be confident that they have a shared secret key.
5. Key distillation: Alice and Bob perform an error correction protocol to correct any errors in their shared key, and then they implement a privacy amplification approach to limit the quantity of data that may have been obtained through eavesdropping.
6. Key verification: Alice and Bob check that their final shared key matches exactly, ensuring that no information was lost or intercepted during the exchange.

By following these procedure, Alice and Bob can create a shared secret key that is only known to them and cannot be read by a third-party.

3.6 Key Sifting

This protocol uses two bases—one of which is a diagonal basis and the other is a rectilinear basis—to produce four polarization states. The rectilinear basis encodes logic 0 as a photon with a 0° polarization and logic 1 as a photon with a 90° polarization. According to the diagonal basis, logic 1 is symbolized by a 135°-polarized photon, while logic 0 is symbolized by a 45°-polarized photon. The polarised photons are delivered from Alice (Sender) to Bob (receiver) across the quantum channel [13, 15].

Figure 6 illustrates generation of sifted key with an example. In the quantum transmission channel, Alice randomly generates a sequence of 15-bits and creates polarized photons which are a sequence of random bases and sent those qubits to Bob. Before sending them to Bob, these qubits are applied to Hadamard and Pauli-X gates. Bob chooses a random sequence of bases to measure with Alice's bases along with random bits accordingly to his random bases [13].

In the Public channel exchange, Bob sends his random bases to Alice. Alice reports matched bases with their respective positions to Bob. Now, a sifted key is generated successfully [13].

4   Results

The proposed methodology is implemented using IBM Qiskit framework [17] for simulating the results. It provides Quantum Computer Lab which offers a strong framework for creating quantum key distribution (QKD) protocols using quantum gates like Pauli X gate and Hadamard gate. Following are the illustrations of our simulation results showing each step of this protocol starting from server's generation of sequence of random bits to establishment of secure communication with a shared secret key between server(sender) and user (receiver).

1. Server generates a random sequence of 100-bits.

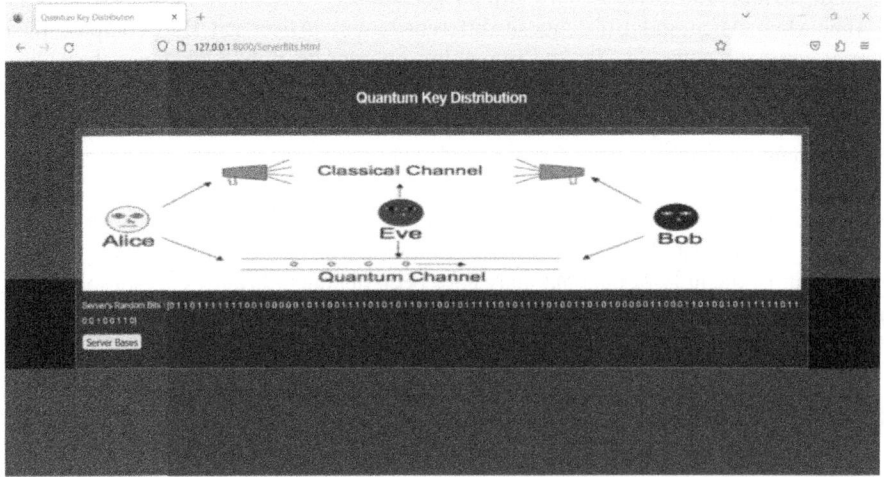

Fig. 1. Server's Random bits

2. Server chooses random bases to convert bits to qubits and sends to User.

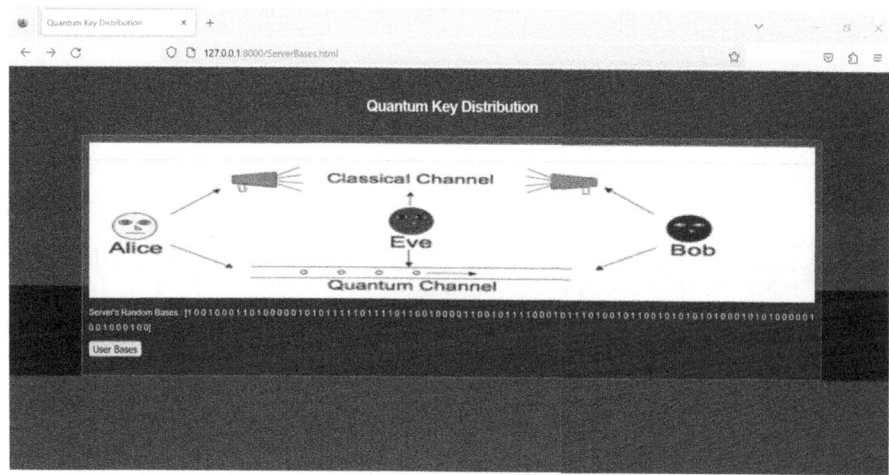

Fig. 2. Server's Random bases

3. User generates its random bases for 100 qubits.

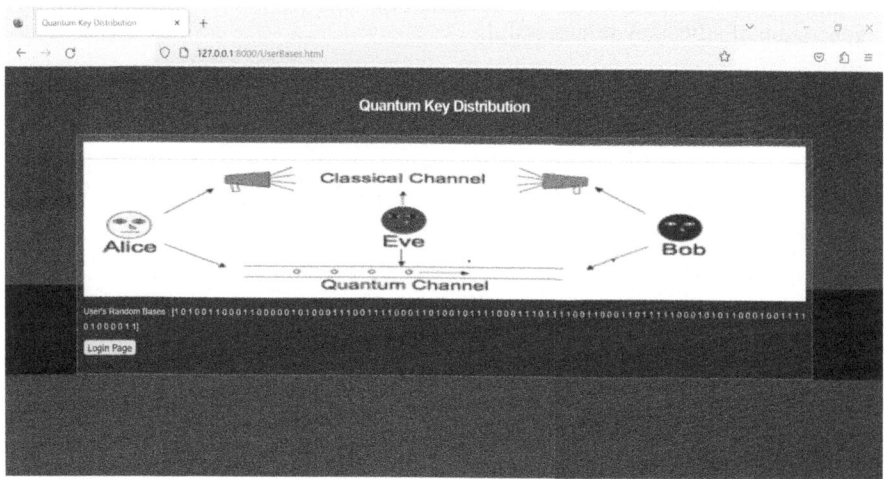

Fig. 3. User's random bases

4. User registration

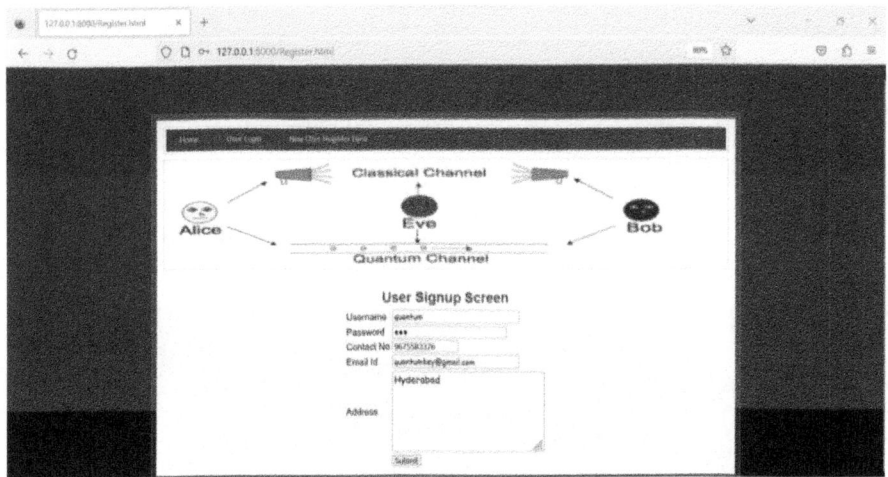

Fig. 4. User Registration

5. User logs in and the communication between server and user starts. Server measures the bases sent by user. They both generate their secret keys based on the matched bases. After removing garbage bits and if both server key and user key are same then generation of sifted key is successful.

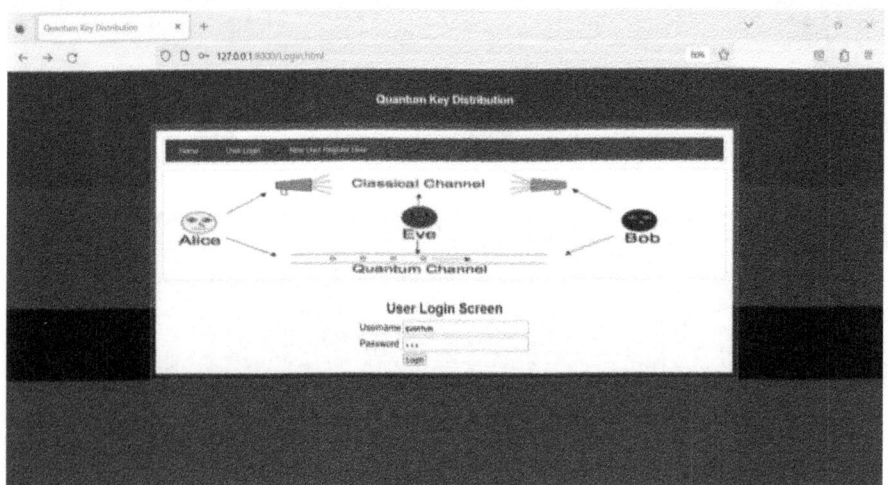

Fig. 5. User Login

6. Shared Key: Sifted key generation is successful. Since shared key is established which is in the size of 15 bits and they can have a secured communication.

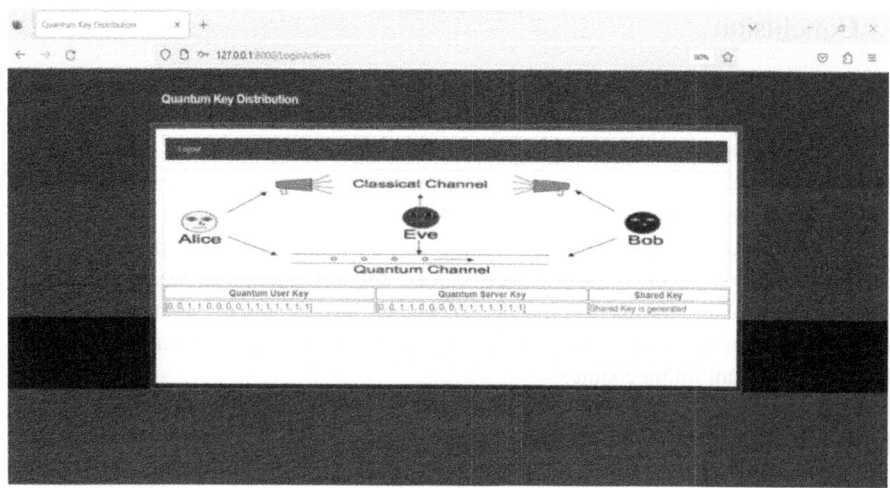

Fig. 6. Shared Key

5 Analysis

From the results it is clear that a secure and authenticated communication channel can be established between user and server following the QKD protocol. QKD protocol offers perfect secrecy by ensuring that the key cannot be known by any kind of third-party which can intercept and measure all the qubits transmitted between the parties. Server has generated random of 100-bits and 100-bases and User measured his random sequence of 100 bases with Server's. The advantage of QKD is it allows the generation of long keys in contrast to the classical which are limited by the length of the key that can be shared through the communication channel [14].

We used Pauli-X and Hadamard gates in our protocol. We applied Pauli-X gate to encode the qubit with the value of the classical bit being transmitted. i.e.; if the corresponding classical bit is 1, the X gate is applied to the qubit to flip its state from $|0\rangle$ to $|1\rangle$. This is because the state $|1\rangle$ is orthogonal to the state $|0\rangle$, which makes it easier to distinguish between them during the measurement stage of the protocol. While measuring the bases, if the base is 0 then the qubit is measured in Z-basis and measured and if the base is 1 then the qubit is first transformed to X-basis by applying Hadamard gate and then measured in Z- basis. By applying the Hadamard gate, the qubit is placed in a superposition of the Z-basis and X-basis, so Bob's measurement is equally likely to yield 0 or 1, regardless of which basis Alice used.

After the server sends the qubits to User they are measured against user bases and a shared key is generated by using the matched bases and removing the garbage bits from bits that were measured in different bases by sender and user. Therefore, a highly secured communication channel is established between server and user which is resistant to attacks from any third-party.

6 Conclusion

Our simulation results show that the proposed implementation of QKD using Pauli-X and Hadamard gates established a successful shared secret key between two-parties. Thus attaining information reliability over web. Qiskit programming offers a strong framework for creating quantum key distribution (QKD) protocols, such as using a Pauli X gate and a Hadamard gate. Qiskit provides an easy-to-use interface for simulating the behavior of quantum circuits and testing the performance of QKD protocols under different conditions, such as the presence of noise and errors in the quantum channel. By using Qiskit, researchers and developers can explore the potential of quantum computing for secure communication and cryptography, and build new applications that leverage the power of quantum mechanics.

QKD is currently a very new and expensive technology, and its actual application confronts a number of difficulties despite its theoretical security guarantees. These include the requirement for specialised hardware and the susceptibility of various QKD methods to side-channel assaults or attacks based on faulty components. Although QKD is a promising technology for secure communication, outside of specialised applications, it is not yet extensively employed. Even said, there is still a lot of research being done in this field, and quantum technology advancements may one day make it more useful for everyday use.

References

1. Biswas, C., Haque, M.M., Gupta, U.D.: A modified key sifting scheme with artificial neural network based key reconciliation analysis in quantum cryptography. IEEE Access **10**, 72743–72757 (2022)
2. Calderaro, L., Stanco, A., Agnesi, C., Avesani, M., Dequal, D., Villoresi, P., Vallone, G.: Fast and simple qubit-based synchronization for quantum key distribution. Phys. Rev. Appl. **13**(5), 054041 (2020)
3. Kumar, A., Dadheech, P., Singh, V., Poonia, R.C., Raja, L.: An improved quantum key distribution protocol for verification. J. Disc. Math. Sci. Cryptograp. **22**(4), 491–498 (2020)
4. Mehic, M., Nemec, M., Rass, S., Ma, J., Peev, M.: Quantum key distribution: a networking perspective. ACM Comput. Surv. **53**(5), 96 (2020)
5. Park, B.K., Woo, M.K., Kim, Y.S., Cho, Y.W., Moon, S., Han, S.W.: User-independent optical path length compensation scheme with sub-nanosecond timing resolution for a $1 \times N$ quantum key distribution network system. Photonics Res. **8**(3), 296–302 (2020)
6. Yan, B., Li, Q., Mao, H., Xue, X.: High-speed privacy amplification scheme using GMP in quantum key distribution. IEEE Photonics J. **12**(3), 1–13 (2020)
7. Zhou, T., Shen, J., Li, X., Wang, C., Shen, J.: Quantum cryptography for the future internet and the security analysis. Secur. Commun. Netw. **2018**(1), 8214619 (2018)
8. Wanqing, W., Sun, C.Y.: Semi-quantum key distribution with two classical users (2022)
9. Adhikari, T., Ghosh, A., Khan, A.: quantum resistance for crypto- graphic keys in classical cryptosystems: a study on QKD protocols. In: 12th International Conference on Computing Computation and Networking (2021)
10. Wiesner, S.: Conjugate coding. ACM SIGACT News **15**(1), 78–88 (1983)
11. Bennett, C.H., Brassard, G.: Quantum cryptography: public key distribution and coin tossing. In: Proceedings of the IEEE International Conference on Computers, Systems and Signal Processing, Bangalore, India, (IEEE, New York), pp. 175–179 (1984)

12. Wootters, W.K., Zurek, W.H.: A single quantum cannot be cloned. Nature **299**(5886), 802–803 (1982)
13. Padmavathi, V., Vardhan, B.V., Krishna, A.V.N.: Provably secure quantum key distribution by applying quantum gate. Int. J. Netw. Secur. **20**(1), 88–94 (2018)
14. Shor, P.W., Preskill, J.: Simple proof of security of the BB84 quantum key distribution protocol. Phys. Rev. Lett. **85**(2), 441 (2000)
15. Padamvathi, V., Vishnu Vardhan, B., Krishna, A.V.N.: Quantum cryptography and quantum key distribution protocols: a survey. In: IEEE the 6th International Conference on Advanced Computing (IACC), pp. 556–562 (2016)
16. M. A. Nielsen and I. Chuang, Quantum Computation and Quantum Information, 10th Anniversary Edition, Cambridge University Press, 2002
17. IBM Quantum (2021). https://quantum-computing.ibm.com/

Author Index

O. Castillo et al. (Eds.): PerSOM 2023, LNICST 517, pp. 381–382, 2024.
https://doi.org/10.1007/978-3-031-66044-3

GPSR Compliance

The European Union's (EU) General Product Safety Regulation (GPSR) is a set of rules that requires consumer products to be safe and our obligations to ensure this.

If you have any concerns about our products, you can contact us on ProductSafety@springernature.com

In case Publisher is established outside the EU, the EU authorized representative is:

Springer Nature Customer Service Center GmbH
Europaplatz 3
69115 Heidelberg, Germany

The manufacturer's authorised representative in the EU is Springer
Nature Customer Service Centre GmbH, Europaplatz 3, 69115 Heidelberg,
Germany. If you have any concerns regarding our products, please
contact ProductSafety@springernature.com

Printed and bound by CPI Group (UK) Ltd, Croydon, CR0 4YY
24/04/2026
02096374-0001